MORE THAN COURAGE

MORE THAN COURAGE

SICILY, NAPLES–FOGGIA, ANZIO, RHINELAND, ARDENNES–ALSACE, CENTRAL EUROPE

The Combat History of
The 504th Parachute Infantry Regiment
in World War II

Phil Nordyke

ZENITH PRESS

First published in 2008 by Zenith Press, an imprint of MBI Publishing Company, 400 1st Avenue North, Minneapolis, MN 55401 USA.

Zenith Press titles are also available at discounts in bulk quantity for industrial or sales-promotional use. For details write to Special Sales Manager at MBI Publishing Company, 400 1st Avenue North, Minneapolis, MN 55401 USA.

To find out more about our books, join us online at www.zenithpress.com.

Designer: Chris Fayers

Library of Congress Cataloging-in-Publication Data

Nordyke, Phil.
More than courage : Sicily, Naples-Foggia, Anzio, Rhineland, Ardennes-Alsace, Central Europe : the combat history of the 504th Parachute Infantry Regiment in World War II / by Phil Nordyke.
    p. cm.
  ISBN 978-0-7603-3313-6 (hbk.)
  1. United States. Army. Parachute Infantry Regiment, 504th. 2. World War, 1939-1945--Campaigns--Western Front. 3. World War, 1939-1945--Campaigns--Italy. 4. World War, 1939-1945--Regimental histories--United States. I. Title.
  D769.348504th .N67 2008
  940.54'1273--dc22
                            2008006488

Printed in the United States of America

Contents

Acknowledgments

Many individuals contributed to making this book possible, and I am deeply appreciative of their assistance. My wife, Nancy, spent long hours with me at the National Archives, the 82nd Airborne Division War Memorial Museum, the Donovan Research Library, and other archives, finding information and veterans' accounts.

My literary agent, Gayle Wurst of the Princeton International Agency for the Arts, believed in the project from the beginning, as did Richard Kane, the managing editor of Zenith Press. I appreciate their faith in me. I want to thank Steve Gansen for shepherding this project through the editing process.

A number of archives contained valuable information that made this book possible. I want to thank Doug McCabe, Curator of Manuscripts, Robert E. & Jean R. Mahn Center for Archives and Special Collections, Vernon R. Alden Library, Ohio University, Athens, Ohio, for providing the large volume of materials and veterans' accounts from the Cornelius Ryan Collection.

I want to extend my gratitude to Dr. John Duvall, Museums Chief, and Betty Rucker, Collections Manager, who made available the vast wealth of the Ridgway–Gavin Archives at the 82nd Airborne Division War Memorial Museum at Fort Bragg, North Carolina.

I want to thank Ericka L. Loze, librarian at the Donovan Research Library at Fort Benning, Georgia, who provided monographs of 504th Parachute Infantry Regiment veterans from the library's massive collection.

Several members of the staff at the National Archives helped me locate many documents, combat and hospital interviews, and awards files used in the book. The dedicated men and women of the National Archives do so much to preserve the country's historical documents, and they all deserve our thanks.

My thanks to Father G. Thuring and Frank van den Bergh with the Liberation Museum in Groesbeek, the Netherlands, for freely sharing information about Operation Market Garden.

I owe an enormous debt to Don Lassen and his *Static Line* publication for so much of the contact information for the veterans I interviewed. My gratitude also goes to Jim Megellas and T. Moffatt Burriss, veterans of the World War II 504th Parachute Infantry Regiment, whose great books about the regiment served as inspiration for me to write this book.

This book would not have been possible without the first-person accounts of the veterans of the 504th Regimental Combat Team. Many such veterans, among them Fred Baldino, Charles Battisti, Edwin Bayley, Bill Bonning, Reneau Breard, Charles Butler, Landon Chilcutt, Al Clark, Harry Corbin, Ed Dodd, Ray Fary, Pat Fusaro, Roy Hanna, Leo Hart, Harold Herbert, Donald Herndon, John Holabird, Tom Holliday, Mike Holmstock, Shelby Hord, Walter Hughes, Francis Keefe, the Reverend Delbert Kuehl, Bill Leonard, Joseph Lyons, Carl Mauro, Francis McLane, Louis Orvin, Ross Pippin, Edward Ryan, Ed Sims, Harold Sullivan, James Ward, Obie Wickersham, and George Willoughby, openly shared their accounts, their time, and vital information for the book, for which I am profoundly grateful.

Numerous families and friends of the 504th Regimental Combat Team, as well as other authors and historians, contributed additional veterans' accounts and information. I am deeply indebted to Dutch author and historian Jan Bos for sharing the veterans' accounts used in his superb book, *Circle and the Fields of Little America: The History of the 376th Parachute Field Artillery Battalion of the 82nd Airborne Division during World War II*. Mike Bigalke, Bob Burns, Alex Kicovic, Jim McNamara, Steve Mrozek, Terry Poyser, Mrs. Leonard Trimble, Peter Turnbull, Frank van Lunteren, Brandon Wiegand, and Robert Wolfe contributed many of the veterans' personal accounts, for which I am extremely appreciative.

In some cases, I have made minor changes to the personal accounts to correct grammatical and spelling errors, to put the action in chronological order, to omit unnecessary information, and to create consistency in unit designations, equipment, and other terminology. However, the first-person accounts are always true to the veterans' original words.

It is to all of the officers and men who served as the Devils in Baggy Pants with the 504th Regimental Combat Team during World War II that this book is dedicated.

Introduction

The 504th Parachute Infantry Regiment and its supporting units, the 376th Parachute Field Artillery Battalion, Battery C, 80th Airborne Antiaircraft (Antitank) Battalion and Company C, 307th Airborne Engineer Battalion, were one of the greatest fighting forces ever assembled. Its combat record is spectacular. No American parachute regiment fought as many days or under as many differing circumstances during World War II. It served 281 days in frontline combat and made combat jumps at Sicily, Salerno, and Holland, fought in the rugged mountains of Italy, made a beach landing at Anzio, endured brutal winter combat in the Belgian Ardennes, and made assault crossings of the Waal and Rhine Rivers. Units of the regiment were awarded four Presidential Unit Citations for actions during the fighting at Salerno, Anzio, Holland, and central Germany.

Lieutenant Edward F. Shaifer, Jr., believed several factors made the 504 a legendary fighting force with a stellar combat record. "Its morale was unshakable and its experience broad. Few fighting teams with the same lengthy time in action had participated in as much heavy fighting under such varied conditions, and suffered as few casualties. Consistently, the unit had fought, often cut off and surrounded, in some of the most critical spots of the war. And, often outgunned by opposing artillery, it had met the best troops the Germans could pit against it, surrendering not a foot of ground, defeating each in turn with an average disproportionate casualty rate of ten to twenty percent to that of the enemy, a truly remarkable record. . . . The members of this regiment were exceptionally fine soldiers."[1]

GENERAL JAMES M. GAVIN, WHO COMMANDED the 505th Parachute Infantry Regiment and later the 82nd Airborne Division during World War II, described the 504's commanding officer, Colonel Reuben H. Tucker, as "a tough, superb combat leader . . . probably the best regimental combat commander of the war."[2]

Other Allied units had tremendous respect for the regiment's combat prowess. The division intelligence section of the U.S. 3rd Infantry Division, which fought alongside the 504 at Anzio, wrote the following: "On the beachhead these parachutists have caused worry and wrinkled brows only in the enemy camp. They have shown themselves particularly qualified at night patrolling and on many occasions have tackled larger numbers of Krauts than they themselves had, usually to the Kraut's disadvantage.

"Their motto is 'Strike-Hold' and to date, they have done all of that and more."[3]

The enemy feared the presence of the 504 paratroopers. A diary found on the body of a German officer at Anzio read, "American parachutists—devils in baggy pants—are less than one hundred meters from my outpost line. I can't sleep at night. They pop up from nowhere and we never know when or how they will strike next. Seems like the black-hearted devils are everywhere."[4]

The paratroopers of the 504 were some of the toughest, best, most aggressive soldiers that America or any country has ever fielded. Despite fighting against some of the best troops of the German Army—the Hermann Göring Panzer Division and the 1st, 9th, and 10th SS Panzer Divisions—the regiment never lost.

Chapter 1

"I'm Going To Be A Paratrooper"

The young men who volunteered for the airborne came from almost every imaginable background and had many different reasons for volunteering. Ross S. Carter, from Duffield, Virginia, was one of the few enlisted men with a college degree. "Every level of society had its representation among us. Senators' sons rubbed shoulders with ex-cowboys. Steelworkers chummed up with tough guys from city slums. Farm boys, millionaires' spoiled brats, white-collar men, factory workers, ex-convicts, jailbirds, and hoboes joined for the thrill and adventure of parachute jumping. And so, the army's largest collection of adventurous men congregated in the parachute troops.

"The thing that distinguished us from most other soldiers was our willingness to take chances and risks in a branch of the Army that provided a great, new, almost unexplored frontier. In other days paratroopers would have been the type to sail with Columbus, or the first to seek out the West and fight the Indians."[1]

One of the early volunteers for the airborne, Reuben H. Tucker III, exemplified that spirit. At the time Tucker said, "I have no definite reason for joining up as a parachutist except that I like excitement and adventure and I always like to participate in something new and different. You might say I like to 'pioneer.' "[2]

Tucker, called "Tommy" by his family, grew up in Ansonia, Connecticut, one of six children in a working-class family. He was an avid athlete and Boy Scout, and at age thirteen, courageously pulled his younger brother and a friend from a frozen pond, for which he received an award from the Boy Scouts. Tucker's high school classmates nicknamed him Duke.

Upon graduating from high school in 1927, he worked as an apprentice to his father in a brass mill for about a year. Tucker, whose ancestors on both sides of his family had served in the military as far back as the Revolutionary War, then decided to embark upon a military career and left to attend Millard's West Point Preparatory School in Washington, D.C. In 1929 he passed the entrance exams but did not receive an appointment. He moved to Wyoming for a year and worked on a surveying crew before receiving an appointment to West Point in 1930. There, Tucker excelled in football, hockey, and lacrosse, but within a year, he washed out because of a failing grade in mathematics. Determined to succeed, Tucker took private tutoring and then passed a demanding two-day series of exams and was readmitted, graduating in 1935, number 186 out of a class of 277. The following day, he was married at the chapel at West Point.

Lieutenant Tucker's first assignment was with the 9th Infantry Regiment, stationed in Texas. He then was transferred to the 33rd Infantry Regiment in Panama.

Tucker volunteered for parachute duty and became an original member of the 502nd Parachute Infantry Battalion in June 1941, where he served with a young Captain James M. Gavin.

Theodore L. Dunn was born in Meridian, Mississippi, and graduated from the U.S. Military Academy in 1925. As a young officer, he served from 1929 to 1932 with the 45th Infantry Regiment in the Philippines, then returned to the United States. He attended the army's tank school in 1932 and subsequently was assigned to the 66th Infantry Regiment. Beginning in 1937, he served in Panama with the 14th Infantry Regiment and two years later was stationed at Fort Snelling, Minnesota, with the 7th Tank Company. Major Dunn volunteered for Parachute School in July 1941, graduating in September.

As America saw the looming war clouds gathering, it began rapidly expanding the military services, including the fledgling parachute units. The young men who volunteered to become paratroopers took many paths. Louis E. Orvin, Jr., joined the National Guard in Savannah, Georgia, in 1939 at age seventeen. "When I joined, the recruiting sergeant said, 'What's your date of birth?'

"I told him, 'March the 20th, 1922.'

"He said, 'Who told you that?'

"I said, 'My mother.'

"He said, 'That's wrong, you were born in 1921.' I was eighteen years old, right off the bat.

"On September the 15th of 1940, we were mobilized. I was still going to high school when we were mobilized. The battery commander asked me if I wanted to get out. I said, 'Well, I'd like to stay in, but I think I had better get out and finish school.'

"He said, 'Well, turn your name into the battery clerk.'

"I turned my name in, but they never let me out. They let his two sons and their best friend out, but they didn't let me out. So I stayed twenty-six months at Fort Jackson, South Carolina, in the artillery, going up and doing maneuvers in the hot summertime and sitting out there by the guns. I was an operator and I took firing data and gave it to the gunners. I just got tired of it.

"I just happened to see a paratrooper walk across the street in Columbia, South Carolina, when I had a pass one day. I liked the looks of the uniform and the way he carried himself. So, I said, 'That's what I want to do.'

"I asked for a transfer to the paratroops.

"They said, 'You'll have to take a bust to private and pay your own way from Fort Jackson to Fort Benning.' I was a corporal—acting sergeant.

"I said, 'O.K., that's a deal, I'll take it.' "[3]

Joseph C. Watts joined the army on March 26, 1941, at the Federal Building in Los Angeles, California. "With the approval of my parents, I enlisted on my eighteenth birthday for the adventure, romance, and travel soldiering offered. I was bused to Fort MacArthur on 27 March. Here, we waited clearances and assignments. Orders for several of us were to the Hawaiian and Philippine Departments. I wanted to go overseas, but being in the service with my parents' permission, my requests were denied. So, I requested assignment to the then forming paratroops, but previous service was required."[4]

Instead, the army assigned Watts to a chemical warfare company, and he trained at an Army Air Corps base, March Field, in Riverside, California. In November 1941, Watts volunteered for a chemical warfare service job at an air force base, at Nichols Field, on the Philippines. On December 3, 1941, Watts and about thirty other chemical warfare soldiers joined a field artillery battalion aboard the SS *Etolin*, bound for the Philippines, with a stop in Hawaii. "According to the map, we would arrive in Pearl on 7–8 December and Manila Bay the day before Christmas."[5]

Watts was seasick for the next few days of the voyage, but began to get his sea legs under him and was looking forward to the stop in Hawaii. "Seven December dawned bright and clear. I awoke on deck hungry and made my way to the galley for powdered eggs, sausage, toast, and coffee. I returned to my usual place on the deck tarp, just below the radio room. The morning was warming up very nicely. About 0900 hours, Jaworski, the card players, and I saw the door to the radio room bang open and the operator flew down the gangway, sliding down the banister by his hands on the rail, without his feet touching a single step, a piece of paper clutched in his hand.

"Shortly thereafter, we noticed our ship was paralleling a ship's wake about three hundred yards to the north. We then realized it was our own wake and we had turned and were going east now, instead of west. The boat drill alarm clanged, scrambling us for our compartments. A few of us knew something was up, because of the ship's wake.

"Over the load-hailer compartment, commanders were ordered to the mess area for a briefing. We just milled around among the six-high canvas bunks—mine was on top—until [Sergeant] McNamara returned. He called us together and asked for quiet. 'Men, this is no shit, this is no drill, the Japs have bombed Pearl Harbor! We're at war!' "[6]

Robert W. Zost was serving in a mule-drawn pack howitzer unit at Fort Bragg when the United States entered World War II. "I volunteered for the original Parachute Test Battery in the early part of 1942. We, one hundred eighty of us, went through one of the first jump classes at Fort Benning, Georgia, and were assigned seven C-47s (Douglas DC-3s) for the purpose of developing a systematic method of dropping the 75mm pack howitzer by parachute, assembling this gun on the ground, and assemble a four-gun battery into firing position. After about a year, we perfected the drop by disassembling the gun into seven parts; six were secured beneath the plane, and the seventh part, the wheels, were strapped together with parachute and pushed out the door manually.

"Most of these men from the Test Battery became part of the 456th Parachute Field Artillery Battalion, and about this same time, I was sent to the Officers Candidate School at Fort Sill, Oklahoma. While at school, the 82nd Airborne Division moved to Fort Bragg. I became a second lieutenant in the field artillery. Ironically enough, they assigned me back to the 456th. However, General Maxwell Taylor, who interviewed me for a possible 'general's aide' position, discovered that I was assigned to the same unit that I was as an enlisted man. He explained the fraternization possibility of old buddies, or between officers and enlisted men, and suggested I be sent to the 376th [Parachute Field Artillery Battalion]. I reported to Colonel Wilbur Griffith. There, I became one of the junior officers of A Battery."[7]

Many men assigned to rear-area jobs saw volunteering for the airborne as a way to get into the action. Private Lawrence H. Dunlop had been drafted in October 1941 and had trained as medical technician. "Right after Pearl Harbor, I was sent to Biloxi, Mississippi. Here, we opened a new hospital at Keesler Air Force Base. I did not intend to become a bedpan jockey and was working in the laboratory, blood typing thousands of new recruits. So I decided to get out of there. I signed up for the new Parachute Training School. About the first of May, 1942, I had to borrow money to go to Fort Benning, Georgia, from the Red Cross. We [privates] were only making twenty-one dollars a month."[8]

Like many others, Milton V. Knight wanted to contribute directly to winning the war. "I was a post motor sergeant at Camp Shelby, Mississippi, in charge of the post motor pool. I didn't feel like that was a very exciting duty, so yeah, I volunteered. Everybody that was in the parachute troops volunteered—there were no people in there that didn't want to be there."[9] All enlisted men and noncommissioned officers, such as Sergeant Knight, who volunteered for the Parachute School had to take a paper-bust to the rank of private.

Still others left civilian jobs and school to join the paratroopers. When Thomas J. McCarthy, from Worcester, Massachusetts, turned twenty-one years old, he made up his mind to join the service. "I tried the various branches and I wanted to get into the marines, but I was half an inch too short. I never had an inclination to join the air corps, they weren't my style. One day I was working, I was laying brick at that time. I wasn't too far from the post office in Worcester. I put my tools in my tool bag and I said to the boss, 'Hey Frank, I'll be back later.' I walked up Madison Street to the post office and walked into the recruiting office. There were some other guys there and they said, 'You might want to join the army.' Strange as it may be, [the recruiter] looked at me and he said 'What branch are you thinking?'

"I said, 'I'm going to be a paratrooper.'

" 'Right over here,' he said.

"I never got home. I still remember it because I had thirty-five cents in my pocket. They sent me to Fort Devens. I called collect from there to tell my mother I was in the army. She didn't quite believe it. But, I was in the army, alright.

"At my best, I was five feet five and half inches and about 128 pounds. I didn't have an inferiority complex, but everything was always an uphill fight. So, I figured I'll would start at the top and work down—what the hell.

"If there was something better than that, I didn't know what it was. I don't think I gave an awful lot of thought at that age of any of the dangers or any of those things were involved. I looked forward to it as more or less some kind of an adventure, jumping out of one of those planes. That sounded like a pretty good idea for an afternoon."[10]

Reneau G. Breard, from Monroe, Louisiana, was between his junior and senior academic year at Louisiana State University on December 7, 1941. "I had a date that afternoon, and when all of this was in an uproar, we were at the picture show. We came out of the show and heard everything going on.

"I was only a freshman in ROTC at LSU. I had had three years of CMTC [Citizens Military Training Camp] during the summers. It was four weeks of training. We did rifle marksmanship, drills, and firing weapons—we were firing the Springfield rifle and the 60mm mortar.

"In December, at Christmas '41, when I came home from Baton Rouge, I had a telegram arrive about the same time I did. I had been taking correspondence courses, and they told me that if I could finish those in the next three weeks, I could go before [an army review] board. If I passed the board, I would have to pass the physical to become a second lieutenant.

"I completed those [correspondence courses] and went back to LSU on time. They called me and told me they wanted me to go before the board. So, I took the bus from LSU to New Orleans and went before the board and passed it. They said to go home and wait for orders for a physical. I asked them about college, and they told me I would be called up immediately. I went ahead and talked to the professors at college, then went on home. By the latter part of February, nothing had happened, so I called back down there and talked to the registrar. They said come back and take your midterm exams late. So I did, and I passed them. Then, I packed my clothes and came back home.

"Then about April, I went to Barksdale Army Air base at Shreveport and had a medical exam and I passed that. They said go home and wait. I waited until the tenth of June, and then they called me. I got my commission in the summer of '42.

"I got on the train in Monroe, and the next morning I was in Anniston, Alabama. They had trucks out there—they were moving soldiers everywhere. I went on out there to Fort McClellan and reported in. They put me in an IRTC [Infantry Replacement Training Center] company, and they were taking draftees through eighteen-week training. They were in their tenth or twelfth week. They were out in the field, and I went out and met the company commander, and he told me they were coming in, in a couple of days, and he would like for me to go ahead and instruct on the light machine gun. I had never seen one.

"I went back in and got a gun and a manual from the supply sergeant and took it over to my hut. I just took the manual and stayed up with it for most of the night, and took it apart and put it back together. I was supposed to teach taking it apart and putting it back together. It was eight hours [of instruction], and I did pretty good, I guess. They had three sergeants there to help me.

"We had so many green second lieutenants just out of college that they had an officer school there. About the first of September, we went through the whole thing—the weapons, the drill, everything. It was good because of the physical training. They had a certain way they wanted it done. After about six weeks of it, with those draftees, I kind of knew what I was doing.

"One of the boys [in the officer school] left about the first of September and went to the parachute school. He came back and married a nurse at Fort McClellan, and I was his best man. He told me about jump school.

"So after he got married, me, the company commander, another officer, and two sergeants put in for the parachute school. I had been trying to go to the officer basic course at Fort Benning, and I would apply every month, but nobody was going—they had such a backlog. So, I went ahead and joined the parachute school and was going to go after I got out of parachute school.

"I had a physical—we sent in the physical with the request. The doctor said, 'They'll never take you, but I've got to approve you.' I had had an operation when I was eight years old. A car had run over me. I had scars on that leg.

"When we got to Fort Benning, probably a hundred of us, we took a physical and we went through naked. The doctors were looking at my appendicitis scar. I had had one just before I went to LSU and it was still raw. They looked up where the doctor who had done the operation got his degree. It was Tulane. I said, 'Do I pass?' and they said, 'Yes.' So, I went on through the line."[11]

IN FEBRUARY 1942, THE 82ND INFANTRY DIVISION was reactivated, having fought with distinction during World War I. One of its men, Sergeant Alvin C. York, had been the most decorated and famous American enlisted man of the war. The division had been nicknamed the All-American Division during the First World War, because its men were from every state in the union. On

August 15, 1942, near the end of its training at Camp Claiborne, Louisiana, the division's commanding officer, General Matthew B. Ridgway, announced to his troops that the 82nd Infantry Division would become an airborne division. At the time, Private Wesley E. Pass was home on a ten-day furlough. "On return I found myself in Company B, 325th Glider Infantry. I had never been up in an airplane. Shortly after, they asked for volunteers to go to parachute school. I reasoned that I'd rather be in a plane with a parachute than in a glider without one. After seeing the gliders after landing, I had made the right choice. The extra money and the shiny boots helped.

"I joined the 376th Parachute Field Artillery Battalion after graduating from jump school. The four weeks at Fort Benning were the hardest weeks I have ever experienced: push-ups and double time were rough."[12]

When the train carrying Private Darrell G. Harris pulled into the station at Fort Benning, he grabbed his barracks bag and made his way off the train. " 'You'll be sorry' was scrawled in the dirt, and several troopers with crutches and leg casts stood by awaiting the arrival of the troop train. This was a typical greeting for would-be paratroopers to the jump school at Fort Benning."[13]

The four-week course at the Parachute School at Fort Benning was one of the most demanding in the U.S. military at that time. The course was divided into four one-week stages—A, B, C, and D. In A stage, the candidates were pushed to the limits of their physical endurance. Private Lawrence C. Warthman also had decided to volunteer for the Parachute School instead of becoming a glider trooper. "The first week was mostly physical exercises, running, hand-to-hand combat.... We had to do many push-ups.... Seemed as though they tried every way to make one quit."[14]

In B-stage, the second week, students continued the physical training in the mornings, followed in the afternoon with instruction and practice in handling the parachute's risers to guide it; the proper ways to tumble to absorb the shock of landing, known as parachute landing falls (PLFs); and exiting a plane using a mockup of a C-47 doorway. The instructors at the Parachute School were legendary for weeding out those without courage and an iron will to succeed. Instructors would order pushups for the slightest infraction, real or imagined. One day during B-stage, Private Louis Orvin was performing one of the exercises to practice parachute landing falls: right-front tumbles and left-front tumbles. "We had a gadget where you would climb up and hang on a bar and slide down this cable. While you were sliding down this cable, he'll holler and tell you to do a right body turn or a left body turn. When you got to the end and hit the dirt, you jumped up and stood at exaggerated attention.

"He was talking to another instructor at the time. He told me to do a right body turn. I did a right body turn. I was standing at attention and he said, 'Give me twenty-five pushups.'

"I said, 'Sergeant, what did I do?'"

"He said, 'I told you to do a left body turn and you did a right body turn.'"

"I said, 'Sergeant, you told me to do a right body turn, and I did a right body turn.'"

"He said, 'If I told you to do a right body turn, you did a left one. If I told you to do a left one, you did a right one. Give me twenty-five.'"

"So I said, 'Yes, sir!' "[15]

The instructors took particular pleasure in punishing officers. One day, during B-stage, Lieutenant Reneau Breard was caught leaning against the wall of one of the sheds as his class was practicing landing falls. "There was a sergeant named Wall and he made me run around the area twice saying, 'Sergeant Wall is on the ball. He caught me leaning against the wall.' Then you gave them fifty pushups after you ran."[16]

C-stage simulated each aspect of a parachute jump. It was at this time that Private Warthman realized the reason behind all of those pushups during the previous two weeks. "First, there was the wind machine, an airplane motor and propeller that created the air. We were put in a harness and would lie on the ground, face down. Two men would hold the parachute up to catch the air. When everything was ready, they would turn on the machine. It would drag one; we would roll over on our backs and come up on our feet, then run around and collapse the parachute. If you were not successful, it would drag you."[17] It took tremendous strength, using the arms' tricep and the chest's pectoral muscles—the precise muscles that the endless number of pushups during the previous two weeks had targeted—to keep from being dragged and to collapse the parachute.

The thirty-four-foot tower was probably responsible for more students washing out of parachute school than any other single factor. At the top of the tower was a platform with a mockup of a C-47 doorway. A steel cable ran inside the platform and down from the top of the doorway diagonally to the ground. The student wore a parachute harness with a static line attached, which he would hook up to the cable. On command from an instructor, he would exit the doorway in the proper form and manner. The student would drop twelve feet before the static line caught him, whereupon he would slide down the cable to a point where a mechanism tripped a release on the static line and the student fell into a pile of sawdust, where he executed a PLF, then quickly recovered to stand at attention. Private Warren J. Le Vangia was one of many troopers who felt that the tower was the most frightening aspect of jump school. "For some reason, the mock jump from the thirty-four-foot training tower was the worst part for me. Looking at the ground from that height looked more dangerous than twelve hundred feet ever did."[18]

The 250-foot towers simulated the height and rate of descent of a parachute drop. Each tower had four arms, aligned to the points on a compass, only three of which were used simultaneously, avoiding the arm facing into the wind because of the danger on that side of being blown into the tower itself. The A-tower consisted of a buddy-seat attached to each arm. Two students would ride the seat to the top, then would suddenly descend at the speed of a parachute drop to the ground.

On the B-tower, students suspended from a parachute canopy by their harnesses experienced a descent from the top of the tower at the same rate of as a real parachute drop.

The C-tower was the most frightening for most troopers and was particularly memorable for Private Warthman. "It was a device with elastic straps, the harness was equipped with a ripcord release. We were strapped in a face-down prone position. They would pull us to the top and then tell us to pull the [D-ring attached to a] ripcord. We would fall about 15–20 feet, then the elastic straps would give us a jerk similar to the opening shock of a parachute, then the cable would let us down at the speed of a falling parachute. Do not drop the [D-ring attached to the] ripcord, that is more push-ups."[19]

On the final tower, D-tower, a parachute suspended by cables to keep the canopy deployed was attached to the student's harness. The student and the open parachute ascended to the top of the tower and then released. The student used the parachute's risers to guide the parachute as an instructor on the ground with a megaphone communicated adjustments to the student during the descent.

During each afternoon that week, students received instruction in packing parachutes. Private Warthman recalled an incident that emphasized the absolute criticality of packing every chute precisely as instructed. "We had been double-timing around the airfield and out on the drop zone. Everyone was ready to drop. It had all been planned, but we did not know that. The instructor had us fall out for a break. At that time, a C-47 appeared over the drop zone. The instructor said, 'I think we are going to see a jump.' At that time the jumper came out, the parachute immediately tangled into a streamer, and the jumper plunged to earth, hit the ground in a cloud of dust with a loud thud, bounced about ten feet, and lay still. The instructor said, 'what you have witnessed was a streamer. How many want to go look?' Some got sick. He said, 'We will all go look.' It was a dummy. We all had a laugh and double-timed back."[20]

On Friday, each student packed the parachute that he would use for the jump on Monday, giving him all weekend to worry about whether he had done it correctly. On the following Monday, the first day of D-stage, and the final week, Lieutenant Breard made his first qualifying jump. "They divided us up into so many people, and we'd walk through these elongated buildings with seats on either side. They'd put a plane outside of there and they would come get you. I went in there and sat down and looked across and there was a friend from Monroe, an engineer officer. He had graduated from VMI [Virginia Military Institute] two years earlier. I was glad to see him.

"I guess I was nervous—I guess everybody was on that first jump. I went out, and I counted one thousand, two thousand, three thousand, and the damned thing opened. I looked up and checked my canopy. There was a boy right near me, and he was yelling so much. So, we all started yelling, 'Geronimo!' We jumped from about twelve hundred feet, so we had a good ride down. I was ready to go the next day."[21]

Private Warren Le Vangia had never been in an airplane until the Monday of D-stage. "When the red light in the C-47 turned green, my stomach did too. As the third or fourth man in line, I barely had time to think as I shoved my static line forward on the cable and went out the door. I think that the memory of that first jump always stays with every paratrooper. My memory is of the incredible blast of wind, the falling, the thought that I did not do everything that I had been taught, remembering to count just as I heard and felt the parachute open and knowing that I had started to count too late. After checking the canopy, I found the windsock, heard the instructor with the bullhorn yelling at me, climbed a riser to turn into the wind, and hit the ground very, very hard. With the instructor screaming that I hadn't turned quickly enough, I just sat there for a moment and grinned at him. When he stopped yelling and grinned back—I knew that in spite of the moment of terror when I left the plane—that I was really a paratrooper—all the way!"[22]

Private Leo M. Hart had a very different experience on his first jump. "I really felt exhilarated on the first jump, and as I was coming down, I thought, 'Oh gee, this was something I could do, because this was such a wonderful experience. I'm ready to do this immediately.' I would have gone back up in five minutes.

"But I think overnight, as you gave it more thought, you became more concerned about the second jump. And I think I was more anxious during the second jump than the first jump, much more so.

"The jump that I really, really recall was when I led the stick—that was my last qualifying jump. We had a jumpmaster who stood with us while we were waiting, who warned us for the green light. I remember he was singing these little songs that were all gruesome and telling me, 'Look down, find that ambulance, and keep it in your mind, because he's waiting for you.' I'll never forget that pleasant conversation we had before I led out."[23]

The students made five qualifying jumps, one daily from Monday through Friday, and graduated on Saturday. At the graduation ceremony, each received a certificate documenting the successful completion of the Parachute School course, and shiny new silver wings were pinned to their chests. For the first time, the new paratroopers would be allowed to wear their jump boots outside the training area and blouse their trousers to show off those boots. Each trooper worked to put a mirror shine on his boots. Private Hart felt that the instructors during jump school "were strict and they were difficult, but I think they did an excellent job of bringing us through the training. I thought jump school was a great experience."[24]

The percentage of officers and men in Lieutenant Breard's class who made it successfully through the course was typical. "Out of the class of about a hundred, we had probably fifty officers and fifty enlisted men. We ended up with about 45 percent who made the grade."[25]

Private Milton Knight felt that the tremendous effort required to become paratroopers had been worthwhile. "The training period was pretty damn tough. It was go from daylight to dark, and a lot of times after dark. It took as much as you had and then some, to get through this thing. But when you got through it, you were fit to do whatever needed to be done, physically and mentally.

"The thing that distinguished Airborne soldiers from the rest of the army and so forth, I think, was the fact that we were all volunteers; we volunteered for the duty and the esprit de corps was much higher than in any other unit that I know of, except maybe the marines.

"The thing that made us a cut above the rest, I think, was the training that we went through to become what we were."[26]

THE 504TH PARACHUTE INFANTRY WAS FORMED on May 1, 1942. Major Reuben Tucker was one of the cadre of ten officers and eighty-six enlisted men, primarily from the 504th Parachute Infantry Battalion, assigned to lead the formation of the regiment. "Colonel [Theodore L. 'Ted'] Dunn was given command of the regiment and started to build the splendid outfit that was the regiment: Captain [Julian A.] Cook, Captain [Charles W.] Kouns, Captain [William] Colville, Captain [William R.] Beall, Major [Leslie G.] Freeman, Major [Warren R.] Williams, and Major [Reuben H.] Tucker.

"The months of May and June were devoted to training the cadre. An intensive schedule was followed so that the cadre was well prepared to receive the newcomers during the first week of July.

"Our training was interrupted somewhat by the moving of one battalion at a time to the Alabama area, but by the 19th of August, the entire regiment was in Alabama.

"August 15th we were incorporated in the All-American 82nd Division."[27]

Private Milton Knight joined Headquarters Company, 1st Battalion, the day after graduating from Parachute School, July 31, 1942. "When you got into our outfit, everybody was the same. You didn't have any ethnic disagreements. Everybody was treated alike and as long as you did your job—as long as you did what you were supposed to—hell, it didn't make any difference if you were German Jew or American or South American or Italian or what. We were all together in the thing and we did for each other just like we were supposed to.

"We were like a big family. We looked out for each other—we did things for each other that you'd do for your own brother. The NCOs took care of the men under them. The officers took care of the men under them, and a lot of times, the NCOs took care of the officers."[28]

Knight rose rapidly to the rank of sergeant. "I had the S-2 section. An S-2 section were the people that gathered information, interrogated prisoners, went on patrols to make reconnaissance of the area, and things like that. In the section, I had all foreign-speaking soldiers to do the interrogation work—I had Germans, I had Italians, and I had some people in there that spoke more than two languages. I had one guy that spoke seven languages. I had some very good people. We got along well and had a lot of fun in our unit."[29]

One of the original members of Company C, Private Ross Pippin, described the training in the Alabama Area—a training area across the Chattahoochee River from Fort Benning— as "intense and rugged. Some marches were over twenty miles or more in a single day. We were also given a lot of weapon training. We were taught how to operate our weapons in the dark. There were some times that I really thought I had made a mistake by joining the paratroopers, and then I would see some scrawny little guys who wouldn't quit, and I thought to myself, 'If they can make it, so can I.' At the end of the training, I was beginning to appreciate it more and more."[30]

Private Louis Orvin graduated from Parachute School in August 1942, just as the 3rd Battalion was being formed. "At the graduation, we went to the theater, and there was a general on the stage and he got up and told us, 'I know you men are very proud of accomplishing this feat of jumping out of an airplane. But, I'm here to tell you that you have just finished 1 percent of your training—the other 99 percent is regular infantry. The rest of your training, you'll train just like regular infantry, but you'll have less equipment to do it with.'

"It was like sticking a pin in a balloon—we were so proud of being paratroopers. He was right—we learned that.

"We went to the Frying Pan [area south of Fort Benning] and we stayed there for a week or two, and then they formed units. They put me in I Company of the 504. I was a charter member."[31]

Early on, because every enlisted man who had graduated from the Parachute School was a private, men were given an opportunity to demonstrate their leadership qualities for possible promotion to corporals and sergeants to lead the squads. Private Orvin had an advantage over many of the others, having spent twenty-six months in the artillery, some of it as a corporal. "The instructors would call different people out and tell you, 'You give the next group of calisthenics.' When it was my turn, I gave the commands to do a few exercises and then when I got finished I said, 'Stand At Ease.' The instructor said, 'No, no, that's wrong.'

"I was a smartass. I said, 'Sergeant, if you'll look on page thirty-four of your training manual for calisthenics.' I knew exactly where it was.

"He said, 'Oh, oh, yeah, that's right, that's right.' I don't think he knew at all. After that, they made me a corporal and then it wasn't long before they made me a sergeant and put me as head of the third squad, which was the mortar squad. But, they thought since I had had artillery training, that that would help. But there is nothing similar [between] a mortar and a 105mm cannon."[32]

When the 3rd Battalion, under the command of Major Leslie G. Freeman, joined the regiment in the Alabama Area in the third week of August, the formation of the 504 was complete.

ON AUGUST 16, 1942, THE 376TH PARACHUTE FIELD ARTILLERY BATTALION was activated under the command of Major Paul E. Wright. The cadre for the battalion came from the original Parachute Test Battery. When Captain Frank D. Boyd joined Headquarters Battery, he found its composition, weapons, transport, and operating procedures to be different from the field artillery battalion of the 35th Infantry Division, with which he had served previously. "Howitzer batteries in the 376th had about 100 men and officers at full strength. Headquarters and Headquarters Battery had nearly 150, of which probably 20 were officers. It was the largest of the five. It had the largest motor pool and transported most supplies for the battalion. One of the battery's responsibilities was communications. In addition to net control radio stations and telephone switchboards, it provided equipment and personnel for all liaison officers and some forward observers. Forward observers attached to infantry battalions came from the gun batteries. These staff officers and their sections were in Headquarters Battery: S-1, personnel records; S-2, intelligence, including surveying; S-3, operations, fire-direction center; [and] S-4, supply. The medical detachment of two surgeons and eight or ten men was attached to Headquarters Battery for supply and administration, just like a platoon within the battery. The battalion adjutant worked closely with all sections, preparing the necessary order for their operations. We also had a parachute maintenance section (riggers) whose job it was to pack parachutes after jumps and salvage them from battlefields or drop zones.

"The battalion included three batteries of four 75mm pack howitzers each, a headquarters battery, and an antitank/antiaircraft battery. The 75mm pack howitzer was a modification of the old mountain howitzer that could be taken apart and transported on pack mules. We took it apart and dropped it by parachute then tried to find all the components and put it back together once we were on the ground.

"The only real difference was in the axle and wheels. Our howitzer had a high-speed axle for towing behind jeeps, and the wheels were much smaller and had pneumatic tires. The mountain howitzer had larger wheels with wooden spokes and iron-band tires. At the beginning of the war, it was the only gun in the U.S. Army arsenal that could be taken apart into pieces that could be dropped by parachute. Our problem was finding all the parts after we were on the ground. Parts of the howitzer occupied five bomb shackles [underneath the C-47s,] and the sixth contained ammunition. Other planes carried additional ammunition. The loads were released by the jumpmaster. Each battery had equipment parachutes of a different color for identification, when collecting their equipment. Equipment chutes were made of rayon, personnel chutes were of silk. The one bundle that would not fit into the bomb shackles beneath the C-47 was the wheels. We strapped a pair of wheels, one on either side of a heavy plywood box containing the breech-block, tied it to a parachute, and kicked it out of the door. I have deep affection and respect for that little gun. It could not demolish stone buildings nor bridges, but it was deadly against enemy personnel.

"The main reason we had large gun crews was that the howitzers had to be moved by manpower until jeeps could be brought in by glider. Each gun section had six ropes, called 'prolongs' with which they pulled like Volga boatmen. Two other men held up the trail by placing the tail spike through the lunette. Two men pushed from the muzzle end and four pulled the ropes. These four also made themselves useful in bringing up ammunition. One of them was used to pass ammunition from the fuse-setter to the loader. Initially the gun crews operated without protection, but as time allowed, they were dug into gun pits. We seldom had access to sandbags. Each section had a corporal (gunner), who set the sight, a number one cannoneer, who fired the piece on command, a loader and a fuse-setter.

"All three of the howitzer batteries (four guns each) and most of headquarters battery personnel were paratroopers. The antitank/antiaircraft battery and some of the service personnel (motor pool, supply, et cetera) rode the CG-4A gliders. The AA-AT battery initially was equipped with a 37mm anti-tank gun that was not effective against anything more heavily armored than the lightest tanks. Later those guns were replaced with a high-velocity 57mm gun. It could not penetrate heavy armor but could jam turrets and knock off tank tracks. The antiaircraft platoon was equipped with single-mount .50-caliber machine guns. They carried both the regular ground mounts and a light, unstable anti-aircraft mount that was little more than tripod holding a vertical 'gas pipe' with the gun at the top. It shook badly while being fired.

"D Battery had two fighting platoons, one antiaircraft and one antitank. The third platoon was headquarters and service, the latter being supply and transportation. The antitank platoon had 57mm 'rifles.' They were low-silhouette weapons, mounted on two wheels and towed by jeeps. They were very accurate, but would not pierce heavy armor. Our gunners aimed at tank tracks or the junction of turret and body. A hit there froze the mechanism, so that the turret could not be rotated. If they could then knock off a track the tank was disabled. The infantry then went out after dark and completed the wreckage with thermite grenades. The 57mm gun was American made [and] had a longer range and greater accuracy than the British six-pounder. The three gun batteries each had two .30-caliber machine guns with ground mounts, only for the protection of the battery command posts.

"D Battery was the antiaircraft/antitank battery. Fewer than half of its men were parachutists. It had the usual battery headquarters administrative and supply and maintenance people, but the majority of the men were divided between the large AA and AT platoons. The AA men were jumpers because their .50-caliber machine guns could be dropped by parachute. The 57mm A.T. guns had to come in by glider, and their crews were not parachutists. Some of the supply and maintenance people in Headquarters Battery were not parachutists. I cannot remember the battalion's total authorized strength, probably something around 650 men and officers."[33]

DURING THE FIRST MONTHS OF THE REGIMENT'S EXISTENCE the command and staff positions were a revolving door, as officers were promoted and moved to fill new openings as each of the three battalions were formed. By September 1, 1942, the regiment's officer assignments had settled somewhat, with Dunn's regimental staff consisting of Major Tucker (executive officer); Lieutenant Harry J. Cummings, S-1 (personnel); Captain William Colville, Jr., S-2 (intelligence); Captain Charles W. Kouns, S-3 (plans and operations); and Captain G. R. Cox, S-4 (supply).

The commanding officer of Headquarters Company was Captain William E. Hornby. His executive officer was Lieutenant Fred W. Vance, who was also the regiment's gas warfare officer. Lieutenant H. C. Hupperick commanded the regimental demolitions platoon.

Service Company's commander was Captain Edward N. Wellems, who was also the regiment's parachute maintenance officer. The adjutant was Lieutenant Mack C. Shelly, and the munitions officer was Lieutenant William A. B. Addison.

Captain F. S. Swift, the regimental surgeon, commanded the 307th Airborne Medical Company detachment assigned to the regiment. Because of a shortage of parachute-qualified surgeons, there were only two battalion surgeons at that time, Lieutenants F. G. Sheehan and Kenneth I. Sheek.

Major Warren R. Williams, Jr., was the commanding officer of the 1st Battalion, with a staff of Captain George W. Rice, executive officer; Lieutenant

S. E. Powers, S-1; and Lieutenant Willard E. Harrison, S-2 and S-3.

The 2nd Battalion was commanded by Major D. A. DeArmond, with Major Daniel W. Danielson, executive officer; Lieutenant P. E. Allemandi, S-1; and Lieutenant Arthur W. Ferguson, S-2 and S-3, as the battalion staff.

Major Leslie G. Freeman commanded the 3rd Battalion. Captain Julian A. Cook was the executive officer; Lieutenant Forrest E. Richter, the S-1; and Captain Abdallah K. Zakby, the S-2 and S-3.

IN SEPTEMBER, GENERAL RIDGWAY AND MEMBERS of the 82nd Airborne Division headquarters staff visited Fort Benning to make a parachute jump and to evaluate Colonel Dunn and the newly assigned 504th. Dunn staged a demonstration jump for the group, one of whom was the division signal officer, Lieutenant Colonel Frank W. Moorman. As the paratroopers gathered their parachutes, Moorman saw Dunn turn to the division chief of staff, Colonel Maxwell D. Taylor, and say, "Well that's it."[34]

Taylor replied, "What do you mean, that's it? They haven't *done* anything."[35]

Moorman knew that "Taylor meant they hadn't made any tactical maneuvers on the ground—no military achievement, merely the jump itself. There was this definite feeling that the job ended with the jump."[36]

Colonel Taylor believed "everyone was too jump-happy. There was too little emphasis on infantry tactics."[37]

WHEN PRIVATE LAWRENCE WARTHMAN ARRIVED AT FORT BRAGG with Battery B, 376th Parachute Field Artillery Battalion, the battalion initially slept in tents in the motor pool area. "We and all our personal belongings were put through a de-bugging process. They did have bed bugs at Fort Benning. After going through this process, we were placed in barracks, two stories. One building housed one battery. We started our training in Fort Bragg around 30 September 1942. We trained hard all this time. We would run five miles every morning before breakfast; about all our time was in the field firing the pack 75s and on the rifle range. We made several jumps, of which I made most of them. I liked jumping and would volunteer for all of them."[38]

On October 1, 1942, the 82nd Airborne Division began moving from Camp Claiborne, Louisiana, to Fort Bragg, North Carolina. On October 14, 1942, the 504th Parachute Infantry Regiment joined the 82nd Airborne Division at Fort Bragg. There, it joined with the 376th Parachute Field Artillery Battalion, Battery C, 80th Airborne Antiaircraft (Antitank) Battalion, and Company C, 307th Airborne Engineer Battalion to form the 504th Regimental Combat Team. Shortly after the arrival of the regiment, an inspection was held for General Leslie McNair's Army Ground Forces staff, in which two of the three battalions failed.

On October 20, 1942, the commanding officer of the 376th Parachute

Field Artillery Battalion, Major Paul Wright, transferred to command the 320th Glider Field Artillery Battalion. The executive officer, Captain Robert H. Neptune, took over as acting commander of the 376th the following day.

By Thanksgiving 1942, the 504th Parachute Infantry Regiment's company-level officer assignments had settled somewhat. In the 1st Battalion, Captain William R. Beall commanded Company A (Able Company), Captain Willard E. Harrison commanded Company B (Baker), Captain Jack M. Bartley commanded Company C (Charlie), and Lieutenant William A. B. Addison commanded Headquarters Company.

In the 2nd Battalion, Captain Stanley M. Dolezal commanded Company D (Dog Company), Captain Arthur W. Ferguson commanded Company E (Easy), Lieutenant Melvin W. Nitz commanded Company F (Fox), and Lieutenant Malcolm A. Nicholson commanded Headquarters Company.

Among the 3rd Battalion's company commanders were Captain Lawrence P. Johnson, Company H (How); Captain George M. Warfield, Company I (Item); and Herbert C. Kaufman, Headquarters Company.

As a result of the poor inspection performance and other factors, General Ridgway relieved Colonel Dunn of command on December 16, 1942, for his "inability to achieve results" and promoted his executive officer, Lieutenant Colonel Reuben Tucker, to replace him. Because Tucker was only thirty-one years old at the time, one of the youngest regimental commanders in the U.S. Army, it took Ridgway another six months to obtain Tucker's promotion to the rank of colonel. Lieutenant Colonel Frank Moorman described Tucker as "a wonderful athlete and soldier—fearless, dedicated. A gung-ho combat officer, exactly the kind of fellow you want when you go to war."[39]

Major Leslie Freeman was promoted to regimental executive officer and was replaced as 3rd Battalion commander by Captain Charles W. Kouns, who was soon promoted to major. The 1st and 2nd Battalions remained under the command of Majors Warren Williams and D. A. DeArmond, respectively.

Shortly after taking command of the 504, Lieutenant Colonel Tucker issued a message to the officers and men of his regiment, in which he alluded to the previous problems while still motivating them with words of encouragement:

"Since the organization of our splendid regiment, we have covered a great deal of ground together, and have taken part in various types of training. Now, we stand on the threshold of combat against Tojo and Schickelgruber. I feel we are all ready and anxious to get in there and do our part. Things have not always run smoothly, and we have had our share of obstacles to overcome. However, in actual battle similar obstacles will arise, and together with the din of firing will form what is called the 'fog of war.' When that condition arises, it will be the man who has kept his head during training, and carried out his mission regardless of obstacles, who will do the same thing in war.

"Together we have built a team which need bow its head to no one, friend or foe. There are still points to be smoothed down, and subjects to be polished up, but I know we have what it takes, and when the history of this war is written, the name of the 504th Parachute Infantry will be printed in deeds that will live forever in the memory of men.

"It is your regiment. Everything you say or do reflects on it's standard, and by the same token, any glory or commendation it may receive belongs to you.

"No one has ever been prouder or happier to command any unit than I am to command this regiment. I consider myself very fortunate to have all of you, officers and men, working with me. Let's all of us pull together and remember one thing. There isn't any enemy that can beat us, and when the time comes, if God wills that we should fall on the field of battle, be sure that we get at least ten enemy lives for every one of our own."[40]

Tucker immediately initiated tough training for the regiment. Private First Class Warren Le Vangia was an original member of Company D. "We spent months in the field with more basic infantry training, weapon firing, unit coordination, and maneuvering from company to regiment. In addition to many day parachute jumps, we also made many night jumps. Not knowing when you would hit the ground and not being able to prepare for landing at the right moment increased sprains and fractures. Being either very tough or very lucky, I had none of either."[41]

Upon his return to Company I at Fort Bragg after hospitalization with a jump injury in the Alabama Area, Private Edward P. Haider quickly discovered Colonel Tucker's emphasis on tough training. "We were back to double-timing it everywhere we went. We made day jumps, we made night jumps, we learned about a variety of weapons, and spent a good deal of time on the target range.

"One morning at 0600 we were mustered out with packs and rifles and began a three-mile march to a nearby lake. North Carolina is known for its mild winters—well, this was not one of them. It was about fifteen degrees out; you can imagine how we all felt. Our commander, a man named Captain [George M.] Warfield, was one tough guy—but fair with all of us. He was a good leader. At the lake, he kept marching and walked right in, clothes and all, saying, 'Follow me across!' This was when we all thought he had flipped his lid. We thought, 'That water is cold!' But we all followed him right into the lake and started across.

"We devised our shelter-halves (which is one-half of a pup tent, buttoned together along the top) with our rifles so they floated in the shelter half and we, with Mae Wests (which was the common name of our flotation vest), practically swam across the lake. When we reached the other side, about a quarter of a mile swim, our clothes began to instantly freeze on us as soon as we were out of the water. Captain Warfield's idea for keeping warm was to double-time it back to the barracks. As soon as we got there, we all took hot showers to try and warm up."[42]

One of the Company I officers particularly impressed Private Haider. "One of our platoon leaders, a second lieutenant [Henry B. Keep], was from Pittsburgh, Pennsylvania. His family was well-to-do; they apparently had a lot of stock in Pittsburgh Steel. One day, he noticed that we sure waited a long time for buses to get into town. Fayetteville was about ten miles away, and the city buses were our only means of transportation. One day, the lieutenant was in town and he up and buys a brand new Buick. According to what we heard, the lieutenant walked onto the showroom floor and shelled out the cash for his new black 1942 Buick. He said we could all use it for trips to town whenever we wanted.

"The Buick was used many a night to go Charlie hunting. Charlie, you see, had a tremendous taste for beer. We often found ourselves going from one Fayetteville tavern to the next till we found Charlie. It usually didn't take too long to find him. Two of us would go in, and with one of us on each side of Charlie, we'd literally drag him out to the Buick. Upon getting him back to the barracks, we'd throw Charlie right in the shower, clothes and all, and then we'd put him to bed. Yell—he sure could holler at us. Next day he never knew what took place the night before. Charlie was really a wonderful guy—he was our platoon's sniper. Charlie grew up in a rural area, where he developed his shot by doing a lot of hunting—he was a very good marksman.

"The times seemed to bring out the best in some people. When you were lucky enough to get some time off, Lieutenant Henry would always make sure you had enough money to cover the fare home and a little extra just for spending money. He was very generous toward the men in the company. . . . One Saturday night, he threw a company party, a big dance with all the trimmings—snacks and soft drinks for everyone. He had several loads of girls brought in from the local college. The lieutenant arranged for trucks to transport the girls to the base and then back again to their school. We got the trucks all cleaned up and made sure the girls had benches to sit on.

"Lieutenant Henry was in a class all by himself. He was the most generous person I had ever seen or met. On one occasion, just before we went overseas, we were going to hold a uniform inspection. They wanted to make sure no buttons were missing, no rips in the clothes or any tears. All the replacement clothes any of us needed were paid for by the lieutenant. He always seemed to go above and beyond for us—no matter what it cost him. Before we left to go overseas, Lieutenant Keep gave the Buick as a gift to another lieutenant, so his wife would have transportation while we were gone.

"Once during our stint at Fort Bragg, Lieutenant Henry invited all the officers in our company to his home in Pennsylvania for a weekend. We couldn't wait to ask them what their weekend was like. From what we heard upon their return, they had a wonderful time. No one wanted to come back to Bragg."[43]

While training at Fort Bragg, Private Fred J. Baldino, with Company A, met a young man who had grown up in Germany and immigrated to the United States. "[Private First Class] Theodore H. Ted Bachenheimer was teaching an intelligence section that I was assigned to. Ted had in his possession a German Army manual and was teaching us the methods of the German Army. He was assigned to Headquarters Company, 1st Battalion."[44]

On January 4, 1943, Major Wilbur M. Griffith took command of the 376th Parachute Field Artillery Battalion, and Robert Neptune, now a major himself, returned to his prior position as battalion executive officer.

In March 1943, at the recommendation of General Ridgway, Major William P. Yarborough replaced Major DeArmond as commanding officer of the 2nd Battalion. Yarborough, one of the early pioneers of the airborne and a 1936 graduate of the U.S. Military Academy, had joined the 501st Parachute Infantry Battalion as commanding officer of Company C in late 1940. As test officer for the Provisional Parachute Group, he had designed the jump boots, jumpsuit, and parachutist qualification badge—the highly coveted jump wings. As executive officer of the 2nd Battalion, 509th Parachute Infantry Regiment, he had participated in the first U.S. Army combat jumps in North Africa in November and December 1942.

After the 505th Parachute Infantry Regiment made history on March 29, 1943, by making the first regimental-sized mass parachute jump near Camden, South Carolina, the 504th planned a regimental jump near Myrtle Beach, South Carolina, for the following day. However, as the regiment's planes approached, a thick fog came in from the Atlantic Ocean, enveloping the three drop zones and forcing cancellation of the jump, much to the disappointment of the regiment's troopers.

The units of the 82nd Airborne Division ceased training exercises on April 1, 1943, to prepare for movement overseas. In early April, officers attended briefings to prepare for the movement. Lieutenant James E. Baugh was the motor pool officer with Headquarters Battery, 80th Airborne Antiaircraft (Antitank) Battalion. "The preparation to get aboard the train was meticulous. We were not to talk to anyone; neither would we divulge the identity of our division or unit. Our shoulder patches that were emblazoned with the AA square patch with the airborne crest had to be covered. We were told that the railroad coaches in which we would be traveling would have all the shades pulled. When the train stopped, our personnel would not be permitted off the train. The battalion would travel as a unit, being under the command of [Lieutenant Colonel] Raymond E. Singleton. We would be supplied with K-rations aboard and our canteens would be filled prior to boarding the train. The trip north would require about two days."[45]

Chapter 2

"Another Hellhole"

On April 17, 1943, the 504th Regimental Combat Team and the other 82nd Airborne Division units began moving by train from Fort Bragg to Camp Edwards, Massachusetts, in strict secrecy. When Private Henry "Hank" D. Ussery, Jr., with Headquarters Battery, 376th Parachute Field Artillery Battalion, arrived at the Fort Bragg train station in the early morning hours, he knew that something significant was transpiring. "We had covered our 82nd Airborne Division insignias and all other things that showed in any way that we were paratroopers. We did not know in any way where we were going or when we would arrive."[1]

That same morning at Fort Benning and Fort Mitchell, near the Alabama Area, troop trains carrying replacement personnel of EGBs 447 and 448, pulled out of the train stations. Private Francis W. "Mac" McLane had been picked up by MPs while on furlough in Columbus, Georgia, a few days before and "placed under restriction—no explanation. On Monday morning, I was on a troop train bound for a port of embarkation, which was Camp Shanks, New York. I found out that I had 'volunteered' to go overseas with the 82nd Division. It was so secret that I wasn't allowed to write home."[2]

As the train carrying the 80th Airborne Antiaircraft (Antitank) Battalion chugged northward, Lieutenant James Baugh and the other glider troopers of Headquarters Battery sat in their blacked-out passenger car. "As the afternoon passed into night, we settled down after eating our K-ration and other knick-knacks that we picked up at the PX [post exchange]. We attempted to sleep, but there was little rest during the night. The continuous thud and bumping of the wheels across the tracks disturbed our rest. By early the next morning, I was able to peep out around the shades, and it was evident we were approaching Washington, D.C. We were served hot coffee with our ration, and the train finally came to a stop at the station in Washington. Everybody was all excited that by chance the president or a member of his staff would board the train for a few words of welcome and a send-off with gusto. This, of course, did not happen, and it was really understandable, with the large number of troops on the march and being transported through Washington. I wanted to leave the train to pick up a newspaper I saw on the newsstand, but I had to be satisfied with one passed around in the coach. As we stayed for a while, perhaps an hour there, I began to feel a sense of urgency to everybody in view. They were rushing about the train station and streets; the traffic was very heavy. This made us feel that we must be a part of an important undertaking. It was difficult to see the whole picture of the world from the vantage point of a railroad car."[3]

The train carrying Private William R. "Bill" Leonard, an EGBer, arrived at the Washington, D.C., train yard during the middle of the night. "While they were exchanging engines, quite a few men took off for home—went AWOL [absent without leave]. All companies were missing men that night."[4]

When Lieutenant Baugh's train left Washington, D.C., "going north to Philadelphia, then to New Jersey, I was impressed with the immensity of our country. I had never been north before. I was a Southerner with roots back to the Civil War and beyond. My grandfather had fought in Northern Virginia and sustained a serious wound in the Battle of the Wilderness. The size of the buildings in this part of the country was impressionable. The train picked up speed in New Jersey, and as it was approaching New York, the speed was slowed. The tunnel under the Hudson (the Holland) was the signal that we had in fact crossed into the city of New York. The tall buildings were an impressive sight, surpassing anything seen in Washington. There was a pause at the station in New York City, and I could tell there were many rail lines, and they were all busy. Aboard the train there was a bustle of activity, with all sorts of instructions about the next leg of our journey that we would be going toward Boston. At no time was I fully informed of our ultimate destination. We all thought we would be debarking in New York City, because from there, most embarkations took place for overseas service.

"As our train entered New England, I could fancy the stories about the early settlers in Massachusetts and Connecticut. From my point of vantage in the train, I saw weather that was comparable to winter weather in Georgia. It was misty, rainy, and cold. I would think that down home the farmer would be planting cotton. As we approached the coastline the fog was evident. The train slowed as we approached the Boston area. I wondered if we would stop here, but no—we were told we would proceed to a military base used for staging out on 'Buzzards Bay.'

"The military base was Camp Edwards. Along the coast and out on Cape Cod, the train was very slow. We would be given assignments that we would only be at the area about seven days. I would remain with the headquarters detachment and supervise the vehicles, unless they were sent in ahead. My small group had already prepared to board ship.

"The train finally came to a stop, and we prepared to detrain. As our transportation arrived, we were driven to the billets on the small enclave, which was near a small town. The name of the waterfront was called 'Buzzards Bay.' The whole area was unimpressive and not especially prosperous. There were stores, shops, and churches, and a cemetery not too far from where we stayed. Our daily meetings with the commanding officer consisted of fragments of projected schedules; we were to leave the staging area and proceed to our next stop, which would probably be New York City. There was nothing definite about this. I think the higher-up officers did not want to be definite about anything for fear that this would be a tip-off that would endanger our crossing."[5]

After arriving at Camp Edwards, Major Robert Neptune, the 376th Parachute Field Artillery Battalion's executive officer, worked hard to get the last preparations completed before departure to the port of embarkation, "issuing clothes, taking up clothes, re-issuing, getting vaccinations and shots. Some of our lads came across some engineers wearing jump boots. They got a gang and overpowered the engineers, took their boots, cut off the tops and gave them back.

"On 26 April I received orders to entrain for POE [port of embarkation]. The following day the loading of the train was a riot. General [Charles L.] Keerans was in the way. He thought the men could put their full equipment and their barracks bags in their watch pockets and comfortably walk aboard. The G-1 fouled up the detail too by getting less cars for us than we were admittedly required. The train ride to New York was uneventful."[6]

On the afternoon of April 27, Lieutenant Baugh boarded the train carrying his battalion. "The train ride to New York was well planned, with even more security precautions than our trip from Fayetteville to Buzzards Bay area. The time to depart was in the evening, which set our arrival time at least midnight or after. I had done all the preparing I personally could over the past week we had been in our staging area. April was about to become history, but due to the inclement weather, we were all in a hurry to leave. The train was just an ordinary train with the windows [shades] pulled, and we entered and took our seats."[7]

From there, the troopers boarded a ferry for Staten Island. Private Ussery struggled under the heavy load as he walked up the gangplank to the ferry. "It was plenty tough trying to carry two bags (A&B), plus all your field equipment and rifle. From here, we arrived in Staten Island, New York . . . a lonely trip . . . one a fellow can never forget. It seemed like hours before we arrived on the island, but actually it was only a few minutes. A million thoughts ran through my mind on that night. As we stepped off of the ferry, a fellow tried to help me off with the bags. I appreciated the hand but almost fell anyhow. The Red Cross was waiting on the pier with a pack of cigarettes and a doughnut. The doughnut tasted wonderful, especially after carrying those darn bags from the pier right onto the boat and, what a boat: the *George Washington*, a German boat converted into a troop transport. One of the largest of its kind."[8]

Private Arthur Foster, a member of EGB 448, stood on the main deck of the *George Washington* after the last of the troops were loaded aboard, awaiting the ship's departure. "At the next dock, another ship was loading, apparently the 103rd Station Hospital, to which my future wife was assigned. When the nurses came on the deck, the troops on our ship all went to that rail (at least all those on deck) and the ship actually listed far over, to the point where the watch officer came on the loud speaker and directed us to move away from the rail."[9]

Major Neptune was also standing on the main deck when the *George Washington* slowly pulled out of New York harbor in the early morning hours of April 29, 1943. "I got my first look of the Statue of Liberty. That is a beautiful and impressive monument. Our convoy was large. The battleship *Texas* was among our escort. A number of oil tankers were in the convoy. I wondered if my old fraternity brother who was a navy lieutenant, [Hubert] 'Hoot' Gibson, might be aboard one of the vessels. The following day Champ and I were in charge of organizing troops and training them in boat drill for abandoning ship. This seemed very important to us and we took it quite seriously. The problem was to get the troops out of the below decks to topside (boat deck) as quickly as possible in event of a torpedo attack. Champ and I learned that ship's compartments for troops from stem to stern. We even found one compartment that the transport commander did not realize existed in the ship. We had some fun over that. The voyage across the ocean was the maiden trip for the refitted *George Washington* as a troop ship."[10]

The accommodations aboard the ship followed a caste system of sorts, based on rank. Neptune felt sorry for those of lower rank. "The ship was huge, but only half big enough for the troops on board. Accommodations for the officers were poor, but for the men they were deplorable. The food the first day was good. B-1, where the junior officers were quartered was a 'hole.' "[11]

Lieutenant Reneau Breard was one of those junior officers. "There were about eighteen hundred in EGB 448—both officers and enlisted men—I guess we had three hundred officers. They had so many people that they would put half of them in the hold and half of them on the deck. In twenty-four hours, they would change over. We had about eight men to a compartment. It was so hot down there."[12]

Private Ussery and the other enlisted men with Headquarters Battery, 376th were "put in the G-1 compartment, a compartment that was pretty low down [in the ship]. In fact, we were so low down that we were under the water line and plenty stuffy too.

"We ate breakfast at 6 a.m. and again at 9 p.m. After dark, any man caught smoking on deck was put in irons. You were not allowed to smoke below, except in the latrine, and the latrine was so crowded you could not get there, so no smokes. After about four days out to sea, a very bad disease broke out: diarrhea. The trip was plenty miserable from there out. The latrines were packed day and night."[13] Ussery termed the voyage as "thirteen days of living hell."[14]

Major Neptune was surprised that more men didn't get seasick. "It was beautiful sailing weather. Practically no one got sick from motion. The poor men got sick from the lousy food. Their chow line to feed two meals a day ran from 6 a.m. to 10 p.m."[15]

The food and even the eating arrangements followed the same caste system, as Lieutenant Breard soon discovered. "They had standing room for the enlisted men to eat. Of course, sloppy people would drop stuff and it wasn't the best deal for eating on a ship."[16]

The unequal treatment of the men and the officers naturally bred resentment among some of the enlisted men, such as Private Ussery. "A few of the fellows were lucky enough to eat with the crew. These men did not suffer. The rest of us ate such as one boiled egg, fish, and about a half canteen cup of coffee to drink. You could not eat the food, so you had a slice of bread and a cup of coffee to do until nine that night. The food was a little better that night, but not much.

"One day I was down by the officers' mess around meal time and had the pleasure of seeing some real food. After seeing this, I said to myself, 'What the hell am I going over to fight for?' Then I thought again of my family and what a wonderful country we have (outside in civilian life)."[17]

On the morning of the third day, May 1, Major Neptune felt the *George Washington* glide to a halt as "her engines broke down and the convoy went over the horizon, leaving us rather lonely. However, it was daylight and we got going and caught the rest before dark.

"One day an airplane of the battleship went out and crashed into the sea. The vessels did not turn back, and I believe that the pilot was not saved. On 8 May, we were in particularly dangerous water now and had a number of submarine scares. One submarine was reported sunk by our destroyer escort. This night our motors went out again. It was quite dark and the convoy glided on away from us. We seemed to be floating helplessly for hours. I was on the deck when a vessel pulled alongside. A message through a megaphone asked, 'What is the matter?' Our message told the inquirer that the motors were capable of giving us only one knot per hour (the rest of the convoy was making twelve!). The escort messaged, 'I will stand by you.' Golly, that was welcome news, for it seemed we were ripe bait for a sub. The next morning we caught the convoy.

"On 10 May we saw Casablanca, French Morocco. There was little evidence of any battles here. A few ships sunk remained visible in the harbor. We were all anxious to disembark, but that too was quite a problem, with full packs, arms, and 'A' bags. It was dark by the time the battalion was completely unloaded. We marched on foot to Camp Don B. Passage. What a march. It

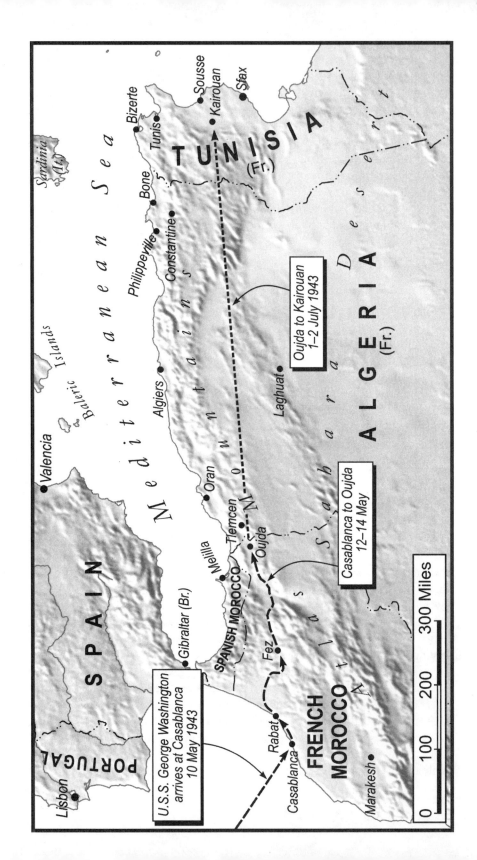

Oujda to Kairouan
1–2 July 1943

Casablanca to Oujda
12–14 May

U.S.S. George Washington
arrives at Casablanca
10 May 1943

PORTUGAL

Lisbon

SPAIN

Valencia

Baleric Islands

Mediterranean Sea

Sardinia (It.)

Bizerte

Tunis

Bone

Philippeville

Constantine

TUNISIA (Fr.)

Sousse

Kairouan

Sfax

Desert

Algiers

Oran

Tlemcen

Melilla

Gibraltar (Br.)

SPANISH MOROCCO

Oujda

Laghuat

ALGERIA (Fr.)

Sahara

Mountains

Atlas

Fez

Rabat

Casablanca

Marakesh

FRENCH MOROCCO

0   100   200   300 Miles

was a five-mile torture with those heavy packs, especially after the twelve days of inactivity and rotten food on the ship. Camp Passage, we found upon our eventual arrival, was a field worked over by a bulldozer I guess to somewhat level the ground. We had made camp by midnight. The ground was rough and cold, but somehow we slept.

"We spent the following day improving our camp and discussing the Arabs. How odd they were. Their filthy appearance prompted us to eject them from our camp area. Their love of chewing gum was colossal. One Arab girl would invite a soldier to her hut for sexual intercourse for a stick of chewing gum. While they were indulging, a sister of the Arab girl would go find a MP and snitch on the business for a stick of gum from the MP."[18]

That morning, Lieutenant T. Moffatt Burriss, with Headquarters Company, 3rd Battalion, saw Arab civilians coming in the encampment. "The Arabs swarmed all over us like roaches over food. They wanted to trade with us or, preferably, to steal. They were particularly interested in our sheets, mattress covers, cigarettes, and chocolate. For these things they offered trinkets and fresh food—dates, exotic bread, and meats of dubious origin.

"We were to post guards twenty-four hours a day in order to keep them from stealing everything we had. Theft was so common that we came to regard the Arabs with almost as much ill will as we did the Germans."[19]

On May 12, Major Neptune received an order to lead an advance party to Oujda, French Morocco, the following morning. "So we would all get to see the city of Casablanca, I took the whole detail to town that night. We spent an hour seeing the town and returned to camp. One of my men stumbled into an officer's bar and sure enough, got to talking to navy Lieutenant Hubert Gibson from Oklahoma. He had been in our convoy. (Hoot was my Pi Kappa Alpha fraternity brother at Oklahoma University).

"The following day we made a motor trip to Oujda with the advance detail from each battery. The overnight bivouac was at Fez. A big Air Corps water truck helped us a lot. We moved on the following day and out to the field to where the division camp was to be.

"14 May: As usual, no one was in charge. There was no one person to get the answers needed. Captain Al Trefny and I had lots of headaches for a couple of days, trying to get set up. The 505th Infantry officer, who was supposed to be the 'Division' officer in charge, disregarded all units except the 505th. Sorry b-----d! He fixed everything for the 505th and gave the rest of the troops the run around."[20]

A couple of days after arriving at Camp Don Passage, Private Hank Ussery, with Headquarters Battery, 376th, and other enlisted men received passes to go into Casablanca. "This pass expected to be a wonderful trip, but turned out to be just the opposite. All the good places to eat in were for officers only, and the rest were closed until five that evening. Things were [priced] so high and unreasonable an enlisted man did not have a chance. Casablanca was a horrible nightmare . . . you could have had a better time in camp talking to your buddies and playing cards."[21]

On May 15, the 504th left Camp Don Passage by train for Oujda. As Lieutenant Burriss, with Headquarters Company, 3rd Battalion, waited aboard the train carrying his battalion to begin moving, he noticed an Arab at one of the open windows offering to buy a mattress cover. "A sergeant obliged. The Arab handed the money through the window and clutched the mattress cover, which was partially hanging out the window. At that moment, as the train started to move out, the Arab tried to pull out the cover. However, the sergeant had tied one end to the seat. When the train picked up speed, it dragged the Arab along with it. He turned a flip and let go of the cover. Scrambling to his feet, he chased the train for a few moments, shook his fist, and cursed in Arabic. Most of the soldiers laughed and jeered at him because Arabs had cheated or stolen from virtually all of them during their stay in Casablanca."[22]

Private Arthur Foster, with EGB 448, arrived at Oujda after a four-day journey in a 40 & 8 freight car. At the train station there, he saw his first German prisoners. "They laughed at us, because we were on our way to the war, while for them the war was over and they were going to the States."[23]

When he arrived at the camp near Oujda, Captain Adam A. Komosa, the commander of Headquarters Company, couldn't believe the contrast of the area. "The camp site chosen was typical of sites for American training camps. On one side of the town there were the beautiful rolling plains, ankle-high grass which looked like a soft green carpet flowing gently over the hills and blending into the beauties of the mountains on the left and the Mediterranean on the right. So the camp was located on the other side of the town, in the middle of the worst dust bowl on the continent of Africa. It was located in a desolate, sterile, rocky, dusty, heat seared valley, which seemed 'nowhere in North Africa' instead of the censor's 'somewhere in North Africa,' found on the letterheads of these troops so recently from the States.

"Oujda brought the regiment the first taste of extended field conditions. Troops lived in long, straight rows of pup tents, interspaced with slit trenches. They squatted on the ground and ate from mess kits at the field kitchens. They bathed, shaved, and washed in their helmets and learned the meaning of water discipline They washed their clothing in wooden tubs or in halves of discarded oil drums. They gave each other haircuts.

"In addition to the scheduled jumps in tricky winds, there was the worst epidemic of dysentery ever imagined in a latrine orderly's nightmare—and jumps, scheduled or unscheduled, were made all through the day and night. Men on guard wore entrenching tools as 'standard equipment.'

"Despite the climatic conditions, the camp at Oujda was to become the greatest parade ground the regiment and division had graced to date. We were to be the proud recipient of virtually every dignitary in northwestern Africa. The proud 82nd paraded before fifteen Allied generals in less than a month."[24]

Having endured the difficult living conditions on the trip across the Atlantic and the hot, dusty, cramped ride from Casablanca, Private Hank Ussery, with Headquarters Battery, 376th, had hoped that Oujda would be different, but he found it to be "another hellhole. If you were not suffocating from the heat and dust, the asps or snakes got you. You would burn up until around four in the afternoon, then the wind gave you a little relief, but dust came with it and what a dust! At night lizards and bugs ran over you all night. This place was strictly no fun. In the daytime you were not permitted to remove your shirt for a sun bath except for one hour, from 11:30 to 12:30. Out of this hour, you must eat with shirts on. Passes were finally given again, to Oujda this time.

"Oujda, a very small town with a Red Cross recreation hall, provided about the only recreation you had. Once a week there was a movie which was a special treat for anyone, especially after being away from movies so long. In Oujda you could walk the streets and see some of the most distressing sights among the Arabs. They were half naked and very filthy. As you walked the streets you could just say to yourself 'Thank God for a wonderful country like we have.' Some would have scars in their heads and on their bodies. Even tiny infants were in this condition. It was really a pitiful sight. After walking the streets until you were dead tired, you went back to the trucks and waited to leave for the camp."[25]

Sergeant Milton Knight, with Headquarters Company, 1st Battalion, found that sand permeated everything and was one of worst factors that contributed to everyone's misery. "Hell, it was everywhere—in your food, in your blankets, your clothes, and your boots. It was just a fact of life that you had to learn to live with—we did it."[26]

Private Clayton W. Blankenship, with D Battery, 376th, adapted to the living conditions as best he could. "We slept in pup-tents and cooled our drinking water by using the Arab jugs and letting these sweat. I also buried my canteen in the daytime after leaving it out at night. I sure missed the U.S. of A. and all the beer, milk and soft drinks, hot dogs, hamburgers and fries."[27]

As the 82nd Airborne Division began training at Oujda for a night parachute operation, the planning for the invasion of Sicily had been underway for quite some time. General George S. Patton, Jr., commanding the Seventh Army, which would be making the invasion, wanted both the 504th and 505th Regimental Combat Teams to parachute into Sicily on the night before the seaborne landings to block enemy forces from attacking them on the beaches the following morning. However, there was a shortage of transport aircraft and American troop-carrier forces were also supporting British airborne operations on the southeastern end of the island. British General Frederick "Boy" Browning, General Eisenhower's airborne adviser, attempted to have the majority of the aircraft allocated to British airborne forces for the operation, while General Ridgway did the same. In the end, only enough aircraft were allocated for one reinforced parachute combat team. Because Colonel Gavin was senior in rank and because Ridgway deemed the 505th Regimental Combat Team to be more combat-ready, the 505th, reinforced by the 3rd Battalion, 504th, received the assignment of making the first mass combat jump in U.S. military history.

When Colonel Tucker learned of this he was furious. He felt his men had trained just as hard and that he and his staff had a regiment that was the equal of the 505th. It was a bitter pill for Tucker to swallow. "To make the situation worse, Ridgway had to steal one of my battalions and give it to Jim for the jump."[28]

Because of his responsibility as the regiment's Headquarters Company commander, Captain Adam Komosa received a briefing about the upcoming operation shortly after arrival at Oujda, because so much of his company would be involved in preparing the regiment for the mission. "Allied headquarters had us slated for a night airborne operation on Sicily. A night parachute operation had never before been attempted by any army; so organization and training offered many new problems. The many intangible and indefinable difficulties of fighting at night in hostile territory, when every object appears to be and often is the foe, had to be overcome. Rapid assembly of the troops and reorganization after landing by parachute appeared to be the greatest problem.

"Training began at night—compass marches by small groups, organizing in the dark, from simulated parachute drops and glider landings, moving across country at night and organizing positions, digging foxholes, laying wire, [and] preparing minefields by the light of the moon. Emphasis was placed on training in judo, demolitions, commando fighting, and the use of the knife. All this worked well, but bayonet practice at 2 a.m. was a little too unique to bring enthusiasm.

"It was too hot to sleep in the day time and as a result, the troops became exhausted."[29]

One serious deficiency that Captain Komosa recognized was the joint training exercises by the airborne and troop carrier forces. "An air corps liaison officer was attached to the 82nd Airborne Division headquarters, but he was not used to the best advantage. He did not operate as an integral member of the division staff and was not in a position to coordinate plane requirements, et cetera.

"An airborne liaison officer was later attached to the 52nd Troop Carrier Wing. He was made assistant A-3 and proved a real value to the unit in its planning and training.

"The spirit of cooperation between the 82nd Airborne Division and the 52nd Troop Carrier Wing was excellent; however, the inadequate organization proved the stumbling block. Cooperation alone was not enough for the closely knit teamwork required.

"The 52nd Troop Carrier Wing arrived in the theater qualified for daylight operations and parachute drops over familiar terrain, but unqualified for night operations. At the start of the training program, the wing did night formation and navigation flying with navigational lights. After becoming proficient with navigational lights, the formation flying was done without navigational lights and resin lights. Occasionally, the air corps was used to work with the 509th Parachute Infantry Scout Company for DZ (drop zone) and resupply exercises. However, the wing did not fully appreciate the value of these projects and used most of their training time to fly large formations and token drops, which had little operational value.

"Very little real effort was put forth by the 52nd Troop Carrier Wing to check the location of pinpoint DZs at night. Equipment containers were made available in an effort to get the 52nd Troop Carrier Wing to drop simulated loads on a DZ on practice flights. Very few times were containers used to check the DZ location by the navigator and the jump signal by the pilot. Air photos, for training aids in the location of DZs by night pilotage were not used in the majority of training flights.

"Training of a practical nature was difficult under the existing setup without a control command over the 52nd Troop Carrier Wing and the 82nd Airborne Division. Despite the necessity of such a step, a full-scale rehearsal of the operation was not conducted. Final training was further hampered because the air corps wing over the final three weeks was engaged in shuttling troops and supplies to advance bases."[30]

When Captain Komosa received a briefing of the enemy situation, there was no mention of two German panzer divisions on the island. "Information of the enemy indicated that the entire island of Sicily had been prepared for defense. Towns, consisting almost entirely of stone buildings, were reported organized as centers of resistance. All beaches were reported protected by batteries, pillboxes, barbed wire, and mines. Roads were understood to be blocked by anti-tank obstacles. Strength of the defenders was stated to be somewhat between 300,000 and 400,000 men.

"The plan for the invasion of Sicily provided for landings to be made on the southeastern extremity of the island, with British and Canadian forces on the east coast and American forces on the south coast. The American assault forces were to consist of the 3rd, 1st, and 45th Infantry Divisions, with attached units, which were to land in the Licata, Gela, and Sampiere vicinities, respectively, and parachute troops from the 82nd Airborne Division, which were to land inland from Gela.

"The plan of invasion called for one parachute combat team of the 82nd Airborne Division to drop just north of an important road about seven miles [north]east of Gela, between known large enemy reserves and the 1st Division's beaches, with the mission of preventing these reserves from interfering with amphibious landings.

"The assaulting paratroopers were the 505th Combat Team, commanded by Colonel James M. Gavin, reinforced by the 3rd Battalion, 504th Parachute Infantry Regiment, and their mission was thus stated in Field Order # 6, issued by the II Corps.

"'(1) Land during the night D-1/D in area N and E of Gela, capture and secure high ground in that area. (2) Disrupt communications and movement of reserves during night. (3) Be attached to 1st Infantry Division effective H plus 1 hours on D-Day. (4) Assist 1st Infantry Division in capturing and securing landing field at Ponte Olivio.'

"In compliance with Field Order # 1, of Force 343 (Seventh Army), the division devised a movement table, under which the 504th Parachute Infantry Combat Team, as a second lift, was alerted for movement the evening of D-Day; or, in the event of negative instructions at that time, the evening of D plus 1, or any day thereafter."[31]

The 61st Troop Carrier Group would transport the 3rd Battalion, 504th, and lead the other serials of the 505th Regimental Combat Team into Sicily. The 3rd Battalion, code-named the 505th's "X" Battalion, under the command of Lieutenant Colonel Charles W. Kouns, would land on DZ "Q" on the northern end of the airhead and block the road south from Niscemi to Gela.

The second lift, the 504th Regimental Combat Team, consisting of the 504th Parachute Infantry Regiment less the 3rd Battalion, commanded by Colonel Tucker; the 376th Parachute Field Artillery Battalion, commanded by Lieutenant Colonel Wilbur M. Griffith; and Company C, 307th Airborne Engineer Battalion, commanded by Captain Thomas M. Wight, would parachute on either the night of D-Day or D+1 into the area secured by the 505th Regimental Combat Team.

Colonel Tucker's regimental staff consisted of Lieutenant Colonel Leslie G. Freeman, executive officer; Captain Harry J. Cummings, S-1; Lieutenant Fordyce Gorham, S-2; Major Emory S. Adams, Jr., S-3; and Major Julian A. Cook, S-4. However, Adams had been temporarily detached from the regiment by General Ridgway and assigned to assist General Mark Clark's chief airborne planner, Major Charles Billingslea, with planning the division's Sicily operation. Captain Adam A. Komosa commanded Headquarters Company.

The 1st Battalion was commanded by Lieutenant Colonel Warren R. Williams, Jr. The 2nd Battalion was under the command of Major William Yarborough.

Colonel Tucker was not told that powerful German armored forces awaited them in Sicily. General Omar N. Bradley, one of the few U.S. generals with the security clearance to know of the existence of Ultra and its information, was disturbed by the knowledge he had of the German presence in Sicily: "Owing to the extreme secrecy of Ultra, we were not allowed to pass this information on to the lower echelons or include it in our circulated intelligence summaries.

If we were asked if there were Germans on the island, we had to lie and say, 'There may be a few technicians.' This was a cruel deception on our own forces, but necessary in order to protect the secrets of Ultra."[32]

The Hermann Göring Fallschirm Division was deployed just north of the 82nd's drop zones and the landing beaches, in a perfect position to attack the paratroopers and the beach landings by the U.S. 1st Infantry Division. It was composed of paratroopers (*fallschirmjägers*) and in the process of converting to an armored division. Although understrength, the division had significant armored strength, with over 131 tanks and assault guns (including a company of seventeen Mark VI Tiger I tanks), armored artillery, and reconnaissance units with many half-tracks and flak-wagons.

After a final review and parade for Generals Eisenhower and Clark on June 16, the division broke camp on June 21 and began movement to its staging areas near Kairouan, Tunisia. Troop trains transported most of the troopers aboard 40 & 8 boxcars. After one of the stops along the way, Private Reed S. Fassett, with Battery A, 376th, saw Private Paul D. North running alongside the train, and as he attempted to step up into the boxcar he missed a step. Fassett saw him fall "under the train as it was pulling out, just at dark. He lost both legs and both arms. First Sergeant Ira Adams, myself, and three or four other men placed North on a stretcher. I reached under the engine on the rear of the train and picked up one foot, I do not know who got the other pieces of Paul North. We all carried North up into town to a doctors office. Sergeant Adams and the doctor stayed in the room where we took North, the rest of us were in a small room or hall; Sergeant Adams came out in a few minutes and told us North had died. A second man killed during this trip was sitting on the top of the brakeman's shack on the rear of the train, when a low hanging wire or cable caught him and jerked him off the moving train. I do not recall how fast we were moving at this time, but this man hit the ground between the rails, striking his head on the rail and caving in [the] side of [his] head and face. After the train had stopped, a number of us ran back about a mile or more. To all indications, the man was dead. One man who knew him stayed with him, and the rest of us returned to the train, and we went on towards Kairouan."[33]

When his train arrived outside of Kairouan, Staff Sergeant Leonard D. Battles with Headquarters, 376th, was hoping that the battalion's new encampment would be an improvement over Oujda. "Kairouan was more of the same, like before, sand everywhere, in everything you ate, slept and it was still hot. Dysentery was a way of life. Morning reveille formations were never completed. There were more troops hurrying to the latrines than standing roll call formation. Best relief at Kairouan was the slight breeze we would get from the ocean, hot, but at least a partial relief."[34]

When the 504th arrived at its new bivouac location near Kairouan, Captain Komosa and his Headquarters Company troopers began to prepare for briefings of the regiment's units for the upcoming operation. "The regimental combat teams were bivouacked in a huge arc around the city in scattered olive groves and cactus patches. This area was also very dusty, and the scorching heat was unbearable.

"Within 275 short miles lay the enemy in Sicily, nervously waiting for the invasion which certainly would come soon. The troops began to sense the nearness of the battle. Situation huts were set up immediately and conferences were held concerning the pending attack on the iron-muscled underbelly of Festung Europa.

"Training was as usual 'continuous,' with both day and night exercises. Troops got up at 0430 and started at 0600. They got madder and meaner."[35]

Like almost all of the enlisted men, Private First Class Lawrence Dunlop, with H Company, was still unaware of the specifics of his company and platoon's mission. "Sand tables were erected, and each company and platoon made replicas of certain missions in the sand. We knew a jump was coming."[36]

As the regiment prepared for their first combat jump, the chaplains held religious services. Private Joe Watts, a company runner with Fox Company, didn't take any chances. "Making friends with the regimental chaplain and the company medic were high on my list of the right things to do. It was always the prospect of close combat that brought the 'believers' out in droves. That was the only time participation reached nearly 100 percent."[37]

ON THE EVENING OF JULY 9–10, THE PLANES of the 3rd Battalion, 504th, attached to the 505th Regimental Combat Team as the "X" Battalion began taking off from its airfield near Kairouan. The battalion would be the first serial in the formation and would jump south of Niscemi at the same time the 1st Battalion, 505th serial would drop to the south.

As the serials neared the island of Malta, they were met by a strong headwind, breaking up the V-of-V formations. The troop carrier aircraft, flying the route using specific timings and headings, were dispersed and the timing disrupted, forcing most of them to be off course.

From the door on the left side of the aircraft, Lieutenant Roy M. Hanna, commanding the Headquarters Company light machine gun platoon, could see the coastline of Sicily and the Mediterranean Sea a short distance out from his plane. "The pilot turned on the red light designating to me that we had five minutes before the jump. We stood up, had our equipment check procedure, and I was standing in the door as we approached the town of Gela. I would guess that our altitude was about eight hundred feet, because the scheduled jump height was five hundred feet. Suddenly we were in the center of what could best be described as a large Fourth of July fireworks celebration. Puffs of smoke and fireballs began to appear near our plane, and tracers could be seen headed our way.

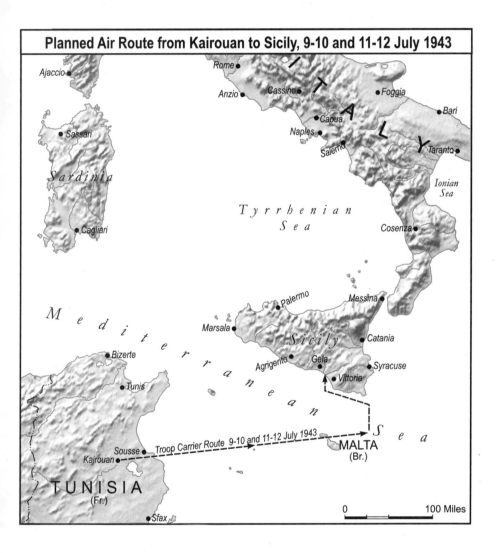

Planned Air Route from Kairouan to Sicily, 9-10 and 11-12 July 1943

"Our pilot must have decided that it was time to get out of there, because he put the plane in a bank and steep-climb mode that was so severe that I had to hang on to the sides of the open doorway to keep from falling down or out.

"Very shortly thereafter, the green light came on over the doorway indicating that it was time to jump. Before leaving North Africa, I had been given a landmark of a small lake [Lake Biviere] that was to indicate that we were near our jump area. I could not locate the lake, but decided that the pilot was better oriented than I, and so out we went.

"Our machine guns and ammunition were packed in bundles and fastened to the carriage underneath the C-47. The bundles each weighed 350 pounds and were carried by a twenty-four-foot parachute, compared to our twenty-eight-foot chute that supported a man and equipment of about two hundred fifty pounds. These bundles were released by the C-47's crew chief shortly after we started jumping.

"This was the highest jump I ever made—must have been up at least two thousand feet. My chute opened and I was drifting in a bright moonlit sky. As I drifted in the breeze like a feather, I tried to keep track of our equipment that was dropping very rapidly straight down. I made my first tree landing in an olive tree. I didn't know how high I was off the ground. But after cutting off a few parachute suspension lines with my switchblade, my one foot touched the ground, indicating that I was only a couple of feet off of the ground. I unhooked myself from the parachute harness and stood there listening. The night was completely silent except for some dog barking some distance away. I started walking in the direction of where I assumed my men were.

"Suddenly, I was halted with our password, 'George.'

"I replied, 'Marshall.'

"After I identified myself, the rifleman said, 'I'm sure glad you are friendly, because I can't get this M1 assembled.' I didn't recognize this soldier, but found out after questioning him that he had just been assigned to H Company a few weeks before as a replacement. I put the man's M1 together, loaded it, and sent him in the direction of where I thought my men should be. I went in search of our machine guns. I searched for our machine guns for what seemed to be a long time and finding nothing, went in search of my platoon. During the next several hours I collected a total of seven of my platoon. And so, the eight of us walked up to the top of a small hill, rested, and waited for daylight. I knew we were in Sicily, but had no idea where."[38]

Staff Sergeant Louis Orvin, with Company I, was the jumpmaster of his plane. He kept glancing at his watch as the scheduled time for the jump approached. "We hit the land, and the plane banked and went back out over the water. That's when I said to the crew chief, 'Ask the pilot if everything is O.K.'

"He went up front, and he came back and said, 'The pilot said to tell you he would give you the light when he's ready for you to jump.'

"I had never done that before, so I said, 'Maybe my watch is wrong, I just misread it, or whatever.' Finally when the red light came on, I said, 'Stand up and hook up.' All of the men behind me did that.

"I was standing in the door and looking down at the water. The green light came on, and everybody behind hollered, 'The green light's on—go!' I reversed my hands to brace, instead of putting all five fingers [of each hand] outside the door like you were supposed to. I stood there braced in that door so I couldn't get pushed out.

"I had told the crew chief to release my equipment bundles when the green light came on. So they were probably in the water. When I [saw that the plane] finally hit the land and I counted, 'One thousand one' until I got up to, 'One thousand five.' I jumped, and it took forever to get around, and I looked around and couldn't find anybody. I finally landed in a vineyard and rolled my chute up and hid it under some vines.

"I walked out to a road and I walked in one direction for probably thirty or forty minutes. I don't know exactly how long it took to find anyone, but it was at least two hours. I was walking down a road and I heard a noise in some bushes, so I jumped into the ditch on the opposite side, and I said, 'George.' Nobody answered and I said, 'George.' Nobody answered . . . so then I took the safety off of my Tommy gun and I said, 'George!'

"Somebody said, 'Is that you, Sergeant Orvin?' "[39]

Sergeant Orvin had found seven of his men. They had landed near the town of Noto, sixty miles from their drop zone, on the southeast side of the island in the British sector.

Private Darrell Harris, with the 3rd Squad, Demolitions Platoon, which was assigned to support the 3rd Battalion, landed several miles from the drop zone. "Our mission, as demolitionists, was to place charges on a certain bridge and be prepared to blow it in case of a German counterattack. We jumped with twenty-eight quarter-pound blocks in our demolition kits, and more explosives were to be dropped in our equipment bundles. In order to expedite assembly after landing, we were issued clickers, or what we used to call 'crickets.' The code was something like, if you met someone in the dark you couldn't recognize, you were to click twice and await the proper response, which would be three clicks. I believe we also had a password that night consisting of 'George' as the challenge and 'Marshall' as the response. We all were new at combat on that first jump, including the air crews, and the jump did not work exactly as planned on the sand table. Very few of us landed on our intended drop zone, and we were not able to accomplish our primary mission."[40]

Only a few small groups of paratroopers from the 3rd Battalion landed near their intended drop zone, "Q," south of Niscemi. They would be some of the first to oppose the drive by the Western Kampfgruppe of the Hermann

Göring Panzer Division moving toward the beaches to drive the U.S. Army's seaborne forces into the Mediterranean Sea.

Private First Class Shelby R. Hord, a machine gunner with Company H, came down near a chateau-like building that sat on high ground overlooking the road that led southeast out of the town of Niscemi. The locals referred to the stone fortress as the Castle Nocera. Hord landed like a ton of bricks in the darkness. "I hit a big stone pile that the farmer had put on the side of the hill and knocked myself out cold. I had three brand-new men that had just come from the United States as replacements. I had only had them [in my machine gun squad] for a few days. These three men kept asking me what was the password. They patted me on the face. I was out cold, then when I finally [woke up and] realized what they were saying . . . I said, 'What are you carrying your parachute for? One of you is dragging one. You go and you bury them right now.'

"They came back, and I saw that all of the company's equipment had landed on the side of this hill. The four of us brought all of that stuff [and] put it around that wall of that home that was up there. It was the closest place and was the highest place, to protect ourselves. In front of the house, I dug in the machine gun overlooking the hill and then one over by the rocks. We knocked on the door and told the people to leave. To the left of the door they had a beautiful flower garden. We put the eight 60mm mortars in the flower garden. Finally Lieutenant Ferrill came."[41]

Arriving with another seventeen men, Lieutenant Willis J. Ferrill began to get the force organized, and "by 0900, had assembled twenty-four enlisted men. A strong position was set up on the high ground at Castle Nocera, three miles southeast of Niscemi. A patrol sent out to contact the rest of the battalion, encountered a company of German antiaircraft. In the engagement two Germans were killed and two captured, but the patrol was forced to withdraw to the defensive position."[42]

During the flight to Sicily, Company H trooper, Private First Class Lawrence Dunlop, had thought about saving something to commemorate his first combat jump. "I had it in my mind to cut the small pilot chute, which helped pull out the main chute, and save it for a souvenir. I was a crazy young paratrooper. There was no shooting at us as I came out the door, and I looked at the ground coming up at me. It did look like the area where I supposed to be, but it was not. I landed in some bushes, stayed quiet for a few minutes, and then I pulled in my chute, and got hold of the pilot chute [and] cut it off with my brass-knuckle trench knife. I tucked it inside my jacket, and then I started to worry about Germans. I was all alone, and I had to find my .30-caliber Browning machine gun, which was in one of the six big bundles under the plane that were dropped. Then, I heard some noise, stopped, listened, and said, 'George—George' A few seconds later, I heard someone say, 'Marshall.' This was the password. Staying alert, I waited to see who had responded to the password. It was my squad leader, Sergeant [Robert A. 'Red'] Tague. We were both glad to see each other.

"We now went on and bumped into four or five other troopers of our plane. We found all our bundles, except one. I was happy to get my machine gun and a few cans of ammo. In a short time, a few more guys came in, and now we had about fifteen guys.

"H Company First Sergeant [Edward W.] Sneddon was now our ranking leader. We didn't know where the hell we were or where to go. So, Sneddon said we better hold up until daylight. We dug in among some trees, on a rise, and put out some outposts. Then he picked out [Private First Class Henry E.] Ferrari, who spoke Italian, and a couple of other guys, to go to a house and get some information. After a while, they came back, and with them were two Sicilians, carrying two large platters of egg and tomato omelets and two of those large wicker covered jugs of vino. Man, did we bite into that food.

"Just before daybreak, we could make out a lot of black smoke and noise in the distance. Sergeant Sneddon said, 'There's some action over that way. Let's get going.' So we started off in single file. We only went a short ways and we saw some men in khaki shorts. 'Jerries!' someone said.

"Sneddon said, 'Spread out, sneak up behind the olive trees, and give them hell.'

"Once they spotted us, we opened up. Firing into tents and anything that moved. In a few minutes, we found out there were Jerry machine guns firing at us and we knew there were too many of them for us. So we took off . . . the Germans after us."[43]

As they did, Dunlop and the others commandeered a nearby truck. "It was [Sergeant Kenneth E.] Brady who got in and started to drive. We tossed a tall, blond German on the truck, who was wounded, and went bumping down a cart path. The truck hit a bump, I fell off the side, and the truck stopped. I had landed in a prickly pear tree, spines sticking into me. We had to keep going. I got my machine gun, and we went a little ways and had to stop. We were pooped.

" 'Have to shoot it out with them!' someone shouted.

"I set the machine gun down behind a flat rock. There was no cover. 'This is it,' I thought.

"The Jerries were still shooting, but not at us. They must have bumped into some other troopers.

"We kept on going and next, we came to where there was a small boy and his jackass. We took the jackass and put our heavy stuff on it. The boy wouldn't leave us."[44]

One group of troopers landed about a mile and a half from the 3rd Battalion's objective, a road intersection code-named "X." Lieutenant James C. Ott assembled a group of fifteen men, including some jump-injured troopers. He assumed the battalion had landed on the drop zone and set out to cover the right flank. Ott led his men "north towards a house, found that the occupants were friendly, and left four injured troopers there. [I] then oriented [myself] in relation to Niscemi by questioning the Italians. From about 0200 of 10 July, [we] patrolled the area to the east and got exact bearings for the road to Niscemi."[45]

The 3rd Battalion commander, Lieutenant Colonel Charles W. Kouns, landed about three miles southeast of Niscemi, near an east-west secondary road that led to the town, where he assembled nine men and positioned the force on a nearby hill. "Lieutenant Ott's planeload was dropped near me. We immediately came under fire from the Hermann Göring Division. The next day, Lieutenant Ott and two bazooka men destroyed several tanks and fired pointblank at two personnel trucks, killing about forty Germans."[46]

Landing within a mile and a half of Niscemi, Lieutenant George J. Watts, with Company G, "had assembled fifteen men by 0830, and had moved to a strategic hill and set up all-round defensive positions which were maintained July 10–11."[47]

MOST OF THE 3RD BATTALION SERIAL WAS DROPPED far to the southeast of DZ "Q." Lieutenant Peter J. Eaton, commanding the 81mm Mortar Platoon, Headquarters Company, 3rd Battalion, landed a couple of miles northwest of Biscari. He took charge of three planeloads of troopers that had landed in the same vicinity, and by sunrise had gathered all of the equipment and men he could find and started moving west toward Niscemi.

The 3rd Battalion executive officer, Major William R. Beall, found himself "with one medical officer (Captain William W. Kitchen) after jumping beside an Italian garrison. Surrounded by enemy who were hunting us in the dark, we withdrew to a vineyard to figure our location and attempt to round up more men. About 0200 10 July, we heard machine gun fire about two hundred yards away and carbine return fire intermittently for one hour, and knew other troopers were in the vicinity."[48]

Despite being horribly misdropped and badly outnumbered, paratroopers, individually and in small groups, were wreaking havoc on the Italian and German reinforcements moving toward the beach landings. They laid impromptu ambushes and formed roadblocks, which held up the counterattacking forces during the critical first hours when beach landings are always most vulnerable.

Moving west toward Niscemi, Lieutenant Eaton was leading about forty-five men when around noon his "scouts encountered two Italian cars towing 47mm antitank guns. They killed the occupants and took the guns. With this added equipment, positions were set up, and manned, with [the captured antitank] guns covering the roads toward Biscari. About 1230, a column of

Italian motorized infantry, with an eleven-ton Italian tankette in the lead (estimated at a battalion because it occupied about 2,200 yards on the Niscemi-Biscari highway) [approached]. Sergeant [George H.] Suggs of Headquarters Company and seven other men of that company manned these guns, of which they had no knowledge. Bore-sighting them, they fired them like veterans. Sergeant Suggs and his men knocked out the tankette with their Italian 47mm antitank guns and so disorganized the foe with their fire, backed by our 81mm mortars, that they retreated in confusion.

"Believing that the enemy force, after reorganization, would be too large and possess too much firepower for our own weapons, which were carbines, [we] destroyed the enemy equipment and withdrew to the south."[49]

Major Beall had landed in the British sector and spent the previous hours of darkness hiding out from Italians who had been hunting them down. Beall was determined to attack the Italians as soon as he could get some help. "About 07:30, 10 July, an advance patrol of Canadians came up. They gave me their positions. . . . I asked for help to attack the Italian garrison, but was not able to secure it, because the Canadians had another mission, that of establishing and protecting the beachheads in another zone. I worked back to the beach and got assistance. The garrison was taken with Canadian assistance a little later. One Italian officer and twenty enlisted men were captured, and six paratroopers were released, having been imprisoned by the Italians. I continued my search for more men, and with what I rounded up, went back to the beach."[50]

ABOUT THREE MILES SOUTHEAST OF NISCEMI, Lieutenant Willis J. Ferrill and twenty-four enlisted men, mostly from Company H and Company I, had gathered at a stone chateau-like structure called the Castle Nocera that stood on some high ground overlooking the road that ran south from Niscemi. Leaving his dug-in machine gun position around 200 p.m., as everyone was eating lunch, Private First Class Shelby Hord went down to a nearby creek to get some water. "A battle started and there was about forty to forty-eight men—Italians—firing at us. There were three machine guns.

"They were good soldiers. I watched them move from a position that was about fifty yards from me . . . move up this little ridge that was a little higher than the house was, about two to three hundred yards from that house. This one group, [consisting] of a machine gunner, the assistant, and a rifleman came running [toward me]. The farmer had made a big, high dirt furrow around one of the trees that wasn't far from me. They ran [and took cover behind the furrow] and were maybe twenty-five feet away from me. I just picked up my hand grenade and threw it in there. I waited a few moments and I slowly walked by and I realized they were dead. Then I went to this next terrace where the farmer had a road going up to the next terrace, where there was an olive orchard."[51]

With his carbine in one hand, Hord made a couple of attempts to climb the steep terrace wall, before finally getting to the top. While doing this, he had accidentally put his carbine in the dirt as he used that hand for leverage to climb the steep dirt wall. As he climbed over the top of the terrace ledge, he came face to face with an Italian officer, just yards away.

The Italian officer, shocked to see an enemy paratrooper in the midst of his force, momentarily froze. Hord raised his carbine and pulled the trigger. Nothing . . . it was jammed . . . fouled by dirt from the climb up the ledge. With quick thinking and lightning speed, Hord pulled back the slide on the top of the chamber of his carbine, grabbed a loose round from his jump pants pocket, shoved it into the chamber of his carbine, pushed the slide forward, aimed, and fired at the officer. The officer was hit with the armor-piercing round, but didn't fall. Immediately, Hord repeated the process. After he fired a second time the officer was still standing. Again, he shoved another round in the carbine. "I shot him three times before he fell."[52]

The firing cleared the jam in Hord's weapon, and he continued his one-man assault on the Italian force. "By the time I got up on the next terrace, [there was] a young man with his feet just a foot or two from me. It was a rifleman protecting the flank of the two machine guns. I was on my knees, and I put my gun up, and I started shooting him. The poor man turned over and he put his hands up in prayer. I had no recourse . . . I shot and killed him. And then I started shooting where I could see the machine guns."[53]

Hord relentlessly fired at the Italians manning the machine guns and at the riflemen who were supposed to be protecting them. Simultaneously, Company I trooper Private Thomas E. Lane killed an additional four Italian riflemen who were protecting the machine guns, during the four-hour firefight.

Hord fired clip after clip of ammunition into the Italian positions. "Then all at once, their machine guns stopped. They just picked up their dying and wounded. They were good soldiers; they didn't drop one gun, except their machine guns and the machine gun ammunition. They took what they had to, and took care of their wounded. They went over the side of this hill, which was the top part of it, and were gone.

"We came and took those three [Italian] machine guns and placed them in the right side in the back of the castle. We put enough ammunition there that no one would have to worry about anything for about three days. No one would have to bring anything to them. We dug them in just below the crest."[54]

For his initiative and extraordinary courage in the face of a numerically superior force, Private First Class Shelby R. Hord was awarded the Distinguished Service Cross.

As the fighting at Castle Nocera was in progress, Private First Class Lawrence Dunlop and his group of troopers were approaching. "Sometime after noon, we came to a rise, and there was a lot of shooting going on. We spread out again and could see down a hill to a large place on another hill. There were cows grazing. Some were dead. There were no bullets coming our way, so we figured whoever was in the big place was having a battle with someone on the other side. So, we just went down the hill and joined the troopers there. There were about ninety men there, so our group made it over a hundred.

"Our small group was put right out on the defensive line. I believe I was on the north side. The ground went out from the side of the farm about twenty feet, then sloped way down and up again to another hill. It was good digging there, and I had a well-dug foxhole in a short while. I set up my machine gun and was ready for business. Sergeant Brady was on my right about twenty feet away. Private Huckins was on my left, about the same distance."[55]

BY THE AFTERNOON OF JULY 10, THE EASTERN KAMPFGRUPPE of the Hermann Göring Panzer Division had begun to move south to attack the U.S. 45th Infantry Division's beachhead. This powerful armored force consisted of the 1st Panzer Grenadier Regiment, one armored artillery battalion, and one heavy panzer company, consisting of seventeen Mark VI Tiger I tanks, each weighing sixty tons and mounting an 88mm main gun.

By the following morning, the number of paratroopers defending the stone chateau had grown to almost sixty, as men had drifted in during the previous day and night. At around 1:00 p.m. Lieutenant Willis J. Ferrill, commanding the force at Castle Nocera, was able to contact Lieutenant George Watts by radio, and Watts led approximately sixty troopers to the chateau to join Lieutenant Ferrill's force.

Private First Class Shelby Hord put twelve Hawkins mines in the road around a curve, in order to at least slow down any armor that approached the chateau.

BACK IN TUNISIA ON JULY 11, THE TROOPERS of the 504th Regimental Combat Team made final preparations for the jump scheduled for that night, drawing ammunition, rations, and parachutes. Most of the men in Sergeant Milton Knight's Headquarters Company, 1st Battalion S-2 section, were armed with M1 rifles and Thompson submachine guns, even though the table of organization and equipment (TO&E) called for most of them to be armed with carbines, a weapon notorious for jamming and inaccuracy. "Our carbine was, to my way of thinking, a toy. I told my men, 'I don't care what the table of organization says we're supposed to carry. All I want you to do is carry what you can use, and I want you to have enough ammunition for that thing to last us for the estimated time of the mission, whatever it is. If it's three days or if it's three weeks, I don't want you to come up hollering, 'I don't have any ammunition.' "[56]

Captain Adam Komosa and the other officers of the regiment made final inspections of their units before loading the planes. "The basic load of combat equipment for the individual parachutist was checked. The bundles and equipment were complete, and the aircraft were dispersed according to the parking plan at the departure airfields. The equipment bundles were raised and hooked into the para-packs under the bellies of the planes.

"Plane loads were lined up near their respective planes. The chutes of each individual were checked by each plane jumpmaster. The troops then emplaned thirty minutes before takeoff.

"The planning for the final takeoff had been complete and thorough, which, with the execution of the final plans, were probably the outstanding features of the entire airborne operation. Bundle and para-pack loading, dispersal arrangements and parking plans all went off like clockwork.

"Allowance was not made for the time required to inform all shipping and shore batteries of the impending flight. Ground units beyond the 1st Division knew nothing of the operation. The 504th RCT was familiar with the situation or countersigns of units on the flanks of the 1st Division area.

"The African sun, like a bloody curious eye, hung on the rim of the world as one hundred and forty-four planes coughed into life, spewing miniature dust storms across the flat wastes of desert airfields.

"Thin aluminum skins of C-47s vibrated like drawn snare drums and, as paratroopers sought their predesignated seats, they wrinkled their noses at the smell of gasoline and lacquer that flooded the planes' interiors. The takeoff proceeded in three-plane V formations as planned. Flights, squadrons, and groups assembled at rendezvous points. By dusk, the planes were airborne, and the formations started flying their course for Sicily."[57]

Chapter 3

"The Sky Was Full of Tracers And Bursting Shells"

The 52nd Troop Carrier Wing flew a similar route as the 505th Regimental Combat Team two nights before. The drop zone was the Farello airport behind the 1st Infantry Division's positions. The 1st Battalion serial was in the lead, followed by the 2nd Battalion and the 376th Parachute Field Artillery Battalion.

After his plane took off from the airfield near Kairouan, Staff Sergeant Leonard D. Battles, with Headquarters Battery, 376th, felt it climb to altitude then begin making wide sweeping turns. "As far as I remember it was a clear, calm night, with a little moonlight, so that (it seemed forever) we were aware that we were in a giant circling pattern, with more and more planes joining us all the time."[1]

Private Albert B. Clark, with Company A, was sitting near the open door of his plane talking to the crew chief as the 1st Battalion serial approached the island of Malta. "Suddenly, I noticed a fighter plane behind the three-plane echelon to our left. I made the comment, 'What the hell, did we pick up a fighter escort tonight?'

"His reply was, 'What do you mean?'

"My reply was, 'Well look, there is a fighter in behind our buddies over there.'

"He took off to see the pilot, came back shortly, and said, 'The skipper says that it isn't ours. We have 'Jerry company.' We patiently watched, and presently he took off. Why he didn't shoot us down out there, we could never figure out, but we were very thankful for that fact."[2]

Lieutenant John S. Thompson, a platoon leader with Company E, stood in the door of his C-47 as it flew toward Sicily. "The 2nd Battalion was flying in a tight V-of-Vs as we flew over a calm Mediterranean Sea. As we neared the island of Malta we could see a long convoy of ships edging their way toward the coast of Sicily."[3]

As the serials made a left turn and then a second left turn, Company D trooper, Sergeant Warren Le Vangia, could see Malta in the distance "just after dusk, visible off to the right as the flight dog-legged toward the island of Sicily. We flew very close to the water for most of the way. About fifty miles from the island, we stood, hooked our static lines to the cable, checked equipment of the man in front of us, and prepared to jump. The flight climbed to about 750 feet. Most of the men unhooked and left their reserve chutes under the seat, as they would be of no use at this height."[4]

Captain Willard E. Harrison, commanding Company A, was the jumpmaster in his plane. "I flew in the leading plane of the first serial and reached the coast of Sicily near Punta Socca at approximately 2230 hours, thence flew in a northwesterly direction along the coast toward Gela. The left wing plane flew just over the water line, and the squadron of nine planes continued perfect formation up the coast at an altitude of approximately nine hundred feet. We encountered no fire of any kind until the lead plane reached Lake Biviere, when one .50-caliber machine gun, situated in the sand dunes several hundred yards from the shore, opened fire. As soon as this firing began, guns along the coast as far as we could see toward Punta Socca opened fire, and the naval craft lying offshore, both towards Punta Socca and toward Gela, began firing antiaircraft guns."[5]

Private Albert Clark, with Company A, waited for the red light to flash on as antiaircraft fire began to rake the formation. "I was fine until we stood up and hooked up and then became airsick. As we approached our DZ, the crew chief was holding a bucket for me, to keep from making the floor slick and causing us to fall. Someone made a comment about the sparks coming out of the engine. I looked and said, 'Sparks hell—those are tracers coming up from the ground.' About that time a shell burst under the plane and I hit my head on the top of the [inside of the] plane. I will admit I was never so scared in my life as I was at that time, not even since then.

"There were a lot of fires on the DZ, and we thought it was nice of those on the ground to light up the area for us. Little did we know that while we were in the air, the Germans had launched an attack and pushed our troops [back] and had fallen back themselves. So, instead of landing behind our own troops as we expected, we actually landed in between the lines. We were surrounded by machine gun fire—there were red tracers on one side of us and green tracers on the other side. The fires we had seen were German tanks that were knocked out by direct fire from 75s and 105s at seventy-five to one hundred yards.

"I remember that the sky was full of tracers and bursting shells, along with a number of planes going down in flames."[6]

Another Company A paratrooper, Sergeant Tom McCarthy, just wanted to get out of the plane. "I can remember going out of that door and saying to myself, 'Just like watching the fireworks on the Fourth of July.' Except they're bouncing all around me. I said, 'Oh, boy, glad to get to the ground.'

"We were badly disorganized. I didn't join my unit for two days from the time I landed. I was disoriented when I first landed, because it was dark. I wasn't too sure where I was, but I knew what to do—take care of myself and head for some high ground so I could see."[7]

Major Robert H. Neptune, executive officer of the 376th Parachute Field Artillery Battalion, was the command liaison with the 504th Parachute Infantry Regiment and was jumping with regimental headquarters personnel as part of the 1st Battalion serial. "I was on board of Colonel Reuben Tucker's plane when we jumped into Sicily. There were seventeen or eighteen paratroopers in the airplane scheduled to jump. I think it was seventeen, because prior to jumping, the procedure was a 'count off' order and with Colonel Tucker at number one and me to be the last one out, my recollection is that I was number seventeen.

"Thirty seconds after I got out of my seat, it seemed all hell broke loose. Ack-ack was going off all around and tracer bullets were tearing through the plane. This was it, boy. I was not afraid. For some reason I felt secure. I joked with a lieutenant beside me and hooked up my static line. Just then a gob of shells came up through the seat I had just left and tore out through the top of the big transport airplane. They also tore up the seat next to mine. The airplane would lurch back and forth, and we had to hang onto our static lines to keep balance. The captain, Air Corps (not the pilot) asked the colonel if he was going to jump into this and was promptly told 'Hell yes, our orders are to jump on Sicily, take us back over the island.' This was after turning away from the island and the first ack-ack fire. There were three casualties in our plane before we jumped. In such a case, the casualty is unhooked and laid over on the seats, and the stick closes up.

"One senior officer who was wounded was Major Cook (at that time S-4 supply officer of the 504th). Whether Cook (seriously wounded) returned to Africa with the airplane or jumped, I do not recall. Colonel Tucker jumped, by insisting that the pilot who wanted to avoid the severe flak and not return over the drop zone (which was the airport at Gela) must again seek to get the airplane over the designated drop zone, which he courageously did do, after three passes back and forth over the area. The flight through the AA fire seemed endless and actually was rather long, because the pilot made three shots at the drop zone before he finally found it.

"Finally, the spot was hit and out we went, into the moonlight. My main interest was still the opening of that parachute, and when it opened with its usual neck-breaking jerk, I felt relieved. I was floating peacefully, alone—that ground down there was Sicily—about thirty seconds away yet. My main interest still was to get down without breaking an ankle or leg, at least to be in sound physical condition. The ground was nearing, so I prepared for the landing and took it in stride with a front tumble. Oh boy, I was not hurt, and a great hurdle was gone. I lay still a moment and listened. All was quiet, I struggled out of my parachute harness, looked about me and saw no one. I then made an answer to a seemingly sudden call of nature. That completed, I began looking for other troopers from my plane, picked up a couple, determined a direction, [and] started for the assembly point. Just then some tanks came around a corner, fifty yards away; we hit the dirt, sneaked our way to some bushes. Then I was scared. I pulled my pistol, cocked it, and lay motionless with my finger on the trigger guard. Three tanks buzzed by without seeing us and opened up with machine gun fire on another planeload a couple hundred yards away. We crawled down a ditch to an assembly point where we joined the rest of the combat team, within our own lines, awaiting orders and without having joined in a real fight."[8]

The pilot of one of the C-47s struggled to keep his plane in the air as it was hit by antiaircraft fire. "A shell smashed into the starboard side of the fuselage and knocked out a hole about four by six feet, while a fragment from the shell split the aluminum and every rib from hole to rudder. Passing through the plane, the fragment ripped off a door as a second ack-ack blast carried away a portion of the left stabilizer.

"The airplane spun at a right angle and nearly pulled the controls from my grasp. For a second I didn't realize what had happened, then finding myself out of formation, I began violent evasive action. I saw three planes burning on the ground and red tracers everywhere as machine gunners sprayed us as if spotting a flight of ducks.

"Meanwhile, I had cut into a less dangerous spot to give the parachutists a fighting chance to reach the ground. But I've got to hand it to those boys; one who had been pretty badly hit by shrapnel insisted on leaping with the others, although he had been ordered to remain in the plane."[9]

Private Keith K. Scott with Headquarters Company, 1st Battalion, had just received the order to stand up and hook up when "just over the beach we ran into AA fire. Our plane kept diving and banking. The pilot passed the word down the line to jump on the red light. At the time the word reached Lieutenant [Richard F.] Mills, the red light flashed on. We started out. Just as I got to the door, our plane was hit. I was knocked back against the opposite side of the ship. I finally got out."[10]

As the 2nd Battalion serial flew along the coastline, Lieutenant John Thompson, with Company E, looked on in disbelief as "a sea of red tracers wound their way up through our formation, and we wondered why and of what origin they came. Some of the planes had been hit, and the formation scattered in many directions as we flew over the coast. We were flying very low now, and one plane on our left went down in flames. Looking out of the door, I found that there were no other planes in sight, and we were all alone in the air.

"The pilot sent back word that he thought we had just flown over our DZ and wanted to know if we should return by circling around and coming in from the water over the east coast. I told him to circle around and as soon as we hit the coastline to give us the green light. As soon as we were over land again, the green light went on. Picking out what I thought was a good jump field, out we went."[11]

The plane in which Company F trooper, Private Joe Watts, was riding "began taking flak and flat-trajectory fire while still over the ocean. I just wanted to get out of the plane and onto the ground as fast as possible.

"I always felt that if I was given time to land and thirty seconds to orient myself, no enemy could kill me. So, I felt it was necessary to leave the plane—it was the target, not me.

"We stood up and hooked up as soon as we understood we were receiving fire, and this happened when one of our guys got hit, first in the foot, then in the buttocks, through the aircraft floor or deck. We jumped as soon as we were over land, without regard for the DZ and without a conference with aircraft crew."[12]

Jumpmaster Lieutenant Edward J. Sims, a platoon leader with Company F, watched helplessly as "a gradual buildup of fire—red tracers from below were engulfing our formation. I felt a shimmy go through our plane, and then pandemonium reigned as antiaircraft guns of our own forces, at sea and on the beaches, were blasting our slow-flying aircraft. As my plane flew through the heavy flak, I could hear the hits as they penetrated. From my door position, I scanned the sky for other planes, but could see only those going down in flames.

"My plane developed a distinct shudder and banked away from the flak with one engine starting to sputter. I had my men stand up and hook up then, before going forward to talk with the pilot. I instructed my platoon sergeant to get the men out fast if the plane started to go down before I returned.

"From the pilot I learned he had lost the formation and had a damaged starboard engine. We decided since there was land below, that he would stay our present course and allow me a few seconds to return to the door, then turn on the green light. We both realized that with the heavy load he had, it would be difficult for him to fly back to North Africa. I rushed back to the door, yelling to my men to get ready to jump. As I arrived, the red light came on, followed within seconds by the green light just as I hooked up. I immediately released the equipment bundles from under the plane, then jumped into darkness with my men following."[13]

The plane carrying Lieutenant A. C. Drew and his stick of Company F troopers was badly damaged by antiaircraft fire. "The pilot of my plane gave me the warning twenty minutes out from the DZ. After the red light came on, he had to give me the green light in about one minute, due to the plane being on fire.

"We jumped into a steady stream of antiaircraft fire, and not knowing that they were friendly troops. About seventy-five yards from where I landed, plane Number 915 was hit and burned. To my knowledge, only the pilot and three men got out. The pilot was thrown through the window. Another plane was shot down on the beach, and another plane was down burning about one thousand yards to my front.

"There were four men killed and four wounded from my platoon. Three of these men were hit coming down, and one was killed on the ground because he had the wrong password. After landing, we found out this had been changed to [a challenge and response of] 'Think' – 'Quickly.' The antiaircraft fire we jumped into was the 180th Infantry of the 45th Division. They also were not told we were coming.

"We tried to reorganize, but found we didn't have but forty-four men, including three officers. We searched all night for the rest of the men. After accounting for them, we took care of the dead and wounded and started toward our objective. We arrived at the 504th CP at 0200, July 12, 1943."[14]

As his Company D stick waited for the green light, Sergeant Warren Le Vangia felt the plane shake violently as a burst of flak exploded nearby. "Two of the men in my plane were hit with fragments of flak that tore through the thin-skinned C-47. We unhooked them, laid them on the seats, and prepared to jump when the red light turned green. I could look down at an angle through the door and one of the side windows, and it appeared that thousands of guns were firing at us from below. Tracer fire streamed around us, and exploding shells rocked the plane. I could no longer see other planes beside us in the moonlight as before, when the firing stopped. The pilot had broken formation, as had most of the flight, and must have completely lost the objective drop zone. When the green light went on, we jumped out into the blackness below."[15]

THE THIRD SERIAL, THE 376TH PARACHUTE FIELD ARTILLERY BATTALION, was the last into Sicily. Staff Sergeant Leonard Battles, with Headquarters Battery, was in Lieutenant Colonel Griffith's stick. "Our plane was in the front position. I could look down and could see the reflection of moonlight off the water, so I knew we were still off-land and we had not stood up or done the equipment check. Suddenly I looked forward in the direction we were going towards the island and saw this stream of fire coming upward, and we seemed to be flying into it or over it."[16]

From his position near the doorway, Battles "noticed other firing from the ground. I suppose it was along the beaches away from us. As soon we stood up and hooked up, I was then able to look back and to the left of me, and I believe our pilot also saw what destruction was going on out over the water. I could see, now that I was in a standing position, all the planes that were just exploding in the air behind us, some of them not exploded, but going down in a stream of fire behind them. I am sure that the planes I saw, exploded in the air, must have been from the firing batteries and were carrying ammunition in their payloads. I only had a short time to see all the carnage going on back there, but all I could think of was my best friend in one of the firing batteries, Sergeant Verne D. Bailey. My fears were right, for a few days later I learned from Lieutenant [Gorman S.] Oswell (he was graves registration officer, in addition to his other duties), that indeed Sergeant Bailey (Tuck) was one of the unfortunate ones lost. I heard that his body has washed up on the beach. I only saw six or seven planes destroyed in fireballs before I jumped.

"We flew past or over this fire, and after what seemed forever, the 'go' light came on."[17]

Captain Paul D. Donnelly, with Headquarters Battery, was on the same plane. "Our battalion commander, Griffith, was first man out of the plane; he followed the daisy-chained door bundles. One of the radio section men was there to help push out the bundles. As battery commander of Headquarters Battery, I was next to go. My first sergeant, Ed Theeck, was clean-up man, the last to exit. He was probably the last division man to see Brigadier General Charles Keerans alive. The plane had been hit by AA fire. We could hear it rattling around in the little cabin in the rear of the airplane. We were too close to the ground for the second bundle to deploy its chute. Captain Tony Bartolina, our S-2, carried a sack of gold coins. I do not remember the monetary value. He jumped with it on his person."[18]

Like every other trooper that night, Private Hank Ussery, with Headquarters Battery, just wanted to get out of the plane. "The sky lit up like the Fourth of July. It sounded like there was rain hitting the plane. I looked out the window and saw Number 4 plane burst in mid-air . . . one man got out alive. I noticed our left motor spitting out flames. About this time, the captain gave the order, 'Hook up.' By this order, we hooked our fifteen-foot static lines to a cable running through the plane. The next order was, 'Is everybody ready?' All the boys sounded off good and strong 'Yes.' Then he said 'Let's go.' Everybody bailed out. It seemed like every tracer bullet was coming straight into you. I landed in an olive grove, somewhere around Vittoria, Sicily.

"As soon as I landed I lay flat on my back until I got my chute off and looked around for the light flashes. We were supposed to assemble around a flashlight that was flashed by our battalion commander. All of a sudden I heard some noise over further in the grove. This noise turned out to be two of my buddies . . . one a medic and the other, a wireman. We took our chutes and rolled them up and threw then under some bushes, as we did not have time to dispose [of] them as we should. We assembled and some of us laid down and tried to get some sleep, but there was no sleep for any of us. We were just a bunch of kids.

I was only twenty-two years old and naturally, being our first combat, we were all afraid of not knowing where we were or what we were going to do."[19]

On board one of the Headquarters Battery planes, Lieutenant Bill Roberts, Jr., heard somebody "hollering to get down on the floor to avoid shells that were coming through the plane. We were over water, probably three or four hundred feet elevation. We stayed in this friendly fire for some time, then the next thing we heard was that we were returning to Africa. We all wore parachutes and equipment, food rations, et cetera. [Lieutenant] Tom Shockley was in command of the paratroopers; however, the pilot was in command of the airplane, and it was his decision to return to Africa with the load of men."[20]

Lieutenant Shockley, the Headquarters Battery executive officer and assistant communications officer, was the jumpmaster on that plane. "I was standing behind this bundle, peering out the open door trying to get our bearings and noticed that our landfall area's sky was filled with shell bursts and tracer bullets, which seemed so intense as we flew into it, I could spot occasional huge explosions in the air around us. Later, I learned they were planes of our serial being shot down from the sky. Our pilot took evasive action, but we did not get the green light to bail out. I unhooked and worked my way to the cockpit and inquired of the pilot, a captain, as to why we did not receive the green light. My pilot replied, 'First of all, I do not know exactly where we are or where the drop zone is. Secondly, we were getting our asses shot off, and I would not let a dog jump into the flak and ground fire. As captain of this plane, I will take responsibility for disobeying our order, 'do not return anyone in the plane unless wounded.' He then took the plane down to tree-top level and headed toward the coast and the sea. We hit the naval element that opened fire, banked right, and flew the entire line of ships at wave-top level, and all ships were firing at the plane. We made it back to Tunisia with the riddled ship; we had no serious wounded aboard."[21]

As Battery A neared Sicily, Private First Class Stanley Galicki, Jr., looked up and down the inside of the plane at the faces of the other troopers in his stick. "I believe that Sergeant [William B.] Bill Martin was our jumpmaster. As far as I remember, the following men [were on board]: [Privates First Class Robert A.] Bob Otto, [Benjamin] Ben Vincent, George [E.] Markwardt, Arthur [H.] Coppinger, [Albert G.] Gene Albott, and [Antonio] Tony Avilla. We all carried carbines, a couple of hand grenades, fifty rounds of ammunition, a knife, and two days of rations. When we were approaching Sicily, I could see the burst of antiaircraft shells. I knew the navy was there, and I thought the burst was a flare to lead us to our target. I soon found out it was not a flare, but shells bursting all around us. The plane began to vibrate. We got the signal to jump, and when I got to the door, the plane was banking and the nose was pointing downward. I was the last person to leave the plane. The plane was banking to the left when I jumped out of the door. My parachute opened, and I hit a small tree immediately. I do not think I was in the air more than two seconds. I had no trouble getting out of my chute and hitting the ground. There was a lot of shooting. I think the troopers that were there already thought we were the enemy. We heard some small gunfire, but it stopped when someone yelled we were American GIs. They soon realized who we were and stopped firing. There were two other troopers, and we headed back to the rear. It took several hours to get our unit together and get ready to fire our guns."[22]

As Lieutenant Robert Zost, with Battery A, stood in the door waiting for the green light to lead his stick out of the plane, his "first thoughts were how was it possible for an airplane to fly through that curtain of fire power. . . . I was amazed, appalled, [and] knew instantly that it was our own ships, shooting at us. I got my men up and hooked up as the red warning light came on. We flew a short distance over land, and when the green light came on, it was like jumping into a bottle of ink.

"My stick was one of the very fortunate to land in the intended drop zone . . . just north of Gela. It was incredibly quiet and dark on the ground. I saw burned-out tanks, both American and German—there had been a tank battle there that very afternoon. The first person I met was Captain [Theodore P.] Gmeiner. Together we started to walk down a dirt road looking for others of our battery. We knew that there existed a massive foul-up and a dreadful mistake on the part of the superior officials.

"We came upon an American tank and were challenged by a GI in the turret. . . . However, when the gunner in the turret shouted 'George,' Captain Gmeiner returned with 'Washington.' Click-clack, went the gunner's machine gun as he advanced a round in the chamber and cocked the gun. 'Marshall, Marshall!' I yelled, 'Don't shoot, we are American GIs.' That is about as close as a call as we had that night after hitting the ground. Actually, the password system was a sort of a joke— it was difficult to keep track of dates, [and the troopers experienced] forgetfulness and a 'I don't give a damn attitude.' Usually, when you were challenged by 'who goes there,' the answer was 'it's me, you son-of-a-bitch, don't shoot.' "[23]

With lots of practice on the first two serials, the American gunners below were getting deadlier as the low, slow flying C-47s came over. They badly shot up the plane carrying Technician Fourth Grade James F. Crosbie's Battery B stick. "We experienced hellish antiaircraft fire as we approached the beach and the DZ. Our C-47 had one through the navigator's compartment, killing him. One man was KIA in the plane. They shot out the left engine, put one through the right wing, and shot off most of the tail."[24]

As Battery B came into Sicily, Private First Class Neil L. D'Avanzo's stick received the command to stand up and hook up. "As we were sounding off with equipment check, all hell broke loose, tracers all over the place, antiaircraft shells bursting around us, and then the pilot pulled back the yoke and climbed for altitude and also turned east to get away from the hostile fire. When he climbed, the jump stick was thrown to the rear of the plane, and the crew chief was yelling for us to get out. We shouted back that we could not get to the door if the pilot did not level off; as it was, if we did get to the door, we would get hung up on the tail or at least hit it as we went by. The pilot leveled off a bit, and we got to the door by pushing and pulling and went out, never mind position, just get out. When my chute blossomed, I knew I was way up there, because of the time that had elapsed; I did not know how high until I came through the cloud cover. At night, it is hard to tell water from clouds, so you hang on and wait. I was slipping as much as I could to get on the ground as fast as possible; tracers and flak were still coming up, but it was mostly to the west. After getting on the ground, I started looking for other men from the stick, forget about the equipment that was supposed to be dropped, who knows where that went. I finally ran into Corporal [Theodore C.] Johnson, Sergeant Laiter, [Private First Class Raymond J.] Ray Bence, Eaton, and [Private First Class Claude H.] Campbell near dawn the next day."[25]

Battery C suffered more casualties than any other battery in the battalion. Corporal Roy F. Pack saw the plane in which he had initially been assigned until thirty minutes before takeoff get hit. "It was flying on our left wing and got a direct hit and exploded. In the plane were a lot of good friends. C Battery took the brunt of the antiaircraft fire. Our plane was also hit. I was slightly wounded in my upper left arm."[26]

As Private First Class Larry Reber's C Battery plane approached the killing zone, "suddenly light attracted our attention. You could see the flames. We were not the first in. There were already planes ahead of us. There was a lot of firing going on. We came in at the tail end of a German bombing raid on the invasion fleet, lying offshore. The planes were fired upon and the firing never stopped. Our airplane was hit. We were all standing and our static lines were attached to the cable in the plane. No one was wounded by the flying shrapnel going through the airplane. Suddenly our plane dove and dove so hard you could see the full shadow of the C-47 on the ground. I thought by myself, 'This is it, we are going to crash.' But the pilot of the plane managed to zoom up in the air. I did not know how high we went, but it was steep enough that the equipment, piled up in the door, moved backwards. The equipment was part of the cannon. When the plane leveled off, we all scrambled to the equipment to get it out of the door, and we could follow.

"I remember one incident with a guy named Corporal [Val L.] Renshaw, who was a member of our stick. I remember the airman [crew chief] in the rear of the plane near the door, asked. 'Are your guys going to jump, because the stuff is flying all over.' We got the equipment piled up, and when the green light turned on, we kicked it out of the door.

"Corporal Renshaw, sitting on top of the equipment bundles answered, 'What the hell you think we came here for.' The bundles and Corporal Renshaw went out of the plane. I was the last man in the stick to get out of the plane. I was in the back of the plane. Suddenly there was a hold-up and I wondered what happened. There was a man named [Private Roy F.] Jenkins, who had been plastered against the outside of the plane. In the confusion, his static line had wrapped up around his neck. . . . Many hands grabbed him and pulled him inside the plane. The static line was unwrapped, and then Jenkins jumped out of the door, followed by the remainder of the stick.

"I do not know how high we were. We all jumped from the plane. Suddenly a C-47 was flying towards us. The plane was below us. Everybody had the same story. Everybody in my stick had seen this plane and had the same story about it. We all thought that we were drifting towards this plane, which was actually some one thousand feet below us. I think that this plane was heading back to Tunisia.

"I remember how dark it was inside our plane, while we were over the Mediterranean Sea. But when we jumped, it was as bright as during daylight. There must have been a fire going on inside the plane, near or in the cockpit. My sergeant, Sergeant [Henry F.] Johnson, later confirmed that our plane was shot down. We were concerned about the crew, whether the plane returned or not. Our sergeant made inquiries about it.

"I drifted down and prepared for the landing. I hit the ground very hard. I always had troubles with my helmet liner. My helmet came loose on landing and slipped down over my eyes. I thought I was blind. The first thing I walked into was a mule that was staked down. I remember that there was a circle eaten all around the animal. The ground was bare.

"My task was to retrieve the breech block of the howitzer. I had to find it and then return to the others of my stick. Then suddenly, I heard a noise and saw an infantryman, believe he was walking around. I acted brave, much more brave than I actually was. I challenged him and asked him, 'Hey soldier, have you seen parts of a cannon around here?'

"He answered, 'Hell no' and took off as fast as he could. We did find the howitzer and started to assemble it. We then hid it in a haystack, and the following morning we joined friendly troops, walking on the road."[27]

Private First Class Russell T. Long, a radio operator, had been transferred from C Battery to Headquarters Battery only a week earlier. "The entire communication section of C Battery was shot down over Gela with no survivors. But for the grace of God, I would have been in that plane."[28]

Lieutenant Alphonse J. "Chick" Czekanski was the jumpmaster of his D Battery stick. "Someone or something caused me to turn around, and I saw someone jump from the airplane. The man jumped out of the door behind me. Then I saw the crew chief, rank of sergeant, coming towards me. He was also heading to the door. I stopped him and asked him what was going on. The man then asked me, 'Don't you know, the airplane is on fire?' The sergeant passed me and jumped out of the door. This was the signal for us to leave the plane as soon as possible. Luckily, the plane was over land, and everyone got out of the plane, including the crew. At that time, we were some fifty-five miles from the drop zone. The fire was caused by antiaircraft fire. I presume that the airplane had crashed."[29]

Some of the paratroopers who jumped were killed in the air, and still others shot upon landing. One plane crashed with five officers and fifteen men from Headquarters and Headquarters Company on board. Fifteen of the twenty survived, including Lieutenant Colonel Leslie Freeman, executive officer of the 504th, along with two other officers and twelve men. Eleven of the fifteen survivors were wounded.

Another plane carrying three officers and fifteen men of Headquarters Company, 2nd Battalion, crashed with the jumpmaster, Lieutenant Mack C. Shelly, standing in the door. Shelly was thrown clear of the wreckage and miraculously survived. All of the other occupants of his plane were killed.

Four of the planes shot down carried one officer and thirty-two troopers from Battery C, 376th Parachute Field Artillery Battalion. One of the four crashed into the sea with nine troopers aboard. From the other three planes, five men deployed their reserve chutes and survived. Two additional survivors crawled out of the wreckage of their plane. Three men were thrown clear as their planes crashed. The 376th lost a total of twenty-four killed and eleven missing. The 316th Troop Carrier Group that had transported the 376th lost twelve of the thirty-five planes that took part in the operation that night.

Approximately 60 of the 144 planes were damaged, with 23 shot down—6 of those before the paratroopers on board could jump. Other planes returned to Tunisia with four dead and six wounded paratroopers aboard. Eight planes returned without giving their troopers the opportunity to jump. The disastrous friendly fire incident had cost the 504th R.C.T. a total of eighty-one killed in action, sixteen missing, and 132 wounded. An estimated sixty aircrew of the 52nd Troop Carrier Wing were killed and another thirty wounded.

CAPTAIN FRANK BOYD, A LIAISON OFFICER WITH HEADQUARTERS BATTERY, 376th, "jumped into Sicily with [Lieutenant] Colonel Warren Williams of the 504th and saw no one from the 376th, except my three men for three or four days. When I did get back to the battalion, I was told about the disaster of Lieutenant [William W.] Laing's plane and that [Charles A.] Marenghi was the sole survivor. He had been just behind Lieutenant Laing in the stick. Two or three others had got out of the plane, but the plane was too low to allow time for their chutes to open. They were dead on the ground from the impact. The plane burned with the rest of the men and Lieutenant Laing in it. I believe it

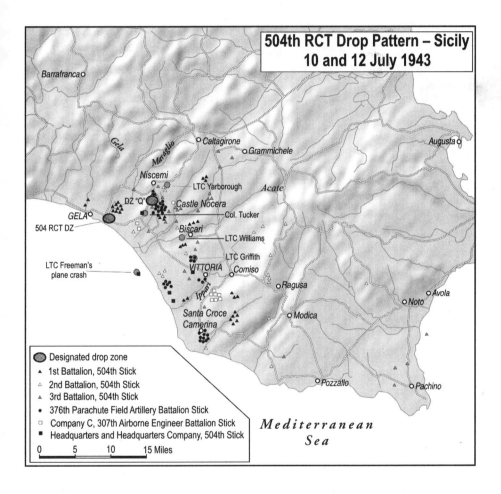

504th RCT Drop Pattern – Sicily
10 and 12 July 1943

Barrafranca

Gela

Maraglio

Caltagirone

Grammichele

Augusta

Niscemi

LTC Yarborough

Acate

DZ "Q"

Castle Nocera

GELA

Col. Tucker

504 RCT DZ

Biscari

LTC Williams

LTC Griffith

LTC Freeman's
plane crash

VITTORIA

Comiso

Ippari

Ragusa

Avola

Noto

Santa Croce
Camerina

Modica

⬤ Designated drop zone

▲ 1st Battalion, 504th Stick

△ 2nd Battalion, 504th Stick

▲ 3rd Battalion, 504th Stick

● 376th Parachute Field Artillery Battalion Stick

□ Company C, 307th Airborne Engineer Battalion Stick

■ Headquarters and Headquarters Company, 504th Stick

0   5   10   15 Miles

Mediterranean
Sea

Pozzallo

Pachino

59

was Lieutenant [Gorman S.] Oswell who told me about it. Laing's Bronze Star for valor was awarded posthumously, of course, probably to his family."[30]

Private Keith K. Scott with Headquarters Company, 1st Battalion, landed near a couple of burning enemy pillboxes. "We started to assemble in an orchard when the artillery opened up on us. That didn't last long. We assembled and found out that one man, Corporal [Stanley J.] Len, had broken his leg. We wrapped him in a chute and hid him in a vine patch. We left him with two riggers.

"Lieutenant [Richard F.] Mills got his bearings and told us what the score was. We had dropped fifteen miles from the right DZ, in enemy territory. We got our weapons and marched down the road. We heard somebody yelling and a whirring sound like an auto stuck in the mud. I don't know why, but we marched right into them. We walked across a bridge. As we reached the end [of the bridge], we heard someone yell, 'Halt!' It was the Heinies.

"Mills said, 'Ground equipment and jump over the bridge.' He no sooner said that than they opened fire on us. We ran into a vine patch and hid. They shot flares in the air and tried to pick us off. They tossed grenades and fired their guns into the patch. Privates [Alvin H.] Boggs, [Arthur M.] Wright, and I were cut off from the rest. We started to run and were chased and fired on. We lost Wright somewhere. Boggs and I hid in a cane brake for an hour or two."[31]

Sergeant Warren Le Vangia, the D Company operations sergeant, came down miles from the drop zone. "Fourteen of us gathered together in our first hour on the ground, and we seemed completely alone and had no idea where we were. Sounds of gunfire and flashes in the distant sky indicated that we were many miles from where we should have been.

"An hour after that, I killed my first two Germans by emptying a twenty-round clip of my Thompson through the windshield of a truck. To this day, I can remember my stomach churning as I looked at the faces and took their papers and a dispatch case. Only a couple of my very scared and inaccurately fired rounds had hit them—but I was pretty horrified at what I saw and what I had done. In later times, when I was being fired at, it seemed easier. These two Germans had no idea they were even in danger when they died. I can't get over that—ever.

"We picked up another couple of guys later from another company and at dawn hid in a small building in high ground."[32]

After landing, Lieutenant Edward Sims, a platoon leader with Company F, assembled his men. "I sent patrols in opposite directions on a nearby road to look for signs and landmarks. One patrol located a road sign indicating that Augusta was forty kilometers. This was sufficient to allow me to locate our general position on the map as being southwest of Augusta, Sicily and about twenty-five miles from where we planned to land in the vicinity of Gela. Also, we were several miles behind the Axis forces opposing the beach landing of the U.S. 45th Division. I had fourteen men with me, so we moved in a southwesterly direction, on roads and cross-country, toward Gela. At one point, we had a short firefight with a small German force, but they soon fled. Later, we spotted a company-size German force moving north, but since they did not see us, we held our fire and let them pass. Our next contact was with advance elements of the U.S. 45th Division. They opened fire on us, and for a few moments the situation was dangerous. We had a tough job trying to convince them that we were U.S. paratroopers."[33]

One stick of Company E troopers, led by Lieutenant John Thompson, landed on the southeastern coast of Sicily. "We hit the ground very quickly, and with no casualties, assembled and immediately sent out three groups of four men each in different directions to gain information and find out where we were. Two hours later, the three groups had returned. One group had six German prisoners. These prisoners were part of thirteen Germans who were surprised down near the shore, and seven had been killed in resisting. With no one able to speak German, we decided to take them along with us. Knowing that we were on the eastern part of the island, and knowing that our objective, in the vicinity of Gela, was on the central part of the island, we decided to head west along the coast, moving at night and resting in the daytime. Traveling was difficult, having to climb over one stone wall after another, and the terrain was mountainous."[34]

BY THE MORNING OF JULY 12, PRIVATE FIRST CLASS SHELBY HORD was going into his fourth day without sleep, since the night of July 8. "That morning about 10:00 Lieutenant Ferrill said, 'Shelby, you have not had any sleep in three days. They've got nice bedrooms up there. You go up there on that second floor and you get in bed and get some rest. Get in one of those nice beds.' There was a nice bathroom next to me, bathtub and everything . . . just like you'd find in a nice hotel. I turned the covers back, then I went and looked out of the window, and just looked down that valley that was in the rear of the building. All at once I could see one of those Mark VI [tanks] coming up the road around the bend. I watched two more Mark IVs come, and I went running down and I got a hold of Lieutenant Ferrill.

"Lieutenant Ferrill said, 'Shelby, I'll go into the flower garden and I'll tell those men to fire [the mortars] almost as quickly as they can simultaneously, and you go around and you tell those men [on the line] what's going to happen: when they hear the puff of those mortars to open fire on them.' "[35]

Accompanying the three tanks was an estimated battalion of German infantry. The force was moving north, retreating after the fighting at Biazzo Ridge. Strangely, the German infantry column stopped. As Hord stayed low, moving from man to man, he kept an eye on the German infantry on the road. Then he saw something that astonished him. Hord could hardly believe this stroke of good fortune. "They had taken a break right in front of us! The tanks had gone way up and around this hill and were gone. So we opened up at the same time the mortars opened up. We fought about two or three hours."[36]

Private First Class Lawrence Dunlop was dug in on the north side of the hill overlooking the road. "There was a good small-arms battle going on. I didn't see anything to shoot at with my machine gun, but just before dark, we saw a German tank emerge over the hill opposite us, about four hundred yards away. It fired a round at us. The shell hit right in front of Sergeant [Kenneth E.] Brady on my right. Brady was killed. Huckins, on my left, got hit on his forehead. I was showered with dirt."[37]

When Hord saw one of the German Mark IV tanks returning, "I called the bazooka man over and I said, 'Now I want you to try and shoot that damned tank.' And damned, his first round hit and knocked everything off the back where they put all of the baggage. I guess [the tank commander] thought there was more power over here, so he moved [the tank] out of the way. Then he came back, and in the bushes you could see him under the trees, with his glasses trying to estimate what was going on. Then he and another tank that had come hit a couple of machine gunners in the holes. I know we lost those men. They lobbed a couple of shells into the center of the house, and they came down into the stairwell. There was a wounded man there that got wounded in the face, and we didn't have a medic. I don't know why we didn't carry him down into the wine cellar, but we didn't.

"Lieutenant Ferrill was in the deep cellar trying to get help for us. We had a big radio, and we were trying to [contact] whoever was coming our way, hopefully it would be the 'Big Red One.' I tried to watch the front [of the chateau]. I'd run down and tell him what was going on, then I would run back and take care of my job. Then a couple of [German] officers came up with white flags and asked us to surrender. This soldier said, 'Like hell we are,' and he shot both of them dead. Then the battle really started and went on for the rest of the day, all the way until dark and then everybody stopped shooting."[38]

That night, Private First Class Dunlop, at his machine gun post, "could hear the Germans shouting orders among their dead and wounded.

"Later, I found out that First Sergeant Sneddon, my H Company leader, had been killed. During the battle, he was worried that the men on the outpost didn't have enough ammo, and wanted to bring some down to them. He had been told that they were all right. But, he insisted and picked up some grenades and some BAR ammo. Someone also said there was a Jerry out there who had the road coming up the hill [to the farm] covered with a Schmeisser. First Sergeant Sneddon took off down the hill, and sure enough—Brrp—Brrp—Brrp—the Jerry got him.

"The next morning, we could see many dead Germans out in front of us. I was amazed the German medics had treated almost all their men. This Hermann Göring outfit was a topnotch unit, as we of the 82nd found out again, and again.

"As I had some medical training, I told one of our officers that I would gladly help out the medics, for I learned that we had eighteen badly wounded troopers. So, he said O.K. Our wounded were in the wine cellar, and I went there and saw Huckins with a bloody bandage on his head. So, I removed the bandage and washed his face, then replaced a clean bandage to his forehead. In this battle, we lost four troopers and had about eighteen badly wounded. I think the Germans lost ninety or more."[39]

That same day, Lieutenant Colonel Charles Kouns, the 3rd Battalion commander, was captured. "We [had] operated alone for three days, and finally had to surrender in a house surrounded by Jerries and Italians.

"After considerable interrogation, I was sent to an Italian POW camp at Capua, Italy. On August 27th, I was sent to Chiete, where I remained until October 2nd. On October 3, while enroute to Germany, I jumped the train and remained at large for nine days, when I was recaptured at Riva. Italian civilians were nice to me during the nine days of liberty. I was transferred to Moosburg, Germany, where I was kept in solitary confinement for twenty days. While enroute to Luckenwalde, I cut my way out of a freight car and escaped near Munich. I bribed civilians for food, but could get no aid otherwise."[40]

BACK IN SICILY, MAJOR WILLIAM BEALL, the 3rd Battalion executive officer, who had rounded up some paratroopers that had landed in the British zone, had spent the night of July 11 on the beach. On the morning of July 12, together with nineteen troopers, Beall "left by RAF crash boat to rejoin the unit, and stopped enroute at coast towns to pick up United States paratroopers."[41]

By 5:30 p.m. on July 12, the 504th Parachute Infantry Regiment had managed to assemble a total of 37 officers and 518 men present for duty. The 1st Battalion, with 221 present, was under the command of Lieutenant Edson R. Mattice. The 2nd Battalion totaled 187, under the command of Captain Stanley Dolezal. Only fifty-nine of the 3rd Battalion troopers had assembled with the regiment and were commanded by a Lieutenant Stewart. Headquarters and Headquarters Company only had sixty-seven and were under the command of Lieutenant Carl W. Kappel. The medical detachment had twenty-one present, under the command of Lieutenant Kenneth Sheek.

Lieutenant Thompson, with Company E, having been badly misdropped the previous night during the friendly-fire disaster, led the men from his stick and six German prisoners west across southern Sicily, trying to find friendly forces. "In our two days of walking we observed many more enemy troops, at a distance, moving north. On the third day, we came across a field strewn with parachutes. These parachutes had been used by members of the 505th CT and some men were lying quite still in their harnesses, evidently not having a chance to get out of them.

"Upon coming to a crossroad, we saw three pillboxes commanding all the road entrances. There had evidently been a stiff fight there, for there were about twenty bodies of paratroopers in the vicinity of the pillboxes, also many enemy dead.

"Later in the afternoon we came upon a battalion CP and were informed that it belonged to the 45th Division. Here we turned over our prisoners for interrogation. We found that these Germans were part of a force that had the mission of laying mines along the coast. At this CP we were able to find that we were fifteen miles southeast of Ragusa, which was on our way to Gela.

"Later that night we arrived at Ragusa and met several paratroopers from the 504th CT who were on their way to Vittoria, where the 2nd Battalion was assembling. We took these men along with us, and early the next morning we arrived at the 2nd Battalion CP, where we met [Major William] Yarborough [the 2nd Battalion CO] and Jack Thompson of the *Chicago Tribune*. They informed me that only one-third of the battalion had reported in so far, and it was believed that the rest of the regiment had landed on their designated DZ at Gela."[42]

Shortly after dawn on July 13, at the Castle Nocera southeast of Niscemi, Private First Class Shelby Hord could see that the Germans had pulled out during the night, after the savage fighting of the previous day. So, he went down the hill to take a look around. "The poor Germans were dead in that field as far as I could see, and then on the other side of the road there were dead Germans, and then on the hill across from us there were dead.

"In the distance I could see the 'Red One' that stands out on a man's shoulder–you could see it was a 1st Division combat patrol. They came and talked with me and said, 'Do you realize that you guys have killed almost four hundred men?' One of the men told me it was 386 dead [Germans] that they had already counted, and they haven't counted some of the ones up closer [to the chateau]."[43]

THAT SAME DAY, MAJOR WILLIAM BEALL, the 3rd Battalion executive officer, and a number of paratroopers who had been misdropped in the British sector and shuttled to the American sector by boat, landed at Scoglitti. Beall "reported to bivouac area west of Vittoria (505th Combat Team CP) with Captain [William] Kitchen, one other officer, and forty-eight enlisted men from various organizations. At Vittoria, I was told that Lieutenant Colonel Kouns, the battalion commanding officer, had been captured and I was in command. I proceeded to organize the remainder of the battalion preparatory to continuing operations. We assembled a total of four officers and ninety enlisted men."[44]

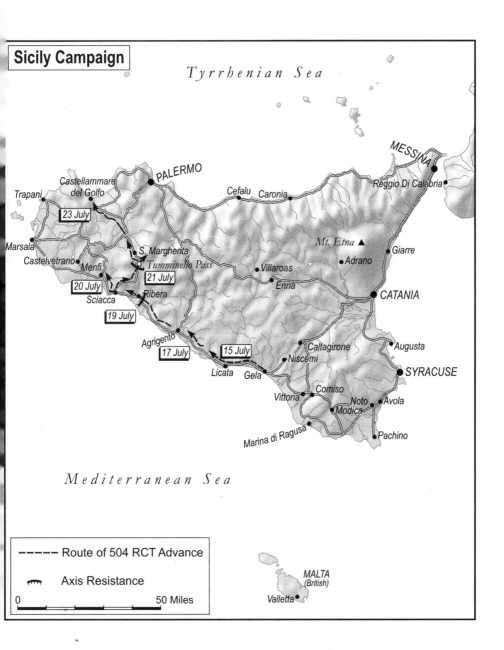

Sicily Campaign

Tyrrhenian Sea

Mediterranean Sea

MESSINA

Trapani
Castellammare del Golfo
PALERMO
Cefalu
Caronia
Reggio Di Calabria

23 July

Marsala
Castelvetrano
Menfi
S. Margherita
Tumminello Pass
Villaroas
Enna
Mt. Etna ▲
Adrano
Giarre

20 July

21 July

Ribera

Sciacca

19 July

CATANIA

Agrigento

17 July

15 July

Licata
Gela
Niscemi
Caltagirone
Augusta

SYRACUSE

Vittoria
Comiso
Noto
Modica
Avola

Marina di Ragusa
Pachino

----- Route of 504 RCT Advance

〜 Axis Resistance

0   50 Miles

MALTA
(British)

Valletta

The 3rd Battalion was returned to control of the 504th Regimental Combat Team on July 13. The entire combat team had suffered grievously over the past three days, losing a battalion commander (Kouns), every company commander, and all first sergeants except one. Over the next few days, the regiment and its supporting units reorganized as troopers continued to arrive.

The 504th RCT, now reorganized, moved from the Gela assembly area at 6:00 a.m. on July 17 in preparation for spearheading an advance up the western coast of the island. On the night of July 19, the 504th RCT, led by the 2nd Battalion, with the 82nd Armored Field Artillery Battalion and Batteries A and B of the 83rd Chemical Mortar Battalion attached, moved west from Realmonte, reaching Montallegro by 3:00 a.m. By 9:00 a.m., the 2nd Battalion had advanced to the Platani River; by 10:15 a.m. the Maggazolo River; and by noon the town of Ribera. By 9:00 p.m., the 504th RCT was stopped by an order from corps at a phase line about halfway between Ribera and Sciacca. The major obstacle was a blown bridge at the Canne River. A detachment of the 307th Airborne Engineer Battalion commanded by Lieutenant Colonel Robert S. Palmer solved this with the rapid construction of a temporary bridge strong enough to support heavy vehicles, completing it early on the morning of July 19.

At 6:00 a.m. on July 20, the 2nd Battalion continued to lead the regimental combat team in the advance to Sciacca. As Lieutenant Edward Sims led his Company F platoon up the road toward Sciacca, they were strafed by German fighter aircraft. "We did take up dispersed positions and opened fire, but all of the planes continued to fly south. As we approached Sciacca, I was leading with my platoon when I noticed smoke rising from the road ahead, so I dispersed my platoon into firing positions and went forward to check out the smoke. The road had been mined with antitank mines, and a two-wheeled cart, driven by an old man with a young child, had set off one mine, killing both of them and the mule that was pulling the cart. To our left on the crest of a small rise were a number of pillboxes with white flags being waved from the gun ports. We advanced cautiously and flushed out a large group (about one hundred) of Italian soldiers who wanted to surrender. After disarming them, they were sent, under guard, to our rear. We cleared Sciacca, then headed for Marsala."[45] The day ended with a total of approximately one thousand prisoners taken at the cost of only two casualties during the advance.

On July 21, with Company F once again in the lead, Italian infantry supported by a battery of 75mm guns and two 90mm guns ambushed the paratroopers. When the Italians opened fire, Lieutenant Sims and his troopers were advancing along the road that ran through the Tumminello Pass. "We were forced to make a frontal assault when a strong [Italian] force caught us by surprise and opened fire on our column. This turned into a long, hard firefight, with a number of casualties on both sides."[46] As Company F assaulted the Italian positions frontally, a flanking movement was undertaken, resulting in the surrender of all of the Italian personnel and weapons. Company F suffered six men killed and eight wounded in the attack.

During the fifteen-mile advance on July 21, the division added 1,515 enemy soldiers to the POW cages while suffering a total of fourteen casualties, all from Company F. With all of the prisoners, the 1st Battalion S-2 section chief, Sergeant Milton Knight, had someone in the section who could interrogate them in just about any language. Knight would simply say, "'Hey, Bachenheimer or Tuzollino or Schneider or Coccia, I got a German prisoner here, I got an Italian prisoner here, or I got a Pollock here or whatever. What we need to do is to interrogate these people and find out what information we can get from them so I can make a report to the colonel.' So, that's how we handled that."[47]

During the advance up the western side of Sicily, Private First Class Lawrence Dunlop, with Company H, walked almost the entire way from Gela, carrying his .30-caliber machine gun. "My feet were so sore, and my buddy [Private James H.] Legacie, a BAR man, was hurting, too. So we dropped off the side of the road and sat down in a vineyard, took our dusty jump boots off, and tried to take care of our feet. We would reach up and grab a grape, but they were not ripe yet. We figured we would grab a ride on some vehicle and catch up to our company. Along came a half-track—it stopped—an officer yelled to us, 'What outfit you soldiers in?'

"We said, '504 Parachute Infantry.'

"The officer said, 'You guys hungry?'

"'Yes, sir,' we said. He threw down a box of ten-in-one rations. We had heard about them, but we had never had any. I knew the box contained a can of bacon, and my mouth was watering. Legacie and I opened up the box, and I got the can of bacon. One of my prize possessions was a Coleman stove. I probably stole it somewhere. Now, how were we going to cook it? Out came my entrenching tool. I shoved it into a sandy soil a few times, wiped it on my backside, lit the stove, and cooked the bacon on the shovel. Man, did that taste good."[48]

Colonel Tucker led the 504th Reconnaissance Platoon into Castellammare del Golfo on the afternoon of July 23 and persuaded the commander of the Italian garrison to surrender. Captain Adam Komosa, the commanding officer of Headquarters Company, was glad they were entering the town from the inland side. "The defenses were strong. The shoreline was rocky and sharp. All beaches were mined. Coastal guns were covered by small arms and automatic weapons; all approaches were covered, except those inland. The defenses were all pointing out to sea.

"The approach to Castellammare was a winding road on the face of a steep bluff. An anti-facist reported this road as being prepared for demolition. He disclosed the position of the charges to the engineers before they could be blown. Approximately ten tons of explosives (similar to TNT blocks) were tamped with sandbags underneath the road in a tunnel three feet square and twenty-four feet in length, with electric detonation leads running up to a farm-house several hundred yards from the road. These charges were immediately neutralized and removed by [Lieutenant Wesley D.] Spike Harris and his men of Company C, 307th Engineers."[49]

The rest of the combat team arrived the following day after trucks became available from the 505th at Trapani. The 504th then moved to Castelvetrano to begin occupation duty.

THERE WERE A NUMBER OF COMMAND CHANGES during and after the campaign in Sicily. While Lieutenant Colonel Warren Williams continued to command the 1st Battalion, General Ridgway relieved Major William Yarborough of command for allowing his 2nd Battalion to be ambushed at the Tumminello Pass. Major Daniel W. Danielson, the executive officer, replaced him. Major Emory "Hank" Adams replaced Lieutenant Colonel Charles Kouns as commanding officer of the 3rd Battalion.

Chapter 4

"Retreat Hell!
Send Me My 3rd Battalion"

On July 29, 1943, General Ridgway received word that the 82nd Airborne Division would conduct an airborne operation as part of an amphibious landing scheduled for September 9 in the Bay of Salerno on the western coast above the toe of the Italian boot. On August 2, Ridgway and some of the division staff flew to Fifth Army Headquarters to discuss the operational plan. General Mark Clark's new airborne planner was newly promoted Lieutenant Colonel William Yarborough, whom Ridgway had recently relieved of command.

Yarborough's plan called for Ridgway's two parachute regiments to drop on the north side of the Sorrento Mountains, to block the north end of the mountain passes and prevent two German panzer divisions in the Naples area from reinforcing German forces defending the Salerno Bay area. The 325th Glider Infantry Regiment would make an amphibious landing at the town of Maiori to forge a quick linkup with the parachute forces. This plan was fraught with risks and problems. Ridgway got Clark's assurance that he would get at least three weeks of training for the 504th and 505th to work with the troop-carrier forces and for amphibious training for the 325th. After the meeting, Ridgway assigned Brigadier General Maxwell Taylor, the division artillery commander, as a liaison to General Eisenhower's Headquarters in Algiers, in order to keep an eye on Yarborough.

There was little time to apply improvements from the lessons learned from the Sicily operation. The most critical issue was dramatically improving the accuracy of night parachute drops. Sergeant Milton Knight was the S-2 section chief with Headquarters Company, 1st Battalion. "After the fiasco in Sicily, the Troop Carrier Command of the air force and the [Army] Ground Force

Headquarters (Airborne) began to look for a better way to deliver troops to the DZ. They came up with the concept of pathfinders—troops going in before the main body of troops were to arrive to mark the DZ and set up a limited defense for the DZ.

"We, the S-2 section and communications section of the 1st Battalion of the 504, were the original pathfinders. So we went back to Comiso and Agrigento [airfields in Sicily] and started working on this system of delivering troops on target."[1]

A pathfinder school was organized at Comiso airfield. The primary electronic gear consisted of a transmitter device, code-named Rebecca, mounted in sixteen special pathfinder C-47s, and a responder homing beacon, code-named Eureka, used by the pathfinders on the ground. The return signal from the Eureka would guide one pathfinder plane in each serial to the drop zone. Communications specialists from the 504th, 505th, and the attached 2nd Battalion, 509th, trained on the use of Eureka, thus becoming the original U.S. Army pathfinders.

After returning from Sicily, Sergeant Tom McCarthy, with Company A, had been selected for mountain training in anticipation of the mountain warfare in Italy. "They were training guys to be mule skinners. They picked me to go to mule skinning school. I didn't like that at all, I was a city kid, and I already knew about those miserable damned mules. They're the meanest animals in the world. That wasn't my style to roll over.

"I had a friend in A Company named [Private Robert W.] Pappy Fogle. Pappy was a real cowboy—came out of Texas. He was picked for pathfinder school, and he didn't like that at all. That wasn't his style.

"I said, 'Well Pappy, why don't we just change? You be a mule skinner—I don't want anything to do with that. I'll be a pathfinder, gladly.'

"So, I became a pathfinder, just like that. It was good duty.

"Plenty of jumping. . . . I think we jumped a half a dozen times. The training wasn't too much. They had some lights—you would jump with that package or you would jump with the radar package. The radar package looked like a barracks bag, only it was slimmer. It was strapped to your leg. When you got out of the plane, you'd release it and it would hang down below your leg. The good thing about it, it would take you down where you wanted to go, because there wouldn't be any oscillation."[2]

Sergeant Milton Knight and his S-2 section would provide the security element of the 1st Battalion, 504th, pathfinder team. "Colonel Chuck Billingslea was the CO of the ground element and Colonel Joel Crouch was the CO of the troop carrier. Lieutenant [William S.] Jones was CO of the S-2 section, and I was second in command. I don't recall who had the communications section, but it might have been Lieutenant [William W.] Magrath. Sergeant [William

W.] Bullock was his second in command. Sergeant Regis J. Pahler jumped the Eureka sending unit.

"It wasn't a very complex operation—first jump, set up the equipment, set up the defenses, and wait for the main body of troops to arrive."[3]

Sergeant McCarthy's assignment was the security team. "My job with the squad was to engage as quickly as we could, so that if we were getting any opposition, we had them occupied while the lights and radar could get underway."[4]

McCarthy and the other security-team troopers decided to jump with their weapons assembled, instead of unassembled in Griswold cases, in order to be able to engage the enemy more quickly.

Because Ridgway's parachute forces were still in Sicily performing occupation duties, and the troop-carrier forces were located in the Kairouan, Tunisia, area, no joint training could take place until the parachute elements of Ridgway's forces could be returned to Kairouan. The 504th and 505th Regimental Combat Teams also had to integrate around one thousand replacements to compensate for the casualties incurred during the Sicily campaign. After training in Kairouan, the plan was for the troop-carrier forces and Ridgway's parachute elements to move to the closer airfields in Sicily a few days prior to the operation.

On August 18, formal orders arrived for the operation, code-named Giant I, which by that time had become even more ambitious. The plan now called for the 504th and 505th RCTs to jump northwest of Naples near the Volturno River, even farther away from the landings at Salerno. The amphibious operation by the 325th RCT would also change to a landing at the mouth of the Volturno River. There was precious little time to prepare. Having only twenty-four trucks available, the division moved its troops, weapons, and equipment by shuttles to airfields and returned to Kairouan, Tunisia, on August 19 and 20.

On the night of August 28–29, a test conducted near the town of Enfidaville, Tunisia, using the new electronic equipment and lights was successful. Specially selected and trained aircrews flying the sixteen C-47 pathfinder aircraft outfitted with Rebeccas were able to pick up the Eureka beacon about twenty miles out and were effectively guided to the location of the equipment. A high-frequency radio beacon called 5G that was susceptible to jamming was also tested and was not as effective as the Rebecca-Eureka gear. The pathfinders employed Aldis lamps and Krypton lights, which were supposedly capable of being visible from twenty-five miles away, to mark the location. The lights passed the test satisfactorily. On August 30 a second test used a small number of paratroopers to actually jump on the drop zone, the planes guided by the pathfinder equipment. An extrapolation of the test indicated that if a mass jump had been executed, over ninety percent of the paratroopers would have landed within a mile of the drop zone, a huge improvement over the Sicily jump.

Unknown to anyone in the division, General Eisenhower had been conducting top-secret talks with an emissary of the Italian king since shortly after the overthrow and arrest of the Italian dictator, Benito Mussolini, on July 25. The new Italian government was prepared to sign a separate surrender and join the Allies in fighting the Germans. Eisenhower demanded that the Italian government announce the surrender before the Allies invaded Italy and order Italian forces not to fire on Allied forces once the landings began. The Italian government wanted an Allied airborne landing near Rome, to protect the government from German retribution once the surrender was announced.

The emissary told Eisenhower that Italian troops could protect three airfields around Rome so that additional forces could be air landed, would provide transportation for the Allied forces, and would help fight German forces that would surely be sent to take over Rome. Eisenhower was suspicious of the emissary and of the commitment of the Italian government to stick to any deal that was negotiated. Nevertheless, on September 2, Eisenhower decided to take the 82nd Airborne Division away from General Clark's Salerno invasion force for the airborne operation near Rome. The new plan, code-named Giant II, entailed parachuting the 504th and 505th onto Italian-held airfields on the night of September 8, and air-landing the remainder of the division, including the 325th Regimental Combat Team, at the airfields held by the paratroopers and the Italian forces. The 325th RCT, already loaded on its assigned LSTs in Bizerte, was ordered to disembark.

On September 3, the Italian government's emissary, Giuseppe Castellano, signed an armistice, with a commitment stipulated in the agreement for the Allies to land forces near Rome to protect the Italian government. That same night, Ridgway, Taylor, and numerous other officers met with Castellano to discuss the planned airborne operation. Already skeptical, Ridgway and Taylor became convinced during the discussions that they could not rely on the Italians to take on the Germans, which would mean certain destruction of the division.

Ridgway argued and succeeded in getting the scale of the initial parachute jump reduced to a regimental combat team, less one battalion for the initial drop. If the drop went well, reinforcements would follow on succeeding nights.

He also argued for a secret mission to Rome to determine the capability and commitment of the Italian government and military forces before the execution of the operation. The mission was approved with one condition—the mission could not commence until twenty-four hours before the operation, so that if the emissaries were captured, the Germans would not have time to extract details of the plan and implement actions in time to counter the drop. General Maxwell Taylor and Colonel William Gardiner, an intelligence officer with the 51st Troop Carrier Wing, volunteered for this very dangerous assignment.

On September 4, Ridgway flew to his advanced command post at Bizerte to work on planning of the operation. He chose Colonel Tucker's 504th RCT, less the 3rd Battalion, for the initial drop.

On September 6, Company H, 504th; the 319th Glider Field Artillery Battalion; D, E, F, and Headquarters Batteries and the medical detachment of the 80th Airborne Antiaircraft (Antitank) Battalion; the 2nd Platoon, Company A, 307th Airborne Engineer Battalion; and two platoons of the 813th Tank Destroyer Battalion loaded on one LST and three LCIs at Bizerte. The amphibious force sailed the next day for the Tiber River with the mission of sailing up the river and linking up with the airborne forces near Rome.

At 4:00 a.m. on September 7, General Taylor and Colonel Gardiner left Palermo, Sicily, aboard a British PT boat for the small island of Ustica, forty miles northwest of Sicily. There, they transferred to an Italian corvette, which took them to the Italian mainland. They both decided to wear their uniforms and carry their pistols, so that if the Germans caught them, technically they would not consider them as spies.

At about 6:30 p.m. they landed at Gaeta on the western coast, about seventy-five miles from Rome. Before disembarking from the ship, they took off their caps, ruffled their hair, and disheveled their uniforms. Armed Italian guards were placed around them to give them the appearance of being P.O.W.s to anyone observing them leaving the ship. General Taylor "knew the kind of treatment we'd get if the Germans did nab us. It had been arranged that if any questions were asked when we were first taken ashore, we were to be described as American aviators who had been shot down in the Mediterranean, and picked up by the corvette as prisoners."[5]

A waiting car drove them to a small side road outside of town, where they transferred to a Red Cross ambulance with frosted glass windows that allowed them to look out, but prevented anyone from being able to see into the back of the vehicle. They passed through six roadblocks and only saw four German soldiers during their drive into Rome. They arrived in Rome around nightfall and were taken to a building across the street from the War Office. They used their trench coats to cover their uniforms as they moved quickly from the back of the truck into the building. They had rooms in a wing of the building entirely blocked off with armed guards posted at each end of the corridor. They enjoyed a superb dinner a short time later with Colonel Salbi, the chief of staff to General Carboni, commander of the Italian Army corps in the Rome area. The Italians, totally unaware of the impending airborne operation, were planning to take the emissaries to meet with General Carboni the next morning. After dinner, Taylor and Gardiner insisted on seeing General

Carboni immediately, which was hastily arranged. Carboni arrived at about 9:30 p.m. for the meeting.

Taylor's patience was tested as the Italian general "launched upon an expose of his views of the military situation in the Rome area. Since the fall of Mussolini (he said), the Germans had been bringing in men and supplies through the Brenner Pass and also through Resia and Tarvisio, with the result that their forces near Rome had greatly increased. There were now twelve thousand Germans, principally parachutists in the valley of the Tiber who [had] heavy equipment, including one hundred pieces of artillery, principally 88mm. The panzer grenadier division [near Rome] had been raised to an effective strength of twenty-four thousand men, with fifty light and one hundred fifty heavy tanks. In the meantime, the Germans had ceased to supply the Italians with gas and munitions so that their divisions were virtually immobilized and had only enough ammunition for a few hours of combat. General Carboni's estimate of the situation was as follows:

"If the Italians declare an armistice, the Germans will occupy Rome, and the Italians can do little to prevent it. The simultaneous arrival of U.S. airborne troops would only provoke the Germans to more drastic action. Furthermore, the Italians would be unable to secure the airfields, cover the assembly, and provide the desired logistical aid to the airborne troops. If it must be assumed that an Allied seaborne landing is impossible north of Rome, then the only hope of saving the capital is to avoid overt acts against the Germans and await the effects of the Allied attacks in the south. He stated that he knew that the Allied landings would be at Salerno, which was too far away to aid directly in the defense of Rome. He stated that General Reatta shared his views.

"It was apparent that regardless of the soundness of General Carboni's information and views, he displayed an alarming pessimism certain to affect his conduct of operations in connection with Giant II."[6]

Taylor and Gardiner asked for an immediate meeting with Marshal Pietro Badoglio, the Italian head of state, and were taken by General Carboni to the marshal's private villa, arriving around midnight. They waited while Carboni met privately with Badoglio, and about fifteen minutes later were taken in to meet with the marshal, where he greeted them warmly.

Taylor asked, "Was Marshal Badoglio in accord with General Carboni in considering an immediate armistice and the reception of airborne troops impossible of execution? The marshal replied that he agreed with Carboni and repeated much the same arguments. I asked if he realized how deeply his government was committed by the agreements entered into by the Castellano mission. He replied that the situation had changed and that General Castellano had not known all the facts."[7]

After some more discussion in which General Taylor emphasized the seriousness of the situation for the Italian government, Taylor agreed to send a statement of the Italian views signed by Marshall Badoglio to Eisenhower's Headquarters in Algiers along with his own message recommending cancellation of Giant II. Badoglio agreed, and with the message in hand, the group returned to the quarters in Rome, where General Carboni arranged for immediate transmission of the two messages. At 8:00 a.m. on September 8, Taylor and Gardiner received confirmation that their messages had been received in Algiers.

Taylor waited most of the morning for a reply. "At 11:35, as no acknowledgement of the message recommending the cancellation of Giant II had been received, the code phrase 'Situation Innocuous' was sent off. This had not been sent initially, as its use had been reserved for the case of an Italian refusal to transmit a request for cancellation. It was used in this instance to save time, as the encoding of longer messages was taking as much as three hours."[8]

By September 8, the division's parachute and glider forces had been flown from Kairouan to several airfields in Sicily and were prepared for the operation, with the 504th Regimental Combat Team, less the 3rd Battalion, scheduled to begin taking off at 5:45 p.m. That afternoon, at the airfield in Sicily, Private Joe Watts, with Company F, was aboard his plane ready for takeoff. "Our 1st Battalion aircraft were in the air and forming up to fly to Italy when jeeps came screaming onto the tarmac among the 2nd Battalion taxiing aircraft. Bagdoglio had renounced the armistice terms—he needed more time. The Rome operation was canceled."[9]

Taylor's mission had narrowly avoided what would have been a disaster for the 504th. With the cancellation of the operation, the seaborne force that was to sail up the Tiber River to link up with the airborne forces changed course for Maiori, Italy.

Lieutenant Edward Sims, now a platoon leader with Company H (after leading a platoon of Company F in Sicily) was aboard one of the navy LCIs and was briefed on the change in plans for the seaborne force. "Company H was given a new mission to land at Maiori, Italy. We had to coordinate, by radio, with the U.S. Rangers who would land in the same area on September 9, 1943."[10]

The next morning, September 9, at 3:30 a.m. the Fifth Army, under General Mark Clark, began amphibious landings near Salerno, Italy. The landings were over a wide area, with a gap of seven miles between the British X Corps on the left and the American VI Corps on the right. The ranger force came ashore on the northern side of the Bay of Salerno at Maiori to protect the far left flank of the Allied beachhead. The rangers were supported by the attached Company H, 504th; the 319th Glider Field Artillery Battalion; D, E, F, and Headquarters Batteries and the medical detachment of the 80th Airborne Antiaircraft (Antitank) Battalion; the 2nd Platoon, Company A, 307th Airborne Engineer Battalion; and two platoons of the 813th Tank Destroyer Battalion.

Lieutenant Robert S. Hutton, a forward observer with the 376th Parachute Field Artillery Battalion, accompanied the 319th Glider Field Artillery Battalion. "They had no assigned forward observers, so I volunteered to go with them. There were, I believe, six of us from the 456th and 376th Parachute Field Artillery.

"We landed there with no opposition. We joined the Rangers at the Chiunzi Pass."[11]

The German 16th Panzer Division opposed the main landings, where they had fortified the beaches with zeroed-in artillery and mortars, mines, barbed wire entanglements, and pre-sighted machine guns. They had an armored counterattack force waiting in reserve.

The new U.S. 36th Infantry Division met heavy resistance as it came ashore. At about 7:00 a.m., the Germans counterattacked all landing beaches with armor and infantry. The German armored attack was thrown back only through the employment of every weapon available to the landing forces. However, by the end of the day, the American and British forces had driven inland between three and five miles. Only on the extreme right flank of the 36th Division was the situation precarious.

On September 10, the Allied beachhead expanded, while the Hermann Göring Panzer Division arrived to reinforce the 16th Panzer Division. That evening, Lieutenant Ed Sims went ashore with the 82nd Airborne Division's seaborne force. "We landed unopposed on the narrow stone coastal area near Maiori, which is nine miles west of Salerno and part of the Sorrento Peninsula. After landing, we moved inland and went to the mountains, where we seized some high ground near the Chiunzi Pass area, including a vital tunnel. Two battalions of U.S. Rangers moved north to positions that commanded the Pagni-Nocera Pass. Another battalion moved into the Amalfi area.

"My platoon occupied positions at the tunnel on the right flank of the company. The company commander borrowed a truck from a local citizen to use for mobility in order to cover the wide area (about five miles) we had to defend. Our company strength at that time was about one hundred twenty men. This rugged mountain area was not difficult to defend, because the heavy equipment of the Germans was restricted to road use. There were two roads that had to be considered: one from Gragniano through the tunnel, and the other through Sorrento and Amalfi. It was our job to prevent German forces from using these roads to get through to Salerno."[12]

The following day, September 11, the 36th Infantry Division pushed into the hills overlooking the beaches, moving east through Altavilla, occupying the strategic Hill 424 east of the town and capturing Albanella to the south. To the left of that division, the U.S. 45th Infantry Division's 179th RCT drove east from Persano toward Ponte Sele, which lay in the hills.

By the evening of September 11, a dangerous situation existed along the boundary between the U.S. and British forces, where a gap appeared as the American left flank advanced east and the British right turned northeast. Also by that evening, the German 26th Panzer Division, 29th Panzer Grenadier Division, and elements of the 15th Panzer Grenadier Division arrived to strengthen the German defenses, now totaling five powerful armored and armored infantry divisions ready to drive the Allied forces into the sea.

During the night, the Germans infiltrated around Hill 424 near the town of Altavilla, in the 36th Division sector. At dawn on September 12, German infantry and tanks struck Hill 424 from three sides and finally from the rear. The Germans broke through to take Altavilla, cutting the 1st Battalion, 142nd Infantry Regiment in two, and surrounding Company K, 143rd Infantry Regiment.

With the hard-pressed British unable to protect the 45th Division's left flank, the Germans drove down the highway north of Persano, with eight tanks leading a battalion of infantry. This powerful force struck the rear area and attached units of the 179th RCT, then, turning northeast, hit the rifle companies from behind, forcing the regiment into a perimeter defense. Other strong forces overran British forces in Battipaglia. The Germans were now in a position for a concerted push the following morning west from Altavilla and south from Persano across the Salerno plain, with the goal to meet at the Sele River and drive toward the beaches.

To relieve the pressure on the beachhead and cut off German reinforcements, Fifth Army directed the 82nd to execute the previously canceled operation, Giant I, with a jump northwest of Naples. Ridgway also received an order to drop the 2nd Battalion, 509th Parachute Infantry Regiment (still attached to the division), near Avellino, Italy, to block the mountain pass there. The orders stipulated that the jumps were to take place that night, September 12. Ridgway replied that the Avellino drop could be made on the night of September 15–16 and that the Giant I operation could not take place until the night of September 14–15. Ridgway also indicated that because no suitable drop zones were available northwest of Naples, the operation could be executed at Capua, northeast of Naples.

On the morning of September 13, the 325th Glider Infantry Regiment and the 3rd Battalion, less Company H, were loaded aboard nine LCIs at Licata, Sicily. The seaborne force began the voyage to the mouth of the Volturno River northwest of Naples to land and quickly link up with the parachute elements.

Ominously that same morning, the Germans unleashed a combined-arms attack that struck the 36th and 45th Divisions with massive sledgehammer blows that sent both divisions reeling back toward the beaches. The situation quickly became critical as German tanks and infantry hit several rifle companies from the rear and surrounded the headquarters of the 1st Battalion, 157th Infantry Regiment. The German forces pushed hard and penetrated precariously close to the beaches.

General Clark ordered his chief of staff to prepare a plan for evacuating the beachhead. The U.S. and Royal Navy ships offshore fired salvo after salvo into the oncoming German armor and infantry with devastating effect. On shore every man and weapon available were thrown into the fight against the relentless German advance.

General Clark, having already committed his floating reserve, the 45th Division, turned to the 82nd Airborne Division for help. Around noon, he wrote a letter to General Ridgway and gave it to a pilot with a reconnaissance squadron, which was operating from a dirt airstrip near Paestum, ordering him to deliver the letter personally to General Ridgway and nobody else. The pilot immediately returned to his P-38 and took off for Sicily with the letter.

At around 1:30 p.m. Colonel Gavin was working at division headquarters at the Licata airfield when the P-38 landed. Gavin met with the pilot, who asked to see General Ridgway. "He had an urgent message for the division commander and refused to give it to anyone else. I talked to him on the field, but finally had the chief of staff radio General Ridgway, who had taken off for Termini."[13]

Ridgway had only been in the air about fifteen minutes, on his way to conduct an inspection of the division's forces, when "the navigator of my C-47 came back and told me that there was an urgent message for me back at Licata. He had no information as to who the sender was, nor what the nature of the message might be. This presented quite a problem of decision, for I was on fairly urgent business of my own. However, some sixth sense must have told me that this thing was important, for I gave orders to return. We landed at Licata about 2:00, and there I found a tired, begrimed P-38 pilot bearing a personal letter from Mark Clark.

"Even through the formal official phrases I could read my old friend's deep concern. The gist of the message was that unless we could get help to him and get it there fast, the landing in Italy might be turned into another Dunkirk. It was absolutely essential, he wrote, that we drop strong forces within the beachhead area that night.

"Word was sent at once to Troop Carrier Command, and I took off immediately for south central Sicily, where Reuben Tucker's fine 504th was in bivouac. To Tucker and his staff I quickly outlined the plan. Within two hours the men were assembling at their aircraft in full combat gear. Maps were spread over the tail surfaces of the C-47, and there on the field the units of the regiment were given their missions."[14]

At the Comiso airfield, Lieutenant Reneau Breard, a platoon leader with Company A, had received a warning order earlier in the afternoon to be prepared for action. Then, "Williams got the officers together and told us we were going to drop at Salerno to reinforce the Fifth Army."[15]

Private Albert Clark and the rest of Company A received a "short briefing just before boarding the planes, to let us know that we would be jumping in as reinforcements—that a German detachment, with tanks, was moving down a canyon on the north end of the beachhead and that we were to stop them. If not [able to stop them], we were to fight a delaying action, to allow them to evacuate as much of the beachhead as possible. When we got pushed back to the beach, [we were] to start swimming and they would try to pick us up."[16]

General Ridgway was worried about a repeat of the friendly-fire disaster that Tucker's troopers experienced over Sicily, especially with such a short amount of time to coordinate with friendly naval and ground forces within the beachhead area. "Plans for lighting the drop zone came with Clark's letter. The troops on the ground were to fill oil cans with sand soaked with gasoline, arrange the cans in a big 'T,' and as the first drop plane drew near, the 'T' would be lighted. Every plane would spill its stick to fall on this flaming beacon. We also had Clark's assurance that along the corridor we would fly, not a gun on the ground would fire. Eight hours after the pilot had handed me General Clark's letter, planes of the 52nd Troop Carrier [Wing] were lifting from the Sicilian fields, carrying the 504th Regiment, plus Company C of the 307th Airborne Engineers."[17]

Dropping ahead of Tucker's paratroopers to guide the planes to the drop zone would be the 504th's pathfinder teams, the first pathfinders to make a combat jump. Behind the pathfinder teams, the main-force serials took off from several airfields in Sicily. Lieutenant Chester A. Garrison, the S-1 of the 2nd Battalion, was the jumpmaster on his plane. "The course was along the north Sicilian coast to Italy, up the west Italian coast to the designated drop zone at Paestum."[18]

In one of the three pathfinder planes, Sergeant Regis J. Pahler, with Headquarters Company, 1st Battalion, jumped with the Eureka "strapped to my right leg and with a quick release attachment [leg bag], which was to be implemented as soon as my chute opened. The plane from which my radar team jumped was jumpmastered by [Lieutenant] Colonel Charles Billingslea. As our plane approached the DZ, a flaming cross was ignited on the ground as a signal to us. As soon as the green light went on, out we went. No sooner had our chutes opened, when the troops on the ground began firing at us. I could hear the bullets whistling around me and could see tracers clearly. At this time, a loud voice below bellowed, 'Cease fire, you ___ers, they are American troops,' but this did not stop the firing. Instead of releasing the seventy-five-pound Eureka from my right leg, I hit the ground with silk in my hand and the Eureka still attached to my leg. Momentarily, I thought that I had a broken leg, but that was not the case. I set up the Eureka immediately, and with Colonel Billingslea beside me, we could hear the planes triggering in on the set."[19]

In the three-quarter moonlit night, soldiers of the 36th and 45th Divisions stood up in their foxholes and cheered as first they heard the low roar of C-47s, then saw the dark silhouettes of C-47s in the distance as parachutes filled the night sky. Sergeant Pahler watched the awesome spectacle overhead. "The main body of troops began to jump right over the set. What a beautiful sight to behold!"[20]

As his plane came in low over the mountains, Lieutenant Garrison could see the drop zone marked with the flaming gasoline drums. "A 'T' designated the field clearly. We jumped at 2335, assembled on the blinker, and moved to the road where trucks were waiting. We were the first elements of the regiment to arrive, with the exception of the pathfinder group, which we met on the field."[21]

The 1st Battalion serial dropped shortly after the 2nd Battalion. Lieutenant Reneau Breard, an assistant platoon leader with Company A, was concerned about a repeat of the friendly fire disaster that had occurred over Sicily. "We didn't fly over the navy at all. We came up from the south. We stayed over the sea. The south end of the Bay of Salerno juts out, so we flew over that; and when we came over that we could see the drop zone. We dropped between six and eight hundred feet."[22]

After landing, Colonel Tucker was taken to a house a few hundred yards from the drop zone, where he, his regimental staff, and his battalion commanders were briefed on the situation. Lieutenant Colonel Warren R. Williams, 1st Battalion commanding officer, told his S-3, Lieutenant John S. Lekson, to accompany him to the briefing. Shortly after Lekson arrived at the house, "a lieutenant colonel [Wiley O'Mohundro] of VI Corps began to review the situation in the VI Corps sector. He told of the troops that had been cut off at Altavilla, and of a gap that existed in the VI Corps line into which the regiment, led by corps guides, would move. The regiment would 'hold to the last man and last round.' Troops were to be warned that men of the 36th Division would undoubtedly be drifting through the lines.

"Then Colonel Tucker made his assignments. The 2nd Battalion would defend the left sector; the 1st Battalion, the right, extending up the slope of Mount Soprano."[23]

Within an hour Colonel Tucker's force was assembled, consisting of the 1st and 2nd Battalions; Company C, 307th Airborne Engineer Battalion, less the 1st Platoon; and detachments of the 307th Medical Company and the 82nd Reconnaissance Platoon. One 2nd Battalion, Headquarters Company stick, and one D Company stick were missing from the 2nd Battalion, while five planeloads of Company B troopers were missing from the 1st Battalion serial.

As THE 504TH WAS PARACHUTING NEAR PAESTUM, the 1st Platoon, Company C, 307th Airborne Engineer Battalion and the 2nd Battalion, 509th Parachute Infantry Regiment (which was attached to the 82nd Airborne Division)

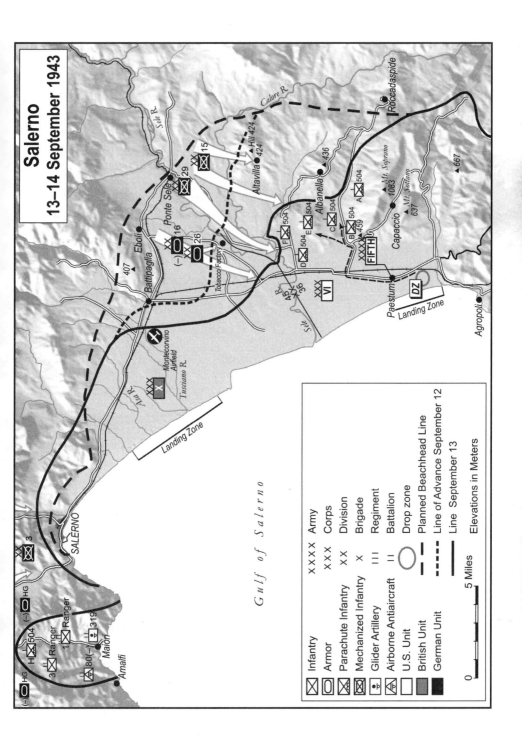

Salerno
13–14 September 1943

Gulf of Salerno

Infantry	XXXX	Army
Armor	XXX	Corps
Parachute Infantry	XX	Division
Mechanized Infantry	X	Brigade
Glider Artillery	III	Regiment
Airborne Antiaircraft	II	Battalion
U.S. Unit	◯	Drop zone
British Unit		Planned Beachhead Line
German Unit		Line of Advance September 12
		Line September 13
	▲	Elevations in Meters

0   5 Miles

jumped near Avellino, about fifty miles to the north. Their mission was to interdict enemy reinforcements. The 2nd Battalion, 509th, objective was a chokepoint for German traffic moving to the Salerno beachhead area—the town of Avellino, through which three key highways passed. The first stick of the 1st Platoon, under the command of Lieutenant Wesley D. "Spike" Harris, was supposed to jump southeast of Avellino, in a valley eight hundred yards northeast of Serino to blow bridges along a road that led to Highway 88, which ran south from Avellino to the town of Salerno. The second and third sticks, under the command of Lieutenant William W. Kellogg, were to jump closer to Avellino, southeast near Santa Lucia.

Instead, all of the units were badly misdropped. The second and third sticks of the 1st Platoon of Company C, 307th, had the worst drop northeast of Paternopoli, over twenty miles northeast of Avellino, far from their drop zone. The first stick was dropped to the south of its drop zone, landing around southeast of Solofra, some four miles from their drop zone. Worse was the fact that the stick was badly scattered, with Lieutenant Harris only able to locate two of his fifteen-man stick.

AFTER THE BRIEFING AT VI CORPS HEADQUARTERS, Tucker was met by General Clark, who told him, "As soon as assembled you are to be placed in the front lines."[24] Inside the Salerno beachhead, Colonel Tucker replied, "Sir, we are assembled and ready now."[25]

To the south near Paestum, Lieutenant John Lekson, the 1st Battalion S-3, returned from the briefing and boarded one of the waiting trucks. "Then came an order to move out. North and then east toward Mount Soprano went the convoy until, some eight miles from the drop zone, it halted. The position to be defended was a flat valley floor and the north slopes of Mount Soprano."[26]

Tucker's men were trucked part of the way, but then marched up to the assigned area, and were dug in by 3:00 a.m. Company A was assigned the right flank on the northern slope of Mount Soprano facing east, their line running down to the valley floor to an east-west road that was the boundary with Company C. The valley floor, for which Company C was responsible, was a very poor defensive position with virtually no natural terrain obstacles to an enemy advance. The Company C position tied in with 2nd Battalion on its left that occupied a hill called Tempone Di San Paolo. The 2nd Battalion's line extended north from Tempone Di San Paolo, where it tied in with the 45th Division. At dawn, the two battalion commanders made a personal reconnaissance of their respective battalion lines in order to make adjustments as necessary.

MEANWHILE, FAR TO THE NORTH, LIEUTENANT KELLOGG set out to find his troopers. "Equipment bundles of only the second stick were dropped. All men, with the exception of Private First Class [Harold E.] Fries assembled on these and obtained twelve TNT bags, twenty M1A1 mines and fuses, one light machine gun, and 1,500 rounds of ammo, in addition to their other equipment. Three small German tankettes were observed reconnoitering the jump field, so Staff Sergeant [Noel E.] Morrison was detailed to use fourteen of the mines to prepare for them. One patrol of four men and Sergeant [Paul D.] Kratsch was detailed to search for Private First Class Fries. They were unable to find [him] at the end of an hour, so we moved out. We left the jump field after one tankette had been destroyed by a mine and the other two retreated. We marched south-west until 0700, and it had become too light to move safely. In this march, we cut seventeen different telephone lines and used one-half of our TNT to blow three towers in a high-tension line. When we cut the line, we noticed that a large German cross on a mountain behind Chiusano was extinguished; within an hour, the lights were burning again. We then used four more of our TNT bags to wreck two towers and short and burn the lines between Chiusano and the point at which the Germans had made the repairs."[27]

Kellogg and his engineers hid out near Paternapoli during the daylight hours of September 14. With their special training and explosives, Kellogg and his engineers planned to inflict great damage as they made their way toward friendly lines.

TUCKER'S TROOPERS NOW OCCUPIED THE GAP the Germans had torn in the 36th Division line, where the Germans were expected to exploit. Word was passed to expect an attack later that morning. In the predawn darkness, the two battalions put out listening posts and patrols toward Albanella in order to gain advanced warning of any German assaults.

Midmorning of the 14th, the missing troopers from Company B arrived in the 1st Battalion command post area. Two of the company's planes had experienced problems on the ground prior to takeoff. With no spare planes, they were forced to distribute the troopers among the planes still on the ground. As Lieutenant Lekson was getting some administrative work done, he heard that the five Company B planes had taken off about an hour after the 1st Battalion serial. "Probably due to an insufficient briefing, the pilot of the lead plane gave B Company a green light over the mountains some six miles south of the drop zone. Upon landing, Captain [Charles W.] Duncan failed to recognize any landmarks and decided to form a perimeter with his group of four officers and eighty men. When dawn came this group could see the Paestum beaches to their north. At once, they moved off toward the beaches. Near the regimental drop zone they were able to obtain truck transportation and a guide who led them to the battalion defense position.

"With the coming of B Company, C Company moved to the north and B Company filled in the center of the battalion sector, astride the road, tying in with A Company on the right."[28]

The missing D Company planeload also reported in to the 2nd Battalion during the morning. So, other than about seventy-five jump-injured troopers, the two battalions were at full strength. As the morning progressed, the Germans began concentrating some strength for an attack against the 2nd Battalion sector.

Lieutenant Chester Garrison, the 2nd Battalion's S-1, responsible for maintaining the battalion's unit journal, kept apprised of reports coming into the battalion command post during the day. "Fifteen tanks have been sighted to our front . . . six have been knocked out by artillery."[29] The Germans continued to probe the 504th line afterward, but the artillery barrage evidently discouraged German plans for an attack in the 504th sector that day. During the night of the 14th, Tucker's two battalions and the attached units continued to patrol aggressively, as much as three miles forward of their lines.

At 11:00 p.m. that evening, the LCIs transporting the 325th RCT and the 3rd Battalion (less Company H), arrived on Red Beach in the 36th Division sector and began unloading their men and equipment. Most of the men had to wade ashore.

DURING THE NIGHT OF SEPTEMBER 14–15, LIEUTENANT KELLOGG and his misdropped troopers moved out and "continued the course southwest as soon as dusk fell; crossed one small river with German patrols on both sides, and found a standard gauge railway with many communication lines. We removed one length of rail from a curve and cut all of the communication lines. We went into bivouac at 0600 about one mile northeast of Castelvetre.

"Numerous German patrols were spotted during the day, and convoys were observed going through Castelvetre."[30]

In the 504th sector, Colonel Tucker called an 11:00 a.m. meeting with his 1st and 2nd Battalion commanders and their company commanders. Tucker briefed them on an attack that was to begin at 3:00 p.m.; the 1st Battalion objective was Hill 424 east of Altavilla, while the 2nd Battalion was assigned to capture Hill 344 and another, known as the unnumbered hill, to the south of Hill 424. The 1st Battalion, 505th would screen the regiment's right flank.

Around noon on the 16th, the 2nd Battalion S-3, Lieutenant John Lekson, received reports relayed from a couple of patrols that had returned after daybreak. "While C Company prepared to move, its combat patrol returned. They had much to report. They had engaged in three firefights. Considerable enemy artillery and mortar fire had fallen on them. However, the resistance seemed so scattered that it was deemed unimportant. A regimental patrol reported that some forty enemy tanks were located on the reverse slope of a hill about a mile and a half southeast of Altavilla."[31]

In the short time he had been at the Salerno beachhead, Lieutenant Lekson had learned from 36th Division officers how the Germans were taking full advantage of the terrain features in the hills. "On the slopes of the hills were intermittent streams, dry now, that had cut deep gullies into the slopes. Numerous additional erosion features such as dips and gullies marred the hillsides. Many of these had steep sides and narrow bottoms. Trails that went from Albanella to Altavilla followed north on noses jutting from the hill mass. These trails dipped through draws and gullies and often formed defiles as they did so. Lining the trails were trees and stone walls. In places, the trails moved along terraced levels with drops on one side and walls on the other. A profusion of minor footpaths and trails joined the main trail.

"Cognizant of the terrain and affected by the heavy American artillery, the Germans had adopted a set of peculiar tactics to hold the hills. Occupying only certain features with outposts and observation parties, the enemy would be alerted as American troops entered the hill mass. From their covered positions would come the enemy main force, which after locating the American forces would maneuver through gullies and ditches to hit the American forces from all directions. Often they were not detected until they were on the positions. With these tactics the enemy had driven out the previous 36th Division attackers."[32]

Just before 3:00 p.m., Tucker's two battalions marched east in a column of companies, with each company in a tactical column of twos. Lieutenant Chester Garrison, the 2nd Battalion S-1, moved out with Headquarters Company. "The march went across country, ploughed fields, and up a very steep hill. The terrific heat of the day and the stiffness of the walk, together with the excessive weight of the equipment, were too much for the men. They could not keep up with the rate of the march, particularly the [81mm] mortar platoon, several of whom passed out along the way."[33]

Otto W. Huebner was the Company A operations sergeant. "The march to the objective was long, hard, and tiresome. The winding trails were narrow and rocky, with overhanging brush in many places, which made it difficult to follow. From the last positions on Mount Soprano to Albanella, the distance was four miles, and yet that was only about half the way to the company's objective. Near Albanella, enemy artillery shells began to drop on the column. It was more harassing than harmful, but it slowed the column down considerably. Gaps began to show between men, and it became very difficult to keep contact. The company commander, Captain Willard E. Harrison, told the point to move faster because the column was behind schedule."[34]

The 1st Battalion found Albanella undefended and moved on toward their objective, with Company A in the lead, followed by Company C, then Company B, with Headquarters Company bringing up the rear. As Company A turned north toward Altavilla and Hill 424, Sergeant Huebner suddenly heard and saw firing up ahead. "As the 1st Platoon reached a creek just north of Albanella, two enemy machine guns opened fire on the point, without inflicting a casualty, but caused the front of the column to take cover. It was easy to observe the fire, for the enemy was using tracer ammunition, and the fire was about five feet off the ground. The 1st Platoon leader, Lieutenant [Donald F.] Horton, put his 60mm mortar into action and knocked out the machine guns in quick order.

"After this short action, the column continued to move again, but at a much slower pace. The men were very tired and began to lag. About this time the enemy artillery began to fall with greater intensity and accuracy. Calls for medics from wounded men in the column could be heard frequently.

"The officers and NCOs had to move up and down the column to get the men to their feet and keep them moving. The men had a tendency to lie down when the artillery came close and not watch the individual in front of him, thereby losing contact. The battalion commander, Lieutenant Colonel Warren R. Williams, and Captain Harrison, the company commander, came up to the point many times and directed the route. About 2200, word came up the column to the company commander that most of Company C and all of Company B had lost contact. Lieutenant Colonel Williams, who was still with Company A, gave the order to Captain Harrison to move anyway to the objective."[35]

AS THE REGIMENT MOVED TOWARD ITS OBJECTIVES near Altavilla, Lieutenant William Kellogg and his engineers "spent the night until 0100 looking for a convoy park, which the Italians had said was around: we were unable to locate the dump, so we moved through the German-held town of Castelvetre, cutting another power line and all communication lines. We encountered one German patrol and were searched all night by a German observation plane, which dropped flares. We bivouacked in the mountains southwest of Castelvetre, and the men ran out of food and water."[36]

AT HIS NEWLY ESTABLISHED FORWARD COMMAND POST in Albanella, Colonel Tucker tried without success to reach his two battalions by radio. Frustrated, Tucker set out to find them in the dark, taking with him his command group, fourteen engineers from Company C, 307th Airborne Engineer Battalion, and about twenty troopers of the 505th who had been picked up during the advance into Albanella. As they moved through the darkness, the group was subjected to shelling by German artillery. Journalists Richard Tregaskis, Cy Korman, and Reynolds Packard, along with photographer Bob Capa, caught up with Tucker's group strung out along a drainage ditch next to a farmer's field on one of the trails. It seemed that the Germans had a spotter nearby, because the German artillery fire bracketed the group. Tregaskis heard Tucker say, "We better get out of here. They're getting the range. Let's go."[37]

Tregaskis followed the colonel's lead. "We jumped up the bank and sprinted across the field and up a hillside. With the motion of our running, we saw a farmhouse bouncing in the moonlight; that would be our immediate objective. We saw another ditch, as the bouncing image of the farmhouse grew larger. We scrambled into the ditch, panting. We were just in time. The shells came again and exploded between this trench and the ditch we had just left.

"The firing lulled, and in a few seconds when thought comes back again, and motion, when the concussion has done its work and gone, Lieutenant Colonel [Leslie] Freeman, the regimental executive, and Major [Don B.] Dunham, came clumping over the no-man's land between the two ditches. They had stayed behind to care for Captain Tom Wight [commanding officer of Company C, 307th Airborne Engineer Battalion], who had been hit by the last shell. He was beyond care. A fragment had struck him squarely in the back."[38] Tucker and his group then moved out again searching for the two battalions.

After the break in the column, the 1st Battalion staff was trying to assist the company commanders in reestablishing a cohesive force in the darkness. Lieutenant Lekson, the S-3, together with Captain Charles Duncan, the commanding officer of Company B, found the break in the column. Lekson listened as the executive officer and the 3rd Platoon leader of Company C explained what had happened. "Their story was brief. Men had fallen asleep. A man looking up saw that the man who had been before him was no longer there. As he called back, he frantically tried to find the column in front of him with no success. The platoon leader, upon hearing the commotion, had sent out a two man patrol north on the trail and had reported the break to the C Company executive officer, who was marching at the rear of C Company.

"As I awaited word from the contact patrol, a quick check was made of the forces. The 3rd Platoon of Company C was still on the trail; tied in behind it was B Company, followed by Headquarters Company. Ahead somewhere [were] A Company and C Company with the battalion commander.

"Soon the contact patrol was back. They had gone north on the trail a short distance, but had neither seen nor heard anything. It was decided that I would command this force until contact had been established. The 3rd Platoon of C Company would furnish the point. The march was resumed, and the point had gone several hundred yards when machine pistol fire from the left of the trail stopped it. My orders to the point commander were to swing off to the right toward the high ground; bypass the Germans; and when the point got on the hill, halt, and the column would close in.

"The point swung off to the right of the trail and to the east without returning the fire of the machine pistols. It dropped down into a steep gully and then climbed up the fairly steep slopes of the hill. When it reached the top, I ordered the point commander to guard the north side of the hill. As B Company came up, it was swung to the west and south [sides] of the hill. Headquarters Company was routed to the east and southeast. As Headquarters Company moved in, it was found that the 81mm mortar platoon was completely missing.

When we met to discuss the situation over the only map, Captain Duncan's, it was decided that Hill 424 was farther to the north. The march would be resumed again."[39]

The two platoons and headquarters group of Company C led by Captain Albert E. "Ernie" Milloy had lost contact with Company A during the long halt. Captain Milloy decided to try to regain contact; leading his men east off of the trail and then north along the western slopes of the hills and valleys, looking for Hill 424. At approximately 11:00 p.m., Milloy and his men found a well on the northwestern slope of the unnumbered hill, south of Hill 424. While his men filled their canteens, Milloy sent a patrol led by Lieutenant James E. Dunn across the dark valley below to the north to reconnoiter Hill 424. While Captain Milloy was waiting with his men for the patrol to return, Colonel Tucker and his group found them.

The patrol returned, informing Milloy and Tucker that Company A was not on the hill and that only a few Germans held it. Dunn and his men had also found a route to the top of hill that avoided the Germans occupying it. Tucker decided to take the hill with the force he had, fully expecting the remainder of the 1st Battalion to arrive on Hill 424 shortly afterward.

The two platoons of Company C and Tucker's group moved out around midnight and found the hill undefended. They immediately formed a perimeter defense and began to dig in. As this was in progress, a German patrol walked into their perimeter. The situation in the dark was confusing, with both sides not wanting to shoot their own men, yet having to react to the split-second movements of their enemies. Richard Tregaskis, the journalist, was caught in the middle of the confusing cat-and-mouse, life-and-death game being played out in the dark. Tregaskis heard somebody shout, " 'Keep your hands up—high!' Turning fast, I saw Major [Don] Dunham at a nervous crouch leveling his .45 at three Germans, who had their hands up. They had thrown their guns on the ground. I helped to frisk them. They were sturdy, muscular men, wearing the usual square-visored khaki caps of the German infantryman. The prisoners were taken over to the center of the open spot atop the hill, and told to sit down on the open ground.

"From the opposite side of the hill, behind us, we heard the rapid, 'Brrd-ddt-t-t-t, brrdddt-t-t-t, brrdddt-t-t-t' of a German Schmeisser machine pistol, firing in short bursts. Lines of white tracers blinked across the sky. Then we heard the heavier-toned, slower-paced firing of our own automatic weapons, and a few rifle shots.

"[Major] Dunham, dragging his Tommy gun, crawled up the slope to the bare crown of the hill. He kept low, for somewhere on the other side of the hill, very close, according to the sound, snipers lurked. Don was looking for human game, and he moved like a practiced hunter. I watched his feet, and the one knee bending and unbending like the rocker arm of an old side-wheeler, disappear over the crown of the slope.

"A trooper crawled back, and reported, 'Freeman and Richter got hit.' But they had not been badly wounded. It had begun to look like we were cut off on three sides."[40]

Tucker's attempts to contact both battalions by radio continued to be unsuccessful. Two messengers were sent out to find them, but both were killed a short time later.

After discovering the break in the column, Sergeant Otto Huebner helped get Company A moving again. "After proceeding a short distance we came directly into a German occupied position, which surprised us as well as the Germans. The small detachment of Germans gave up without a fight. By this time the company knew we were getting deep into enemy territory. As the point came to a small hill, three or four enemy machine guns opened fire. Everybody hit the ground and it looked as if we were going to have a rough firefight. As the men lay on the ground, word came down the column to fix bayonets and get prepared to charge the enemy positions, which were only about fifty yards to the front. The only real concealment one had was the deep darkness of the night. The squad leaders managed to get their squads into a skirmish line.

"Then a voice rang out along the line, 'Let's Go!' The men got on their feet and took off hooting and yelling like a tribe of Indians on the warpath. The Germans took off on the double without a shot fired on either side. Total captured: one small, skinny medic, and he was too scared to run.

"After the company reorganized, we moved on toward the objective and shortly thereafter came to a hill. The company commander, with a small party, reconnoitered the hill, and on his return summoned the platoon leaders. He told them this was the objective and then gave the company defense orders. He ordered the platoon leaders to prepare an all-round defense, close to the crest of the hill, with the 1st Platoon on the forward slope, 2nd on the left, 3rd on the right, tying in all the way around. This was about 0200 hours, 17 September."[41]

When Lieutenant Lekson found out that his force was on the wrong hill, he and the other officers pulled in their outposts, awakened others, got everyone on their feet, and started north trying to find Hill 424. Lekson put the force in single file, with Company B leading, and moved toward the hill to the north, some five hundred yards away. After reaching that hill, he sent a patrol to the east and one to the north with instructions to find Lieutenant Colonel Williams while and he and Captain Duncan reconnoitered to the north. When Lekson returned to the hill, the 2nd Battalion commander, Major Daniel W. Danielson, had arrived and informed him that they were standing on the unnumbered hill that was his battalion's objective, and that his battalion would arrive on the hill shortly.

At about 1:00 a.m., as Lekson was getting his force ready to move north, the patrol from Company B that had reconnoitered the trail to the north returned. "Its leader, Sergeant Gerald [M.] Murphy, reported that he had contacted Colonel Tucker near a well on the next hill north. Colonel Tucker's message was, 'Bring the battalion down here at once.' As rapidly as the column could, it moved out with Sergeant Murphy leading the point. Somewhere, after the column started, a platoon of Company C, 307th Airborne Engineer Battalion, had tied in behind Headquarters Company. In addition, some twenty men of B Company, 505th Parachute Infantry, the flank security, had joined the column. At 0200 he halted at a well below the hill and said that this was where Colonel Tucker had been. The S-2 and I, reconnoitering along the trail, ran into Lieutenant Colonel Williams, who had just left A Company as it moved up the hill."[42]

After conferring with Williams, Lekson led his force up the hill and joined the defense with Company A. While the men who had been with Lieutenant Lekson dug in, a patrol was sent out to find the 81mm mortar platoon that was still missing.

As the 1st Battalion was trying to find Hill 424, Lieutenant Chester Garrison and Headquarters Company, 2nd Battalion moved through the darkness toward the battalion's objectives, the unnumbered hill and Hill 344. "About 2100, we moved slowly to our high-ground objective, which we reached about 0200, after numerous stops. Artillery fire was directed at our column throughout the night. The battalion dug in on the high ground assigned to us. The 1st Battalion was to the hill north of us. F Company and most of the 81mm mortar platoon became detached from us in the dark and were somewhere to our rear."[43]

As of 4:00 a.m. on September 17, Colonel Tucker, on Hill 424 with his regimental headquarters command group and part of Company C, was still not able to make contact with either of his battalions. Even though two men sent earlier had both been killed, the regimental S-3, Major Don B. Dunham, and the operations sergeant, Jack Furst, volunteered to try to find the 1st Battalion. About five minutes after they left, troopers on Hill 424 heard German burp gun fire. Approximately ten minutes later, Furst made it back to the perimeter and reported to Colonel Tucker that Dunham had been killed. Major Dunham would later be posthumously awarded the Distinguished Service Cross for his heroism.

At dawn, Company C trooper, Corporal Ross Carter, got his first look at the scene of heavy fighting earlier between the 36th Division and the Germans. "Cadavers lay everywhere. Having seen only a few corpses in Sicily, it was a horrible experience for us to see dead men, purpled and blackened by the intense heat, lying scattered all over the hill. The body of a huge man, eyes bloated out of their sockets, who lay dead about twenty yards from me,

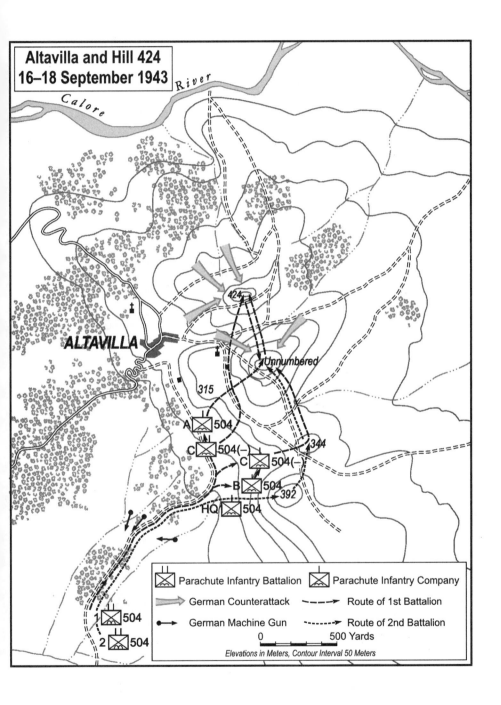

Altavilla and Hill 424
16–18 September 1943

River

Calore

ALTAVILLA

424

Unnumbered

315

A 504

C 504(–)

C 504(–)

344

B 504

392

HQ 504

1 504

2 504

Parachute Infantry Battalion   Parachute Infantry Company

German Counterattack   ------▶ Route of 1st Battalion

German Machine Gun   ------▶ Route of 2nd Battalion

0   500 Yards

Elevations in Meters, Contour Interval 50 Meters

had swollen and burst. First lieutenant's bars were on his shoulders. His pistol belt with open compass case and empty binocular case bore witness to the quality of our equipment: the Krauts had looted them. A broken carbine lay by the body."[44]

As Carter surveyed the carnage around him, Captain Milloy, the Company C commander, sent a patrol from Hill 424 toward Altavilla to the west. At the base of the hill, the patrol spotted a German self-propelled gun and light tank. The patrol returned and asked for a bazooka to take back down the hill and try to knock out the German armor. After obtaining the bazooka, the patrol moved down the hill once more when it encountered a German combat patrol, which drove the patrol back up the hill.

A second patrol sent by Milloy to the north ran into a large number of German infantry advancing toward the hill. A firefight broke out as the patrol attempted to make it back up the northern slope of Hill 424, killing one trooper before they got back to the perimeter.

A short time later, the German tank and self-propelled gun west of Hill 424 opened fire on the Company C foxholes on the western slope. The Company C troopers could hear German infantry moving toward them up the slope. When the Germans got about seventy-five yards away, the troopers opened up simultaneously with deadly accuracy, decimating the German infantry before they could take cover or maneuver. Corporal Ross Carter took careful aim with his Tommy gun, making sure each burst found its mark. "Since only a few of our machine guns and automatic rifles had reached us, it was up to the riflemen and Tommy gunners to hold off the assault. The boys lay in their holes around the top of the hill and calmly squeezed off shots. American riflemen were always among the best in the world, and our Legion[45] riflemen were among the best in the army. In about thirty minutes the attack was broken up."[46]

The survivors withdrew down the hill as the two German armored vehicles increased their fire. After pulling back, the Germans fired on the troopers' positions on the hill from three sides with small arms and machine guns in an effort to pin them down and inflict casualties.

Shortly after dawn, seeing troop movement on the hill to the north and believing that they might be friendly troops, the 2nd Platoon of Company A was ordered to investigate. From his foxhole, Sergeant Otto Huebner with Company A observed the scouts leave the perimeter defenses ahead of the platoon. "As the lead scout, Private First Class Ralph R. Young, went down the crest about two hundred yards, he spotted troops to his front. Thinking they were friendly troops, he did not take cover and was fired upon and killed. The platoon leader, Lieutenant [Mearle D.] Duvall, went out to help him and was hit in the legs with shrapnel from a mortar shell."[47]

Lieutenant Lekson instinctively moved over the crest of the hill, where he saw the two men lying below. "Captain Harrison ordered the 1st Platoon back into their foxholes. As they covered him, he ran out and brought back the platoon leader [Lieutenant Duvall], under both friendly and enemy fire.

"Shortly after 0800, we observed enemy troops moving from the edge of Altavilla into the valley toward us. As Lieutenant Colonel Williams and I watched this force of some seventy-five to one hundred Germans moving, another smaller enemy force appeared from the south edge of Altavilla and swung around Hill 315. As the Germans approached within three hundred yards of B Company, our men opened fire. The Germans broke into small groups that moved forward from bush to bush and terrace to terrace.

"Lieutenant Colonel Williams ordered troops on the east edge of the perimeter into position facing [west toward] Altavilla. Enemy artillery began to fall on B Company and into the [perimeter].

"By this time, some fifty men, including about six automatic riflemen, were firing at the enemy. As the Germans sought cover, the 60mm mortar of the 2nd Platoon of B Company drove them out into the open. The 60mm mortar squad leader, Sergeant Douglas Morehead, was directing the mortar fire from the crest. His mortar crew was some fifteen feet behind him. From down on the forward slope, Lieutenant William [A.] Meerman, 3rd Platoon leader, B Company, was calling out targets to Morehead. As the German attack slowed down and then dropped back, Lieutenant Colonel Williams ordered the mortar to stop firing. It had expended much of its ammunition, and resupply was not certain.

"Enemy artillery concentrations of thirty to forty rounds each and mortar fire hit the slopes of the hill. Then a mist began to gather in the valley, obscuring Altavilla and parts of Hill 424. The battalion waited.

"Though the mist did not last more than a half hour, it seemed much longer. The troops on the forward slope were tense, and word was being passed back and forth to watch for enemy infiltrations.

"When the mist thinned, an enemy tank opened fire on the hill. At the northeastern edge of Altavilla, on the road that ran east along Hill 424 could be seen three German tanks. All three tanks soon began to fire into foxhole after foxhole along the northwest slope on the hill. The tanks first fired on the foxholes on the western edge of A Company, then along the 2nd and 3rd Platoons of B Company.

"A direct hit on a bazooka position of the 2nd Platoon, B Company, blasted two men out of the position. The platoon leader of the 2nd Platoon of A Company and his aid man ran down. They were joined by the 1st Platoon leader and his platoon sergeant. Another shell burst wounded the A Company platoon leader before the bazooka team could be evacuated. On the right flank of the 2nd Platoon, B Company, was a company strongpoint dug in among a cluster of trees. Two shell bursts killed six men there.

"As the tanks fired, a German attack was launched from the northwest along the draw against the 1st Platoon of A Company. In a short firefight, the German force was driven back with some loss. Though the German tank support had hit the battalion northwest perimeter hard, the 1st and 3rd Platoons of A Company had not been affected by the tank fire.

"While the tanks had been active, the artillery observer had gained radio contact. Soon, VI Corps artillery was firing on Altavilla and on the tanks. As the German tanks and infantry withdrew, enemy artillery began to pound the hill.

"I, with a command post detail, moved to the aid station to collect ammunition from the wounded. Some of the troops had reached a critical low in small-arms [ammunition]. In the aid station were some twenty wounded. About ten had been killed so far in the morning's action."[48]

Two hills to the south of Hill 424, Lieutenant Chester Garrison, the 2nd Battalion S-1, saw a plane coming toward the hill from the west. "About 0830 a P-38 flew over, dropping two bombs in the D Company area, killing five men . . . Private First Class John C. Di Rienso, Private James E. Lechner, Private First Class John C. Le Count, Private John J. Monti, and Private James H. King, Jr."[49]

Still unable to contact the two battalions, and seeing movement that appeared to be friendly troops on the unnumbered hill, Colonel Tucker decided to withdraw to the unnumbered hill to the south about 9:30 a.m. Shortly after the attack on the unnumbered hill was broken up, Tucker with the two platoons of Company C and Regimental Headquarters began coming into the perimeter of the 1st Battalion. After a conference with Lieutenant Colonel Williams, Tucker ordered Hill 424 retaken. Company A would lead the assault, with Company C following, and Company B would take over the defense of the unnumbered hill. At the same time, Tucker sent a radio message to the 2nd Battalion, which was occupying the hill to the south, to move to occupy the hill that was the present 1st Battalion position.

About 10:30 a.m., Sergeant Otto Huebner moved out with Company A, led by the 2nd Platoon. "They passed down the gully and started up Hill 424, when a machine gun opened fire, killing three men instantly. The 3rd Platoon, which was in the rear of the column, moved around the west side of the hill in a flanking movement, attacked the [enemy] position, and eliminated it quickly.

"The 3rd and 2nd Platoons abreast moved up to the top of the hill at once, with the 1st Platoon following. As the platoons reached the top of the hill, Captain Harrison ordered the 2nd Platoon to move to the right, 3rd to the front, and 1st to the left."[50]

Lieutenant Reneau Breard, the assistant platoon leader of the 1st Platoon of Company A, quickly advanced toward the top of Hill 424. "We went up there and it was unoccupied, the place was full of dead 36th Division people. As we went over the hill, we found the Germans coming up to reoccupy it."[51]

Sergeant Huebner helped to get the company deployed. "Just as the platoons were moving to the crest in their sector, a strong force of Germans started moving over the crest on the opposite side. Company A immediately set up a hasty defense.

"One advantage the company had was the fact that we were on the hill while the main German force was still climbing. As for surprise, both were stunned, but the Germans threw the first punch.

"Every man hit the ground and scuffled about seeking any kind of cover or concealment. After a few seconds elapsed and men gathered their wits, each man who could bring fire to bear on the enemy opened up without being told. This caused the enemy to hunt for cover, and as the men noticed how effective their fire was, they seemed to gain confidence and the company's firepower really increased. For the first ten minutes, it was each man for himself; but after a short time the men began to coordinate and give each other a little mutual [fire] support. By this time, the officers and NCOs began coordinating the company's fires.

"Finally, the 1st Platoon drove the Germans back over the crest and closed in fast, taking up positions along the crest. The 1st Platoon then swung part of its fire to the right in front of the 3rd Platoon, causing the Germans to withdraw in that sector. Every step the Germans would take backward, the company would take forward, using every possible means of cover. Finally, the company with all three platoons abreast held the entire crest of the hill. The fires soon ceased; the attack was repelled, but the company suffered eight casualties, though the enemy suffered many times more.

"Immediately, the company commander ordered a hasty defense set up in a moon-shape design, with the 1st Platoon on the west overlooking Altavilla, the 3rd Platoon to the north, and the 2nd Platoon to the east, all tying in. Company headquarters [was] to the rear and center of the company, and a couple of small security positions [were] to the rear facing the unnumbered hill for rear security."[52]

For the first time since arriving on Hill 424, Company A trooper Private Albert Clark took time to notice the view to the west. "We found out why the Germans wanted this hill so badly. It had a perfect view of the beachhead, and they could see everything that went on down there. There was a small airfield that fighter planes were using. When one started to take off, they would send a couple of shells."[53]

While the officers and noncoms got the company reorganized, Sergeant Huebner scrounged what he could from the scene of devastation around him. "The sight on the hill was an unpleasant one. This was the same place that the 1st Battalion of the 142nd Infantry, 36th Division, four days previously was finally forced to withdraw [from] after great losses were inflicted on both sides.

"The hill was infested with scattered dead Germans and American soldiers, supplies, and ammunition. There were machine guns still in their original emplacements, rifles, packs, clothing, ammunition belts, machine gun [ammunition] boxes, and stacks of 60mm mortar shells scattered all over the hill.

"The ammunition was gathered up and distributed through the company as soon as possible. The platoons began digging positions in their sectors. Foxholes dug by the 142nd Infantry were improved and used in many cases. Slit trenches were also used in many instances instead of foxholes, because the hard ground made digging difficult.

"The officers and NCOs directed the exact spots of positions. We tried to arrange them to cover the most likely enemy approaches, have each position give mutual support to the one on the right and left, with observation, fire, and depth in that order of priority. To add firepower, the machine guns that were left on the hill by the 142nd were put in the platoon positions.

"It was about 11:00 now and the men were still digging their positions, when enemy tanks began to shell the hill. One could hear the tank fire; about a second later, the shell would burst. The men dug deeper because the fire was extremely accurate, causing many casualties.

"The tank fire continued on without a letup. The men were quite hungry about this time, for they had not had any rations since the day before. A few were lucky enough to find a little bread and jam in the dead Germans' packs. Water was also scarce. There was a well down the draw to the northwest, about two hundred yards, but every time anyone would go for water, they would either get in a firefight or be shelled.

"The company radio operator had finally gotten through to battalion on the unnumbered hill. Lieutenant Colonel Williams, the battalion commander, told Captain Harrison, the company commander, that Company C would be on their way to help.

"It was impossible at this time to evacuate the wounded, but the company medical personnel were doing a fine job of taking care of them. Their greatest assistant was the little morphine syringe.

"The shelling increased, with mortar and heavy artillery falling, and everyone stayed low in his hole. At noon, the shelling became almost unbearable. It was so bad that the sides of the foxholes began caving in. The air was thick with smoke and dust from the bursting shells, and then—all quiet.

"The quiet period continued for only a minute, as heavy enemy machine guns began blasting away from the front of the 1st and 3rd Platoon areas, supporting a German assault force approaching the positions.

"The men ducked their heads in the foxholes to escape the machine gun fire. A couple of alert squad leaders immediately noticed the machine gun fire, approximately two feet off the ground in most places, and yelled to the men to get their heads up and start firing, which they did. The platoons laid down a heavy base of fire, with every possible weapon being fired. The 60mm mortars were employed singly with each platoon. The 1st and 3rd Platoon mortars began laying down fire within a hundred yards of the frontline positions traversing back and forth.

"The company radio operator finally managed to communicate with battalion again on the unnumbered hill, and the company commander requested artillery support."[54]

Lieutenant Lekson was at the 1st Battalion command post on the unnumbered hill when a radio transmission from Company A on Hill 424 was received. "Captain Harrison radioed a request for artillery to Lieutenant Colonel Williams. He had spotted two tanks in the churchyard north of Altavilla. Relaying the message to the forward observer, Lieutenant Colonel Williams asked if Captain Harrison could adjust."[55]

As the assaulting German infantry climbed the slope of Hill 424, Sergeant Huebner hoped that the VI Corps artillery fire would not be too late. "When the company opened up its final protective fire, it momentarily stopped the assault. After a few minutes of hesitation, the Germans began rushing the positions in groups, while another group would support by fire, but for some reason their fire was inaccurate.

"In the 1st Platoon, a Private [First Class Peter R.] Schneider, of German [birth] and who spoke German well, began shouting orders to the Germans in their native tongue [and] caused a considerable amount of confusion, making it possible for his platoon to pick them off. This still did not take away their aggressiveness, for they continued the firefight and moved forward by leaps and bounds.

"Soon, the hand grenades flew like snowballs from both sides, but for every shot or grenade from the Germans on the 1st and 3rd Platoon positions, they received two back. The officers and NCOs were up in the front foxholes firing with the men. Heavy artillery began falling on the hill, only this time it was falling in the middle of the enemy position, which was deeply appreciated by the company, because shortly after, the attack seemed to become disorganized and easier to control by fire. Before long the Germans began to withdraw down the crest. Once the 2nd Platoon leader had to yell at a couple of men to get back in their foxholes, for they began to pursue the enemy. The company had killed approximately fifty Germans, but had suffered almost half that number in casualties.

"The squad leaders now checked on their men, redistributed ammunition, and reported in detail to the platoon leader. The platoon leaders did the same and reported to the company commander. Evacuation of the wounded was still impossible, and the best place for them was in their foxholes.

"For the next few minutes everyone on the hill thought the attack started all over again due to the fact that in the 2nd Platoon area on the east, a small-arms firefight began. We didn't know if the Germans were getting aggressive again or not, but it was only a five or six man patrol trying to penetrate the lines. They were repelled without much trouble.

"Shortly after this small firefight, the enemy started shelling the hill again. Much to our delight, Company C had just come up the hill to help. The battalion commander and his CP group were with them, including the battalion medical officer. The medical officer was needed greatly and performed miracles, including two amputations, with his meager stock of medical supplies.

"The battalion aid station was set up in a gully near the battalion CP. Evacuation of the wounded was still impossible, and to add to the evacuation problem, a heavy concentration began falling on the hill, including air bursts, which caused many additional casualties."[56] Corporal Fred Baldino was dug in near Lieutenant Ned E. Wall, the Company A executive officer, and First Sergeant Edwin L. Rouse. "A tree burst killed Ned outright and wounded First Sergeant Rouse. He screamed all night, but was dead in early morning."[57]

To the southwest, at around 11:30 a.m., Lieutenant George F. Taliaferro, the 1st Battalion S-4, was in a truck headed toward Hill 424. "Major Robert B. Acheson [regimental S-4] was in charge of a train of five one-quarter-ton 4x4 vehicles which was on its way to the position occupied by the 1st Battalion, with a cargo of ammunition requested by radio by that battalion. Major Acheson, without regard for his own safety, and with little information of the tactical situation, went forward on foot to reconnoiter the route of advance of the train, which was moving by bounds. The train reached Hill 315, and was able to proceed no further, because of enemy artillery, mortar, and small-arms fire. At this point, Major Acheson went forward on foot, under fire, to locate the 1st Battalion. While moving along the slope of Hill 315, Major Acheson was wounded in the right chest by a rifle ball and received a severe shell fragmentation wound in the right arm, later necessitating the amputation of the arm."[58] Major Acheson succeeded in getting the critically needed ammunition through to the 1st Battalion and was later awarded the Distinguished Service Cross for his bravery.

Late that morning, radio contact was finally established between Tucker's command post and the 2nd Battalion, and Tucker ordered the battalion to move north one hill. Lieutenant Garrison helped get the 2nd Battalion command post ready to move. "At 13:00 the battalion began to move forward to the hill originally assigned to them, but which had been held by the 1st Battalion. We moved out with E Company in the lead, F Company, Battalion CP, Headquarters Company, and D Company. Another climb; it took at least three hours to get everybody there."[59]

After arriving, the 1st Battalion command group organized an all-around defense of Hill 424. Company A was shifted to cover the west and northwest side of the hill, while Lieutenant Lekson assisted in getting Company C deployed. "C Company was placed in position along the north side of Hill 424, tying in with A Company on its left.

"The next German attack, about 1500 hours, struck against A Company from the west slope of Hill 424 and against C Company from the northwest. The attack was preceded by a heavy artillery and mortar preparation that lasted almost an hour. Again, enemy machine guns covered the advance of an estimated two German companies. The Germans coming up the slopes could be seen as they got within three hundred yards of the riflemen's positions."[60]

Company A trooper, Sergeant Otto Huebner waited in his foxhole on the western slope as German panzer grenadiers moved relentlessly up the hill. "The Germans began advancing by fire and movement, taking advantage of the cover afforded by the good approaches. They were hitting all three platoons of Company A with the main force coming up the west slope.

"Due to the shape of the hill mass, it was impossible to lay down a good final protective line. The field of fire was very limited, in places only fifty yards. One outpost was cut off and later eliminated, while the other fought its way back, giving the company very little notice of the attack. With the large volume of fire the enemy was laying down, it sounded as if the entire German Army was attacking.

"Mortar targets were picked and fired upon as close as fifty yards in front of the troops. Its fire was very effective and most valuable in disorganizing assaults.

"In one squad of the 3rd Platoon, the BAR team was killed and four or five Germans penetrated that area. Fast thinking NCOs grabbed a couple of men from the two-man foxholes, charged the penetration area, killing all the Germans. The platoon sergeant jumped in the BAR position and took over command.

"Frequently, potato masher grenades would be thrown, but unless they went off in the foxhole, they had little or no effect. One dropped in a foxhole with a man, but he jumped out, and when the grenade went off, he jumped back."[61]

Lieutenant Reneau Breard was now leading a platoon of Company A, when the 1st Platoon leader, Lieutenant Stanley J. Whitman, was wounded by mortar fire. Breard and his men poured fire down on the German infantry at close range with devastating effectiveness. "It was just a good old infantry fight. We were on top looking down."[62]

For a few moments, it appeared to Sergeant Huebner that the hill might get overrun if they couldn't get artillery support, and get it soon. "The company commander kept calling back to battalion for artillery fire. The [battalion] commander said the only kind he could get was from the naval boats off the beaches, and it was very dangerous to fire so close to friendly troops. The company commander said he had to take the chance, and the battalion commander agreed.

"The firefight continued on, and in its second hour casualties began mounting on both sides. The word was passed along for the men to get deep down in their holes as the navy began firing.

"The shell bursts, landing on the northwest slope, seemed to rock the entire hill. The foxholes cracked like glass, and the topsoil around [them] sprinkled into the foxholes with every burst. One could hear terror-stricken screams coming from the Germans along the slope of the hill, which made one's backbone quiver."[63]

Lieutenant Breard and his platoon were positioned on the northwest slope, closest to where the naval rounds were impacting. "I thought they were going to cave my hole in."[64]

As Sergeant Huebner peeked over the lip of his foxhole, he could see the German infantry being decimated by the massive, earth shaking explosions. "A few Germans still tried to come forward, but the bombardment disorganized them completely, and before long the enemy withdrew. The hill was still ours, although Company A suffered twenty more casualties during that attack. The Germans suffered many, many more."[65]

When the 2nd Battalion arrived on the unnumbered hill, it relieved Company B, which moved out to rejoin the 1st Battalion, as fighting still raged for Hill 424. From the crest of Hill 424, Lieutenant Lekson watched Company B cross the saddle between the two hills. "As it started to cross along the east slope of the saddle, several rounds of enemy artillery fell along the column. As men lay in a narrow sunken trail, some one hundred rounds fell. Before a lull in the firing allowed the group to cross the saddle, two officers had been wounded and some fifteen men killed or wounded. The company commander estimated that some forty or fifty tanks, between one thousand and two thousand yards away, had shelled his company. Most of the rounds that fell seemed to be armor piercing."[66]

After arriving on the unnumbered hill, Lieutenant Garrison helped set up the 2nd Battalion command post. "The artillery became particularly stiff about 1700. One barrage was constant for two minutes. Colonel Tucker set up in our Battalion CP area . . . many of the regimental staff were casualties. About 1730 a messenger came through with information that we were to return to Albanella. This was much to our disgust, as we [had] the hill and [were] not suffering undue casualties."[67]

General Mike Dawley, commander of the U.S. VI Corps, had received no information regarding Tucker's two battalions all day. Fearing the worst, and correctly believing that Tucker and his men were now surrounded, Dawley had sent a runner to Tucker with a message instructing him to try to break out while he could still do so.

Colonel Tucker ignored the order to retreat to Albanella; his troopers had captured the two hills and they were going to keep them. That night, Headquarters Company wiremen ran a sound-powered phone line to Tucker's command post and General Dawley was patched through. Tucker explained the situation, and Dawley suggested that his two battalions retreat because they were cut off from other friendly forces. Colonel Tucker replied, "Retreat hell! Send me my 3rd Battalion!"[68]

Chapter 5

"The Germans Were Always On The High Ground Looking Down Our Throats"

In the mountains north of the Salerno beachhead, Lieutenant Kellogg and his NCOs got his stick of 1st Platoon, Company C, engineers prepared to move out. "Three German patrols had been sighted during daytime, but we were not discovered. We broke camp at dusk and continued southwest through the mountains and climbed Mount Taggiano. We bivouacked on the southwest slope, overlooking Highway Number 7, and the Tavernole intersection and bridge. German convoys were observed moving in both directions, to and from Avellino. German guards were on all known water holes. No water or food was available."[1]

AT 12:01 A.M., ON SEPTEMBER 18, COLONEL TUCKER'S 3rd Battalion, less Company H, was relieved from attachment to the 325th RCT. Companies G, I, and Headquarters Company, 3rd Battalion, supported by the 1st Battalion, 325th moved out to break through to the regiment. As they walked in column across the valley floor, Staff Sergeant George Leoleis, a platoon sergeant with Company I, heard incoming enemy artillery. "We scattered and tried to crawl between the rocks, but soon realized that this was even worse, because as the shells exploded, the chips from the rocks became shrapnel. I figured that they could not reload and traverse as fast as we could run. I yelled to the men nearby to drop their packs and pass the word that we would make a run for it. The men passed the word to all the men, and then I yelled, 'Go, go, go!' and all joined in, yelling, 'Go, go, go!' and everyone moved like 'big birds' as the saying goes. We kept running as fast as we could; it seemed that the Germans had hundreds of guns, because the sky lit up, bursts fell everywhere, the men kept running and falling, picking themselves up and running again and again. We finally turned [behind] one of the hills and out of range. I still don't know how we survived, but I believed that run saved most of us. (We did not run away from the Germans, but toward them.) After catching our breath and taking count of the men we had left, we moved on Hill 344. . . . Everyone distinguished themselves, knocking out position after position."[2]

About 3:00 a.m., the battalion broke through German resistance to occupy Hill 344 and contact the 2nd Battalion on the unnumbered hill northeast of Albanella. At dawn, a Company A combat patrol moved out from Hill 424 to contact the enemy. They moved through the ruins of Altavilla and then about a mile north, returning two hours later without finding any Germans. A second combat patrol was then sent north to gain contact with the Germans. A mule train carrying supplies arrived early that morning, providing the first meal for most of them in the last forty-eight hours. During the afternoon, the second combat patrol returned without contacting the enemy. After establishing outpost security, most of the men were finally able to get their first real sleep in almost seventy-two hours. For his leadership and heroism during the capture and subsequent fighting for Hill 424 and the surrounding area, Colonel Reuben Tucker was later awarded the Distinguished Service Cross.

NEAR AVELLINO, WHILE THE REMAINDER OF HIS MEN HID, Lieutenant Kellogg led four men on a scouting mission. "This party found a way across Highway Number 7 and a good location to use our remaining six mines and two TNT bags. The location was a very well defiladed single-span concrete-arch bridge.

"This night the twenty-seven men crossed to the southwest side of the road and the north side of the bridge, and took up defensive position upon a heavily wooded slope. Sergeant [Warren G.] Hayes, Sergeant [Paul D.] Kratsch, and I took up a position by the bridge, which was well covered by our men's fire [if we were spotted]. We allowed one serial of a convoy to pass unmolested and then mined the bridge with three mines (U.S. M1A1) and two TNT bags with pressure-type firing devices, and connected the five explosives with Primacord. We then withdrew and waited.

"The first truck of a serial went through the bridge and the second vehicle hit the mines. This vehicle was a troop-carrying truck headed for Avellino. Two armored personnel carriers arrived at the bridge and shot machine guns all around the hills attempting to draw our fire. Everything subsided in a half hour, and we had three mines left. The procedure was repeated, and another troop carrier was blown up. Within four minutes, two Mark IV tanks were at the bridge and fired 75s into the hills—we still had no definite targets, so we did not betray our positions. A company was observed starting to envelop our flanks, but we were well protected by heavy brush.

"During the resulting confusion, we withdrew to the top of the mountain, and the German patrols became mixed up and fired into each other. We then changed course to the west, and the only other enemy resistance was a plane dropping flares. We went into bivouac at 0700 after finding a water hole.

"Score: two German troop carriers and an estimated twenty-four German casualties."[3]

DURING THE PREVIOUS EIGHT DAYS, COMPANY H, attached to the ranger force, had held the railroad tunnel and Chiunzi Pass against almost daily German attacks. During that time the German force was estimated to outnumber the ranger force by as much as eight to one. Providing invaluable support to Company H and the rangers in repulsing the attacks was the 319th Glider Field Artillery Battalion, while the D, E, F, and Headquarters Batteries of the 80th Airborne Antiaircraft Battalion protected Maiori and relieved the Rangers on outpost duty.

There was little activity on September 19. The 36th Infantry Division relieved the 504th that morning, while Company H continued to hold the Chiunzi Pass.

That same day, the 3rd Battalion (less Company H) was trucked to the beach near Paestum, then at 3:00 p.m. the following day boarded LCIs and LSTs and sailed to Maiori, landing about 6:30 p.m. The 3rd Battalion made the long, hard climb up to the Chiunzi Pass to relieve their own Company H troopers who had been holding the pass and the key railroad tunnel against German attacks since arriving there on the night of the 10th of September.

Lieutenant Edward Sims and his Company H platoon had defended the railroad tunnel, denying German forces a route south to attack the left flank of the beach landings. "During the ten days we defended in this area, the Germans made a number of attempts to get through, but were repulsed. They did get a few small patrols into our position and on one occasion, took two of my men prisoner. During part of the time in this position, we received supporting fire from a 4.2-inch Chemical Mortar unit and from the 319th Glider Field Artillery Battalion."[4]

As part of the ranger force, Company H; the 2nd Platoon, Company A, 307th Airborne Engineer Battalion; the 319th Glider Field Artillery Battalion; D, E, F, and Headquarters Batteries, and the Medical Detachment of the 80th Airborne Antiaircraft (Antitank) Battalion were later awarded the Presidential Unit Citation for this action. This was the first of several awarded to units of the 82nd Airborne Division during World War II.

BY THE NIGHT OF SEPTEMBER 19, LIEUTENANT KELLOGG and his engineers were exhausted and hungry, having not eaten for three days. "We moved down to San Stefano del Sale at dusk and obtained food and rested that night, after discovering that Avellino was still in German hands. We bivouacked at San Stefano del Sole"[5]

The following evening, September 20, one of the Lieutenant Kellogg's troopers, Private Dale H. Wood, had injured his leg on the jump. Wood hadn't told anyone and had moved through the mountainous terrain with the group, carrying his heavy load as a member of a machine gun crew. His injury had worsened to the point that he could no longer keep up. Kellogg "sent Private Wood to [an Italian] hospital. We observed a large concentration of German troops moving back into the valley of Santa Lucia. They went into bivouac and started stringing wire. We moved out south, going about two hundred yards above the German bivouac area, and attempted to cross the valley at Santa Lucia; but ran into heavy concentrations of German troops. We bivouacked at 0300 on the west slope of the mountain east of Santa Lucia."[6]

The area around Avellino had been the site of the jump by the 2nd Battalion, 509th Parachute Infantry Regiment, the prior week and was thick with German troops still hunting them. Kellogg and his men moved out again at dusk on September 21, and "went further south down the valley through a small German bivouac area. We were surprised by an airplane flare in the middle of the bivouac—there were no casualties, but we were forced to retreat to the hills by large German patrols. We bivouacked on the mountainside above San Sossio—no food and water."[7]

The following night, Kellogg led his men south along the mountains. "We arrived at the top of a mountain at 0700 in the morning, and were bombed by American planes at 0730, before we had finished digging in. We found a sheep wounded by the American Air Force and cooked it . . . still no water. We were bivouacked at the top of a mountain between San Sossio and Volturara.

"We obtained water and found a potato field. The men rested all day and tried to regain strength. Our patrols discovered that the Germans had moved from Volturara, with only patrols left in the hills. The men were now considered too weak to fight. There was continual artillery fire."[8]

That day, the 376th Parachute Field Artillery Battalion sailed from Sicily to join the 504. One of the troopers on board was Technician Fourth Grade James Crosbie, with Battery B. "We sailed from Termini, Sicily, on an LST to the Salerno beachhead on September 23, 1943."[9]

On the 24th of September, Kellogg's men "continued to rest, and fourteen men went to try to find food. A British bomber flying over exploded in the air. Two men parachuted down, and I was able to rescue Sergeant J. L. McAninch, R-78612, 24th Squadron, SAAF [South African Air Force]. During our rescue, our positions were bombed, and the chute of the sergeant caught a stick. The sergeant had his foot almost shot off and was badly burned all over. I used morphine, sulfanilamide powder, and sulfadiazine tablets to administer first aid. All water this day went to the sergeant. The other aviator was captured by the Germans. We kept the same bivouac. Patrols of our men found that Germans had moved bivouac close to Avellino. There was continued heavy artillery fire."[10]

MAJOR WILLIAM R. BEALL, THE EXECUTIVE OFFICER of the 3rd Battalion, was acting as the battalion commander, while Major "Hank" Adams recovered from malaria. Sergeant Robert M. Tallon Sr., with Headquarters Company, 3rd Battalion, was digging his foxhole on a hillside on the evening of September 24, when Beall and his aide approached. "Beall had his orderly construct the major's foxhole into the side of a terrace with about four feet of soil on top of it. This would prevent shrapnel from hitting him when we were attacked with aerial artillery [bursts].

"About 2230, a shell hit about thirty feet from me. Moments later a runner from one of the line companies, lost in the dark, fell into my foxhole, saying he had a message for Major Beall. I said, 'He's just a few feet away,' and then I called in a low voice, 'Major Beall?' No answer . . . Then I called again . . . No answer. Suddenly my heart seemed to jump into my throat as I thought about the dirt on top of the major's foxhole.

"As quickly as I could, I scrambled over to his foxhole. It had caved in and buried him under four feet of dirt. I called for help and medics. We dug as fast as we could with hands and helmets."[11]

Lieutenant Moffatt Burriss, the 3rd Battalion S-2, was nearby. "I was one of those who started digging with his hands as I tried to reach the major in time."[12]

After digging frantically in the darkness, they uncovered Major Beall. Tallon could tell that they were too late. "When we reached his body, we didn't need the medic to tell us that he was dead."[13]

Burriss could sense the sadness that the battalion felt as the news spread of Beall's suffocation. "His death was a great loss to our unit. He was an outstanding soldier—a leader whom we had confidently followed into battle."[14]

Major Hank Adams returned from the hospital a few days later to resume command of the 3rd Battalion.

THE FOLLOWING DAY, SEPTEMBER 25, LIEUTENANT KELLOGG "obtained food for my men and water for all, including the wounded [air]man. We attempted to cross the valley of Santa Lucia with the wounded man, but were driven back by artillery fire. Patrols found that the Germans had withdrawn from Santa Lucia."[15]

As the Allied forces approached, Kellogg's group was subjected to "bombing, strafing, and artillery fire all day [on September 26]. I attempted to find a doctor for the wounded man and food for the men. Sergeant [Paul] Kratsch and four men discovered the location of a German patrol. The German patrol moved before we could get our men to capture it."[16]

THAT SAME DAY, THE 504TH AND 505TH RCTs began moving from the vicinity of Castelcivita to the Sorrento Peninsula, and the division command post was established at Maiori. There, General Ridgway took command of a task force, consisting of the ranger force and the parachute elements of the division. The Eastern Force was commanded by Lieutenant Colonel William O. Darby, the ranger force commander, and included the 504th. Colonel James Gavin commanded the Western Force, consisting of the 505th. On the night of September 27, the Eastern Force began a push through the Chiunzi Pass. The Western Force supported this main effort with a push north from the Agerola-Gragnano tunnel. Both forces were lightly opposed and reached the Sarno Plain the following morning.

EXHAUSTED, HUNGRY, AND THIRSTY, LIEUTENANT KELLOGG and his men set out again on the evening of September 27. "We moved out of the Volturara area and attempted to take Sergeant McAninch to Montello, which we had heard was in the hands of the English. We had to abandon Sergeant McAninch at an Italian house, after carrying him over one mountain. The men were in bad physical condition. It rained all night and we continued on course to Montello. We encountered four German patrols, which were making much noise. They fled in the dark woods, so we had no targets. We sighted no friendly troops. . . . No food, no sleep, no water."[17]

The following evening, Kellogg and his engineers, nearing the end of their endurance, moved out at dusk toward Montello. "At 2200, we ran into a patrol of Company C, 1st Battalion, 7th Infantry, 3rd Division at Montello. We aided in taking a German patrol and were relieved at 2400. We guided patrols to Sergeant McAninch."[18]

Through the leadership of Lieutenant Kellogg, his 1st Platoon, Company C, 307th Airborne Engineer Battalion troopers had destroyed power and telephone lines, a railroad track, a tankette, two personnel carriers, and killed at least twenty-four of the enemy. For his extraordinary leadership and heroism in bringing the men in his platoon through miles of mountainous terrain, infested with enemy troops, Lieutenant William W. Kellogg was awarded the Distinguished Service Cross.

ON SEPTEMBER 28, LIEUTENANT COLONEL CHARLES BILLINGSLEA joined the 504th as regimental executive officer, replacing Lieutenant Colonel Leslie Freeman, who had been wounded during the fighting on Hill 424. From September 28 to 30, the 504th and 505th RCTs converged on Castellamare. At noon on the 30th, the 3rd Battalion, 505th, led the advance along the highway to Torre Annunziata. The following day, the battalion once again moved out in trucks around noon, escorting General Mark Clark and General Matthew Ridgway into Naples. The 504th and the remainder of the 505th RCTs followed, occupying the city and conducting patrols before nightfall.

When the 504th arrived in Naples, they found that the retreating Germans had destroyed much of the city's infrastructure. Shortly after arriving in Naples, Private First Class Reed S. Fassett, with Battery A, 376th, heard a series of explosions in the distance. "Several of us went to see just what happened, and on the way there, we were told what had occurred. Naples did not have potable water. The Germans had put sewer water in fresh water mains, so it could not be used for useable water. No electricity, no food until [the arrival of] tons and tons of American flour and other ingredients for turning flour into usable food (bread). Water lines were laid on top of the ground to various points in the city for military and civilian use, and bakeries were reopened. It was necessary to have guards at water points and at the bakeries. I saw one woman very badly cut-up with a broken gallon jug, because she tried to cut into the waiting line. I also saw a woman who appeared to be pregnant get in the bread line and another woman pulled a knife and slit the first woman across the abdomen. I held my breath until I saw feathers fly; the pregnancy turned out to be a pillow. I have never seen such warm weather turn so cold as in Naples."[19]

Sergeant Albert Clark and the rest of Company A occupied "an abandoned school building near a bombed-out railway station. It was a pretty devastated area."[20]

Other units, such Private First Class Neil D'Avanzo's Battery B, 376th, were billeted in a museum. "I believe it was just off Via Napoli. It was a big place and had a balcony on the side street that was almost a block long. We used to sit on the low wall and throw 'bon-bons' down to the children that sat on the curb across the street, but more important was the warehouse that was on the corner. We found out that stored in the warehouse were 25,000 bottles of cherry brandy. Now, when you have so many goodies so close, you have to find a way to get to it. Guards had been posted at the main doors on the next block, but the battalion kitchen was set up against the rear wall of the warehouse, and someone made the suggestion that if there was a hole in the wall of the warehouse, we could get to the brandy. We figured that the best place for a hole would be behind one of the big GI stoves. We moved a stove out and made a nice two-foot hole for access and cleaned up all the debris. For the three weeks or so that we were in Naples, that hole was one of the best kept secrets of the war."[21]

Other troopers, such Sergeant Milton Knight's S-2 section, took advantage of the Italian-speaking troopers' connections. "[Private Frank T.] Tuzollino's family came from Naples to the United States way back in the immigration days, and we found some of his relatives, and so did we find [Private First

Class Anthony] Coccia's relatives. When we found these people, man, we had it made! We didn't have to eat so many C-rations then! We'd get some flour and stuff from the mess sergeant and take it to them, and they'd make spaghetti and whatever for us. We had a pretty good time while we were there."[22]

On October 7, a powerful time bomb left behind a false wall in the main post office building by the retreating Germans exploded, killing or wounding upward of one hundred people, primarily civilians. The 307th Airborne Engineer Battalion immediately began searching for, finding, and disarming any other time bombs and booby traps.

The following Sunday morning, October 10, many of the troopers were sleeping late in various public buildings in Naples where they were been billeted. General Ridgway was attending a church service when he heard the sound of a huge explosion in the distance. Ridgway and his aide left the church and found the location of the explosion—an Italian Army barracks housing Company B, 307th Airborne Engineer Battalion. "I will never forget the tragic sight. Arms and legs of American soldiers, killed in their sleep, were sticking pitifully out of the rubble on the second floor. We were never able to establish definitely whether some of the engineers' own demolitions went off by accident. I still believe, though, that it was the result of a German booby trap."[23]

All 307th engineers not buried in the explosion risked their lives in the resulting fire and cave-in of the building to pull badly injured and dead Company B troopers out of the rubble until everyone was found.

When word spread of what had happened to the engineers, Lieutenant Reneau Breard, a platoon leader with Company A, and others in his building took action to prevent the same thing. "We went down in our cellar and we cut off every wire we could find, trying to make the building safe."[24]

General Mark Clark wanted to keep the 82nd Airborne Division as part of his Fifth Army for the drive north to Rome and beyond. However, General Dwight D. Eisenhower had decided to use the division to spearhead the cross-channel invasion planned for the coming spring. Clark asked for and received permission to retain the 504th RCT on a temporary basis, promising to return them to the division in time to participate in the cross-channel invasion. Ridgway was bitterly disappointed that the 504th would not accompanying the rest of the division. "I wrote General Clark the strongest letter I could devise, asking for their return.

"'Dear Wayne:

'I leave in your hands another part of me—that portion of the division remaining temporarily under your command. These officers and men, like all the other members of the division, have given without reserve of all they have to the Fifth Army. When you appealed to me, personally, on the afternoon of September 13, 1943, for immediate help, the division instantly and wholeheartedly responded, accepting without thought of self the unusual hazards involved.

'Now this division sees a major part of itself about to be left behind when it moves to another theater. Its officers and men view this separation—temporary as it is promised to be—with live concern. Eighteen months and an untold amount of devoted effort have gone into the building of this team. It has been tested in and out of battle. It has worthily met all those tests. It has developed a spirit and a soul of its own and no member of the division could view its participation without a sense of personal hurt.

'I therefore bespeak earnestly your personal attention in safeguarding the interest of these units and helping to bring about their early return to their own division.'

"General Clark's reply was brief and to the point. 'Dear Matt,' he wrote, 'I need them.'

"I could not blame him. No commander would willingly give up troops who fought with the skill and dash and fire of the 504th. But I needed them, too, for reasons not only of military necessity, but for sentimental reasons. They had been part of the 82nd from its earliest days. They were, as I told Clark, part of me."[25]

General Clark hated to see the division leave his command. "In the latter part of November 1943, the Fifth Army lost some of its finest fighting men when the 82nd Airborne Division departed for the United Kingdom, where preparations were being made for the 1944 cross-channel invasion of France. General Ridgway came around on November 18 to say goodbye, and I promised to see that the 504th Regiment of his division, which was remaining for a while with the Fifth Army, rejoined him in due course. He was an outstanding battle soldier, brilliant, fearless, and loyal, and he had trained and produced one of finest Fifth Army outfits."[26]

Ridgway directed Brigadier General Maxwell Taylor to keep pressure on Clark to expedite the return of the 504th to the division.

The regimental staff underwent a change when Lieutenant Colonel Leslie Freeman, the regimental executive officer, who had been wounded on Hill 424, returned from the hospital. Because Lieutenant Colonel Charles Billingslea had replaced Freeman after he was wounded, Colonel Tucker assigned Freeman to command the 3rd Battalion, and brought Lieutenant Colonel Hank Adams back as regimental S-3.

Lieutenant Colonel Warren Williams and Major Daniel Danielson continued to command the 1st and 2nd Battalions respectively.

CLARK IMMEDIATELY PUT THE 504TH TO WORK, attaching the regimental combat team to the U.S. 34th Infantry Division. On October 27, 1943, the 504th RCT moved by truck from Naples to Alife, in the Apennine Mountains.

Lieutenant Ed Sims, a platoon leader with Company H, was briefed on the combat team's mission after arriving at Alife. "Our job was to protect the

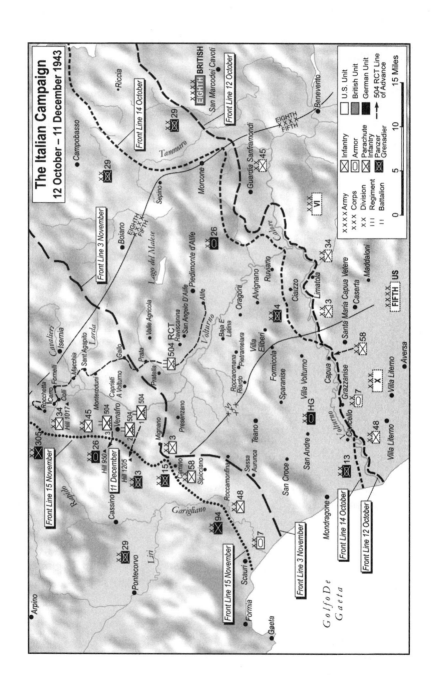

The Italian Campaign
12 October – 11 December 1943

right flank of the U.S. Fifth Army and to maintain contact with the British Eighth Army on our right. We were restricted to movement by foot and had to carry our equipment and ammunition. The few mules we had were a big help, but progress was slow in these treacherous mountains. The numerous booby traps and destruction of trails made it more difficult. German resistance was sporadic."[27]

The Germans were using delaying tactics and minefields to slow the advance, while waiting for winter weather and the completion of the Gustav Line behind them. The weather in the mountains had turned bad, with cold temperatures, overcast skies, intermittent rain, and mist as the 2nd Battalion approached Gallo. On the night of October 30, a four-man patrol led by Italian-speaking Private Robert Finizio went into the town of Gallo to contact the local priest. Lieutenant Chester Garrison, the 2nd Battalion S-1, was at the command post, located a short distance down the valley in the town of Latino, when the patrol returned. "[Private Finizio] gained the information that the German vehicles had left town as it had grown dark; also, that a fifteen-man machine gun squad was believed to be in the hills. An engineer patrol [had] set up mines on a small bridge on the road leading out [of] the opposite side of town."[28]

The following morning at 5:00 a.m., the 2nd Battalion's S-2, Lieutenant Virgil F. "Hoagie" Carmichael, led a patrol into Gallo to check out the town. At 8:30 a.m., the 2nd Battalion advanced into the town, with Company D on the left and Company F on the right in a skirmish line. The battalion encountered no enemy resistance until the forward elements reached the far side of the town, where they received machine gun fire, wounding one man.

For the next twelve days, the 504th RCT moved through the steep hills and mountains, and north along the Volturno River valley. The terrain was so rugged that mules were used almost exclusively to carry ammunition, rations, water, and other essentials to Tucker's troopers. Patrols penetrated deep into enemy-held territory as the combat team moved north, clearing the towns of Monteroduni, Sant'Agapito, Macchia, Fornelli, Cerro, Scapoli, and Rocchetta as they moved up the valley.

The artillerymen, such as Corporal Ted Johnson, with Battery B, 376th Parachute Field Artillery Battalion, found the combination of mud as a result of incessant rain, steep hills, gorges with fast-flowing streams, and few roads to be daunting for movement of the battalion's 75mm pack howitzers. "The going was rugged, and we moved position to position in constant rain and mud. The Germans were always on the high ground looking down our throats."[29]

The 504th troopers, like Sergeant Milton Knight, with Headquarters Company, 1st Battalion, admired the 376th Parachute Field Artillery Battalion, whose troopers had struggled through the mountainous terrain to provide artillery support for the infantry. "We loved our little artillery unit. They weren't very big—little old pack 75s that had a range of about eight thousand yards. But when we needed them, they were there for us, and we used them, and they did a good job for us."[30]

On the morning of November 11, Lieutenant Payton F. Elliott, a platoon leader with Company H, received orders to conduct a reconnaissance patrol. "Our battalion was holding the east bank of the Volturno River on both sides of Colli. The enemy held Scapoli and Hill 1017 and had patrols, though no large forces in Montaquila.

"My platoon was given the mission of sending out a daylight patrol. It was to start from Colli and was to determine if the enemy was holding Hill 1017 and, if so, in what strength; it was also to determine if the hill was mined. The platoon consisted of thirty-two men, two rifle squads and one 60mm mortar squad. I sent out one rifle squad on this patrol. They followed the stream valley (R. Acquoso). There was an open field running along this stream, with a grape vineyard on the hillside above the field. They moved in squad column along the edge of the vineyard, keeping in the shadows. They found a wire running along the side of the hill, generally parallel to their route. This wire had a sign on it saying, 'Mined' in Italian. (We later discovered that the area inside the wire was mined and believe the sign was put up by Italian civilians as a warning to other Italian civilians who might be grazing sheep or goats in that neighborhood.) The patrol got about a mile and a half from Colli when they were fired on by a sniper located on a nose of the hill to their front. They could not get around this in daylight, so they came back to Colli and reported.

"Our company was then ordered to make an attack, as a reconnaissance in force. We were to start that same night at 2200. Our mission was capture Hill 1017 if possible, but if that was not possible, to determine the hostile strength and the caliber and locations of [the enemy] guns. The company order directed that the company would move to the base of the north slope of Hill 1017 in columns of platoons, my platoon leading. On arrival at the base of the hill, the 1st Platoon was to form on my right, and we were then to launch the attack on the signal of the company commander, who would then be in the interval between the two platoons.

"The enemy was shelling Colli when we started to move out, so I had my platoon start out in single file, with twenty yards between men. It was a moonlit night, so the men could keep in contact. We waded across the Volturno River, which was waist deep. After we got across, I reformed the platoon with the 1st and 2nd Squads abreast at about fifteen yards interval and the mortar squad following in rear at about the same distance. All squads were in squad column. The 1st Platoon followed us in the same formation at about thirty yards distance. I was in front of my platoon, and the sergeant [Charles R. Hawkins] who had led the daylight patrol followed me at about four yards, guiding me. We moved out without incident to the same point which the daylight patrol had reached.

"Just beyond the spot where the daylight patrol had been fired upon, we came to a barbed wire entanglement along the front of the vineyard. I had the wire cutters passed up to me, and I cut a gap through the entanglement. The sergeant assisted me, holding the wire to keep it from making a noise. The platoon moved through the gap in single file, and I had it resume its formation on the other side.

"We then moved up through the vineyard. The leading man of the rifle squad on the right was a man who had had demolition training at Benning, the only one in my platoon. About twenty-five yards beyond the entanglement, he spotted an S-mine. I halted the platoon and sent back word of this immediately to the company commander, who came forward at once to join me. We decided to go 'by the left flank' for about thirty yards and then resume our original direction. Just as we started to the left, the sergeant about four yards behind me stepped on a mine and was killed. Another man was badly wounded, and three others were hit. I can't account for the fact that I wasn't hit—it must just have been my lucky night. All the men, and myself, dropped to the ground and watched carefully to the front and flanks, expecting the Germans to fire on us or attack us. The company aid men came up, gave first aid to the wounded, and made stretchers out of raincoats. The company commander then ordered us to withdraw. So twelve men carried back the wounded, while the remainder of the platoon followed as a rearguard. The demolition man, although wounded in the heel, said nothing about it, but preceded the platoon and located a safe route so we would not hit any more mines.

"The next afternoon, we moved out again, my platoon again in the lead. This time, we were to move up Hill 1017 considerably to the east of where we ran into the mines the night before. We had three engineers with mine detectors attached to the platoon. They worked ahead of us to clear a path, marking the edges of the path with white tape. The platoon followed close enough behind so that we could cover them all the time with small-arms fire. The engineer in the lead moved around a large boulder and discovered two Germans fast asleep behind it. He captured them and brought them back to the platoon. They were pretty scared and when questioned, told us that the east slope of the hill was heavily mined, but the north slope of the hill had some areas which were not mined. We backed out immediately and moved around to the north side of the hill, taking the two PWs with us as guides. They guided us, and we found an area there which was apparently clear of mines, as they had said. We started up the north face. After we got up a ways, we captured two more Germans who were on outpost. They also told us there were no mines around and pointed out on the ground the locations of two machine gun nests. We worked around, hit the two machine gun nests from both flanks, and captured both. We took several more PWs here and killed ten or twelve of the enemy. One machine gun was a heavy barreled, air-cooled gun; the other was a regular German light machine gun.

"Company I was then pushed around to our right to outflank the enemy on top of Hill 1017."[31]

Lieutenant Willis Ferrill was one of the Company I platoon leaders. "My platoon was one of the leading platoons. We operated in small parties because the climbing was so difficult. The immediate party with me consisted of four enlisted men, two other officers, and myself. After we had climbed quite a while, we heard someone talking in a low voice, just off to our left front. I thought it was probably the party on my left, so I called out, 'What outfit are you from?' Somebody said something in German, and we heard people moving around as though to surround us. We hit the ground and took up positions in generally a circle, so we could cover in all directions. In a few minutes, the enlisted man nearest me and myself both saw a couple of men moving down the hill as though to get behind us. He used his rifle, and I used my Tommy gun, and we think we got one or both of them. We heard the rest of them scrambling off, so we waited a few minutes and then started up again.

"About 2130, we reached the top of Hill 1017, without having encountered any more Germans. We found what appeared to be a whole German company bivouacked there; they were lying on the ground and had no foxholes or prone shelters. They only had one or two sentries awake. We moved cautiously for a few minutes, sizing up the situation, and then attacked—just the seven of us—firing everything we had and yelling bloody murder. We killed one of the sentries, and the rest of them just ran like frightened sheep. It was five hours later before any more of our men got up there. The Germans counterattacked at daylight, but by that time, there were enough of us up there to beat them off."[32]

Private Francis W. "Mac" McLane was a member of another small party of Company I troopers to reach the top of Hill 1017 along with Lieutenant Ferrill's party. When McLane and the other troopers "got to the top of the mountain, we saw a very pretty meadow, a tent, and a large supply dump with stacks of boxes of food and ammunition. [Sergeant Lloyd V.] Engebritzen covered me while I crossed the meadow looking for a good spot for a defensive position. I was halfway across when I came face to face with a Jerry who was running toward me. I fired without a thought, just a reaction. He called, 'Nicht schiessen,' but it was too late. I didn't have to shoot him, but I couldn't think fast enough to avoid it. I think he had been manning the machine gun at the head of the gully and was coming for more ammunition.

"The men from the gully came up and joined us. They were Lieutenant [Henry B.] Keep, Lieutenant [Robert C.] Blankenship, and Corporal ['Red']

Evenson. We had found a round depression edged by small trees—a perfect spot for defense. A column of Krauts came up to, and around our position. They didn't see us, but we couldn't engage them because they held one of our boys prisoner. He had a strong Arkansas accent and, for our benefit I'm sure, talked very loudly all the time. They headed down the hill and were taken care of there. We waited until we collected ten more people. It was getting late in the day, so we headed for the peak at the end of the ridge that we were on. The fifteen of us got credit for the capture of Hill 1017."[33]

After Company I captured Hill 1017, the Germans mercilessly shelled Companies H and I with artillery and mortars over the next three days. Private McLane and the other men holding the hill "had been without food or water for several days. We spread out shelter-halves to try to catch rainwater. We could only catch a sip or two. The hunger subsided, but the thirst was unbearable."[34]

Three days after the hill's capture, Company C moved up in a torrential rain to relieve Companies H and I on Hill 1017. When Corporal Ross Carter, struggling through the mud, reached the Volturno River, he couldn't believe what he saw: "A crude bridge consisting of two Manila ropes with planks tied between. There were no wires or ropes to cling to. The Volturno churned through the gorge as if speeded by hydraulic pressures. If a man tumbled into that angry stream, nothing could save him from drowning.

"We had to stick to the center of the path because the S-mines were still planted on the sides. When we rested, we had to sit in the center, down which a fair-sized stream of water was pouring, or else run the risk of springing a mine. The rain trickled down our necks and into our boots. We didn't mind the rain though as much as usual since our tails were continuously wet anyhow from sitting in a brook."[35]

After Company C relieved them, Companies H and I moved down Hill 1017 to a rear-area encampment. By the time Private Mac McLane's Company I group reached the crossing on the Volturno River, the continuous rains had greatly swollen the river, making it impassable. "So we had to make a wide detour to get back to Colli. We headed north across a plowed field. Every step [we] sank into mud halfway up to our knees. It was getting dark and we were exhausted from the effort.

"When we found a big barn, we made the most of it. We covered the windows with blankets and built a fire in the middle of the floor. It was like heaven. We were in enemy territory, but it was worth the risk."[36]

Meanwhile, up on Hill 1017, Corporal Carter spent a miserable night. "At three in the morning my platoon was ordered to take up positions near the crest of the hill. At four, it began to rain. We rigged up a crude tent in the dark and crawled into it. By this time, the water had soaked through even our epidermis.

"Wild Bill [William A. Murray] started to cuss. He was seldom moved to blasphemy and invective, but when he got going his artistry made the best of us take off our hats in admiring astonishment."[37]

At dawn the next morning in the valley, Private Mac McLane continued the journey to Colli. "We found a main road and traveled in the direction we wanted to go. There were German oil bottles and assorted trash along the sides of the road—all the labels were in German. We came to a group of small buildings, obviously having been recently occupied by the Krauts. Lieutenant Blankenship asked me to take a patrol out to the north to find out where the Krauts were. He said, 'Don't try to contact them, just get as much information as you can, and above all, try to scrounge a meal for us somewhere.' We hadn't eaten in four days."[38]

On November 18, Corporal Carter and another man with him descended Hill 1017 to get water for his squad. On the way back up the hill, shrapnel from a German artillery barrage struck the water jug they were carrying, breaking it. Carter wearily reached the top of the mountain where "bad news awaited us. A captain and two radio operators from the 376th Parachute Field Artillery Battalion were on top of the mountain observing for their guns. Since Krautheads were not firing at the mountaintop, the captain is reported to have said, 'Hell, I'll give them a target so I can find out where their guns are.' He stepped out into an open space where the Krautheads could see him. They dropped a mortar barrage that killed the captain, Lieutenant [Lyle] Nightingale, our first sergeant [Albert Henry, Jr.], one radio operator [Sergeant William C. Jones], and severely wounded three other men.

"Next afternoon, donkeys were brought up on the mountain to carry off the dead men. The wounded had been carried down the night before. Ernie Pyle wrote about the beloved captain who came down the mountain on a donkey with his men hating to see him go.

"First Sergeant Henry, the last to be carried down, was one of the best men who ever served his country. We stood looking at Henry, whose short, black, curly-haired blood-matted head hung on one side of the donkey and his shrapnel-mangled legs on the other. More than one man had tears in his eyes as Henry disappeared around a bend."[39]

THE 456TH PARACHUTE FIELD ARTILLERY BATTALION, less Batteries C and D, sailed from North Africa on November 17 to join the 504th RCT for combat in Italy. Lieutenant Ed Sims, with Company H, was thankful when he got the news that the 504th RCT was going to be relieved. "On November 23, 1943, the entire regiment was replaced by the 133rd Infantry and went into two weeks reserve near Ciorlano. During the period we had an exceptional Thanksgiving dinner."[40] It was to be a short-lived rest.

On December 9, 1943, the same day the 82nd Airborne Division arrived in Belfast, Northern Ireland, the 504th RCT received orders to get ready to move. Corporal Ross Carter was hopeful at the news. "Since we hadn't been re-equipped, we thought, and rumor confirmed it, that our mission in Italy was completed and that we were going to England to rejoin the 82nd. Rumor was wrong as usual. Although we didn't all have entrenching tools, and our shelter-halves were worn out, and some of our guns were in bad shape, we got into some trucks and went driving through the rain. It always rained when we went anywhere. If the Legion would drive through the Sahara in the driest season, I bet a cloudburst would fall on it. We got off the trucks under the rocky slopes of the biggest mountain we ever saw in Italy and set up a bivouac in some olive trees. Dozens of 105[mm] howitzers and 155[mm] long toms and other breeds of howitzers were all around us. They fired day and night. A man had to be stone deaf to get any sleep. Plenty of tanks were all around. It looked like something big was going on, something bigger than anything we'd seen so far."[41]

The regimental command post was set up in the town of Venafro on December 10. That night, Lieutenant James Megellas arrived as one of the group of replacements who reported to the 504th regimental headquarters command post, located in the cellar of a house in the town. "We reported to the regimental commander, Colonel Reuben Tucker, who was seated behind a desk in a dimly lit room. He was an impressive looking man who had a deep voice and wasn't given to small talk. As he welcomed us, he talked about what we would be up against: rugged terrain and a determined enemy giving up ground only grudgingly and at a high price. The sounds of incoming and outgoing artillery permeating the air made the briefing short. For me, I had found a home after eighteen months of frustration trying to become part of a combat unit. I could not have been assigned to a better fighting unit than the 504th Parachute Regiment."[42]

Megellas and Lieutenants Richard G. LaRiviere and Peter Gerle, Jr. were assigned to Company H. Megellas "was sent to the 3rd Platoon, then being led by Staff Sergeant Michael 'Mike' Kogut, who reverted to platoon sergeant. Mike was an original member of the 504th, a combat veteran of the jump in Sicily; the landings at Salerno, Maiori, Chiunzi Pass, and Naples; and the cross-ing of the Volturno River. It was my good fortune to be with him during my baptism of fire. I learned from him some of the tricks of staying alive and how to lead men, not command them. At six-foot-three, Mike was an impressive figure, but his stature was based on the respect his men had for him more than his physique. As a replacement officer in combat for the first time with a lot to learn, I relied heavily on Mike's advice and assistance. Being an officer and a platoon leader did not automatically command the respect of the men. It had to be earned, and that could be done only by leading."[43]

The next day the 3rd Battalion was ordered to relieve the 3rd Ranger Battalion, which had suffered 50 percent casualties and was still fighting on Hill 950. The 2nd Battalion was to reinforce the 1st Battalion of the 143rd Infantry on Mount Sammucro, designated on the combat maps as Hill 1205. Private Mac McLane, with Company I, gathered his gear and began the long walk to the top of Hill 950. "We walked through a narrow pass into a moonscape—a bowl of a mountain in front of us, covered with boulders and rocks. There was not a speck of anything green and growing. Artillery had pounded the life out of it. On our right was a peak shaped like an upside down ice cream cone. The whole area was echoing with the screech and explosions of hundreds of shells. It was obvious that this was not a neighborhood in which to raise children. The ice cream cone was to be ours—Hill 950. The bursting flowers of flame could be nothing but hand grenades, which meant very close contact with the enemy. We started up. My old friend, Engebritzen, was waiting for me, but we hadn't gone far when a grenade exploded next to his thigh, giving him a very nasty wound. After calling for a medic, I moved on. It was so steep that you had to use your hands as well as your feet."[44]

At 5:30 p.m. on December 11, the 2nd Battalion began their approach march to Hill 1205, the highest elevation facing the German Gustav Line, with a clear view across the valley of the abbey on Monte Cassino. The mountain overlooked the town of San Pietro that would be the scene of fierce fighting in the days to come. At about 6:45 p.m., Lieutenant Chester Garrison, the S-1, and rest of the battalion turned off of the road and began the long slog up "a long, muddy torturous trail. The night was as black as could be, with a mist setting in early and turning to rain. When at 0300 a place was reached where the ascent was possible only by pulling oneself up by a long rope, the battalion stopped for a few hours' sleep. Loose and rolling rocks also hampered the climb. In the dark, it was almost impossible to find a nook or cranny large enough to lay down on a level. Most of the men slept where they were able to sit and still keep from sliding down the mountainside."[45]

As the 1st Battalion followed the 2nd up Hill 1205, Company A platoon leader, Lieutenant Reneau Breard, heard an explosion ahead of him in the column. "Somebody ahead of me had a grenade go off in his pants pocket. I thought it blew his leg off. But, he survived. . . . I don't know how in the hell he did. We had a Cajun medic from south Louisiana named Polette, and he took care of him and got him evacuated. He never did come back to the unit."[46]

After a very long and difficult climb, Company I trooper, Private Mac McLane reached the crest of Hill 950. "I got to the top where my squad was digging in. How do you dig in on a forty-five degree slope of solid rock?

"[Private First Class Leo P.] Muri, [Private William R.] Leonard, [Staff Sergeant George] Leoleis, and [Private Dwight] Goodwin had found spots, but before I got located, [Corporal 'Red'] Evenson found me and said that

[Lieutenant Robert] Blankenship wanted to see me on top. I thought we were on top, but there was a shelf on the other side that furnished positions for twelve to fourteen men.

"The Krauts were throwing 'egg' grenades in such numbers that we were holding our rifles in a way that we could bat them off—like you bunt a ball in baseball. As if the Krauts didn't pose enough trouble, Lieutenant Blankenship was suffering from an attack of malaria. The enemy had a 170mm gun in the valley below us, and between attacks, would shell us. Evenson and I found a position behind a boulder that was close to the officers, but gave us a good field of fire."[47]

That night, a heavy German counterattack to capture Hill 1205 fell on the 1st Battalion, 143rd Infantry, but was repulsed. The 1st and 2nd Battalions of the 504th arrived to take over the northern half of Hill 1205 before dawn. When Lieutenant Breard, with Company A, arrived at the top of the mountain, he found a barren, boulder-strewn surface. "You couldn't dig a hole; there was nothing but rock. You just had to build rocks around you."[48]

At about 4:00 a.m. on Hill 950, Staff Sergeant George Leoleis and fourteen other Company I troopers were still trying to dig in around the rocky summit. "I glanced up and saw a shadow moving up and down in front of me. I looked away and right back to make sure my eyes weren't playing tricks on me. Sure enough, I made out a form in the skyline; I was just below the crest and he stood right out. I continued to make noises as if I was still digging and I tapped the men on either side of me and nodded toward the shadow. By now, he was almost within [hand]shaking distance of me. I now moved my rifle across my lap while still making noise with the small shovel I had. I then pointed my rifle at him while holding it in one hand and fired. He gurgled and went down. At the same time, I yelled as loud as I could, 'Here they come!' Then all hell broke loose. They came at us, right over the top, which the two men and I were holding. The three of us were on our knees and firing from the hips as fast as we could reload. Then they rushed us, and the knives came out, we were in a fight for survival, one, two, three, then five. We could not even take one step back, because we would have gone over the cliff that was at our backs. When the [hand-to-]hand fighting ended, the rest of the Germans fell back and started to throw potato-mashers (hand grenades)."[49]

During the German attack that night, Private McLane "took very careful aim at the muzzle blast of their automatic weapons. The distance was like one hundred yards, or less. They set up a machine gun in front of us and Evenson knocked it out with a rifle grenade. Toward morning, he got hit in the face and had to leave. He had been like a rock, and I sorely missed him.

"Near dawn there was a lull in the firing, and I must have dozed off, when I heard several excited voices saying that the Krauts were flanking us. It took a while for my eyes to adjust to the light. I counted five helmet tops moving above a niche in the rocks. I had no way of knowing how many had already passed. The captain told me to get some help and stop them. I had to start from the extreme right of our position and go to the extreme left, maybe one hundred feet distance. On the way, I tried to enlist help, but didn't have any success. I asked a very young, white-faced kid to give me some covering fire.

"His reply was, 'I was told to face that way.' (Not in my direction.) I had no time for extended debate. I ran to a bald slope and hit the ground in the prone position. This was the saddle that gave access to both the front and rear of our position . . . the most vulnerable part of our defense. The first Jerry started to run up the slope toward me; his gaze was riveted above me. This guy looked exactly like my brother! I was completely shaken. What the hell was he doing here? The Jerry didn't have my type of problem. He dropped his gaze and saw me. He snap fired his P-38 [pistol]. The bullet hit the dirt about a foot from my head. Brotherly love notwithstanding, I had to consider my priorities, and I shot him. The other Krauts were trying to shoot, but I shot them before they could pull a trigger. They tried to do a 'jumping jack' (popping up from dispersed positions). This exaggerated popping up gave me time to hit each one as he showed himself. They gave up trying to outshoot me and tried the same tactic with grenades. This was even more futile, as they were exposed longer. I had no idea how many there were, but the last three gave it up and tried to run back to their positions. I ran parallel to them and got all three before they made it. This turned out to be a very messy business, as I couldn't shoot accurately while running over rough ground. I won't go into detail, as it was not a matter of which to look back upon with pride. I couldn't be sure, but I think the rest of the Jerries just watched. I don't believe anyone even shot at me. After this, the Jerries seemed to have lost heart. I could see helmet tops moving around aimlessly, and I tried to get in a shot."[50]

Shortly after the last German attack ended, Staff Sergeant Leoleis crawled out of his hole and down the hill to see if he could find where the German attacks were being staged. "I stopped to check the first guy I shot from the hip. I flinched a little when I saw that my first shot hit him right in the nose and tore half his face off."[51]

Private McLane crawled back to the shallow hole he had scratched out of the rock-hard hill. "The Germans and we were exhausted. They had quit firing and prisoners were coming in. Private First Class [John E.] Schultz, the BAR man, had performed extremely well all through this battle. His position had been about five yards below and to the left of me. He spoke German and interrogated the prisoners who came in.

"These men had been on the Russian front and had been sent to Italy as sort of a rest area. It wasn't what they expected. They were terrified by our marksmanship. Many of their dead had been shot squarely between the eyes;

our firepower was too much for them to cope with. This seemed strange to me, because the whole German system was always based on firepower—more automatic weapons, higher rates of fire. Their weakness may have been that these fast-firing weapons climbed too much, and much of their power was wasted. The estimate of German loss of men was 150 killed—our loss around forty-five."[52]

From December 12 to 14, the Germans subjected both Hill 950 and Hill 1205 to intense artillery and mortar fire, while snipers infiltrated at night and, from hidden positions among the boulder-strewn ridges, took a deadly toll. Anyone appearing to be an officer or NCO was targeted. On December 12, Company G officers Captain George Watts and Lieutenant James C. Kierstead, as well as Lieutenant Frank W. Gilson, with Company I, were all killed. Artillery and mortar fire was directed at the suspected positions of the enemy snipers. Patrols also hunted these snipers, often resulting in the elimination of the snipers, but usually at the cost of more men. On December 14, Lieutenant James G. Breathwit led a Company G patrol to clear snipers from the saddle between Hill 950 and Hill 1205. The German snipers, hidden among the rocks, waited as the patrol got close and then opened fire, killing Lieutenant Breathwit, who reportedly was wearing second lieutenant bars on his shoulders and had a painted stripe on the back of his helmet, indicating his rank.

Lieutenant Joseph W. Lyons, with the newly arrived Battery B, 456th Parachute Field Artillery Battalion, spent two weeks as a forward observer on Hill 1205. "The guns were always in the valleys, and the OPs [observation posts] on high ground. These actions were the classrooms for the 456. The outfit molded into an outstanding battalion. We all looked like 'Willie and Joe.' "[53]

On December 14, the 504th was ordered to assist in seizing the high ground overlooking the valley behind the town of San Pietro. Specifically, the 2nd Battalion on Hill 1205 was assigned to attack across a deep saddle and capture Hill 687 to the west, while the 3rd Battalion would send a strong combat patrol from Hill 950 to the northeast to grab Hill 954.

On the night of December 14, as the 2nd Battalion S-1, Lieutenant Chester Garrison, brought a group of replacements up Hill 1205, "the battalion moved forward in column at 2015 with E Company in the lead. The head of the column went down the far side of the mountain, reaching its objective. Contact between E and D Companies was lost, and E Company proceeded alone without knowledge of the loss of the rest of the battalion. The battalion CP group never cleared the ridge. When they got into a firefight and realized their loss of contact, Lieutenant [Walter S.] VanPoyck gave the company orders to return to their starting position on the ridge. They did not discover any of the rest of the battalion until they reached this position, as Major [Daniel] Danielson had given the battalion orders to return there. The battalion stayed in this position for the remainder of the night. The 1st Battalion moved into the area which the 2nd Battalion had used, putting their CP in the locality of the 2nd Battalion CP.

"The [2nd] Battalion remained along the ridge [of Hill 1205] all day in preparation of a night attack. It moved out at 1845 in the same order of march, in column with E Company in the lead. It was again pinned down by fire on the northwest side of the mountain. Heavy casualties [resulted] from artillery, machine gun, mortar, small-arms, and grenade fire."[54]

Caught in the rocky low ground in front of Hill 687 with little cover and no way to dig in, the 2nd Battalion was once again forced to withdraw before dawn back to Hill 1205. They had suffered fifteen killed and seventy-five wounded in the two attacks.

Lieutenant Garrison once again made the trip to the bottom of Hill 1205 and brought more replacements up the hill. "Additional rations and ammunition were picked up by each man at the supply dump at the end of the mule trail, only half way up."[55]

Private First Class Harry A. Corbin was a new replacement, assigned to Company C, 307th Airborne Engineer Battalion. "They wanted me to carry supplies up the mountain. I got a couple of cases of C-rations. We had a file of about fifteen men loaded with stuff. The only way to get it up there was with manpower. We started up that mountain and it was dark. The Germans started shelling us, I guess with mortar shells. So we all ducked down. We had to stay about three or four feet from the guy ahead of you to be able to see him. So when we ducked down, there was a little gully there where water had washed down the side of the mountain, so I jumped into that, which was a couple of feet from where we were walking on the trail. There was another soldier lying there. I waited a couple of minutes. I didn't hear [anything], and the shelling finally stopped. The guy kept lying there. I shook him and said, 'Hey, we better get going.' The guy was dead—stiff as a board. The group had taken off. It was pitch dark and I didn't know which way they went. I got my boxes of rations and started going up the hill and made my own path.

"I finally got up there, and there were some soldiers along the trail who were coming back down, carrying bodies. They showed me where the trail was to get up there. The troops were coming down off the top at the time we were going up. But they were still sending us up there. I climbed on up to within about thirty or forty feet from the top. There, it went almost straight up. They had a path to weave around between the boulders. Finally, I put one of my boxes down because I couldn't climb that part with two boxes, because you had to have an extra hand. So I got up and the only people up there were four or five guys like me who had just come up. The top of Hill 1205 was like a bulldozer had flattened it. You could stand up there and see Monte Cassino down below about two or three miles."[56]

On the morning of December 16, the Protestant chaplain of the 504th, Captain Delbert Kuehl, overheard a trooper mention that there were some wounded 2nd Battalion troopers in no man's land on the other side of the ridge from the site of the previous night's attack. Captain Kuehl talked with the medics, and they agreed that they couldn't leave the wounded out there to die. Kuehl and the battalion surgeons and medics decided to go get them in broad daylight. "We found in the medics supplies a tattered Red Cross flag, put it on a stick, took some folding litters, and started over the mountain to the German side.

"We all knew that if the German troops were from the fanatical SS, or if they couldn't figure out our purpose, we wouldn't be coming back.

"As we started down the open slope, a machine gun opened up, with bullets hitting beside us and spraying us with bits of rock. We thought, 'This is it.' All they had to do was traverse that gun slightly and we would have been wiped out. Then the firing stopped.

"We found a number of our wounded men. We put some on litters and dragged others across our shoulders, and struggled back over the rugged slope—back to our side of the mountain."[57]

That same morning Lieutenant Garrison put the replacements to work hauling more supplies instead of assigning them to rifle companies. "They far excelled any expectations in their willingness and stamina to do their utmost to aid the battalion on the forward slope. The climbing and re-climbing with loads of supplies on their backs was extremely exhausting. Captain [Robert N.] Johnson, [commanding Headquarters Company, 2nd Battalion,] with an enlisted man, made his way back safely over the exposed rocky mountainside to get some water for the men. They returned to the forward position without drawing any fire by 0900. Captain Johnson was shortly afterwards killed in his foxhole by an almost direct hit of enemy artillery. A terrific barrage was laid down on the battalion lasting about two hours and forcing the personnel to seek refuge and slight protection of the saddle to the rear of their prepared positions. Numerous casualties were inflicted [on the battalion]."[58]

One of the replacements carrying supplies that morning was Private Jack L. Bommer, who would later be assigned to Headquarters Company as a wireman. "Rocky [Private Rockwell R. Easton] and I became close friends the first day I was with the 504 in Italy, on a trail going up Hill 1205. Enemy mortar fire was following the trail down the hillside perfectly, curve for curve, bend for bend. I was carrying a five-gallon water can on my backpack, and I fell to find cover. In doing so, I lost my helmet and was in the middle of the trail with no cover at all. Shells were [exploding] within five feet of me, and all of a sudden, I felt 'something' fall on me. That 'something' remained on me until the barrage moved downhill. I felt the 'something' move from my back, and a voice said, 'I think its okay now! Let's get the hell out of here!' The 'something' that I felt save my life was Rockwell Easton."[59]

Also on December 16, falling rocks severely injured Major Danielson's knees and he was evacuated. Major Melvin S. Blitch, Jr., the 2nd Battalion executive officer, replaced him.

On December 17, a sniper shot and killed Lieutenant Peter Gerle, one of three replacement officers assigned to Company H a short time earlier. Later that day, another of the Company H replacement officers, Lieutenant Jim Megellas, was ordered to take his platoon and capture Hill 610, about three hundred yards to the front, which was being used as a base by German snipers and forward observers. Megellas led his men down the trail, watching for mines as he went. "We reached the base of Hill 610 and started climbing to the crest. At about the halfway point, an explosion and a flash appeared in the center of the column. The call went out: 'Mines,' then 'Scannell is hit!' The platoon froze in place."[60]

Caught in a minefield on open ground in front of Hill 610, they were incredibly lucky that the Germans had withdrawn the previous night, or it could have been a bloodbath. The platoon moved forward very slowly, with each man stepping on the same ground as the man ahead, all the while carefully looking for the telltale signs of mines: tripwires and disturbed ground.

Megellas got his men to the top of the hill without incurring additional casualties. "Before we took up defensive positions, we made a fine-toothed-comb search for enemy mines left behind. I learned to look for and trace a trip wire, often concealed, to an armed and activated mine, but more importantly I learned how to disarm and render it ineffective. On Hill 610 I developed a healthy respect for German antipersonnel mines, the silent killers.

"Scannell's body was left where he fell. After dark, the mules coming up with water and rations would take his body back to Graves Registration. I had joined the company only a short while before and was not familiar with most of the men, but I will always remember Private [John R.] Scannell, the first man killed in a platoon I led. He would not be the last."[61]

The 1st Battalion relieved the 2nd on the evening of December 17. After reaching the summit of Hill 1205, Captain Ernie Milloy, the commanding officer of Company C, reported to Major Warren Williams, the 1st Battalion commander. Milloy received an order to take his company forward one thousand yards in front of the battalion's main line to establish a line of outposts. "The position may have looked good on a higher headquarters situation map, but on the ground it was nearly untenable. The ground was barren and too rocky to dig in, and we were literally under the gun muzzles of the Germans. Any movement on our part immediately drew heavy fire."[62]

That following night, Company A succeeded in capturing Hill 687. Lieutenant Reneau Breard spent a restless night with his platoon waiting for the inevitable counterattack. A strong German force hit Breard and his men around dawn the next morning. "The Germans came up [the slope] and we held them off."[63]

The 504th held on to the hard-won hills for another two weeks. The weather and enemy artillery continued to take their tolls. The morning report for the 2nd Battalion on December 20 indicated three officers and twenty-four enlisted men in Company D, while Company E had four officers and only ten enlisted men, and Company F only two officers and twenty-eight enlisted men. Even Headquarters Company, 2nd Battalion, reflected the attrition: eight officers, but only sixty-nine enlisted men. Lieutenant Breard saw the strength of Company A slowly dwindle over those bitterly cold days and nights. "It was so damned cold, people just had to quit . . . it was exposure. I think we got down to about fourteen men in the company. I think that on Christmas Day they gave us these tankers' uniforms. I threw away my wet blanket."[64]

For Private First Class Leo Muri, with Company I, the approach of Christmas was depressing. "We were all wondering if we would be relieved by Christmas. The rumors were sure running wild in the company—all about being relieved. Well, it was just about Christmas, and there were four of us who were on the side of the hill to prevent any Jerry patrols from coming through the gap in the line. We had located an old goat house, which we made our home, and [it] helped to keep us warm. Of course, the goat house was lousy with ticks and lice, but by this time, we were all suffering with the damned things anyhow. So it was on Christmas Eve [that] I was standing guard outside the goat house as we took turns watching while the others slept. I think this was just about one of the saddest times overseas, as I stood there cold and disgusted, thinking of the folks at home. There was snow on the hill for Christmas, but our dinner was the usual can of stew or beans, which was brought up to us by donkeys."[65]

Private First Class Russell Long, a radio operator with Headquarters Battery, 376th Parachute Field Artillery, spent a couple of weeks on Hill 1205 as part of a forward observation team. "I spent Christmas Day on Hill 1205, and although we did have a field day at Jerry's expense, who wants to be killing even the enemy on such a day."[66]

The 504th was officially relieved on December 27, but it took a few days before the rifle companies left their positions. Lieutenant Breard and the remnants of Company A, occupying Hill 687 out in front on Hill 1205, were some of the last to be relieved. "We came off of that mountain on the 31st. When we pulled out of there, I decided I'd go back over the mountain, 1205, and get my [60mm] mortar . . . we had left it up there. [Sergeant Bernard E.] Karnap, one other person, and I went; and we got up there and got that mortar. We were so damned tired . . . it was dark and everything . . . we were just worn out. So we said to hell with the mortar. I just left it up there.

"We went down the mountain and found a little ration dump with ten-in-one rations. We built a fire and we had bacon, chopped eggs, and I don't know what all in there. It was good! Then we took a nap and started off again, and got down to the bottom and passed a kitchen on the road. It was an artillery unit down there, and they were frying pork chops. They gave us pork chop sandwiches. They let us sleep in their beds, until the damned one-five-five's went off on a fire mission. We got up and got the hell out of there.

"It was the morning of the 1st of January when we got back. I think we were about the last to get back. Somebody saw us and gave us a ride. We caught up with the regiment and came on back to Naples."[67]

Since December 11, the 504th Parachute Infantry Regiment had suffered fifty-eight killed; Company C, 307th Airborne Engineer Battalion, had two men killed; and the 376th Parachute Field Artillery lost three men killed. The 504th Parachute Infantry had 226 wounded and many more evacuated for illness and injuries.

An exhausted and depleted 504th RCT moved to the town of Pignatoro, about twenty miles south of Venafro. It was welcome relief for men like Corporal Shelby Hord with Company H. "They gave us a bath, sprayed us with DDT, and gave us clean clothes."[68]

On December 30, Captain William Roe took command of Company D. On New Year's Day 1944, the men of the 504th RCT were fed a special dinner. Christmas packages and mail from back home were passed out and opened. The 504th RCT again moved to the suburbs north of Naples on January 4, where they continued to rest, refit, take on replacements, and get troopers back from hospitals.

Chapter 6

"Seems Like
The Black-Hearted Devils
Are Everywhere"

A fter another two weeks, the 504th RCT prepared once more for combat. Despite receiving some replacements and troopers returning from hospitals, the regiment was still understrength. The 1st Battalion would go into combat with only 445 men and thirty-four officers, while the 2nd Battalion had a total strength of 481, and the 3rd Battalion only 450 men and officers. The initial plan was use the 504th RCT to make a parachute jump to support amphibious landing at Anzio on the western coast of Italy, about fifteen miles southwest of Rome. The landings were code-named Operation Shingle and were designed to draw German reserves away from the Gustav Line, which was proving to be a tough and costly obstacle in the Fifth Army's drive toward Rome.

Concerns about a parachute landing alerting German forces to the amphibious landings caused the planners to decide to bring in the 504th RCT with the seaborne forces. On January 20, the 504th troopers received briefings regarding the amphibious operation.

AT AROUND 9:00 A.M. ON JANUARY 22, THE 504TH RCT followed the 3rd Infantry Division ashore on the southern end of the Anzio beachhead, landing almost without incident. However, a low-flying German plane swept over the LCIs unloading the regiment and dropped a bomb, hitting the LCI unloading Company G. Surprisingly, the only soldier killed by this attack was not from Company G. Private First Class Henry E. Ferrari, an H Company trooper who came in on that LCI to act as an interpreter for G Company, died of his wounds a week later.

Also on that LCI was Lieutenant Robert S. Hutton, a forward observer with the 376th Parachute Field Artillery Battalion. "I was blown into the water along with my forward observer members and several infantrymen. I lost my whole crew. Two of my men were seriously wounded. I was hurt in the knee and evacuated to a hospital in Naples. It was not serious, and I was back to my battery in a few weeks."[1]

The LCIs were anchored just off the beach and had ramps on each side that were lowered so that troopers could exit the ship. After the German plane started to turn to come in for another run, Private First Class Leo Hart, with Company F, began scrambling down the ramps to get off of his LCIs. "When I stepped off that thing I went completely underwater. I hit bottom and I followed my nose, straight ahead. The only thought I had was, 'Please keep walking straight ahead.' It was just a few steps and I was back [above the surface]."[2]

On board the LCI unloading Company I, Private First Class Leo Muri could hear his buddy, [Private] "Francis Keefe calling, and he was getting ready to dive overboard. So as I dashed over to the rail, there were some men who had been thrown overboard and no lifejackets. We threw ours in and dove overboard to help them in. I swam like I had never swam before. The wounded were brought to shore all right, and the craft was burning.

"We had lost a lot of ammo and equipment, so Francie and myself decided to swim to the burning craft and salvage a machine gun and some ammo. But just as we almost reached the burning craft, the ammo began to explode. So we turned around and headed back to the beach and started to join the rest of the company, with not a weapon between us."[3]

Private First Class Harry Corbin, a Company C, 307th engineer, was carrying a BAR and several bandoleers of ammunition. As he neared the ramp, Corbin could see the men below dropping into the water over their heads as they stepped off of the ramp. "I didn't want to go down that ramp. I asked them, 'Give me a life preserver,' and they wouldn't give me one. When I stepped off of that ramp, I went straight down and hit the bottom. I started trying to walk, but had run out of breath by that time. So I held on to the tip end of the barrel and took the butt of that BAR and jammed it into the bottom, pushed real hard, and my face just barely came out of the water, and I caught a breath and went right back again. 'I'm a goner,' I thought. I started walking as much as I could then. So then I held on to the tip of it and pushed it again. I came up again, stuck my head up and got another breath of air and saw which way the shore was. You just went up and down like a yoyo. I did that about four or five times. About the time I got out in the middle, here came these fighter-bombers strafing the beachhead. The bullets came down all around us, just like in a movie."[4]

After getting ashore, the 504th RCT moved to a wooded area a short dis-

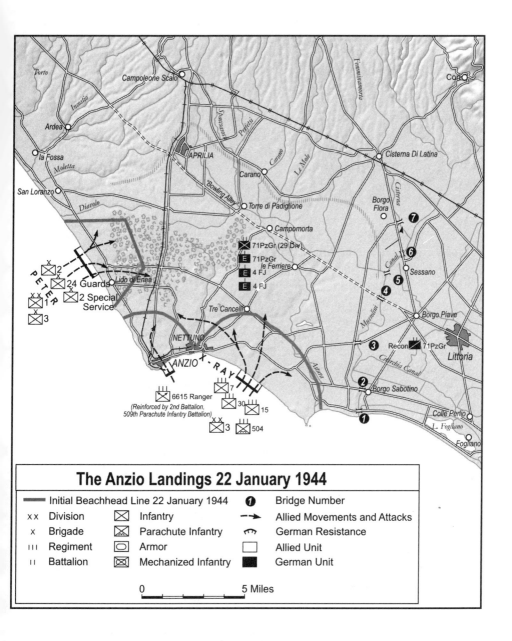

The Anzio Landings 22 January 1944

▬▬▬ Initial Beachhead Line 22 January 1944	❶	Bridge Number
xx Division	⊠ Infantry	—▶ Allied Movements and Attacks
x Brigade	⊠ Parachute Infantry	⌒ German Resistance
ɪɪɪ Regiment	◯ Armor	☐ Allied Unit
ɪɪ Battalion	⊠ Mechanized Infantry	■ German Unit

0   5 Miles

tance inland, got organized, and went into corps reserve. Instead of driving inland and cutting the main highway running south from Rome to deny the Germans their main supply line, the commanders ordered the Anzio invasion force to dig in on its initial objectives. The commanders expected swift and heavy armored attacks once the Germans learned of the extent of the landings. It was to be a tragic blunder and would cost many Allied lives as a result.

On the afternoon of January 23, the 3rd Battalion received an order to push east to seize and secure a 3,300-yard line along the east side of the Mussolini Canal on the right flank of the invasion beachhead. Company G had the assignment of capturing Bridge Number 0 at the mouth of the canal and Bridge Number 1 to the northeast, while Company I would attack and capture Bridge Number 2 to the northeast, on the left flank, near the town of Borgo Sabotino.

Private Bill Leonard was getting ready to eat when he heard the order for Company I to move out. "I bet 90 percent of us were caught eating our first five-in-one rations in many weeks. We threw on our horseshoe [bed]rolls and packs, grabbed a hand full of food, and fell in line with the rest of the platoon with my M1 rifle over my right [shoulder] and machine gun over and on top of my left shoulder. [Private] Don Emmett and I were going to trade off carrying the machine gun."[5]

Company I troopers Private First Class Leo Muri and his assistant gunner had lost their machine gun during the landing. "At this time, Francie [Private Francis X. Keefe] and myself were scouts. My buddy, Francie, is quite a guy, afraid of nothing and we worked rather well together—always sharing the same foxhole and getting into scrapes together—always managing to find our way out.

"We were two of four men who went ahead of the company to see if there was any enemy ahead and how far the company could go before meeting the enemy. The company was to wait along the road until our patrol was finished and we returned with the information. But we had just been gone but a few hours when the company received orders from higher up to move on. We had finally reached the enemy, hiding out in the woods along the road the company was coming up. We started back to warn them, but it was too late. The boys were coming up the road walking right into the trap set for us."[6]

Moving down the road with the main body of Company I, Private Leonard heard Lieutenant Robert Blankenship tell "everybody to 'shut up—be quiet.' Within seconds there was a call to halt. And at the same time, shots were fired ahead of our column. Everybody ran to the gullies and the open field, then returned fire. We had no idea that there was anybody around except us before that moment. Lieutenant Willis Ferrill was ahead of me approximately nine men. He was shot right through the helmet—center front—into his brain. He never knew what hit him."[7]

Staff Sergeant Louis "Lukie" Orvin was near the point of the Company I column when the Germans ambushed it at about 7:30 p.m. "It was dark and they just opened fire. Lieutenant Ferrill was killed . . . he was a good officer. We jumped into the little ditches on each side of the road. Then we crawled back far enough where we could get out of the ditches and spread out to the sides. We stayed there all night."[8]

Company G captured its two bridges without incident and put out patrols to its front. At about 1:30 a.m. that night, a patrol from the 3rd Platoon was fired on by two enemy machine guns.

At 5:30 a.m., a platoon of Company H and a section of bazooka teams were ordered to move to Bridge Number 2 to stop enemy armor from crossing the canal. However, at about that time, about two hundred German infantrymen supported by four tanks attacked Company I west of Bridge Number 2, forcing it to withdraw about one thousand yards. Colonel Tucker ordered the remainder of the 3rd Battalion to attack and relieve the pressure on Company I. At 6:30 a.m., Company H moved to attack the German left flank.

Soon after the Company H attack began, it lost its new company commander, Captain Melvin W. Nitz. Lieutenant Ed Sims, the executive officer, took command and kept the company moving forward in the attack. "Here for the first time, we were fighting German paratroopers, and they were a formidable fighting force, but outnumbered."[9]

By 8:00 a.m., the fighting intensified as Company I, after reorganizing, surged across the flat terrain, closing with the German infantry as Company H poured rifle, automatic weapons, bazooka, and mortar fire into the enemy infantry and tanks. Private First Class Muri and the other Company I troopers were "mad as hell at what happened the night before, and we went like wild men across the fields on the side of the road as the tanks came up the road, keeping well up with us."[10]

Staff Sergeant George Leoleis and the 3rd Platoon charged forward in a skirmish line, firing from the hips, through the fields on the left side of the road when five tanks arrived to support the Company I attack. "The lead tank was putting shells into each house as we got to them, and you could see some men run out of them. We came across some drainage trenches and received some fire. [Private First Class Harold E.] Gustafson was nearest to the trench. 'Hey sarge, they're over in the trench.' I motioned to him to go to his right, I went to the left, and both jumped in and finished them off.

"We continued across the field until we came up to this house that was sitting back about one hundred yards off the road. We approached it cautiously and we received more fire from there. It seemed all the action was on our side (how lucky for us). We ducked in one of the many trenches that the farmers were using to water their fields (they came in real handy) and returned their fire. One of the men had a walkie-talkie, and I yelled to him, 'Tell them to put a couple of shells in that damn house.' He waved to me with an okay sign. We were about fifty yards from that house, and I motioned to the men near me that when the lead tank fires, we would all rush to the house at the same time."[11]

Just seconds later, Leoleis heard the tank open fire. "The shell hit the second floor and we were up and running as fast as we could and firing at the same time. Harold and I hit the front door and [Private First Class Howard C.] Barksdale dove through the window. There were four of them inside and were somewhat stunned by the tank shell. We were all firing as we went in, and all four went down. One man went upstairs to check, and a couple of other men joined us. 'Hey sarge, come up here.' So I ran upstairs while the other men waited downstairs, catching their breath.

"Harold was up there. 'Look down there.' He pointed out the window.

" 'Where?'

" 'Down there,' and he pointed to a trench that was a good three hundred yards away. Then [Private Albert] Ferguson came up. Well, what do you know, our friends from last night—four machine gun emplacements. They were hidden pretty good. They too were using the trenches the farmers had dug for watering their fields. They were waiting for our guys. Tanks or no tanks, they would kill a lot of men. They were set up on a curve in the road that went left, and they wouldn't be spotted until our guys were right on top of them. They might be able to get a tank or two, because they had Panzerfausts with them.

"We watched them for a few minutes and wondered what to do. 'Where's the walkie-talkie? I asked Barksdale.

" 'Not here, sarge.' To try to warn the guys by the road was no good; they were too far away. I decided to try and pick them off from up here, since they didn't know we had taken the house from their men. We had perfect vision of their positions. We were high and looking down on them; that's why they had left those four guys here, to protect their flank. Harold had a submachine gun, so he was no use—too far for that. Barksdale and I had rifles (M1s) that I had a lot of faith in. (Although as a platoon sergeant, I was supposed to carry a sub, I liked the rifle. The only time I ever carried the sub was when I went on night patrols, because that's when you are close, and you could spray a lot.)

" 'Sarge, that's a long shot, and they're lying down, which makes it even harder,' Barksdale said.

" 'It's too late now anyway,' I said. 'Barksdale, you take that window and I'll take this one.' I made sure I had a full clip to start with and Barksdale started to shoot just ahead of me, but his gun jammed. He tried to eject his clip, but it wouldn't come out. I then told Harold, 'Here, take my bandoliers and have the clips out and hand them to me as fast as I can use them.' I took a deep breath, took aim, and started firing as fast as I could. One after another the empty clips pinged out of the breach, and just as fast [I] reloaded and emptied my rifle again and again. I could see the Krauts jerk as they were hit and lay down flat against the banking. They did not know where they were being hit from. I traversed from one to the other and then back again. I could see dirt fly when I missed, and that gave me a clue as to where I was aiming. I must have fired over a hundred rounds; my rifle was so hot I could barely hold it. I felt a hand on my shoulder, 'I think that's it,' Harold yelled. 'You got them all.' "[12]

As Staff Sergeant Orvin moved forward with his men, naval gunfire shook the ground. "At first, the rounds started falling behind us. I don't think we had anyone hit. Then they got the right range on it and started firing up toward the canal."[13]

The powerfully built Private Bill Leonard, carrying his .30-caliber machine gun and M1, moved forward on the right flank of the Company I attack. "We were pursuing Germans running down the back slope towards the canal. I was kneeling in a gully shooting all of them who were too scared to retreat back down the road."[14]

Some of the fleeing Germans were cut down as they tried to escape across the canal, leaving approximately forty-five dead strewn over the flat ground. Private First Class Muri and the other Company I troopers had their blood up and were in hot pursuit. "We weren't satisfied at just getting up to the canal. A group of us crossed the canal to rack up the Jerries who had managed to escape to the other side. Upon reaching the other side of the canal, we laid on the bank and shot Jerries as one shoots targets at a shooting gallery; because of the open fields the Jerries had to run across, they didn't have much of a chance against us, and we took advantage of it."[15]

After expending the ammunition for his machine gun, Private Leonard left it behind. "Peter Moss and I came upon an Austrian-German lying on his stomach with the gun barrel in his left hand. I turned, but not fast enough. Moss put one in his head and two more in his chest. 'Well, he won't be playing dead anymore,' he said. The Austrian-German had on a pair of tanker's boots and a pair of yellowish green coveralls. He was over six feet tall.

"We headed for the canal. There, we called back, 'Watch out for us.' We climbed the first eight-foot bank, then over the top, and across the canal—the water was only waist deep—then we hauled ass up the next six-foot bank and over it. We walked up to another Austrian-German. We couldn't get him awake or to turn over. I yelled, 'Alles ist kaput!' He grabbed for his gun, but he received two slugs into his head.

"Someone said, 'Look in back of us will ya?' Emmett and I hurried back to a six-foot hole some ways back. There were three corporals and one sergeant. Two were awake and moved for a half-foot or so, before they were all dead. We emptied two clips into them. We cut collar insignias off of their uniforms.

"We walked and sometimes trotted from one or two Germans lying on the ground [to others], trying to get them up and awake. Most were lying on their stomachs five to ten feet apart from each other. Some thought we were going by them and would wait until [they thought] we went by and then they would grab their rifles and finish us off. But that's what we were waiting for. Many, hearing the shots close by, pushed and shoved their buddies next to them, so we wouldn't kill them. Quite a few turned over after our first three kicks. But still, quite a few grabbed their guns and tried to get away. We walked up to a pair of twins, only about seventeen years old. It was hard at first to get those two to roll over. Shooting into the ground beside one's head made both jump up and take notice. Before we kicked our way down approximately two hundred yards, we had taken some forty prisoners. God only knows how many we tried to get awake and march off as POWs. We knew as soon as we turned away they were going to kill us.

"As we went to others lying along the bank, it was an eye-popping view, just in back of us. But there were at least a dozen Austrian-Germans lying heads up. They might have knocked us off while we were only forty or fifty yards away—us trying to get their comrades awake and standing up. This gully [was] about four feet deep—in it were eleven Germans and one Austrian-German corporal [who] were playing dead.

"Slightly in back of me, a German half rose [up] with a trench knife. I hit him with the butt of my rifle and shot him in the head. Moss kept going up the gully approximately 150 yards, making sure they were all dead. Emmett got two—playing dead—gave them hard kicks in their asses to get them to stand up.

"On my right, we were slowly looking for bullet marks or holes in their bodies. There, down at my feet, was a fat one. As I raised up my rifle to pound his butt, he raised his hands and said in English, 'Please don't shoot me.' I told him to ask his friends to sit up so we wouldn't shoot any of them. He called to each of them. The fifth one stayed still. I walked over to him, then I felt his pulse, which was good. I saw the Iron Cross on his jacket front. He was called again—but nothing. So I [fired], fifteen feet away—hair and eyeballs flew. The fat boy yelled something. I pointed it at him. Up went his arms again. He, in a halting voice said, 'They'll come along nicely.'

"Moss and Emmett gathered up all of the abandoned rifles and put them in piles for our POWs to carry over and across the canal up to the road for souvenirs. The fat boy told me he and his father left New York in 1936 to go to Germany. They had walked around sixty miles [since] two days ago. That's why they were all tired."[16]

As Company I fired from the canal bank, Company H crossed the canal and again struck the enemy left flank. The Germans reeled from the onslaught, leaving another forty-six dead behind.

Private Leonard and his buddies marched their prisoners back across the canal. "That's when I went over to Lieutenant [Willis] Ferrill's body. I knelt down and closed his eyes. This one bastard had the guts to snicker and laugh openly

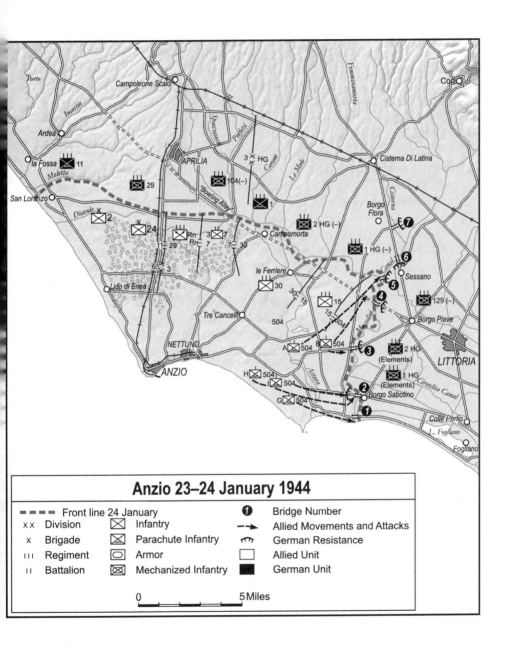

Anzio 23–24 January 1944

▪ ▪ ▪ ▪ Front line 24 January		❶	Bridge Number
x x Division	⊠ Infantry	→→	Allied Movements and Attacks
x Brigade	⊠ Parachute Infantry	⌒	German Resistance
۱۱۱ Regiment	⊡ Armor	☐	Allied Unit
۱۱ Battalion	⊠ Mechanized Infantry	■	German Unit

0   5 Miles

while I was covering Ferrill's body with a raincoat. I reached over and grabbed my rifle, pointing it at him, [and] twice shot the snickerer. We made two of his buddies carry him over to the road trees, where there lay four or more we had shot out of those twenty-foot trees the night before during their ambush."[17]

Lieutenant Colonel Freeman ordered the battalion to pull back to the canal and reorganize. Two platoons of Company G defended Bridges Numbers 0 and 1, while Company H took over defense of Bridge Number 2. Examination of the enemy bodies by the battalion and regimental intelligence sections revealed that the regiment was again opposed by veterans of the Hermann Göring Panzer Division.

Beginning that same morning, the U.S. 3rd Infantry Division began a drive toward Cisterna to the northeast. To cover the right flank, Company B was ordered to seize and blow Bridges Numbers 3 and 5 across the Mussolini Canal, near where a tributary canal joined it. During the attack, automatic weapons fire from overwhelming enemy forces pinned down Company B, which was unable to reach either bridge. Next, a platoon of Company A supported by a platoon of tanks and 57mm antitank guns manned by troopers with Battery D, 376th Parachute Field Artillery Battalion, providing cover fire, made a second attempt to take the bridge. After a four-hour fight, the Company A platoon, supported by the tanks and antitank guns, forced the Germans across the canal and captured Bridge Number 5. Company A squad leader Sergeant Albert Clark ordered his men to dig in along the canal. "We had just got dug in well when they started hitting with very heavy artillery fire and personnel attacks."[18]

The next afternoon, January 25, the entire 504th Regimental Combat Team made a diversionary attack at 1:30 p.m. to draw German forces opposing the 3rd Infantry Division. On the left flank of the regimental sector, the 1st Battalion attacked east across the Mussolini Canal on the tabletop-flat ground toward the town of Sessano. German heavy artillery opened up as Sergeant Milton Knight and his Headquarters Company, 1st Battalion S-2 section moved forward during the attack. "I heard the gun fire, and I looked at my watch, and we hit the ground. I looked at my watch again, and to me [it seemed like] the shell had gone over us. [Private First Class Anthony] Coccia and I were in a little defilade, a little hole in the ground, and as I raised up to start off again, the damned shell exploded right over us. It tore my pack off my back, it hit me in the arm and shoulder—shrapnel—and it killed Coccia instantly. He was lying right under me. That was a traumatic thing for me because I had been lying right on top of him, and he got killed and I didn't. . . . It took me a little while to reconcile that.

"[Private First Class] Ted Bachenheimer was sent from regimental headquarters to take my place as S-2 section sergeant when I was wounded at Anzio and stayed with me in the S-2 section when I returned to duty."[19]

From several well-dug-in strongpoints, superior numbers of German infantry supported by 20mm antiaircraft guns, tanks, and flak-wagons raked the 1st Battalion troopers, pinning them down on the open ground west of Sessano. The battalion didn't have armor support east of the Mussolini Canal. Any tank attempting to move to the top of the canal dike to fire in support would be silhouetted, and the Germans would immediately knock it out. With no means of dealing with the German armored vehicles, which kept out of bazooka range, the battalion commander, Lieutenant Colonel Warren Williams, ordered a withdrawal to the east bank of the Mussolini Canal, which was executed in an orderly manner, despite the heavy enemy fire. The battalion had inflicted severe casualties while losing six killed, twenty-three wounded, and nine missing. That night, Company C, 307th Engineers laid minefields in front of the battalion's dug-in defensive positions on the east bank of the canal.

In the center of the 504th sector, the 2nd Battalion, supported by three tanks and the 376th Parachute Field Artillery Battalion, made the main attack across the canal, driving east toward the town of Borgo Piave, a couple of thousand yards to the east of the canal. Intelligence previously gathered indicated that the town was lightly held by low-quality troops with no tank support. The intelligence report also indicated that no enemy tanks would be able to reach the area for at least eight hours once an attack began.

At 1:25 p.m., the 75mm pack howitzers of the 376th opened fire, and five minutes later Company D moved forward behind a rolling barrage. As Company D advanced, the 376th lifted the artillery concentrations and laid them down farther ahead. The Germans quickly realized that the rolling barrage meant an infantry attack was coming, and began firing their own concentrations into Company D and then lifting their fire. The Germans intended to give the impression to Company D that the artillery fire was friendly. This ruse was successful, as Company D held up while the liaison officer contacted the 376th and ordered it to fire on the objective only. This left Company D with almost 1,500 yards of flat, open terrain to cross without the protection of the rolling barrage. Company D quickly pushed forward, running toward the north side of the town, but was pinned down by 20mm antiaircraft fire from the town and from Germans positions to the north. Company E swung to the right and moved into the town.

From his position near the bank of the canal, Lieutenant William J. Sweet, Jr., the 2nd Battalion S-3, saw enemy armor moving down the road toward Borgo Piave, with Company D pinned down in the fields on both sides. "The enemy then counterattacked from the north and east of the town, cutting D Company off from the rest of the battalion and into two parts, and isolating E Company in the town. Five tanks and eight half-tracks mounting 20mm guns were used by the enemy, and our troops had no antitank protection at all. Our three tanks were rendered ineffective by the banks of the canal and a desire not

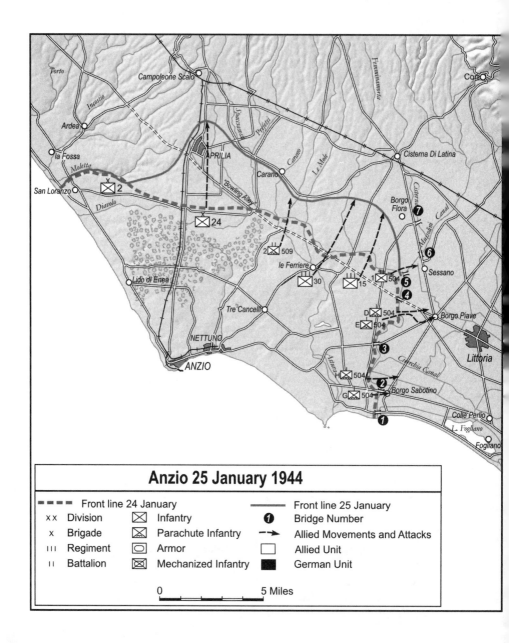

Anzio 25 January 1944

Legend:
- ▬ ▬ ▬ Front line 24 January
- ▬▬▬ Front line 25 January
- xx Division
- x Brigade
- ⊥⊥⊥ Regiment
- ⊥⊥ Battalion
- ⊠ Infantry
- ⊠ Parachute Infantry
- ▭ Armor
- ⊠ Mechanized Infantry
- ❶ Bridge Number
- ➝ Allied Movements and Attacks
- ▭ Allied Unit
- ■ German Unit

0 _____ 5 Miles

to get on top of the banks of the canal for fear of high-velocity [enemy antitank] fire. Major Blitch ordered F Company to pick up some antitank weapons and get D Company out of their situation. It was getting dark by the time F Company could bring any pressure to bear on the situation, as all the antitank weapons were left with the regimental supply in the rear and had to be brought forward.

"E Company was having a bad time in town. They had been hit hard twice by three medium tanks and two flak-wagons, plus about two companies of infantry. Lieutenant [Hanford A.] Files [Company E commander] at last withdrew to the west side of town and set up a perimeter defense on the three roads leading towards the canal. The town was being shelled by [our artillery as a result of us] using the 536 radio [link] to the CP and then relaying the directions through the normal channels. By these means the companies held out until 2020, when they left an outpost of a platoon in position, and F Company covered the area where D Company had been cut in two, as the remainder of the battalion withdrew. F Company withdrew at 0200 to their old positions on the west side of the canal.

"D Company had only twenty-eight men left when they returned, and their company commander [Captain William Roe] was still missing. But the missing men from the company continued to drift in all night long, until at 0845 the following day they had a total of forty men and officers. E Company held the outpost for the day, with only an occasional exchange of artillery fire. They withdrew the evening of the 26th under cover of darkness.

"Captain Roe came in at 0845 on the 26th with nine more men. He had gone all the way through Borgo Piave and had tried to hold the enemy from entering the town from Littoria and the northeast. He had no idea what had happened to his company when they had been hit, as he was with the point at the time. All he was concerned with was why no one had come to help him hold the enemy off.

"While our battalion had suffered heavily, the enemy had been hurt too. He had lost two dual-purpose 88mm guns, three flak-wagons, and one medium tank in the fight, and three other vehicles to mines left in the area. Three prisoners were taken and an estimated one hundred killed or wounded in the action."[20]

Company D suffered the majority of the 2nd Battalion casualties. After all of the troopers exfiltrated to the 2nd Battalion line, the company had only fifty-eight men and officers present for duty. There were twenty-nine missing in action, the majority of whom were captured.

On the right flank on the morning of January 25, Company H repulsed an attack by two platoons of infantry, supported by artillery. The company then jumped off at 1:30 p.m., crossing the canal and advancing 1,500 yards to the east from Bridge Number 2 against light enemy opposition. Company G to the right crossed the canal and advanced east against light resistance to capture the town of Borgo Sabotino, losing two men killed. The following morning the battalion was ordered back across the canal, where it held the 3,300-yard line running south along the Mussolini Canal from Bridge Number 2 to the sea.

The 504th was understrength when it landed at Anzio, and the attrition from the attacks as well as enemy artillery and mortars continued to reduce the strength of the regiment. The attrition in Sergeant Albert Clark's Company A platoon was fairly typical. During the attack on January 25, Clark's platoon was reduced from thirty-two to twenty-nine; "the next night twenty-seven; the next night nineteen; then eleven; and finally down to nine men. Then we started getting a few [of our wounded] back. One day I got three men. One still had a hand in a cast. The next morning, one of them was killed by artillery fire."[21]

Private First Class Darrell Harris with the Demolitions Platoon was assigned a temporary duty that no one wanted. "It was during Anzio that I saw more dead bodies in a brief period of time than in all my other combat experience. One of our judge advocate (lawyer) officers was assigned as GRO (grave registration officer) for a part of that campaign, and I was assigned as his aide. It was our job to pick up dead bodies, both American and German, and transport them back to the beachhead cemetery at Nettuno. We had a jeep with a utility trailer with which to do our work, so there was not much dignity in those soldiers' last ride. Except for the levees on both sides of the canal, the terrain in our sector was very flat and under German observation. For this reason, when there were bodies to be picked up near the canal, we would ease up under cover of darkness with the jeep engine barely above idle, recover the bodies, and ease back out, hoping not to attract any German artillery fire. One night, we had driven almost to the bank of the canal and loaded three German bodies into our trailer. When we started to drive off, I looked in my rearview mirror and saw one of the German soldiers rise out of the trailer. Drawing my forty-five, I got out of my jeep in a hurry, but once we stopped there was no further movement. It turned out that, unnoticed by us in our haste and in the darkness, this man had somehow become entangled in a down telephone wire, one end of which was still attached to the pole. When we moved out, this wire had drawn him partly out of the trailer. It gave us quite a start until we determined the cause, because we were quite certain that soldier was dead when we loaded him into the trailer.

"We saw sights such as a trooper who got hit by a 20mm shell from a flak-wagon. The shell had exploded inside his chest, blowing most of his lungs apart and leaving his heart exposed, but intact. Once, I picked up a friend of mine, [Private First Class] Quentin T. Newhart, who was from California. Newhart had been on machine gun outpost the night before. When we picked him up, he was grasping a book of matches in his left hand, and he had the top of his head blown off. One of the prime rules of an infantry soldier is to never strike a match when you are on the front lines at night, because it can attract sniper or mortar fire. The soldier had broken that rule and paid for it with his life.

"On one occasion we had to dig up some troopers who had been buried in a shallow grave by the Germans. When we pulled them out, we found that one of the troopers had his ring finger cut off. On another occasion, we went to the site where a German crew had covered their half-track with a haystack for camouflage. Our mortar crews had spotted them, however, and laid in a few rounds of incendiary shells which burned the haystack, half-track and all. When we recovered those German bodies, they were literally cooked, and they were puffed up like sausages. As we picked them up, their skins would split open and juices would spew out.

"It was at Anzio, too, that I saw my first American woman killed by enemy fire. A nurse at the beachhead hospital had been killed by an artillery shell. I think the sight of this one young woman lying there dead devastated me more than all the other dead bodies I had seen."[22]

ON THE NIGHT OF JANUARY 28–29, a group of combat engineer trained replacements—twenty-three enlisted and five officer replacements—landed at Anzio. Among the officers were Lieutenants John A. Holabird, Michael G. Sabia and Melvin C. Ullrich. Holabird and the others disembarked from their LST at a blacked-out pier and were loaded into waiting blacked-out trucks for the journey to their destination. "Twice we were almost hit by incoming shells—we jumped out of the trucks, crawled into the ditches—then got back into the trucks. We reached the command post of C Company. Our reception was hardly warm. C Company already had a full contingent of officers by the table of organization. But I guess they saw that with our addition, the present officers wouldn't have to lead as many patrols or mine-laying operations. So, we were at least part of the 82nd Division.

"Captain Spike Harris was a tall, red-faced, New Mexican-Texan. He looked like a real cowboy Western man. The other officers turned out to be friendly and interesting."[23]

Lieutenant Ullrich and about a third of the enlisted men were assigned to the 1st Platoon, which was led by Lieutenant Travis T. Womack. Lieutenant Holabird and another third of the enlisted men were assigned to the 2nd Platoon, under the command of Lieutenant Ralph W. Hendrix. Lieutenant Sabia and the remaining third of the enlisted men were assigned to the 3rd Platoon, led by Lieutenant Patrick J. Mulloy. The replacements were then taken to the houses where their assigned platoons were bivouacked.

On the morning of January 29, Colonel Tucker ordered an attack by the 1st and 2nd Battalions for the early morning of January 30. "The mission was to secure the right flank of the 3rd American Infantry Division, who were attacking to link up with the rangers, who were to seize the town of Cisterna. The LD [line of departure] for the assault was a tributary canal running into the Mussolini Canal. The jump-off time of the attack was 0100 hours."[24]

Upon receipt of the order, Lieutenant William Sweet, the 2nd Battalion S-3, began developing the battalion's plan for the attack. "We received the assignment, along with the 1st Battalion, to act as right flank protection for the 3rd Division in an attack to the northeast on the night of 29–30 January. The two battalions were to move northeast along the Mussolini Canal, covering the area to the first main road on their left, or an area of about two thousand to three thousand yards. The plan of action was to attack in a column of battalions with the 1st leading and peeling off along the canal until they were used up, then the 2nd would take over doing the same until the objective, Highway 7, had been reached. The leading battalion was to have five medium tanks in direct support. Each battalion had its own artillery forward observers.

"The battalion was scheduled to move by shuttle from the bivouac area to a forward area and placed along the road in movement order. This action took three hours, or until about 2100, as only four tanks were available for movement. A new CP was set up in the house at the crossroads of Strada del Piano at the head of the column. The troopers were along the main road in the order from front to rear; E, F, HQ, and D. The battalion would cross the canal to the front, some three hundred yards to the east of the road bridge, follow the 1st across country, and take up the attack when the 1st had been completely committed, taking over the five tanks at the same time. The highway bridge [to cross the canal to the east] was denied to us, as the 3rd Division had priority on the road.

"The battalion moved out early through some confusion and moved into the 1st as they were moving out. This caused some delay and a great deal of confusion. As a result, the battalion was late in getting to the canal. Crossing the canal proved to be a great hardship, as it had to be waded, and the night was cold. More delay and confusion was experienced. There were supposed to have been planks across the canal, but they had either been broken or lost, and the few that remained were not enough to accommodate the battalion."

However, the 1st Battalion was able to reach the line of departure on time and moved out at 1:00 a.m., advancing northeast, with Company A deployed on the right, Company C on the left, and Company B following in the center. Lieutenant John N. Pease, the Company A executive officer, moved out with the company's reserve platoon. "During the early phases of the attack, one platoon and A Company headquarters became separated in the darkness. I took charge of the other two platoons and continued on toward the objective."[25]

Captain Ernie Milloy and his Company C troopers were assigned a crossroads to cut the elevated road running north from Sessano. "We left the LD at approximately 0100 hours and advanced rapidly to the crossroad just north of

Bridge [Number 6]. There, at 0200 hours, a firefight developed. Our company radio failed, and we were temporarily out of contact with the battalion CP. At 0400 hours, Lieutenant Colonel Williams arrived in our sector, personally leading a group of medium tanks. At dawn, the enemy activity increased to a high pitch; we were receiving a devastating [20mm] fire from our rear, which was causing heavy casualties."[26]

Colonel Tucker, as usual, was up front and observed the fighting by Companies A and C. "Small-arms fire, mortar fire, and artillery fire became intense. Groups of enemy which had been bypassed during the night advance in the maze of irrigation canals began to fire into the rear of the assault companies, who by this time were fighting for the north-south road into Sessano. A dual 20mm cannon some two hundred yards south of the battalion headquarters group laid direct fire into the group and upon the supporting tanks, the lead tank of which was engaging a machine gun to the east. Lieutenant Colonel Williams, realizing that this fire was not only pinning down the battalion CP group, but causing heavy casualties in Company B, unhesitatingly climbed aboard a second tank which was buttoned up, while 20mm shells bounced off alongside him. He attracted the attention of the tank crew and accurately directed the tank's fire, which knocked out the dual gun.

"In the meantime, a heavy firefight was in progress about two hundred yards to the east of Company C positions, and Company A was fighting for the row of houses along the road. Lieutenant Colonel Williams led a composite force of tanks and infantry up the road and moved in upon the enemy from the north, toward Bridge [Number 6]. During this time, from four to five machine guns in the houses were spraying the roads and fields. In addition, SP [self-propelled] artillery and mortars were pounding the route of advance on the road. 20mm guns from the south of the [Mussolini] Canal were also putting grazing fire into the area. Despite this fire from two directions, Colonel Williams led the tanks on foot and directed the fire of both tanks and infantry from a completely exposed position.

"Company A then reported that it was engaged in an extremely heavy action with numerous local counterattacks, which were mounting in intensity. Company C was now also engaged in a firefight. Intense artillery fire was interdicting the area. Lieutenant Colonel Williams immediately committed Company B, his reserve company, which he personally led toward Bridge [Number 6 across the Mussolini Canal]. After a fierce assault upon the houses from which the enemy was engaging Company A, his force broke through to the bridge."[27]

Sergeant Landon M. Chilcutt, acting as a scout, led Company B toward Bridge Number 6. "When we got to the bridge, we heard the Germans shouting, and then the bridge blew. We moved on to two other bridges that we had to take."[28]

Colonel Tucker observed Lieutenant Colonel Williams committing "Company A to secure the canal bank and blown bridge. He then contacted his tank force and swung toward Bridge [Number 7] and the houses nearby, which were being hotly contested. Deploying the armor against the houses along with a portion of Company B, Lieutenant Colonel Williams started for Bridge [Number 7] on foot, alone.

"The fight around the houses and bridge increased in intensity. Enemy artillery fell with increasing rapidity. The assaulting troops were taking casualties and were hard pressed. With utter disregard for his personal safety, Lieutenant Colonel Williams joined this group and with his command radio was able to obtain additional supporting artillery fire and was able to direct the deployment of reinforcements at the most critical juncture in the battle."[29]

As the fighting reached a crescendo, the 2nd Battalion moved up to assist the 1st Battalion. Lieutenant Sweet was with the 2nd Battalion headquarters group, advancing just behind Companies E and F. "The going was slow, as nearly every house was defended, and the enemy small-arms fire from the canal banks kept the troops down low in their advance. A system was worked out whereby the troops would advance until fired on from a house or strongpoint, then the tanks would move up, blast the defenders out, to be taken by our troops. The further the advance continued the more fire was received from the right flank. At last, E Company had to be committed to clear the dike along the Mussolini Canal, [east] of the 1st Battalion. F Company took up the lead, using the same tactics, and advanced fairly well until they hit a strongpoint. Here the enemy did not break from the tank fire, and the tanks were unable to advance or flank the position. The company had to flank, and reduce it from the east and rear.

"While F Company was doing this, the rest of the battalion was left strung out in a column along the road, and we got our first taste of the Germans' Nebelwerfer, or 'Screaming Meemies.' The entire column was shelled for about ten minutes by this fire and then hit by 88mm or antiaircraft fire. Several men from D and Headquarters Companies became casualties, and the column was spread into the fields. E Company forced the Germans across Bridge Number 7 and experienced the same thing as the 1st Battalion. The Germans blew the bridge as soon as they had withdrawn across it.

"F Company reduced the [strongpoint] position and took twenty-five prisoners, then moved along the road to Fosso di Cisterna. Here the Germans blew Bridge Number 8. Now it was apparent that the enemy had decided to deny us any crossings for armor in the area, so a race started for Bridge Number 9. Before D Company could get well under way with the tanks, the Germans blew that one, leaving us with no armor crossings of the Mussolini Canal or of Fosso di Cisterna."[30]

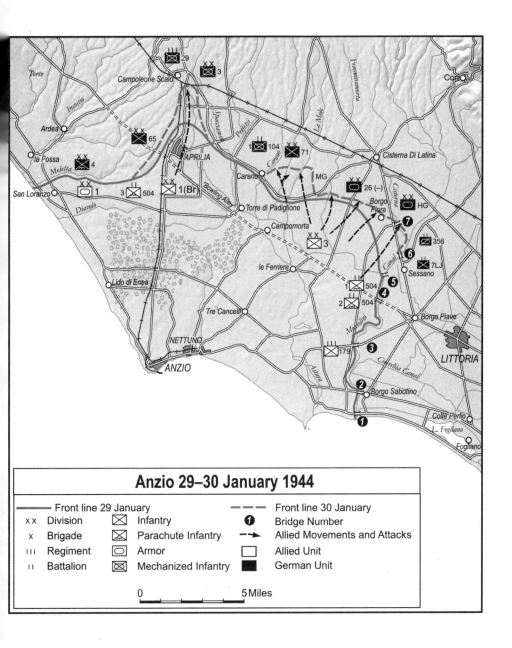

Anzio 29–30 January 1944

——— Front line 29 January		- - - Front line 30 January	
xx Division	⊠ Infantry	❶ Bridge Number	
x Brigade	⊠ Parachute Infantry	--→ Allied Movements and Attacks	
ꟾꟾꟾ Regiment	▢ Armor	▢ Allied Unit	
ꟾꟾ Battalion	⊠ Mechanized Infantry	■ German Unit	

0   5 Miles

Colonel Tucker watched as troopers with Companies B and E cleaned out the area around Bridge Number 7. "Out of the houses adjacent to Bridge [Number 7], over one hundred Germans were taken.

"About 0800 hours, a sizeable enemy counterattack was mounted against Company A's positions. This was eventually beaten off, and the line was restored. By 1030 hours, all objectives had been taken and secured, thus accomplishing the mission.

"Although suffering heavy casualties, the 1st Battalion accomplished a most vital and difficult mission. A determined enemy was forced to withdraw from strategic positions with heavy casualties. Over one hundred prisoners were captured. Numerous machine guns, four 20mm cannons, and three flakwagons were put out of action."[31]

Colonel Tucker recommended Lieutenant Colonel Williams for the Distinguished Service Cross for his heroic leadership during the attack, but Williams was eventually awarded the Silver Star.

THAT EVENING, THE 3RD BATTALION was relieved of its position on the Mussolini Canal by an entire regiment—the 179th. The battalion was assigned to protect the right flank of the newly landed U.S. 1st Armored Division on the north side of the beachhead, tying in with the British 1st Infantry Division's sector to the east. The British had been attacking up the main Anzio-Albano road, and a dangerous salient was developing. By the evening of January 29, the British 1st Division had driven the Germans back, reaching the edge of Carroceto, and capturing the town of Aprilia, including a German strongpoint at the community center building, which the British referred to as "The Factory."

TO THE SOUTH, ALONG THE MUSSOLINI CANAL, the Germans commenced a heavy artillery barrage at 8:00 p.m. on January 31, in preparation for an attack against the 1st Battalion. During the attack, a group of approximately twenty Germans penetrated one of the Company A outposts and threatened its right flank. Staff Sergeant Robert J. Lowe took two men and moved over two hundred yards across flat terrain under intense enemy fire and engaged the enemy force that had overrun the outpost. In the ensuing firefight, Staff Sergeant Lowe received a wound in the right side, but he and the other two troopers wounded fourteen enemy soldiers and took four prisoners, in recapturing the outpost position. Staff Sergeant Lowe received the Silver Star for his gallantry and leadership.

That same night, Major Blitch, the commanding officer of the 2nd Battalion, was evacuated to the rear with shellshock.

AFTER SEVERAL PLANNED ATTACKS WERE CANCELED, the 3rd Battalion was detached from the 1st Armored Division and attached to the British 24th

Brigade on February 1, 1944. The 24th Brigade, meanwhile, had reached but not captured the town of Campoleone against tough German resistance, while the 1st Armored Division cleared the railroad embankment northwest of Carroceto. The salient was now three miles deep and between a mile and a mile and a half wide.

By February 2, however, the offensive by the U.S. 3rd Infantry Division to capture Cisterna and by the British 1st Division and U.S. 1st Armored Division to take Campoleone was spent. The one hundred thousand troops of the VI Corps were ordered to go over to the defensive in anticipation of a German counteroffensive, preparing defensive positions on February 3, 1944.

On the night of February 3–4, the Germans began a major attack to pinch off the salient in the Factory area in a double-pincer assault to cut off and then destroy the entire British 3rd Brigade. One prong, west of Aprilia, drove south into the salient toward Carroceto. The other prong of the pincer pushed south to the east of Aprilia. The plan was for the two pincers to then turn and drive east and west to link up just south of Aprilia, then attack south from Aprilia down the Anzio-Albano road all the way to the sea. The 3rd Battalion was positioned almost precisely where the Germans planned for the two pincers to meet.

Around 11:00 p.m., the Germans infiltrated between the positions of the 3rd Brigade and struck the British from the rear. About 11:30 p.m., the 3rd Brigade headquarters passed through the 3rd Battalion positions as they withdrew to avoid being overrun by the German infiltration attacks.

At around midnight on February 3–4, the Germans unleashed a massive artillery and mortar barrage on the base of the British salient to prevent reinforcement of or escape from the salient. Unknowingly, the German barrage fell largely on the 3rd Battalion positions. At about that same time, Lieutenant Ed Sims, commanding Company H, received an order to block the Anzio-Albano highway in case the expected German attack broke through the British positions. "My company was given the mission to straddle the Albano Road north of Carroceto to help support the withdrawal of British troops. Soon after getting my company in position, British troops started passing through our lines going to the rear."[32]

The withdrawal of the British 3rd Brigade continued throughout the day, as Sims kept his men on alert for a possible enemy assault once the Germans realized the British were withdrawing. "They completed their withdrawal as darkness set in. Within the hour, a strong German force attacked our position, but we responded with devastating fire, to include heavy artillery fire, which disrupted their attack, causing them to stop and withdraw. I was sure they would try again, so I had my platoon leaders locate the British units on our flanks. I was rather disgusted to learn that they were several hundred yards behind us on an old railroad embankment. I then moved my company back to the same embankment in order to have contact on my flanks with the British. During this move, my company was subjected to enemy artillery fire, and I was hit in my lower leg by a fragment. I felt the wound was not serious, so had local treatment and continued to supervise the occupation of our new position, which was accomplished before daylight on February 5, 1944.

"Shortly after daylight, the Germans increased their shelling of our position. Numerous rounds landed in my command post area, causing everyone to seek shelter. I jumped into a large, open slit trench next to a building, and two men came in behind me just as an explosion took place directly above the hole. The fragments came into the hole, killing the two men with me [Staff Sergeant William C. Kossman and Private First Class John A. Bahan] and I was hit in the right shoulder. The trench caved in on us, and after digging out, I was taken to the hospital near Anzio. That evening the hospital was shelled by German artillery, so I located my clothes and equipment, got dressed, and hitched a ride in an ambulance back to the front line and my company."[33]

On the night of February 5, the Germans began probing the defenses of the British and the 3rd Battalion, looking for a vulnerable spot. Staff Sergeant Louis Orvin was leading his Company I platoon, because almost all of the officers in the company were casualties. "I had my platoon dug in on the left flank of the Factory in a ditch perpendicular to the road. We heard a tank coming down the road, and I told the bazooka man to get ready. When we saw this vehicle, it turned out to be a half-track. [The bazooka man] fired and hit the thing right at the radiator or the engine, because it burst into flames. A couple of guys jumped out and started running. I had a Thompson submachine gun, and I opened fire on this guy on the right and he fell. They teach you with a Thompson submachine to fire three rounds at a time . . . quick bursts. I pulled that [trigger] one time and then I pulled it again, and I had emptied a clip.

"I went up there and walked around the half-track. There was one guy lying on the side of the road that was dead. I rolled him over, and he looked like a young kid. Of course, I was just a young person myself.

"A little bit later the company commander told me to send out a patrol down the road. So I told Sergeant [George] Leoleis, 'Don't go too far. Just go down there beyond that half-track and see what you can find. Don't stay out there too long.'

"He found the other guy on the other side of the road that I had shot. Evidently I had hit him, and he had died while he was running. We stayed in the holes all night long. I checked on my positions later on that night, when I heard Leoleis firing his M1. A German patrol had been coming up. He was a big strong guy. He would fire that thing, and it would sound like an automatic pistol.

"I saw a man lying down on the side of the bank. Leoleis said, 'Don't bother him, he's dead.' He had been shot in the head. I don't know why he had his head up that far out of the ditch."[34]

The Germans lit the night sky with flares, hammering the British and American positions with a terrifying artillery barrage, reminiscent of World War I. The following day, February 6, was a relatively quiet day in the 3rd Battalion sector as the Germans regrouped for yet another attack. The British used the respite to reorganize, dig in, and strengthen their new positions.

On February 6, Lieutenant John Holabird, with the 2nd Platoon, Company C, 307th Airborne Engineer Battalion, received an order to construct a footbridge across the Mussolini Canal in the 2nd Battalion sector to facilitate movement back and forth. "We went as quietly as possible to an engineer storage lumberyard to get a load of lumber—then unloaded it on the side of the C Company house most shielded from the enemy mortar fire. Then we crept up to a levee close to the canal where the bridge was needed to have a 'look-see.' We tried to guess the width of the canal and the depth of the water without getting shot at.

"We returned to C Company and proceeded to make plans for the bridge. We figured about nine little trestle bents, connected by 2x10-inch planks spanning about nine feet—so the bridge would be about eighty or ninety feet long. We built the bents, loaded them on the truck, with 2x10 planks for walkways and 2x4s for handrails."[35]

On the 7th, German artillery fire increased once again, and intelligence sources warned of a renewed offensive that night. The same night, Lieutenant Holabird and a squad of engineers drove the truck loaded with lumber to the Mussolini Canal to construct the footbridge. "Building a bridge in the water in daylight is a big problem—in the dark it is an entirely bigger problem. But the biggest problem of all was that every time one used one's hammer, there was a hail of fire—like stirring up a hive of bees.

"But somehow, we got going—anchored one bent on the near shore and went out ten feet with bent number two—nailed a plank down, then waded out with number three—and so on—nailing diagonal bracing to steady the bents and nailing handrails to the top of the bents—all the time trying to concentrate on hammering because of the return fire. The Germans sent up flares, at which point we all stood like statues and tried to look as much like a bridge as possible.

"Somehow, we got the damn thing built—no one was killed or wounded, and my sergeant told me later that he had tacked a sign on the entrance, 'Holabird Foot Bridge.' What an honor!"[36]

About 7:00 p.m. on February 7, on the north side of the beachhead, the 3rd Battalion was ordered to move south of Carroceto to act as a counterattack force. The British 1st Scots Guards replaced the battalion on the north side of the town. Shortly after arriving, Company H was ordered to move west of the overpass to help the 5th Grenadier Guards. They were only told that the Germans had broken through and were moving toward the beach, and they were to locate, engage, and stop the lead elements with a total of two officers and twenty-five men. They initially made contact with some of the British soldiers who were in full retreat. Company H continued to move forward past the British and down the slope of a hill to an old railroad embankment. The company took positions on the embankment, while the two officers, Lieutenants Jim Megellas and Richard LaRiviere (known as "Rivers") moved forward to conduct a reconnaissance, leaving a sergeant in charge. They soon found themselves in the very midst of German infantry moving toward the railroad embankment. The Germans were shouting their locations to each other as they moved in order to maintain contact in the darkness. Megellas and Rivers moved quickly back to the railroad embankment, where their men were already engaging the German infantry.

Megellas took the entire 1st Platoon of just six men with him to try to locate friendly forces on their flanks. "I was the lead man in the patrol as we headed up the high ground to our left while the platoon sergeant, Sergeant Thomas Radika, brought up the rear, keeping the patrol together. When we reached the crest of the hill, I noticed a sharp drop on the other side: a cliff steep enough to protect our immediate left flank from an enemy attack. At this point, a German machine gun opened fire from high ground across the roadbed on the silhouetted targets we presented. It was almost point-blank fire. We hit the dirt, and I gave the command to turn around and crawl back down the hill to the company position behind the embankment.

"Because I had started out leading the patrol, when we turned around and started going back downhill, I found myself bringing up the rear. I soon caught up with Sergeant Radika going downhill. He lay motionless, his arms and legs still in a crawling position. I crawled alongside, exhorting him to get going: 'Radika, that's machine gun fire.' As I shook him I noticed that the left side of his body had been ripped open by enemy bullets. He had been killed instantly."[37]

With the cliff protecting the company's left flank, Megellas took his five remaining troopers back to the company, then led another six-man patrol that moved behind the railroad embankment to check out the area on the right flank. They followed the embankment until it intersected a road, which they crossed, and continued moving east about one hundred yards, along the base of a hill on their left. They heard Germans talking behind the hill, trying to regroup in the darkness before continuing their advance.

Megellas quickly deployed his small force at the base of hill and waited. "As soon as we were set, the Germans, in what I estimated was a platoon-sized force, stormed over the top of the hill and straight toward us, not knowing we were positioned just below them. In the patrol, I was armed with a Thompson submachine gun; one soldier had a Browning Automatic Rifle; and the other five carried M1 rifles. We held our fire until the Germans were within close range, then we opened up with rapid fire. A large number fell with the first outburst before they could take cover and attempt to fire back. Confused and not knowing the strength and location of the force that had hit them, they retreated and took cover behind the hill."[38]

Megellas and his men reloaded and waited for the next attack, which didn't come. "We could hear the anguished cries of the wounded while their buddies were attempting to retrieve them. The Germans we fought at Anzio were highly trained, combat hardened, disciplined, and well led. The Germans at Anzio, like the troopers of the 504th, would risk their lives if need be to retrieve their dead and wounded, a mark of good troops."[39]

Megellas continued to lead his six men east, searching for any friendly forces. After about one hundred more yards, he and his men repeated the same ambush on another platoon of Germans coming down the hill toward them. The Germans fired flares attempting to locate them and dropped a mortar barrage all around them. After this ended, the patrol moved about another quarter of a mile without contacting any friendly forces. The patrol then returned to H Company, which had been heavily engaged stopping repeated assaults by German infantry during the two hours they had been gone. Megellas "placed the Browning Automatic Rifle man, Corporal John Granado, on the high ground to our right with orders to dig in and shoot anything that approached from the direction of the enemy. We placed Privates [Lawrence] Dunlop and [Sylvester J.] Larkin with their machine gun in the draw to our left, with the field of fire being the [rail]roadbed, in the event that the Germans attempted to storm over the road to engage us in hand-to-hand combat.

"The Germans continued an attempt to dislodge H Company from its entrenched positions with mortars and automatic fire. A few Germans were able to penetrate to the other side of the embankment from us and were lobbing grenades over the road and into our position. Meanwhile, we were lobbing grenades back at the Germans on the other side of the embankment. It was during this engagement that I suffered a flesh wound that would immobilize my left arm.

"We came through the night without further casualties while repelling every German effort to overrun our position. The break of dawn found a small force of two officers and twenty-four men still entrenched behind the roadbed and determined to hold the position against any odds."[40]

Before dawn on February 8, the 3rd Battalion prepared to counterattack with Companies G and I to break through the German forces surrounding H Company. A little after 6:00 a.m. on February 8, Lieutenant Roy M. Hanna, with Headquarters Company, reported to the 3rd Battalion command post as ordered. "At the time I was in command of the battalion machine gun platoon and was in support of Company G that was engaged with the enemy on another flank of the operation. The battalion commander, Lieutenant Colonel Leslie G.

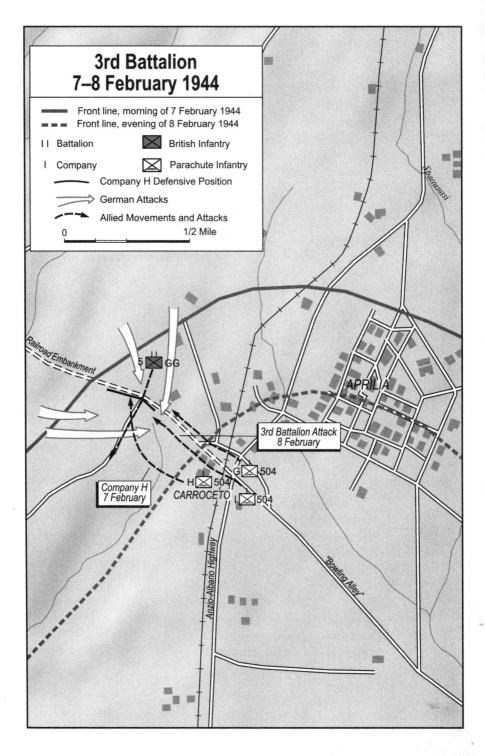

3rd Battalion
7–8 February 1944

Front line, morning of 7 February 1944

Front line, evening of 8 February 1944

I I Battalion   British Infantry

I Company   Parachute Infantry

Company H Defensive Position

German Attacks

Allied Movements and Attacks

0   1/2 Mile

Spaccasassi

Railroad Embankment

5 GG

3rd Battalion Attack
8 February

APRILA

Company H
7 February

G 504

H 504
CARROCETO

I 504

Anzio-Albano Highway

"Bowling Alley"

Freeman, relieved me of my duties and reassigned me as the company commander (temporary) of Company I. Company I had lost all of its officers (eight) and about forty percent of its enlisted personnel either killed or wounded and taken back to rear-area hospitals.

"My first action was to withdraw the company to the reverse side of the railroad embankment, out of direct line of enemy fire, and had all of the men fix bayonets. This was the first and only time I had to give such an order."[41]

With Company I on the left and Company G on the right, Hanna led what was left of I Company northwest along the railroad bed to break through the German forces surrounding H Company. Staff Sergeant Louis Orvin didn't even know the name of the officer who was leading the company. "We went up this road. I was on the right-hand side, and I had a lieutenant that was on the left side. I had a squad behind me, and he had maybe a few more men than a squad behind him. The lieutenant got up to a house on the left side of the road. He ran around a corner and got shot in the chest. He came running back, and he collapsed."[42]

Lieutenant Hanna had suffered a critical wound. "It was between two ribs on the upper right side of my rib cage, into the top part of my lung, down through the lung and exited between two lower back ribs. After being shot, the right lung filled up with fluid, which stopped it from performing its normal function. Thus, because of oxygen starvation, I simply passed out."[43]

Staff Sergeant Orvin quickly took over. "I called for two men to come up behind me. One of them [Private Robert L. Fetzer] got right behind me and he stepped on a mine. He went up in the air and he fell down into the road. The road was cut probably six to eight feet deep at the crest of the hill.

"I told the last man to go back and get somebody with a stretcher. I wanted to get Fetzer out of there. I called for our medic that was with us. I said [to the platoon medic, Private Stanley E. Christofferson], 'Chris, Fetzer is down there in the road. I'm going to run across this road. If they shoot at me, you don't do anything. But, if it's clear, you get down there and see if you can help him.' Well, he just jumped down there.

"When I ran across the road, I rolled the lieutenant over and saw where he had been hit in the chest. I said, 'You're going to be all right. It went right through you.' But, I couldn't see where the bullet came out. I just wanted to make him feel better. I took my Thompson submachine gun and tried to spray a haystack behind the building where he had gone around the corner. I figured somebody might have been up in that haystack. But the Tommy gun wouldn't shoot. I gave it all of the intermediate action [to clear the jam]. Then I threw it down and picked up his pistol.

"I had sent one man named [Corporal Ernest E.] Emmons up ahead of us; I said, 'Emmons go down the road about a hundred or a hundred fifty yards as an outpost. If any more Germans start coming, you don't do anything but come back and let us know. Just stay down there about two minutes.'

"Emmons went down the road. As he turned around to come back, there was a German standing in the road that he had bypassed. He just ran through that German with his bayonet. He came on back.

"In the meantime, I started telling the guys we were going to withdraw. The lieutenant had regained consciousness, and he got up and headed back down the road. He was a good lieutenant."[44]

At 9:00 a.m., the attack was called off until dusk, but it had managed to draw the attention of the Germans away from H Company. Meanwhile, Lieutenant Megellas awaited the next German attack. "Surrender was never an option. The Germans knew where we were, and if they wanted us, they would have to come and get us. Before they did, we would take a lot of them with us."[45]

Corporal John Granado, dug in on the extended right flank with two other Company H troopers, Privates Richard R. Ranney and William W. Reiley, tried to stay low in his hole, as German infantry was close by, on the other side of the railroad bed. "You could hear them. During the day, they were shelling with those airbursts, because they knew we were over here. One of the guys got hurt—got stuff in his tail end from shrapnel."[46]

At 7:00 p.m., Companies G and I resumed the assault. Despite his terrible wound, Lieutenant Hanna continued to lead Company I. However, Hanna's collapsed lung was depriving him of oxygen, and when he exerted himself during the attack, he passed out again. "This passing out happened probably three or four times over the next few hours."[47]

That night, the Germans attempted to finish off Company H by attacking the company's right flank and driving straight down its defensive line from right to left. Corporal Granado and two other troopers were holding the extended right flank of the thinly held line of Company H and weren't in contact with the rest of the company. "We were on a knoll, up high. We were [dug in] down about a couple of feet. It was blacker than an ace of spades. You couldn't [even] see yourself—it was dark. All of the sudden they started firing—I got hit in the hand and in the throat. We returned some fire, but we couldn't see anything—you couldn't see a thing."[48]

Lieutenant Hanna and his Company I troopers, together with the remnants of Company G, fought to link up with Company H, but an enemy strongpoint in three farmhouses held up the attack. Firing from the bank of a two-foot-deep ditch running parallel to the abandoned railroad embankment, Staff Sergeant George Leoleis and some of the Company I troopers kept the Germans in the first house away from the windows. "I then yelled to the men, 'The next step you take is over the bank. I don't know if there are any more mines; we're rushing the house, go, go!' I yelled as loud as I could, and all of us firing and yelling, jumped out of the ditch onto the road and rushed the house. We broke in the front door and some of the windows. We went in firing from the hip and sub[machine guns] crackling. There were ten Germans in there—none walked out. A few of the men hit two other houses nearby and cleaned them up. Some Germans were seen running through the open fields. This short but effective action by I Company (or should I say what was left of I Company) broke the ring around H Company and allowed them to walk out of the trap."[49]

Lieutenant Hanna sent a runner to tell Lieutenants Rivers and Megellas to fall back while they covered the withdrawal. Megellas and LaRiviere ordered their men to withdraw. However, Corporal Granado and two troopers holding the right flank were fighting a desperate and furious battle to hold the company's right flank that lasted about an hour.[50] "The Germans appeared to be everywhere, infiltrating all around us. We had no contact with the company and were unaware that we were pulling back. We never got the word."[51]

At the end of the hour-long firefight, Corporal Granado and the other two troopers "were out of ammo. They were all the sudden right there—there must have six or seven.[52]

"The Germans overran the outpost and took us prisoners. We were taken back through the attacking forces and the German lines. We passed through what had been the British lines, where we saw a lot of dead British soldiers. A lot of them were killed in their foxholes. The Germans took us to a big farmhouse and from there to a POW camp."[53]

After ordering the men to withdraw, Megellas went down the line toward the right flank to tell Corporal Granado and Privates Ranney and Reiley to pull back. "I made a hurried search of the area, but to no avail. The Germans had attempted to penetrate on our right, and I assumed they had become casualties defending our right flank. But, because I could not find any bodies, we listed them as MIA. I later recommended Granado for, and he received, the Distinguished Service Cross."[54]

AFTER THE WITHDRAWAL OF COMPANY H WAS ACCOMPLISHED, a runner arrived with a message for Lieutenant Hanna. "Just after dark, our mission being completed, we received orders from battalion headquarters to withdraw to a more advantageous position."[55]

Private Bill Leonard and Corporal Albert R. Al Essig covered the withdrawal of Company I with Leonard's .30-caliber machine gun, which he had set up in an advantageous position. "Essig said, 'Here they come,' and as the dark forms came across the road, he shot them down in bunches. Many never got a chance to throw their hand grenades our way. We were told to try and hold a coal pile, up on our right. But with all the coal being blown sky high, we chose some other walled-in place to knock off the Germans as they came running around the corner. We changed from one place to another, better one, as there had been close, near misses as groups came tearing in fast, heading right for us. We tried not to let any Germans get on our right flank at any time. Finally, around 3:30 a.m., we were told to pull back to the houses in the rear, another three-quarters of a mile back, to take a position on the company's right. We took turns digging a huge, three feet by four feet wide, three feet deep hole by the break of morning."[56]

After the mission was accomplished, and only then, did Lieutenant Hanna allow the medics to evacuate him. "I got a ride to the British tent hospital, where I remained for three days. From there, a trip by ship to a large general hospital in Naples, where I spent the next sixty-two days."[57] Lieutenant Roy Hanna would later receive the Distinguished Service Cross for his incredible bravery and inspiring leadership during the attacks to relieve Company H, despite being critically wounded.

Staff Sergeant Orvin also went to the aid station after the withdrawal. "I had a little bit of shrapnel and some rocks and stuff in my neck underneath my helmet. Captain [William W.] Kitchen took the tweezers to get the rocks and shrapnel out of my arm and neck. I asked Captain Kitchen, 'How is Fetzer?'

"He said, 'We don't have Fetzer.'

"I said, 'Well, I sent for two men to bring a stretcher back. I want to take a patrol back to get Fetzer.'

"Captain Kitchen asked [the medic] Christofferson, 'How is Fetzer?'

"He told Captain Kitchen that he had lost one of his legs, and he had shrapnel all up in his groin, and he was probably already dead by that time from bleeding to death. So Captain Kitchen said, 'No, we can't send anybody up there to try to get him out if he's already dead. Chances are he would be dead.'

"Evidently, I had stepped over the mine. You could just see the top of something metal in the clay. He came right up behind me and took the whole blast of that mine when he stepped on it.

"Then Captain Kitchen told me, 'Sergeant Orvin, take off your boots.'

"I said, 'No sir.'

"He said, 'What? I told you take off your boots.'

"I said, 'If I take my boots off I can't put them back on.' I had trenchfoot. I didn't know that was what it was. My feet were swollen because we had to stay in those drainage ditches. That area was reclaimed land that had been underwater, and Mussolini had ordered dikes built and had it drained and made it farmland. We were walking in those drainage ditches in water and it was cold, and so I had frozen feet.

"He said, 'Go back in that room back there and take a nap.' This little house had two or three rooms to it, and he had several mattresses.

"I went back and woke up the next morning, and I walked out the door. They had a stack of M1 rifles outside the door. I said, 'Can I have one of these guns?'

"They said, 'Take your pick.' So I picked up an M1 and I kept that rifle for the rest of the war."[58]

The 3rd Battalion continued to hold part of the frontline positions in the critical Carroceto sector, rotating the rifle companies back as battalion reserve until relieved by British forces on February 15, 1944. By that time, the battalion consisted of about one hundred men and officers. The 3rd Battalion would be awarded a Presidential Unit Citation for the critical role it played in stopping the German breakthrough in the northern sector.

On the Mussolini Canal, the fighting settled into static warfare reminiscent of World War I. Major Robert H. Neptune was the executive officer of the 376th Parachute Field Artillery Battalion, which was dug in behind the 504 and supporting their defenses along the canal. "We were mined in and dug in on the canal banks and almost at the mercy of considerable German artillery, because the Alban Hills were occupied by the Germans, and they were looking down our throats. We were on the small flat areas of the beachhead. One pleasant event, even though it involved hostile fire, was our success in moving a howitzer out of our regular firing position at night and firing counterbattery fire on enemy positions and then immediately moving the howitzer and crew safely away to another area. German artillery responded with hundreds of rounds on that vacated position without damaging us in the least. This we repeated many times, with continuing success."[59]

Private First Class C. L. Tackel was a radioman with Company F. "It was a gopher's life. We had to stay in our holes all the time during daylight. The Germans had a lot of self-propelled guns, tanks, and flak-wagons across the canal from us, and they'd shoot at just one man if they saw him get out of his hole."[60]

As the 2nd Battalion was about to be relieved by U.S. Army Rangers on the morning of February 16, it was hit with 20mm antiaircraft direct fire as well as a heavy artillery barrage at daybreak. Company D was hardest hit, with three killed and eight wounded, including Captain William Roe, who was wounded in the arm by shrapnel. Lieutenant James D. Simmins, acting as F Company commander since Captain Beverly T. Richardson had been wounded by enemy artillery on February 2, was killed, Lieutenant William Sweet, the 2nd Battalion S-3, was sent to Company F as commanding officer on February 18.

On February 21, Platoon Sergeant Bernard Karnap, leading an eight-man Company A combat patrol about three-quarters of a mile northwest of Sessano, ran into an enemy machine gun nest. Karnap told his men to take cover, and he single-handedly moved forward and wiped out the position. As he did so, a twenty-man German patrol approached. Karnap opened fire on them with his Thompson submachine gun, killing or wounding approximately twelve of the enemy and causing the others to flee. Karnap ducked into an outhouse, where he quickly reloaded his Thompson, then dashed back outside under fire to retrieve information identifying the enemy unit off the body of one of the enemy dead. Karnap finished off the machine gun nest by tossing a couple of hand grenades into position to destroy the machine gun. Then he returned to his men and led them safely back to friendly lines while under long-range small-arms fire. Karnap received the Silver Star for his heroic leadership.

The Germans both feared and respected the 504th as fierce warriors. While going through the pockets of a dead German officer looking for intelligence, a trooper found a diary and turned it over to the regimental S-2 section. They translated a passage in the diary that read, "American parachutists—devils in baggy pants—are less than one hundred meters from my outpost line. I can't sleep at night. They pop up from nowhere, and we never know when or how they will strike next. Seems like the black-hearted devils are everywhere."[61]

Word of this quickly spread through the regiment. Tucker's troopers considered the term "Devils in Baggy Pants" a badge of honor, and adopted it as the 504th's nickname.

Chapter 7

"The Regiment Was Probably At The Peak Of Its Fighting Efficiency"

One of those troopers who did so much to strike fear into the Germans was Private First Class Ted Bachenheimer, who would become a legend in the regiment. Corporal Fred Baldino, with Company A, had met him while attending an intelligence class that Bachenheimer had taught at Fort Bragg. During the Anzio campaign, Baldino got to know him much better. "Ted seemed to find his niche in recon. Ted just loved to go out on patrols behind enemy lines—most of the time by himself, and he would bring back prisoners.

"I, as a corporal at that time, along with fourteen others, went out on a patrol with Ted leading the way. We slowly made our way through a German minefield. I remember one newcomer to the front saying, 'Look, we are going through a German cemetery, look at the crosses down there.'

"I told him, 'Cemetery, hell.' Those crosses had 'Achtung, Minen' written on them. Somehow, we got through that minefield unscathed. Soon we were in German territory and were walking quietly when we heard some guttural voices. We all laid flat. About twenty yards away, we could faintly see about a platoon of German soldiers. They were evidently relieving their outposts with fresh troops. After they passed on, Ted told us to stay put, and he walked up to the outpost and asked the two German soldiers inside the foxhole for a light for his cigarette. When they went to do so, Ted calmly told them they were surrounded, and he took them prisoner. We headed back to our own lines, and Ted got ahead of us with the two prisoners, and we lost sight of him.

"Meanwhile, someone did not tell our own artillery that we were out there, and we started to get artillery shells coming down around us. If that was not bad enough, every third or fourth one was a phosphorous shell. Now, we had been under German artillery fire before, but when it comes to firing for effect, it is hard to beat the American artillery. Those shells were dropping all around us, but the worst thing that happened was some of the guys got their jumpsuits scorched.

"On the way back, we came to a ditch along the side of a road and laid down, as we had to wait for two stragglers. As we lay there waiting for them to catch up with us, we heard German boots marching down the road—probably a non-com checking on his men. We had every intention of letting him walk past, but one of the men took the safety off his M1 rifle, making a sound of 'click.' The German looked over at the ditch and said, '*Was ist los?*' Well, every man in the ditch let loose with everything they had.

"Our stragglers, by now on the other side of the ditch, later told us they saw rifle fire coming out of the German's back. Soon, it seemed that every outpost in the vicinity was firing weapons in our direction. Luckily, we were lying down in the ditch. After a while, we slowly made our way back to our own lines."[1]

Major Melvin Blitch was again evacuated to a hospital in Naples at 9:45 a.m. on March 1, and was replaced as 2nd Battalion commander by Lieutenant Colonel Hank Adams, the regimental S-3. Major Edward Wellems was assigned as the 2nd Battalion executive officer. That night, the battalion received eight new replacement officers: Lieutenants John C. Barrows, George H. Furst, and Vance C. Hall, Jr., were assigned to D Company; Lieutenants Robert V. Heneisen, Carl Mauro, and James H. Nelson went to E Company; and Lieutenants Stuart McCash and Richard W. Swenson to F Company.

Lieutenant Mauro had been a technical sergeant and one of the dreaded instructors at the Parachute School back at Fort Bragg before being sent to Officer Candidate School. Now, he was just another replacement officer. Mauro had had a harrowing introduction to the Anzio beachhead in getting from the LCI on which he arrived at the port of Anzio to the 2nd Battalion. "As we approached the docking area, we were attacked by speedy, low-flying German fighter planes that came out of nowhere. Planes from both camps arrived almost simultaneously, and the conflict above the harbor lasted only a few minutes—long enough to scare the hell out of us—sending us diving under the trucks on deck or below deck. Our antiaircraft guns surrounding the port and our planes drove off the enemy before they could inflict much damage. 'Jerry' was not going to make anything easy for us.

"When enemy aircraft was first sighted, our fleet of landing craft reversed their engines and pulled back out to sea, scattering in the process. After the enemy planes were driven off, our landing crafts went to the wrecked docks, where our small contingent of replacement personnel disembarked as quickly as possible. We were not a large group—fifty or so—men destined for various fighting units already entrenched several miles inland.

"We walked away from the docks as quickly as we could, carrying every-thing that we owned in our pockets, which were extra large on parachute pants; hooked onto our web-belts; and in the overflowing, bulging, musette bags we had strapped to our shoulders. It was only a double-quick route-march to the nearby beach where, instinctively, we immediately began to dig in! We were out in the open. 'What a dumb place to tarry,' I thought. But I would learn that there was no place to hide on Anzio. But, as everyone else, I started to dig a slit trench in the sand, for lying prone and not a foxhole to stand in. At least the digging was easy.

"We were victims of the 'hurry up and wait' scenario. We wanted to get out of there! We heard artillery and cannons and saw signs of shelling in the water, but nothing real close. Fortunately, only a half hour later, but it seemed much longer, we were on our way again, happily, thinking foolishly, that it would get better.

"Small groups of replacement personnel were led in various directions to join Darby's Rangers, the 3rd Division, or other units. Some of the paratroop-ers may also have gone to the brilliant 509 Parachute Infantry Battalion, which was not a component of the 504.

"The paratroopers in my group, now fewer than ten, moved off the beach and through Nettuno, following a battle-hardened guide who had been sent to lead us to a lightly wooded area. We trudged through Nettuno on the east side of Anzio, because the 504 Combat Team was guarding the right flank of the whole beachhead. Like Anzio, Nettuno was demolished; it was all rubble and ruins. No civilian nor civilian metropolitan activity was observable; the destruction was complete. War was the only open business.

"Meanwhile, we heard intermittent gunfire. Shells were flying over our heads towards the ships that had brought us in. We got a brief glimpse at the large hospital complex near the beach; hundreds of pyramidal and other shaped tents with huge red crosses painted on the canvas that could be seen from miles away. This medical complex got the name 'Hell's Half Acre' because of the constant shelling it received—just like the rest of the beachhead. Several nurses were killed there from enemy fire.

"We stopped in a wooded area to wait for darkness before being led to our new assignments; it was about an hour before dark. At various places around us, I could see our 155mm howitzers and other guns, well-camouflaged with netting above them and well dug in. At Anzio, artillery was king . . . LSTs fulfilled the insatiable demand for artillery shells. We watched the artillerymen methodi-cally dueling—sending heavy projectiles towards the Germans in the distance. We probably sent them two for every one they sent our way. This was my first view of ground combat, though it was between well separated antagonists. It was raucous and frightening, but exhilarating; it made my heart beat faster.

"Though they were out of our sight, we could hear other friendly guns not too far away. The firing and the noise intensified. At the same time, we heard the crashing, incoming fire from German artillery, tanks, and possibly large mortars coming from far away—not exactly bursting on top of us, but striking fearfully close. It made me wonder if we would be the target for each of the next incoming rounds. I began to ponder whether I would be able to react bravely to this deafening onslaught.

"No one had time to notice or advise us; no one came to tell us what best to do. Except for our guide, a private, we were leaderless and ignorant. Our small group of replacements officers was hugging the shaking earth, lurking behind trunks of small trees that had been already scarred by shrapnel from previous bombardments. We expected to move on soon, as it was [getting] dark, thinking that by then the cannonading would abate. None of us, maybe unwisely, had even attempted to dig a foxhole.

"We new recruits huddled closer to each other than was prudent. The awesome din caused us to bunch together, believing that proximity provided security. There was no place to hide and we couldn't run.

"Certainly, I was scared, but not as much as two terrified officers in our group. They were unashamedly on their knees, praying out loud. They begged God, if their lives were spared they would willingly sacrifice an arm or a leg, right here and now; any injury that would cause them to be evacuated immediately.

"Just before darkness fell, a few Luftwaffe fighter planes zoomed into a squadron of American planes that were flying above our heads—eight or ten in all. The rendezvous didn't last long, but this aerial conflict was the only dogfight I saw during the war. Now, we had a brawl in the air; a duel of artillery on the ground; and German shells were tracking down our naval guns off the beach. We had an unsolicited three-ring side-seat for a variety-show combat-cacophony.

"After a long hour in the midst of this dueling artillery fracas, the action abated, and our guide led us, in the dark, to the 504 regimental headquarters. Here, we eight new officers were met by the regimental intelligence officer, 1st Lieutenant Louis A. Hauptfleisch, and quickly taken to the 2nd Battalion command post, nearby."[2]

From there, Mauro was taken to the command post of Company E, which was in reserve at the time. There, he was introduced to Captain Walter Van-Poyck, the commanding officer, and the company exec, Lieutenant Hanford Files. Mauro thought VanPoyck "looked like handsome Errol Flynn, the popular movie star. He was a thin, short guy and wore a small mustache and walked a little bow-legged.

"Van was a university graduate and worked for Eastern Airlines in Miami, Florida. He enlisted in the army in 1941 and was commissioned a second lieutenant in 1942. He volunteered for parachute duty and was a member of the original 504 regimental cadre."[3] Lieutenant Mauro was assigned as assistant platoon leader of Lieutenant John "Jocko" Thompson's 3rd Platoon.

On the night of March 3, Easy Company moved up to take over a sector of the defense line on the Mussolini Canal. There, at a meeting of the company's officers, Lieutenant Mauro met "1st Lieutenant William E. Sharp, Jr., leader of the 2nd Platoon. Sharp really presented a humorous picture: a short guy; heavy beard; handsome; wore really baggy pants; web-belt hanging low on his hips, because he was wearing two pistols and ammo clips; his camouflaged-with-netting helmet was too large and fell down over his thick eyebrows. He reminded me of the stereotypical gunslinger cowboy I used to see in the movies. He was a jolly, young fellow, a gung-ho paratrooper aching for battle. He was a shy, gentle, kind person. He nodded his head continuously and grinned as he talked or listened. I would soon learn that he had gone out on more patrols than any officer or enlisted man. He was always ready to go—he would do as much as any man. His men let me know that Lieutenant Sharp was their paradigm of intelligent courage and daring.

"We all called him 'Sharpie,' and possibly it was his patrols that inspired that literary, dead Anzio-German to have written in his diary those now pro-verbial lines about the ubiquity of American paratroopers in no-man's land: 'devils in baggy pants.'

"VanPoyck set up his command post and gave his lieutenants some brief, routine orders. We talked briefly with our sergeants, and they led a squad at a time, crouching, to their defensive positions along the Mussolini Canal. We replaced some tired and bedraggled rangers of the 4th Battalion who had pre-viously relieved E Company men at these approximate positions."[4]

On March 4, the 504th received a large group of badly needed enlisted replacements to fill its depleted ranks. One of them, Private First Class James L. Ward, was assigned to Company H. "My first night there was in a farmhouse between the lines (no-man's-land). The shelling was tremendous . . . an awful way to spend your first day on the line. I was glad to leave that farmhouse.

"My first combat experience began while on a ten-man patrol just beyond the Mussolini Canal. [Robert A.] "Big Bob" Harris [six feet four inches tall], with his BAR, was number one in line. I was right behind Bob, and Ray [L.] Walker was in the middle of the line. We were moving along a ditch parallel to a farm road when a Jerry machine gun opened fire. This gun was directly across the road from me, probably fifteen or twenty feet away, and firing to my rear. I hit the ground and almost immediately, a potato masher struck me on my right leg. Several seconds later, the second grenade landed a few feet away. I didn't have any luck finding either of the grenades, which I intended to throw back. It didn't take long either to realize that the grenades were duds, or maybe landing in six inches of water caused them not to explode. In a few seconds, I threw a grenade which landed exactly as planned, right in the midst of them.

I could hear them shouting, scrambling around trying to find it . . . must have been three or four of them. I was looking at any moment for that grenade to come back my way. That was the longest five seconds I had ever known.

"We sent out patrols almost every night. It took a while to get used to the dead Germans which we had to look at until we were released several weeks later.

"I first met Chaplain Delbert Kuehl when Ray Walker and I were dug in on the Mussolini Canal, manning a .30-caliber light machine gun. On this particular day, shortly before dusk we observed a soldier moving in our direction. He was carrying an M1. When he arrived at our position he said, 'We're going to have a prayer meeting.' No one will ever know how much it meant to have our chaplain there with us. You'd never know where or when Chaplain Kuehl would show up. It seemed like he was always around when you needed him most.

"It rained almost every day in the spring at Anzio. Ray Walker and I usually kept our machine gun covered with a raincoat, but this particular day we left the gun uncovered and walked down to a farmhouse nearby where we saw smoke coming from the chimney. Thought we might thaw out for a while. Lieutenant Rivers charged in the farmhouse and screamed, 'Who in the hell is on that machine gun up there?'

"Ray and I said we were. I never knew a man could get that angry. He said, 'You two SOBs get that gun down here, field strip it, and I'll be back in ten minutes to check it.' I think we did it in five minutes. We were taught that your weapon comes first and should have known better."[5]

On March 8, Captain Beverly Richardson returned from the hospital and reassumed command of Company F. That night on the Mussolini Canal, Lieutenant Carl Mauro was "standing there quietly with Jocko and Captain VanPoyck, in the dark, behind our line of gun emplacements on the bank, in a melancholy mood. A few moments before, word had preceded his arrival: Private Edward W. Nolan had been killed while on night patrol in front of our line. A member of his patrol had hurried back ahead of the others to inform the men on the firing line and VanPoyck that his squad was bringing in the body; this time, one of our own.

"Four men struggled quietly over the embankment and placed the heavy body on the cold ground in front of Van, the company commander. The men were silent; they would give Captain VanPoyck the details later. They, as I, must have thought, once more: there, but for the grace of God, I would be. At a time like this, I learned, there is not much to say; it was better to not dwell upon it. I could only look briefly and sadly on the inert object.

"A couple of hours earlier, a vibrant Private Nolan was among his buddies, laughing and talking, while putting burnt cork soot on his juvenile face. He made certain that he was wearing or carrying nothing that would shine in the moonlight, bang, crunch, creak, tinkle, or rattle as he crouched and crawled in the silent darkness. Nolan made certain he had grenades, his brass-knuckles-handled paratrooper assault knife, and a pistol; he wore a black wool stocking hat rather than his protective but clumsy steel helmet.

"Now, he was a cold 'body' dead and silent forever. Captain VanPoyck had the boys take the body to battalion headquarters, after it was covered with an army blanket. The Graves Registration unit would take over from there.

"Nolan was the first 'friendly' body (someone I knew) that I encountered in the field of combat. I had known this young, brave paratrooper, if only briefly, and that made a difference."[6]

Lieutenants John Thompson and Mauro were standing down near the bank of the Mussolini Canal behind the embankment that served as the Company E front line in mid-March listening to German planes bombing in the distance. Mauro had spent just a couple of weeks on the line, but the effects were already evident. "He [Thompson] said, 'Why are you shaking?'

"I replied, 'I'm not shaking!'

"He said, 'You're not moving, but you're shaking.' That's what unceasing bombing made us do—shake in our boots, made our skin crawl.

"I had lost track of Lieutenant John Holabird [Company C, 307th Airborne Engineer Battalion], who was one of my best war-friends, so I was more than delighted to hear his voice outside our trench-home, on the banks of the emaciated Mussolini Canal. Jocko and I were in our den one mid-March midnight when tall Lieutenant Holabird hastened along the muddy path between the canal and our dugout. The high embankment protected him from the sight of German machine gunners, out front, less than shouting distance away.

"Holabird knew that, because he and his compadres were just out in little no-man's land installing trip wires and flares that would be activated by probing, creeping Krauts who were determined to sneak up on us to toss potato-masher grenades or make a capture. They too were ordered to bring 'back a body.'

"Our regiment depended on the engineer company that was attached to us to do the dirty work; they were skilled at it. The engineers went out front and cleared enemy mines, barbed wire, and booby-traps so our patrols could move about. They also did the reverse: set up our own mines, barbed wire, and booby-traps to deter the enemy. They devised and placed tripwires that, when touched or stretched, would activate our flares, sending them skyward to illuminate acres of ground. This, of course, is what patrols wanted to avoid most of all."[7]

On the night of March 17–18, a forward observer team with the 376th Parachute Field Artillery Battalion, consisting of Lieutenant Harold A. Stueland and his wireman, Technician Fifth Grade Jack W. Blake, reported to the battalion command post to receive orders for a company-strength diversionary patrol the following night. Lieutenant Stueland was briefed on a mission "to attack the town of Sessano to wipe out the strongpoint and retire after creating enough diversion to relieve pressure on critical portions of the line.

"Our line was along the Mussolini Canal. Between us and the German lines was an open, flat area about one thousand yards wide. A road from Bridge Number 5 across the canal to Sessano bisected our sector. Small houses lined the road. Extensive minefields, known and unknown, spotted all over the open ground. Small drainage ditches ran parallel to the canal at right angles to the road.

"The main center of the enemy strongpoint was near the crossroads of the town. Double apron wire and minefields surrounded the outskirts of the town in a semicircle. Two known machine guns were sited to fire grazing fire down the road and along each side of it. One house on the outskirts had three machine guns. At night, two were downstairs and the other in the second story. During the day, another was located in a deep dugout somewhere in front of it [the house]. The entire sector was covered with interlocking bands of fire from other guns on either flank—grazing fire. Mortars were zeroed in along the road and outside the wire.

"C Company, 504th Parachute Infantry, was to move from the canal bank after dark, go parallel to the road until the farthest outpost house was reached. From there, the route lay at right angles to the road for about six hundred yards, skirting a known minefield. On the town side of the minefield an irrigation ditch ran back towards the road, passing within a few yards of the enemy wire. This was the place selected for the breach.

"Artillery fire was to try to roll up the wire and blast a hole in the minefield, the craters to be utilized by the initial attacking element. As soon as they were inside the enemy defenses, the rest of the company would pour through and kill or capture the enemy. The plan was to hold the town for an hour to draw enemy troops and then retire to our own lines.

"During the afternoon of March 18, 1944, I adjusted 155mm howitzers on the minefield and wire before the strongpoint in Sessano. During the adjustment, one round struck the house known to contain three machine guns, demolishing half of it. Lieutenant [Howard L.] Frohman, a new officer replacement, requested permission to accompany the FO [forward observation] party on the attack for the experience. The battalion CO granted his request.

"About dusk, the artillery party left the protection of the canal to lay wire ahead of the infantry for the initial phase. We reached the farthest outpost house just as machine gun fire swept the road and area. Fire was adjusted to silence the gun. When the rear of the infantry company passed across the exposed road, Lieutenant Frohman and I followed, laying wire. I left the wireman and a phone there to call for artillery on the machine gun covering the road, in case it opened up again.

"When we reached the shelter of the drainage ditch on either side of the large minefield, I took up my position at the side of Major [Julian] Cook. The initial attacking elements were heard by the enemy and fired on by mortars, Panzerfausts, and machine guns. The sound of their feet in the muddy ditch was clearly audible. When they hit the ground and crawled, their automatic weapons were fouled beyond use. Replacements [for the automatic weapons] were brought forward, and the attack was resumed. Our bazooka teams were firing at the flashes of machine guns, but enemy mortars caused many casualties, and the attacking platoon set off booby traps and flares.

"I recommended close artillery support to cover the sound of our movement and make the enemy keep their heads down. Major Cook agreed, so I adjusted one battery, each gun individually. The enemy fire died abruptly and was only resumed when rushes were being made. We were so close to the enemy that a great volume of artillery fire was impractical. As it was, some of our rounds landed within twenty-five yards of the ditch. A percentage of hits were scored on the observable bulk of enemy-occupied buildings. At one time, the sound of falling tin kitchenware caused a snicker that almost gave away the position of the reserve element.

"The tip of the moon began to come in view, so on orders of the regimental commander, the attacking force prepared to withdraw. I called for a battery right at ten-second intervals and another battery to cover the machine guns covering the road and last half of the return route. Under cover of the close artillery fire, the company withdrew down the drainage ditch. When the end of the column carrying the dead and wounded passed, I informed the FDC [fire direction control], and brought the fire down a trifle closer. Lieutenant Frohman and I withdrew [and] checked in at the outpost house, giving information of the exact location of the troops. No enemy fire was delivered from the time we started evacuating until we reached the safety of the canal bank.

"I tied into the wire and reported our location again. While cutting, tying, and tagging the line, the infantry company disappeared in the dark. Hurrying to catch them, Lieutenant Frohman and I got off the narrow path into an unmarked minefield and were both wounded. Lieutenant Frohman could not walk. I got help [and] led them into the minefield and out again with the stretcher. Lieutenant Frohman was evacuated that morning to a clearing station.

"The attack did not penetrate the defenses of the strongpoint, but the diversion it created, drew reserves from critical portions of the line. . . . Mission accomplished."[8]

AFTER SIXTY-ONE DAYS AT ANZIO, a tired, decimated 504th RCT was relieved on March 23, leaving the beachhead the next day aboard LSTs for the port of Pozzuoli, then to Bagnoli, a suburb of Naples, where it rested before leaving for England. The regiment had lost 120 killed, 410 wounded, and 60 missing in action, while having inflicted estimated losses of ten times those numbers on the enemy. While there, General Mark Clark conducted a review of the regimental combat team and presented Lieutenant Colonel Freeman, the 3rd

Battalion commander, with the Presidential Unit citation for its actions in stopping the German breakthrough near Carroceto.

On April 5, Technician Fourth Grade James Crosbie, with Battery B, 376th, received an assignment to get the battalion's new base camp in England ready for its arrival. "An advance detail made up of a few men from the 504, 376, and 307 set sail on the LST Number 384 for Wales. From Naples, Italy, [we proceeded] to Palermo, Sicily, to Bizerte to Oran to Port Talbot in Wales."[9]

On April 10, the 504th RCT boarded trains for Naples, arriving at Garibaldi Station, then marched to the harbor, where it boarded a converted South African liner, the *Capetown Castle*. Also on board for the journey was the British Irish Guards regiment. The following morning the ship sailed for England.

Lieutenant John Holabird, with the 2nd Platoon of Company C, 307th Airborne Engineer Battalion, felt sorry for the enlisted men, due to their accommodations. "The officers were in cabins. The enlisted men were in hammocks, which they slung every night—then had to be taken down each day because they ate in the same room. The British Guards regiment had a sergeant's mess in the main dining room—our men felt very much discriminated against."[10]

Corporal Ted Johnson, with Battery B, 376th Parachute Field Artillery Battalion, was one who felt that discrimination. "We had fish and boiled potatoes for one of our [daily] meals. The British (whom we called 'Limeys') even made us pay for tea in between the meals, which we thought was cheap or shoddy."[11]

Staff Sergeant Leonard Battles, with Headquarters Battery, 376th, sailed to England with the battalion's artillery and vehicles. "The name of the British ship was the *Empress of India*. We slept in hammocks [and] existed on tea, marmalade, and corned beef. The ships sailed in convoy; the voyage took about ten days."[12]

On April 22, the 504th Regimental Combat Team arrived in England. Lieutenant Carl Mauro had joined Company E as a replacement during the fighting at Anzio in early March. "The wharves of Liverpool, where we docked, were a beautiful sight to the battle-weary veterans. The red rooftops of the Liverpudlian homes and buildings shone brightly in the spring sunshine. We were entering another world, different from Naples, Anzio, Sicily, and North Africa. We were entering a domain more like America."[13]

As the *Capetown Castle* pulled into the harbor, the sight of Liverpool attracted most of the troopers, like Corporal Ted Johnson, to that side of the ship. "When we arrived at the dock, everyone moved to that side, and the ship began to list. The captain of the ship ordered half of us to the other side to right the ship."[14]

The 504th RCT disembarked from the ship that night, and carrying their equipment, weapons, and barracks bags, the troopers marched through the quiet streets of Liverpool to the train station. There, they boarded trains for the overnight trip to Leicester, arriving the following morning. The 504th Parachute Infantry Regiment was billeted at nearby Evington, the 376th Parachute Field Artillery Battalion at Hinckley, and Company C, 307th Airborne Engineer Battalion, at Ullesthorpe.

Technician Fifth Grade Wesley Pass and the rest of Headquarters Battery, 376th, were "billeted in an ex-roller rink in Hinckley. England was on double-summer time, so they could tend their gardens. It was not to our liking, as bed check was at midnight, and it did not get dark until eleven. I had a couple of lady friends, so I'd take my shirt off or one boot, get in bed, and pretend to sleep until after the officer of the guard had made guard bed check, and zip, away we go. I had a soft spot for the English and enjoyed the few months in Hinckley."[15]

Like just about every other trooper, Staff Sergeant Leonard Battles, also with Headquarters Battery, 376th, enjoyed his new surroundings to the fullest. "In Hinckley I did what every one of us did: fraternization with the local population in the pubs. I had a 'girl' like all others, and I lived as though each day was the last. I had very little money for free spending, but managed somehow to buy a bicycle. I was free from the early evening on each day, only having to be able to show up for duty the following morning. This was the advantage of living in our own house.

"As I was in the battalion headquarters (as personnel clerk in the sergeant-major's office), I was shut off from the rest of the battalion. They were each individually quartered in different areas around the town. I lived in a house that we had set up as battalion headquarters right in the town itself. I had my own office there; the wire chief, the communications center, colonel's office and I, myself, had the job of typing orders, court-martial and such, so I did not have personal contact with my fellow troopers, only when some papers would come through concerning their activities."[16]

General Gavin, the assistant division commander, visited the 504th shortly after its arrival and felt that with the replacements available in England to bring it back up to strength, it could participate in the Normandy jump. Colonel Tucker and many of the 504th officers and men wanted to get in on what they all knew would be an historic invasion.

General Gavin approached General Ridgway with the proposal of substituting the veteran 504th for either of the untested 507th or 508th Regiments. However, Ridgway decided to leave the 504th out of the invasion plans and hold them in England as division reserve because "they were so badly battered, so riddled with casualties from their battles in Italy, they could not be made ready for combat in time to jump with us."[17]

This angered and disappointed both Gavin and Tucker. Gavin felt that "the 504th was one of the very best and would have made a tremendous difference to the division."[18]

Only five days after arriving in England, Major Robert Neptune, the executive officer of the 376th Parachute Field Artillery Battalion, was transferred temporarily to the 456th Parachute Field Artillery Battalion as executive officer for the upcoming cross-channel invasion. "Because only in late April 1944 had I arrived from severe combat in Italy, I did not relish the idea of being handed the assignment as executive officer of an outfit scheduled for almost immediate combat: Normandy. But [Brigadier General Francis] Andy March, the general, insisted that the newly formed 456th Parachute Field Artillery Battalion needed a combat-experienced officer, and apparently General James Gavin suggested that it be me. I was slightly acquainted with a number of the officers of the new unit, but the officers junior to me did not appreciate the insertion of an outside senior officer between the commanding officer, Lieutenant Colonel [Wagner J.] D'Alessio, and them, when promotion from within the unit would have moved several of them along toward higher rank. But the cool relationship rather quickly dissipated, and all of us did our utmost to prepare for the imminent invasion, just a few weeks away. As the executive officer of the battalion, I counseled when my counsel was sought or when I felt it was critically needed, but restrained substituting my judgment for that of either the commanding officer or the individual officers of the unit. We got along fairly well, and I stayed 'out of the way,' independently taking care of the duties as executive officer."[19]

SHORTLY AFTER THE 504TH ARRIVED IN ENGLAND, a call went out for volunteers for an extremely hazardous mission. So many troopers stepped forward, that they had to turn most away. Sergeant Tom McCarthy was a veteran of Company A and had served with the original pathfinder team organized in Sicily. McCarthy's attitude was typical within the regiment. "I volunteered just because, after the Italian campaign, which was savage fighting, we were over there in England, sitting down. They were going replace the best regiment in the division with a green regiment? We were going to sit behind and listen to that crap? I said, 'You go ahead, but if McCarthy can get in there, he's going. It's the main bout and I'm going one way or the other.' "[20] McCarthy "took a paper bust when I volunteered, so I went as a private."[21]

The 504th volunteers weren't informed of the nature of the mission. Lieutenant John T. Joseph, the commanding officer of the 507th pathfinder teams, was one of the few who knew of the nature of the assignment. "During the latter part of the training period, it was decided to provide pathfinder teams with security elements. For this purpose, one officer and twelve enlisted men from the 504th Parachute Infantry Regiment (all combat veterans) were attached to [each of] the 507th and 508th pathfinder teams. Inasmuch as the 505th had had previous combat experience, they provided their own security. The officer in command of the security detachment accompanied the regimental pathfinder leader."[22]

The pathfinders had been training at an airfield at North Witham. It had evolved far beyond the first pathfinder school in Sicily. Each of the regiments had provided six officers and fifty-four enlisted men, forming a provisional pathfinder company. Lieutenant Joseph and "all potential pathfinders were 'handpicked' from a large group of volunteers. Training consisted mainly in practical work—dropping with equipment and organizing drop zones and landing zones for airborne operations. Special emphasis was placed on night operations.

"As training progressed, new ideas and practices were developed. A standard operating procedure (SOP) was set up to control the training and insure coordinated action in combat. The strength of the pathfinder teams was two officers and twelve enlisted men (team leader, assistant team leader, light section leader, seven light men, two Eureka operators, and two assistant Eureka operators).

"Three pathfinder teams, each representing a battalion of one regiment, were flown to a drop zone in three planes flying in a tight 'V' formation. All pathfinder troops dropped on the approximate center of a jump field.

"Immediately after assembly on the ground, the regimental pathfinder leader (usually the senior officer, who was also in command of a battalion pathfinder team) selected the location for the 'T' of lights carried by his team and ordered them set up. Simultaneously, he dispatched the two remaining teams to their general locations, one forward and one to the rear of the base position. The distance between 'T's was usually about seven hundred yards. As the teams moved away from the base position, the light section leader laid assault wire. Each team set up its lights and Eurekas and installed sound-powered telephones so that voice communication was available between the battalion teams and the regimental pathfinder leader.

"The regimental pathfinder leader controlled the use of navigational aids by telephone. This permitted the dropping of each battalion on different sections of the drop zone without losing control and aided considerably the problems of assembly. The regimental commander was certain (assuming the pathfinders were able to complete their missions) of having communications with his battalion commanders at the very outset of the operation.

"Training along these lines was supplemented by additional work in map and aerial photograph reading, physical training, and assembly problems. Colored TE-122 flashlights were used in conducting pathfinder assembly problems. Red, amber, and blue lights were employed, each designating the assembly point for one team. The center teams (the team commanded by the regimental pathfinder leader) was always designated as the base team to which other teams reported upon assembly. The assistant team leader for each battalion was equipped with a light that was raised fifteen feet into the air and aided the main elements in assembling. This light, known as the McGill light, was set up at the battalion assembly point as soon as the battalion serial approached the drop zone. This greatly facilitated the assembly problem, for the light could easily be seen for several miles. A red light indicated the 1st Battalion area, an amber light the 2nd Battalion area, and a blue light the 3rd Battalion area.

"This type of training continued up to the time of the invasion. After pathfinders jumped on and set up drop zones, main elements of the regiments followed them in to carry out complete tactical problems. The pathfinder teams attained a high proficiency in organizing jump areas. Under favorable conditions, twelve minutes were all that [it took] to organize a field from the time the first pathfinder left his plane until the last light or Eureka was set up."[23]

Company C trooper Private First Class William D. Dan Serilla was also one of those volunteers selected. "From the 3rd Platoon, there was [Private First Class Thomas L.] T. L. Rodgers and myself, and from the 2nd Platoon, [Private] John [F.] Esman, a demolitions man. Out of all the volunteers who came forward from C Company, we were the three chosen.

"We underwent a training period of about two weeks, which consisted of night jumps, where we practiced setting up the lights and radar on the DZ."[24]

Private McCarthy and the other volunteers received only the information required to carry out their mission, but not the location of the objective, nor the timing of the operation. "The pictures we studied showed a farmhouse being used as a garrison by Kraut troops near the DZ. We were to attack the farm and keep them busy while the light and radar teams did their jobs."[25]

Lieutenant Thomas A. Murphy with Headquarters Company, 3rd Battalion, would jump with the 2nd Battalion, 508th team, and Lieutenant James H. Goethe with Company A, would jump with the 3rd Battalion, 507th team. This select group totaled only twenty-six men and officers of the 504th.

General Gavin also selected a few 504th officers as part of his staff for the Normandy operation. "Lieutenant Thomas Graham and Captain Willard Harrison were picked for their combat experience and reputation for toughness and courage in combat."[26] Tucker also told Gavin to take another trooper from the 504th. "Tucker insisted that I allow him to come along, saying he was the toughest soldier he had in the regiment—and that was saying an awful lot. This man wore a gold earring in one ear and didn't do much talking, but he had a reputation for being a very rough character indeed."[27] That man was Lieutenant Donald Crooks, who commanded the 504th Reconnaissance Platoon.

The 504th executive officer, Lieutenant Colonel Charles Billingslea, would jump as an observer. Captain Harrison would act as Gavin's field assistant.

On the evening of June 3, 1944, McCarthy received the briefing of their upcoming mission. "We never got briefed until we were just about ready to go in. Then, the maps came out and the locations came out. The instructions as to how it was going to work—they showed us where we were going, what we were going to, what the objective was. For my part, our objective, in that jump, it was to clear a farmhouse, which was an established barrack."[28]

Now, the pathfinders knew where the invasion would take place—the Cotentin Peninsula of Normandy, France—but they still didn't know when.

On June 5, Private First Class Serilla and some of the other pathfinders received an unexpected bonus, after being restricted to the airfield since their arrivals. "Esman and I were called to the commander's office, where we were both issued a seventy-two hour pass to London, with no reason at all. We both were under the impression that we were being closely spied upon, as we had been under confinement while we were here at North Witham.

"Esman and I arrived in London and checked into the King Edward Hotel."[29]

At approximately 10:30 p.m. that night, nine planes carrying the 82nd Airborne pathfinder teams began lifting off from their airfield at North Witham, bound for Normandy.

Private McCarthy was assigned to Chalk 13, along with Lieutenant James Goethe, with Company A; and Privates First Class Thomas L. Rodgers with Company C; John D. Dickinson with Headquarters Company, 1st Battalion; and Arthur Caton, Jr., with Headquarters Company, 2nd Battalion. After clearing the coast of England, McCarthy looked down and saw "the armadas down in the channel. I mean there were ships and ships and ships forever. . . . You thought about how big it was. The reality was beginning to come to you. This is the biggest thing that ever happened to me. Now, what? What really are we getting into?"[30]

After passing over the west coast of the Cotentin Peninsula, the red light flashed on, and McCarthy and the others on his plane stood up and hooked up. The planes carrying the pathfinder teams began to receive small-arms fire as they approached the drop zone. When the green light flashed on, Lieutenant John Joseph, the jumpmaster, went out the door, followed by his stick. As McCarthy felt the sudden jerk of his chute opening. "I looked down and saw that we were not heading for the big field, but were going to land right on top of that German garrison in the farmhouse. The pilot had given us the light too early, and we were coming up short.

"It was a full moon and with the clouds having moved off, we were coming in low—perfect targets. I could see the Krauts running around shooting at us with small arms."[31]

As McCarthy floated down "one of the bullets from the small arms creased my head, and I came down a little dazed, but I kept an eye on those birds doing the shooting, and did a little swearing at the pilot, who was now heading for home.

"The Krauts weren't organized, thank God; they were scared, too! I remember seeing Rodgers go down, he was a big guy from C Company—a BAR man. He landed right inside the courtyard of that farmhouse. I landed outside the walls of the place, near a well. I remember hearing the BAR going and then the sound of a Kraut burp gun, and it was over. I struggled out into the field, and that's when I saw those two Krauts who had been shooting at me. I disposed of them with a grenade, and moved off to find the rest of the stick."[32]

In that courtyard, Private First Class Thomas Rodgers killed or wounded twenty-five Germans and knocked out a machine gun that had pinned down several members of his stick. Later Rodgers was posthumously awarded the Distinguished Service Cross for his actions that night.

Back in London, on the morning of June 6, Private First Class Dan Serillo was awakened at the hotel. "At daybreak, the church bells were ringing and car horns were blowing. Rushing outside, [we met] two American MPs [who] asked to see our passes, and that is when we were informed of D-Day."[33]

CORPORAL EDWIN M. "MIKE" CLEMENTS was one of the replacements arriving in England fresh from training in the United States to fill the depleted ranks of the U.S. airborne divisions. "We docked in Liverpool in the dead of night. It was raining and foggy, and it took us over two hours to unload, collect our two huge duffel bags, and get on the trucks that would take us to our assigned units. Except, that my two bags could not be found, and the trucks couldn't wait. Even though the bags were heavily labeled and marked with my name, rank, and serial number I never saw them again, including the beautiful monogrammed Dopp kit and a number of other personal items that my parents had thoughtfully sent with me. So, off I go to win the war with a small musette bag containing shaving stuff, a bunch of dirty underwear, and a few pair of socks. We unloaded while it was still dark. I was told to find a cot in a twelve-man tent. All I knew was that I was in the 82nd Airborne Division and we were in a camp near the city of Leicester. It was pitch dark, and I was cursed loudly, since I woke two men by stepping on them. Finally, I found an empty cot and without undressing—except for my boots—fell on the cot and slept. In the morning, I awoke to the usual sound of reveille and found that I was now a part of the 1st Platoon, B Company, 1st Battalion, of the 504 Parachute Infantry Regiment.

"I quickly found that my squad leader was a young man whose name was Jerry Murphy. Murphy put me in touch with the company supply sergeant, one of the more memorable characters in B Company. The role of the supply man was to keep the company supplied with everything they needed on and off the line. Sergeant [Charles J.] Hyde heard my sad story and very quickly supplied me with almost everything I needed in terms of clothing and equipment.

"Murphy, although acting as squad leader, was still a private, though he was in a job which called for sergeant's stripes. I had come over with the two stripes of a corporal on my sleeve, which apparently created a bit of a problem. Later that day, it was resolved when I was told to report to the company commander.

"Captain [Thomas B.] Helgeson could have served as a perfect role model for a World War II parachute officer. Not tall, but wide-shouldered, thin-waisted, and flat-bellied, he was also blonde and blue-eyed. His uniform was spotless, his boots glistened, and he came to the point quickly. 'Corporal Clements, your rank and training entitle you to fill the job of an assistant squad leader of a rifle squad, even though you have never been in combat. I am sure you would not feel comfortable leading a squad of combat veterans who have been in combat in Sicily, Salerno, and on the Anzio beachhead.' He didn't wait for my response. 'Therefore, I am demoting you to private, immediately. You are dismissed.'

"This was the unit—or what was left of it—that I joined in Leicester. In fact, there were not a large number of troopers who had jumped into Sicily and lasted through all the campaigns that followed. Attrition was supposed to be offset by replacements, although the numbers always fell below what which constituted full strength. Some of the men in B Company had seen little or no action, arriving when the unit was in a reserve position, but I was fortunate in that my platoon sergeant, William P. (Knobby) Walsh, had been with the regiment since it was activated. He had come over with the regiment prior to Sicily, fought through all the major campaigns and had achieved relatively high rank—first sergeant—which he kept for only a short time. Knobby had difficulty dealing with fools and incompetents, regardless of rank, and didn't mind saying so. This led to a unique situation that had Knobby giving up his stripes when the company was off the line (not in contact with the enemy), but getting them back when the unit went back into combat. Knobby was the platoon sergeant of the 1st Platoon when I arrived, and some said that was a sure sign that a mission was in the offing."[34]

AFTER THE 82ND AIRBORNE DIVISION RETURNED FROM NORMANDY, the training regimen of the 504th increased in intensity to integrate the replacements and get the regiment in fighting shape. The veterans of the regiment were bored by the repetition of drills and training they now knew by heart. Many of the old timers found ways to minimize their exertion. Private First Class Joe Watts "stripped a light machine gun of its heavy barrel, barrel extension, and bolt to lighten my load for a training road march in England. I was caught and given twenty-four hours' pack-drill: four hours after supper each night for six nights, marching with a pack loaded with bricks, carrying a heavy 1917A1 [water-cooled] machine gun with cradle and tripod. The punishment was fair and added to my physical conditioning."[35]

The 3rd Battalion's new commander, Major Julian Cook, had taken command of the battalion on the way from Italy to England in April. "During the course of training in England, the men resented having to train—being combat veterans already—failing to remember that new men had joined the battalion. One day, in talking to the NCOs of the battalion, I gave them hell about the kind of job they were doing and made the point of saying, 'Remember, in combat I won't be there to correct your mistakes, as I do in training.' Maliciously or otherwise, the men twisted this around to imply I was afraid of combat."[36]

Unfortunately, because of a lack of suitable land in England for firing ranges, the 376th Parachute Field Artillery Battalion was unable to conduct much training. Captain Frank Boyd was the command liaison officer with Headquarters Battery, 376th Parachute Field Artillery Battalion. "We did practically no training in England. There are a few areas suitable for maneuvers. We did make one practice jump and drove in convoy to Sennybridge, Wales, for a week of firing on the artillery range there."[37]

However, the great complexity of operations of an artillery battalion meant that experience in combat was highly valued. The 376th had more combat time than any artillery battalion in the division.

Because the 504th was again part of the 82nd, one of the temporarily attached regiments would have to be transferred out of the division. It was determined that the 507th would be transferred to the newly formed 17th Airborne Division. The 508th would remain attached to the 82nd.

On August 11, at Leicester, a ceremony was held to commemorate a change of command of the 82nd Airborne Division. Brigadier General Jim Gavin would be taking command of the division, and General Ridgway would shortly take command of the newly formed XVIII Airborne Corps. For Ridgway, it was an emotional moment. "I suppose a prouder division commander never lived than I, as I watched that magnificent division swing past the reviewing stand."[38]

On August 16, 1944, General Gavin assumed formal command of the 82nd Airborne Division.

By mid-August, the Allied armies on the continent had broken out of the Normandy lodgment, encircled and destroyed most of the German forces west of the Seine River, and were driving rapidly toward the Seine and the German border beyond. The major obstacle to the drive was a shortage of gasoline. Troop-carrier aircraft were being utilized by General Bradley to ferry gasoline to keep the tanks rolling east.

On Tuesday, August 29, 1944, Gavin attended a conference at the headquarters of British General Frederick Browning, commander of the British 1st Airborne Corps. Gavin was briefed on a planned airborne operation. "We were given a mission of participating in a proposed landing north of Tournai [Belgium] to seize and hold the crossings of the Escaut River to prevent German withdrawal. The drop was to take place Sunday morning [September 3] about 8:30. Participating were the Poles, British, and 101st Airborne Division. Plans were pushed, orders prepared, ammo and chutes issued, troops dispersed at the proper airdromes, all by dark Friday evening. It was raining and continued to rain more. The U.S. armor continued to drive the Germans back, actually threatening to get to our DZs before Sunday.

"They did, Sunday morning, besides the weather was lousy. Knowing the armor was going to beat us to it, General Browning changed our missions to seize and take over Lille, Roubaix, Tournai, etc., so as to assist the armor in its passage—a hell of a mission for airborne troops. But General Browning was not to be denied, and for some unexplainable reason, the high command was hell bent on getting the First Allied Airborne Army into the fight, whether or not the commitment was decisive or even sound.

"Well, Sunday morning [September 3], I was called to Moor Park, General Browning's headquarters, and given a new mission. We were to jump on the west bank of the Meuse, opposite Liège [Belgium] to again block the retreating Germans—the historic Liège gap. By now the troops were aware of the apparent lack of necessity of our participation in this type or role, or so it seemed. Again, weather intervened and was conveniently and also typically lousy. The British ground troops were overrunning our DZ and LZ areas in addition.

"Consequently, by Sunday night the mission was called off, we reverted to the U.S. XVIII Corps, and back home we came, a bit wetter, but hardly the wiser."[39]

Gavin was in London on September 10, when he received a phone call around 4:00 p.m. notifying him of a meeting two hours later at General Browning's headquarters. "I took off, arriving a few minutes late for the meeting. It was conducted generally by Browning and had to do with a new plan envisioning a drop for the 82nd to seize bridges at Grave and Nijmegen and the high ground between Nijmegen and Groesbeek. That the plan would go through was all agreed to, [and] Browning was to command it and had it all set up. The troop-carrier lift was not set, however."[40]

The plan was part of a British operation devised by British Field Marshal Bernard Montgomery, code-named Market-Garden. General Lewis H. Brereton, commanding the First Allied Airborne Army, wanted to make the drop on September 14, less than four days away. But because of the disposition of troop-carrier aircraft ferrying gasoline to Bradley's forces, the date was delayed until Sunday, September 17, less than seven days away.

Three airborne divisions would drop and land by glider behind German lines in southern Holland to seize bridges over canals and rivers and hold them until the British Second Army could drive north from the Dutch-Belgian border over the bridges and turn east into the plains of northern Germany. From there, the Second Army would seize the industrial center of Germany— the Ruhr Valley.

The 101st Airborne Division would drop south of the 82nd just north of the city of Eindhoven and seize two canal bridges at Son and Best, and two

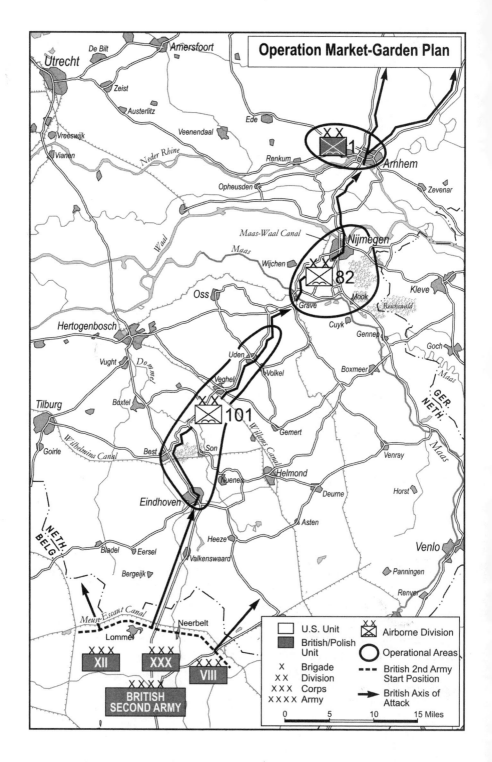

Operation Market-Garden Plan

bridges to the south of Veghel, and drive south through Eindhoven to link up with the British XXX Corps, spearheading the British ground force assault. The British 1st Airborne Division with the Polish Airborne Brigade attached would drop north of the 82nd and capture a single bridge over the Rhine River at Arnhem, some sixty-four miles deep in enemy territory.

The 82nd Airborne Division's assignment would be extremely complex, requiring aggressive execution. Jumping fifty-three miles behind German lines, the division would seize four major river bridges and five canal bridges, including both the longest single-span bridge (the Nijmegen highway bridge) and the longest bridge (Grave bridge) in all of Europe. In order to protect the route of the British Second Army, the division would also need to hold high ground east and southeast of Nijmegen and the landing zones southeast and northeast of Groesbeek for glider landings. The frontage of the division's area was enormous and the objectives ambitious. Only an elite veteran division could hope to accomplish the mission.

The work by Gavin's staff to put together the plan in six days was nothing short of spectacular. Colonel Robert H. Wienecke, the chief of staff, wasn't even aware of the operation until the evening of September 10. "I had gone up to visit the 505th Parachute Regiment on 10 September, and returned to find the division commander (Gavin) and the G-3 (Norton) had gone to Allied Airborne Headquarters for orders. By midnight we had our draft order ready."[41]

Lieutenant Colonel Walter F. Winton, Jr., assistant chief of staff, intelligence (G-2) and his staff developed a number of intelligence reports, including one entitled "Weather; Sun and Moon Tables" that provided information regarding climatic conditions typical for the month of September in Holland, a table showing the times for the rise and fall of the sun and moon, and the effect of weather on enemy operations. An intelligence report entitled "Background Information" gave the division general information about Holland, and the Nijmegen area in particular, such as population, the government, the language, attitude of the population, and even an assessment of the Dutch police. The G-2 section formulated an assessment of the terrain in three documents concerning the terrain around the Nijmegen area. The first, entitled "Preliminary Tactical Study of the Terrain," covered topography of the area, critical terrain features, and tactical effects of the terrain. The second, "Tactical Study of the Terrain," included more detail regarding the topography, such as statistics of the Maas and Waal Rivers and military aspects such as obstacles. The third, "Evaluation of Terrain for Airborne Landings: Nijmegen Area," covered suitability for parachute glider landings.

The importance of the bridges required a separate report entitled "Bridge Data," which described the type of structures, the dimensions, the materials used for construction, and the width of the water. Each bridge was assigned a number, which would be used as a code to refer to them during radio conversations. The discussions could take place in the clear without the Germans knowing which bridge was being discussed until it was too late. The lock bridge on the Maas-Waal Canal at Heumen would be referred to as Bridge Number 7, the bridge at Malden was code-named Bridge Number 8, the bridge at Hatert was designated as Bridge Number 9, the Honinghutie rail and road bridges would be Bridge Number 10, and the Grave bridge would be Bridge Number 11.

The G-2 staff formulated a very important document outlining security entitled "Counterintelligence." Section I dealt with security measures to be taken prior to the operation covering the planning, period after receipt of orders, movement to the departure fields, the time while sealed in at the departure fields, the briefings and the subsequent period prior to takeoff. Section II covered actions required once in Holland to maintain operational security. These activities included the arrest of known enemy agents, collaborators, and sympathizers; seizure of enemy communication centers for the purpose of obtaining documents, codes, cipher devices, and other records; seizure and impounding of civilian mail and telegrams; protection against sabotage of local public and private installations; and assistance in civilian movement control, among many others.

A plan for the G-2 staff's intelligence operations prior to takeoff and subsequently while in Holland was entitled "Intelligence." This plan detailed the types of information that the G-2 staff would seek to obtain, such as the type and location of enemy defenses, reconnaissance, prisoners of war, captured enemy documents, and supplies of maps and aerial reconnaissance photographs.

Intelligence regarding the German forces was contained in an intelligence document entitled "Order Of Battle Summary," which attempted to estimate the enemy's situation in general and specifically in the 82nd's operational area, the strength of German antiaircraft defenses, the perceived enemy strength by specific panzer and infantry divisions, and potential replacements and reinforcements that the Germans might be able to bring into the battle. The report stated that the German Army was beginning to recover from the terrible defeat in Normandy a month earlier. It asserted, "There is no doubt that the enemy has made a remarkable recovery within the last few days, at any rate in the 21st Army Group area."[42]

More ominous was the information in the report regarding the presence of forces around Nijmegen. "It is reported that one of the broken panzer divisions has been sent back to the area north of Arnhem to rest and refit; this might produce some fifty tanks."[43]

The report went on to say, "Photographs, together with ground reports from Dutch sources, indicate the main direction of German movement is northwest to southeast; not only is the 347 Division down from the north, but it is definitely established that many of the SS training units which were near Amsterdam are now quartered in the excellent barracks in Nijmegen. It is estimated there are four thousand of these SS troops; moreover, troops are also reported in St. Canisius College and the Marienboom Girls' School. There is little doubt that our operational area will contain a fair quota of Germans, and an estimate of a divisional strength in this area may not be far wide of the mark."[44]

The report used Supreme Headquarters Allied Expeditionary Force (SHAEF) estimates of German troop and tank strength as of September 1 on the Western Front. SHAEF identified forty-two German infantry divisions that totaled approximately 130,000 men. The report estimated the strength of the panzer and panzer grenadier divisions to be approximately 45,000 men in thirteen divisions.

Of particular concern to the G-3 Plans and Operations group was German armored strength. The "Order Of Battle Summary" stated, "The present tank strength is about 250 tanks. The maximum that can be expected in the way of reinforcements is 350, with a possible fifteen thousand troops, making a total strength in panzer troops of six hundred tanks and sixty thousand men."[45]

Lieutenant Colonel Jack Norton, commanding the G-3 section, had an incredible task to accomplish in a very short time frame. This would be the largest, most complex airborne operation ever attempted. The 82nd would have to seize enough of the four bridges over the Maas and Waal Rivers and five bridges over the Maas-Waal Canal to create a corridor for the British ground forces, while taking high ground east and southeast of Nijmegen that dominated the bridges over the canal. In addition, the division had to be concerned about an armored attack coming from the nearby Reichswald, a forest on the German border, just a few miles east and southeast of Nijmegen. Finally, the reported SS troops and refitting panzer division required that the division wipe out any German forces in the immediate area and be concerned with a possible armored attack from the Arnhem area to the north.

There wouldn't be enough paratroopers in the initial drop on September 17 to capture all of the division's objectives. Therefore, General Gavin had to prioritize the objectives. "This mission, of course was discussed at great length with the British airborne corps commander (General Browning). About two weeks prior to the receipt of the mission by the 82nd Airborne Division, it had been planned that General [Robert F.] Urquhart's British Airborne Division would do the job. They had, therefore, devoted considerable study to intelligence reports and to the terrain. The Nijmegen-Groesbeek high ground was the only high ground in all of the Netherlands. With it in German hands, physical possession of the bridges would be absolutely worthless, since it completely dominated the bridges and all the terrain around it. The understanding was therefore reached with British corps headquarters that it would be absolutely imperative that this high ground be seized.

"It is a basic concept of airborne tactics that an airhead must first be established, from which further tactical operations can be conducted. This high ground provided ideally such an area. I personally considered it the key to the accomplishment of the entire mission and thought that even if we were driven off the low ground around the bridges, if the high ground could be held, ultimately the Second Army could accomplish its mission.

"The Grave bridge was considered the most important, and one regiment was committed to it. There was where the first link-up would be made. The bridges over the Maas-Waal canal were to me an obvious necessity, based on my experience in the past, particularly the bridges over the Merderet River in Normandy, when I lost a major part of the 507th Parachute Infantry because of my lack of foresight in seizing bridges that would enable us to maintain some tactical integrity within the division.

"It was obvious that we had to get bridges across the Maas-Waal Canal. Our G-2 estimate of the situation indicated that the major German reaction would be from the Reichswald, up the main highway via Mook and Molenhoek to Nijmegen. If the Germans succeeded in driving in here, we were in serious trouble. Seizure and retention of the bridges in strength on the canal would add to the defensive strength opposing such an enemy effort. Due to the tremendous sector that the division was to hold, it was first considered best not to attack the Nijmegen bridge until all other objectives had been captured and the division well reorganized and well in hand."[46]

Because there would be no time for rehearsals, the planning process would not have the benefit of lessons learned during the preparation phase normal to most offensive operations, and would, therefore, take on especially critical importance. Working almost continuously day and night, Lieutenant Colonel Norton and his staff, in conjunction with Gavin and the other staff sections, finished the planning for the operation in an astounding three days, a truly remarkable accomplishment. On September 13, 1944, Lieutenant Colonel Norton issued operational orders on behalf of General Gavin.

All three of the division's parachute infantry regiments would drop south and east of Nijmegen on September 17. The 504th would land south of Nijmegen, where it would capture the key bridges over the Maas River at Grave and over the Maas-Waal Canal. The 505th would jump south of Groesbeek to capture the town and the high ground between the town and the Maas-Waal Canal. The regiment would also establish blocking positions south and east of Groesbeek to protect against attacks from the Reichswald, a short distance to the east, and along the Nijmegen-Gennep road to the south. The 508th would land southeast of Nijmegen and seize the high ground and establish roadblocks south and east of the city, and upon the completion of these objectives, move to capture the bridges across the Waal River in Nijmegen. The 376th Parachute Field Artillery Battalion would land by parachute and support the division's parachute regiments, initially in direct support of the 505th and prepared to support the 504th to break up enemy counterattacks. Companies B, C, and the newly formed D, 307th Airborne Engineer Battalion, were assigned to security for the division command post. The pathfinder team for the 325th would mark the landing zones for the glider landings on subsequent days. The remainder of the division artillery, the 80th Airborne Antiaircraft Battalion, and Company A, 307th Airborne Engineer Battalion, would arrive by glider on D+1. The 325th would land on D+2 and assemble in the division reserve area. The other elements of the division would move by water, then over land to join the division.

The plan for Operation Market (the airborne component of Market-Garden) called for 7,250 paratroopers of the 82nd Airborne Division to be flown to Holland by the 50th and 52nd Wings of the IX Troop Carrier Command in the first lift, September 17. The armada would consist of 480 planes carrying paratroopers in eleven serials, followed by one fifty-plane glider serial. Each wave of nine-plane V-of-Vs in the parachute serials would fly at five-second intervals.

Pathfinders would mark only the drop zone at Overasselt for the 504th. Two planes carrying the pathfinders would depart from the airfield at Chalgrove, and they would jump at 12:47 p.m. General Gavin, concerned about the possibility of German armor hidden in the Reichswald and that pathfinders marking the drop zones would give them an early warning, decided not to have the drop zones for the 505th and 508th marked.

Following the pathfinders, the 505th and elements of division headquarters would jump at DZ "N" southeast of Groesbeek. The 504th would jump at DZ "O" north of Overasselt, north of the Maas River, a couple of minutes after the 505th began jumping. The 3rd Battalion would lead the regiment, arriving at 1:13 p.m. The 1st Battalion would follow, jumping at 1:15 p.m. The 2nd Battalion, less Company E, would jump at 1:17 p.m., with Company E at the rear of the serial jumping southwest of the Grave bridge at the same time. Elements of Headquarters and Headquarters Company and Service Company would jump with each of the three battalion serials.

Companies B, C, and D, 307th Airborne Engineer Battalion, would jump next at DZ "N" and provide security for the division command post. The 508th serials would follow the engineers and jump at DZ "T" northeast of Groesbeek. The 376th Parachute Field Artillery Battalion would follow the 508th and jump at DZ "N" at 1:40 p.m.

The twelfth and last serial of fifty C-47s towing gliders would bring in Battery A, 80th Airborne Antiaircraft (Antitank) Battalion, elements of division headquarters, division artillery headquarters, the 821st Airborne Signal Company, the 82nd Reconnaissance Platoon, a forward air controller team, and a British SAS Phantom detachment.

The whole operation would take one hour, and only thirty-nine minutes from the arrival of the first battalion-sized element until the glider serial. The commanders and their staffs of each regiment, and artillery, engineering, and antiaircraft battalions used the divisional orders to formulate detailed operational plans and assign unit missions to their companies and platoons.

The command structure of the 504th had undergone a number of changes after Italy. The regimental staff was now composed of Lieutenant Colonel Warren Williams, executive officer; Lieutenant Louis A. Hauptfleisch, S-1; Captain Fordyce Gorham, S-2; Major Mack Shelly, S-3; and Major William Addison, S-4.

The 1st Battalion was commanded by Major Willard Harrison, with Major Abdallah Zakby, executive officer; Lieutenant G. F. Crockett, S-1; Captain James Goethe, S-2; Lieutenant John N. Pease; S-3; and Lieutenant George F. Talliferro S-4. Captains Charles Duncan, Thomas Helgeson, Albert Milloy, and Roy E. Anderson continued to command Companies A, B, C, and Headquarters companies.

The 2nd Battalion was commanded by Major Edward Wellems, with Major William Colville, executive officer; Lieutenant Chester Garrison, S-1; Lieutenant R. A. Stribley, S-2; Captain Adam Komosa, S-3; and Lieutenant Ross I. Donnley, S-4. Captain Robert J. Cellar commanded Headquarters Company, with Captain Victor W. Campana commanding Company D, Captain Walter VanPoyck commanding Company E, and Captain Beverly Richardson commanding Company F.

The 3rd Battalion was commanded by Major Julian Cook. His staff was composed of Captain Arthur Ferguson, executive officer; Lieutenant Thomas F. Pitt, S-1; Lieutenant Virgil Carmichael, S-2; Captain Henry Keep, S-3; and Lieutenant Thomas T. Utterback, S-4. Headquarters Company was commanded by Captain Warren S. Burkholder, G Company was commanded by Captain Fred E. Thomas, H Company was under the command of Captain Carl Kappel, and I Company's commanding officer was Captain T. Moffatt Burriss.

ON THE MORNING OF SEPTEMBER 15, THE 504TH RCT moved by truck to the airfields. As Lieutenant Alphonse "Chick" Czekanski, with Battery D, 376th Parachute Field Artillery Battalion, waited for the truck convoy to leave Hinckley, many of the town's citizens gathered to wish them good luck. "A great many of the people just stood by and cried."[47]

After the units arrived at the airfields and were sealed in, the officers were briefed on the operation, followed by the non-commissioned officers and enlisted men. Lieutenant Jack Valentic was the executive officer of C Battery, 376th Parachute Field Artillery Battalion. "We were told of the operation and where we were going by the battalion command personnel. We were briefed on landmarks and other checkpoints we would cross. We were briefed about the drop zone and our assembly point. We were all quite familiar with the Groesbeek area. We had many briefings and sand box discussions as to the mission and the area."[48]

Colonel Reuben H. Tucker III, holding a folding stock carbine, prepares to board his C-47 for the flight to Sicily, July 11, 1943. *U.S. Army photograph, courtesy of the 82nd Airborne Division War Memorial Museum*

Two 504th PIR troopers fire a .30-caliber machine gun during the fighting in the mountains of Italy, December 18, 1943. *U.S. Army photograph, courtesy of the National Archives via Martin K. A. Morgan*

A trooper with Company C, 307th Airborne Engineer Battalion, uses a metal detector to sweep for German landmines during the advance of the 504th RCT in the Apennine Mountains. *U.S. Army photograph, courtesy of the 82nd Airborne Division War Memorial Museum*

Personnel with the 307th Airborne Medical Company, attached to the 504th RCT, and ambulance drivers with Service Company, 504th, carefully remove patients from an ambulance. Both of these units performed heroically to save as many lives as possible during the fighting in the Apennine Mountains. *U.S. Army photograph, courtesy of the 82nd Airborne Division War Memorial Museum*

The 376th Parachute Field Artillery Battalion fires one its 75mm pack howitzers in support of the infantry in the Apennine Mountains. *U.S. Army photograph, courtesy of the 82nd Airborne Division War Memorial Museum*

Dug-in positions of the 504th PIR are visible along the Mussolini Canal, with the fighting positions along the top of the embankment and dugouts behind it. *U.S. Army photograph, courtesy of the 82nd Airborne Division War Memorial Museum*

Private First Class Theodore Bachenheimer's exploits behind German lines are legendary among the troopers of the 504th PIR. *U.S. Army photograph, courtesy of the 82nd Airborne Division War Memorial Museum*

Wounded troopers from the 504th RCT aboard a ship after being evacuated from the Anzio beachhead. *U.S. Army photograph, courtesy of the 82nd Airborne Division War Memorial Museum*

Nineteen of the twenty-six 504th troopers who served as security for the pathfinder teams of the 507th and 508th Parachute Infantry Regiments during the Normandy combat jump were photographed on June 5, 1944. *Courtesy of Dave Berry*

The 1st Battalion, 504th PIR serial passes over the flooded area along the coast of Holland, September 17, 1944. *U.S. Army Air Corps*

The 504th PIR jumps on Drop Zone "O," just north of the Maas River, near Overasselt, Holland, September 17, 1944. *U.S. Army Air Corps*

The 376th Parachute Field Artillery Battalion drops on DZ "N," September 17, 1944. *Photograph by Stanley Weinberg, courtesy of Ann Weinberg*

An aerial view of the Grave Bridge across the Maas River and the ancient town of Grave, with the old walled fortifications. The concrete pillbox and flak tower guarding the southern approach can be seen along the left side of the road as it curves toward the bridge. *Photograph by British RAF 541 Squadron, courtesy of Frits Janssen*

An aerial view of the Heumen lock bridge (Bridge Number 7) across the Maas-Waal Canal. *U.S. Army photograph, courtesy of the Cornelius Ryan Collection, Alden Library, Ohio University*

The drawbridge and control house on the man-made island of the Heumen lock bridge, captured intact by Company B after a fight that lasted into the night. *Photograph courtesy of the Cornelius Ryan Collection, Alden Library, Ohio University*

The 504th PIR objectives on the north side of the Waal River, the railroad bridge (lower center) and the highway bridge (lower right). Fort Hof van Holland can be seen in the left center of the photo. The dike road from which much of the German direct fire emanated runs from the upper left of the photo to the south side of Fort Hof Van Holland and under the railroad and highway bridges. *Photograph by British RAF 541 Squadron, courtesy of Frits Janssen*

The 376th Parachute Field Artillery Battalion broke up an attack by eleven enemy tanks as gliders landed on LZ "N," September 18, 1944. *U.S. Army photograph, courtesy of the Cornelius Ryan Collection, Alden Library, Ohio University*

One of the courageous 504th troopers who was killed in action during the Waal River assault crossing, September 20, 1944. *Courtesy of the Cornelius Ryan Collection, Alden Library, Ohio University*

This German 75mm antitank gun positioned between the railroad and highway bridges north of the Waal River had a clear field of fire on any vehicles that crossed the bridges. The 3rd Battalion, 504th PIR, took out this antitank gun during its attack west to capture the highway bridge. *Courtesy of Jerry Huth*

The Germans used concrete blocks as a roadblock on the ramp at the north end of the highway bridge. German antitank guns covered the opening. Two German wooden flak towers are visible above the concrete blocks. *Courtesy of the Cornelius Ryan Collection, Alden Library, Ohio University*

Captain Carl Kappel, commanding Company H, attended a briefing for officers that afternoon. He listened with the skepticism of a veteran to "the usual old-men-too-weak-to-pull-the-trigger and ulcer battalion stories. I remember the colonel [Reuben Tucker] giving us the rundown on what we could expect, then looking up at us and saying, 'And don't you believe a word of it.' "[49]

Captain Kappel felt confident that the regiment could carry out its assigned mission. "The regiment at this time was probably at the peak of its fighting efficiency. For the first time since the invasion of Sicily it was able to have an extended period of time for rest and relaxation in congenial surroundings, and an opportunity to train and fit replacements into the organization prior to combat. Morale, always high, was of the best. All units were slightly overstrength.

"Assuming H Company was typical . . . About fifteen percent were original members of the company, two-time unit citation winners; seventy-five percent were combat experienced; and about ten percent replacements, but were combat experienced during the latter days of Anzio. Five of the officers had been company commanders, and three had handled more than one company in heavy action. All were ready for action and anxious for airborne action. Approximately four percent had Allied decorations, ninety-five percent had Purple Hearts, and all had Combat Infantry Badges."[50]

At the briefing, Captain Kappel and the other assembled company and battalion commanders learned the specifics of the 504th's mission and the missions of every company in the regiment. "Bridges 7 and 8, across the Maas-Waal Canal, at Malden and Heumen, the highway bridge at Grave, and the division area west of the Maas-Waal Canal were assigned to the 504 Parachute Infantry. The 504 Parachute Infantry assigned Bridge 7 and 8 to the 1st Battalion; Bridge 11 at Grave to the 2nd Battalion. The 3rd Battalion was to clear all enemy movement on the Grave-Nijmegen highway and be prepared to assist the 1st and 2nd Battalions, or both.

"One enemy battalion was known to be in Grave and one battalion was believed to be protecting the bridges across the Maas-Waal Canal. The 3rd Battalion plan of attack was to drop east of Overasselt on Drop Zone 'O,' and reorganize and assemble in the nearby wooded area in SOP [standard operating procedure] perimeter assembly; Battalion Command Post in the center, Headquarters Company three hundred yards north, G Company three hundred yards south, I Company three hundred yards east, and H Company three hundred yards west.

"G Company was to block all enemy movement on the Grave-Nijmegen highway with roadblocks at Lunen and Alverna. I Company was to clear the enemy from their portion of the battalion sector from East Wijchensche Ven, establish roadblocks at Diervoort, and contact 1st Battalion in the vicinity of Diervoort. H Company was to eliminate all enemy resistance in the drop zone, screen the assembly of the battalion, establish roadblocks at Mary's Hoeve, and become the battalion reserve upon movement of G and I Companies to their assigned sector.

"The plans were detailed and thorough, as they must be in an airborne operation. Everything must be right the first time. As soon as a unit is committed it must be able to take care of any contingency that might arise. It is too late then to go back for anything that might have been overlooked."[51]

The 2nd Battalion was assigned the mission of capturing the top-priority Grave bridge. Captain Walter S. VanPoyck, the commander of Company E, was a veteran of Sicily, Salerno, and Anzio. "I had a strong premonition I wasn't going to make it back. My battalion was given the mission of dropping one rifle company [south] of the Maas [River], in the vicinity of the town of Grave to secure the southern end of the Grave bridge and to establish a roadblock on the road south of Grave leading to Eindhoven. The remainder of the regiment was to drop east of the Maas.

"Our battalion commander, [Major] Ed Wellems, called us three rifle company commanders together, and we drew lots for the mission. I lost, and my company, Easy, was tapped for the job. On the surface, it looked like a very sticky one.

"After the Sicily and Salerno night drops, I personally welcomed a daytime jump. I knew we'd be more vulnerable to ground fire, but I felt the control and assembly advantages in daytime outweighed this. My basic fear was that of jumping too late, landing in the Maas, or too close to the bridge to allow mobility of deployment for our two-fold mission.

"My men hoped this would be our last mission. I never personally felt that the war could end by winter."[52]

Private Hubert A. Wolfe, with Company B, had gone through the same preparations for the previous jumps that had been canceled, so "we still didn't know whether we were going to jump or not. They had set up a big tent with big tables down the middle of it, with maps all over the tables. They had us all go through there and check it and try to put it to memory."[53]

Private First Class Thurman I. Clark, a glider trooper who had been a member of D Battery, 376th, since it was organized, was assigned to antitank protection for the battalion. "We had four .50-caliber machine guns with anti-aircraft mounts. Individual soldiers were armed with .30-caliber carbines, and there were some bazookas for anti-tank protection. We did not take the 57mm guns to Holland. We were using only the bazookas. George Pringle and I were assigned as bazooka men in our platoon.

"Before the Holland invasion we were sealed in at the airport in England for two days and nights. Then our Captain [Richard C.] Barrett told those of us going by glider to return to Hinckley and bring in the vehicles by ship. We went back and got the trucks and jeeps to Portsmouth."[54]

Early the next morning, September 16, Captain Kappel oversaw the Company H preparations for the following day's operation. "Each man was issued a 1:25,000 map of Groesbeek and vicinity; a 1:100,000 map of the Netherlands; a partial pay in Netherlands, Belgium, and German currency; and a Gammon grenade with plastic explosives. As soon as the grenades were fashioned, they were collected and kept in platoon piles. Two K rations and one D-ration were drawn. The basic load of ammunition had been issued prior to arrival at the departure base.

"The remainder of the morning was free for men to write letters, visit Red Cross mobile units, and check personal equipment. The afternoon was spent loading and checking bundle-release mechanisms, [and] loading and tying of bundles. All bundles had been rolled, loaded, and marked in accordance with regimental SOP prior to movement to the departure fields. Generally, individual weapons, including BARs and one-half the total of rocket launchers, were carried in the hands of the individual. Crew-served weapons were dropped in containers.

"The 300 radio was to be carried by the radio operator in a leg bag, with one spare battery. The 536 radios, less batteries, were jumped in the leg pockets of the jumper. The batteries were carried in the same pocket. One set of spare batteries were carried in the field bag (musette bag) of the jumper. Extra batteries for all radios were dropped in the communication bundle.

"Sound-power telephones were carried in the leg pockets. EE8 telephones were carried on the jumper. Each platoon carried one half mile, and company headquarters carried one mile of WD 130 assault wire. In addition, four miles of WD 130 was carried in the communication bundle.

"Motion pictures were held in the evening concurrently with pilot-jump-master conferences, CO meetings, and rehashing of each plan of action. The succession of command with the battalions and companies was published in special orders prior to departure to the airfields."[55]

Private Philip H. Nadler from New Jersey, with Company F, gathered around a sand table with the troopers in his platoon, while his platoon leader, a young lieutenant, conducted the briefing. "With a pointer in his hand he threw back the cover of the sand table and said, 'Men, this is our destination,' and pointed to a sign on the table—'GRAVE.'

"I recall my crack to him. 'Yeah, we know that. But what country are we dropping into?' "[56]

Chapter 8

"Let's Get Across
The Bridge"

In the predawn hours of Sunday, September 17, from airfields all over south-eastern England, 1,094 U.S. and British heavy and medium bombers took off to bomb German flak positions, airfields, and barracks in Holland in preparation for the airborne landings. The deafening roar of bomber engines shook furniture and windows in homes and buildings all over that part of England. The U.S. Eighth Air Force sent 872 B-17 Flying Fortress bombers, escorted by 147 P-51 Mustangs, to hit 117 German targets that lay along the troop-carrier routes. The British dispatched 85 Lancaster, 65 Mosquito, 48 B-25, and 24 A-20 bombers, accompanied by 53 Spitfire fighters to attack German defenses on the coast of Holland and barracks at Nijmegen, Arnhem, and Ede.

Lieutenant Hanz K. Druener was a replacement and new platoon leader with Company D. "I was somewhat anxious, not having been in combat before. However, training with my platoon, which included many troopers and non-commissioned officers who had participated in combat jumps, had the effect of [my] looking forward to the operation. Some of the combat-experienced personnel mentioned that previous combat had been conducted at night. However, they felt that our superior air cover would keep German fighters out of the sky. In addition, they felt that the problem of reassembling would be made much easier during daylight hours."[1]

Just prior to boarding their plane, Private Nicholas W. Mansolillo, with Headquarters Company, 1st Battalion, was approached by his best friend, Private John T. Mullen. Mansolillo listened as "he told me his life would end during the operation. He had a strong premonition that his number was up. A lot of guys say a lot of things at times. In most cases it's just talk, nothing to take serious. But in John's case, the way he talked made you believe it. I felt nothing I could say could change his way of thinking. For deep down inside me, I believed with him."[2]

As they boarded their assigned C-47s, Tucker's paratroopers saw hundreds of airplanes beginning to fill the sky. This would be Company B trooper Private Mike Clements' first combat jump. "Because of our heavy and cumbersome loads, almost all of us needed some help in boarding. This was provided by the crew chief who, along with the pilot and co-pilot, made up the crew of the C-47. After another interminable wait, the engines were started, and we took our place in the long line of C-47s awaiting take-off."[3]

The two pathfinder planes leading the division into Holland lifted off from Chalgrove airfield at 10:25 a.m. and flew a direct course for Holland and DZ "O."

At Cottesmore airfield, forty-five C-47s carrying the 1st Battalion and elements of Headquarters and Headquarters Company began taking off at five-second intervals, climbing to altitude, and vectoring to form up into the nine-plane V-of-V formations, each carrying a company. Private Clements was both excited and anxious as his plane taxied, waiting for its turn. "Take-off began with the familiar roar of the two engines. We began to move slowly down the runway, and I said a special 'Hail Mary,' because take-off in a fully loaded C-47 was always critical. We spent at least an hour finding our place in the huge armada over England before settling on a heading, which would take us to our respective drop zones.

"Every now and then I would peek out the tiny porthole windows. The first thing I saw were P-51 fighters—a lot of them—swerving in and out of the formation."[4]

At the same time, forty-five planes carrying the 3rd Battalion and elements of Headquarters and Headquarters Company were taking off from Spanhoe airfield, followed by another forty-five planes transporting the 2nd Battalion and the remaining elements of Headquarters and Headquarters Company. The plane carrying Corporal Jack L. Bommer, with Headquarters and Headquarters Company, "was only five or six minutes in the air when across from me and behind the men facing me, the emergency hatch sprang open. The force and air pressure was terrific. We thought the two closest men would be sucked out into space. They managed to grab hold of something and secure themselves. There was a seemingly long [intercom] radio conversation between the pilot and crew chief and the rumor spread—we would have to drop out of formation and land back in England. Chatter commenced and thoughts formed as to what we would do. Then, it happened—with a beautiful 'flip' of the tail end of the C-47, the pilot slammed the hatch door down and secure. We continued on course. At this point, mixed emotions became 'really' mixed. The remainder of the trip was made up of cat-naps, reminiscing, thinking both aloud and silently, and just looking."[5]

Nine planes carrying Company C, 307th Airborne Engineer Battalion, took off from Balderton airfield as part of the battalion serial. The last parachute serial, the 376th Parachute Field Artillery Battalion, lifted off from Fulbeck airfield in forty-eight C-47s. As Sergeant Jack Alexander, Jr., with D Battery, sat alone with his thoughts, his plane turned onto the runway, where the pilot applied the brakes and revved the engines. Alexander felt the plane thrust forward as the pilot released the brakes and the C-47 rolled down the runway. "There was a constant loud roar as the plane took off and others moved to the runway. Once airborne, the sound changed into a drone as planes took their positions in the flight and started for Holland."[6]

Flying on a precise timetable, the planes circled as other C-47s joined the formation of V-of-Vs comprising the serials. Each of the division's serials flew a course southeasterly to an assembly point over the city of March in Cambridgeshire. There, the division's serials rendezvoused with the transport planes carrying the British 1st Airborne Division, bound for Arnhem. The 101st Airborne Division flew a more southerly route to their drop zones north of Eindhoven. The massive, one-hundred-mile-long, airborne armada flew low over the green countryside and centuries-old villages of eastern England as the civilians below waved to the troopers. The immensity of the largest airborne operation in history became apparent to most once they were airborne and could see serial upon serial of transport planes and gliders, protected by more than 1,500 fighter escorts and fighter-bombers. The spectacle of more than 4,700 aircraft filling the skies was unforgettable.

The huge armada cleared the coastline of England at Aldeburgh and flew out across the North Sea toward the coast of Holland. As the 3rd Battalion serial approached the flooded areas of the Dutch coast near the Walcheren Islands, German antiaircraft fire rose up to meet it. Underneath one of the planes carrying sixteen troopers from Company H, an equipment bundle was hit by flak and caught fire. The bundle contained Composition C, a highly explosive and flammable substance used for demolition and to make Gammon grenades.

Inside that stricken plane, eighteen-year-old Private George Willoughby, who had lied about his age and had enlisted in the army at age fifteen prior to Pearl Harbor, was jumping number two after his platoon leader and was seated across from the open door of the plane. "I could see out. It was only a short time before I could hear the crack of small-arms fire and see puffs of antiaircraft gunfire.

"Shortly after, the plane started filling with smoke. As I looked across the plane, I noticed Lieutenant [Isidore D.] Rynkiewicz had been hit in the left knee and Hatfield, the BAR man, was hit on the back of his hand. To my right, a trooper was on the floor of the plane. I think it was [Private First Class Everett R.] Rideout.

"I remember saying, 'Let's get the hell out of here' and we started standing up. The air force sergeant dove out the door of the plane. Within seconds, the plane was so full of smoke you could not see anything. Some men near the cockpit of the plane started coughing, and we were pushing for the door.

"At that time, myself and others fell through the floor of the plane. We were hooked up, and when my chute opened, I could smell flesh and see skin hanging from my face and hand. I had released my rifle when the flames burned my hands."[7]

Up ahead in the serial, the 3rd Battalion S-2, Lieutenant Virgil "Hoagie" Carmichael, watched anxiously from the door of his C-47 for signs that the paratroopers on board were able to exit the burning plane. "I counted the chutes as they left the plane and saw that after the camouflaged chutes, one white chute came out, which we figured to be the crew chief. Immediately after the white chute left the plane, the plane nose-dived over and apparently at full throttle, at about a forty-five degree angle, plowed into the water, which flooded the land below. Upon impact, a white chute billowed out through the front of the plane."[8]

The troopers owed their lives to the courageous pilot and crew of the C-47. Captain Bohannon of the 34th Squadron, 315th Troop Carrier Group, piloted the plane that crashed. Lieutenants Felber and Martinson and Sergeants Epperson and Carter also died.

Badly burned, Private Willoughby looked for any dry area below on which to land. "I looked down and saw that there was only a small strip of land along the road that was not flooded. I started working my chute to land near the road. When I landed, I rolled over and pulled my .45-caliber pistol from its holster, and pointed it in the direction of a man near me. He put up his hands and shouted, 'Hollander.' I realized he was friendly, so I put my pistol back in the holster, got out of my chute, and crossed the road to see if I could help any of the other men that had landed in the water.

"I saw [Private Donald F.] Woodstock had landed in water about waist deep. As he walked in the direction of the bank where I was standing, he stepped off into a deep trench about four to six feet wide that was around the flooded area. He came up shouting a few choice words, and I helped him to dry land. We took off our packs and placed them behind a small house that was empty. Then we started checking on the others. Everyone had done a good job landing on dry land or near the edge of the flooded area.

"We assembled in the small house. Lieutenant Rynkiewicz and Hatfield were in the house next door. The air force sergeant and others went upstairs to keep a lookout for Germans, while the Dutch people took care of our burns. Both of my hands and my face were wrapped with gauze, and I looked like a mummy. I could only see out of my right eye. I held my hands up along my chest because it was painful when they were lowered to my side.

"It wasn't long before a truck came down the road with some German soldiers in it. They stopped between the house that Rynkiewicz and Hatfield were in and the house we were in. They dismounted and some came in the direction of our house. One of the Germans threw a potato-masher type grenade at the window. It bounced off and [shrapnel] struck the one in charge in the leg. He jumped around like he had a broken foot. Someone waved a white piece of cloth out the window, and we were taken out of the house. We were loaded on the truck and driven to a small town, where we were herded into a building and questioned by a German officer. I was hurting so bad I moved to the side of the room and lay down on the floor. It was getting late in the afternoon by the time the questioning was over. We were loaded onto an old, school-type bus and traveled all night, arriving in Utrecht [Holland] the following day."[9]

The only troopers from Lieutenant Rynkiewicz's stick to escape were Everett Rideout and Private First Class Walter P. Leginski, who were hidden by the Dutch Underground.

Company H platoon leader Lieutenant Jim Megellas, who had witnessed the tragic loss decided to take no chances. "I gave the order 'Stand up and hook up' to my stick, and we stood hooked up, ready to go for almost forty-five minutes prior to the actual jump. The purpose of this command, of course, was to have the stick on the ready should the plane be hit. This period of forty-five minutes was a long, agonizing wait for my stick."[10]

Private First Class Landon M. Chilcutt's Company B stick did the same. "When we hit the coast of Holland, the flak began, and twenty minutes before we jumped, we stood up and hooked up as a [pre]caution."[11]

As the 3rd Battalion serial crossed the Dutch countryside, Sergeant Albert A. Tarbell with Company H, saw one of his best friends very nearly die from enemy antiaircraft fire. "We were carrying on a conversation with 1st Sergeant Michael Kogut, who was seated directly across from us, and the next instant he was lying on his back in the middle of the aisle with a funny expression on his face and wondering how he got there.

"A bullet had come through the seat and on into his chute, missing him, but the impact threw him to the floor. A few seconds later we reached our DZ, and he jumped with the chute."[12]

The leading serial, carrying the 3rd Battalion, approached DZ "O" just north of the Maas River. Captain Arthur W. Ferguson, the executive officer, stood in the door of his plane, carrying part of the 3rd Battalion staff. "The Maas River, Grave-Nijmegen bridge, and the city of Grave came into view. The pilot throttled down, the wind screeched and tingled against my face as I looked down and out, every nerve crying out for action. Passing over the river and the dike, [I saw] purple smoke rising up from the drop zone (a signal from the pathfinder group who had preceded us by twenty minutes). [I was] looking back into the plane and signaling the troopers, who were now hooked up and ready to go, that we were right on target. Large, round, black balls of smoke appeared with ear-splitting explosions around the plane. The green light flashed on—'Go!' I yelled toward the men, at the same turning and stepping into space. A feeling of relief came over me—everything going according to plan."[13]

Private Paul A. Mullan was jumping third on board one of the nine planes carrying Company G. "As we got near the drop zone, we ran into more flak. It sounded like throwing gravel on a tin roof. We were getting lower. Lieutenant [Charles A.] Drew was standing in the door. He stepped back and said to Hoff [Sergeant Henry C. Hoffman], 'If I get hit, push me out or drag me out of the way, and don't jump until you get the green light. And if he gets hit (he looked at me), you know what to do.'

"I said, 'Yes sir.'

"We were almost ready to go, when I hit Hoff. He looked back and I said, 'Hoff, I'm scared.'

"He said, 'You'll be okay when you get in the air.' "[14]

As Corporal Earl S. Oldfather, with Company G, shuffled toward the door, he "had to release the bundles because I was in the middle of the stick. Thinking about doing that at the right time kept my mind off of the jumping. I released the bundles O.K. and landed right beside them."[15]

Most of the paratroopers landed on the flat, soft, freshly plowed Dutch farmland. However, Company G trooper, Sergeant John R. Duncan, sustained one of the few jump-related injuries. "We landed in an apple orchard near Grave. My chute went into a tree, swinging me into a gully, and I landed on one leg, then my back and head. Later [I] learned I had a fractured ankle, torn ligaments in one knee, and a fracture of pelvic bones."[16]

Not wanting to risk losing or damaging Company G's SCR-300 radio in an equipment bundle, Technician Fifth Grade Stanley S. Stencel jumped with the behemoth radio strapped to his leg.

As his parachute opened, Lieutenant Louis A. Hauptfleisch, the regimental S-1, could see the buildings below. "I unfortunately landed on top of a building in the village of Overasselt. I crashed through the tiled roof top and suffered leg injuries as a result."[17]

Upon landing, Lieutenant Colonel Warren Williams, the regimental executive officer, observed the civilians coming out of Overasselt to the drop zone. "The Dutch civilians were delighted to see the Americans. They formed work parties to help us assemble and move equipment from our supply bundles and resupply drops. The house next door to the 504 command post was converted into a temporary hospital, and Dutch women assembled voluntarily to help care for the casualties.

"Approximately four hours after the drop, two Dutch women came into the CP with soup and boiled eggs for the staff. They stated although they did not have much to provide, they were sure that we didn't have time to cook lunch and they did not want us to go hungry."[18]

As the serial carrying the 1st Battalion approached DZ "O," Staff Sergeant Frank L. Dietrich, the jumpmaster of his Company C stick, stood in the door looking ahead for the drop zone. "The green light came on, and Pierson, a replacement with no previous combat, hit me on the shoulder and yelled, 'The green light's on, the green light's on!' He continued to hit my shoulder and yell until we reached the proper spot and I jumped. My arm was so sore I could hardly raise it later on."[19]

Private Mike Clements, with Company B, was making his first combat jump. "Almost without warning, the familiar commands began. I didn't know we were that close to the drop zone, but we pulled ourselves up and began checking our equipment. Normally, when the plane was on its final heading to the drop zone, it would slow down and begin losing altitude. Instead, we seemed to be increasing speed and the plane was pitching and yawing. It was becoming very difficult to keep from falling. In fact, the plane was taking evasive action and was still searching for a heading which would take us to the proper drop zone. Finally, the last command but one was given, 'Stand in the door.'

"We shuffled forward, anxious as always, once the commands began, to get out of the airplane. I was carrying my rifle [strapped under the bellyband of the parachute] at port arms and I wanted to make sure not to get it caught in the door. 'Go!'

"Stumbling, lurching, trying desperately to stay close to the jumper immediately ahead of me, I finally reached the door and dived out. I realized immediately, with the opening shock, that I had jumped at the highest speed and lowest altitude ever. I swung under the canopy maybe twice before I hit the ground. Fortunately, it was a plowed sugar beet field, and it only took seconds for me to realize that all my limbs were intact."[20]

As he exited the plane, Company B trooper Private Hubert Wolfe could see "all of the C-47s coming in, the sky was almost black in some areas. At the drop zone, we were coming in very low—we were 440 feet off the ground. It was useless to even carry a gasmask or a reserve chute. We [had] left them in the plane."[21]

Private First Class Landon M. Chilcutt, with Company B, "came in backwards and landed in a tree. I was straddled [over] a limb, so I had to get out of my gear. If I had landed six inches on the right of the limb, I would have been singing soprano."[22]

Private Nicholas W. Mansolillo, with the 81mm Mortar Platoon, Headquarters Company, 1st Battalion, was jumping number sixteen and concerned with landing in one of the canals or rivers. "Remembering past experiences of the Sicily jump . . . I started to make some plans in preparation for a water landing. I thought of leaving some of my gear behind in the plane, but it seemed that I needed everything. Under the conditions and circumstances, I came to one conclusion: I would take off my reserve, leave it in the plane, and mention it to no one, for if word got to our mortar officer, who was sitting by the jump door, he would order me to leave it on regardless of what my plans were.

"The warning light flashed on, and the order came down to stand up and hook up, and check equipment. As each man checked each other's gear, I put my plan to work. For now, it was only a matter of moments before the green light would flash and send us on our way. With 'sixteen OK' sounded, I made my move. In a flash, off came my reserve; I grabbed my static line hook. No sooner had I done that, the green light flashed, we started our move for the door. My scheme had worked. It was too late now for anyone to change my plans.

"As I headed for Dutch soil, my reserve was headed back to England. We made a good landing–our entire stick landed on solid, dry land a good distance from the river. I was sure happy and relieved it happened this way, for I sure had my doubts about making a river landing. It sure had me worried."[23]

One of the few tragedies of the jump occurred when an equipment bundle struck and killed Private Max D. Edmondson, with Company A.

A couple of minutes following the 1st Battalion jump, the 2nd Battalion serial approached, with only D, F, and Headquarters Companies jumping on DZ "O." Company E had the special mission of attacking the southern end of the Grave bridge and would jump south of the Maas River. This was Company D platoon leader Lieutenant Hanz Druener's first day in combat. "After jumping out of my aircraft, I landed in a field and next to a cow, which kept sniffing me while I was trying to get out of my chute. As I was trying to get out of my chute, I looked skyward and saw a C-47 hit by enemy antiaircraft fire and burst into flames before the paratroopers could get out."[24]

Captain Victor W. Campana, the commanding officer of Company D, also witnessed the stricken plane crash. "On the way to battalion assembly, I observed a C-47 hit by antiaircraft fire flying even and level with the right wing on fire and then slowly go into a final spin with two or three men falling out. I did not see chutes open."[25]

As he landed, Company F trooper Private Philip Nadler badly sprained his ankle. "My boot heel was torn off, and the leather lace had broken across each set of [eyelet] holes, except the top two sets."[26]

The 2nd Battalion serial was placed last in the 504th drop to prevent any errors associated with the Company E drop south of the Maas River and the Grave bridge. For that reason, Company E was the last nine-plane V-of-V of the 2nd Battalion serial. Captain Walter S. VanPoyck, commanding Company E, had just one concern about the jump: "My basic fear was that of jumping too late, landing in the Maas, or too close to the bridge to allow mobility of deployment for our two-fold mission."[27]

Lieutenant John S. Thompson was the commanding officer of the 3rd Platoon of Company E. "My plane, which was on the extreme right of the V-of-Vs, started to idle its motors as we neared our DZ south of Velp. When the green light came on, with everyone in readiness to jump, I noticed that we were directly over a group of buildings and decided to wait a few seconds and jump on a field just southwest of the Grave bridge, which I could plainly see a short distance away. The remaining eight planes jumped on the prescribed signal. As we flew on, the town of Grave could be plainly seen with its high walls surrounding the buildings. Several vehicles were moving north along the highway towards the bridge.

"Then, out we went! The bridge was directly to our front. The jump was without incident, although spasmodic firing could be heard from the town. Assembly of men and equipment was accomplished quickly, although two of the men had landed in a drainage canal and had quite a hard time getting out.

"Radio contact with the company was immediately tried, but we could not get through. Seeing that we were very close to the bridge and that this was our primary mission, I sent a messenger back to where the company was assembling and told Captain VanPoyck that we were proceeding toward the bridge."[28]

Meanwhile, VanPoyck was getting his company assembled and attending to one of his men. "When we jumped, [Private First Class Curtis C.] Morris suffered a malfunction—a streamer. He was alive when I got to him. Dutch farmers came out to assist him, as we had to move forward.

"Shortly after the drop, we were pinned down in a ditch, under fire from the town of Grave. A young Dutchman emerged from the farmhouse directly behind us carrying two pails of milk, which he proceeded to dole out in spite of the fire."[29]

The seventh serial, consisting of Companies B, C, and D, 307th Airborne Engineer Battalion, jumped at DZ "N" at 1:21 p.m. Private First Class Harold G. Herbert was a BAR gunner with Company C. "All of the flak was taking place—we were anxious to get out of the plane. When the green light came on, we were out, and it wasn't too long before we hit the ground. I don't know exactly what altitude we jumped at, but it wasn't as high as we usually jumped. We got together pretty fast on the ground."[30]

As Herbert and the other engineers were assembling, the Dutch civilians "brought out ice-cold milk out to us to drink. They were good people. They wanted to do anything they could for us."[31]

As the 376th Parachute Field Artillery Battalion serial approached DZ "N" less than twenty minutes later, Lieutenant Robert Hutton, with B Battery, saw the green light flash on. "The crew chief tried to jump us early, and I refused as we were not at the drop zone yet. Our sand table briefing was perfect, as I recognized the drop zone as soon as we reached it."[32]

When the planes carrying Corporal Theodore C. Johnson's Baker Battery "reached our drop zone, we had difficulty pushing out a big door load that had to go before we jumped. We finally got it out, and then we went out. My chute opened, and I was on the ground. The C-47 must have lost altitude because of our problem with the door load.

"We were darting all over looking for our 75s, which were scattered. We were experiencing airbursts and small-arms fire. I cannot remember how long it took to find and assemble our 75s, but it was done before nightfall. We dug ourselves in and lined our holes with parachutes, which helped keep us warm. I woke, lifted my head, and drew small-arms fire. Also, right on the edge of my hole was a shiny artillery shell half imbedded in the ground. It was either a dud or an armor-piercing shell. I got out of there in a hurry. Shortly afterwards, we were pinned down by heavy shelling."[33]

Private First Class Pat A. Fusaro, with Battery A, was almost killed on the jump when "another trooper landed on my parachute and collapsed it."[34] When his parachute canopy collapsed, Fusaro hurtled to the ground. "First thing I felt was pain in my back—I had a broken tailbone—pain from my back down both legs to my feet. It took me a bit longer to catch up with my outfit."[35]

Corporal Clayton Blankenship was a D Battery squad leader of a .50-caliber machine gun squad and jumpmaster of his plane. "I was the first man out after I rolled a machine gun out. The rest followed. My personal landing was OK, but I was afraid [of] getting hit before I reached the ground. We were not very high and got down quickly. Those pilots deserve a lot of praise flying us in. They are a class bunch of guys. I had jumpmaster training, so I guess that is why I went first. The last one out was our officer in charge, Lieutenant Alphonse J. Czekanski."[36]

Lieutenant Czekanski was the executive officer of D Battery. "One of the equipment bundles hit me in the back and dislocated my left shoulder, I could not use my left arm and I landed with very little control, thereby breaking both legs. I had hit a barn, but I did not break my legs until I bounced off the barn and hit the ground. After being wounded in Holland, I was put on a stretcher by two of my aid men, and they took me to a house in Groesbeek, where I stayed for two days. One of the medics was [Private First Class John B.] Chavez and he was the first man to come to my aid. A woman of about fifty years gave me a glass of water and a drink of Dutch gin."[37]

Private Walter A. Barbour, with Headquarters Battery, 376th, "was one of the last men to leave the plane at the Groesbeek drop zone. The plane I was in was hit seconds before I made my exit. I have never been sure how many got out of the plane. The time was about 1:00 p.m. Our drop zone was under small-arms fire and machine gun fire from the forest at the edge of the field. After the fire was silenced, I proceeded into Groesbeek, joining up with Major Robert Neptune, our executive officer, and [Private First Class] Frank Habyan and the rest of our liaison team."[38]

Lieutenant Robert A. Lally and others with Headquarters Battery "assembled at the perimeter of the drop zone. Colonel Griffith was brought in on an ammunition cart. We set up temporary headquarters and started establishing communications with the batteries, forward observer teams, and the 504th Parachute Infantry Regiment. There was small-arms fire going on outside the perimeter of the drop zone, but we received none. We then proceeded to this big house, where we set up headquarters, including an aid station, the fire-direction center, and the communications center."[39]

Corporal Arthur A. Fransosi, with Headquarters Battery, landed without incident. "My lieutenant and myself went to get our equipment pack, which was a few hundred yards from us, and went by a trooper lying on the ground who had hurt himself on landing. We told him we'd send a medic back, and he said, 'Just roll me on my stomach and I'll crawl.' "[40]

AFTER OVERSHOOTING THE DROP ZONE AND LANDING CLOSER to the Grave bridge than the remainder of E Company, Lieutenant John Thompson immediately set out with the men he had to capture it before the Germans could destroy it. "We started out working our way down various canals, wading in water up to our necks. By this time, firing from the town and various buildings around us had increased considerably, and there was now fire coming from a camouflaged flak-tower on the southern approach to the bridge. As we neared the bridge, we could see German soldiers running to and from a power plant, which was fifty yards due west of the bridge. These men made several trips to the power plant, carrying something in their arms. We waited until their third trip and then raked the ground between the bridge and the power plant with machine gun fire."[41]

The balance of Company E, under the command of Captain Walter Van-Poyck, assembled almost a mile southwest of the bridge. After landing, Lieutenant Carl Mauro helped get the men assembled and ready to move out. "I was Lieutenant [Patrick C.] Collins' assistant platoon leader at this time. We were the 1st Platoon. I got my men to join him and the rest of our platoon. Lieutenants William Sharp, Jr., and James 'Arky' Nelson had the 2nd Platoon ready. Lieutenant John H. Murphy [, Jr.] when he returned from the hospital (he had been wounded and hospitalized in Italy) became Jocko's assistant platoon leader (taking my place, which I held since March when I joined the 504 at Anzio) was at the head of the 3rd Platoon, less the men who were at the bridge with Jocko. VanPoyck and Lieutenant Hanford A. Files, his company executive officer, organized the company headquarters. We were ready to go. Van put Collins in the lead because of his experience. I followed him, being somewhere in the middle of our platoon. The remainder of Company E followed us in company formation and columns of four at double-time (a fast trot). I couldn't see the bridge but was positive Collins knew [where it was] and would lead us there. Captain VanPoyck knew, because he had consulted his map and gave orders where to go; but he remained near the rear of the company, leading company headquarters and where he could see most of his men who were running in front of him.

"In spite of our heavy loads, we were making good time. Fortunately, we didn't have a great distance to run, and in about twenty minutes or so, I would guess, we reached a juncture in the road near a small apple orchard."[42]

At the road junction, Lieutenant Collins halted the 1st Platoon. His platoon sergeant was Staff Sergeant Alek Misseres. "Lieutenant Collins wanted to see the best approach to the bridge. At that time, there was a lot of sniper fire coming from the right, probably the outskirts of Grave. Lieutenant Collins saw a ditch leading [north] from this point to a small canal. This ditch was partially filled with water, and they waded right through it to the canal (this was the 1st Squad only). The 2nd Squad went through some high weeds on the flat ground [to the left] and got pinned down there. The 2nd Squad began to work its way into the ditch. Lieutenant Collins went over to the ditch to try to stop the 1st Squad until the rest of the company caught up. The 1st Squad had gone too far for him to catch them.

"The 2nd Squad got into the ditch and the 1st Squad, under Sergeant Arley Staley, sent back a runner, Private [Louis H.] Tuthill, who met Lieutenant Collins in the ditch. The whole company, minus the 1st Squad and Lieutenant Thompson [and his stick], was strung out behind Lieutenant Collins at 1430 [hours].

"The 1st Squad, led by Sergeant [O.] Staley, began to meet machine gun and rifle fire at the junction of the canal and the ditch. Sergeant Staley set up his machine gun at the junction and returned the fire. The Germans were firing from the right, from the buildings outside Grave. "[43]

There was an embankment about three feet high and three feet thick which separated the north end of the ditch and the canal, which ran perpendicular to the ditch. Staff Sergeant Misseres, in the lead with the 1st Squad, decided to conduct a reconnaissance to find a covered route north of the canal toward the bridge area. He crawled over the embankment and into the canal as bullets passed a few inches over his head and struck the ground to his right. The water in the canal was three to six feet deep, and the current flowed about one and a half miles an hour toward the closed end of the canal to the left. Misseres waded across the canal and ordered Private John M. Lawler, armed with a BAR, and two other troopers to cross the embankment and cross to the north side of the canal to cover the approach to the front. Misseres then waded down the canal to the left for about seventy-five to a hundred yards, where he found a route toward the bridge—a ditch which began about seventy-five yards north of the canal. He hollered back to Private Lawler to bring up the rest of the 1st Squad to join him. With Sergeant Misseres in the lead, the squad crawled across the open ground from the canal to the ditch, which contained about three to six inches of water.

Meanwhile, the 2nd Squad moved up the ditch south of the canal, with Private Tuthill in the lead, followed by Lieutenant Collins. When Tuthill crawled over the embankment at the end of the ditch and into the canal, a German opened fire on him with a machine pistol from the east, but missed. Three Germans armed with machine pistols and a machine gun crew, now alerted that others would probably be crawling over the embankment, opened fire on Lieutenant Collins as he followed Tuthill over the embankment and into the canal. Collins waded about twenty yards to the left as Private William A. Maney crossed the embankment and joined Collins in the canal. Next, Corporal Taylor Isaacs jumped over the embankment and into the canal, but halted there as the canal was getting crowded. Private Tuthill, up ahead in the canal, saw the rear of the 1st Squad and crawled out of the canal and across the open ground to join the rear of the 1st Squad, where he passed the word up the single-file column for the squad to halt.

After waiting about five minutes, Sergeant Misseres called back to ask if it was OK to proceed and received no answer. He then checked on the twelve troopers and had them check their weapons to make sure they were not fouled by mud and water. Including Misseres, the squad had a light machine gun, a BAR, ten M1 rifles, and a Thompson submachine gun. The 1st Squad had still not suffered any casualties. Receiving no further instructions, Sergeant Misseres decided to continue moving up the ditch toward the bridge.

Meanwhile, the rest of the 2nd Battalion had landed on or near DZ "O" north of the Maas River, about a mile from the Grave bridge. Company F, followed by Company D, moved along a road that ran from Overasselt roughly parallel to the river and intersected the Grave-Nijmegen road just north of the bridge.

Lieutenant Martin E. Middleton, the platoon leader of the 1st Platoon of Company F, led a combat patrol of thirty-five men ahead of the main body with orders to secure the north end of the bridge. Middleton and his men used cover as much as possible to get close to the approach to the bridge. Along the way, they picked up nine prisoners and encountered some fire from a 20mm antiaircraft gun, which they silenced when Private First Class Artie M. Bledsoe hit a house with a bazooka round in the direction from which the fire was coming.

Colonel Tucker was moving with the 2nd Battalion as it approached the bridge. "[We] met snipers along the way, from houses along the route. The Germans at the end of the bridge were in a flak-tower built here. This had about a platoon of Germans, and on the northeast bank two more 20mm emplacements manned by Germans. Also, [we] met 20mm fire as we got up to the bridge; fire was coming from the south side, from four 20mm emplacements. . . . There was fire coming from the edges of Grave—machine gun, 20mm, and small arms.

"Advanced elements reached the bridge at approximately 1345, and the main part of the 2nd Battalion got there about 1430. . . .

"There was a hell of a time picking up snipers, especially one hidden in a barn and firing out the door. Couldn't pick up the smoke of his shot or anything."[44]

The majority of Company F arrived near the north approach to the bridge, where Captain Beverly T. Richardson led them up the dike and they engaged German 20mm antiaircraft guns positioned between the dike and the river. These guns were firing up at anyone who appeared on the dike or near the bridge ramp.

Private Philip Nadler, with Company F, had twisted his foot on landing and was limping badly as he climbed the dike wall. "We got up on the dike, on the lip of it, and were firing down at the Krauts between the river and the dike. I had practically no view of the bridge from where I was. In fact, I had practically no view of anything. I know my fire at the Krauts between the river and the dike wasn't too effective. You had to crawl part way on the road running along the dike to get a decent shot, and I wasn't too anxious to poke my head up too high."[45]

A light machine gun team set up near Private Nadler on the dike. The machine gunner lay on the dike and poured .30-caliber fire down on the Germans dug in on the flood plain between the dike and the river. Nadler looked over at the machine gunner, who was "firing away, when a bullet hit him, I think, in the left shoulder and went horizontally down his body and out his right buttock. I wondered how the hell they were ever going to evacuate the guy. He was in pretty bad pain."[46]

Nadler began to work his way down the backside of the dike toward the bridge as the battle continued. "The fight lasted two to three hours."[47]

Thompson had the only force close to the bridge on the south side of the Maas River. "As we worked our way along the canal, we were surprised to see two large trucks coming down the highway from Grave towards the bridge. My leading scout fired at the leading truck, killing the driver. The truck careened off the road with the German soldiers scrambling to get out. The second truck stopped, and the soldiers in it jumped out and deployed themselves along the opposite side of the highway. By this time, my men had taken up the firing at these Germans. It was evident that these Germans were endeavoring to escape rather than to engage us. But it was unfortunate that we had deprived them of their transportation. They had taken up firing at us by now, but at the same time they were withdrawing one by one in an easterly direction along the southern bank of the river. We continued to work our way along toward the bridge, and we now approached the flak-tower, which was very well camouflaged and fortified. Firing from this flak-tower still continued, but the fire was now going over my men's heads. My bazooka man [Private Robert McGraw] worked his way into range and fired three rounds, two going through the slits at the top of the tower. The gun then ceased firing. We were by now very close to the bridge. I sent seven men around the left to reconnoiter the area and the power plant and then work their way over to the bridge. When we overran the power plant, we found four dead German soldiers and one wounded. All they had been carrying was their personal equipment and blankets. I took the remaining seven men and worked my way over to the highway on the right. All communication wires were cut leading across the bridge and a roadblock was set up on the southern approach."[48]

Sergeant Roy E. Tidd then led those seven men against the other flak-tower. When they got close enough, Tidd rushed the tower ahead of his men, as the Germans concentrated machine gun fire from several directions on him. He single-handedly captured the second flak-tower, killing one of the crew and wounding the other three.

On the northern side, Lieutenant John E. Schaeffer, with Company D, took the ten men with him, moved around the right flank of Company F, and engaged the dug-in German positions around the bridge. They moved west across the Grave-Nijmegen road and then worked their way across open ground to a point west of the northern approach.

Schaeffer then charged a machine gun nest protected by two riflemen who poured fire at him as he came directly at them. Coming to within a few yards of the German positions, he opened fire and wounded several of them, capturing all six. He then waved his men forward to guard the prisoners.

While Thompson's men fired a 20mm antiaircraft gun from one of the captured flak-towers across the river at the Germans manning the flak-tower on the north side, Schaeffer assaulted it. Upon reaching it, he found one German dead, and he captured two others. He climbed to the top of the tower, where he noticed that Germans were setting up a mortar in a field. He then turned the newly captured 20mm gun on the German mortar crew. Lieutenant Schaeffer's actions opened the way for D and F Companies to reach the northern end of the bridge, and he was later awarded the Silver Star for his heroism.

As Private Nadler arrived at the northern bridge approach, he noticed one of his fellow Company F troopers, Private Henry D. Covello, get up and run ahead of the others onto the bridge. Nadler couldn't believe what he was seeing. "He was standing there, waving his rifle back and forth. He'd been firing, because I could see the smoke coming out of the barrel.

"'Come on!' he shouted. 'Let's go! Let's get across the bridge!'

"It seemed to me there was still some firing going on across the bridge and in the town itself. I wasn't going to cross any bridge. I figured some idiot with a plunger might be lurking around somewhere, just waiting for his chance. I stayed put. Covello was shouting to come, on and finally my platoon leader shouted to Covello, 'Get down, you damned fool, before you're killed!' "[49]

As Thompson and his troopers consolidated their hold on the southern approach to the bridge, Sergeant Misseres and the 1st Squad, 1st Platoon, of Company E came to the end of the ditch, where it formed a junction with a trail. There, Misseres saw men in the vicinity of the flak-tower on the south side of the bridge, but couldn't determine whether they were friendly or enemy. Misseres then noticed another ditch, which led in the general direction of the bridge. They moved into the ditch, with Misseres in the lead, followed by Private Lawler with his BAR, and the light machine gun. The squad came to a large hedge running north-south, so they spread out along the west side of the hedge. Staff Sergeant Misseres left the squad and ran across the open ground and found Lieutenant Thompson and his troopers. Misseres called back to the 1st Squad leader, Sergeant Staley, to bring up the squad to the power plant, where they joined forces with Thompson's stick.

Back in the canal to the south, Lieutenant Collins ordered the 2nd Squad to stay where they were while he made a reconnaissance. He then waded in the deep water to the left for about fifty yards. He saw the open ground to the north, now under fire from machine guns, and believed the company would suffer too many casualties if it crossed the open ground. He passed the word back to withdraw back down the ditch to the road junction. However, Captain VanPoyck countermanded this order, and the 2nd Squad remained in the ditch.

The three troopers in the canal were drawing a lot of long-range automatic weapons fire. Corporal Taylor Isaacs, in the canal just north of the ditch, crawled over the embankment and told the 2nd Squad leader, Sergeant Robert Lemery, and the 1st Platoon's mortar squad leader, Sergeant Alton G. Machost, about the fire they were receiving in the canal. Lemery and Machost set up the 2nd Squad machine gun about ten yards behind the junction of the ditch and the canal, and opened fire on the church steeple in Grave and the base of a windmill from which German machine gun fire was coming. This suppressed the fire temporarily, allowing Private William Maney to crawl out of the canal and across the open ground toward the south end of the ditch.

Now, Lieutenant Collins was alone in the canal and receiving fire, which forced him to go underwater. When he came up for air, the enemy would open fire on him again. Collins was now too exhausted to get out of the canal.

Back down the ditch, Lieutenant Carl Mauro saw Private Maney approaching. "He said, 'Lieutenant Collins is in trouble, and he ordered me to get my ass out of there before I got killed.'

"Sergeant Machost and his squad were at the crest of the embankment peeking over the road and directing fire across the river and also towards Grave. With this fire-cover, I left the ditch and moved in the direction from which Maney had come.

"I had to cross the open ground for about sixty yards. I did this on my stomach, using my knees and elbows to propel my body forward, as we were taught to do in basic training.

"Still lying on my stomach, I came to the edge of a deeper channel, which was a canal. There was Lieutenant Collins up to his armpits in water. 'Get the hell out of here!' He yelled at me. 'You'll get killed!' I saw and heard evidence of weapons fire from somewhere popping all around him and me, too, I guess. I was oblivious to it.

"I said, 'I'm not leaving here without you!' The banks were steep and slippery. He was fatigued. He couldn't get a foothold or grab anything to pull himself out, nor did he seem to have the determination to do so—a very unusual attitude for such an exemplary, courageous soldier.

"Collins had been wounded in Italy and hospitalized before he joined E Company again in England. Shortly before this Holland mission, he had broken his arm on a night practice jump in England and was hospitalized again. He insisted on rejoining E Company and the 504 for the airborne mission: he came out of the hospital to do it; he wasn't going to stay behind in England. He was already in frail condition before the jump. The twenty-minute run to the road junction near the apple orchard which he led, and his immediate aggressive approaching action in attacking the bridge had to completely fatigue him. Collins was too exhausted to work himself out.

"I didn't know it, but Sergeant Machost was only a minute or so behind me. I was glad to see him when he crawled up to me. I asked Collins to hold out his M1 rifle so we could reach it. He did so. While on our bellies, because we didn't dare to even get to our knees, the sergeant and I pulled on the rifle until we could grab Collins by the arms and drag him out of that swirling pool of water.

"Collins was a stout 220-pound, six foot five cowboy-turned-paratrooper. Now, he was inert and absolutely exhausted and offered little assistance. He was dead weight as Sergeant Machost on one side of him and I on the other—all of us on our bellies, knowing we were targets of enemy fire—dragged Lieutenant Collins and his M1 rifle, inch-by-inch across sixty yards of soft, level ground."[50] Lieutenant Mauro and Sergeant Machost and the exhausted Lieutenant Collins eventually reached the safety of the ditch, where other Easy Company troopers had been firing to provide cover for them.

With Thompson's men in control of the southern approach, Lieutenant Martin Middleton, on the other side of the river, led Company F across the bridge, moving double time in single file across on the right side of the bridge road. Bullets whipped through the air, buzzing like swarms of bees as they ran. Private First Class Leo Hart fully expected it to be blown at any moment. "The bridge was all metal. Bullets were ricocheting everywhere off of that old thing."[51]

They reached the south side without any serious casualties, where they made contact with Thompson and his men. Just as they got back to the ditch with Lieutenant Collins, Lieutenant Mauro saw a green flare go up near the southern end of the bridge. "It was our prearranged signal that the bridge was now under American control. When we saw the flare just above our heads, we all were relieved and cheered lustily."[52]

As Thompson was discussing the situation with the Company F officers, he heard the sound of fast-approaching vehicles. "We were surprised to see two automobiles tearing down the highway towards the bridge from the vicinity of Grave. As they neared the bridge, my BAR man could not resist the temptation and fired directly through the windshield of the leading vehicle, killing the driver. The second man in the vehicle tried to escape by running over the embankment, but only got half way. The second vehicle tried to turn around and head back toward Grave, but did not succeed. Three Germans were killed in this vehicle. The remainder of E Company in the meantime had started working their way down toward the proposed site of the roadblock south of Grave. There was plenty of firing coming from that direction.

"With the bridge well in our hands, it was the mission of D Company to pass over the bridge and send heavy patrols into the town of Grave. I was to follow D Company into the town to give them any help that they might need, and after the town was taken, I was to proceed on to where my company CP was located. D Company proceeded into the outskirts of Grave, where they ran into heavy machine gun and mortar fire. These positions were overrun, and D Company was split into three large patrols to enter the town from different directions. Darkness was now falling, and there was only small-arms fire coming from the center of Grave. I was given the mission of setting up a defensive position on the southern outskirts of Grave, straddling the main highway leading into the town."[53]

Captain VanPoyck led Company E south to establish a roadblock a thousand yards south of Grave at De Elft, at a junction of the main highway and a dike road. The platoon sergeant of the 2nd Platoon, Staff Sergeant John G. Branca, Jr., helped to get the main roadblock defenses organized. "Demolition men (six) were attached to the 2nd Platoon from Headquarters Company, 2nd Battalion, under the leadership of Sergeant [Juliust.] Maneth [Jr.,] and they set up a roadblock of sixteen mines, the bazooka section (three) under Sergeant Augustine V. Coppola. Lieutenant John H. Murphy, Jr. assistant platoon leader of the 3rd Platoon, organized the roadblock defenses on the left side of the road.

"Before putting in the roadblock at De Elft, a German officer and non-com in a motorcycle came up the road from Grave, attempting to go through De Elft and were fired on by Private John W. McGarrah and Staff Sergeant Coppola with their Tommy guns. Both Germans were killed. The roadblock was then established.

"Captain VanPoyck ordered the 2nd Platoon to move to the east side of the road along the dike and set up defenses for the night. Lieutenant [James H.]

Nelson and Lieutenant [William E.] Sharp took the 1st Squad across the road. At the end of the dike, they saw a large concrete block, but they didn't know whether it might be a blockhouse, pillbox, or what. Lieutenant Nelson took Private First Class Lyman D. Brainard, bazooka man, and Private First Class Paul A. Kunde on the north side of the dike, ready to blast the concrete block. Lieutenant Sharp took Corporal Jack E. Abrams, assistant squad leader, 2nd Squad, along the south side of the dike to close in on the block. About halfway between the east end of the dike and the road, Lieutenant Sharp found and cut a communications wire, which was running from north to south and probably connected the German garrison at Grave. They found the block to be a pillbox, but undefended."[54]

Just before dusk, Captain VanPoyck heard a tank approaching. "Our mission provided for our relief at the roadblock by British armor moving north on the Eindhoven road. Simultaneously, one of my men shouted, 'Hold your fire, it's a Limey.' The tank was covered with camouflage netting and branches, with the commander standing in the open hatch. I casually walked toward him, to our great relief. Simultaneously, as he realized I wasn't German, I realized he wasn't British. He fired a cannon round at me, which passed close to me and shattered a tree at my right rear."[55]

As the tank opened fire, Captain VanPoyck jumped into a nearby ditch as the German tank commander "reversed his tank, spraying our positions with machine gun fire. [Privates First Class Lyman Brainard and Paul A. Kunde] snapped off two bazooka rounds; one missed, one hit and caromed off without detonating. He successfully escaped around the bend of the road."[56]

The tank fire wounded twelve enlisted men. Lieutenant John Murphy, Jr., "was wounded in the chest and arm and knocked flat to the ground."[57]

Tragically during this brief firefight, Captain VanPoyck saw his executive officer, Lieutenant Hanford A. Files, get hit and mortally wounded. "He was killed just a few feet from me."[58] The death of Lieutenant Files, a great athlete and standout member of the 1942 UCLA rowing team, shocked everyone in the company.

The highest-priority objective for the 82nd Airborne Division, the Grave bridge over the Maas River, had been captured by the 2nd Battalion at a cost of just one killed and fifteen wounded. The objective for the 1st Battalion was the capture of the bridges over the Maas-Waal Canal and establishment of contact with the 508th and 505th Parachute Infantry Regiments. Company A, commanded by Captain Charles W. Duncan, was assigned to a support role. The 1st Platoon was assigned to lay down a base of fire to assist Company C in the mission of capturing Bridge Number 8. The 2nd Platoon had the mission of defending the 1st Battalion command post. The 3rd Platoon was given the assignment of providing fire support for the Company B mission of capturing Bridge Number 7. Upon landing, Captain Duncan sent sixteen troopers under the command of Sergeant Mitchell E. Rech towards Bridge 8, because the 3rd Platoon leader, Lieutenant Robert C. Currier, was rounding up the remainder of the platoon on the drop zone. Duncan sent Lieutenant Robert Wheeler, with eight other 2nd Platoon troopers to Bridge Number 7.

Captain Ernie Milloy, commanding officer of Company C, got his officers and men assembled on the DZ, and together with sixteen additional troopers attached from Headquarters Company, they moved out toward Bridge Number 8, which crossed the Maas-Waal Canal near Blankenberg. Along the way, they picked up a misdropped Company B mortar squad and brought them along.

Speed was the key to capturing the bridge, so Milloy moved his company directly to the bridge via the road. "The company moved out in platoon columns northeast by north along a secondary road until it was within one thousand yards of Bridge 8. At this point, a platoon of Company A, which had landed east of the drop zone, cut across the company's line of march, drawing small-arms fire from the bridge.

"Germans on the road southwest of the bridge were firing. The company moved north two hundred yards and set up mortars and a base of fire. While the 2nd Platoon, under Sergeant William L. Reed, built up a support position, the 1st Platoon was ordered to make a frontal assault on the bridge down the road to Dijk. As the 2nd Platoon put down a base of fire, the 1st Platoon started up and ran into [Capt. Roy E.] Anderson, [the] Headquarters Company commander, and his BAR men pinned down by enemy fire.

"The 1st Platoon moved up faster than expected under fire, and the base of fire was stopped when one of the noncoms reported that the 1st Platoon had reached the woods west of the bridge. As the 1st Platoon reached the woods, I moved forward with the 2nd and 3rd Platoons. As they swung right, the 3rd Platoon was pinned down by sniper and automatic fire. Staff Sergeant Frank Dietrich, 3rd Platoon sergeant, sent word back that the platoon could not move. I crawled up to the 3rd Platoon, then sent word for the 2nd Platoon to move up.

"At 1615 hours, just as Staff Sergeant Fred E. Gonzales, 2nd Platoon sergeant, 2nd Lieutenant Milton L. Baraff, 3rd Platoon leader, and the 2nd Platoon BAR team dashed toward the bridge, the bridge went up in smoke."[59]

With Bridge Number 8 blown, the capture intact of Bridge Number 7 took on critical importance. Company B, commanded by Captain Thomas B. Helgeson, was assigned Bridge 7, the southernmost bridge, where it crossed the Maas-Waal Canal at one of the locks, due east of the Grave bridge. Captain Helgeson got his men assembled quickly and set out for the bridge, along with an attached light machine gun section from Headquarters Company. The 3rd Platoon led the way, with two scouts, Privates First Class Harris V. Duke and Herman C. Wagner, about a hundred yards to the front. The 2nd Platoon followed, then the 1st Platoon, and company headquarters. Each platoon had flank guards deployed to the right and left. Captain Helgeson chose the most direct route to the bridge. "We traveled along a paved road due east, with a ditch of about two by two feet on each side of the road. The route was interspersed with dense apple orchards."[60]

About three hundred yards from the bridge, apple orchards lined both sides of the road, providing some cover to within about one hundred fifty yards. The ground rose slightly the last one hundred yards before the bridge, making the bridge itself about twenty feet higher than the surrounding terrain. The ground to the left of the road approaching the bridge was elevated about three feet, and the ground to the right of the road dropped off, providing defilade all the way to the dike and the bridge.

As the 3rd Platoon approached to within one hundred yards of the bridge, the fifty or so Germans guarding the bridge opened fire with rifles and machine pistols. Private Hubert Wolfe, who had broken his foot on the jump, was limping badly as well as carrying the added weight of his BAR and ammunition. "We came down the road, and a house and barn were off to the left. There was enough of a ditch there that when they started firing we had a little cover we could get into that. I jumped into the ditch."[61]

One of Captain Helgeson's NCOs didn't make it to the ditch. "Sergeant Lawrence [F.] Blazina was killed on the road. Machine gun fire was coming from a house on the island, cutting branches of trees on the road. Technician Fifth Grade [Raymond G.] Larabee and Private First Class Ralph W. Jetton [both with Headquarters Company, 1st Battalion] fired four bazooka rounds at the house, but none went off. They fired four rifle grenades (two smoke, two HE). The HE exploded, but the smoke did not."[62]

Private Wolfe set up his BAR and opened up on the Germans in the house on the island. "I had one guy with me as an ammo carrier. They [the rest of the platoon] were all moving out along that ditch. It was a two-story house, and there were Krauts upstairs. Every once in a while, this one Kraut would peek out of a corner where the curtains were and fire off a few rounds at us. I don't know that he ever hit anybody. Every time I saw the curtain move, I would run a clip through that BAR—I had twenty rounds. I think I did hit him."[63]

Captain Helgeson watched the lead elements of Company B begin to close in on the bridge, despite the intense fire. "Initially, Lieutenant William Meerman, 3rd Platoon, had his men closest to the bridge, about one hundred yards away on the left side of the road. Lieutenant Meerman was pinned down behind the elevated ground to the left side of the road and protected against machine gun and rifle fire coming from the bridge and the island. This elevated ground had a row of barbed wire [about three feet high], which ran from the road for about five hundred yards along the canal bank.

"The ground dips down on the right side of the road. The 2nd Platoon, led by [Lieutenants Maurice Marcus and Harry Cummings], got into this depression. A group of eight men led by Lieutenant Marcus and Corporal [Charles

E. "Butch"] Nau, with Lieutenant Cummings met no opposition and went on to the dike and placed a light machine gun at the point where the barbed wire began at the dike. The machine gun manned by Pritchard, [Private Charles] Piazza, and [Sergeant] Shelton W. Dustin covered the bridge. A second machine gun was set up midway between the barbed wire juncture with the dike and the road along the dike, also covering the bridge.

"Lieutenant Marcus decided to get across the bridge. Marcus, Cummings, and eight men did so at about 1500 [hours]. Lieutenant Marcus gave the signal to move, and the machine gun at the juncture of the dike and the barbed wire fence opened fire. The men crossed the dike, which was about five meters high, [and] ran across the sloping ground in defilade, firing as they went, at the house and the bridge.

"While Lieutenant Marcus and the others were going across the defilade, I ordered twenty-six men of the 1st Platoon to the top of the dike. where they occupied German-dug holes. The purpose was to build up a base of fire to cover the crossing. All men fired at the crossroads beyond the bridge and down the road. They had three BARs besides the machine guns already set up. Lieutenant Richard A. Smith was in charge of the 1st Platoon and had Corporal Francis J. Cleary as runner.

"At the same time, I ordered one squad of the 3rd Platoon, under Lieutenant Meerman on the other side of the road, to move forward as far as possible and build up a base of fire. One machine gun was placed about ten yards from the road on the elevation, firing at the house on the island. [Meerman] also put one BAR about twenty-five yards from the road around the curve of the elevation to fire the same mission. Another light machine gun was put at the edge of the orchard under Private First Class Clark M. Comin, Jr., to fire on the same mission.

"I ordered Lieutenant Henry C. Dunavant, executive officer, to move his two mortars behind the houses on the right of the road and fire on the house on the island. The mortar observer, Private Lee [W.] Cox, went to the junction of the road and the dike and directed mortar fire. They fired about twelve rounds, which pinned down the enemy."[64]

Knowing that it could be blown at any moment, Lieutenant Marcus and his men stormed the bridge. From his position, Captain Helgeson saw them reach a flight of concrete steps that led from their cover behind the dike up to the bridge. "Lieutenant Marcus, Lieutenant Cummings, and Corporal Nau got to the steps, then the corporal went up the steps, ran across the bridge."[65]

Corporal "Butch" Nau led the assault force forward, firing as he ran across the bridge. The Germans concentrated their automatic weapons fire on Nau as he came toward them, the bullets cutting his jump suit. Corporal Nau overpowered six German guards, quickly killing or wounding them before they could blow the bridge.

The remaining Germans on the bridge took refuge in the control house on the manmade island that lay in the center of the lock bridge. Captain Helgeson watched Nau cross, and "when he got halfway over, Lieutenant Marcus started across. When Nau reached the end of the bridge, Lieutenant Cummings started across. There was fire on them all the time, but they didn't know the direction from which it came.

"Technician Fourth Grade Onie A. Burnett, radio operator, started across, and he and Lieutenant Cummings caught up with Marcus. Just as Burnett caught up he was hit in the neck. Burnett then handed the radio to Marcus and ran back across the bridge. He was hit at the other end of the bridge, this time fatally.

"Lieutenant Marcus turned left to get to a sand pile on the northeast side of the road and was seriously wounded, falling in front of the pile, pinned down. The ground here again, was in defilade. Nau was in a hole in this corner.

"Sergeant Jerry M. Murphy and two men attempted to cross the bridge by running across, but Murphy was killed at the far end of the bridge. The other two men were not wounded—[Private Ernest R.] Farmer and [Private First Class Joseph A.] Eggrie. The Germans seemed to be picking off officers and noncoms. Lieutenant Hewitt also ran across. Sergeant [James R.] Lowe, with the 2nd Platoon, attempted to cross and was pinned down midway, but dashed on over after awhile.

"In the meantime, six men from the 3rd Platoon, under Lieutenant Meerman and Sergeant Dustin, got across the dike and built up a base of fire along the road leading to the bridge and covering the island enemy positions."[66]

As this was occurring, Privates Louis Costa and Elmer C. Pankow, with Headquarters Company's regimental demolition platoon, believing that the Germans in the control house might blow the bridge at any moment, decided they had to act immediately to prevent the destruction of the bridge. Costa and Pankow, attached to Company B, with the mission of removing all demolitions found on the bridge, saw that they could not cross the bridge, which was still under fire from the Germans in the control house. Privates Costa and Pankow noticed a half-sunken rowboat on the near bank of the canal and took off for it. As they did, enemy machine gun and rifle fire opened up on them. Costa and Pankow got into the boat and began rowing across the canal while under fire from the far bank. Upon reaching the far side of the canal, they climbed up through the girders of the bridge to the demolitions, where they quickly cut the wires leading to the charges and removed the blasting caps from the explosives. After they finished, they came down the girders to the rowboat and began rowing back to the near bank. As they did, enemy fire sank the boat, forcing them to swim the remaining distance.

From his position, Captain Helgeson observed Lieutenant Meerman and

Sergeant Dustin leading an attack on the control house at about 1700 hours. "They, with nine men, moved across the road behind the powerhouse, intending to assault the positions. They got around the corner of the powerhouse and met heavy fire from the enemy positions, so they retired behind the powerhouse again.

"There were three men across the bridge. At 1630 to 1700, Lieutenant [Richard A.] Smith took across a boatload of six men and a medic. They were fired at during the crossing, but no casualties were suffered. There were then eleven men on the far side, and they were pinned down at the crossroads beyond the bridge."[67]

Upon reaching the far side in the boat, Private First Class Robert D. Stern spotted the badly wounded Lieutenant Marcus, still lying on the sand pile. "When [Private Nelson F.] Hudson and I went out there to help him, I told Hud stay back, 'It's too hot out here.' So I went out on my hands and knees and I asked Marcus, 'Where are you hit?' And I don't know if he told me or not; anyway he was hurting, so I took his first aid kit off his helmet and gave him a shot of morphine. About that time, [Private Fred] Grainger, our medic, came out. I told him to stay back.

"And he came out anyway—and I remember this very clearly—he kneeled down a little on one knee and with the same motion took his helmet off. He [said,] 'Where are you hit, sir?' A shot rang out and he was shot right through the head, killing him instantly. And he fell sort of on Marcus, so I got down and I lay on my stomach. The only thing that was keeping [me] from getting any closer to the ground was my zipper. Every time I moved, I got shot at. So I laid still and didn't move. And every once in a while they'd take a pot shot, and the sand would hit me in the side, and when they missed me, they put more bullets in Grainger. We were there it seemed like all night; it must have been afternoon and getting toward dusk."[68]

At about 6:00 p.m., Captain Helgeson sent an eight-man patrol "under Sergeant [John W.] Kellogg to the houses on the west side of the canal on the north side of the bridge. The patrol got there, occupied the houses, and fired on the island.

"Lieutenant Meerman and Sergeant Dustin with nine men waited until 1930 (dusk) for the attack. The German positions were fired on by rifle fire. The men were in defilade and in the darkness and weeds, so there was little return fire. They came out from behind the powerhouse on its right hand side and moved into a skirmish line. They infiltrated west along the bank so they could throw grenades into the German positions. Private Edward Schultz fired rifle grenades at German positions while other men moved and took a German machine gun position.

"Sergeant Dustin threw a Gammon grenade through a window into the house and another at a German who came up from a nearby dugout. He called on those in the dugout to surrender—there were two officers and ten or twelve noncoms, plus five civilians in the dugout.

"A young boy in civilian clothes came out and said the officers and noncoms were afraid to come out, lest they be shot. Sergeant Dustin went down after them and got one officer who could speak English to call on his men in the house and other positions further north to surrender. He did, and they came out with their hands up. They got between thirty-five and forty prisoners. It was then about 2300. One man, [Private Edward J.] Schutt, was killed. There were no wounded. Six killed and one wounded for the whole operation."[69]

Shortly after dark, Private First Class Robert Stern decided it was safe enough to evacuate the wounded Lieutenant Marcus. "[Private Nelson] Hudson or [Private First Class John T.] Hogan, [Jr.]—I don't know which one it was—we got Marcus and dragged him back across the road down in the ditch, and then there were others that were down there [who] put him in a rubber boat and took him back across the canal."[70]

For their extraordinary heroism in the capture of the first bridge across the Maas-Waal Canal, Corporal Charles Nau was promoted to sergeant, and he and Sergeant Shelton Dustin were both awarded the Distinguished Service Cross. Privates Louis Costa and Elmer Pankow received promotions to private first class and were awarded the Bronze Star for heroism in disabling the demolitions on the girders of the bridge. With the capture of the Grave bridge and the Heumen lock bridge, the 504th had secured the vital bridges that would allow the British XXX Corps to advance to Nijmegen once they reached the southern edge of the 82nd Airborne Division's area of operations.

That night, Private Mike Clements' Company B squad took up positions east of Bridge 7 to defend the approaches against a possible enemy counterattack. "[Private Carmine S.] Iaquinto and I and the rest of the squad were told to dig in front of the dike. Instead, following Iaquinto's lead, we dug in on top of the dike, which was about twelve feet tall. This time we dug a two-man hole so that we could take turns sleeping during the night. We had just finished digging when our platoon leader showed up to check our positions. 'You don't have a flat field of fire,' he said. 'You will have to re-dig that hole in front of the dike.' Then he left. Of course, he was right. He was pointing out that if attacked, we would be firing down at our targets, instead of straight across. It took us another hour to dig a new hole, and by this time, it was quite dark. In front of us was a broad, flat field with many interlocking barbed wire fences. I opened up a can of rations when I realized that I hadn't eaten since the day before. Since I was very tired, but not sleepy, I took the first watch (two hours) so that 'Ikey' could sleep. We would then alternate sleeping and watching all night long. So, with my rifle cocked, fully loaded, and the safety 'off,' I waited for the attack, and waited, and waited. I did this all night long, even when I was supposed to be sleeping."[71]

Chapter 9

"Somebody Has Come Up With A Real Nightmare"

Upon landing, the 3rd Battalion cleared the area in and around DZ "O." The battalion then pushed north and west, establishing strong roadblocks on the Grave-Nijmegen road, and forming a perimeter from the Maas River at Neder Asselt extending roughly parallel to the Grave-Nijmegen road, which was within the perimeter.

Company G, with 132 men and eight officers, together with an attached section of machine guns from Headquarters Company, 3rd Battalion, and three attached medics, moved out in column formation to the northwest, with the mission of establishing roadblocks on the highway between Grave and Alverna, a secondary road to the west of the highway, and one near Eindscheestraat. The company encountered sniper and small-arms fire, but otherwise had no significant opposition.

After landing, the Company H commander, Captain Carl Kappel, and his planeload moved out to the 3rd Battalion assembly area. "The group was fired on several times, but the enemy would immediately withdraw on a run. Many empty uniforms were found at positions, indicating the local defense forces were intent on escaping by mingling with the civilian population. At the company portion of the battalion assembly area, all sticks were assembled and reports were being compiled. (The SOP for H Company was that each jumpmaster have one copy of the plane-loading manifest, with name, rank, and serial number of each jumper. In addition, each platoon leader carried copies of his platoon manifest, and company copies were carried by the company commander, executive officer, and first sergeant. Upon assembly, the jumpmaster of each aircraft forwarded one copy, with appropriate notations, to headquarters section. These copies were the basis for the morning report.)"[1]

After checking in with the battalion, Captain Kappel moved out with his men to establish roadblocks at Mary's Hoeve on the road that ran from the

Grave-Nijmegen highway to Overasselt. There, Kappel received word that the 2nd Battalion had captured the Grave bridge. "At 1700 hours, H Company moved forward to block any movement from Eindschestraat, and along the Grave-Nijmegen road. The 2nd Platoon was responsible for Nederasselt and the area to the [Maas] river; the 3rd Platoon was responsible for the area from Nederasselt to the Grave-Nijmegen road; the 1st Platoon forming the perimeter rear. The area was occupied without incident."[2]

Upon landing, Company I, commanded by Captain T. Moffatt Burriss, moved out toward the company's objectives. The 1st Platoon dispatched a patrol to the north, where it captured four Germans and set up a block on the road from Bridge Number 9 at Diervoort. The company observed approximately seventy-five Germans defending Bridge Number 9 and spotted a flak-wagon to the north of the Wijchensche Ven lake, but encountered no enemy south of the lake.

Private First Class Leo Muri and his Company I squad's objective was a hospital. "As soon as we assembled, we headed for a hospital which we had been shown on a map. We were to take this hospital—which we were in doubt as to whether or not it was a hospital—and get all the transportation we could get ahold of. We cut all communication wires, found out the hospital had been burned, picked up a civilian car—the only one we could find—and went to find the rest of our company. This all happened just three hours after the jump. So now Francie [Private Francis Keefe] and myself were in a field trying to milk a cow (he didn't know how to milk either). But we managed to get our helmets full and [the milk] was very refreshing."[3]

AFTER LANDING, LIEUTENANT ROBERT ZOST, a forward observer with Battery A, and others collected the equipment bundles. "Shortly after landing, Lieutenant Hugh [W.] Wylie and I were on a small road. It was a dirt road or hard gravel, retrieving our equipment that was dropped separately. I was engaged in gathering some maps that were rolled up in an empty cartridge (75mm) case, and Lieutenant Wylie was on the other side of the road, about ten feet from me. He was loading 75mm shells on a cart, pulled by a single horse. The cart had only two wheels. I vaguely remember the farmer or owner of this horse and cart was in front of the horse, possible that he was just holding the horse steadily; at any rate, giving an air of cooperation. Everything at this particular time was at a frantic pace; we had always been trained to race against time. The goal was to assemble the guns and get into firing position.

"I heard a muffled explosion and snapped my head around to see Lieutenant Wylie whirl and scream. He flung himself face down into the ditch beside the road. I rushed over to him, rolled him over, face up, and knew instantly that one of his hand grenades that was carried in the right side pocket of his jacket had exploded. His jacket and lower clothing almost tore off [during the explosion], exposing a sight so horribly startling, gruesome, and appalling, that it is indelible in my mind. He screamed at me 'Shoot me, shoot me.' I knew that he knew what had happened in the last few seconds of his life. I tore open a first aid kit and injected a morphine tube. The morphine came in a small tube, much like a miniature toothpaste tube. It was about one and a half inches long, the needle was built in the end, and you simply uncovered the needle, inserted, and squeezed the tube. However, I was having trouble finding a clear area in his upper arm, and the clear morphine was running out of another wound, so I quickly injected a second dose. This entire ordeal lasted probably thirty seconds; his eyes closed, his face turned white, and he died. I covered his face with part of his shredded jacket.

"I AND I ALONE, WAS WITH HIM WHEN HE DIED. I admired Hugh Wylie immensely. I was really in awe of him. He stood tall and straight. He one day informed me that he graduated from the University of Ohio and was the cadet colonel of the ROTC. He treated me as his equal, and I, at the time, a high school drop-out. He loved cars and talked a lot of his '38 Chevrolet."[4]

Lieutenant Gorman S. Oswell, with Headquarters Battery, "was the grave registration officer for the 376th Parachute Field Artillery Battalion. With regard to the deaths of Lieutenant Hugh Wylie and Private Herbert [W.] Smith, both were accidental. One, that of Lieutenant Wylie, was very foolish and the other, that of Private Smith, a pity.

"While still in England as a part of our preparation for the invasion of Holland, we were issued two hand grenades. Most of us simply taped them to the D-rings on our parachutes or pack harness. Lieutenant Wylie, however, for some reason unknown, taped his with a fragile paper tape, pulled the pins, and placed his grenades in the side leg pockets of his jump suit. These live grenades survived the flight over and the opening shock and descent to the ground, but when Lieutenant Wylie hit the ground, he apparently tumbled and rolled. In any event, the tape on the grenade . . . in his right pocket broke. The cap blew off and the grenade exploded, tearing away the right side of his body from the chest down. He died instantly. As I was the grave registration officer, in addition to my other duties, I was called to the scene. Needless to say, I was somewhat nervous about Lieutenant Wylie pulling the pins in England and the fact only one grenade had exploded. I gingerly poked around and found the second grenade. The tape was intact, but sure enough there was no pin. I found an open area, broke the tape, threw the grenade, ducked, and it exploded harmlessly. By the way, a friendly Dutch farmer with a horse and wagon helped me load and transport the body to the burial site.

"Private Smith, unfortunately, was walking down the center of the landing zone, oblivious to the fact that a silent resupply glider was making a landing behind him. Since the glider pilot had no way of warning Private Smith, and since he was committed to the landing and could not swerve without jeopardizing his load of personnel and/or equipment, he continued his landing. Private Smith was hit on the back of his head by the glider wing and also died instantly."[5]

After landing, Captain Frank Boyd, with Headquarters Battery, 376th, made his way to the predetermined location of the battalion command post. "Lieutenant Colonel Wilbur Griffith actually broke a foot on the jump. Father van Heuvel had brought him in to his command post. I was present when Captain [John R.] Mickley put a 'walking' cast on it. For that first day, at least, the colonel traveled about the battalion in a wheelbarrow, borrowed from some Dutchman. We all thought it was funny and the colonel enjoyed it, too.

"The 376th seldom operated more than one aid station, but for some of the days we were in Holland, I believe we had two. We did have two doctors. Most battalions had only one. They were Captain Henry C. White and Captain John R. Mickley. I remember that at one time when we had two aid stations (D+2 or 3) the one Captain Mickley was operating [was] in a farm house, a place called Knapheide."[6]

After getting their 75mm howitzer set up and ready to fire, Corporal Roy Pack and his C Battery, 376th, gun crew set to work building a bunker in the woods near Groesbeek. "The bunker was roomy and would sleep four of us. It took a couple of days to dig the bunker. We then cut logs to cover the hole. The whole thing was then covered with dirt and brush."[7]

Meanwhile, the 376th command liaison officer, Captain Frank Boyd, checked the systems required for the battalion to operate. The operations of an artillery battalion were extremely complex, and any mistake could cost the lives of the infantrymen it supported. Boyd worked with each battery to register the battalion's guns. "BP was base point, the initial point of registration in a target area, usually some prominent terrain feature. ChP or CP was checkpoint. We usually had several in areas where we did much firing. They were registration points like a base point but scattered over the target area. We used them for reference in identifying new targets. The fire direction center had the data (elevation and deflection settings) used to hit the checkpoints and a forward observer might locate a target by telling FDC, 'From check point four to right 800, add 400.' Those were yards. Add meant increase the range by 400 yards.' To decrease range he said, 'Drop.' The 301, 302,' et cetera are concentration numbers. 301 was probably the first one fired in Holland. If a target reappeared at the same place, the forward observer had only to say, 'Repeat concentration 301.'

"FDC was the firing direction center. 'A 345' meant that the 'A' Channel on the battery's [radio] set was on frequency 345, the battalion command frequency. 'B 303' meant that 'B' channel was on the 303 frequency. It is used for radio messages within the battery. 'B 295' was division artillery frequency for communication with 376th and the other three artillery battalions. SCR-694 was the battalion command set (more powerful) for communications with Division Artillery. 'B 275' was the frequency of air observation with both battalion headquarters and FDC. 'B 330' was the liaison net with the LNO's to the three 504th battalions. Battery forward observers operated on the same frequencies as their batteries. Lieutenant Roy also was FO [forward observer] for C Battery, Zost and Dunn for A Battery, and Lieutenant Powers for B Battery. D Battery had no forward observers."[8]

ON THE EVENING OF SEPTEMBER 17, Private First Class Willard M. Strunk, with Headquarters and Headquarters Company, was sitting in his slit trench when Private First Class Ted Bachenheimer approached, riding a bicycle. "Bachenheimer [had] returned from Nijmegen, where he had attacked the Germans at the railway bridge on his own. He said he needed two men who could ride a bike. Because there were no men in the platoon who could ride a bicycle, I, a farmboy from Kansas who had never ridden a bike before, volunteered. [Private First Class William] Bill Zeller and I went to Nijmegen with Ted. And after the first shot from a sniper, I became the best biker in the whole country. Ted took us to the headquarters of the Underground in a transformer factory. At their request, Ted took charge over there."[9]

From September 17 to 20, Bachenheimer and the two other troopers operated in Nijmegen in the very midst of a couple of thousand German troops. Bachenheimer skillfully directed the efforts of the Underground to gather intelligence regarding enemy strength and their positions and get that information to elements of the 82nd Airborne Division. Bachenheimer personally led many of the patrols during that period.

BY MIDNIGHT, THE DIVISION HAD ACHIEVED almost all of its objectives while suffering few casualties. The 504th had captured the Grave bridge and Bridge Number 7 over the Maas-Waal Canal intact, providing a land route for British forces to link up with the division, in the most critical missions of September 17. It had also established a perimeter to the northwest across the Grave-Nijmegen road. The 505th Parachute Infantry Regiment had cleared Groesbeek and the high ground to the west; established a defensive perimeter from the Gennep-Nijmegen road near Riethorst to Horst, to defend against attacks from the Reichswald; and had cleared the Landing Zone "N" for the next day's glider landings. The 508th had captured the high ground at Berg-en-Dal, established a perimeter that ran north from Kamp to Wyler, Germany, cleared Landing Zone "T" for glider landings the following day, and had driven to within a few hundred yards of the Nijmegen highway bridge. Of all of the major objectives, only the capture of the Nijmegen bridges over the Waal River remained, and there was optimism that this objective too would fall in the morning.

At the Champion command post that evening, General Gavin received situation reports regarding the day's action. "During the night all three parachute regiments reported they had the situation well in hand."[10]

THE MORNING OF SEPTEMBER 18, CAPTAIN WALTER VANPOYCK, commanding Easy Company, met with the farmers who had taken care of Private First Class Curtis Morris, who had suffered a streamer during the jump the previous day. "The farmers delivered his body to us in a casket, draped in his chute and covered with flowers. Morris had died without regaining consciousness."[11]

VanPoyck and some of his headquarters personnel went into Grave, where "the local Boy Scouts conducted a short parade to the town hall, escorting several female collaborators, whose heads had been shaven and marked in pitch with a swastika."[12]

Later that morning, the citizens of Grave and the local farmers congregated at VanPoyck's roadblock on the highway south of town. "So many Dutch civilians offered to help us, we couldn't handle all requests. We supplied them with German arms, and they patrolled constantly, bringing back valuable information and rounding up prisoners. All this precluded patrol activity on our part, to a great extent. One Dutch lad, about sixteen, joined us rather permanently, and we outfitted him as best we could. He was a constant inspiration."[13]

That same day, Lieutenant Harry H. Price and a couple of troopers with his Company I platoon "patrolled further north to Nijmegen, contacting the 508th, which was fighting for Bridge Number 10. Due to the fact that we had such a small patrol, we came back to our original position and reported to the battalion commander [Major Julian Cook].

Later that afternoon, Company A was sent north to defend Bridge Number 10, with the 1st Platoon defending the east side and the other two platoons defending the west side.

During the afternoon, gliders carrying the division's artillery and antitank units arrived at landing zones east of the Maas-Waal Canal, and 131 Eighth Air Force B-24 Liberator bombers dropped 258 tons of supplies from an altitude of three hundred feet. Captain VanPoyck marveled as the "Dutch people scrupulously collected all bundles and chutes and delivered them to us in a school courtyard, not taking one item for themselves. We issued rations to those obviously in need, but they did not request them."[14]

The following morning, September 19, Sergeant Earl Oldfather was on guard with six other Company G troopers in the town square of Wijchen. "A Hollander with an American jumpsuit on stopped and asked to see an officer. I took him to Lieutenant [Charles A.] Drew [2nd Platoon leader]. He wanted some of us to go with him to pick up some pro-Nazi. So, six of us went with him. We rode in a Terraplane driven by the lord mayor of Overasselt. The Holland paratrooper rode on a motorcycle taken from another pro-Nazi. The guy we

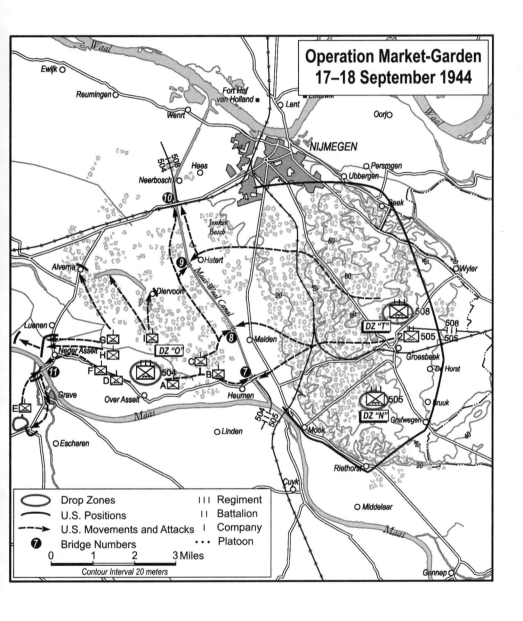

Operation Market-Garden
17–18 September 1944

Legend:
- Drop Zones
- U.S. Positions
- U.S. Movements and Attacks
- Bridge Numbers
- ||| Regiment
- || Battalion
- | Company
- ••• Platoon

0   1   2   3 Miles

Contour Interval 20 meters

picked up was a lord mayor, put in by the Nazis. He was sitting at his desk when we walked in—an elderly man. We found papers showing he belonged to the Nationalist Socialist Party. He had a young daughter who cried when we took him away. The people put up the Holland flag and sang their national anthem—quite a touching scene. We went to another village and picked up seven or eight more pro-Nazis. We put them in a fire truck. It broke down, so we pulled it with the Terraplane, then it stopped. While the Terraplane was being fixed, we were taken to a house and fed sandwiches, headcheese, eggs, ham, and all the milk we could drink. We got back to Wijchen just in time to move out into a woods and dig in."[15]

At about 9:30 a.m. the same morning, Captain Fred Thomas received word "from battalion that the first British armored car preceding General Dempsey's tanks crossed the Grave bridge. A little later, they passed our company CP."[16]

Lieutenant James "Maggie" Megellas, a platoon leader with Company H, watched the British column pass through his company's sector. "For at least twenty-four hours, British armor crossed the bridge, bumper to bumper. I had never seen such a display of strength or force, nor had I realized so much armor existed on our side. It was indeed an awesome display of might."[17]

It was critical that British ground forces link up with the British 1st Airborne Division, as German forces were pressuring them greatly in the Arnhem area.

That afternoon, the 2nd Battalion, 505th, attached to the British Grenadier Guards Regiment of the Guards Armoured Division, made a two-pronged thrust into Nijmegen to capture the two huge bridges across the Waal River. The British commander halted the attacks on the southern approaches of both bridges in order to clean out the German forces defending the area between the two bridges before making the final assault on the bridges.

General Gavin knew that quick and bold action was required to capture both bridges before the Germans could reinforce the defenses or demolish the bridges. He therefore proposed to General Brian Horrocks, the commander of the British XXX Corps, a daring plan to make an assault crossing of the Waal River to capture the northern ends of both bridges. Horrocks agreed to the plan and instructed his staff to have the boats brought up immediately. Gavin wanted to make the crossing in the predawn darkness of September 20, but Horrocks couldn't assure him when the boats would arrive, only that they would be brought up as quickly as possible.

On the evening of September 19, Colonel Tucker "was informed by division headquarters that the 504th was to make an assault crossing of the Neder Rhine and to establish a bridgehead on the north end of the road and railroad bridges. I was directed to contact British XXX Corps at General Horrocks' headquarters, where I would meet a British armored commander who would support the 504th crossing with tank fire. The division directive to me said to make the crossing 20 September, establish the bridgehead, and to contact the

British armored [forces]. This was not a written order, but was given to me by [Lieutenant Colonel] Jack Norton, Division G-3.

"At this time, my 2nd Battalion covered the bridge from Grave, plus other crossings, the 1st Battalion was over along the [Maas-Waal] canal, the 3rd Battalion was in a reserve position north of the Grave bridge toward Nijmegen. My CP was in the same general area. I sent an alert to the battalions telling 3rd Battalion they would make the crossing and fan out to the west, well in front of the road bridge. First Battalion was to follow 3rd Battalion to complete the arc of the bridgehead, and the 2nd Battalion, when available, would support the crossing by fire. The C Company, 307th Engineers, would assist with assault boats, which would be delivered at the crossing site."[18]

Later that evening, there was a large meeting at the Champion CP. Assembled were General Gavin, British Generals Browning and Horrocks, officers of the Guards regiments and divisional staff, the 82nd divisional staff, and Colonel Tucker and his regimental staff.

An observer at this meeting, Colonel George Chatterton, commander of the British Glider Pilot Regiment, noted that the British officers were wearing "corduroy trousers, chukka boots, and old school scarves. They seemed relaxed, as though they were discussing an exercise, and I couldn't help contrast them to the Americans present, especially Colonel Tucker, who was wearing a helmet that almost covered his face. His pistol was in a holster under his left arm, and he had a knife strapped to his thigh. Tucker occasionally removed his cigar long enough to spit, and every time he did, faint looks of surprise flickered over the faces of the Guards' officers."[19]

Gavin laid out his very bold plan to the assembled officers. "Speed was essential. There was no time even for a reconnaissance. As I continued to talk, Tucker seemed to be the only man in the room who seemed unfazed. He had made the landing at Anzio and knew what to expect."[20]

Browning was "by now filled with admiration at the daring of the idea."[21] He immediately granted permission to Gavin to proceed with the assault crossing.

Gavin's plan was to launch the boats in the Maas-Waal Canal close to where it empties into the Waal River. This would provide a covered position from which to load the boats and time for the men to become familiar with the boats before they left the canal to cross the river. Gavin wanted to use every artillery piece the division and the British could employ to shell the opposite side of the river, together with direct covering fire from the British tanks and Tucker's 81mm mortars and machine guns to cover the crossing. And finally, Gavin wanted the crossing to be made under the concealment of a heavy smokescreen.

At the conclusion of the conference, Colonel Tucker left and returned to his command post to brief his staff. At 6:00 a.m. the following morning, he ordered Captain Wesley D. "Spike" Harris, the commander of Company C, 307th Airborne Engineer Battalion, to report to the regimental command post.

Tucker informed Harris of the mission and ordered him to take a party to reconnoiter the best place for the crossing.

Harris returned to his command post and briefed his staff. He ordered Lieutenant Michael G. Sabia to contact British engineers to get a demonstration of the assembly of the boats to be used in the crossing. Lieutenant Sabia commandeered a motorcycle and drove south along the highway toward Eindhoven to locate the trucks carrying the boats. Harris ordered Lieutenant John N. Bigler, the 2nd Platoon leader, to brief the company and make boat crew assignments. Harris then set out on the reconnaissance with Lieutenants John Holabird, Thomas McLeod, Patrick Mulloy, and Melvin Ullrich; Staff Sergeants Anthony J. DePolo and Noel Morrison; Corporal James A. Jacobs, and Private Max E. Albert. They moved to the Dutch Underground headquarters building in Nijmegen.

After briefing Captain Harris, Colonel Tucker left the regimental command post. "Early in the morning I went to XXX Corps and met General Horrocks and was introduced to Lieutenant Colonel [Giles] Vandeleur, who would support us. He and I took off with one of his armored cars and a small security group."[22]

Colonel Tucker was driven to the Dutch Underground headquarters building in Nijmegen, where he joined Captain Harris' party. "Suffice it to say we traveled in Nijmegen mostly by foot, trying to locate a house, roof, or any raised point from which we could see the crossing area. We never found one until we came up to the crossing site about noon."[23]

Arriving at the power plant, Lieutenant Holabird, the assistant platoon leader with the 2nd Platoon, accompanied his commanding officer, Captain "Spike" Harris, to the ninth floor to take a look at the river and where they were going to cross. "When we were briefed for the assault crossing, we took it as a joke. We couldn't believe anyone could be serious about it. I saw that huge railroad bridge looking right down on us. Suddenly, it came across that this was not a joke; that we were going to paddle those flimsy boats across, and at that moment, I would have liked to have been any place in the world, except there. I still hoped or believed the mission would be called off before we left; that we would wait around there until dark and then be sent back."[24]

Captain Harris and his party selected a point along the south bank of the river between a factory on the east and the power plant on the west. Lieutenant Thomas McLeod, the assistant platoon leader of the 3rd Platoon, told "Captain Harris our assembly area offered pretty good cover, but that it was a long walk across pretty open territory to get to the launching site."[25]

Meanwhile, at the regimental bivouac in a wooded area south of Nijmegen, Captain Fred Thomas and his officers awakened Company G about 5:30 a.m. "After a breakfast of cold K-rations, we moved to another battalion assembly area on the outskirts of Nijmegen. Our mortar ammo was all loaded in the old Dutch car we had, so several of the men were left to bring it up to the battalion assembly area. We arrived at the area at about 0900 and were placed in company areas and told to prepare for the river crossing attack. Ammunition and grenades were drawn from supply, and all unnecessary items were turned in, along with the few bedrolls in the company and the blankets that we had been able to dig up."[26]

At about 9:10 a.m., Major Julian Cook and the S-3 officer, Captain Henry Keep, briefed the 3rd Battalion company commanders. As Staff Sergeant Robert M. Tallon, Sr., the battalion operations sergeant, listened, "it sounded impossible—utterly impossible. I kept thinking over and over, 'This is suicide. This is just plain suicide.' "[27]

When Lieutenant Roy Hanna, the Company G executive officer, heard the plan, he thought it was "pure craziness. I knew damn well we'd never have to do that; not in broad daylight anyway."[28]

The 2nd Battalion would lead the regiment into Nijmegen. Company F was left in position defending the Grave bridge area, and Company E was assigned to take over the defense of Bridge Number 10. Lieutenant Chester A. Garrison, the 2nd Battalion S-1, woke up at 7:00 a.m. after spending a cold night in a foxhole without a blanket. "Major [Edward] Wellems and Captain [Herbert H.] Norman went to regiment to get the situation. [Major William] Colville moved out the battalion (Headquarters and D Companies) by 0800 in column of twos, well separated. Sixteen German planes suddenly appeared along the line of march, flying very low. However, the men were well dispersed and able to take cover under the high, full trees and in house doorways. There was some strafing about a mile down the road. Progress was very slow and had numerous halts while the advance elements of D Company probed the way along the streets of the Nijmegen suburbs."[29]

The 3rd Battalion commander, Major Julian Cook, was already at the crossing site with the regimental officers. "The battalion was late in getting up to the river crossing site, so I went down to bring them up. In fact, I picked the exact spot for them to enter the area and stood on a couple of strands to make the barbed wire stay down, so they could hurry up and get lined up for the crossing. I tried to have a word for each man, and practically the entire battalion filed by me."[30]

Company D was assigned to clear the southern bank of the river and to provide overhead supporting fire for the assault. Lieutenant Edward T. Wisnewski's platoon was in the lead. Lieutenant Hanz Druener was the assistant platoon leader. "I was with the lead platoon for the simple reason that I was the only one of the unit that could speak German. I got up on the riverbank. There was a little jetty by the factory building with an enclosure open to the top [toward the river]. I got out on the jetty to look the situation over. It was pretty quiet. Suddenly, I saw across the river some people moving, and we were told there was a lot of partisans. We all carried these orange cloths with us. So I stood up there and waved the orange cloth I had, expecting they would wave back from across the river. Unfortunately, those weren't partisans; they were Germans. They fired back across the river toward us and pinned myself and one of my radio people down on the jetty for about two hours.

"We couldn't move, and in the process of pinning us down, they killed my immediate superior officer, Lieutenant Edward Wisniewski. We put the Red Cross flag up to get to him, but the Germans wouldn't let us. Wisniewski was lying about forty to fifty yards from me. After he was hit, I could hear him moan. We tried to get some medics out there, but every time they moved, the Germans would either hit one of them, or they couldn't make it out there. Wisnewski lay out there for about the same length of time I would say that I was pinned down."[31] Wisnewski, gravely wounded, would die five days later, on September 26, 1944.

The loss of Lieutenant Wisniewski was particularly tough for Company H platoon leader Lieutenant Jim Megellas. " 'Pollock' as he was nicknamed, was one of my closest friends, and we had gone through jump school and then overseas together."[32]

Seeing what happened to Wisniewski steeled Lieutenant Megellas' resolve. "As we were grouping behind the protected dike alongside the river prior to the assault, all of us prepared in our own way to meet our maker. It did not seem militarily or humanly possible to accomplish such a suicide mission. I remember asking my buddy and closest friend, 1st Lieutenant Richard G. LaRiviere, to contact my mother for me if he survived and I did not. His request to me was along similar lines."[33]

FROM THE NINTH FLOOR OF THE POWER PLANT, the commander of the 3rd Battalion, twenty-seven year old Major Julian Cook, looked through binoculars at the terrain and German positions that awaited his men across the four hundred-yard-wide Waal River and thought to himself, "Somebody has come up with a real nightmare."[34]

The 3rd Battalion operations officer, Captain Henry Keep, arrived moments later. "Everyone gasped when they saw the width of the river and the lack of protection. Once across the river the situation appeared little better. What greeted our eyes was a broad, flat plain void of all cover or concealment. The first terrain feature which would offer us assistance was a built-up highway approximately eight hundred yards from the shore, against the bank of which we would have our first opportunity to get some protection and be able to reorganize. I knew it would be every man for himself until the embankment was reached. We could see all along the Kraut side of the river strong defensive positions, a formidable line both in length as well as depth—pillboxes, machine gun emplacements, and what was really wicked looking, one or two Dutch forts between the place where we were landing and the two bridges.

"A 20mm was firing at us as we took all this in from the tower. While here, the plan of attack was formed. We were to cross the Waal and land at a point two miles down the river (west) from the [highway] bridge, fight our way across the broad expanse of field on the other side, and make for the road embankment, where we would momentarily reorganize before pushing on. After regrouping there, we would turn to the right (or east) and attack parallel to the river, overcoming all resistance and mopping up strong points in the two-mile area we had to take before reaching the bridge, which obviously we would capture by coming at it from the rear. While all of this was going on, another part of the division would wrest from the Kraut what remained in enemy hands of Nijmegen on the friendly side of the river. We were to shoot a flare as soon as both bridges were taken, and the British armor would cross."[35]

Along with the other 3rd Battalion officers in the power plant, Captain T. Moffatt Burriss, the Company I commander, looked across the river through his binoculars. "We could see enemy machine gun positions along the dike and also on the flat terrain. We observed mortar and artillery units behind the dike and 20mm guns on the railroad bridge."[36]

As the regiment prepared for the crossing, troopers of the 376th Parachute Field Artillery Battalion arrived to support the crossing. The battalion's command liaison officer, Captain Frank Boyd, with Headquarters Battery, had the vital responsibility of relaying firing requests and adjustments from the forward observers to the battalion fire-direction center. Wanting a house with a view of the river, he stepped inside the house where the regimental command post was located. "There was not room for even my small section in it, so we went into the house just east of it. It was a larger house, brick I believe, but possibly stone. It faced the Waal River, and we entered through a large room at the west end that apparently was made to house livestock. It had a huge door, and near the east end of this room, a few steps went up into the kitchen. Another stairway went to the stone-vaulted cellar below the kitchen. The owners of the house must have left only minutes before we arrived. I sent two of my men through the house, and they reported that no one was there. Aside from that brief inspection, we never went beyond the kitchen. On the stove we found a large pot of pork chops, cooked and ready to eat. We took the pot to the west door and passed them out to the infantrymen on their way to the river.

"The only members of the 376th who [would make] the original river crossing were Lieutenant Whitney S. Russell and Privates Richard [P.] Barr and Richard Martin. The third [enlisted] man, Scott, had been killed minutes earlier.

"Scotty was killed just before the team got to the house where I had installed my liaison section. The others came in that house after the artillery concentration that killed him. I told Russell that I would take my section and go over in his place, but he said that they would rather go ahead and keep busy than to sit around and think about Scotty. He also declined my offer to give him one of my men to replace Scotty [Private First Class Robert M. Scott].

"Light tanks of the King's Own Yorkshire Light Infantry had been popping in and out of the woods all day, doing nothing but drawing German artillery fire that knocked out my telephone line at least six times. Lieutenant Russell and his section were crossing an open field between those woods and "my" house, when Scott was hit. The tanks, of course, were back out of sight by the time the concentration arrived. A large part of Scotty's chest and abdomen was blown away, and he died almost instantly."[37]

Lieutenant Robert Hutton, with Battery B, 376th, would watch the "crossing of the Waal River from the power plant at Nijmegen. I was the forward observer on top of the plant."[38]

Because there weren't enough boats to carry the entire battalion, the plan called for Company H, Company I, and part of the Headquarters, 3rd Battalion, to cross in the first wave, with three Company C, 307th Airborne Engineer Battalion, engineers per boat to row the boats back to the south shore to pick up succeeding waves. The second wave would be Company G and Headquarters Company, 3rd Battalion.

Lieutenant Roy Hanna still couldn't believe the crossing would actually take place. "We went about the whole thing rather casually, as if convinced there was no sweat—we'd never be asked to go, anyway. I poked my head up over the dike to take a good look, and what I saw wasn't very reassuring—just flat water and flat land on the other side."[39]

Captain Carl Kappel, the commander of Company H, kept reminding himself that there would be plenty of supporting fire to cover the crossing. "Tanks of the 2nd Irish Guards would support the crossings by fire from positions on the dike. The 2nd Battalion, 504 Parachute Infantry, would support the crossings by fire from positions along the dike. The 376 Parachute Field Artillery was in direct support, to be supplemented with all available British artillery [which was] arriving constantly. All artillery was to fire a ten-minute concentration on the target area. Dive bombers and rocket-firing Typhoons were to bomb and strafe from 1445 to 1455. The area [was] to be smoked at 1455 by artillery and mortars. (75mm howitzer and 81mm mortar [fire was] not as satisfactory as desired.) Tanks were to fill in blanks of the smoke to the limit of their capacity. H-Hour was set at 1500 hours."[40]

Captain Keep and the 3rd Battalion staff left the ninth floor to brief the men. "As we wound our way down the twisting stairs of the tower, no one said a word. All our thoughts were identical. How could this operation succeed? At least three-quarters of the battalion would be killed, and the rest would drift downstream. It was a humanly impossible undertaking. However, it had to be

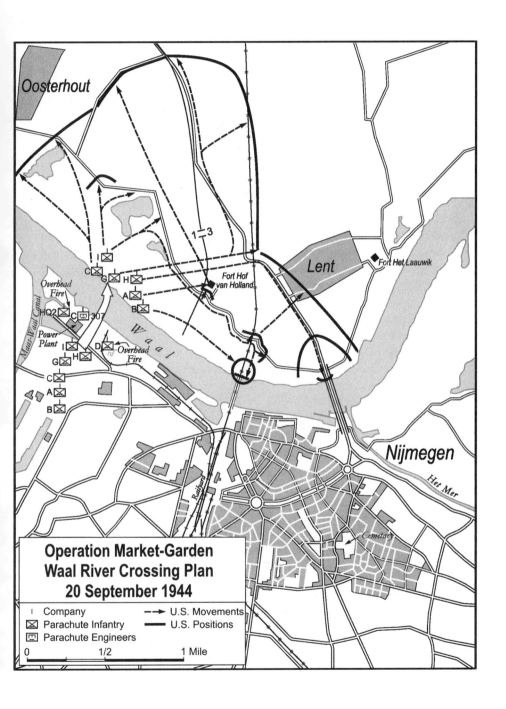

**Operation Market-Garden
Waal River Crossing Plan
20 September 1944**

I Company	- - → U.S. Movements
⊠ Parachute Infantry	—— U.S. Positions
⊡ Parachute Engineers	

0   1/2   1 Mile

Oosterhout

Lent

● Fort Het Laauwik

1–3

Fort Hof
van Holland

*Overhead
Fire*

HQ2

C ⊡ 307

*Power
Plant*

*Overhead
Fire*

Maas-Waal Canal

W a a l

Nijmegen

Het Mer

Cemetary

C ⊠
G ⊠
H ⊠
A ⊠
B ⊠
I ⊠
C ⊠
D ⊠
G ⊠
H ⊠
I ⊠
C ⊠
A ⊠
B ⊠

[done] soon and quickly; the bridge must be taken; the road to Arnhem must be opened up.

"In the meantime, the men had been brought to a defilade position behind the bank we had to cross to get to the river. We proceeded to organize them in boatloads, and then we waited until H-Hour, all huddled together behind that bank. Some men slept. Others talked in little groups. Fortunately, none of them had seen what we'd seen from the tower. However, all of us officers told our boatloads the general picture. 'Don't be surprised,' I told mine, 'if you meet an awful lot of fire as we start carrying the boats out on this bank. No matter what happens, we have to cross the river, and the boats must go back to pick up the next wave.' "[41]

When the 504th Protestant chaplain, Captain Delbert Kuehl, heard the plan, he asked Major Cook for permission to cross with the first wave. "We were on a suicide mission, and my men didn't even have the choice to volunteer. Since they had to go, I chose to go, too."[42]

Company I trooper Private Francis Keefe noticed that "it was quiet throughout the company as we waited for the boats to arrive. We were all wondering what they would look like. There was little conversation—everyone was looking at each other. I was confident about myself, but was concerned about the others, as I had been through attacks before. I knew we would have C Company engineers with us. They were like part of the regiment."[43]

Then Keefe heard the familiar low rumble, punctuated by squeaking sounds as a column of tanks of the Irish Guards approached. "I didn't realize that the tank support would come right down to the road where we were. There were quite a few of them. The road was wide. They turned and faced north and backed up as far as they could to leave room for the trucks to come down with the boats.

"First, Lieutenant [Harry F. 'Pappy'] Busby started telling different squad leaders who was to go into what boats. I spoke to Lieutenant Busby, saying that I wanted to go in the same boat as [Private First Class Leo] Muri, since we were always together in this kind of situation. We got into a heated argument. . . . I would go into the boat I was assigned."[44]

As the time neared for the attack, Lieutenant Virgil Carmichael, the 3rd Battalion S-2, noticed Lieutenant Busby standing nearby, "taking out a Camel cigarette, lighting it with a valued Zippo lighter, and throwing the pack away and throwing the Zippo away, saying that he would have need of them no more."[45]

At 2:45 p.m., the artillery and the 81mm mortars of Headquarters Company, 2nd Battalion, opened up on the German positions on the far side of the river, pounding them for ten minutes. Staff Sergeant Kenneth S. Nicoll was a forward observer for the 81mm mortar platoon. "My platoon leader, Lieutenant [Lauren W.] Ramsey, [had] told me to get on top of the power house and start firing my mortars at the Germans. When I got up there, the

German artillery spotted me and my buddy [Sergeant Charles L. Warren] and started throwing 88 shells at us. But we stayed behind the smokestack and really pounded the mortars on those positions they were preparing for our assault across the river."[46]

As he waited, Lieutenant Megellas heard fighter-bombers approaching from the south. "British Typhoons flew across the river, strafing the entire north bank with bombs, rockets, and automatic fire. The Germans responded with a devastating barrage of antiaircraft fire. Rivers and I watched in awe from our concealed front-row seats as the planes attempted to neutralize enemy resistance. More awesome, however, was the amount of fire the enemy threw up. The sky was black from puffs of exploding shells. The 'ack-ack' was so thick that you could have walked on it. Paddling across the river was going to be bloodier than anticipated."[47]

Captain Keep anxiously glanced down at his watch every few seconds. Then he heard the sound of trucks approaching. "The trucks with twenty-six flat bottomed boats arrived ten minutes before 3:00. There was a mad rush to get them unloaded, and then we all stood around the boats to which we had been assigned."[48]

When the canvas tarps on the backs of the trucks were pulled back, Lieutenant Holabird was momentarily stunned. "The boats were flat-bottomed, with low canvas covered sides and bottoms. They looked pretty flimsy to me. But they were heavy; they had to be to carry sixteen men. We unloaded the boats off the trucks that brought them up and set them on the ground."[49]

The engineers took wooden staves attached to the plywood bottoms, swiveled them up, and secured the canvas sides to the staves of the nineteen-foot boats as the 3rd Battalion troopers stood by in disbelief.

Private First Class Walter E. Hughes, with Company I, had more than enough knowledge to be frightened. "My initial shock at seeing those boats being unloaded from the trucks was of complete horror. As a seaman before the war, [I knew that] no one in their right mind would use boats like that for a swift running river. I believed everyone would drown before we reached the other side. Could I get rid of my equipment fast enough if the boat foundered? Could I swim with boots on? I never even thought about the Germans who would be looking down our throats."[50]

Chaplain Kuehl asked the engineers how they were to be propelled. "By canoe paddles . . . like we were voyagers going on a trip. I couldn't believe our commanders were serious. British engineers used these [boats] as floats in building a pontoon bridge; they were not intended for river crossings under fire."[51]

Megellas was wondering whether the boats could even make it to the other side. "Here we were, thirteen paratroopers with our individual weapons, crew-served weapons, ammunition, and packs—preparing to squeeze into a nineteen-foot canvas boat propelled by an armful of paddles. By any standard, the boats would be dangerously overloaded. I wondered if we could stay afloat even without enemy resistance."[52]

When the engineers finished assembling the boats, Company C, 307th engineer, Lieutenant John Bigler, responsible for loading and embarkation of the boats, together with the 3rd Battalion officers, double checked the assignments of each man to a boat. Then, the engineers and troopers piled their weapons and gear into the boats and carried them to the staging point.

Even though he had been with the engineer reconnaissance party, Lieutenant Patrick Mulloy, the 3rd Platoon leader, got his "first look at the stretch of water we would have to cross. I can remember thinking that it was a long way across. Most of us had had some training for assault crossings, using pontoons, and I suppose I drew a certain amount of confidence from that. But the fact remained we were supposed to row across a wide open stretch of water looking right down the barrels of German guns."[53]

As the time for the assault crossing neared, Colonel Tucker ascended the steps to the ninth floor of the power plant. "I went up in the tower with [Lieutenant Colonel Giles] Vandeleur [commanding the 2nd Armoured Battalion, Irish Guards Regiment] and he had a radio to contact his tanks, which were drawn up beside the buildings at the edge of the river."[54]

At 2:55 p.m., British tanks, the regiment's mortars, and the 376th Parachute Field Artillery fired smoke and white phosphorous shells to lay a smoke screen on the north side of the river.

Private First Class Alfred J. Hermansen, with Headquarters Battery, watched as the smoke rounds from the 376th landed. "Our intent was to cover the crossing with smoke rounds. The wind favored the Germans that awful day, and our effort went for naught."[55]

Third Battalion Headquarters and one section of Headquarters Company, 3rd Battalion, machine guns would cross with the rifle companies in the first wave. Staff Sergeant Robert Tallon was the 3rd Battalion's operations sergeant. "A young fellow, about eighteen years old, a replacement—I didn't even know his name—struck up a conversation with me as we were waiting to load onto the boats. He was so very concerned about whether he would know how to use the items in his first aid kit if he were wounded. He kept repeating his questions about when to use the tablets, the powders, the ointments."[56]

Captain Keep waited by his boat for the signal to go. "The tanks were in position, the dive bombers came and went, the ineffective smoke screen was laid, we waited by our boats. Suddenly, a whistle was blown. It was H-Hour. Each boatload hoisted their boat onto their shoulders and staggered out across the flat top of the bank. Our job had begun."[57]

With the sound of the whistle, the machine gun platoon of Headquarters Company, 2nd Battalion, and the machine guns and BARs of Company D cut loose with overhead fire on the enemy positions on the railroad bridge deck and the dike road and Fort Hof Van Holland across the river.

The troopers of Companies H and I, and Major Cook and the 3rd Battalion staff, with their boats loaded with weapons and gear, began crossing the open, flat ground in front of the dike. Captain Kappel, the commander of Company H, and his boat were in the lead coming over the flat ground toward the dike. "The routes leading to the water from our position couldn't be seen, and they were not reconnoitered, because as we went over the dike, we ran into a large, chain-link type of fence with a couple of strands of barbed wire on the top that blocked our way.

"I was mad as hell. I took a Gammon grenade out and threw it against one of the pipe supports, and Megellas did the same on the next support. Our combined weight against the fence pushed it down, and we were able to go on down toward the river.

"We had lined up intending to go over the dike laterally separated, but ended up being more or less funneled down to the river by the fence and the terrain."[58]

Captain Keep and his boat crew struggled to get their boat across the flat ground, over the dike, and into the water. "The weight of the boat seemed imponderable; our feet sank deep into the mud. We must have caught the Krauts by surprise, because the first one hundred yards there wasn't a round fired from the enemy side of the river.

"Then suddenly, all hell broke loose. We had run halfway across the flat-topped plateau prior to reaching the drop, when Jerry opened up with everything he had—light machine guns, mortars, 20mm guns, artillery, and rifles. As if in a rage at our trying anything so dangerous, he was throwing everything he possessed at us.

"I don't think I have ever been prouder of our men. Not one of them faltered. In spite of the withering, murderous fire, they lumbered on, sinking ankle deep in the soft sand under their cumbersome boats. Here and there men would fall, but their places would only be taken by others. I felt as naked as the day I was born on that exposed spot."[59]

Lieutenant Tom McLeod, the assistant platoon leader of the 3rd Platoon of the Company C engineers, reached the riverbank and together with Major Cook and the other men, put the boat into the water. "I was outside [of the boat] with another fellow from my platoon, Sergeant [Robert] Mistovich, and we were trying to hold the boat for them. It was an awfully poor spot—very muddy and difficult to get a footing. When the boat sank in the mud, I shouted for everybody to get out. They got out, the major included, and we pushed the boat out farther. Mistovich and I held it, waist deep in the water, while they got in again. I got in the bow, and Mistovich climbed in the back, and we started off."[60]

Lieutenant Carmichael was with one of the boats in the center of the column. "Fire came from across the river and from gun positions to our right on our side of the river, and from all along the railroad bridge, and from the old Fort [Hof] Van Holland. It was about one hundred yards from the top of the dike to the water's edge, and about one-third of the way down was a small escarpment, which was about three and a half feet high.

"As I moved out from behind the fence, there was a continuous hail of bullets, with small geysers of earth popping up everywhere. There would have been no need to have dodged one way or the other. As each boat reached this small escarpment, the men were unable to walk and carry the boats past it. The men in front of each boat would lay the boat down and then jump off the bank, and after that, each boat was almost automatically put on the shoulders of the men, and they literally ran to the water's edge with it."[61]

The Company C engineer officer in charge of coordinating loading of succeeding waves, Lieutenant John Bigler, moved to the forward slope of the riverbank, where he could best observe the crossing. He remained there through the operation, despite the almost unbelievable volume of enemy machine gun, 20mm, mortar, and artillery fire directed on the loading area.

When Private First Class Bill Leonard and the Company I troopers carrying one the boats reached the edge of the water, the squad's machine gun crew got into the front of the boat. "We helped them get in and put them up front, [Privates] Don [Emmett] on the left and George [E. Ham] on the right, with my machine gun. It was a frightful sight, trying to watch us all trying to get aboard at once. We never had any instruction at all, nor had anyone seen these darned things before."[62]

As they neared the riverbank, Sergeant Albert Tarbell, with Company H, started to wade into the water holding his share of the boat. "I saw our CO, Captain Kappel, take his harness off with pistol and throw it in the boat. I unconsciously did the same, not knowing why. The CO jumped into the water, and it wasn't until then that I realized one of our men [Private James H. Legacie] had fallen in and was drowning. The captain saved him."[63]

Sergeant Tarbell and others reached out and pulled them both into the boat and then the troopers began paddling toward the far shore. "The current was very swift and it seemed like no one had ever used a paddle in our boat. Maybe it was just from the confusion of receiving fire from three sides. It looked like it was raining from the way the bullets were hitting the water. I wondered how anyone could survive. I never realized one could count cadence for the fellows to paddle by, and at the same time say your prayers. But, I did."[64]

Lieutenant John Holabird and a squad of his 2nd Platoon, Company C, 307th Engineers, were assigned to cross the river and make their way to the bridges with the assault companies and look for and neutralize demolition charges on the bridges. After carrying their boat to the water, Holabird got his men aboard. "I got in and shouted, 'Everybody paddle like hell!' I sat back and tried to steer. We all tried to crouch, but I took one look at the sides of the boat and didn't think crouching was going to do much good. I remember feeling that my helmet at that point seemed like a beanie."[65]

When Captain Keep's boat reached the drop-off of the dike "we let the boats slide down to the beach and ourselves slide alongside of them. We pulled our boat quickly across the short beach, and everyone piled in. By this time, the situation was horrible. The automatic and flat-trajectory fire had increased, and the artillery was deadly. Men were falling right and left. In everyone's ear was the constant roar of bursting artillery shells, the dull wham off a 20mm, or the disconcerting ping of rifle bullets.

"After a false start, we got stuck in a mud bar, and several of us had perforce to get out and go through the extremely uncomfortable process of pushing off again. We found ourselves actually floating, but in the wrong direction. The current was taking us away from the bridge. Everyone grabbed a paddle and frantically started to work. Most of the men had never paddled before, and had it not been for the gruesomeness of the situation, the sight might have been rather ludicrous. With all our strength, we would lunge forward, only to miss the water completely. Gradually we got our boat moving in the right direction"[66]

As Lieutenant Virgil Carmichael and the Headquarters, 3rd Battalion troopers with him launched their boat, there was bedlam. "Bullets were flying everywhere. Our boat started going around in circles. When I was young I had paddled a canoe quite a bit on the Tennessee River, and I knew how it was supposed to be done. So I slipped over to the left rear of the craft, took a paddle from one of the men, and kept the boat steered straight for the other shore."[67]

From the ninth floor of the power plant, Colonel Tucker watched the first boats push off the southern shore. "In less time than it takes to tell, all hell broke loose—enfilade Kraut MG fire from under the shore abutment of the railroad bridge, 88 fire, and small-arms fire.

"Vandeleur had laid down smoke over some Kraut gun positions, and his tanks fired at numerous targets. I would tell him what I wanted, and he would relay it to his tanks. His fire was most effective, and although I had been promised considerable artillery support, little if any, ever materialized and the tank fire was our support."[68]

The Germans began to find the range with their artillery and mortars. Machine guns on the railroad bridge brought plunging fire down on the troopers. Private Francis Keefe, in the front of his boat carrying Company I troopers, saw 20mm antiaircraft guns on the railroad bridge about a thousand yards away firing a continuous stream of high-velocity shells that exploded in airbursts among the men trying to get their boats straightened out and headed for the far shore. "It was like a continuous streak of lightning, which we knew from Italy. It hit one of the boats in front; that too went into a spin."[69]

Private First Class Leonard was aboard that stricken boat. "We were about one hundred yards out when a 20mm gun was able to zero in on us. Two guys to my side were hit. I grabbed [Corporal Al] Essig on my left and pulled him from hanging in the water, inside [the boat], with blood on his shoulder and face. At that instant, [Private First Class Leonard G.] Trimble on my right was hit badly, too. We had to pull and hold him from falling into the river, also. I tried to hold them both from falling back into the water by their harnesses. Another fifty yards, we were hit so badly, we went out of control and headed downstream. After a few minutes, we righted our craft."[70]

When Private First Class Trimble was hit, "one of the grenades on my left shoulder was struck and exploded. I received a machine gun slug in my right arm. I received shrapnel in my mouth, knocking out my front teeth, lower lip, and it broke my nose. I received flak in my shoulder and my left leg. I was hit in the face, shoulder, left leg, and had a compound fracture of the right arm."[71]

Staff Sergeant Louis Orvin, with Company I, glanced back to his right rear and saw Germans on south side of the river, below the railroad bridge, "shooting grazing fire down the river. Whatever they shot down the river, it would bounce off the water and ricochet and go through the sides of the boats. You'd see men in boats get hit, stand up, and fall over and drown. You couldn't save them . . . you couldn't stop for them.

"Sergeant Darrell [D.] Edgar—a bullet evidently went through the side of the boat and hit the stock of his rifle and went into his groin."[72]

Private First Class Harold Herbert and two other engineers with the 2nd Platoon of Company C, Privates Donald R. Rodman and Max E. Albert, were in the same boat. Herbert was furiously paddling the boat. "There was so much fire—not only small-arms fire, there were mortars coming in. We didn't have enough paddles for everybody, so they were using the butt ends of their guns to row the boat. The farther you went, it seemed like there was more fire. You just had to keep going."[73]

Private Louis P. Holt had tried to get in a boat with Lieutenant Megellas and twelve men earlier, but there wasn't room, so he jumped into another. Sergeant Tarbell was frantically paddling, when we looked over at the boat carrying Private Holt at the very moment it took a direct hit. "To this day, I can still see the look on Private Louis Holt's face as our eyes met."[74]

Casualties began to mount as airbursts from 88mm and 20mm guns rained shrapnel on the helpless men in the boats. Chaplain Kuehl, rowing in one of the crowded boats, heard the sickening thud and explosion of a 20mm shell. "The man next to me had the middle part of his head blown away, so that his skull dropped on what was left of his lower face."[75]

Others, such as Company C engineer Lieutenant Patrick Mulloy, the 3rd Platoon leader, used all of their concentration, despite the carnage all around them, to focus on reaching the opposite shore, to the exclusion of all else. "I fixed my eyes on the opposite bank, and I don't think I took them off it the entire way across."[76]

Captain Keep heard a low grunt behind him. "I turned around . . . and found someone taking the place of a man in the rear of me who had just received a 20mm in one shoulder and out the other.

"The water all around the boats was churned up by the hail of bullets, and we were soaked to the skin. Out of the corner of my eye, I saw a boat to my right [get] hit in the middle by a 20mm shell and sink. Somewhere to my left, I caught a glimpse of a figure topple overboard, only to be grabbed and pulled back into the boat by some hardy soul. Large numbers of men were being hit in all boats, and the bottoms of these crafts were littered with the wounded and the dead. Here and there on the surface of the water a paddle floated, dropped by some poor casualty before the man taking his place could retrieve it from the lifeless fingers. By now, the broad surface of the Waal was covered with our small canvas craft, all crammed with frantically paddling men. It was a horrible picture, this river crossing. Set to the sound of a deafening roar of omnipresent firing, this scene of defenseless, frail canvas boats jammed to overflowing with humanity, all striving desperately to cross the Waal as quickly as possible, was fiendish and dreadful. We were soaked, gasping for breath, dead tired, and constantly expecting to feel that searing sensation as the bullet tore through you. I wanted to vomit; many did."[77]

The 3rd Battalion operations sergeant, Robert Tallon, sitting on the left side of his boat, paddled frantically, with the frightened young replacement who had asked him how to use the items in his first aid kit before they began the crossing, sitting on his right doing the same. "All of a sudden, the kid on my right groaned and slumped over in my lap. I looked down at him and knew he had been hit in the chest. It had gone in the front and come out the back. There was no question about it—he was dead, very dead. The bullet had come out almost exactly between his shoulder blades.

"To our left, a mortar scored a direct hit on a boat. There was a geyser of water and I could see men being blown out and up in the air. The boat just vanished."[78]

Company H platoon leader Lieutenant Jim Megellas also saw it happen. "Halfway across the river, a mortar or artillery shell hit the boat carrying one half of my platoon, and the boat sank at that point."[79]

Sergeant Jimmie S. Shields' boat, carrying Company H troopers, only had a couple of paddles. "I was paddling with the butt of my Browning Automatic Rifle, while others were using the butts of their rifles. Some without paddles used their hands. Anything to keep the boat on a northward course."[80]

Private First Class James Ward, with Company H, was rowing hard when his boat took a hit. "Our boat's helmsman, a 307 engineer who was seated in the stern, took a hit. At once, we lost control and the boat headed down river.

Being a farm boy from the Louisiana bayou country and seated a few seats away, I assumed the helmsman's position and managed to restore steerage."[81]

The boat carrying Lieutenant Tom McLeod "got out in the middle [of the river] and began going around in circles. I was trying to get straightened out when the major shouted, 'Come on there, let's try to paddle together.' "[82]

Lieutenant Carmichael could hear Major Cook in the boat beside him. "As he struck the water with his paddle, you could hear him say, 'Hail Mary, full of grace,' repeating it over and over again as he paddled as hard as he could toward the other shore."[83]

Despite all of the noise, Company I trooper, Private Francis Keefe could hear troopers in boats to his right shouting " 'Heave—ho.' It was like a race—we were trying to get to the other side as soon as possible.

"A 20mm was firing at one of the boats that was in the left front of us, which had slowed down. We rowed right underneath the lightning, which I figured if I stood up with my hand, I could have touched it. That's how continuous it was. If the elevation of the gun was brought down, it would have cut us in half."[84]

Captain Burriss, commanding Company I, was at the rear of his boat, sitting next to an engineer [Private First Class Willard Jenkins]. "Suddenly, I noticed his wrist turn red. 'Captain,' he said, 'take the rudder. I've been hit.' Just as I reached for the rudder, he leaned forward and caught a 20mm high explosive shell through his head, a round that was meant for me.

"As the shell exploded, I felt a stinging sensation in my side. I'd caught some of the shrapnel, though I felt no real pain. I grabbed the rudder and tried to steer the boat. At that moment, the upper part of the engineer's body fell overboard; and when the current hit his head and torso, the drag swung the boat upstream. 'Straighten out! Straighten out!' the men in the front of the boat shouted.

"I couldn't. His feet were caught under the seat, and his body was acting as a second rudder. I was finally able to reach down, disengage his feet, and push him overboard. As I watched his body float downstream, I could see the red blood streaming from what was left of his head. When the engineer in my boat was hit in the head, the explosion had splattered his blood and brains on my right shoulder, neck, and helmet. Also, my jacket was soaked with blood from the shrapnel wound in my side. Apparently, I looked a bloody mess."[85]

Chapter 10

"I Have Never Seen
A More Gallant Action"

Watching helplessly as machine gun and rifle bullets, white-hot shrapnel, and 20mm antiaircraft shells tore into the flesh of their buddies—horribly wounding, maiming, and killing them—the fear among the paratroopers changed to a rage that spurred them on to the far shore to exact revenge on the Germans.

Private First Class Walter J. Muszynski, a light machine gunner with Company I, sitting in one of the lead boats, put his machine gun on the bow of his boat and started engaging Germans dug in near the riverbank. The Germans opened fire on his boat, wounding two men, but Muszynski kept up his fire on the dug-in German positions.

In the lead Company I boat with Captain Burriss, Private First Class Leo Muri was sitting "in the front of the boat and had a machine gun resting on the bow and shooting like hell. Everyone was yelling at each other to row faster, and the canvas [was] ripping. Men who were hit, rolled to the center to give more room to those still able to paddle."[1]

The boats neared the far shore and began touching down as they were raked with automatic weapons fire as Germans on the railroad bridge poured enfilade fire into the boats from the right flank and rear. Meanwhile, enemy machine gunners on the dike road fired at them from the front. At the top of the power plant on the south side of the river, Staff Sergeant Ken Nicoll, a forward observer with the 81mm Mortar Platoon of Headquarters Company, 2nd Battalion, was watching the lead boat through his binoculars as it neared the shore, where one of several dug-in German machine guns was positioned almost at the water's edge. "I remember the first boat getting ashore and one of the boys throwing a Gammon grenade at a German machine gun nest, when one of the Germans jumped up and tried to throw it back. He didn't know it was point-detonating. That cleared a path for them to get up the steep bank."[2]

German fire riddled the boat in which Muri was riding, ripping and tearing holes in the canvas. "It was nothing less than a miracle that saved my life on that boat, and we reached the other side just in time, as the boat went down as we hit shallow water. The wounded crawled out and lay on the beach. The others of us had to advance and keep shooting, as we didn't dare to stop too long to help the wounded."[3]

As the boat carrying Private Francis Keefe was "about forty yards from the shore, I could see a steady stream of machine gun bullets popping on the water coming at us."[4]

Private First Class Bill Leonard and his buddies paddled "straight into the German machine gun and rifle fire [that] we could see and hear, coming directly at us, with the water jumping at least one foot. We were all on our knees and trying to get real low. We were hit so fast we were taken by surprise. [Private] Don [Emmett] was feeding the machine gun ammo by hand to [Private] George Ham, who was pointing it towards the banks of the incoming shore. Again, they got us in range—Don was lying real low, but a large burst came our way, knocking off Don's helmet and a piece of his right ear. And as he got lower, several bullets tore his jacket almost in two, down his back, then into the couple of machine gun ammo boxes, and then my left thigh. There for a moment, I thought someone had hit me with a sledgehammer. I felt into my trousers; I couldn't feel anything but blood."[5]

Instead of fear, Leonard was enraged. "So I stood up, holding on, to give the Germans a good shot. 'Kill me you bastards,' I yelled.

"Minutes later, we were being helped over and out into the low water level. George and Don helped drag and lift everybody out of the craft, which was half full of blood and water. Two other crafts pulled along side—guys being drug, falling out, and helped to get ashore. Mortar shells started to come into our area with terrible accuracy, blowing guys everywhere.

"Since I couldn't walk, I tried my darndest to crawl with my good right leg and my arms in shore, some twenty-five feet. There, I tried to dig in with my helmet. There was too much interference to dig in very deeply, with guys falling on you and others crawling over the top. The one we called Blacky [Private Louis Rassiga] fell on me. The medics grabbed his head and wrapped his brains that were sticking out. Then they tore my pants down. He put some powder on—several packets and then took off to help some of the ones who were getting shot up."[6]

As the boat carrying Lieutenant Harry Busby and part of his platoon reached the shore, a burst of enemy fire raked the boat, wounding Private First Class Matthew W. Kantala, Jr., and killing Busby. "He was right in front of me.

We had [had] an argument about the seat. He wanted to sit in the front and I wanted the seat. He took the seat and he got killed.

"I was hit in the face and hands."[7]

As Lieutenant Patrick Mulloy's boat approached the shore, "something smacked into my side. At first, I thought I had caught one, but the impact was greater than the wound. I had been grazed."

Just seconds later, as the men emptied the boat, Mulloy saw one of his engineers, Corporal Louis F. Gentile, get hit. "Gentile was in a real bad way. He was pretty well torn up, from a[n artillery] shell or mortar [round], I'd say. He was conscious, but only just briefly. The other boats, I noticed for the first time, were pretty well dispersed up and down the bank. I got Gentile out and laid him down, behind some rocks, I think. I remember he was only concerned that everybody else would be alright. There were a lot of other wounded lying on the bank. I felt terrible about Gentile, but I was glad we were across."[8]

As Major Cook's boat neared the shore, "everyone began to jump overboard, as the flanking fire from the Nijmegen bridge was intense. I was just getting ready to get out of my boat when I saw a bubble of air come up out of the water. I hesitated a moment and looked further. I saw a 'bulge' in the water and kept on looking as I saw it move to the shore. The sensation was one of confusion by this thing in the water. Rapidly, the 'bulge' emerged from the water. It was the machine gunner [from my boat], a little fellow who, seeing the others leave the boat, took his two boxes of ammunition, one in each hand and simply jumped into the water and started walking, even though the water was a foot or more over his head. The ammo boxes weighed him down, but he walked out with them. He told me he knew we needed that ammunition."[9]

After crawling ashore, Sergeant George Leoleis, with Company I, paused for a moment to catch his breath, then jumped to his feet. "We started up the banks of the river and cleaned out the Krauts who had foxholes along the riverbanks. We then charged up the banks in the face of homicidal grazing fire, bayoneting the enemy in their foxholes, knocking out their machine gun nest with hand grenades and some trench knife handiwork.

"After we routed them from their foxholes and bunkers at the river's edge, the few remaining broke for cover to some nearby houses on a narrow road."[10]

As they were chasing the Germans, one of the men with Leoleis was hit. "He was right next to me and as he went down, he cried to me, 'Help me.'

"I looked at where he was hit (down by his privates); there was no way to stop the bleeding. No way to put a tourniquet on. I opened a first aid kit and a second one from one of the other men with me—Nestles, [Sergeant Albert] Ferguson, and [Sergeant Harold] Gustafson. I tried to stuff the bandages in the open wound. The hole in front was big, and the blood was just gushing out.

"He realized that he was hit bad and he begged me, 'Please do something.'

"All this time, we were under intense fire from those houses, and the Germans were sensing blood and trying to finish us in that ditch we had jumped into for some cover. Gus, Fergi, and Nestles were keeping the Krauts busy with return fire, while I was helping the wounded man. Within a minute or so of frantically trying to stop the flow of blood, the wounded man looked at me with eyes pleading and not saying anything else—I knew he was gone. Right there, tears came to my eyes. I held him for a split second when a grenade exploded near us. That woke us up and the five of us got down to the business at hand."[11]

After landing, Private Keefe noticed that "some of the troops were lying down—some exhausted or wounded perhaps. I immediately said, 'If we stay here, we'll all die, let's move out.' I made a move, and a kid from Brooklyn, whose name I didn't know, as he [had just come] into the unit two weeks before, moved with me. There was a hesitation behind me; I turned around and yelled, 'Move out or you'll die!' I took off, and everyone let out this unmerciful cry, including myself, and I know my personality had changed. God help anyone in front of us—they would pay.

"After about forty yards we ran into a trench I did not see from the beach. It ran parallel with the beach and the river. We went into the trench, which was over six feet. I looked sideways and saw Lieutenant [Robert] Blankenship in the ditch with us. The trench curved, so we couldn't see past twenty-five yards. I told Blankenship I was going to check out around the curve, but it curved more. I didn't see anyone. I came back and told him that. I then said, 'Let's take a rest.'

"He said, 'No, let's keep going.' We used our rifles to step on to get out of the ditch, and it looked like everyone had their second wind."[12]

A 20mm shell hit the boat carrying Lieutenant Ernest P. Murphy and part of his Company H platoon as it got close to the north bank of the river. "About twenty yards from the opposite shore, the boat was hit and sunk by enemy fire. After reaching shore by swimming, I counted my men, and one was missing. Shortly after, his head popped up out of the water close to shore. I told him to get out of the water, that this was no time to be playing around. The Germans were shooting at us from all sides.

"He said, 'Lieutenant, I can't swim, and I had to crawl on the bottom.'

"We all had to laugh. He was my BAR gunner, and he was loaded down with ammunition and other equipment. This made it possible for him to stay on the bottom and crawl to shore."[13]

Private First Class James Ward, with Company H, struggled to get out of the boat as it touched ground. "We fell on the bank completely exhausted. Some of us, due to a shortage of paddles, had been paddling with rifle butts. Many of us just lay there, too tired to move. The dead and wounded were all around us. I knew that if we didn't get off that beach soon, we would be killed.

I wasn't a hero, I wasn't a leader; I was just a PFC trying to stay alive."[14] Ward shouted for the other men to get off the beach, then jumped to his feet and began running toward the dike.

When Company H squad leader Sergeant Clark H. Fuller landed, he experienced a feeling he had never felt before in combat. "All fear of the past fifteen or twenty minutes that it took for the crossing seemed to leave me, replaced by a surge of reckless abandon that threw caution to the wind. I felt as though I could lick the whole German army."[15]

The boat carrying Company H commander Captain Carl Kappel was full of casualties. "A few yards from the shore, I dropped off the back of the boat and gave a big shove, which drove us into the shore. There were three of us moving. The boat was half-filled with water; most of it was blood."[16]

Of the thirteen Company H troopers in Kappel's boat, six were dead and four badly wounded; only Kappel, Staff Sergeant James Allen, Jr., and medic Technician Fifth Grade Seymour Flox had not been hit. Kappel had left his weapon on the other side of the river, so he picked up a Tommy gun and some ammunition and then told the other two troopers to follow him. "The three of us started running for the first thing to get down behind—a trench or ditch, I believe, at least six hundred yards from the shore. I still hadn't recovered from my swim, and I developed a hell of a pain in my side. Flox, Allen, and I made the trench and got down. I was in terrible pain; they thought at first I had been hit, but I hadn't. We laughed about it, and it was at this point that Sergeant Allen turned to me and said, 'Our luck is still holding out.' "[17]

Lieutenant Megellas and his H Company troopers landed with the first few boats, pausing momentarily to catch their breaths. Then Megellas and his men formed a rough skirmish line. "We had to cross about five hundred yards of flat, open terrain to reach the dike, which was our next objective. The Germans were entrenched on the dike and were raking the open area with small-arms and automatic fire. Since there was no place to take cover, our only alternative was to charge in the face of this murderous fire and rout the enemy from their positions."[18]

After landing, Private First Class Walter Muszynski, with Company I, moved forward, firing his .30-caliber light machine gun from the hip, covering the advance of his squad. The German machine gunners on the dike now shifted their fire from the boats to the troopers in rough skirmish lines charging toward them.

From the ninth floor of the power plant, British Lieutenant Colonel Giles Vandeleur, commanding the 2nd Armoured Battalion of the Irish Guards Regiment, watched the crossing through his binoculars. "I saw one or two boats hit the beaches, followed by three or four others. The men got out and began moving across an open field. My God! What a courageous sight it was! They just moved across that field steadily. I never saw a single man lie down until he was hit. I didn't think more than half the fleet made it across. The boats started back and it was obvious that half of them had been lost."[19]

As his boat neared the shore, shrapnel from a 20mm shell tore into the back of Private First Class Herbert P. Keith, one of the engineers. "[Private Grover F.] Fields helped me out of the boat and onto the bank. A medic dug a hole for me to get in. The medics were the bravest men there—running around trying to help everybody. I laid three hours before being picked up and taken to a first aid station."[20]

Private First Class Keith's position in the boat had meant the difference between life and death. When they were getting into their boat, Keith had "told [Private Herbert R.] Wendland to get in the boat. He said, 'No, you get in.' So I got in. He was the last man in and got killed."[21]

When his boat took a direct hit, killing two other engineers and wounding several troopers in his boat, Staff Sergeant Warren G. Hayes, with Company C, 307th Airborne Engineer Battalion, suffered a painful leg wound. Hayes took command of the remaining infantrymen and got the boat to the north side of the river. As it approached the riverbank, Hayes jumped out under fire and pulled the boat in by himself to save the wounded from drowning. With bullets and shrapnel hitting all around him, Hayes organized a new boat crew and returned to pick up a second boatload. He refused evacuation, and would make six round trips across the Waal River that day. Staff Sergeant Hayes received the Silver Star for his courageous actions.

Private First Class Walter E. Hughes was surprised that so many troopers made it. "Most of us did get to the other side, thanks to the efforts of some very brave 307 engineers, who to me were the real heroes that day."[22]

Only thirteen of the twenty-six boats made it to the north bank of the Waal River. As each of the boats unloaded their troopers, the surviving engineers rowed them back to the southern shore to pick up the second wave. From his position on the south riverbank, Lieutenant John Bigler observed that only one or two engineers were rowing the returning boats, instead of three, due to casualties during the initial crossing. Bigler, aware that those engineers would be exhausted as well, ordered all available Company C, 307th, engineers to man the boats to take the second wave across.

The boat that had taken Captain Burriss and twelve of his Company I troopers across the river was too badly shot up to make the return trip, so a Company C engineer, Private Ollie B. Obie Wickersham, Jr. found another boat. "There was a man [Technician Fifth Grade Harry W. Nicholson, Company C, 307th Airborne Engineer Battalion] lying in the boat—[he] had been shot through the thigh, with a tourniquet on. He said he thought that they had just forgotten about him, and he was just going to lie there and die. I don't know how I did it, but I got him back across the river in that boat. When we hit the [south] shore, he was so happy he gave me a trench knife with brass knuckles."[23]

Despite being hit in the hand by 20mm shrapnel, Private Wickersham made three round trips across the river that afternoon.

After the engineers rowed their boat back to the southern shore, the gravely wounded Private First Class Leonard Trimble's jump boots slipped on the bloodstained plywood bottom as he struggled to get out of the boat. As he did, Trimble saw the forms of three men running towards him in the hail of bullets and shrapnel. "There was never a more welcome sight in my life as these men approached me with their orange armbands, indicating they were Dutch Underground. They took me back to the nearest aid station."[24]

ON THE NORTH SIDE OF THE RIVER, THE 3RD BATTALION S-3, Captain Henry Keep, and his group "moved out across the open field into the fire. In many ways, this was the most remarkable scene of the whole operation. All along the shoreline now, our troops were appearing deployed as skirmishers. They were running into murderous fire from the embankment eight hundred yards away; but they continued to move forward across the plain in a long, single line many hundreds of yards wide. They cursed and yelled at each other as they advanced, noncoms and officers giving directions, the men firing from the hip their BARs, machine guns, and rifles, and steadily they moved forward.

"All this time the 2nd Battalion and the tanks on the other side of the river were giving us marvelous support. Their constant overhead fire into the embankment where the Germans were ensconced was heavy and effective, and somehow, it gave one a feeling of security and warmth, and pride in your buddies, who were helping you out. Because of it, you didn't mind the dirt that was constantly being kicked up around you from the Kraut bullets or the continual whistle of rounds whizzing by you, or the men who grunted and dropped in their tracks on either side.

"Many times I have seen troops who are driven to a fever pitch—troops who for a brief interval of combat are lifted out of themselves—fanatics, rendered crazy by rage and the lust for killing—men who forget temporarily the meaning of fear. It is an awe-inspiring sight, but not a pretty one. However, I had never witnessed this human metamorphosis so acutely displayed as on this day. The men were beside themselves. They continued to plow across that field in spite of all the Krauts could do, cursing savagely, their guns spitting fire."[25]

Lieutenant Edward Sims organized the survivors from his Company H boat and those from another boat, which landed with a number of casualties. "I ordered those who had not been wounded to join my group and then led this combined group of eighteen men in a frontal assault of the dike, [which] was several hundred yards farther north. I carried an M1 rifle and directed the assault forward by bounds, with rapid fire from all, including myself. Enemy fire from the dike was heavy, but the men with me did not falter. Their courage and determination was obvious."[26]

On the left flank, four Company I officers, Captain Burriss and Lieutenants Robert C. Blankenship, Robert M. Rogers, and Calvin R. Campbell, led the way toward the fifteen-foot-high embankment. Several enemy machine guns maintained a crossfire on the troopers as they charged the dike.

Lieutenant Blankenship observed one of the machine guns firing into the left flank of the advancing troopers. He moved across a hundred yards of open ground, drawing the fire of the machine gun. Closing to within fifty yards, Blankenship emptied his M1's eight-round clip, killing the four-man crew. Suddenly, he noticed a sniper concealed just five yards away, firing at his scout. Blankenship lunged at the German barehanded and knocked him unconscious with his fists.

Another I Company trooper, Private First Class Leo Muri, took another machine gun out, killing the three-man crew with a Gammon grenade. Then, he charged and destroyed a second machine gun crew with a fragmentation grenade.

Lieutenant Blankenship's and Private First Class Muri's courageous actions cleared the way and prevented many more casualties. Both received the Silver Star for their actions.

Sergeant Albert Tarbell, with Company H, finally reached the relative shelter of the dike after charging through a hail of 20mm and MG-42 fire. "One of our men, Private First Class John Rigapoulos, a veteran of the pathfinder group into France and of Anzio, was joking to me about getting a Purple Heart for his finger that had just been shot off."[27]

When Staff Sergeant Louis Orvin reached the dike, he attended to the wound of another Company I trooper, Sergeant Darrell D. Edgar, who had received a wound in the groin during the crossing and had charged the dike with the other troopers. "I told Edgar, 'Roll over and give me your sulfa packet.' All it looked like he had was a scratch right up in his crotch. I put the powder on it and laid the bandage on top of it. I said, 'Just stay here until a medic comes.' "[28]

After running all of the way to the dike, Keep was completely out of breath. "For a moment everyone lay on the rear slope of the bank drawing deep full breaths. A few of us stuck our heads up above the top to see what came next; a man had his head blown off. There was little organization at this point. How could there be? Officers found themselves with heterogeneous groups from all platoons and companies. They mustered whatever men were with them—it made little difference who was who—and prepared to go over the top."[29]

When Sergeant Robert Tallon, the 3rd Battalion operations sergeant, made it to the dike, he noticed that they were still receiving enfilade fire, so he and others got down low behind the dike. "I remember a machine gun was firing at us off to the right, probably from around the railroad bridge. The bullets were just skimming the top of the dike road; some even were hitting it. Next to me was another young replacement, a kid probably no more than eighteen or nineteen. He kept wondering where the firing was coming from. Frankly, I did too, because our artillery was supposed to have neutralized it before we got there. I told the kid to forget it; we could do nothing about it, and besides, there was a squad flanking to the right which would take care of it.

"Finally, the kid said something like, 'I'm going to have a look,' and he started crawling up the dike.

"I shouted, 'No!' But it was too late. He peeped over the top and instantly fell back, with a nice, neat, black hole square in the middle of his forehead."[30]

Lieutenant Burriss told the men on both sides of him, "'Use your grenades!' They immediately pulled the pins, and tossed them over the dike. The earth underneath us trembled with the almost simultaneous explosions. Then there was a moment of silence in front, followed by the screams of wounded Krauts. All along the line, other German gunners stood up, ready to surrender.

"But it was too late. Our men, in a frenzy over the wholesale slaughter of their buddies, continued to fire until every German on the dike lay dead or dying."[31]

One of Lieutenant Megellas' noncoms, Sergeant John J. Toman, was hit just above the ear as they closed in on the dike. Reaching the dike, Megellas stopped to bandage the arm of his platoon sergeant, Staff Sergeant Marvin Hirsch, when he looked to his right. "I noticed Sergeant [William H.] White, of I Company, jump to the top of the dike and holler, 'There go those S.O.B.s— after them, men.' With that, Sergeant White and a few men assembled at the dike gave hot pursuit of the fleeing enemy, and as others arrived at the dike, they too took after the enemy.

"Our plan to reassemble at this point obviously went astray, but I believe Sergeant White's ingenuity served to our advantage, since the enemy were not given an opportunity to regroup at alternative defensive positions."[32]

Staff Sergeant Orvin was almost killed as he crossed two wire fences lining the road that ran on top of the dike. "It had metal poles with a couple of strands of clothesline-type wire on each side of the road. I told my men, 'Let's get ready and go across and get on the other side of this dike.' I jumped across and when I did, I had a shovel with a 'T' handle, and that shovel got wound up in that wire. I was lying on my back and I saw tracers were going by. I told myself, 'Be calm.' I grabbed one wire with one hand and then I took my other hand and unwound my shovel, then rolled on off the other side of the dike."[33]

Private Francis Keefe reached for one of his specially modified Gammon grenades, which back in England he "had put British coins in the putty to make it an antipersonnel grenade. I threw one on the other side of the road. It sounded like a bomb going off. Two of the other troopers did the same thing. We immediately went over to the other side of the road. There was a house to our right front about fifty yards from the road or dike. I didn't see it because of the embankment [when I was] on the other side. There was a machine gun firing out of the upper window at the troops coming up from the river. At that time, I saw about six Germans come along a hedge and then run in the back door. This was happening in a matter of seconds.

"Sergeant [Marvin C.] Porter then let out a yell—he was shot in the leg. In a couple of seconds, the man next to Porter was also shot in the leg. They were only about four feet away from me. Lieutenant Blankenship, Muri, the kid from Brooklyn, and someone else were to the right front of them. I was in front of Porter a few feet, when a German about seven feet in front of me seemed to rise right out of the ground. I was stunned that he was that close. Porter must have seen him, because he killed him with a burst from his Thompson submachine gun."[34]

Keefe then mounted a rifle grenade on the barrel and loaded a blank cartridge in the chamber of his rifle to fire at the machine gun in the window of the house as Lieutenant Blankenship moved to help the two wounded troopers. Keefe "had the rifle in position to fire at the window when I was hit in the left wrist. The rifle dropped right down next to Blankenship. He was lucky that the grenade didn't go off. I said, 'Lieutenant, they shot off my hand.' The bullet had hit the bracelet I was wearing, which actually did a lot of damage.

"The kid from Brooklyn came over to help. I told him that in my back pocket there was a first aid packet. He went into the wrong pocket and pulled out my wallet. He said, 'What will I do with this?'

"I told him, 'Throw it away,' and he did. I said, 'Get the first aid packet,' which he did. I was holding my hand and my arm across my stomach. If I moved my left arm, my hand was hanging off. At that moment, I got hit in the upper right arm. Something hit me in the mouth and broke off my front tooth. Muri came over and helped the kid bandage my hand and arm. Then Muri was giving me a shot of morphine when somebody said, 'What do we do now?'

"I said, 'Keep firing at the building.' Blankenship knew we were in a bad position and went over to the other side of the road. Meanwhile, the kid from Brooklyn, who nothing seemed to bother, asked for my .45, and I said, 'Take it, I could care less.'

"I looked down the road and saw a lot of firing. It looked like H Company was doing a lot of firing into the building. Captain Burriss was there with 1st Sergeant [Curtis] Odom and about twelve men from the company. Odom took out his canteen and gave me a drink of water. It was just as if the war had stopped.

"Captain Burriss then told Sergeant [Alexander L.] Barker to take two men, go down, cross the river, and bring back more ammunition. He detailed two other men to help Porter and the other troops get down to the river. I was sitting there staring at the other troops, especially Muri. I was concerned about him, as we [had been] together two months at Anzio [and] neither of us [had] got a scratch (physically). They used to say he was too small and I was too skinny. I guess tears came to my eyes when I realized I couldn't be anymore help and I would never be back.

"It was then Captain Burriss said, 'I'll give you somebody to help you get back. Get yourself taken care of, and we'll see you when you get back.'

"I said, 'You won't see me again.'

He said, 'Well, I will never forget you.' It was nice of him."[35]

About that time, Keefe saw Lieutenant Blankenship returning over the top of the dike road "with a few men to help us get back to the other side of the road. I remember [Lawrence A.] Red Allen grabbed me around the waist and practically carried me over."[36]

Lieutenant Blankenship, Sergeant Porter, and Private First Class Muri then moved out, going after a flak-wagon and a machine gun, which Porter destroyed by firing rifle grenades from a distance of only seventy-five yards. Lieutenant Calvin Campbell took a squad of Company I troopers and moved northwest to attack and destroy another machine gun position.

With the dike overrun, Megellas gathered some of his Company H platoon and set off for Fort Hof Van Holland with one thought on his mind: "It was payback time."[37]

Lieutenant Sims and his eighteen men moved toward the railroad embankment to deal with the 20mm guns on the railroad bridge that had done so much killing earlier. "Lieutenant LaRiviere with a few men moved east to flush out a sniper that had shot and killed one of his men."[38]

Captain Burriss split his men into two groups. "I told [Private First Class] Muri to take his men and head up the dike road. I would follow the hedgerow just north of the road and meet him where the railroad and the [dike] road intersected."[39]

As Companies H and I were assaulting the dike, Lieutenant Holabird and his engineers had landed closest to the railroad bridge and had moved directly toward it in an effort to disarm any explosive charges wired to the bridge before the Germans could detonate them. Holabird and his men fought as infantry in order to get to there. "We started inland, and about 150 yards up from the beach we came across two German pillboxes. We hit them from the side. I took one, and my platoon sergeant, Sergeant William [E.] Kero, took the other. We threw three or four grenades in and then went on."[40]

Captain Keep was with a group of about thirty men, including Major Cook, the 3rd Battalion commander. Keep and his group kept the pressure on the Germans, not allowing them to reorganize. "By squad rushes, we crossed fields, worked our way through orchards and down ditches. From one house to another, we jumped. . . . In our particular bunch, I witnessed countless acts of heroism—all of which deserve decorations, but which of course will remain unknown."[41]

Watching the entire crossing and assault from the power plant, and commenting on the incredible bravery shown by Tucker's paratroopers, British

General Browning turned to the British XXX Corps commander, General Brian Horrocks, and said, "I have never seen a more gallant action."[42]

As ENGINEERS RETURNED THE BOATS TO THE SOUTH BANK to ferry across the second wave, additional engineers and other troopers replaced the engineers who were casualties or too exhausted to continue. Lieutenant Hanz Druener and the rest of Company D had been firing in support of the 3rd Battalion crossing. "Only half of the boats came back, and with a lot of the engineers either killed or wounded, some of my people just volunteered. . . [they] got in and helped row these things back and forth."[43]

The boats arrived singly and in pairs, most carrying back wounded and rowed by one or two engineers, sometimes themselves wounded. Despite heavy concentrations of enemy artillery, mortar, and long-range automatic weapons fire meant to interdict additional crossings, the Company G commander, Captain Fred E. Thomas, kept his company behind the embankment, formed in boatload groups. Thomas observed the returning boats from the front of the dike, and as they arrived, he signaled by hand the number of boats to the next man in a chain he had formed of four troopers that extended over the dike to where the company was waiting. Boatloads were dispatched accordingly.

Crossing in the first boat of the second wave, Lieutenant Roy Hanna, the Company G executive officer, "kneeled in about the center of the boat, on the right hand side, and just started paddling. I think it took me only 455 strokes to get across, I was paddling so damned fast. I can't remember who was in the boat with me, but I know I felt like I was the only one."[44]

Sergeant Earl Oldfather had fought as a member of G Company since the Italian campaigns. "I think the fiercest fighting I was ever in was crossing the Waal River at Nijmegen. How we ever made it in those assault boats with shells landing all around us, I'll never know. Some were plenty close."[45]

Company C, 307th engineer, Private First Class Harold Herbert, was wounded in the hip as he made his second crossing with a load of Company G troopers. Herbert would make the return trip and take another boatload across and return before being helped out of the boat and taken to an aid station. After he was patched up, he returned to the company that night.

Lieutenant Allen F. McClain, III, the commander of the 81mm Mortar Platoon, Headquarters Company, 3rd Battalion, was carrying the base plate of one of the platoon's mortars as well as his personal weapon and gear, as he tried to get aboard one of the boats, but "the additional weight caused me to sink hip deep in the silt-like mud. But for the super strength of Victor [G.] Rosca, a staff sergeant, I might have been left to settle in that slimy mud."[46]

Lieutenant John Bigler, with Company C, 307th Airborne Engineer Battalion, responsible for overseeing the loading of Company G and Headquarters Company, 3rd Battalion, took the place of a seriously wounded engineer and made the crossing with the second wave. Lieutenant Bigler was awarded the Silver Star for his valor.

THE REGIMENT'S PROTESTANT CHAPLAIN, CAPTAIN DELBERT KUEHL, tended to the wounded near the landing area and oversaw their evacuation to the south side of the river. "While giving first aid to a man who had a serious stomach wound, I was hit in the back by shrapnel and fell on top of him. I'll never forget the concern he showed me when he cried out, 'Oh chaplain, did they get you too?' Here's a trooper with his belly torn open and he's sorry about me. That's what made the 504th the unit it was. Never was I prouder than then to be a member of such a fighting force."[47]

Captain Kuehl's presence was inspirational and unforgettable for those who saw him tending the wounded that day. He helped get thirty-five of the wounded ferried back to the south side of the river. Chaplain Kuehl received the Silver Star for his selfless and heroic actions.

One of the 3rd Battalion surgeons, Lieutenant Hyman D. Shapiro, treated some of the wounded and dying near the water's edge. "I had a couple of calls and administered a few injections of morphine. Most of the [wounded] men were in the boats, still, and I told the engineers to take them back with them."[48]

With his badly wounded left hand and right arm, Private Francis Keefe, with Company I, made his way toward the landing area on the north side of the river. "In the distance by the water's edge on the right [was] a congregation of men coming up from the river. About halfway, there were about six bodies strung out. As I got closer, I saw [Private Robert E.] Dority, the medic, attending to one of the men who was lying there. Someone was taking potshots all around him. The dirt was popping up. As I got closer, [the German soldier] started popping them around me. I believe it must have been coming from the wooded area on the other side of the road or dike. Dority yelled to me to get down and then ran over to me.

"When he got there he said, 'You better stay down, or you are going to get killed.' I asked him how the troops were that were lying down. He said not too good. He asked if there was anything he could do for me. I said no. He said he had to get back to the wounded and told me to stay down getting back. I kept low getting back as best I could. As I got close to the group [near the shore], I saw some German prisoners, the protestant chaplain, some wounded, and Sergeant [Alexander] Barker getting into a boat to start across with some of the wounded. It made me feel good that the German prisoners didn't get priority.

"As I got close to the chaplain, I said, 'Why can't [the German prisoners] give some help to the wounded lying above?'

"He said, 'They will be alright.' He was concerned about the German prisoners. I had to get away from there. I walked back to where we had landed.

"Someone was coming down on an angle to the right. When he came closer, I recognized him as Blacky [Private Louis Rassiga]. He had a head wound. We went over to the chaplain and where the prisoners were, and Blacky got into a discussion with the chaplain about the prisoners. He came back to me and wanted to know if I had a gun. He said, 'Let's see if we can find one.'

"I walked about forty yards along the shore towards the bridge that ran into a little inlet which was about twenty feet in from the water, about fifteen feet wide, and about four or five feet deep. I saw Lieutenant [Harry] Busby's body—his legs were still lying in the water. I felt bad about the argument [just prior to the crossing]. I wish I could have gotten down and pulled him out of the water, but it was impossible. I called Blacky and showed him, but he couldn't get down there by himself. The chaplain told me not to worry about it—he would be alright."[49]

THE 504TH HAD PAID FOR THE NORTH END of the two Nijmegen bridges with the blood of troopers like Lieutenant Busby; now they were going to collect. The plan called for Companies H and I to fight their way north along the railroad embankment to where it intersected with the roadway running north from the highway bridge, then turn south and attack toward the north end of the highway bridge with Company I on the left (east) and Company H on the right (west) side of the highway. Company G was to follow and block the highway, protecting the rear of the two assaulting companies.

After crossing the dike, Lieutenant Richard LaRiviere ("Rivers") led part of his 2nd Platoon, Company H, troopers east through ditches to a junction with a secondary road, northeast of Fort Hof Van Holland. There, they cleared two houses and started toward the fort. Suddenly, a German machine gun opened up on them. Rivers and Private First Class John Rigapoulos were kneeling beside one another trying to locate the machine gun when Rigapoulos was hit in the chest with a burst, knocking him over backward, killing him. Rivers and his group overran and occupied a number of German foxholes and then returned fire on the fort. Rigapoulos had jumped in Normandy as one of just twenty-six 504 pathfinders, and his loss would shock Company H.

At this point, Rivers' platoon sergeant, Staff Sergeant James Allen, Jr., Sergeant Theodore Finkbeiner, and ten men split off from the group and headed northeast toward the area of the junction of the railroad overpass and the main road north of the highway bridge. Along the way, a squad of the 3rd Platoon of Company I, led by Lieutenant Edward W. Kennedy, Staff Sergeant Orvin, and Sergeant George Leoleis, that included Privates First Class John P. Ternosky and Walter J. Muszynski, joined them and moved along a ditch which ran parallel to the railroad embankment to within twenty yards of the railroad trestle.

There, Sergeant Finkbeiner stuck his head over the top of the embankment and found himself staring right into the muzzle of a German MG-34 machine gun. "I think he was as surprised as I was. I ducked, but the muzzle blast blew the little wool line cap off my head. My two companions and I tossed some grenades over the embankment, and the Germans tossed some over at us. I heard what I assumed was a command, and several Germans charged us. We repulsed the charge, killing a couple and wounding another."[50]

Moments later, wanting to capitalize on the temporary disorganization of the Germans, who had just been thrown back, Sergeant William Kero, one of Lieutenant John Holabird's 2nd Platoon engineers, rushed to the top of the railroad embankment and began firing his Thompson submachine gun down at them. As he was spraying the stunned Germans, Kero himself was cut down by enemy fire. Sergeant Kero's extraordinary heroism was recognized with the posthumous award of the Distinguished Service Cross.

Meanwhile, Sergeants Allen and Leoleis rushed a house about five yards from the railroad overpass, then motioned for Muszynski and Ternosky to bring up their light machine gun. As the machine gun team reached the house, Allen and Leoleis rushed the overpass.

About that time, some thirty or so Germans got around behind the group and opened fire. Almost simultaneously, a German self-propelled 20mm flak gun pulled up to the junction where the railroad embankment passed under the highway and opened up on the group. Sergeant Allen was hit in the groin by rifle fire and would die later that day from a severed femoral artery. Sergeant Leoleis withdrew to the house, just before the flak-wagon trained its fire on it and destroyed Muszynski's machine gun. Muszynski slipped out of the house and crept up to within fifteen yards of the flak-wagon, and using hand grenades, knocked it out, killing four more of the enemy. Only moments later, as he started back to get more hand grenades from the group, Muszynski was killed by rifle fire. Sergeant Leoleis decided to withdraw to the ditch and await reinforcements. For his courage, Private First Class Muszynski would later be posthumously awarded the Distinguished Service Cross.

Just seconds later, Lieutenant William H. Preston and Sergeant Sus J. Gonzales, both with Company H, arrived and opened fire on the Germans who had gotten behind Finkbeiner's group, killing most of them. Finkbeiner and his group then moved under the trestle to the other side of the railroad embankment.

As this was occurring, Lieutenants Jim Megellas and Ernest Murphy, leading a group of 3rd Platoon, Company H troopers, followed the west side of the dike road and then crossed over and took up positions in defilade between the dike and Fort Hof Von Holland. Megellas' group included Sergeants Leroy M. Richmond, Robert N. Seymour, and James Foley; Corporal Edward E. Jackson; Privates First Class Lawrence H. Dunlop, Robert E. Hawn, and Tommy G. Smiley; and Privates Edward J. Kelly, Sylvester J. Larkin, James H. Rosser, and Everett S. Trefethern. Megellas "saw an opportunity to silence the 20mm antiaircraft guns and machine guns that had rained so much havoc on us when we were sitting ducks. I directed all the fire we could mass at those targets, forcing the Germans to seek cover."[51]

After Megellas and his men suppressed the enemy fire from the fort, they rushed up to the moat surrounding the fort. Sergeant Leroy Richmond pulled off his equipment, swam across the moat, and climbed the sloped earthen wall of the fort as Megellas and his men kept up a covering fire. Megellas watched Richmond look over into the fort. "He began frantically waving his arms, pointing to the Germans inside and motioning us to circle around to the opposite side to a drawbridge, the only entrance to the fort. As he was looking down into the fort, the sound of a German Mauser rifle broke the silence.

"Sergeant Richmond must have been carrying a rabbit's foot. The bullet grazed his neck, but did not seriously wound him. He started back down the incline, swam the moat, and rejoined us. From our position on the edge of the moat, we lobbed hand grenades over the parapet and inside the fort."[52]

Megellas and eleven of his men worked their way around the fort to the causeway on the south side. There, Megellas and the others covered Private First Class Robert Hawn and another trooper as they rushed across the causeway, where they reached the archway leading into the fort's courtyard. Germans in the fort fired at them with rifles and threw hand grenades, while Hawn and the other trooper retaliated with Gammon grenades. As this occurred, Megellas, Murphy, and the rest of the group charged across the causeway and began climbing the sloped, grassy sides of the fort. After Privates First Class Everett Trefethern and James Rosser lobbed Gammon grenades into the gun emplacements, Sergeant Robert Seymour called on the German garrison to surrender, but was wounded by a sniper. A short time later, artillery from the 376th and friendly small-arms fire began to hit the fort. Lieutenant Megellas, thinking the small-arms fire was coming from Company G, dispatched Private First Class Sylvester Larkin with a message requesting that they cease fire on the fort. However, the artillery fire continued, so Megellas decided to withdraw the group to a position north of the fort. "I didn't know how many Germans were inside the fort, but as long as they didn't constitute a threat to our forces still crossing the river or impede our attack on the bridges, I was not concerned. We could move out to help seize the bridges, our principal objective, and let the men of the 1st Battalion coming up behind us take care of them."[53]

As Megellas and his troopers were attacking Fort Hof Van Holland, other elements of Company H moved eastward through a ditch north of the fort, reaching the west side of the railroad embankment. Captain Kappel and his men initially attempted to rush the other side. "All efforts to cross the embankment were repulsed by heavy fire. Grenades were exchanged over the [embankment]. Many machine guns, including 20mm, fired grazing fire along the top of the railway embankment. Men were dispatched south along the top of the railway embankment in an effort to penetrate through culverts or to find an underpass. An unfortunate incident occurred because a group of civilians occupied a concrete shelter under the railway embankment. The attacking force, seeking an entrance through the embankment, found the shelter, believing it to be a passageway and hearing voices, tossed in Gammon grenades and assaulted the position, severely wounding two women, among others. The chamber did not have an exit on the east side.

"In the assault on the embankment, one 88mm antitank gun and one smaller-caliber AT gun, mounted on top of the embankment covering the railway bridge, were neutralized. The guns, dug in, were not physically in our possession, but could not be reached by the Germans as long as we remained within a few feet of them.

"I then directed that the attack be shifted south along the embankment to seize the northern end of the railroad bridge, pass under the bridge, and attack the highway bridge from the west, with the right flank secured by the dike parallel to the Waal. This, if successful, would give us one bridge across the river. The 2nd and 3rd Platoons pressed this attack with vigor and quickly overran the exterior positions."[54]

As Lieutenant Rivers led about a squad of troopers south along the west side of the railroad embankment, they ran into a group of thirty to forty Germans, whom they killed, then continued toward the north end of the railroad bridge.

Captain Kappel and his group of Company H troopers converged on the railroad bridge. "A concrete and steel fort had been constructed within the abutments of the railroad bridge. With one group of six men keeping the embrasures under fire, the remainder of the 3rd Platoon, consisting of eight men, entered the abutment, found the passageways in the dark, and emerged into the fort. The squad leader [Corporal John M. Fowler] leading the assault (only one man could go up the narrow winding steps at a time) was severely wounded, but he killed and wounded several Germans. The remainder of twelve to fourteen surrendered. They were the first prisoners H Company had taken all day."[55] For his valor, Corporal Fowler received a promotion to sergeant and the Silver Star.

PRIVATE FIRST CLASS WALTER E. HUGHES, with Company I, moved along the dike road with a group led by Captain Burriss. "Everyone started toward the railroad bridge, taking out pockets of Germans along the way. I followed Captain Burriss and four or five others, trying to ignore the noise of the firing and mortars, but afraid to blink my eyes, for fear of becoming separated from them or coming upon a German and not acting quickly enough. The constant noise seemed to urge everyone on, 'Finish the job,' I thought, 'and the shooting will stop . . . finish the job and the killing will end.'

"I came face to face with a dead paratrooper on the stairs and thought, 'Some American family back home will never be the same again.'

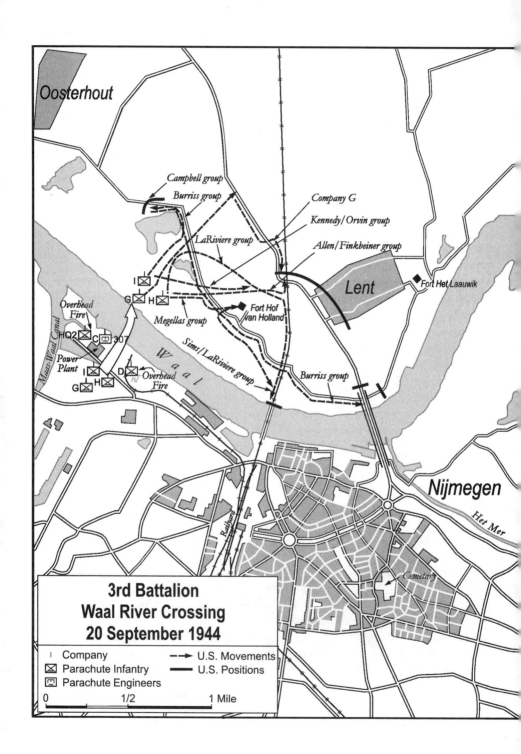

Oosterhout

Campbell group
Burriss group

Company G

Kennedy/Orvin group

Allen/Finkbeiner group

LaRiviere group

Lent

Fort Het Laauwik

I

G H

Overhead
Fire

Megellas group

Fort Hof
van Holland

HQ2 C 307

Power
Plant

I D

G H Overhead
Fire

W a a l

Sims/LaRiviere group

Burriss group

Maas-Waal Canal

Nijmegen

Het Mer

Ratbort

Cemetary

**3rd Battalion
Waal River Crossing
20 September 1944**

I	Company	----▶ U.S. Movements
⊠	Parachute Infantry	▬▬ U.S. Positions
▥	Parachute Engineers	

0   1/2   1 Mile

"Someone said to cut the wires wherever you see them; they are attached to explosives."[56]

After supervising the loading of his company while under intense artillery and mortar fire, Captain Fred Thomas had crossed the river with the last boatload of Company G troopers. "After beaching our boats in the deep end on the enemy bank of the river, we ran forward to the small rise that constituted the levee on that side of the river. Gaining our breath, we moved forward across open, level fields for approximately 450 yards. We began assembling our company, by platoons, next to a raised road. Company G then moved across the road by running one at a time, because the road was under enemy machine gun fire and the house at the far side of the road had been set on fire by an artillery shell. After crossing the road, the company moved forward again through small ditches that ran all around the edge of each field. The company moved forward in a ditch which ran diagonal to the main road from the Nijmegen bridge. Upon reaching the road, the company was stopped by the enemy who were just on the other side of the large railroad embankment. A hand grenade battle began, with both sides tossing hand grenades over the railroad embankment. About seventy-five or one hundred feet to the right, down the road, was a railroad trestle. The Jerries were in the underpass in strong force. It was at this point that the platoon leader of the 2nd Platoon [Lieutenant Steve Seyebe] was killed while rushing the embankment."[57]

The engineers returned once more to the southern shore of the Waal River to take troopers of the 1st Battalion across the river, with Company C crossing in the third wave. The first two returning boats, bullet ridden and littered with the bodies of dead and wounded, arrived on the south bank west of the loading area because the current had carried them down river. Charlie Company troopers rushed down to board them, only to have both of them sink. The next four boats arrived, taking on water from the holes torn in the canvas by bullets and shrapnel, [they] were plugged with pieces of cloth. Private First Class Ross Pippin threw his equipment in his assigned boat and climbed over the canvas side. "By that time there were only a few boats left. Every time a boat landed, the paratroopers would immediately go into action."[58]

Troopers in each boat bailed water while others paddled, as sporadic rifle and 20mm fire continued to make the crossing dangerous. Upon landing, Company C moved out to its objective, establishing a line in an arc extending southwest from the dike road to the riverbank, defending the left flank of the regiment. Captain Ernie Milloy sent Sergeant Edward A. Fox and a group of 2nd Platoon troopers deployed in a skirmish line to the northwest. Next, Milloy dispatched the assistant platoon leader of the 1st Platoon, Lieutenant Robert A. Madruga, with most of the rest of the platoon, also deployed as skirmishers, to the right rear of Fox's troopers. They met little opposition, but did flush out a few enemy soldiers as they moved. Lieutenant Milton Baraff and nine 3rd

Platoon troopers, advancing in a wedge formation, moved into position as the company reserve, with the mortar squads deployed to their rear. By 4:30 p.m., the 1st Platoon was deployed with its right flank on the dike road southeast of Oosterhout and its positions extended southwestwardly, where it tied in with the 2nd Platoon, which extended southward to the riverbank. The 3rd Platoon and the company mortars remained in reserve.

The Company A commander, Captain Charles Duncan, had split his company into thirteen-man-boatload teams, and they crossed in six boats in the fourth wave. An exhausted Lieutenant Tom McLeod, the assistant platoon leader of the 3rd Platoon of the Company C engineers, made it to the north side of the river with his fourth boatload of troopers. "I got out and walked up and down the bank. I saw Corporal Jim Jacobs, a fellow from South Carolina, slumped over in the stern of a boat. He was dead, [but] no one had gotten around to moving him yet. I found another engineer sprawled out flat in the bottom of another boat. He was dead, too, but I can't remember his name.

"One strange thing I remember as I walked up and down the bank was rifles stuck in the ground, bayonet first, marking the spots where men had fallen. Their bodies were lying right alongside, and someone had come along and pushed their rifles into the sand."[59]

As Private Nicholas Mansolillo waited for a boat to cross in the fifth wave, along with a group of other Headquarters Company, 1st Battalion troopers, including one of his best friends, Technician Fourth Grade John T. Mullen, enemy artillery began falling nearby. "Most of us were running for cover. That's when I came across John. I ran right by him seeking cover by a wall, when I heard someone say that that trooper was John. I ran over to him—he was a goner. He lay in a pool of blood. It looked to me like shrapnel got him in the neck. You could see the steam rising from the warm blood. John died—he had bled to death—there was nothing anyone could do to save him. John and I had been together since our days at Fort Bragg."[60]

Upon landing, the 1st Platoon of Company A moved out under machine gun, sniper, 88mm, and 20mm fire to assault Fort Hof Van Holland while the 3rd Platoon moved east along the riverbank to clear the area between the railroad and highway bridges. The 2nd Platoon remained in defilade on the edge of a small lake, which had a low water level, affording good protection against direct fire.

Captain Duncan led members of the 1st Platoon on the assault on the fort, including Staff Sergeant Otto Huebner; Sergeant Homer Henry; Corporal Frank L. Heidebrink; Privates First Class Peter Schneider and Charles Spiegle; and Privates William G. Brown, Edward J. Gaida, Gordon Gould, James E. Tippitt, Robert Washko, and Ignatius W. Wengress. They charged over the dike road, across the causeway, up the grass slopes of the fort, and jumped into the gun positions at the top of the walls. After Schneider called on the Germans to

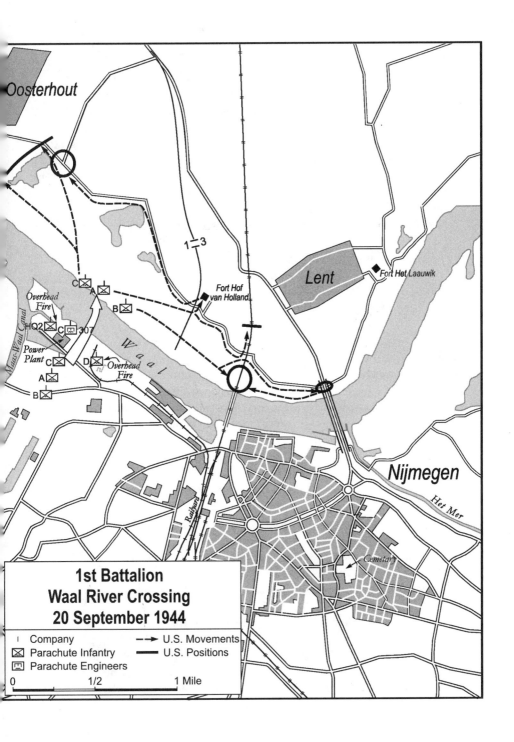

Oosterhout

1–3

Fort Het Laauwik

Lent

Fort Hof
van Holland

C

A

*Overhead
Fire*

B

HQ2

C 307

*Power
Plant*

C

D *Overhead
Fire*

A

B

W a a l

Maas-Waal Canal

Nijmegen

Het Mer

Railyard

Cemetary

1st Battalion
Waal River Crossing
20 September 1944

	Company		→ U.S. Movements
☒	Parachute Infantry	— U.S. Positions
▣	Parachute Engineers	

| 0 | | 1/2 | | 1 Mile |

surrender, eighteen came out with their hands up. Just as this occurred, other Germans outside the fort attempted to retake it. As Private Washko set up his BAR to cover the causeway, he was killed. However, reinforcements in the form of the 2nd Platoon of Company A and some Headquarters Company troopers arrived to secure the fort. With Fort Hof Van Holland secure, the 1st Platoon moved northeast and took up positions straddling the railroad embankment.

As Company B waited for their turn in the sixth and final wave, Private Mike Clements finished two Hershey's chocolate bars and was starting a third. "I had been told that the Germans loved to loot American soldiers for the cigarettes and candy bars, and I was determined to keep this from happening. Finally, my face smeared with chocolate, we moved out into the opening and ran down to the boats. As we loaded up and pushed off, directly in front of us on the other side, we saw the bodies of six German soldiers who had died manning two machine guns placed at the edge of the water. There was not the slightest bit of cover for them—no place to hide—and no opportunity for them to surrender. Behind them was a flat floodplain of approximately three hundred yards. Clearly, they must have known they were in a suicidal position, and I marveled at their bravery."[61]

ACROSS THE RIVER, LIEUTENANT ED SIMS and a small group of Company H troopers moved cautiously toward the railroad bridge. "Resistance at the north end of the railroad bridge was light, and it soon fell into our hands. Next, I ordered a few men to look for explosives and cut all wires. Then, I set up a defense around our end of the bridge. During a hasty search of the supporting abutments, a holdout sniper shot one of my sergeants. He was badly wounded, but he received fast medical treatment and eventually recovered. "Lieutenant LaRiviere and the few men with him joined us—and not a moment too soon."[62]

On the south side of the river at the railroad yard, Company D, 505th Parachute Infantry Regiment, attacked the Germans holding the embankment on the southern approach of the railroad bridge. Fearing their escape route across the river was about to close, the Germans abandoned their positions and fled across the bridge.

Together, Lieutenants LaRiviere's and Sims' group now totaled just nineteen troopers. Rivers saw a large group of Germans trying to escape the trap, coming from Nijmegen north across the railroad bridge toward the small force. "We let them come—two-thirds of the way."[63]

Lieutenant Allen McClain, commanding the 81mm Mortar Platoon, Headquarters Company, 3rd Battalion, was watching from the northern end of the bridge with LaRiviere and Sims. "I estimate there were better than five hundred who started across. We had two machine gun crews and two BARs set up at the end of the bridge. When the Germans were a little better than halfway across, the automatic weapons opened up."[64]

Captain Kappel watched as the Germans attempted to break through the small force of Company H troopers holding the north end of the bridge. "These units made several counterattacks across the bridge, which were easily dealt with. One [German soldier] did succeed in reaching within hand grenade distance of the fort, but was promptly killed. Many Germans, now hopelessly cut off, attempted to escape by jumping from the bridge. The men were shooting them in the air until stopped by me, due to the shortage of ammunition. Two German machine guns were mounted to sweep the long axis of the bridge, and the German situation was now hopeless.

"One of the German prisoners who could understand English, was ordered out on the bridge to tell the Germans to cross to the south side and surrender. He was shot by the Germans pinned on the bridge. They were again swept by machine gun fire, and many leaped from the bridge, even though they were not over the river. None surrendered at this time."[65]

As the two captured German machine guns opened up again on the Germans trapped on the bridge, Lieutenant McClain saw more enemy soldiers "leaping into the swift current of the river below. Some wounded fell through between the ties. Hardened by over two years of combat and the loss of many of my men, I still felt sick at this inhumanity to man. Two hundred sixty-seven bodies remained on the bridge the next morning."[66]

Lieutenant Sims felt differently. "At the time, my men and I were tense and angry because of the strenuous fighting and the loss of so many of our own men during the crossing. We had little concern about destroying the large enemy force opposing us.

"Often in my mind I relive this particular action, and always conclude that this terrible slaughter of humans is not something to be proud of or brag about."[67]

The following day, Private Joseph A. Dickson, with Company C, 307th Airborne Engineer Battalion, counted thirty-four machine guns, two 20mm antiaircraft guns, and one 88mm dual-purpose antiaircraft/antitank gun on the railroad bridge.[68] These weapons had been responsible for much of the devastating fire experienced by the 3rd Battalion during its crossing of the Waal River.

At 5:00 p.m., Captain Kappel tried to radio Colonel Tucker to report that the railroad bridge was in their hands and request that tanks be sent across the railroad bridge. To the north on the main road, near the railroad trestle, the Company G commander, Captain Fred Thomas, received "information over the battalion radio that the railroad bridge had been taken. All of this time, the company was surrounded on three sides by the enemy."[69]

From the dike, across the fields to the railroad embankment, and now at the railroad bridge, Captain Keep, the 3rd Battalion operations officer, had seen dead Germans seemingly everywhere. "I have seen a lot of gruesome sights since this war began, but I have never witnessed such absolute carnage as I did that day. Everywhere, the bodies of Krauts were sprawled grotesquely; in places, they were piled high."[70]

Corporal Jack L. Bommer, with Headquarters Company, 504th, "killed boys not over fifteen and men over sixty-five in their foxholes in the crossing. It was such an operation, everything went so fast and so hectic—it's hard to explain.

"Surrenders—I saw few of—there wasn't time. I did see old German men grab our M1s and beg for mercy—they were shot point-blank."[71]

Below the railroad bridge, Lieutenant Robert Currier arrived with the 3rd Platoon of Company A, where they set up two machine guns and two mortars. Sergeant William J. Schlacter called out in German for enemy soldiers on the bridge abutment and girders below the railroad track bed. Hearing no answer to the surrender demand, and noticing hammering sounds on the steel, they believed the bridge was being prepared for imminent demolition. The Able Company troopers opened fire, killing fifteen German soldiers. Again, Sergeant Schlacter called out to the survivors, and twenty-one Germans surrendered.

As Company B began arriving, the 1st Battalion commander, Major Willard Harrison, not knowing whether the railroad bridge had been captured, ordered Captain Tom Helgeson to take the first three boatloads of Company B troopers to land and attack the north end of the railroad bridge. Lieutenant Richard A. Smith and Staff Sergeant William P. "Knobby" Walsh led the assault element of a squad of twelve troopers eastward toward the railroad bridge, followed by the remaining twenty-five troopers deployed in a skirmish line. However, about four hundred yards from the bridge, two enemy machine guns on the south end of the railroad bridge opened fire, pinning them down.

With the north end of the railroad bridge firmly in their control, Lieutenant LaRiviere told Lieutenant Sims, "You take care of the railroad bridge, I'm going with Burriss."[72]

Captain Burriss led the way east down the dike road toward the highway bridge, making sure they cleaned out the houses located along the dike road as his Company I moved east. "We approached houses on either side. 'OK, let's check each house to make sure no Krauts are inside,' I said.

"I stepped on the porch of the first house and opened the door. More than a dozen German soldiers were sleeping on the floor. One of them, a grizzled veteran, rolled over, opened one eye, saw me, and grabbed for his rifle. When he did, I tossed a Gammon grenade in the middle of the sleeping pile and dived off the porch. The ensuing blast blew out the windows and the door. After the smoke had cleared, I peered inside. There were no survivors."[73]

As Burriss' group moved east along the dike road nearing the highway bridge, enemy machine gun fire from the south end of the railroad bridge and from the north, pinned down the last half of the column. Private Ralph N.

Tison, Jr., set up his machine gun and returned the fire. The leading half of the column forced the Germans to abandon an antitank gun positioned between the two bridges, with fields of fire covering any vehicles attempting to cross either bridge. While Privates Gerald E. Melton, Robert L. Tope, and Young were searching for snipers, they came across another antitank gun, which Melton took out with a Gammon grenade, killing five Germans. Burriss then dispatched Privates Robert J. Yanuzzi and Elvie W. Bartow to bring up the rear of the column, which brought the strength of the force to twenty. Burriss and his group then resumed the drive for the highway bridge.

After Company G arrived at the railroad overpass, Sergeant George Leoleis and four other Company I troopers moved south, crossed the railroad embankment, and dashed to the main road, north of the highway bridge. There, Leoleis and his men cleared a house, killing eight Germans. "We were separated from any other men, but we knew in what direction to head for, down the road toward the bridge. We were now fighting the kind of fight we were trained for, and we were the best at it. No quarter given and no quarter asked."[74]

Pinned down just west of the railroad bridge, Captain Tom Helgeson, Lieutenant Richard Smith, and the troopers of Company B took off on command and ran to the north end of the railroad bridge, where they found Lieutenants Megellas and Sims, with about forty H Company troopers. Company B relieved them and set up a perimeter defense of the north end of the bridge, while the Company H group moved out toward the highway bridge.

Just as British Grenadier Guards tanks and the 2nd Battalion, 505th, were overrunning the southern approach to the highway bridge, the Company I commander, Captain Burriss, and Company H platoon leader, Lieutenant LaRiviere, neared the highway bridge. Burriss sent Lieutenant Robert Rogers and nine of his men around the north approach and up to the road, while he took the other nine underneath. The concrete piers rose almost two hundred feet above to the bridge surface. Strangely, there was no firing around the bridge. Burriss could hear firing around the southern end of the great bridge across the river in Nijmegen. "As I stood beneath the north end, I saw a set of concrete steps that went from the lower road to the main highway at that end. I told [Private First Class Leo] Muri to take some men and cut any wires that they saw around the supporting columns of the bridge. Then I turned to LaRiviere and pointed up the concrete stairway. 'Let's go up!' "[75]

Meanwhile, the other group circled around and came toward the north end of the bridge along the highway. The first men on the bridge were Privates First Class John W. Hall, Jr., and Robert A. Hedberg and Private Norman J. Ryder.

Burriss led the other group up the stairs and encountered one lone German as he reached the road surface of the bridge above. The German surrendered, and Burriss waved his guys up. "LaRiviere and an enlisted man were standing with me at the end of the bridge. I had just told LaRiviere to take some men, start across the bridge, and cut wires, when a German standing high in the girders shot and killed the enlisted man standing between us. LaRiviere immediately wheeled around and shot the Kraut. As the man fell, one of his straps caught in the girders, and he was caught in the steel structure. When we left two days later, he was still hanging there."[76]

Private James J. Musa and the other troopers with Megellas "deployed on both sides of the bridge. The Germans were firing at us from the girders, and there were more [Germans] on the bridge. Some Germans tried to escape the advance of the Allied forces on the south and ran toward us. We held our fire until they were within close range and then opened fire. Some turned around and started back towards the south end trying to surrender. Other Germans were still holding out in the girders of the bridge. We called for them to come down and surrender."[77]

After securing the bridge, Lieutenant Rogers took eight troopers 150 yards up the road north of the bridge and set up a roadblock. Down on the dike road, Lieutenant Robert Blankenship and another eight troopers set up a roadblock about two hundred yards from the bridge.

Lieutenant Megellas and part of his Company H platoon had arrived at the bridge just as the firing subsided. "The highway bridge was littered with German bodies, evidence of the fierce fight that had taken place."[78]

Arriving with Lieutenant Megellas, Captain Kappel quickly organized the close-in defense of the highway bridge. "I Company established a command post in the abutments and dispatched their men to the east. The 1st Platoon of Company H pushed to the north about four hundred yards and occupied positions astride the road. The 3rd Platoon occupied the west side of the bridge. The 2nd Platoon of H Company crossed the highway bridge to the south side. There were many Germans in the girders of the bridge, firing into the area, and many more Germans in the vicinity of the bridge, all disorganized but quite capable of serious trouble, if they realized it.

"The situation at the highway bridge was critical. Although they were in possession of the objective, many of the men were without ammunition. Nearly all were down to the last clip. Messengers were dispatched to the battalion commander, informing him the bridge was in our hands and requesting ammunition. The 300 radio, now with the battalion commander, was the only link with the south side. The 2nd Platoon leader had expected to contact friendly troops on the south side of the bridge, but the infantry had not yet arrived. The battalion commander [Major Cook] and S-3 [Captain Keep] arrived at the highway bridge. They had been promised ammunition to be delivered across the highway bridge. The mortar section of H Company was rounding up prisoners in the vicinity of the bridges and had about one hundred gathered underneath the railroad bridge. They were being collected and guarded by men whose total amount of ammunition was approximately twenty-five rounds.

"Prior to contact being made with friendly units, the tractor-trailer captured by H Company on D+1, driven by the 3rd Battalion supply officer [Lieutenant Thomas Utterback] and escorted by the regimental munitions officer, roared across the bridge, loaded with ammunition. With all men busy and under some fire, it was speedily unloaded by a high-ranking detail consisting of those two men, the battalion commander, battalion S-3, and the company commanders of H and I Companies. The truck returned to our area safely.

"With the resupply of ammunition, the 2nd Platoon of H Company recrossed the bridge, capturing fourteen Germans in the girders, and killing several more. This time, they contacted elements of the 505 Parachute Infantry. Patrols were sent out with instructions to have the 3rd Battalion assemble on the highway bridge and reorganize. A platoon from 1st Battalion, of about twenty-five men, reported in to the bridge and were immediately attached to H Company to strengthen the defense of the bridge."[79]

At 7:15 p.m., as the light faded in the west, Captain Burriss radioed to regimental headquarters that they had captured the highway bridge. About fifteen minutes earlier, the 1st Battalion had cleaned out Fort Hof Van Holland.

On the south side of the highway bridge, the commander of the 2nd Battalion, 505th, Lieutenant Colonel Benjamin H. Vandervoort, had a front-row seat as the Grenadier Guards' Sergeant Peter Robinson's platoon of four tanks began to cross the highway bridge. "As Sergeant Robinson's lead Sherman approached the midpoint of the bridge, from dead ahead, an 88mm antitank gun opened fire. It should have been a mismatch. One or more tanks, knocked out, could block the bridge. Our tanks stopped and returned fire.

"The lead Sherman fired its cannon as fast as it could load and sprayed the road ahead with its .30-caliber machine gun. The 88 fired half a dozen—more or less—near misses, ripping and screaming with an unforgettable sound— past the turret of the tank. In the gathering dusk they looked like great Roman candle balls of fire. Brightly glowing, 17-pounder cannon shots rocketed back along with flashing machine gun tracers. Suddenly, the 88 went silent. One of the tanks' .30-caliber armor-piercing rounds had penetrated the soft metallic end cap of the 88's recoil mechanism, causing the gun to jam. That improbable, long-odds happenstance of good marksmanship and good luck ended the shoot-out on the bridge."[80]

As Robinson's Shermans began to move again, German General Heinz Harmel, commander of the 10th SS Panzer Division, looked through his binoculars from a concrete pillbox northeast of the bridge near Lent. Lieutenant General Wilhelm Bittrich, commanding the II SS Panzer Korps, had been ordered by Field Marshal Walter Model not to blow the bridge. Harmel was determined not to allow the bridge to fall into Allied hands. He didn't want to be brought to Berlin to be executed for allowing the British to cross the Waal River. Harmel watched Robinson's tanks reach the center of the bridge.

Harmel gave the order to the engineer waiting nearby to push the plunger on the detonator. "Get ready. . . . Let it blow!"[81]

Nothing happened. " 'Again!' I was waiting to see the bridge collapse and the tanks plunge into the river. Instead, they moved relentlessly, getting bigger and bigger, closer and closer."[82]

Harmel turned to his staff and said, "My God, they'll be here in two minutes. Stolley, tell Bittrich. They're over the Waal."[83]

Captain Burriss heard tanks coming across the bridge in the fading light. "We couldn't tell if they were German or British, but I think most of us believed that they were Kraut reinforcements.

" 'Let's get off the bridge and over the embankment,' I said, 'until we can tell whose they are.'

"As we waited with Gammon grenades in our hands, two tanks passed within a few feet of us. They were British."[84]

With that, the paratroopers came out of their positions and briefly celebrated with the British tankers. Burriss told the commander of one of tanks, "You guys are the most beautiful sight I've seen in months."[85]

Captain Burriss received the Silver Star for his brilliant and inspirational leadership and heroism in securing the north end of the vital Nijmegen highway bridge.

The highway bridge was firmly in Allied hands. However, German artillery continued to pummel the southern approaches to the highway bridge, preventing British troops from crossing to reinforce the bridgehead.

The British tanks moved cautiously up the road toward the railroad overpass. In the growing darkness on the other side, Captain Fred Thomas's Company G held the west side of the railroad embankment. "All at once, we heard much heavy firing, and a tank broke through the [highway] underpass coming in our direction. At first, we thought it was a British tank that had crossed the bridge, but when the tank that had come through the underpass kept up its machine gun fire and fired its 75 into the orchard on our right, we thought it was a German. The platoon sergeant of the 2nd Platoon threw a Gammon grenade under the tank, and it exploded directly underneath [it]. The tank stopped, and the top opened, and a typical British voice announced that it was a British tank. We were all about the happiest bunch of fellows that ever existed."[86]

At 8:00 p.m., the 1st Battalion commander, Major Willard Harrison, ordered Captain Charles Duncan to deploy Company A facing north, with its right flank on the highway extending southwest to the north of and parallel to Groene Straat, and with its left flank tying in with Company C. At the same time, Company C extended its right flank from the dike road to the northeast a short distance to contact the left flank of Company A. Captain Duncan sent a patrol of five troopers, led by Staff Sergeant Ernest Castle, to contact Company C, then three guides were to return to lead the company to the contact point. At 12:30 a.m., the three troopers returned and led Company A along the defilade of the south side of the dike road. However, when Sergeant John W. Harper, leading the point of the Able Company column, contacted a squad of Company C troopers, he discovered that Charlie Company had not extended its right flank as ordered. Captain Duncan decided, because of the darkness and terrain that had not been reconnoitered, to hold up until morning to move. Major Harrison agreed, and Company A dug around the dike road on the right flank of Company C.

At the railroad bridge, the Company B commander, Captain Helgeson, believing it to be clear of Germans, sent Lieutenant Ralph S. Bird, Jr., and four troopers across the bridge to contact the 505th on the south side in Nijmegen. A short time later, Helgeson learned that the 3rd Platoon of Company A was moving about fifty yards west of the north end of the bridge to place flanking fire on any Germans crossing the bridge from the south. Captain Helgeson dispatched his runner, Corporal Francis J. Cleary, to bring the patrol back before Company A opened fire on them. In the growing darkness, the Company A platoon believed they heard the Germans preparing the bridge for demolition and opened fire. The patrol sought shelter behind the girders until the fire ceased, then made its way back without suffering any casualties. However, a member of the Dutch Underground called on the Germans still on the bridge to surrender, and eighteen came out. Five more Germans remained with their wounded comrades. After sending word for the Company A troopers to hold their fire, Company B troopers moved out across the bridge and took the five Germans prisoner, leaving the wounded on the bridge and ending enemy resistance there.

On the south side of the river at the 2nd Battalion command post, the battalion commander, Major Ed Wellems, received a radio message shortly after the bridges were secured. "Colonel Tucker ordered the remainder of the battalion, which consisted of one rifle company [Company F, which had arrived after marching from Grave at 5:30 p.m.], to cross the river. But a combat patrol [of ten troopers led by Lieutenant William L. Watson sent to clear snipers from the southern approach to the railroad bridge] had picked up 217 German prisoners from the south end of the railroad bridge, and we had nowhere to send them. Due to our guard requirements, we were told to remain in place."[87]

At 9:00 p.m., Major Cook ordered the 3rd Battalion to expand the bridgehead, with Company G on the left pushing north with its left flank east of the highway, Company I on the right pushing east and northeast long the dike road toward Fort Lent, and Company H in reserve. Captain Henry Keep, the battalion S-3, issued the orders to the company commanders. "We attacked one thousand yards to the north to establish an outer defense ring. And so, at 9 o'clock that night our dead-tired men moved out, knowing damn well what they would run into—stiff, bitter opposition on the part of fanatical crack Nazi troops, who were furious at the loss of the vital bridge. Our greatly depleted companies met determined resistance as they pushed forward in the darkness; the fighting was bitter, but by two in the morning we were in position, holding the line assigned to us."[88]

North of the river, Colonel Tucker left his forward command post in a house near the railroad overpass. "I walked down to the main bridge and went part way across it toward Nijmegen, but the girders of the bridge were covered with Krauts who engaged in sporadic firing down on the bridge. Many were shot, while others were rounded up as prisoners. By dark, the 1st and 3rd Battalions were joined up in position. I remained at a farmhouse at the intersection of the railroad and main road that night, and although the British tank commander kept screaming most of the night for close-in security, we had two battalions well out in front of him, and our small group [at the CP] could take care of any group attempting to get at his tanks."[89]

At midnight, a company of infantry of the Irish Guards crossed the highway bridge to take over the close-in defense of the highway bridge. At about that same time, Major Abdallah K. Zakby, the 1st Battalion executive officer, arrived at the division hospital in Nijmegen, having been wounded during the crossing. "I received a burst in my left leg and the palm of my right hand. By then, I had bled quite a bit and developed chills.

"The receiving room was full of wounded men, [with wounds] much more terrible than mine. I was carried to the operating table. A young doctor, whom I had not seen since 1941, and whom I knew well at Fort Dix, New Jersey, operated on me. As luck would have it, the bone was not shattered—just seared—but all my flesh and ligaments in the middle of my left thigh were burned. He put seventeen drains around the leg."[90]

That night in Nijmegen, Private Obie Wickersham and the other surviving Company C, 307th, engineers gathered in the transformer factory. Wickersham was worried about his best friend, Private Herb Wendland, whom he had not seen since shortly before the crossing began. "We were so tired. It was very quiet—very quiet—nothing was being celebrated or anything. We were so beat. There was carpet on the floor, so I crawled underneath a table and I conked out and went to sleep."[91]

THE COST OF THE CAPTURE OF THE NIJMEGEN BRIDGES was steep. So many brave troopers were killed or grievously wounded. Company C, 307th Airborne Engineer Battalion, lost eight killed and twenty-six wounded. The 3rd Battalion suffered twenty-eight killed, one missing in action, and seventy-eight

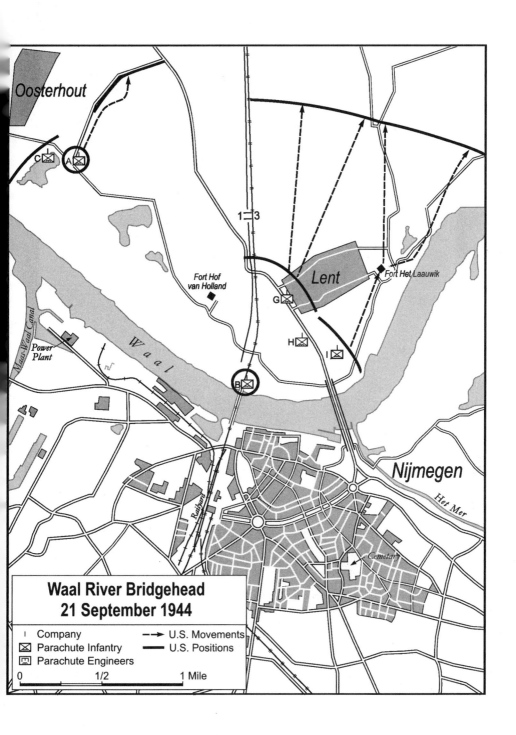

Oosterhout

C⊠ A⊠

1–3

Fort Hof
van Holland

Lent

Fort Het Laauwik

G⊠

H⊠   I⊠

B⊠

Waal

Maas-Waal Canal

Power
Plant

Railroad

Nijmegen

Het Mer

Cemetery

Waal River Bridgehead
21 September 1944

I	Company	– ⟶ U.S. Movements
⊠	Parachute Infantry	▬ U.S. Positions
▦	Parachute Engineers	

0   1/2   1 Mile

wounded. The 1st and 2nd Battalions each lost two killed. Many of the wounded suffered grievously. Sergeant John Toman, with Company H, shot in the head while leading his men against the machine guns at the dike, was evacuated and sent to a hospital in the United States. He lost his hearing and control of his facial muscles and was confined to a wheelchair for the rest of his life. Lieutenant Harry "Pappy" Busby, with Company I, who had the premonition that he wasn't going to make it, died during the crossing of the Waal.

Chapter 11

"Our MOS Was Still, Kill Germans"

At 4:30 a.m. on the morning of September 21, Captain Henry Keep, the 3rd Battalion S-3, received another order from Major Cook to expand the bridgehead. "With the aid of a couple of British SPs and British artillery, we pushed forward another thousand yards. Every inch of these advances was hotly contested; the Krauts had all the advantages. They controlled the orchards, the ditches, the farmhouses, etcetera and it was necessary to wrest every square foot from them."[1]

As the 3rd Battalion attack progressed that morning, a gap developed between Companies G and I. The Germans, intent on recapturing the highway bridge, infiltrated into this gap along a secondary railroad track running east-west north of Lent. At about 7:30 a.m., Company G platoon leader Lieutenant Don E. Graeber spotted them. Captain Fred Thomas, the company commander, was with the platoon on the left flank. Lieutenant Graeber acted quickly and decisively. Leaving his platoon under the command of his platoon sergeant, he rounded up a small force of company headquarters and mortar personnel. An estimated fifty-man German force had taken up positions behind one side of the railroad embankment waiting for orders to move. Graeber led his ad hoc group to within twenty yards of the Germans on the opposite side of the embankment and placed them at intervals to close the 150-yard gap between G and I Companies. Lieutenant Graeber and his improvised force quickly engaged the Germans in a wild and deadly firefight, with both Germans and paratroopers popping up, shooting at anyone sticking their heads above the top of the embankment slope on the opposite side, then ducking back behind their side of the embankment. Both sides tossed grenades over the embankment as the close-quarters fight raged. Lieutenant Graeber constantly moved up and down the 150-yard line, checking on the troopers and exposing himself to enemy fire as he tossed grenades over the embankment. Before dawn, the German force pulled out. For his quick action in stopping this threat to the highway bridge and for his exemplary leadership, Lieutenant Graeber received the Silver Star.

At dawn on September 21, Colonel Tucker attempted to get the British armor moving up to Arnhem. When the British tankers refused to move without infantry support, Tucker requested permission to allow his regiment to move north to the aid of their British paratrooper brothers. "I wanted to move out toward Arnhem, but was ordered to remain right where I was, and a British Dorset regiment would escort the British tanks to Arnhem. Unfortunately, the British tried one road, were blocked by two 88s, [and then] tried another road with the same results, whereas if they had sent elements up all roads at the same time, they probably could have broken through. That's the way our people would have done it, particularly General Patton."[2]

A short time afterward, Gavin found Tucker's command post in the farmhouse at the junction of the railroad and the highway. "Tucker was livid. I had never seen him so angry. He had expected that when he seized his end of the bridge, the British armor would race on to Arnhem and link up with Urquhart. His first question to me was, 'What the hell are they doing? We have been in this position for over twelve hours, and all they seem to be doing is brewing tea. Why in hell don't they get to Arnhem?' I did not have an answer for him."[3]

At about 9:10 a.m., two British tanks supporting the attack of Company I shelled Fort Lent, knocking out some 20mm antiaircraft guns which were holding up the company's advance northeastwardly along the dike road. Company I then resumed the attack, capturing Fort Lent about 11:00 a.m. and then set up a defense line from the north bank of the Waal River to the secondary railroad tracks, where Lieutenant Graeber's force had fought off the German force.

The 3rd Battalion moved out again at 1:00 p.m. to expand the bridgehead once again. The attack met stiff resistance, and by about mid-afternoon, both G and I Companies were running low on ammunition. An ammunition resupply arrived about 5:15 that afternoon. Company G reached its objective on the north side of the intersection of the main railroad embankment and Ressenche Wal by 5:30 p.m., where it fought a heavy battle against Germans entrenched in an orchard there. One platoon of Company I assisted Company G in securing the orchard.

Captain Keep was in communications with the assaulting companies throughout the day. "By late afternoon, once again we had reached our prescribed position, and here we held, determinedly fighting off constant counterattacks. Ammunition was running out and had to be replenished every hour or so."[4]

In the 1st Battalion sector on the morning of September 21, Company A moved out to establish a line on the right flank of Company C. The 2nd Platoon of Company A on the left flank, tied in with Company C, while the 1st Platoon on the company's right extended its line to the highway from Nijmegen to Arnhem. The 3rd Platoon was in reserve in an orchard behind the point where the 1st and 2nd Platoons joined.

About 3:00 p.m., the Germans counterattacked from the town of Oosterhout with a company of infantry supported by two Mark VI Tiger I tanks and a half-track, hitting the Company C sector. Private First Class Ross Pippin watched the enemy force moving toward them. "There was only one thing that saved us. One of the paratroopers in our platoon, Private John [R.] Towle, had a bazooka. All the other bazooka men in our battalion were out of ammunition. He went after these tanks. He would fire at a tank, then slide down the bank to another position and fire at the other tank until he drove off the tanks."[5]

Private Towle fired a bazooka round at nine Germans who were setting up a machine gun in a nearby house, killing them all. Towle then ran back, retrieved more rockets for his bazooka, and then moved over one hundred yards in front of his company's positions. As he knelt to fire on the half-track, a mortar shell exploded close by, killing him. The remaining German force withdrew a short time later. Private Towle had almost single-handedly stopped the counterattack and later posthumously received the Congressional Medal of Honor.

That night at about 10:00 p.m., Captain Henry Keep accompanied Major Cook to the regimental command post. There, Keep listened as "we were told that we were to be relieved at 0600 the next morning. I say, 'relieved;' that was a strange term to use in conjunction with this operation. We were to pull out of our present positions, but no one was to take them over. It had been decided that a close-in defense of the bridge was sufficient and that now, we were no longer needed. It was going to be a ticklish situation. We were to withdraw from our present position with the Nazis hot on our tail as soon as they realized what was going on. Could our companies get back to the security of the bridge without being cut off by the Krauts? We were to receive no assistance of cover from anyone.

"Our company commanders started that night to move their wounded back and other personnel not needed for fighting; and at dawn the infiltration to the rear commenced. It was a very skillfully directed maneuver. One platoon would cover the withdrawal of the other, and then the unit which had just pulled out would stop and perform the same service for its former covering force. Just what we expected occurred. As soon as the Nazis were cognizant of what was taking place, they were breathing hard down our backs. Our troops eventually reached the security of the close-in defense of the bridge by the British, and we moved across this huge structure still littered with the dead we had killed what seemed eons ago, but what in reality was barely two days. We had taken it—our job was finished."[6]

Word spread of the 82nd Airborne Division's great feat of arms on September 20, 1944, as it successfully executed an assault crossing of the Waal River, captured the two Nijmegen bridges, and fought off German counterattacks on its thinly held line at Mook, Riethorst, Beek, and Wyler. The 3rd Battalion was awarded a second Presidential Unit Citation for its heroic capture of the north ends of the two bridges.

The British Second Army, not able to force a crossing over the Rhine River, evacuated the remnants of the British 1st Airborne Division from the north side of the river. Of over 10,000 officers and men that had jumped and landed by glider north of the Rhine, only about 2,400 came back across the river. Operation Market-Garden had failed, but not because of the fighting of the three airborne divisions and the Polish airborne brigade.

Eyewitness accounts by General Browning, Sir Allan H. S. Adair, and General Horrocks made their way to British General Sir Miles Dempsey, commander of the British Second Army, who visited Gavin at the 82nd Airborne Division Champion Command Post on September 23. As Dempsey entered, Gavin saluted and Dempsey returned the salute and extended his hand, saying, "I'm proud to meet the commanding general of the finest division in the world today."[7]

AFTER THE FAILURE OF THE BRITISH TO BREAK THROUGH across the Rhine at Arnhem, the situation in Holland settled into defensive, static warfare. Night-patrol actions and sharp, local attacks by both sides marked the next month and a half.

At 3:00 p.m. on September 21, four hundred C-47s made a poorly executed resupply drop west of the Maas-Waal Canal, in part due to overcast weather conditions. The planes dropped supplies over a six-mile length and a two-mile width, of which only an estimated 60 percent was recovered, with the substantial help of the Dutch civilians.

After the 504th was relieved north of the Waal River on September 22, it moved across the river to division reserve. Most of the troopers, like Company C engineer Private First Class Harold Herbert, had not eaten for a couple of days, as they had long since consumed their rations. "After we got cleaned up, we were able to go into the folks' gardens and get the fresh vegetables. We even made stew in our helmets. That was really good."[8]

While in reserve, the 504th executive officer, Lieutenant Colonel Warren R. Williams, Jr., was one of the regiment's officers who approved a recommendation for a battlefield commission for Private First Class Ted Bachenheimer with Headquarters Company, 1st Battalion, for his heroic actions in working with the Dutch Underground in Nijmegen. "Bachenheimer was recommended for a battlefield commission and directed to report to division for an interview by a board of officers. When he left the 504 CP for division, he picked up a steel helmet with a first lieutenant's bar on it, instead of his own helmet. When he reported to division wearing this helmet, he was sent back for reconsideration."[9]

Major Cook, who had gallantly led the 3rd Battalion in the first wave of the assault crossing of the Waal River, would later receive the Distinguished Service Cross for his heroism. "For the next couple of days, many of the NCOs simply came up and shook my hand and with traces of tears in their eyes, saluted and took off. This action confused me until one of the officers got it out of the men—it was their way of taking back their dirty remarks about me not sticking with them up front in combat. From that day on, I never had any disciplinary problems with my battalion. In nearly eight months of combat, I had only one court-martial case (and that against a relatively new man), no AWOLs, and the fewest incident reports of the 504 PIR."[10]

On the night of September 24–25, the 504th relieved the 508th Parachute Infantry Regiment along the main line of resistance (MLR) from the Waal River south to Kamp, just northeast of Groesbeek. The 2nd Battalion took over the 3rd Battalion, 508th's sector, where Company E defended the brick kilns on the south bank of the Waal River near Erlekom south to where it tied in with Company F, which held Thorensche Molen and a line along dike that ran southwest to the Wyler Meer. Contact patrols covered the area between Company F and Company A on the left flank of the 1st Battalion. Company D was in reserve on Hill 9.2 to the west.

The 1st Battalion relieved the 1st Battalion, 508th, along the high ground overlooking the Wyler Meer and extending southeasterly to where it curved in front of Wyler and tied in with the 3rd Battalion sector just west of Voxhil. The 3rd Battalion relieved the 2nd Battalion, 508th, on the high ground extending just west of Voxhil southwesterly to Kamp. Company G took over the positions on the left, tying in with the 1st Battalion on their left. Company H took over the sector on the right, tying in with the 325th Glider Infantry Regiment near Kamp. Company I, the battalion reserve, was in the woods to the west of the frontline. Companies G and H kept one platoon each in reserve.

On September 25, Major Robert H. Neptune, executive officer of the 376th Parachute Field Artillery Battalion, was promoted to command the battalion. "The division artillery executive officer was Lieutenant Colonel Harry Bertsch, who at the eleventh hour before our departure to Holland, obtained permission to skip the mission for some reason not disclosed. His avoidance of the mission may have been entirely justified, but rumors were to the contrary. Anyway, Bertsch's absence made Lieutenant Colonel Wilbur Griffith the division artillery executive officer and me the commanding officer of the 376th."[11]

However, Major Neptune had almost missed the Holland jump. "A few days before the mission was to be launched, I severely injured my right leg, particularly my knee, in a softball game while sliding in to second base. The battalion physicians, Doctor White and Doctor Mickley, ordered that the injury was such that I could not accompany the battalion on the Holland mission. The knee was badly torn and swollen, with fluid accumulating into a substantial bulb. I spoke to Griff and the doctors and endeavored to demonstrate that I was well enough to make the mission. They agreed that *if* a senior medical officer at a higher echelon would certify that I was fit for combat, I could participate in the mission. I immediately went out to find a hospital unit with a physician who would so certify and came back with the certificate. I had been away from the 376th during much of the previous months, because I had been assigned to the 456th [Parachute Field Artillery Battalion] for the Normandy invasion and campaign, and so in September was delighted to be back with the 376th and did not want to miss any combat in which it served. Thus, it was that I happened to be in Holland with the 376th, when Griff was brought up to artillery division headquarters. My knee healed sufficiently that I managed OK. If I had stayed in England with the bad knee, I might never have been commanding officer of the 376th."[12]

THE MORNING AFTER TAKING OVER THE 508TH POSITIONS, Lieutenant James H. Nelson made a reconnaissance of the area to the front of the Company E positions. "The 508 defensive position which E Company took over was a very poor one, and the field of fire of our left flank extended only about twenty-five yards.

"It was decided to move our left flank forward about five hundred yards, thus giving us a good field of fire and much stronger position."[13]

In the 3rd Battalion sector, Company H set up an outpost in a farmhouse east of Kamp that they would occupy at night. Two brothers served in Company H, Sergeants Daun and William V. "Bill" Rice, who were both fearless combat veterans. Sergeant Daun Rice Z. was on outpost duty in a farmhouse, while his brother was on a patrol to snatch prisoners on the night of September 25–26. At 1:30 a.m., a German patrol approached the house undetected and tossed a hand grenade through the window of the house that Rice and Corporal John A. Beyer were occupying. The grenade dropped between Rice and the wall, exploding and killing Rice.

Sergeant Albert Tarbell was at the company command post when he got the word of Sergeant Rice's death. "Captain Kappel and I went to see Sergeant Rice after he was dead, and Kappel was very overcome [at] that time. He was like a father to all of us. He felt badly if anyone got hurt, and he cried when he saw Rice."[14]

Meanwhile, Lieutenant Virgil "Hoagie" Carmichael, the 3rd Battalion S-2, was waiting for the patrol to return with a prisoner or prisoners for interrogation. "At 5:30 in the morning, the Company H patrol returned to our lines and reported that they had captured a German captain as he stepped outside the house which he occupied to answer the call of nature. They took him quietly and in the dark carried him back to our lines without his comrades ever knowing what happened.

"I arrived on the scene just after the patrol had returned with the German captain, and the H Company men and officers had learned that this very captain had sent out the patrol from his company that killed our sergeant. Our men had a part of a nylon camouflage parachute around the captain's neck, and they were twisting it as tightly as they could, slapping him on the face and beating him. I believe if it had not been for my intervention, that they would have beat the poor man to death right there. I prevailed upon them to turn him over to me, since he was a valuable prisoner, and we might in that way avoid patrols for a day or two."[15]

The prisoner was brought to the 3rd Battalion command post and interrogated by the S-2 section, but refused to talk. Then, Major Cook "interviewed him and knowing that he understood English, I told him I would give him two minutes to start talking or else I would kill him, as he was of no use to me. When the two minutes were up, I dramatically pulled out my .45, and the S-3, Captain Keep, and the S-2, Lieutenant Carmichael, who were on either side of the prisoner, stepped away. For once, I saw real fear in the man's eyes, and he started answering questions and turned out to be of good intelligence value to us.

"He explained he knew from the way the men talked, that he was going to be killed anyway, so why talk. But somehow he got my message that to talk meant to live. Regiment and division never did understand why the man was so willing to talk. They always claimed we didn't know how to handle prisoners!"[16]

At 11:00 p.m. on September 25, a fifteen-man Company G patrol, led by Lieutenant Don Graeber, moved out to occupy Den Heuvel Woods between the main line of resistance and the enemy lines, with the mission of establishing outposts. Graeber decided to swing around and approach the woods from the north, but got lost in the process and returned about 2:30 a.m. to the company command post. Graeber reported his error to the company commander, Captain Fred Thomas, who immediately sent the patrol out again, this time reinforced by a six-man machine gun team from Headquarters Company, 3rd Battalion. This time, they took a direct route to the woods and met no opposition on the way. Prior to entering the woods, Lieutenant Graeber sent five men in to conduct a reconnaissance. They reported the woods to be unoccupied, so Graeber and the patrol moved in and began digging-in a series of two-man outposts around the perimeter of the woods. He positioned three men of an attached machine gun team and their gun on the eastern end of the woods, facing the German MLR. He and four troopers dug a command post position in the center of the woods. At 4:30 a.m. on the morning of September 26, Graeber fired a green flare to signal that the patrol had occupied the objective.

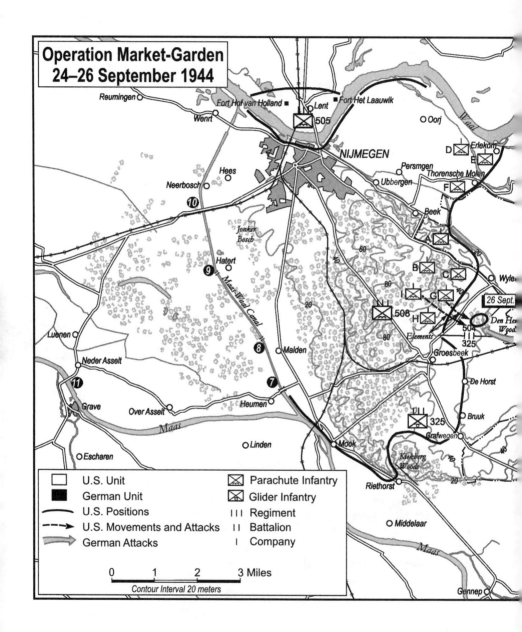

Operation Market-Garden
24–26 September 1944

Reumingen

Wenrt

Fort Hof van Holland

Fort Het Laauwik

Lent

505

Oorj

Erlekorn

D

E

NIJMEGEN

Persmgen

Thorensche Molen

Hees

Neerbosch

Ubbergen

F

Beek

10

Jonker Bosch

60

B

C

Wyle

Hatert

9

40

80

I

G

26 Sept.

Maas-Waal Canal

20

N

508

H

Den Hes Wood

504

Luenen

80

Elements

325

8

Malden

Groesbeek

Neder Asselt

De Horst

11

7

Grave

Over Asselt

Heumen

Bruuk

325

Maas

Grafwegen

Linden

Mook

Escharen

Kieleberg Woods

□ U.S. Unit	⊠ Parachute Infantry
■ German Unit	⊠ Glider Infantry
⌒ U.S. Positions	⁞⁞⁞ Regiment
⇢ U.S. Movements and Attacks	⁞⁞ Battalion
⇨ German Attacks	⁞ Company

Riethorst

Middelaar

Maas

0   1   2   3 Miles

Contour Interval 20 meters

Gennep

Shortly before dawn, a lone German, unaware of the presence of the patrol, walked into the woods and approached Graeber's command post. The unsuspecting soldier started speaking to Sergeant Henry Hoffman, who kept digging with his left hand as he quietly pulled his .45 pistol out and shot the German. This alerted the Germans to the patrol's presence. At dawn, an enemy patrol estimated to be a squad infiltrated through the outpost line and into the woods. Concealed in the tall grass, and wearing camouflage made with cloth from U.S. parachutes on their helmets, the Germans opened fire, seriously wounding Lieutenant Graeber and two others. Private Paul Mullan was one of the G Company troopers who was with Hoffman and Graeber during the firefight. "Lieutenant Graeber was shot in the face with a burp gun. Hoff gave him a shot of morphine."[17]

The Germans were difficult to locate, but were eventually found and all were killed. Another group of about one hundred Germans infiltrated into the farm buildings and the woods between the outposts, and engaged Graeber's troopers.

Sergeant Earl Oldfather and another George Company trooper were dispatched from the MLR to contact Lieutenant Graeber. "Hatcher and I took off for the woods, watching the treetops for snipers. We saw three guys out in the field; one was bailing water out of his hole, the other two were digging. The one picked up his rifle when he saw me—I waved—he put it down. Someone fired at them and they ducked. We reached our men—they were in bad shape, practically surrounded by Jerries. Hatcher and I went back for help. Hatcher said later those men I had waved to were Jerries."[18]

At 8:30 a.m., acting on orders from the 3rd Battalion commander, Major Julian Cook, and his S-3, Captain Henry Keep, Captain T. Moffatt Burriss, commanding Company I, ordered Lieutenant Bernard Karnap to take the seventeen troopers of his 2nd Platoon and deploy them on the Waldgraaf road, west of Voxhil, to await the arrival of three British tanks. The tanks arrived at 10:15 a.m. and moved cautiously toward the Den Heuvel Woods, stopping twice along the way, concerned that Karnap's small force was insufficient to protect them from concealed enemy infantry. The tanks arrived and deployed at the intersection of the Wijlersche Baan and the short road that led to the entrance of the woods, just northwest of Den Heuvel. One tank covered the Wijlersche Baan to the northeast, while the other two covered buildings occupied by the Germans within the woods. Eight of the Company I troopers, led by Sergeant Leon E. Baldwin, turned right at the entrance on the west side and skirted the woods, reaching the buildings. Lieutenant Karnap and the other eight men turned left at the entrance, moving eastward through the northern side of the woods. Karnap sent four of those men to cover his left flank and to ferret out snipers. One of the tanks moved forward and rolled over the barbed wire fence surrounding the woods, and fired twelve high-explosive rounds through an opening in the woods at the farm buildings, driving the Germans to the rear of the buildings. One round inadvertently struck a tree, the shrapnel from the explosion killing a medic, Private Einar Flack.

After expending their ammunition, the British tanks withdrew, taking all of the wounded troopers with them. Karnap's platoon stayed with Graeber's G Company troopers in the woods.

Around 12:30 p.m., Staff Sergeant William D. Sachse and eighteen troopers from the 2nd Platoon of Company G moved to Den Heuvel, where they took up positions on the left flank of the entrance. Sergeant Alexander Barker led troops of the 2nd Platoon of Company I arrived and cleared the south side of the woods and dug in.

At 1:00 p.m., Lieutenant Karnap took five of Sergeant Barker's troopers to clean out the houses within the woods. Karnap knocked out a German machine gun by tossing a Gammon grenade through the window of the farmhouse from which it was firing, collapsing the wall. Karnap left three of his men to hold the farmhouse, then took the other two and moved to clear the other farm buildings. As he moved around one of the buildings he came upon the rear of a three-man German machine gun crew, protected by three riflemen about to fire on Sergeant Sachse and his men. Karnap immediately opened up, killing all of them before they had time to fire. He then positioned Private Solon W. Whitmire, with his BAR, to cover the area. A few moments later, four Germans ran across the road to reach the machine gun that Karnap had just put out of commission. Whitmire cut them down, killing all four before they reached the gun. Having cleared the buildings, Lieutenant Karnap moved to find Sergeant Sachse, whose men had taken nineteen prisoners.

A little before 2:00 p.m., the Germans attacked with a battalion of infantry advancing behind a heavy artillery barrage. At that time, the platoon command post requested tank support. Believing there were too few men to guard them and defend the woods, someone shot approximately ten prisoners. The ferocious fighting lasted for several hours as the heavily outnumbered troopers fought with incredible courage and tenacity.

Upon learning of the attack, the battalion commander, Major Julian Cook, and his S-3, Captain Henry Keep, left the battalion command post for Den Heuvel and ordered reinforcements sent there. Captain Fred Thomas dispatched Lieutenant James R. Pursell and seventeen Company G troopers to the woods. Pursell and his men arrived at the platoon command post in the center of the woods at about 2:30 p.m., where they found a lot of confusion, along with three enemy prisoners, one of whom they forced to point out German positions in the orchard on the north side of the woods. Lieutenant Karnap and eleven troopers assaulted the orchard and by 2:45 p.m. had secured it, capturing twenty-eight prisoners and taking them to the platoon command post in the center of the woods. At the time, the command post was under artillery fire, and the prisoners, using only their hands and feet, quickly scratched out some relatively safe holes.

Lieutenant Pursell moved to the orchard and found seven troopers lying behind a slight elevation, protecting them from enemy fire coming from the east. Just as Pursell arrived, an 88mm barrage began, but inflicted no casualties. It lifted shortly to engage British tanks that were coming up the road to the entrance to the woods. Pursell ordered the seven troopers to move to the elevation and found a light machine gun team and positioned them across the road, where the orchard and the woods met. The seven troopers and the light machine gun opened fire and silenced the enemy fire coming from the northeast. Afterward, Lieutenant Pursell took the seven troopers back to the platoon command post.

At about 3:00 p.m., when three British tanks arrived at the entrance to the woods in a column, an 88mm round knocked out the rear tank. The lead tank moved around the south edge of the woods, with its place at the entrance taken by the second tank. Lieutenant Karnap guided the lead tank to an advantageous position on the southern edge of the woods, where it fired seventeen or eighteen high-explosive shells into a house to the south and into a small wooded area just north of the house. The tank also machine gunned a hedgerow Karnap suspected of concealing enemy troops. When a shell stuck in the breech of its main gun, the tank radioed for the second tank to follow the same route. That tank soon pulled up on the right of the lead tank and shelled the same house with another twenty rounds, then fired about a thousand rounds of fifty-caliber machine gun bullets into a fence. Both tanks then withdrew.

At the platoon command post, Lieutenant Pursell sent Sergeant Sachse and nine men to outpost the north side of the orchard. On the way, a tree burst wounded seven of them, including Sergeant Sachse. The remaining three returned to the command post and informed Lieutenant Pursell of what had occurred. Pursell and a medic took off to find the wounded men, and just as they arrived, enemy machine gun fire also wounded Private Roger E. Chapin, leaving only thirteen men to outpost the north side of the woods. Pursell deployed the men, two to a hole in the original outpost foxholes.

About 4:30 p.m., Major Cook and Captain Keep arrived at the battalion command post, after checking on the situation at Den Heuvel where they were told that casualties were eight KIA and twenty-one wounded, and estimated enemy casualties were at one hundred fifty.

At 7:00 p.m., Captain Burriss sent Lieutenant Robert M. Rogers and seventeen Company I troopers to Den Heuvel to reinforce Karnap and Pursell. When they arrived ten minutes later, one squad of eight troopers, led by Sergeant Curtis L. Sims, was sent to Lieutenant Pursell and the other squad of nine, led by Sergeant George Ham, was sent to reinforce Lieutenant Karnap.

Pursell and Karnap divided the responsibility of Den Heuvel, with Lieutenant Karnap defending the woods to the east and south, while Pursell took the north and east side extending to the farm buildings.

During the night of September 26–27, Lieutenant Virgil Carmichael was at the 3rd Battalion command post when a message was received from the Company H command post that "Lieutenant William H. Preston was killed by one of our guards. Preston was a very good friend of mine, being from Knoxville, Tennessee, and he was a little hard of hearing. One of the command post guards, who was a scared replacement, challenged Preston as he went into his own command post about midnight. The replacement vigorously swore to us that he challenged Preston three times before he fired. However, we always doubted that the man said much more than 'halt.' Anyway, he emptied a clip of submachine gun ammunition into Preston. This man later developed into an excellent soldier and performed good service throughout the rest of the campaign."[19]

During the remainder of the night of September 26–27, Den Heuvel received enemy rifle fire, and a number of German snipers infiltrated. In a close, deadly game of hide and seek, the troopers killed or drove the enemy snipers out of Den Heuvel by around 9:15 a.m. The remainder of the daylight hours passed relatively uneventfully.

IN THE 2ND BATTALION SECTOR, ON THE MORNING OF SEPTEMBER 27, a combat patrol from Company E was sent out to destroy a camouflaged enemy tank which was firing on the company's forward positions. About a hundred yards from the tank, enemy small-arms fire pinned down the patrol. Sergeant William C. Boyle and another trooper volunteered to work around the right flank and attempt to take out the tank with Gammon grenades. As they moved along a ditch, they suddenly encountered at least an enemy platoon in an intersecting ditch. Sergeant Boyle called for them to surrender, which drew bursts of automatic weapons fire. Boyle and the other trooper responded by lobbing their Gammon grenades into the ditch, killing at least four and wounding several others. Sergeant Boyle and the other trooper crawled back for more Gammon grenades and returned to take on the remaining enemy infantrymen.

Meanwhile, a British tank arrived and together with the others in the patrol engaged the enemy tank. Boyle and the other man continued to attack the Germans in the ditch, until they showed a white flag. As Boyle covered them as they filed out of the ditch, four tried to escape but were quickly shot by the two troopers. At this point, the remainder of the patrol moved forward to lend a hand in securing the prisoners. The result of Boyle's and the other trooper's actions were twenty killed, fifteen wounded, and twenty-five prisoners. In addition, the haul included twelve of the new MP-44 assault rifles, an antitank gun, two flamethrowers, and several Panzerschrecks and numerous

A dead German SS trooper, possibly an engineer, lies on the highway bridge, with wires running along the bridge deck behind him. A Very pistol, used to fire flares, lies beside him. *U.S. Army photograph, courtesy of the Cornelius Ryan Collection, Alden Library, Ohio University*

German dead lie all over the highway bridge at Nijmegen. *U.S. Army photograph, courtesy of the Cornelius Ryan Collection, Alden Library, Ohio University*

Two troopers advance across the open, flat ground in Holland as a shell explodes nearby. *U.S. Army photograph, courtesy of the 82nd Airborne Division War Memorial Museum*

Troopers with the 1st Battalion move through Rahier past one of Battery C, 80th Airborne Antiaircraft (Antitank) Battalion's 57mm antitank gun on the way to assault Cheneux, Belgium, on December 20, 1944. *U.S. Army photograph, courtesy of the 82nd Airborne Division War Memorial Museum*

A 504th paratrooper, covered by a buddy, advances across open ground near Bra, Belgium, on December 24, 1944. *U.S. Army photograph, courtesy of the 82nd Airborne Division War Memorial Museum*

Paratroopers with Company H ambushed a German patrol of SS grenadiers near Bra, Belgium, killing several and capturing one. They are shown taking the prisoner back to the main line of resistance on December 25, 1944. *U.S. Army photograph, courtesy of the 82nd Airborne Division War Memorial Museum*

The crew of a Battery B, 376th Parachute Field Artillery Battalion, 75mm pack howitzer fires at German positions on the east side of the Salm River, in support of attacks by the 504th on January 9, 1945. U.S. Army photograph, courtesy of the 82nd Airborne Division War Memorial Museum

Colonel Reuben H. Tucker, III, commander of the 504th PIR (left) receives an oak leaf (second award) for the Distinguished Service Cross. Major Julian Cook, commander of the 3rd Battalion, 504th PIR (second from left) and Capt. Wesley D. "Spike" Harris, commanding officer of Company C, 307th Airborne Engineer Battalion (right), receive the Distinguished Service Cross from Lt. Gen. Lewis Brereton, commanding general of the 1st Allied Airborne Army, at Remouchamps, Belgium, on January 20, 1945. All three displayed extraordinary heroism in leading the assault crossing of the Waal River at Nijmegen on September 20, 1944. *U.S. Army photograph, courtesy of the 82nd Airborne Division War Memorial Museum*

Company G troopers and a Sherman tank from the attached 740th Tank Battalion advance through deep snow along a firebreak near Herresbach, Belgium, on January 28, 1945. *U.S. Army photograph, courtesy of the National Archives*

Troopers with Headquarters Company, 3rd Battalion, move through a heavy snowstorm towards Herresbach, Belgium, on January 28, 1945. *U.S. Army photograph, courtesy of the 82nd Airborne Division War Memorial Museum*

Medics use the wide-tracked Weasels to evacuate the wounded, as well the cases of frostbite and trench foot, in the rough terrain and deep snow near Herresbach, Belgium, on January 29, 1945. *U.S. Army photograph, courtesy of the National Archives*

Sergeant Charles E. Nau, Company B, is awarded the Distinguished Service Cross by General Gavin on March 19, 1945, for his actions during the capture of Bridge Number 7 at Heumen, Holland. The trooper to the left of Gavin is Tech. Sgt. William P. Walsh, with Company B, who was awarded the Distinguished Service Cross for his actions during the attack at Cheneux, Belgium. *U.S. Army photograph, courtesy of the 82nd Airborne Division War Memorial Museum*

Troopers with Company B take a break during the train ride to the Cologne, Germany, area in April 1945. *Courtesy of Bill Bonning*

Staff Sergeant Ross Carter served with Company C from North Africa through the end of the war. As a survivor of so many days of combat, he was one of the refugees from the law of averages. Tragically, cancer would take his life in 1946. *U.S. Army photograph, courtesy of the 82nd Airborne Division War Memorial Museum*

Engineers with the 307th Airborne Engineer Battalion disarm one of the magnetically activated sea mines planted by the Germans along the road to Ludwigslust. *U.S. Army photograph, courtesy of the 82nd Airborne Division War Memorial Museum*

One officer and one enlisted man were selected as representatives from the 82nd Airborne Division to receive the award of the orange lanyard from the Dutch government during a ceremony on October 19, 1945. Lieutenant James Megellas, Company H, 504th (center), was selected as the representative of the division's officers. *U.S. Army photograph, courtesy of the 82nd Airborne Division War Memorial Museum*

The division passes under the arch at Washington Square during the New York City Victory Parade on January 12, 1946. *U.S. Army photograph, courtesy of the National Archives*

grenades. The division recognized Sergeant William Boyle's aggressive actions and leadership with the award of the Silver Star.

At 7:00 p.m. on September 27, Captain Burriss moved the remainder of Company I into Den Heuvel. Lieutenant Edward W. Kennedy and eighteen troopers of the 3rd Platoon relieved Lieutenant Pursell's Company G platoon. The company also included eight company headquarters personnel, eight from the now combined mortar squads, and fifteen machine gunners with Headquarters Company, 3rd Battalion. Company I, together with the attached machine gunners, totaled just eighty-five men and officers.

Captain Burriss assigned the eight mortar men, deployed as riflemen, to the west and southwest portion of the woods. The 3rd Platoon, led by Lieutenant Kennedy, took over the northwest, north, and northeast. The northeast and east were assigned to the 1st Platoon, led by Lieutenant Rogers. Lieutenant Karnap's 2nd Platoon covered the south, southeast, and east. The only "blind spot" was the group of buildings on the east side.

Burriss had wire lines laid for sound-powered field telephones among the platoons, from the platoons to the company command post in the center of the woods, and to battalion. Additionally, the company radio operator had carried in an SCR-300 radio.

Earlier, at about 6:00 p.m., Headquarters Company, 3rd Battalion's 81mm Mortar Platoon had fired a concentration of twenty white phosphorous rounds at the house and small woods southeast of Den Heuvel. The house burned throughout the night, silhouetting any Germans who attempted to infiltrate from that direction. Karnap's men killed six Germans around 9:00 p.m., when they tried to do so.

At 11:00 p.m., Lieutenant Kennedy sent out a three-man reconnaissance patrol, led by Staff Sergeant Louis Orvin to check a blind spot in the line, caused by the farmhouses on the east side of the woods. Orvin led his men to a position close to the farmhouses. "I said, 'O.K., y'all stay here.' I crawled up, and there was a little bit of a mound between the side of this little trail that I was on and to my left. I was standing on a broken-down bush, and it started moving. I looked over and I saw a shadow going across that mound. It wasn't one of my men. I went back; they were still where I had left them. So I came on up, and I threw a hand grenade over in that direction. The hand grenade went off and then a machine gun fired one burst. Then you could hear the Germans giving it immediate action—evidently the gun had jammed. They were raising the [receiver] cover and pulling the belt through. So I told the men, 'Let's get out of here,' and we went back."[20]

At around midnight on September 27–28, the Germans began firing their Nebelwerfers into Den Heuvel to cover an infiltration into the farm buildings. Although another six Germans were killed, they succeeded in setting up

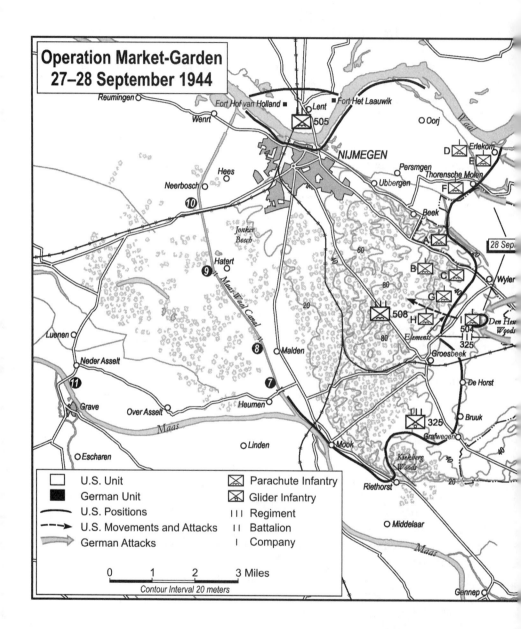

Operation Market-Garden
27–28 September 1944

Reumingen

Fort Hof van Holland ■   Lent   ■ Fort Het Laauwik

Wenrt   505   Oorj

NIJMEGEN   D Erlekom
E

Persmgen
Ubbergen   Thorensche Molen
Hees   F

Neerbosch   Beek

Jonker
Bosch   A   28 Sep

Hatert   60   B   C   Wyler

Maas-Waal Canal   80   G

Luenen   N   508   H   504
Elements   Den Heu
Woods
325

Neder Assett   Malden   Groesbeek

Grave   De Horst

Over Asselt   Heumen   325   Bruuk

Mook   Grafwegen

Linden   Kiekberg
Woods

Escharen   Riethorst

☐ U.S. Unit	⊠ Parachute Infantry
■ German Unit	⊠ Glider Infantry
⌒ U.S. Positions	┃┃┃ Regiment
- - ➤ U.S. Movements and Attacks	┃┃ Battalion
➤ German Attacks	┃ Company

Middelaar

0   1   2   3 Miles

Contour Interval 20 meters

Gennep

282

a machine gun in the upper window on the west side of a barn facing the 1st Platoon sector by 3:00 a.m.

At precisely 5:00 a.m., the Germans fired a massive artillery barrage of approximately two thousand rounds at Den Heuvel, an area of approximately one hundred square yards, within a span of only thirty minutes. During the barrage, German infantry infiltrated through the farm buildings and into the 1st and 2nd Platoon positions. When the barrage lifted, Rogers and Karnap phoned the command post and informed Burriss of their situation.

Staff Sergeant Orvin was sharing a two-man hole with Corporal Russell J. McDermott. "I looked up and I saw somebody running by on each side of us. I asked, 'What's going on.'

"They said, 'The Germans broke through.'

From the east, a battalion of German infantry, supported by three Mark IV tanks, moved in. The troopers of the 1st and 2nd Platoons, knowing the enemy was behind them in the woods as well, opened up on the approaching infantry with a devastating fire, cutting down many of the enemy. One of Lieutenant Karnap's 2nd Platoon squad leaders, Staff Sergeant Leon E. Baldwin, saw an enemy soldier kill one of the machine gunners about twenty yards to his left. The German jumped into the hole and turned the gun in preparation for firing it at Baldwin and the other troopers nearby. Baldwin, without hesitation, jumped from his foxhole and rushed across the open ground as other approaching German infantrymen opened up on him. In just seconds, Baldwin was at the lip of the foxhole, bayoneting the German, then picking up the corpse and throwing it out of the hole. Baldwin jumped into the hole and opened fire with the machine gun, killing and wounding many of the massed German infantry closing in on the woods, even as they focused their fire on him.

Meanwhile, one of the tanks overran the positions in the southern portion of Den Heuvel, firing its 75mm main gun and machine gun at the troopers' foxholes at almost point-blank range. A second tank stopped near the farm buildings and fired into the woods on the north side.

The third tank stopped just east of the woods and fired a number of high-explosive rounds along with hosing down the troopers' positions with machine gun fire. The tank then moved through the woods, penetrating almost to Captain Burriss' command post. "During the artillery barrage, Sergeant Robert [G.] Dew, who was in the trench with me, had received a shrapnel wound in the chest, and Lieutenant [Robert C.] Blankenship suffered a concussion. Dew, a huge, quiet man, lay gasping beside me. He was in a bad way. Two medics, one carrying a stretcher, came running toward us.

"'Put the sergeant on your stretcher and get him out of here!' I yelled, knowing he couldn't last much longer without medical care.

"They nodded, slid into the trench, and expertly rolled the sergeant onto the stretcher."[21]

The two medics took off carrying Sergeant Dew on the stretcher just as a German tank approached the company command post. Captain Burriss contacted Major Cook by radio, telling him of the situation. Burriss received the order to withdraw. "No man moved from his position until I gave the order. By this time, the Krauts had overrun our position; as we withdrew, they were running side by side with my men, both sides shooting at each other."[22]

Staff Sergeant George Leoleis, on the north side of the perimeter, had given his M1 to a young replacement the night before. "Everyone was firing and throwing hand grenades. We were now overrun, and everyone was involved in a death struggle for survival. Not having a rifle, I used my .45 till I emptied that. I then threw it at the next Kraut that came at me, and when he ducked, I closed and used my knife on him. I then picked up his burp gun and used that till the ammo ran out. There were so damn many of them, you just couldn't miss. Another came after me, and again it was a fight to the finish. (I was covered with blood; I didn't know if any of it was mine.) All the men were doing the same thing. The tanks just rolled over people, theirs and ours, and went past us."[23]

Leoleis then looked to his right and saw the troopers on that side of the perimeter falling back. "They were just overwhelmed by sheer numbers. I still remember taking a quick look over to the right side and saw a friend, Sergeant [Alexander L.] Barker, in a fight with three Krauts hanging all over him, trying to take him, and from sheer force of numbers they all went down, and that was the last I saw of him."[24] Leoleis would later learn of Barker's death at Den Heuvel. "It was my privilege to know him."[25]

Staff Sergeant Leoleis picked up a rifle from one of the dead troopers and firing from the hip, moved back. "It seemed that the more you killed, the more there were. (I never saw that many up close, before or after.)"[26]

Staff Sergeant Baldwin took charge of evacuating the prisoners. As he and the prisoners ran, one of tanks drove between him and the prisoners. He remains missing in action, his body never found. For his courage and outstanding leadership, Staff Sergeant Baldwin was awarded the Silver Star, and remains missing in action.

As Staff Sergeant Orvin watched German infantry moving through the woods to either side and to the rear, he heard someone shout, "Get out of here!"

"So I told McDermott, 'Come on, let's go!' We got up and we started running.

"Our company operations sergeant [Robert G. Dew] had been wounded, and a couple of guys had him on a stretcher. The tank came up and fired . . . and just riddled him. The guys had to drop that stretcher with him on it, because that tank just riddled him with machine gun fire.

"Instead of me running over to that road, I stayed to the right-hand side of the road—there was a pretty wide road with big trees on each side. They started shooting at me with a machine gun, and I hit the deck. It was a farm road where the farmers had had a horse and wagons pulling through there. I started crawling in the rut where those wagon wheels had been [worn]. They were way back below me, probably two or three hundred yards. But they were firing at me, and I stayed down and just slithered like a snake. I got out of there."[27]

As the survivors of Company I cleared the west side of the woods, Corporal Edwin S. Westcott walked backwards toward the MLR, firing his machine gun from the hip to cover the other troopers. Westcott's courageous action kept the enemy infantry from pressing the survivors too closely and suppressed their fire as the surviving Company I troopers ran toward the MLR.

During the sprint across the open ground, Burriss tripped and fell. Just as he did, one of tanks fired its main gun. The high-velocity shell passed over Burriss and "blew apart the fellow running in front of me. I scrambled to my feet and continued running. When we got back to the MLR and regrouped, twenty-three of my men were missing. I had lost half of my company while crossing the river, and now I had lost almost half of those remaining—after only eleven days of combat."[28]

Out of the 1st Platoon, only seven made it back, with eleven missing. The 2nd Platoon had twelve missing and only five, those holding the southwest portion of the perimeter, made it back. The 3rd Platoon, the mortar men, and company headquarters troopers except for Dew, escaped uninjured largely because they were on the opposite side of the perimeter.

At dawn on September 28, German infantry, including some armed with flamethrowers, and supported by tanks and self-propelled guns attacked the 2nd Battalion from Erlekom to Thorensche Molen. Lieutenant James Nelson was at the Company E command post when "a report came in from the platoon leader in charge of the left flank defense sector of E Company, saying that enemy infantry with tanks were approaching both the dike and secondary road and that his outposts had already been forced to withdraw. A short but bitter battle ensued."[29]

Private First Class Raymond E. Fary's battery of the 80th Airborne Anti-aircraft (Antitank) Battalion was providing antitank protection for the 2nd Battalion. "The 1st Platoon of Battery C, 1st Gun Section had two 57mm guns, one on each side of [the] Kerkdyk [road], the 2nd Gun Section with two guns near the brickyard. As dawn broke, a German 88 was fired into our immediate area. I jumped into my foxhole as a steady shelling continued, mostly by mortars, for about thirty minutes. Later, a trooper ran to my foxhole and said, 'There's a German tank coming out of the wood line from the right flank.'

"I saw this tank on the dike moving slowly. I ran to get help from the two nearest foxholes, Corporal [Roland] Boteler and [Private First Class] Robert [L.] Atkinson. We ran to our 57mm antitank gun, removed all the camouflage and sandbags, and turned the gun ninety degrees to get it in the direction of the tank. I then threw an armor-piercing shell into the chamber and Boteler fired. The projectile hit the drive-sprocket wheel. The tank stopped dead, the gears were jammed."[30]

The right flank of Company E received intense artillery and mortar fire as approximately two companies of German infantry supported by five tanks attacked. Corporal Joseph J. Jusek, with Headquarters Company, 2nd Battalion, commanding a light machine gun supporting the defenses on that flank, exposed himself to the deadly shrapnel of the rain of artillery and mortar fire to direct the fire of his machine gun team, devastating the German infantry. The enemy tanks moved up—one within two hundred yards—to blast Jusek and his machine gun team, wounding Jusek in the face and shoulder and seriously wounding his three men. Staff Sergeant Ken Nicoll, a forward observer with the 81mm Mortar Platoon of Headquarters Company, 2nd Battalion, was nearby. "Joe Jusek from Chicago was shot right through the eye, and he picked up his machine gun and kept firing at a bunch of tanks that were on top of us. He kept them buttoned up, so we could get them with grenades."[31]

Jusek single-handedly manned his machine gun for over two hours, refusing evacuation until the attack was beaten back. He was later awarded the Distinguished Service Cross for his extraordinary courage under fire.

As the Germans closed on the paratroopers, they opened fire on the infantry, pinning them down. Sergeant Roy E. Tidd, a squad leader with Company E, left his foxhole and ran two hundred fifty yards through intense mortar, artillery, and tank fire to the rear to a British tank. He directed the British tank forward to an advantageous firing position. The houses to the front of the tank were burning fiercely, having been set on fire by the German flamethrower teams to conceal the advance of the attacking force. Tidd took up an exposed position near the tank so that he could effectively direct the fire of the tank. The enemy concentrated mortar, machine gun, and tank fire at Tidd and the tank, but due to Tidd's courageous tenacity in directing its fire of the British tank, two of the enemy tanks were destroyed and two more forced to withdraw. Sergeant Tidd received the Silver Star for his gallantry.

At one of the Fox Company outposts, Private First Class Oscar F. Ladner opened fire on the advancing German infantry. The enemy armor located his position and concentrated their fire on it, wounding him across the cheek and momentarily blinding him. Nevertheless, Ladner remained at his exposed position, delivering deadly accurate fire, even when wounded a second time by shrapnel.

Another F Company machine gun team on the main line of resistance, led by Private First Class Robert D. Maier, moved their gun to the forward edge of the dike and raked the German infantry, pinning it down. A German tank, only a hundred yards away, fired its main gun at their position, wounding Maier and his assistant, Private Joseph M. Koss. The explosion damaged the machine gun, causing it to jam. Incredibly, Maier field-stripped the gun as bullets impacted the ground near him and zipped by his head. Maier cleared the jam and started firing again. Refusing to withdraw to the main line of resistance and the protected side of the dike, and despite his wounds, Maier poured fire into the enemy infantry. Even when a tank round killed Private Koss, Maier remained at the machine gun until antitank fire knocked out the tank and the German attack in that sector fell apart. Privates First Class Ladner and Maier received the Silver Star for their bravery.

From his position, Lieutenant Nelson was able to see that "three enemy tanks and one half-track were knocked out and the enemy completely routed and forced to withdraw, leaving many dead on the battlefield. Our own casualties were two dead [Corporal Arthur J. Lewandowski and Private First Class Kenneth J. Pinney] and six wounded. We had two British tanks supporting us, which accounted for the enemy tanks being knocked out."[32]

Captain Walter VanPoyck checked on the Easy Company medics who, together with a German medic, were treating some of the seventeen prisoners, several of whom were seriously wounded. "Before we could dress their wounds or give them morphine, I had to convince their medical corporal that we weren't attempting to inject them with a poison. They had thought they were attacking British positions. When they learned we were American paratroopers, they were convinced we would murder them. I spoke no German of any consequence, and the medical corporal conversed in French."[33]

Later that afternoon, at the command post, Lieutenant Nelson received a report that an E Company patrol "killed ten Germans and took thirty prisoners, just about one hundred yards in front of our position. These Germans had been hiding in a ditch and, we supposed, had meant to infiltrate through our positions after dark."[34]

That same day, Lieutenant Jim Megellas, with Company H, received an order to report to Colonel Tucker. Megellas was told that "our intelligence had been receiving reports that the division would be attacked on this evening by three divisions of German infantry and two of armor. From all reports, we understood the Germans intended to wipe out our position and all our forces. This was boastfully decreed over a German radio broadcast stating that the 82nd Airborne Division would be wiped out. The entire division was alerted for an attack. We were told to stay in our foxholes and let the German armor pass by us, and then we should engage the accompanying infantry."[35]

Tucker told Megellas that he needed to bring back some prisoners for interrogation. That night, shortly after dark, Megellas led his depleted platoon toward the German lines. "In attempting to get behind enemy lines to secure prisoners, we had to cross the Wyler Meer, which was between our established positions. Since we did not know the depth of this lagoon, we planned to cross at an appropriate footbridge.

"The Germans had accordion wire (barbed wire) stretched across the bridge. I assumed that the bridge or the approaches would also be mined. I therefore ordered my patrol to take cover while I crawled forward, feeling with my fingers for trip wires or evidence of mines. I reached the barbed wire without finding any mines, and then decided to cross over and reconnoiter the other side. In doing so I got tangled up in the barbed wire and ripped my trousers. I was so disgusted with myself that I used profane language. The noise I created caused a couple of Germans to pop their heads out of the foxhole. I immediately realized the enemy was entrenched on the other side of the bridge. I freed myself quickly from the barbed wire and hit the ground. I crawled forward towards the foxholes and called for the enemy to come out with their hands up. Failing to do so, I rolled grenades into the foxholes, which were occupied by enemy soldiers. I killed four of the enemy and captured two others single-handedly.

"I do not know why the Germans did not fire upon me when I was hung up on the barbed wire, nor why they remained in the foxholes while I was rolling grenades in on them. Apparently, they were waiting to be relieved by another patrol, and I caught them by surprise."[36] Megellas personally destroyed a ten-man German observation post, and he and his men captured four prisoners. He dispatched two troopers to take them back for interrogation. Megellas then led his platoon deeper into enemy territory and attacked the enemy main line of resistance, killing a number of Germans at an embankment, before retreating with two more prisoners. The Germans used flares to illuminate the area, looking for Megellas' combat patrol. But, they made it safely back to the 504th lines. For his daring leadership and bravery, Lieutenant Megellas was awarded the Distinguished Service Cross.

From October 3rd until they pulled out, the 82nd Airborne Division sector was relatively quiet. However, the shelling, the sniping, and patrolling continued, seemingly without end. Lieutenant John Holabird, the assistant platoon leader of the 2nd Platoon, Company C, 307th Airborne Engineer Battalion, led "almost nightly patrols—trying to find out what the Germans were up to—while they were finding out what we were up to."[37]

Early on October 3, near Erlekom, Lieutenant Carl Mauro, with Company E, walked to the half-destroyed house that was serving as the command post for Captain Walter VanPoyck, the company commander. Mauro entered the house and walked into the kitchen. " 'Jocko' [Lieutenant John Thompson], recuperating from his shrapnel wound, was sleeping with four or five others in the basement of the house, where everyone believed it was the most secure place to be. A couple of soldiers were frying on the stove, what looked to me like chicken—they said it was fresh domestic rabbit. It looked great and smelled good.

"VanPoyck was writing at the kitchen table, and I told him it looked like he was going to get a good, hot breakfast. Yeah, he was looking forward to that.

"I noticed that Van had just finished addressing a letter to Captain Edward ('Eddie') Rickenbacker—I was surprised. 'Do you know Rickenbacker?' I asked Van.

" 'Know him? He was my boss!' Van said.

"I learned that Rickenbacker, a World War I air-combat ace and household name when I was a teenager, was Van's boss. He was president of Eastern Airlines, where Van had worked as an administrative officer.

"Lieutenant [Edmund H.] Ed Kline, Headquarters Company platoon leader, had sent me in to tell Van about some enemy activity on our front—light and sporadic mortar fire at the time. Kline was ready to retaliate with his 81mm mortars, and Van so advised.

"I wasn't offered any rabbit stew, so I returned to Kline's gun emplacement about a hundred yards in front of the CP house.

"He was holding his retaliation in abeyance, so as to not reveal our gun positions. Kline was not yet certain exactly where his targets would be, and as always, the factor of conserving ammunition had to be considered.

"Soon, Kline thought he could direct his firing proportionally and sought his target carefully and wisely. We had return fire from the enemy mortars, fortunately all misses. A few rounds were fired intermittently from each side. We couldn't see them, and I'm certain they couldn't see us.

"Kline reached a point where he was pretty certain where his target, or targets were. He ordered the gunners to 'fire for effect', which meant they let loose a small but sufficient barrage upon the enemy gun emplacements.

"Then everything became quiet. No return fire. 'We got them that time,' Kline said, 'I think we've knocked them out!' He said, 'Let's go tell Van.'

"Kline and I walked back to the Company CP to tell Van that we were pretty sure we knocked out the mortars that had been firing randomly on our position. Actually, I was also going into the house to see how 'Jocko' was feeling.

"Just before entering the house I opened a small round can of cheese that came with our rations. I took it out of my pocket, opened the can, took off my helmet, and began eating the cheese as I opened the door to the kitchen where Van was.

"At that very moment, I heard a large bang and saw for just a fraction of a second, a light bursting through the kitchen ceiling, and felt myself reeling backward; stunned and falling in the doorway.

"I remained conscious, but felt numbness in various parts of my body. The area seemed hazy and smoky, with many splintered pieces of wood all about me.

"I couldn't see him from where I was lying, but I heard Van say, 'Carl, can you come in here, I need some help.' I told him I was sorry, but I couldn't move."[38]

A German mortar shell had scored a direct hit on the house, and Captain VanPoyck was critically wounded. "I suffered a traumatic amputation of my right leg and a shattered left foot. Corporals [William H.] Gotts and [Harold

H.] Roman, flanking me, each ultimately lost a leg. While busy applying belt and bootlace tourniquets, I remember one of them said, 'I've lost my leg,' and my replying, 'I think I've lost both of mine.'

"My immediate concern was to contact battalion. Lieutenants Mauro, Kline, and [James H.] Nelson, Sergeant [Edgar N.] Dumas, and Corporals [Romeo J.] Hamel and [Amos E.] Overholt were also wounded.

"Lieutenant Nelson, severely wounded when I was hit, ran from our CP for help, to a platoon position. Later, in the hospital in England, a doctor told me it was physically impossible for him to stand on his shattered feet, let alone run on them.

"We were evacuated in a jeep, involving four trips in broad daylight on the dike road, directly under the German gun positions. We flew a Red Cross flag from a tree limb staff, and they held their fire. I was hospitalized two years."[39]

ON THE NIGHT OF OCTOBER 11–12, Private First Class Ted Bachenheimer, with Headquarters Company, 1st Battalion, accompanied a British officer across the Waal River at Tiel, to contact a Dutch family named Ebbens. The mission was to set up a chain of guides to bring British paratroopers, being hidden by courageous Dutch citizens in the Arnhem area, back through enemy-held territory to friendly lines. However, Bachenheimer and the British officer were spotted in civilian clothes by a traitor who informed the Germans of their presence, and they were captured on October 17. Fortunately, both had worn their uniforms on the mission and were captured at night, so they were able to say they had taken off their uniforms when they went to bed. However, the Gestapo tortured, interrogated, and ultimately shot the entire Ebbens family. On October 23, while being taken to a POW camp, Bachenheimer attempted to escape and was shot, ending the life of one of the 504th's most legendary troopers.

THE STATIC WARFARE CONTINUED THROUGH THE MONTH OF OCTOBER as both sides shelled each other at every opportunity. Private First Class Alfred Hermansen, with Headquarters Battery, 376th Parachute Field Artillery Battalion, was a member of a forward observation team supporting Company I. "We were in a defensive position, and our observation post was within a strong point manned by Captain Burriss. We were on a slight ridge covered with brush and small trees, looking down on the Germans occupying the hamlet of Wyler, I would say some three hundred yards or so. As was my custom, each morning, at barely daylight, I would go a little or so to the rear for a canteen of hot water for our groups' instant coffee. This particular morning, before my errand, I decided to check our telescope. I touched neither the tube or the lens, just put my eye to the instrument (it was mounted on a low tripod and viewed from the prone position). There, as clear as ever, looking over a hedgerow was a German looking at something to our left. I could make out the features of his face and the crushed, visored cap he was wearing. He then disappeared, and coming from a nearby spot came four little smoke rings—a mortar battery. Those German guns were positioned a short distance from one of our many recorded checkpoints, and in a matter of minutes a salvo of 75mm shells came whining low overhead, bursting right on target. One brave German medic came through the smoke waving a Red Cross flag at us to ease off. He had work to do. I did my day's work, and before breakfast!"[40]

As the 504th held the high ground along the wooded plateau extending east from Berg en Dal, much of the regimental sector fronted a body of water called the Wyler Meer, northwest of Wyler, Germany. Therefore, a very limited area was available for patrols to bring back POWs for interrogation. During October, as combat patrols entered this small area nightly, the enemy built up its defenses dramatically to the point where every patrol became engaged in firefights and was unable to capture prisoners.

The regiment devised a plan for a daring daylight patrol, hoping that surprise and easier movement through enemy minefields would result in success. The patrol would have to move parallel to the Wyler Meer and the Nijmegen-Wyler road. About 150 yards in front of the regiment's outpost line, the Germans had constructed a roadblock using a dozen felled trees and a wrecked vehicle, with Teller mines sown surrounding the block. An enemy trench line in dense woods across the road from the Wyler Meer covered the approaches to the roadblock with machine guns, rifles, and Panzerfausts. Barbed wire entanglements and five-pound explosive charges with pull-type detonators attached to tripwires strung between trees at varying heights protected the trench line.

The plan called for a carefully coordinated mortar and artillery support plan. At 1635 hours, one 81mm mortar would lay forty high-explosive (HE) rounds in five minutes along the enemy's forward positions, then elevate twenty-five yards and fire another forty rounds, and continue this pattern through the length of the woods, lifting at 1715 hours and firing on Wyler itself. The patrol would follow this rolling barrage as closely as possible. A 60mm mortar would fire continuously on a house containing a machine gun sighted to deliver enfilade fire from the right along the patrol's route. Beginning at 1710 hours and continuing until 1740, fifty-two artillery pieces—one of the division's 105mm and two 75mm artillery battalions, plus two batteries of British 25-pounders and 5.5 inch guns—would fire barrages into Zyfflich, Wyler, Lagewald, and all known and suspected enemy gun and mortar positions. Two entire regiments of British 25-pounder artillery would be on call to isolate the enemy in the wooded area where the patrol would operate from reinforcement from the rear.

The 3rd Platoon, Company A, led by Lieutenant Reneau Breard, was chosen to conduct the patrol. Breard augmented the firepower of his twenty-seven-man platoon with additional automatic weapons and bazookas. The patrol's armament would include eight Thompson submachine guns, three BARs, and two bazookas. Everyone else would carry M1 rifles. The patrol would also carry two rolls of engineering tape to mark paths through the minefield and wire cutters to penetrate the barbed wire entanglements. The regiment scheduled the patrol for October 23.

That day, about three hours before commencement of the patrol, a lone trooper crept forward to reconnoiter the minefield. As he was doing so, he observed three German engineers laying additional mines. He took note of the types of mines before shooting one of the Germans and withdrawing.

At 1635 hours the 81mm mortar opened fire and the patrol, in three squad columns moving abreast, advanced toward the enemy positions under its suppressive fire. The 1st Squad, reinforced by the two bazooka teams, moved forward on the left, along the edge of the woods near the highway, across from the Wyler Meer. On the right, the 3rd Squad moved along the right edge of the woods, with the three BAR gunners dropping off to cover the open ground to the patrol's right flank. Lieutenant Breard led the 2nd Squad up the center, through the woods south of the road. After approximately one hundred yards, the patrol came to the minefield. With the trip wires visible in the light of day, the three squads converged in the center and moved single file, clearing a path through the minefield, cutting trip wires, removing some mines, and marking the path with engineering tape. Midway through the minefield, Breard's platoon encountered the concertina wire, which they cut with the wirecutters.

As the patrol picked its way through the minefield, the 81mm mortar dropped shells on the enemy positions just ahead about every five seconds. Lieutenant Breard watched as explosions flashed in the woods just ahead. "It was just a creeping barrage. We stayed close behind the 81mm mortar—right behind. We cleared that minefield when all of the covering fire was going on."[41]

The three squads moved back to their original formation abreast after clearing the minefield. As the 1st and 2nd Squads approached the roadblock, they engaged in a firefight with the dug-in enemy machine gunners and riflemen. Breard's paratroopers moved from tree to tree, firing as they closed with the enemy. The firepower from the Thompson submachine guns at close range suppressed the enemy fire. The Germans withdrew, taking their wounded with them and leaving seven dead, two MG-42s, and a number of Schmeisser machine pistols.

Corporal Frank Heidebrink, at the 2nd Squad point, moving through the center of the wooded area, suddenly saw two Germans pop up from a spider hole to his right and begin to set up a machine gun. Heidebrink opened fire with his Thompson, wounding one of them in the stomach, a large German paratrooper, who slumped back down in the hole. The other tried to run, but hit the ground and surrendered when Heidebrink fired a burst over the German's head. They pulled another German out of his hole nearby. Breard found the prisoners to be "subdued. They were ready to leave—they'd been mortared to hell and back. We pushed 'em up and got 'em moving. We got them out first. We tried to get the big one [who had been shot in the stomach], but his foxhole was up near the edge of the woods to the right. He was just too big to carry, so we just rolled him down the hill and I heard him groaning—to hell with him."[42]

The daylight was now beginning to fade, and the woods grew darker. The patrol had captured two enemy prisoners and had not suffered a single casualty. As enemy tracers zipped through the woods, Lieutenant Breard fired a green flare, which was the signal for the patrol to withdraw. "The hard thing was getting the three squads back in to go through the minefield. Then when we got back, Heidebrink and I went by and briefed the company commander.

"He said, 'Well, they want you down at battalion.' So, I took Heidebrink down to battalion, and we briefed battalion.

"When we got through, they asked, 'How many men did you lose?'

"I spoke up real fast, 'We didn't have any casualties.' That made 'em feel real good."[43]

The following day, October 24, Private First Class Leo Hart received the word that his F Company platoon would be conducting a combat patrol with the objective of a prisoner snatch that night. "Late in the afternoon, we got the charcoal to blacken our faces, checked our weapons, and got a briefing on what we were to do. It was a simple mission. An outpost was the target, and the surprise was with us. Lieutenant [Vance C.] Hall was to be in charge."[44]

That night Hart moved out with the patrol heading east toward the village of Vossendaal. "We proceeded to within several hundred yards of the outposts and waited as our artillery laid in a cover barrage. After the barrage, word came down to move in."[45]

At about 1:00 a.m. on October 25, the platoon moved forward for about two hundred yards. It was eerily quiet as they silently crept toward the enemy outpost line, when suddenly Hart heard gunfire just ahead. "Two or three members of the raid decided to shoot out ahead. [Private First Class Willard G.] Bill Tess was one that I remember and [Private Joseph] Montbleau was another. Tess asked me to go with him. I recall saying 'Hell no! Take it easy!' He made a rather unpleasant remark. I moved back into position behind Cornelius."

Private First Class Marshall J. Cornelius, Jr., a bazooka gunner with Headquarters Company, 2nd Battalion, had been attached to the platoon for the combat patrol. As Private First Class Hart fell back to his position in the tactical column, "suddenly a burst of enemy machine gun fire cut waist high from my right to the left. I was knocked off my feet. At first, I thought I was hit; but the bullet slammed into my M1, right at the slide. The M1 was useless.

"Everything went dead quiet after this first burst. Then, out of this quiet, I heard Cornelius, who must have taken the burst right in the middle, cry very softly, 'Mama . . . mama . . .' Then, he began reciting, 'Now I lay me down to sleep, I pray . . .' and that was all. I can't express how I felt; but enemy artillery came barreling in, and cover was of the utmost importance from then out.

"We got the prisoner."[46]

Death stalked the troopers everywhere. Even the rear areas were not safe. On October 27, Company A, after being relieved, walked back to retrieve their musette bags in the rear. Lieutenant Reneau Breard wasn't able to find his in the pile. "They had dropped our bags and there was just a big pile of them. We walked up there and got them. There was Panzerfaust in the pile. Somebody had put a Panzerfaust on that truck and they just kicked everything off. This boy by the name of [Private Paul G.] Stinson saw his musette bag and pulled it, and the damned [Panzerfaust] went off, and the blowback just disemboweled him. It didn't blow up. The warhead went one way and didn't go off. We gave him a shot of morphine real fast. He just turned pale and died real fast. I asked him if he was hurting and he said no."[47]

A couple of days later, Lieutenant Breard "went up to battalion and they got shelled. A damned shell came right in the room where we were and exploded. Nobody got hit, but everybody was chalked up. I told them, 'If you're through with me, I'm going back home, out of here.' "[48]

On October 30, Staff Sergeant George Leoleis, the platoon sergeant of the 3rd Platoon of Company I, was preparing to take a patrol out later that night, when another reconnaissance patrol moved out just after dusk. "This patrol consisted of 1st Lieutenant Edward W. Kennedy, Staff Sergeant William H. White, and two other men. . . .

"They were gone about an hour when the two men came back carrying Lieutenant Kennedy as best they could. He had lost his foot just above the ankle. I happened to be in the CP going over some details as to where I was to take my patrol when Kennedy and his men got back. As the two men busted in yelling for the medic, everyone was up asking what the hell happened. I asked about Whitey. The men told us that they were working their way up a draw and then something exploded. When the shock of the explosion wore off, they realized Sergeant White was missing and the lieutenant had lost part of his leg. They put a tourniquet on his leg and carried him back as best they could. After the excitement calmed down and seeing the lieutenant, we asked the two men if they could find their way back to the same place. They said they could. Meanwhile, the two men grabbed some coffee and tried to relax a little. Some men were trying to cheer the lieutenant by joking with him so he could keep his spirits up. Some of the men kidded, 'Hey, lieutenant, you got that million dollar wound.' For him the war was over and at least he was alive and in a few days he would be home. The jeep pulled up and we all wished him well. He shook my hand and wished me luck when I went out to look for Sergeant White.

"They took Lieutenant Kennedy to the first aid station and then to a field hospital. Later, we were informed that Lieutenant Kennedy died when shock set in, after he was operated on to fix his shattered leg."[49]

Staff Sergeant Leoleis led two patrols that night to the location of where the explosion occurred, but was unable to find any sign of Staff Sergeant White, who was later declared killed in action.

At the beginning of November, Lieutenant John Holabird reported to the Company C, 307th Airborne Engineer Battalion command post. "Captain Spike Harris sent me to Colonel Tucker's regimental headquarters, where I kept a file of antipersonnel minefields we had set and were setting so we could turn this information over to whoever relieved us."[50]

The 504th Regimental Combat Team and the rest of the 82nd Airborne Division were relieved by Canadian forces on November 11, and were trucked to Sissonne, France, to receive rest and replacements, arriving on November 15.

Private First Class Edwin R. Bayley was a new replacement who had helped prepare the barracks at Sissonne for the regiment. He had contracted an illness and was just returning from the hospital when he arrived at the camp shortly after the arrival of the regiment. "I had no idea where I belonged or where my stuff was. I went to the barracks from which I had gone to the hospital and found exactly where I had been assigned and where to find my clothes and equipment. I was assigned to Company A, 1st Platoon.

"I went to the orderly room and was surprised to find my arrival was no big deal. They said to go find an empty bunk in the platoon squad room and settle in. That's all there was to it, immediate acceptance by the more experienced troopers, without question of where I came from. Later, I realized that replacements and new arrivals were non-events because they were always occurring.

"Some of the soldiers made close romantic attachments with some of the town girls. We found out that the reason for the short clipped hairstyle of some of the girls was that they had been romantic associates of German soldiers. When the Germans left, the villagers shaved all the hair off these girls' heads so that the public would know that these women were collaborators. The men were advised to be careful about these girls in the event they still had connections equal to spying and German informants.

"Some of the days were spent in training, getting the new personnel integrated with the veterans. There was a lot of free time, with many passes being issued to Paris and many other places. Regimental officers at one time tried to organize a dance and party with nearby WAC [Women's Army Corps] personnel. According to the story, the WAC commanding officer told our colonel that she didn't want her girls associating with his bunch of overpaid killers. His quoted reply was that he decided that he didn't want his men associating with her bunch of underpaid whores, and that was the end of the dance plans.

"The 504 had a very satisfying Thanksgiving. The food service personnel went all-out for that day. They managed to get white tablecloths for every table and prepared a magnificent Thanksgiving dinner with all the conventional fixings. After that, we were looking forward to Christmas.

"According to the reports the men had, all was going well with the war at the front, and it looked as though the troopers might not be needed again. Rumors were rife, though, with plans of jumping into Berlin ahead of the Russians or the outfit being returned to the USA for refitting and assignment to the invasion of Japan.

"Some of the men managed to get a few Christmas tree ornaments, and others of us went to the local woods and cut a small Christmas tree, which we set up in our platoon room. It looked as though there might be a quiet Christmas. Meanwhile, every night and all day Sundays the poker and craps games continued throughout the barracks."[51]

Captain Victor Campana, who had served as the Company D commanding officer during Holland, transferred to Headquarters, 2nd Battalion, as the operations (S-3) officer after the regiment arrived in France. "The training during the stay at Camp Sissonne consisted mainly of small-unit training to include night compass problems, range firing, and road marches. Regimental and division reviews, intermingled with three-day passes to Paris, filled out our program. Christmas was just eight days away, and everyone had visions of a peaceful Christmas holiday, accompanied by that very appetizing turkey dinner, which does not come too often in the army."[52]

As everyone in the 82nd and 101st Airborne Divisions relaxed after their long combat duty in Holland, many caught up on letters home and sleep, and enjoyed good times with their buddies in Rheims and Paris. Many top officers were on leave. No one anticipated the coming cataclysm in Belgium.

Chapter 12

"Far Worse Than
Any Nightmare"

By the evening of December 17, 1944, rumors were swirling about a German breakthrough. In fact, the Sixth SS Panzer Army, supported by the Fifth Panzer and Seventh Armies, had broken through American lines and was driving toward the Meuse River with the intent of turning north to capture the key port of Antwerp. The tip of the spear of the Sixth SS Panzer Army was four of the best-equipped and battle-hardened divisions in the German military—the 1st, 2nd, 9th, and 12th SS Panzer Divisions.

Captain Campana was at the quarters he shared with the regiment's two other battalion S-3s. "On Sunday evening about 2130 hours, word was passed through the officers' quarters that Colonel Tucker had been summoned to division headquarters for an important meeting. Some of the officers who had been listening to the radio during the course of the evening stated that the radio announcer had mentioned a series of German attacks in the Ardennes sector, and possibly that was the reason for the meeting. Many of the officers discredited that assumption and prepared for bed. However, word traveled around again that Colonel Tucker had called a battalion commanders' meeting."[1]

Company A platoon leader Lieutenant Reneau Breard was attending a function in a little theater near the barracks. "The regimental staff wasn't there. Somebody came in, and all of the sudden, the battalion staffs got up and left.

"I went up and rolled my bedroll out and put everything in that bedroll I wouldn't need. I took a shelter-half, a blanket, and my musette bag, and got my Tommy gun. I had the new green jumpsuit, long underwear, OD [olive drab] wool pants, an OD wool shirt, a sweater, a jacket, and an overcoat. I went over to the company to see what was going on."[2]

After hearing of the meeting Colonel Tucker had convened with the battalion commanders, Captain Campana and the other S-3 officers decided to report to their respective battalion headquarters to find out what was occurring. "Lieutenant Colonel Edward Wellems, commanding officer of the 2nd Battalion, arrived at battalion headquarters about 2230 hours. He immediately instructed the adjutant, 1st Lieutenant Chester Garrison, to phone the company commanders for an immediate meeting. He then gave me an overlay and some French road maps. The overlay was very scanty, merely showing the proposed route of march to a general area in the vicinity of Bastogne.

"The company commanders soon arrived . . . Captain Robert Cellar of Headquarters and Headquarters Company, Captain Adam A. Komosa of D Company, 1st Lieutenant William Sweet of F Company, and 1st Lieutenant John Thompson, executive officer of E Company. Captain Felix E. Simon and 1st Lieutenant Ross I. Donnelly, the battalion surgeon and supply officer respectively, were also present. Captain Herbert H. Norman, commanding officer of E Company, was on pass in Paris, as were also 1st Lieutenant [Lauren W.] Ramsey, the 81mm mortar platoon leader, and other key officers and non-commissioned officers.

"[Lieutenant Colonel Wellems said,] 'The Germans have made a breakthrough in the Ardennes sector near Bastogne. Some American units have already been overrun, particularly the 106th U.S. Infantry Division. We move out tomorrow at 0900 hours in ten-ton semi-trailers. Lieutenant Donnelly will issue K-rations and ammunition tonight to the companies. One machine gun, half loaded, will be manned on the cab of each truck in case of enemy air attacks. Lieutenant [Ernest H.] Brown, from D Company, will be in charge of the battalion rear echelon. Each company will leave at least two men behind for the rear echelon. Kitchen will also be left behind initially. All weapons that are in ordnance will be returned to us before we leave.'

"Upon completion of this meeting, the company commanders returned to their respective orderly rooms and started immediate preparations for the move the next morning."[3]

Lieutenant John Holabird was the duty officer for Company C, 307th Airborne Engineer Battalion, that night. "I went to the barracks and 'cheered everyone up' by saying we were leaving at 8:30 a.m. with full field equipment—pack all their junk in barracks bags to leave behind. Then I drove to the neighboring little town to get the officers back to camp. What a night! This was to be a 'truckborne' operation."[4]

Private First Class Ed Bayley, with Company A, was getting ready to turn in for the night when "our company commander came into the barracks and announced that the Germans had broken through. We were told that we would be moving out to combat early in the morning of the 18th. The non-coms were conferring with their squads and platoons. The lieutenants were conferring with the company commander. My platoon sergeant said that I would be the machine gunner, mostly because I was big and strong enough to carry this weapon. I told him to get someone else, as I had no training on the machine gun and didn't know how to set it up and operate it. He got the normally assigned machine gunner out of the prisoner stockade where he was serving time for something he had done or not done. This was rather a suave and smooth character who had a custom-made shoulder holster for a small automatic which he carried inside of his shirt or coat—looked like a professional gunman.

"Late this same night, a bunch of new replacements arrived in camp. They were very tired after being trucked across France in rainy, chilly weather. They had been cheered to some extent as they had been told the 82nd would probably be in barracks for the next month or so, where they would be able to meld with the division, get to know the other men, and get some more training.

"They were shocked and frightened when they were told that they were going directly into combat the next day or so."[5]

Lieutenant Breard "got a hold of the sergeant and told him to get 'em ready. I told him that I would be inspecting the weapons. We didn't have a formation, anything like that. I just went through and inspected the weapons to see what they were carrying.

"In my platoon everybody had their assigned weapons. It was SOP [standard operating procedure] for us to have a basic load of ammunition for the whole regiment. It was underground somewhere nearby. We always did that. We had learned from experience to have that on hand. The 504th Regiment also had in that basic ammunition supply—I don't know how many they had—but they had beaucoup Panzerfausts. We had captured a dump of them somewhere around Nijmegen. We latched onto them real fast and taught one another how to use them. We had a school real fast up in Holland. Every time we would go into a position, we had those Panzerfausts. Those bazookas weren't worth a damn. The Panzerfausts were wonderful. We had two or three in a squad. So, that's what they issued to the supply sergeants."[6]

Private First Class Bayley got his personal gear and extra clothing packed into his musette bag. "We were instructed to go to the supply room and get needed blankets, emergency food rations, and whatever ammunition we could carry. We were told to take plenty, as we would be needing it.

"Early in the morning, those who had been able to get some sleep were awakened, and we all went to early chow. In the company streets were some of the largest open, stake-bodied tractor-trailer trucks we had ever seen. These were to be our transport to the frontline assembly area. Only the officers seemed to have any information as to our destination. We and the 101st Airborne were the only active reserve troops in the theater. We were to leave at 6:00 a.m. on December 18, and be followed that afternoon by the 101. The weather was cold with a wet, heavy mist."[7]

Like all of the troopers in the regiment, Lieutenant Breard and his Company A platoon were miserable standing outside in the overcast darkness, waiting to board the trucks. "It was raining and cold—the wind was blowing—it was just bad weather."[8]

When the troopers began loading into deuce-and-a-half trucks and long-bedded trailers towed by eighteen wheeled tractor-trailers, Private First Class Malcolm Neel, with Battery A, 80th Airborne Antiaircraft (Antitank) Battalion, was one of the last to board his truck. "I was in a 2 1/2-ton, 6x6 truck sitting near the tailgate when I heard one of our guys, looking out at a group of cold, wet paratroopers standing packed into an open semi-trailer, say, 'Boy, I feel sorry for the first Germans those guys get a hold of.' "[9]

As Captain Victor Campana, the 2nd Battalion S-3, climbed into the back of the battalion commander's jeep, which would lead the 2nd Battalion serial, the battalion's troopers boarded the open beds of the semi-tractor trailers. "Approximately sixty men with all their personal equipment, plus crew-served weapons, were loaded into each truck. The 2nd Battalion followed the 1st Battalion serial with a five-minute interval."[10]

Lieutenant John Holabird made the trip in a jeep with four other Company C, 307th Airborne Engineer Battalion officers. "We kept together to keep warm. We had only a very vague idea of where we were going. Some place in Belgium! Who knows where. It was a cold ride—we ate K-rations without stopping—only 'pit'stops."[11]

Private First Class Ed Bayley was a recent replacement, having joined Company A just after Holland. "My platoon was among those climbing into the lead trucks. There was a small area covered with canvas at the front of the truck trailer. I and about four others jumped into the truck real fast and got these choice semi-weather-protected positions. We only got up when really necessary for pee stops and did it over the side while standing in our spots so we wouldn't lose them. It was chilly and misting all day long as we trekked along a one hundred fifty mile drive."[12]

Private First Class Morris "Mike" Holmstock was riding in the back of one of the trucks hauling Company B. "I slept as much as I could. Guys were bitching and moaning. No one knew anything, really."[13]

As the convoy moved into Belgium, Private First Class Tom Holliday, also with Company B, noticed that the roads were clogged with traffic going the other way. "Hell, everything was streaming to the rear, but we just kept going up."[14]

Driving through the rain and sleet, the jeep carrying Gavin pulled into a small, obscure village. "I arrived at Werbomont at approximately mid-afternoon and immediately made a reconnaissance of the entire area. It offered excellent defensive possibilities, being the dominant terrain for many miles from the crossroads of Werbomont. At about 1600 hours, I contacted an engineer platoon at the bridge at Hablemont. The bridge was prepared for demoli-

Movement of the 82nd Airborne Division
to Werbomont, Belgium

LIEGE
Meuse
Verviers
Mons
Sambre
Charleroi
Amblève
Werbomont Arrival Time
Head 1730, 18 Dec. 1944
Tail 1000, 19 Dec. 1944
Werbomont
Trois Ponts
Salm
BELGIUM
Maubeuge
St. Vith
Sambre
Marche-en-Famenne
Ourthe
Mariembourg
Lesse
Houffalize
Sprimont
Meuse
Bastogne
Hirsons
Semois
Our
Vervins
Recogne
LUXEMBURG
Serre
Charleville-Mezieres
Montcornet
Camp Sissone
Departure Time 0900, 18 Dec. 1944
Sedan
Chiers
Luxembourg
Sissone
Laon
Rethel
Ainse
Aisne
Mazagran
Thionville
Vesle
RHEIMS
Meuse
Aire
Marne
FRANCE
Verdun
METZ
Epernay
Suippes
Camp Suippes
Departure Time 0900, 18 Dec. 1944
Moselle
CHALONS-SUR-MARNE
0   10   20   30 Miles

tion, and they reported the Germans were in the immediate vicinity, coming over the main highway from Trois Ponts. At the time, a number of civilians were very excitedly moving west on the Trois Ponts–Werbomont road. They all stated that the Germans had passed Trois Ponts and were 'coming this way.' I made a reconnaissance down the valley from Hablemont to the Amblève River but encountered no enemy or any indication of his whereabouts. One bridge was still intact at Forge and was not prepared for demolition. Upon returning to Werbomont, I asked a lieutenant at that bridge about it, but he appeared to be fully occupied with the means at his disposal of blowing the bridge at Hablemont. At about 1600 hours I left for Bastogne to meet General [Anthony] McAuliffe. I reported to the VIII Corps CP in Bastogne and had a short conversation with General [Troy] Middleton and talked to his G-2 and G-3. At that time the corps CP was preparing to move. The situation was very vague. The 28th Division officers present seemed to feel that their division had been overrun, although they were uncertain of its whereabouts. I met General McAuliffe, gave him his orders that he was to assemble in Bastogne, reporting to the corps commander of the VIII Corps, and I left, moving north and passing through Houffalize shortly after dark. I arrived in Werbomont at approximately 2000 hours and about that time the first large group of 82nd vehicles started arriving. A command post was established and troops disposed as rapidly as they arrived. Drivers and troops were very tired, having by this time been up for two nights. All during the night the staff worked on closing the vehicles into the Werbomont area."[15]

Captain Victor Campana, the 2nd Battalion S-3, was riding in the battalion commander's jeep leading the battalion serial. "About 1900 hours, the 2nd Battalion motor serial came to a halt in the vicinity of Sprimont. The road ahead was crowded with vehicles, almost bumper to bumper. We discovered that we were behind division artillery; somehow or other the artillery serial had managed to insert itself between the 1st Battalion and the 2nd Battalion. After waiting in the cold night for almost two hours in open vehicles, we finally moved on again. However, we discovered that instead of turning south towards Bastogne, we were now headed towards Werbomont. . . .

"The town of Werbomont contained an important road net to the north, south, east, and west, and the retention of this town would prevent the enemy from reaching Liège, which at that very moment the Germans seemed intent upon doing, having no opposition before them to prevent their advance."[16]

The 504th began arriving in Werbomont about 11:30 p.m., after a thirteen-hour drive from their base camp in Sissonne. When Private First Class Ed Bayley, with Company A, climbed off the truck, he and the other new men didn't know where they were or what was going to happen. "We asked our sergeant, who was dispersing us into the woods, if he knew where the Germans were. Those of us facing combat for the first time were worried as to what might be happening. He said the Germans were several miles away. About this time, we heard a .50-caliber machine gun firing. We knew they were not very far away. Two troopers were assigned as buddies. My partner was named [Private Clarence E.] Sonntag, a newly arrived replacement whom I had never met before this night. Most of us tried to get some sleep on the cold, wet ground."[17]

While the 2nd Battalion waited in their trucks behind a group of vehicles near the unloading point, Lieutenant Colonel Wellems went forward to find out where the battalion would move after unloading. Captain Campana was left in charge and "brought the battalion forward several minutes later and halted the serial at a road intersection where other units had been dismounting. . . .

"Lieutenant Furst, the battalion S-2, who had preceded the battalion to Werbomont earlier that day, met us at the dismount point along with company guides. The battalion was given a sector to defend on the high ground about one-half mile northeast of the town. The battalion command post was located in a small wooden shack next to an odorous pigpen and outhouse. By the time the companies were in position, it was long after midnight.

"On the following morning, 19 December, the battalion commander had a patrol from E Company dispatched with instructions to contact American troops located somewhere to our front. Five hours later, the patrol returned and 2nd Lieutenant Sampson, the patrol leader, reported that he had contacted a battalion of the 119th Infantry Regiment, 30th U.S. Infantry Division some three miles to the east of Werbomont. The battalion commander of that unit had been overjoyed to learn that the 82nd Airborne Division had now come up into the lines. He stated that the 106th Infantry Division and the 7th Armored Division were having a difficult task warding off frequent German attacks. The report from this patrol was immediately forwarded to regiment.

"That afternoon, Captain Norman, Lieutenant Ramsey, and the other members of the battalion who had been on pass in Paris, reported to the battalion. On that day also, German armor cut the road between Werbomont and Bastogne in the vicinity of Houffalize, just after the tail of the division column had cleared the town.

"Immediately after dark on 19 December, the regiment received orders to attack east of Werbomont and seize the town of Rahier. The regiment moved off in a column of battalions, each battalion in a column of companies, and each company in a column of twos. The 2nd Battalion was the advance guard. The order of march was F Company, E Company, D Company, and Headquarters Company. F and E Companies each had a light machine gun section attached from Headquarters Company. The 2nd Battalion was ordered to attack, seize, and hold the town of Rahier. The battalion moved out on foot at 1900 hours 19 December. Except for a long six-hour trek over some very hilly terrain, the march was uneventful. There were no enemy in Rahier. The battalion immediately prepared defensive positions to hold the town.

"A perimeter defense was established with the companies disposed in the outskirts of town from right to left as follows: F Company, E Company, and D Company. The battalion CP was set up in town, and the 81mm mortars were located on the west edge of the town. A platoon of Company C, 307th Airborne Engineer Battalion, was attached to us during this movement. Later on, this platoon under Lieutenant [Travis] Womack was given a sector to defend on the left of D Company. I obtained extra hand grenades when requested by Lieutenant Womack, but was unable to get him any automatic weapons.

"After we had arrived in Rahier, we questioned civilians about the location of enemy troops. The civilians reported that many enemy vehicles, about 125 in number, including thirty tanks, had moved through the town that afternoon (19 December) on the way to Cheneux, located on the very high ground about two miles northeast of Rahier.

"This information was passed on to General Gavin by Colonel Tucker when the former visited the unit later that morning [of December 20]. General Gavin then ordered Colonel Tucker to seize Cheneux and the nearby bridge which crossed the Amblève River. . . .

"A patrol from D Company led by Sergeant [Elton R.] Venable made its way towards Cheneux. On the ridge about one-half mile west of the town, they fired on a German motorcyclist accompanied by a small patrol. Sergeant Venable was wounded in the hip during the brief exchange of shots that followed."[18]

Lieutenant Marshall W. Stark, the platoon leader of the 1st Platoon, Battery C, 80th Airborne Antiaircraft (Antitank) Battalion, set up his four 57mm anti-tank guns to defend Rahier, where the 1st Battalion was concentrated. "During the remainder of the morning, considerable firing could be heard and seen in the vicinity of Stoumont, which was in the 30th Infantry Division sector. This town was approximately two miles from the platoon location."[19]

Shortly after noon on December 20, Captain Tom Helgeson, the commanding officer of Company B, was called to the 1st Battalion command post. "The 1st Battalion, 504th Parachute Infantry, was ordered to seize and occupy the village of Cheneux, Belgium. This order was given to the battalion commander at Rahier, Belgium. The battalion commander [Lieutenant Colonel Willard Harrison] issued his order to the company commanders in the battalion defensive area at Rouge Thier, Belgium. One company [Company A] was to seize and hold the village of Brume, Belgium. Two companies [B and C] were to seize and hold the village of Cheneux. The attack on Cheneux was to jump off from Rahier in a column of companies, [the] leading company deployed on either side of the road from Rahier to Cheneux. The attack jumped off at 1400 after an approach march from Rouge Thier to Rahier."[20]

The paratroopers pressed into service an abandoned German half-track armed with a 77mm gun, which had run out of gas at Rahier. Private First Class

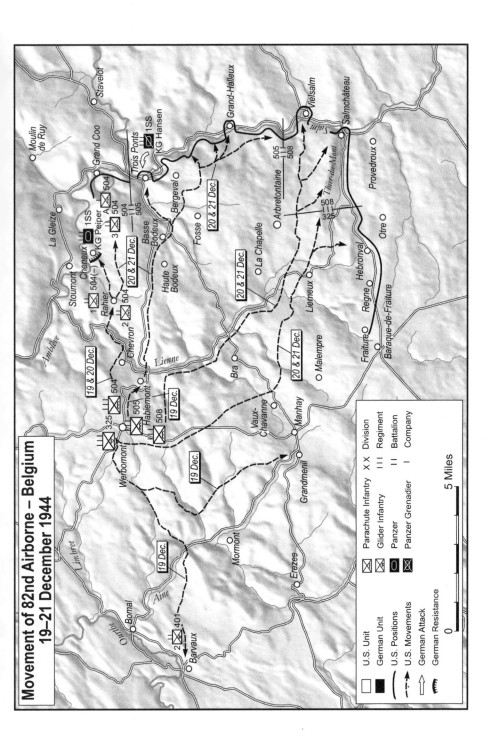

Movement of 82nd Airborne – Belgium 19–21 December 1944

Moulin de Ruy

Stavelot

Grand Coo

Trois Ponts

KG Hansen 1SS

Grand-Halleux

Vielsalm

Salmchâteau

La Gleize

A 504

KG Peiper 1SS

Cheneux

3 504
504
III
505

Basse Bodeux

Bergeval

Fosse

20 & 21 Dec.

S. Salm

505
III
508

Arbrefontaine

Provedroux

Stoumont

Rahier

1 504(–)

504

2 504

Chevron

20 & 21 Dec.

Haute Bodeux

La Chapelle

20 & 21 Dec.

Lierneux

Thier-du-Mont

508
III
325

Otre

Hébronval

Amblève

19 & 20 Dec.

504

Lienne

Bra

20 & 21 Dec.

Malempre

Règne

Fraiture

Baraque-de-Fraiture

19 & 20 Dec.

325 504

505

Habiemont

508

19 Dec.

Werbomont

Vaux-Chavanne

Manhay

19 Dec.

19 Dec.

Grandménil

Lisbyre

Mormont

Erezée

19 Dec.

Ourthe

Bomal

Aine

2 401

Barvaux

	U.S. Unit		Parachute Infantry	X X	Division
	German Unit		Glider Infantry	I I I	Regiment
↥	U.S. Positions	▯	Panzer	I I	Battalion
↥	U.S. Movements	⊠	Panzer Grenadier	I	Company
↥	German Attack				
⌇	German Resistance				

5 Miles

0

Russell P. Snow, a clerk with Headquarters Company, volunteered to drive it, though he had never driven a half-track previously.

Lieutenant Stark received an order to move his 57mm antitank guns to the eastern edge of Rahier along the Rahier-Cheneux road, where they had observation for almost half of the distance to Cheneux. "In addition, at about 1455, I was requested to furnish two men to operate a German 77mm howitzer mounted on a half-track, which had been abandoned somewhere in the area. Prior to this request, one or two test rounds had been fired; and apparently the entire half-track and its gun were in perfect operation condition. At this time, the point of the column was all set to move out and was awaiting the scheduled time to advance. The battalion commander [Lieutenant Colonel Harrison] desired that this reinforcing armor, as he called it, accompany the point during the advance. Therefore, he decided to delay the advance until these two men [Privates First Class Harold Kelly and Harry Koprowski, who had volunteered] were briefed on the operation of the weapon. For two men who had never seen a weapon of this type, other than in pictures, the five-minute interval allotted to me for orienting them was rather brief, and only minimum knowledge necessary for operation could be imparted. Actually, this was the first time that I had ever seen one of these weapons."[21]

The half-track moved forward and came up behind the 1st Platoon of Company B as they were waiting to move down the road toward Cheneux. Private Thomas R. Holliday Jr. got the word for the BAR men from 1st Platoon to come up front. "Captain Helgeson just said, 'Get on that damned half-track.' Nobody briefed [Private Buland] Hoover and I."[22]

Company B moved out with the half-track near the rear of the column, followed by Company C and Headquarters Company, 1st Battalion. About five hundred yards out of Rahier, Company B ran into a squad of German infantry with an MG-42 acting as a screening force for the German force east of them. The scouts out in front of Company B moving along each side of the road assaulted the German squad, killing one and capturing one. The enemy squad made a fighting withdrawal as the scouts kept up the pressure, driving them a thousand yards or so up the road toward Cheneux, where the scouts made contact with the German main line of resistance defending the town.

A half-dozen German armored vehicles were deployed on the road just west of Cheneux. The first vehicle, an SdKfz 234/3 Puma heavy reconnaissance vehicle with 75mm short-barreled gun mounted on an open-top compartment, was positioned in the middle of the road where a secondary road converged, so that it could cover both the main and secondary roads. Just behind it and to the right, an SdKfz 250/7 half-track (with an 81mm mortar mounted) had excellent visibility of both roads and the fields to each side. A 105mm howitzer positioned by a prime mover also covered both roads and the fields to each side. Three SdKfz 250/9 half-tracks, each with one 20mm gun mounted, were behind it parked diagonally to the road to cover the flanks. On both sides of the road were open fields laced with barbed wire fences every fifty yards of so. South of the road the fields dropped off, then rose again to high ground, on which a flak-wagon with a 20mm antiaircraft gun was positioned to pour enfilade fire into any advancing enemy. On ground south of the village, two platoons with four MG-42 machine guns were dug in facing the open field south of the road, with visibility of the high ground north of the road. The ground north of the road sloped upward and was covered by three platoons and six MG-42s dug in north of the village. A flak-wagon, with its 20mm gun, positioned on the north end of the town behind the dug-in infantry, provided overhead supporting fire north of the road. A Puma with a 75mm gun was positioned on high ground north of Cheneux in the event the Americans attempted a flanking movement using the protection of the lower ground to envelop the town from the north. Five more 75mm armed Pumas were positioned beside and behind buildings in the town, where they covered the approaches. It was defense in depth, and the open fields were a perfect killing ground.

Even more ominous was the force manning those guns: the elite 1st SS Panzer Division's Kampfgruppe Peiper, the tip of the armored spearhead of four SS panzer divisions driving toward Antwerp. SS-Obersturmbannführer Joachim Peiper's men were responsible for numerous acts of atrocities against U.S. troops and Belgian civilians, including the infamous Malmédy Massacre. Kampfgruppe Peiper was north of the Amblève River and running low on fuel for their tanks and armored vehicles. They faced elements of the 30th Infantry Division north and east of them. U.S. Army engineers had blown the bridge over the Amblève River south of them, at Trois Ponts. A small bridge at Petit-Spa further east was not sturdy enough to support heavy vehicles and collapsed when a crossing was attempted. Other elements of the 30th Division were holding the only bridge capable of carrying heavy traffic, located at Stavelot. Kampfgruppe Peiper's only hope lay in holding onto its bridgehead across the Amblève at Cheneux, where it could link up with the rest of the 1st SS if a bridge over the Salm River at Trois Ponts or to the south could be seized. The critical bridgehead at Cheneux was defended by the 6th Company, 2nd Battalion, 2nd SS Panzer Grenadier Regiment, remnants of the 11th Company, 3rd Battalion, 1st SS Panzer Grenadier Regiment, and the attached 84th Armored Flak Battalion.

Continuing astride the road, the lead Company B platoon column advanced to within about five hundred yards of Cheneux. Lieutenant Charles Battisti was at the point with the lead platoon. "All at once, ahead of us, this flak-wagon opened up on us, with 20mm antiaircraft guns. These bursts hit the trees above us and around us. Some of the guys on the ground got direct hits; it was very bad. Everybody hit the ditch, and the guys dropped the heavy weapons right in the middle of the road. This sergeant next to me got hit; there was nothing I could do for him. We moved off to the right.

"Captain [John M.] Randles came up and he said to me, 'Damn it, let's get those mortars over here and set 'em up. Let's knock out that flak-wagon.'

"We kept moving up, and some of the men moved forward. Finally, they set up one mortar that we could never zero in. I went off to the left of the road and went up; it was a little bit higher. There was some barbed wire up there, and I went through that. I had the [field] telephone, I was trying to zero in [the mortar], and they shot over [the flak-wagon]. Finally, I came back."[23]

Lieutenant Battisti's platoon deployed in a narrow strip of woods on the right side of the road. Captain Tom Helgeson brought up the platoon following them and deployed them on the left side of the road and prepared to attack the town. "The attack jumped off from the woods four hundred yards from the enemy MLR. The left platoon set up a base of fire to cover the right platoon's advance. The left platoon (the base of fire) was engaged by vicious counterfire. The right platoon was pinned to the ground by devastating crossfire from two 20mm cannons, supported by two MG-42s. Enemy mortar fire swept the two elements of the attack, [wounding[24]] six men and knocking out the company's radio. Through the iron-bound discipline of the men and the forceful leadership of the officers and NCOs panic, disorder, and confusion were prevented. Not a yard of ground was lost at this point.

"The support platoon which had remained in the edge of the woods was ordered to envelop or turn the enemy's right flank. Since none of the forward attacking elements could move, this order was passed back to the support commander via person to person, word of mouth. In the same manner, a captured 77mm self-propelled gun [the half-track manned by 504th troopers] was ordered to go into position between the forward attacking platoons along the road and support the envelopment with fire against the 20mm cannons."[25]

As the captured half-track moved forward on the road, Company B trooper Private Tom Holliday was riding in the back. "We went down this road ahead of the company. When we got down there, they were set up all across this hill. The Krauts had a hell of lot of stuff down there. There were 20mm's zinging all over off of this thing.

"The gun on this half-track didn't stick out more than two feet in front of the shield, and it would only traverse so far. To get our fire all the way across the hill, we had to back up and pull forward to aim the half-track towards where we wanted to shoot."[26]

Meanwhile, Captain Helgeson watched his reserve platoon move out across the high ground north of the road to envelop the German right flank. "The enemy had placed breakthrough guns in depth on his left flank (our right flank) about one hundred yards from his forward lines. These breakthrough guns, one 20mm cannon and two MG-42s, supported by approximately one squad of enemy riflemen, pinned the platoon to a fixed position, despite the vigorousness of the flanking movement."[27]

The gunner on the half-track, Private First Class Harold Kelly, spotted German infantry moving in column around their flank. Private Buland Hoover quickly looked over the side of the half-track and saw a machine gun crew setting up an MG-42 to lay down suppressive fire. Hoover opened up with his BAR, leaving dead and wounded Germans lying in a heap around their gun. Kelly shouted for Snow to adjust the vehicle, then engaged the infantry closing in on their flank with high-explosive 77mm shells, inflicting casualties and forcing their withdrawal. As Kelly was firing the 77mm gun at German half-tracks, flak-wagons, and infantry, one of the 20mm shells fired at the half-track hit the gun and exploded. Shrapnel hit Kelly in the lower lip and chin. The driver, Snow, moved back from the cab and helped move Kelly to the rear of the passenger compartment of the vehicle, then took over as gunner. When the half-track required movement to engage new targets, Snow returned to the cab and adjusted the position of the vehicle, then returned to operate the gun.

After expending all of its ammunition, the captured half-track in which Private Holliday was riding withdrew. "We got the hell out of there. I know we did a lot of damage, because they were close. They were only three or four hundred yards out in front of us. They had the stuff up there to kill us if they had used it. I guess their own half-track doing that must have confused them."[28] The half-track drove back down the road, stopping to let Privates Holliday and Hoover dismount to rejoin Company B.

With the company radio destroyed, the Company B commanding officer, Captain Tom Helgeson, was unable to contact Company C and the 1st Battalion. "The decision was made to withdraw two hundred yards to the edge of the woods, as the present position was on top of a flat knob of land cut with innumerable barbed wire fences. Artillery support was ineffective due to ground haze, and the general position was untenable until the attacking forces could be regrouped for another thrust at the enemy's organized position. Platoons were withdrawn one at a time, covering one another; the slight ground haze facilitated the withdrawal.

"At this time, a company runner reported that contact had been gained with Company C to our rear. Company B was reorganized and set up a perimeter defense in the edge of the woods."[29]

Company C came up and took the left (north) side of the road, while Company B moved over to the right (south) side. At about 6:45 p.m., Captain Helgeson briefed Captain Ernie Milloy, the Company C commander; Captain John Randles, the battalion S-3; and the 1st Battalion commander, Lieutenant Colonel Harrison, on the situation. When Harrison contacted Colonel Tucker and advised him of the situation, Tucker ordered a night attack.

Captain Helgeson listened as the attack order was issued. "The battalion commander ordered Companies B and C to attack abreast, astride the road, Company B on the right and Company C on the left, with two M36 tank destroyers in support on the road. The time for the attack was 1930, with a ten-minute artillery barrage preparation preceding the jump-off time. The companies were oriented and formed into four assault waves—waves fifty yards in depth from each other. The order was given, 'We will take that town!' During the organization of the battalion for the attack, the enemy mortared the battalion assembly area incessantly and fired 75mm AT tracer shells into the area."[30]

Prior to the jump-off time, Lieutenant Marshall Stark, with Battery C, 80th Airborne Antiaircraft (Antitank) Battalion, noticed the two tank destroyers of the 103rd Tank Destroyer Battalion assigned to support the attack, parked some four hundred yards west of Harrison's command post at the first house on the right side of the road as you moved from Rahier to Cheneux. Stark immediately left to inform Harrison. "About half way to the house, I met the battalion commander running toward the rear. He had just learned that the tank destroyers were sitting back in the woods, and he was going after them. I led him back to the commander of the tank destroyers. After a brief, heated discussion between the battalion commander and the tank destroyer platoon leader, in which the latter said little, the tank destroyers were finally moved forward to the edge of the woods, or about one hundred yards. The platoon leader refused to move them any farther forward.

"The situation appeared critical, as many armored vehicles could be heard moving about in the town [of Cheneux]. Since the tank destroyers were of no value, the order was given to move the antitank guns forward so that the road and the broad, open fields north of the road would be covered. On the south side of the road, the terrain dropped off sharply and was considered to be sufficient antitank protection."[31]

Private First Class Charles L. Butler, with Company C, looked so young that he the other troopers called him "Kid." "We were told to fix bayonets. This field was like a pasture separated into sections by barbed wire fences. Sergeant [Ross] Carter noticed that, so he had [Private First Class Raymond D.] Levy and me swap places, because Levy was the shortest person in the squad. That way, Sergeant Carter would be able to help him over the fences."[32]

Private First Class Morris "Mike" Holmstock, with Company B, waited at the edge of the woods for word to move forward. "They said, 'We are going to form a skirmish line, and we're going to go out.'"[33]

At 7:30 p.m., after the artillery barrage had failed to materialize, both companies started moving out of the woods. Company C on the left side of the road advanced over more exposed ground, with barbed wire fences twenty to fifty yards apart. Platoon Sergeant Frank L. Dietrich and squad leader Sergeant George W. McAllister, in the leading wave, had the only pairs of wire cutters in the platoon. The barbed wire was snagging the troopers' jumpsuits as they tried to go over or crawl underneath.

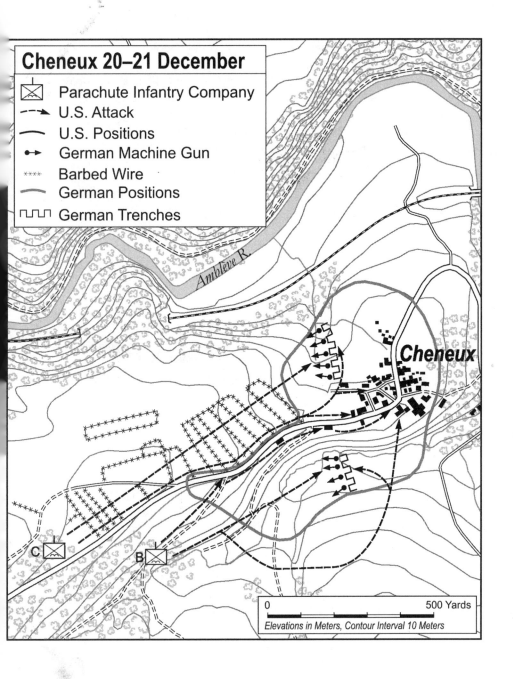

Cheneux 20–21 December

⊠	Parachute Infantry Company
--→	U.S. Attack
—	U.S. Positions
•→	German Machine Gun
****	Barbed Wire
~~	German Positions
⊓⊔⊓⊔	German Trenches

Amblève R.

Cheneux

C

B

0   500 Yards

Elevations in Meters, Contour Interval 10 Meters

Sergeant Dietrich would cut a gap in a fence, and the men on each side would pour through the gap. "Some were no more than twenty yards apart. We kept doing this as quietly as possible."[34]

Holmstock hoped that poor visibility would conceal their approach and they would be able to get close to the German positions without being detected. "It was dark and foggy. You couldn't see more than ten feet ahead of you. We came out of the woods; we didn't know what was in front of us. We couldn't see anything; we were on this open field. I came to a strand of barbed wire, and I stepped over that. We walked a little farther, and I came to another strand of barbed wire, and I said, 'What the hell is all of this?'

"There was somebody that had a box of machine gun ammo. He said, 'Here, hold this for me.'

"I got down on the ground and I shoved the box in front of me and started crawling under this barbed wire fence. And then, All—Hell—Broke—Loose!

"We were pinned down and you could see the tracers going over your head. Fortunately, the road to my left was elevated, and we were on the slant on this open field. We must have been about five or ten feet below the level of the road. The Germans were firing level [with the road] and consequently firing over our heads."[35]

However, in addition to the 20mm antiaircraft fire from the flak-wagons to their left, grazing fire from machine guns to their right front crisscrossed over their heads as Holmstock and the rest of Company B hit the ground. "It sounded like a hundred machine guns going off at once. I could see German tracers going over my head, only inches away. I was scared as hell and lay as flat as I could and prayed.

"That was the longest minute of my life. One of my friends, [Private Melvin D.] Isbel, was wounded in the back."[36]

On the other side of the road, Company C troopers were getting hung up by the fifteen barbed wire fences that stood between them and the dug-in Germans ahead. Moving ahead of the first wave, Sergeant George W. McAllister and Technical Sergeant Frank Dietrich courageously cut gaps in the wire, despite German machine gun and 20mm antiaircraft fire being concentrated upon them. McAllister would receive an oak leaf for his Bronze Star for this heroic action. Company C was now within two or three fences, less than one hundred yards, from the German main line of resistance. Dietrich shouted above the deafening noise, " 'Let's get 'em.' We surged forward and tried to climb the fences. Between the town and the last fence the Germans had at least two platoons with two MG-42s each, with at least three in our sector. We kept going forward and we kept losing people. They just decimated us."[37] In fact, there were three platoons and six MG-42 machine guns as well as four 20mm antiaircraft guns pouring frontal and flanking fire into the Company C troopers as they advanced.

From his position in the ditch on the north side of the road, Private First Class Ross Pippin, a member of one of the Company C mortar squads, observed the company's rifle squads advancing across the high ground to his left. "They were caught in the open and were being cut to pieces by the German machine gunners. There were so many tracer bullets flying back and forth, you could read a newspaper from the light."[38]

The smallest man in Company C was Private First Class Raymond Levy. Lieutenant Charles Battisti, who had been a member of Company C in Holland, recognized Levy. "He was the only Jewish guy in the outfit. They used to give him a rough time, but he could take it. He was carrying [machine gun] ammunition, which was no easy job. A German machine gun was sitting right on the road. This one kid, Levy, ran up behind the gun while we were off to the right and started firing at the first flak-wagon. The machine gun turned around and got him with a burst. I wasn't more than twenty-five yards away from him. He was just burning up from the tracer fire."[39]

When the tracers from the German machine gun hit Levy, they struck a white phosphorous grenade that he was carrying, causing his body to catch fire, illuminating the scene around him. Many of his fellow troopers witnessed Levy's body burning and smoking that night.

On the other side of the road, Private First Class Holmstock, with Company B, lay on the ground and could see 20mm tracers crisscrossing above his head and the buzzing sound of rounds zipping past him, as the Germans used grazing fire from MG-42s without tracers. "You talk about scared, I was scared. I crawled forward a little bit and came across a buddy of mine by the name of [Private First Class] Raymond [R.] Ault, who had a belly wound and was begging me for water. We were always told that if somebody has a belly wound, don't give them water. I called for the medics and I said, 'I've got to go, Ault, I can't stay here. The medics will be up here soon.'

"About that time I heard Knobby Walsh up on the road, yelling for hand grenades."[40]

Staff Sergeant William P. "Knobby" Walsh was the platoon sergeant of the 1st Platoon of Company B. One of Walsh's squad leaders was Sergeant William L. Clay. "Several men, including our platoon leader, were hit. Staff Sergeant Walsh was also hit. Nobody was moving."[41]

Staff Sergeant James M. Boyd was the platoon sergeant of the 2nd Platoon, which was following Walsh's platoon. "The entire company was pinned down by fire coming from about twenty armored vehicles, mortars, and individual riflemen. It was a crucial moment. Men on all sides were being hit."[42]

As Sergeant Clay lay flat, "Staff Sergeant Walsh stood right up and said, 'Come on, let's get 'em men!' He started to run towards the town, and the entire platoon followed him, shouting all the way."[43]

Walsh, followed by his platoon and then the rest of Company B, charged across the open ground as tracers criss-crossed from three directions. As Company B surged forward, urged on by noncoms like Walsh's example and officers like Captain Helgeson and Lieutenant Richard A. Smith, most of the first two waves were shot down by the devastating crossfire from four MG-42s and four 20mm antiaircraft guns. The third wave continued forward, passing through the wounded, carrying the attack forward into the edge of the town.

Sergeant Clay followed Walsh into the edge of the town. "We cleaned out several houses and continued to advance. Staff Sergeant Walsh was the leading man. Suddenly he came back and said, 'Somebody pull the pin out of this grenade, I can't use my left arm.' "[44]

The next time Staff Sergeant Boyd saw Walsh, "he was moving towards an enemy flak-wagon and tossed a grenade into it from a distance of about ten feet. He knocked out the entire crew. I approached him and saw that he had been hit in his left arm and left leg. I suggested that he get his wounds treated, but he answered, 'Later,' and continued to advance through town."[45]

One of Walsh's troopers, Private Edward Focht, passed the flak-wagon Walsh had just knocked out. "Every German in the flak-wagon was either killed or wounded, and we no longer got any fire from that particular vehicle. Staff Sergeant Walsh continued to lead and direct the platoon. I saw that he was becoming exhausted. He finally sank to the ground, all worn out."[46] Staff Sergeant William P. Walsh would later receive the Distinguished Service Cross for his bravery and inspirational leadership during the assault.

Walsh's example inspired Holmstock and many others. "At that point, I lost my fear. There was still a lot of fire going on, but I stood up and I threw a grenade up at a flak-wagon. I ducked, then it went off. Then I made my way up to the road. There was yelling and shooting . . . the heat of battle is something hard to describe.

"I got up to one of the flak-wagons—I remember sticking my rifle into a port in the cab and firing off eight rounds. With those metal vehicles, you don't have to aim at anybody, it is going to bounce around and kill whoever is in there."[47]

Lieutenant Richard Smith led his men in overrunning two armored vehicles and two MG-42 positions. On the edge of town, Smith reorganized his platoon, which was down to just eleven troopers, and died leading them against another flak-wagon and two houses on the edge of town.

One of the medics, Private Theodore S. Watson, braved the enemy fire to go to the aid of the wounded, safely evacuating five men. The medics repeatedly went to the aid of the wounded and dying men, despite the dangers, no doubt saving many lives. Acts of incredible heroism became almost commonplace as troopers, enraged after seeing so many of their buddies hit, individually and in small groups closed with the enemy flak-wagons, half-tracks, armored reconnaissance cars, and dug in infantry, killing them without mercy in their trenches and vehicles.

On the other side of the road, most of the Company C officers and NCOs in the first two assault waves were hit by the savage enemy crossfire of automatic weapons. Lieutenant Wayne M. Fetters, one of the Company C platoon leaders, led his third wave past the wounded and dead, and together with the survivors of those initial assault waves, closed with the three German platoons dug in on the north side of the road on the western edge of the town. Lieutenants Smith (posthumously) and Fetters were later awarded the Silver Star for their heroism and exemplary leadership.

As he charged towards the town Sergeant Dietrich came upon a hole containing one the six MG-42s on that side of the road. "I ran into three men at a machine gun. They were dug in and I was moving. I spotted them about the same time they saw me. I knocked out the guys on the right and left. Rounds struck my hand on the submachine gun grip, and the Thompson stopped firing. I ran to the side and toward him while he was firing at me. I threw the Thompson and hit him in the chest. [Private Orin B.] Guidry came up with his BAR and shoved the muzzle into the foxhole and shot him."[48]

Dietrich's left hand was bleeding profusely, so he gave his pistol to Billy Crip and moved back to get it patched up.

Private First Class Butler got to within a few yards of the German holes. "I went into a prone position. Then I decided to throw a hand grenade, so when I raised up to throw the grenade, I got hit. A rifle or machine gun bullet went through my right thigh. I could feel it, and I tore my pants open so I could apply the first aid kit. Where it penetrated going in it was a nice little round hole with lacerations, and then on the back was quite large."[49]

On the south side of the road, Private First Class Tom Holliday, a BAR gunner with Company B who earlier had been part of the crew of the captured German half-track that had initially engaged the Germans, could see one of his buddies go after one of the flak-wagons mounting a 20mm gun. "[Private] Mike Clements went right upon that damned thing and started on them with a knife. He was wild. He was out of his mind—all of us were. He was something else.

"Everything was collapsing then. The Krauts were surrendering and getting killed. It was just a hell of a firefight. A lot of us shot up all of our ammunition."[50]

As Private Butler lay on his back, badly wounded in the thigh, fellow C Company troopers, Privates First Class Bethel D. Nix and "Wild Bill" Murray, came over to check on him. "Nix and Wild Bill bent down to pick me up, Nix's back was toward the enemy on one side of my body, and Wild Bill was on the opposite side of my body facing the enemy. A 20mm armor-piercing round hit Nix in the back and penetrated, but didn't go all of the way through. I assume there was a ricochet that hit Wild Bill, because apparently it hit him flat and didn't penetrate. It knocked him over backwards, and I can remember his helmet flying up in the air. I said, 'Wild Bill's been hit.' I didn't realize that Nix had been hit."[51]

Company C overran the German main line of resistance, killing twenty or so of the SS grenadiers in savage, hand-to-hand combat. The remainder of the Germans broke and fled into the town. However, Company C had suffered almost seventy casualties. The three remaining officers tried to reorganize the company, but this wasn't possible because the troopers' blood was up, and they continued to carry the fight into the town, individually and in small groups.

On the other side of the road, all of the B Company officers had been hit, and the company had suffered around sixty casualties. The noncoms tried to organize the survivors to carry the attack through the town, but it was impossible as well. The troopers were preoccupied with fighting their individual battles with the enemy. After emptying his M1 into a flak-wagon, Private First Class Holmstock, with Company B, reloaded and started working his way along the ditch on the right side of the road to the first house. "There was a little bit of water in the bottom of this drainage ditch, and subconsciously I was thinking, 'I don't want to have to get down in this, because I don't want to get wet.'

"As I got up toward the first house, the third flak-wagon that I can remember started backing up [from behind a house]. I opened fire, and I guess some other guys did, and he pulled forward behind the house again. So I had to hit that water. . . . I didn't want to be hit.

"I decided to go down my side to the rear of the house. I worked my way down there, and behind the house about ten or fifteen yards the land went off into a steep drop. I was crawling behind that when I saw this flak-wagon from behind the edge of the house, firing. I remember two guys with a machine gun up on the road level above me open fire on the flak-wagon. The flak-wagon returned the fire. When I got up there the machine gun team was gone. I took my shot at the flak-wagon, and he took a shot at me. I had ducked just in time behind this tree, when one of those 20mm shells exploded, and I got a piece of it right above my left eye. I thought at first I was hit by some dirt or something from the tree. When I started to fire again, I couldn't see. I checked myself and I tasted blood. . . . I was bleeding, so I worked my way back to the first part of the house up near the road.

"There was a little room that had had sheep in there, and [we] had converted that into an aid station. I got to the medic, and he said, 'I'm going to evacuate you.' I said, 'No, no, I'm not hurt. I'm just cut someplace.' He cleaned me up and put a patch on my eyebrow."[52]

Holmstock left to return to the fight in the town. "There was a church next to the house and a house behind the church. It looked more like a barn, but it was actually a house. There were some living quarters in there, and some stairs that led up to a room. There was a firefight going on in there. I think we got eight or nine Germans in there. It was like a shooting gallery.

"There were still some Germans in the church. The church had a lot of cemetery stones in the courtyard, and there was some fighting in there. Then we left there and got into the main part of town. I can't tell you what went on in the town. It was just house-to-house and yelling and screaming."[53]

Holmstock described the melee as something "like cowboys and Indians. We slowly picked off the German defenders and then hid until the next victim was found. Everyone had their own private war."[54]

An SdKfz 234/1 Puma armed with a 20mm gun in an open turret positioned two hundred yards away in the town, with good fields of fire, pinned down the remaining troopers as they attempted to move through the town. Lieutenant Colonel Harrison ordered the Headquarters Company, 1st Battalion light machine gun platoon, led by Lieutenant Howard A. Kemble, to advance and engage the enemy vehicle. As Kemble led the platoon across two hundred yards of open ground with his squads spread out north and south of the road, they came under fire from two 20mm antiaircraft guns and a newly committed platoon of SS grenadiers. Kemble and the machine gun crews north of the road set up their machine guns and opened fire on the Puma. The Puma proceeded to knock out five of the platoon's eight machine gun crews.

Then Lieutenant Kemble carried a machine gun forward fifty yards and laid down covering fire while his men dug in. A great deal of enemy fire was concentrated on Lieutenant Kemble, tearing holes in his clothing and ricocheting off the machine gun as he courageously fired five boxes of ammunition. After his men had dug in, Kemble returned to their positions and led them in repulsing two enemy counterattacks. Lieutenant Kemble, mortally wounded during the fighting, was posthumously awarded the Silver Star.

Another officer with Headquarters Company, 1st Battalion, Lieutenant William G. Yepsen, crawled forward with a machine gun left lying by one of the crews that had been hit. Yepsen drew heavy automatic weapons fire that came to within six inches of him as he single-handedly set up the machine gun. He opened fire and took out an enemy machine gun crew, then engaged one of the armored vehicles, firing at the driver's slit, causing the vehicle's crew to button up. Even though his tracers gave away his position, Yepsen courageously continued to fire until mortally wounded by cannon fire.

Private Robert M. Kinney, one of Kemble's machine gunners and an acting squad leader, led his team against one of the enemy flak-wagons through another two hundred yards of open ground swept by crisscrossing grazing fire. Kinney had to cut his way through several barbed wire fences during the advance, exposing himself to even more enemy fire. "The firing was coming from behind an old farmhouse built up on the bank of the road. A half-track had our guys pinned down there, and they were laying it on heavy. One of our boys was shooting a .30-caliber machine gun at that half-track, and I could see the tracers hit it and go towards the sky. I hollered, 'Stop shooting! Whoever is shooting over there, stop! You can't hurt that half-track.' About that time, somebody said [Private Paul E.] Hayden got it."[55] Private Hayden, seeing the seriousness of the situation, had picked up his machine gun and tried to create a diversion by flanking the enemy when he was killed.

Private Kinney "hollered, 'Everybody here, throw me an extra hand grenade.' I took four or five and stuffed them in my jacket. I was wearing one of those tanker jackets, the zipper type.

"I had a pistol and I ran up by the house. I knew I had to go by the door, and I didn't know if there was anybody in there, so I stopped and put three or four shots into the door and went around the house. I was right on the road, and that half-track was on the [opposite] side of the house from where I was. I went around there, and the guys just kept shooting. I threw hand grenades in that thing. It started booming and banging as their ammunition blew up, and they were yelling. Some of the Germans started moving back down the road. I ran back and hollered, 'Somebody bring a machine gun up here, let's get the son-of-a-guns as they are going down the road!' [Roberto] Lopez brought the machine gun up, and we just covered that road with fire."[56]

One of Kinney's machine gun crew, Private L. N. Emmons, crawled toward the MG-42s to the right front, which had been spraying grazing fire across the open ground. The enemy now concentrated much of their machine gun fire on him as he cut his way through a barbed wire fence. Bullets hit all around him and zipped past his head, until he reached defilade behind a small knoll. There, he tossed two hand grenades into one of the machine gun nests, destroying the gun and the crew. Then, jumping to his feet, he rushed the riflemen protecting the strongpoint and killed them all with his Thompson submachine gun. For their courageous actions, Lieutenant Yepsen (posthumously), Privates Hayden (posthumously), Kinney, and Emmons received the Silver Star.

A short time after Emmons cleaned out the enemy strongpoint on the high ground south of the village, Private Tom Holliday, armed with a BAR, moved through the area. "I went around the side of the hill, and there was a damned Kraut taking a shit back there. I guess he just had the shit scared out of him. I took care of two of them like that."[57]

Another trooper, Private First Class Arley O. Farley, a bazooka gunner with Headquarters Company, 1st Battalion, saw the decimation of the light machine gun crews and crawled forward under heavy fire to a position very close to one of the armored vehicles, where he fired his bazooka, destroying it. Private First Class Farley received the Silver Star for his gallant action.

After the Headquarters Company, 1st Battalion, commander Captain Roy Anderson and Lieutenant Kemble were hit, the company's executive officer, Lieutenant Harold C. Allen, came forward and while reorganizing the remaining troopers, was himself wounded. Despite his wound, Allen led two men forward and knocked out a machine gun nest. When heavy enemy fire stopped the advance again, Lieutenant Allen moved forward alone, knocking out a second machine gun nest and killing two SS grenadiers, but received a second wound in doing so. Lieutenant Allen received the Silver Star for his heroic actions.

During the fighting that night, the battalion was close to running out of ammunition. Staff Sergeant Norman A. Angel, the 1st Battalion supply sergeant, repeatedly drove a jeep loaded with ammunition along a thousand yards of road exposed to enemy 20mm, mortar, machine gun, and small-arms fire to deliver ammunition to within fifty yards of the forwardmost riflemen. From there, he personally delivered the ammunition to individuals on the frontline, crawling as much as two hundred yards under fire to reach those on the flanks. Despite enemy fire riddling his jeep, Sergeant Angel continued to deliver the ammunition and later received the Silver Star for his gallantry.

Lieutenant Colonel Harrison brought up every available man. He approached Private First Class Ross Pippin and another Company C trooper, who were part of a 60mm mortar squad. "The colonel had spotted two American tank destroyers and wanted us to go for help. The tank destroyers were hiding in a nearby thicket and didn't want to get into the battle. The colonel turned and said to us, 'I'm giving you a direct order; if these men don't get into the battle, shoot them!'

"I thought to myself, 'I don't want to have to shoot our own men.' After what seemed to be an eternity, they started up their engines and headed into the battle."[58]

As the two tank destroyers moved forward, Corporal Obie Wickersham and his squad of the 1st Platoon, Company C, 307th Airborne Engineer Battalion, deployed on both sides of the lead vehicle as enemy automatic weapons fire converged on it. "[Private First Class Alexander S.] Alex Nemeth and I were right beside the tank destroyer coming into town. We were just firing everywhere, because they were firing at us with their ack-ack and 20mm. The Germans had the prettiest tracers you ever saw. The tank destroyer was firing 90mm rounds. When he fired that 90mm, it would jar you."[59]

The lead tank destroyer fired two rounds at the German Puma reconnaissance vehicle in the town that had inflicted so much damage, knocking it out. This opened the way for the survivors to move from their foothold on the edge of town to begin clearing it. However, Lieutenant Colonel Harrison ordered the officers and noncoms still in the fight to hold up and reorganize into one assault group.

Corporal Wickersham and the rest of the 1st Platoon, Company C, 307th Airborne Engineer Battalion, were deployed on the high ground on the left flank, with some Headquarters Company men to the left of the engineers. "We dug in along a barbed wire fence. We were in slit trenches. The Germans were pretty sharp. These [fence] posts were sticking up. Well, they started popping those posts with 20mms, and they came down on you. That night, I was lying in there, and I had my raincoat slung over my pistol belt. The next morning it was full of little holes."[60]

Harrison positioned three Headquarters Company, 1st Battalion, machine guns on the right flank to cover that approach and put his men into a number of outposts in buildings on the western end of the village.

Company C trooper, Private First Class Albert S. Ianacone, and another trooper manning one of the outposts watched an estimated fifteen enemy troops approach their position. Ianacone waited until they were within ten yards before opening fire. The SS grenadiers returned fire with a machine gun, MP-44 assault rifles, and grenades, painfully wounding Ianacone. However, he tossed a hand grenade into the midst of the machine gun crew, taking out four of the enemy and causing the remaining Germans to withdraw. For his heroism, Private First Class Ianacone received the Silver Star.

Colonel Tucker arrived around 11:00 p.m., and Harrison briefed him on the situation. Harrison requested another rifle company to take advantage of the hard-earned gains. Tucker agreed and contacted the 3rd Battalion, and ordered them to send a company to assault the town.

Company G arrived outside of the western edge of Cheneux about 2:00 a.m. They were briefed on the situation and organized for the assault. Meanwhile, the Germans had regrouped and set up killing lanes of fire for their 20mm guns and machine guns. At 2:45 a.m., Company G began its assault, but 20mm, machine gun, artillery, and mortar fire devastated it, inflicting very heavy casualties. The company received an order to withdraw and went into position to the rear of the 1st Battalion to provide an all-round defensive perimeter.

The Germans continued to pound Harrison's troopers with self-propelled artillery and 20mm fire until 7:45 a.m., when at least a company of panzer grenadiers launched a counterattack after an intense artillery barrage lasting thirty minutes. Fire from two flak-wagons and self-propelled guns swept the thin line of troopers who were dug in to stop the assault. During this time, medic Private Theodore Watson again risked his life to go to the aid of six troopers wounded on the high ground northwest of the town, shielding them with his body, then evacuating each one across 150 yards of open ground under heavy fire. Watson received the Silver Star for his gallant actions.

Private First Class Raymond S. Holsti, with Company G, observing the casualties and Watson's actions, concentrated the fire of his machine gun on the enemy vehicles, which in turn focused their firepower on Holsti's position, seriously wounding him. Despite the grievous wounds, Holsti continued to fire, until a bazooka team succeeded in knocking out one of the flak-wagons and forcing the other to withdraw. Holsti then trained the fire of his light machine gun on the SS infantry until he collapsed from loss of blood. Private First Class

Raymond S. Holsti was later awarded the Distinguished Service Cross for his extraordinary courage under fire.

As the panzer grenadiers ran forward, firing as they came, Harrison's 81mm mortars decimated them, with deadly shrapnel cutting down many of them. This was followed moments later with the addition of a barrage from the 75mm howitzers of the 376th Parachute Field Artillery Battalion, with the shells landing among the pinned-down and wounded German infantry. The attack fell apart, with heavy German casualties. Harrison's battalion continued to hold on to the western portion of Cheneux.

Private First Class Mike Holmstock, with Company B, was drained after fighting all night. "It was now dawn and I was sitting on this little wall with [Private John L.] Johnny Barton, and we said something about the fight, nothing special. Then I looked at him and I said, 'Why are you shaking?' It was actually like he was shivering.

"He looked at me and he said, 'The same reason you are shivering.' I realized that I was shaking. All of the adrenaline had worked off of me."[61]

For the first time that morning, Holmstock looked at the scene around him. "The field was red with blood and broken, smoldering equipment and tires—helmets, packs, rifles strewn about. Dead lay everywhere, and many bandaged wounded were walking about."[62]

As Holmstock was resting with his buddy, tank destroyers drove up to the scene of the previous night's fighting west of the town. "I was up on the road about where Knobby had gotten hurt. All of the fighting had ceased. There were several dead Germans, one in the middle of the road. The tank destroyers that we had hoped for now came forward. 'This was a fine time for you to come, we needed you last night.' I remember the tank destroyer stopped about twenty feet in front of me. I was sitting on the side of the road with somebody. This guy popped up out of the tank destroyer and he said, 'One of you guys drag that Kraut out of the way.'

"We just looked at him and said, 'If you want him out of the way, get out and move him. We're not going to move him.'

"He said, 'If you don't move him, I'm going to run over him.'

"We said, 'Be our guest.'

"So he ran over him.

"Down at the first house they had started to collect bodies of the Germans to stack them up for Graves Registration to come and get them. They called the remaining men of the company, eighteen of us. I said, 'Oh good, they can't use us as a company anymore, maybe they'll put us in the rear.'

"About that time they brought up twenty replacements fresh from England. There was a guy by the name of Gallagher, who made a remark, 'Boy that was nifty last night. It was just like fireworks. Boy that was neat.'

"That really burned me and I said, 'You really think that was nice?'"

"And he said, 'Yeah, that was great.'"

"I said, 'Go clean up that neatness,' and I pointed to the Kraut that was now mangled from the tank destroyer. I said, 'Go take that down to that pile down there with the others.' He went over and grabbed the sleeve and an arm came with it. He started dragging the pieces down—he was sick."[63]

The 504th planned a final attack commencing at 5:00 p.m., to secure the little village and wipe out the German bridgehead across the Amblève River. Supporting the attack would be the attached tank destroyer platoon. The 3rd Battalion, less Company G, moved through the town of Monceau, south of Cheneux. The tank destroyer platoon preceded the attack by systematically blasting each building in Cheneux held by Peiper's men, forcing their withdrawal. Following this, the 3rd Battalion, less Company G, attacked the flank and rear of the Germans in Cheneux by advancing northward over a hill that led to the road between Cheneux and the bridge over the Amblève River to the east.

Lieutenant Jim Megellas led his Company H platoon to the line of departure for the assault from the south. "The terrain around the town was hilly, and as we approached in two columns, with H and I Companies abreast, we were careful to take advantage of available cover to avoid detection from enemy gunners. Behind the crest of a hill just outside Cheneux and the Amblève River, H Company deployed as skirmishers.

"Rivers [Lieutenant Richard LaRiviere] and I were leading our platoons down the barren hill when we were fired upon by enemy 20mm flak-wagons and machine guns. When the Germans opened fire, I was about halfway down the hill heading for the Amblève River. The shrapnel from the exploding 20mm shells initially took a heavy toll in wounded men, forcing those who had just started down the forward crest to seek cover behind the hill. I was at least halfway down the forward slope, so instinctively I charged down the hill in the direction of enemy fire rather than retreating for cover behind the hill."[64] Megellas and five other troopers made it to the bottom of the hill and found concealment near the riverbank.

On the hill, another Company H trooper, Sergeant Albert Tarbell, helped evacuate the casualties inflicted by the 20mm fire, including "a captain with us from Service Company [Jack M. Bartley] who was severely wounded and eventually died. Another of our men was wounded in the leg and yelling like a stuck pig. The officer told him to quiet down, that he was not hit that bad."[65]

Megellas and the five troopers concealed at the riverbank observed the enemy dispositions and waited for an opportunity to get back to the company. Then, Megellas saw eight SS troopers on the opposite bank begin digging an emplacement for an antitank gun to cover the bridge approach. Megellas quietly passed the word, "'Fire on my order, unload your guns, then make a mad dash for it.' In rapid order, we unloaded on those eight unsuspecting Germans. Although a body count was not possible, I am certain they all ended up in the hole."[66]

The six troopers took off through about seventy-five yards of heavy brush near the river as 20mm antiaircraft shells chased them, exploding in the air behind them. About halfway, Private Donald Herndon was hit in the leg and began limping badly. "Lieutenant Megellas picked me up and carried me back to aid station. I spent two and a half months in the hospital in Bath, England."[67] Lieutenant Megellas was awarded the Silver Star for his heroism and leadership in destroying the crew of the antitank gun and saving Herndon's life.

Megellas returned to the Company H position behind the crest of the hill, just as Companies H and I prepared for a renewed assault. "From a map of the immediate area, I was able to determine the coordinates of the enemy positions. Lieutenant Allen F. McClain of Headquarters Company [3rd Battalion] brought up the 81mm mortars and, before resuming our attack on Cheneux, was able to bring fire on enemy positions from the coordinates I had marked on the map."[68] Simultaneously, Companies H and I attacked down the hill as the 1st Battalion, less Company A, with Company G attached, attacked through the town with the tank destroyers, against the enemy rear guard, securing Cheneux and the high ground overlooking the Amblève River.

Corporal George D. Graves, Jr., with the regimental S-1 section, visited the scene late on December 21. "Lieutenant Colonel Harrison, 1st Battalion commander, said the assault across the top of the hill crossed with many barbed wire fences was far worse than any nightmare he had ever imagined. The surrounding terrain was the worst example I had ever seen of what results when a large number of men are out to kill each other. Broken rifles, loose ammunition, countless helmets, bloody GI clothes and bandages, belts of machine gun ammo, mortar shells, all sort of miscellaneous items were strewn about the bald hill and ditches along the sides of the road. Dead bodies were everywhere. Living troopers, glassy-eyed and expressionless, were hugging holes scraped out of the banks bordering the road. The overall scene was so sickening that it made you want to shout out to God: 'Why was all this necessary?' "[69]

The 504th had destroyed or captured fourteen flak-wagons, six half-tracks, four trucks, four 105mm howitzers, and numerous machine guns. A prisoner interrogated by the division G-2 section indicated that the 504th had destroyed five enemy companies. The cost had been steep. The 504th suffered twenty-three killed and 202 wounded. Company B had no officers and eighteen men left, while Company C had thirty-eight men and three officers remaining for duty. The 1st Battalion, 504th (less Company A) and the 1st Platoon, Company C, 307th Engineer Battalion, would later be awarded a Presidential Unit Citation for the fighting at Cheneux.

Chapter 13

"At Times A Person Did Not Care If He Lived Or Died"

On the afternoon of December 22, the 2nd Battalion S-3, Captain Victor Campana received a message at the battalion command post ordering the 2nd Battalion to relieve the 1st Battalion at Cheneux. "On arriving in that town, we saw evidence of the bitter fight which had taken place. German dead and equipment laid strewn on the main road and adjacent fields. A disabled self-propelled gun and tank were on the road. Some of the enemy dead were clad in American uniforms. The battalion took over the defenses of the town and bridge and waited for events to happen. Sounds of brisk fighting on our left flank could be heard, intermingled with tank gunfire. It was the 119th Infantry attacking the Germans at La Gleize with assistance from the 740th Tank Battalion.

"Late that night, enemy planes were overhead, and we thought that parachutists were being dropped. It was later reported that the Germans were trying to resupply their troops in the vicinity of La Gleize, but most of the resupply bundles fell into American hands."[1]

The following morning, December 23, Captain Campana was at the command post at Cheneux, when "the 2nd Battalion was suddenly ordered to move out. The destination turned out to be the town of Lierneux, where we were attached to the 325th Glider Infantry Regiment, commanded by Colonel [Charles] Billingslea. The battalion was placed in division reserve on the high ground some five thousand yards southwest of Lierneux. The 325th Glider Infantry CP was located in the town of Verleumont on the high ground southeast of Lierneux. This move was part of the division plan to hold the Lierneux ridge, since it dominated the road nets at Regne, Fraiture, and Hebronval.

"The battalion of the 325th Glider Infantry Regiment, which was originally in reserve, had been returned to its mother unit when division orders had required the regiment to further extend its right flank to include Regne and Fraiture. This extension was necessitated by the failure of the 3rd Armored Division on the right flank to maintain physical contact with the 82nd Airborne Division. It was imperative for the airborne units, in keeping with orders from XVIII Airborne Corps, that contact be made and maintained with American units in the Vielsalm–St.-Vith area and to provide an exit for their extrication. The U.S. forces in the Vielsalm–St.-Vith area were the 7th Armored Division, the 106th Infantry Division (minus 422nd and 423rd Infantry Regiments), the 112th Regiment of the 28th Infantry Division, and some corps artillery units.

"The 2nd Battalion, 504th Parachute Infantry, immediately prepared and occupied defensive positions astride the Regne-Lierneux road. The battalion CP and aid station were located in two adjacent houses about eight hundred yards to the rear. Shortly afterwards, the battalion commander and I went to the CP of the 325th Glider Infantry for instructions. While there, we heard reports over the radio stating that 7th Armored Division tanks were still coming through the roadblocks.

"That afternoon, 23 December, the enemy attacked and captured the town of Regne. The division commander immediately ordered the recapture of that town, which was accomplished by the 325th Glider Regiment, with the aid of supporting armor. During the recapture of Regne, the regimental adjutant of the 2nd SS Panzer Division was captured with orders for the advance of the following day. These orders were quickly relayed to higher headquarters. That same afternoon, the important crossroads at [Baraque-de-] Fraiture was taken by the enemy."[2]

From the treeline northeast of the crossroads at Baraque-de-Fraiture, Gavin witnessed the final assault by elements of the 2nd SS Panzer Division that overwhelmed the composite force defending it, which included Company F, 325th Glider Infantry Regiment. Now, because the U.S. 3rd Armored Division was unable to secure the road north, nothing stood between the 2nd SS and Manhay. Only a small force of the 3rd Armored Division defended Manhay, and very little defended the road between Manhay and Werbomont. The 82nd Airborne Division was in grave danger of being surrounded, much like the 101st Airborne Division had around Bastogne, except that the 82nd was defending a far larger perimeter and didn't have the supporting armored combat command that the 101st had around Bastogne. Gavin took immediate action to block the road north through Manhay to Werbomont. "I moved to the CP of the reserve battalion [2nd Battalion, 504th] in the region southwest of Lierneux, arriving there at about dark. I issued verbal orders to the battalion commander, Major Wellems, outlining the situation to him and directing him to secure the right flank as far west as Malempré. I then moved without delay via Tri-le-Chesling to Manhay, the CP of the 3rd Armored Division. Here, I found one MP on duty at the crossroads and the town completely abandoned. I then moved without delay to corps headquarters to explain the situation to them and obtain further assistance in holding the main highway, which was out of my sector, but the retention of which was necessary to the accomplishment of my mission.

"By telephone, Colonel Tucker was told to be prepared to move the 504th Regimental Headquarters and one battalion to the vicinity of Lansival, where he would take over the sector on the right of the division. Two TDs [tank destroyers] were moved southwest of the Division CP at Bra at approximately 2200. Upon my arrival there, I learned by telephone from corps that Manhay had fallen to the German attacking forces."[3]

Captain Campana was at the 2nd Battalion command post when Gavin arrived. "Just before dusk that afternoon, the 2nd Battalion, 504th Parachute Infantry was ordered to retake the crossroads at [Baraque-de-] Fraiture. An artillery liaison officer from the 320th Glider Field Artillery Battalion came down to the CP, but could not promise us any artillery support, except possibly from corps artillery. At this time, all division artillery was busily engaged along the twenty-five-thousand-yards sector which was being held by the division. Thus, without artillery support and without armor, the battalion moved out at 1930 hours to recapture a terrain being held by an enemy superior in numbers and firepower. The only prior reconnaissance made was from a map. The outlook was very black indeed, and the battalion commander had accordingly designated his succession of command before we moved out.

"The march was made in silence. We had now turned off the main road and were now approaching the town of Fraiture itself. The battalion commander went into the town ahead of the battalion to obtain as much information as he could from the unit of the 325th Glider Infantry holding Fraiture. Suddenly, Major [William] Colville, the executive officer, received a radio message stating that the attack had been called off. I suggested that this message be authenticated before adopting any action whatsoever. This was done. The message was from the battalion commander, announcing that the attack had definitely been canceled. The entire battalion did an about-face and returned to Lierneux much happier.

"Late that night, the first of a series of long-range patrols were sent to Malempré, four miles to our right, to keep the battalion informed of any possible enemy envelopment on that flank.

"The following day, 24 December, the 3rd Battalion, 504 Parachute Infantry Regiment, minus G Company, was placed in position on our right in the vicinity of the woods Bois Houby and Bois de Groumont."[4]

The 1st Battalion, severely understrength after the vicious fighting at Cheneux, was stretched extremely thin. It was holding a sector along the

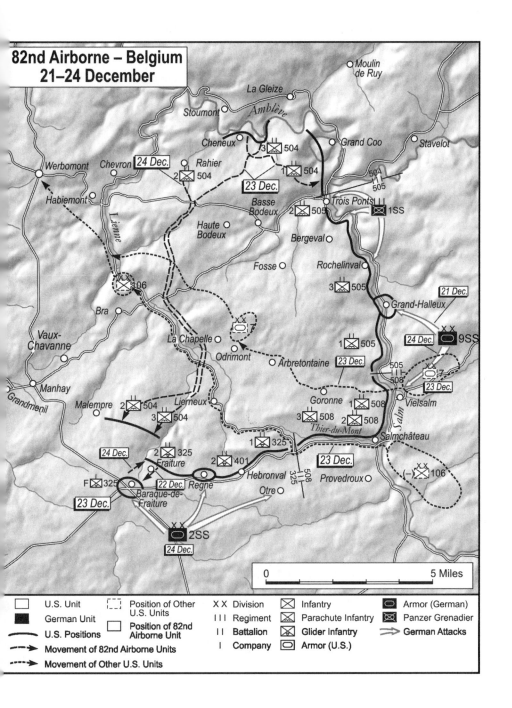

82nd Airborne – Belgium
21–24 December

Moulin de Ruy

La Gleize

Amblève

Stoumont

Grand Coo

Stavelot

Cheneux

3 ⊠ 504

1 ⊠ 504

504
505

Trois Ponts |||

1SS

Werbomont

Chevron

24 Dec.

Rahier

2 ⊠ 504

23 Dec.

Basse Bodeux

2 ⊠ 505

Habiemont

Lienne

Haute Bodeux

Bergeval

Fosse

Rochelinval

3 ⊠ 505

21 Dec.

⊠ 106

Grand-Halleux

Bra

La Chapelle

Vaux-Chavanne

Odrimont

Arbretontaine

1 ⊠ 505

24 Dec.

X X
9SS

23 Dec.

505
508

7

23 Dec.

Manhay

Malempre

2 ⊠ 504

Lierneux

3 ⊠ 504

Goronne

1 ⊠ 508

Vielsalm

Grandmenil

3 ⊠ 508

2 ⊠ 508

Salm

Thier-du-Mont

Salmchâteau

1 ⊠ 325

24 Dec.

2 ⊠ 325

2 ⊠ 401

Fraiture

Hebronval

508
325

Provedroux

23 Dec.

X X
(–) ⊠ 106

F ⊠ 325

22 Dec. Regne

Otre

23 Dec.

Baraque-de-Fraiture

X X
2SS

24 Dec.

0   5 Miles

☐ U.S. Unit	⌐⌐ Position of Other U.S. Units	X X Division
■ German Unit		||| Regiment
U.S. Positions	Position of 82nd Airborne Unit	|| Battalion
Movement of 82nd Airborne Units			Company
Movement of Other U.S. Units		

⊠ Infantry	⬭ Armor (German)
⊠ Parachute Infantry	⊠ Panzer Grenadier
⊠ Glider Infantry	⇒ German Attacks
⬜ Armor (U.S.)	

Amblève River, from north of Trois Ponts to Cheneux, a frontage of more than twelve thousand yards, most of it wooded, hilly terrain.

IN COMMAND of all Allied forces on the northern shoulder of the Bulge, British Field Marshall Bernard Montgomery arrived on the morning of December 24 at the XVIII Airborne Corps Headquarters command post at Werbomont. He told Ridgway that the XVIII Airborne Corps "could now withdraw with honor to itself and its units."[5] He then ordered Ridgway to withdraw the XVIII Airborne Corps, repeating much of the same of what he had said four days earlier, that it was time to "sort out the battlefield and tidy up the lines. After all, gentlemen, you can't win a big victory without a tidy show."[6]

Ridgway had already warned Gavin that a withdrawal might be necessary. Accordingly, Gavin had informed his commanders. "Similar warning orders were given to unit commanders to be prepared to withdraw if necessary to the Trois Ponts–Erria–Manhay line. Early on December 24, therefore, they were directed to make [their] small-unit reconnaissance of the defensive positions, and sectors were allotted and missions assigned. A conference was held at Headquarters XVIII Corps (Airborne) at 1330 hours, December 24th, at which time orders were issued for the voluntary withdrawal to the corps defensive position. Division plans were completed and orders issued during the afternoon to effect the withdrawal starting after darkness."[7]

During the 24th, the 3rd Battalion, less Company G, repulsed a strong enemy attack southwest of Lierneux. At 9:00 p.m. that night, as part of the division's withdrawal, the 2nd and 3rd Battalions moved north to new positions on high ground south of a line running from Bergifaz to Bra to near Vaux-Chavenne. The 1st Battalion was moved to regimental reserve, north of Bra.

Captain Frank Boyd, with Headquarters Battery, 376th Parachute Field Artillery Battalion, was the command liaison with the 504th and spent "the spooky Christmas Eve at the 504th headquarters when the regiment was withdrawing on Montgomery's orders from the salient we occupied. The 307th Engineers were blowing bridges behind us and left us only one over which to withdraw. We had orders to retire to Bra, and Colonel Tucker asked a Belgian civilian if there was a landmark building in Bra that was easy to identify and find. The man told him there was a big, well known chateau on the east edge of the city, and Colonel Tucker said, 'That is my CP.' "[8]

Upon arriving at the vicinity of Bra, the 2nd Battalion S-3, Captain Victor Campana coordinated the establishment of the battalion's defensive system. "The positions occupied by the battalion were as follows: F Company on the right, contacting the 3rd Battalion of our regiment; E Company in the center along the high, wooded ground; and D Company minus the 1st Platoon, on the left in the vicinity of Bergifaz, contacting the 3rd Battalion, 508th Parachute Infantry. The 81mm mortars were set up on the reverse slope of the hill behind

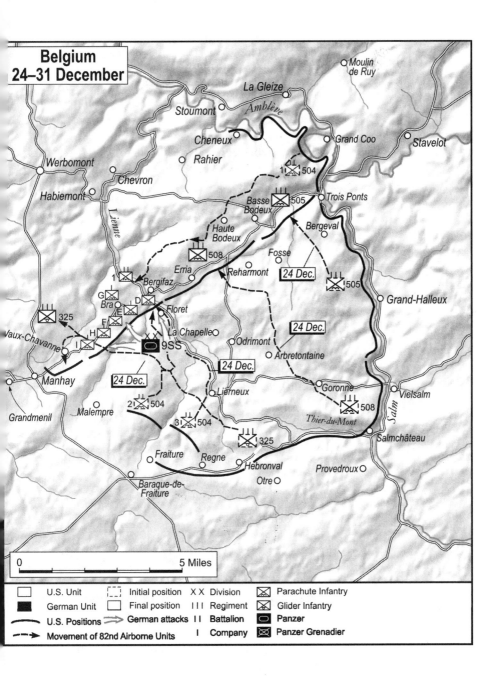

**Belgium
24–31 December**

Moulin
de Ruy

La Gleize

Stoumont

Amblève

Cheneux

Grand Coo

Stavelot

Rahier

Werbomont

Chevron

1⊠504

Habiemont

Lienne

Basse
Bodeux

⊠505

Trois Ponts

Haute
Bodeux

Bergeval

⊠508

Fosse

24 Dec.

Grand-Halleux

Erria

Reharmont

⊠505

Bergifaz

1⊠

G

D⊠

Bra

E

Floret

24 Dec.

⊠325

F

La Chapelle

Odrimont

Arbretontaine

H

Vaux-Chavanne

I

9SS

24 Dec.

Manhay

24 Dec.

Lierneux

Goronne

Vielsalm

2⊠504

⊠508

Thier-du-Mont

Grandmenil

Malempre

Salmchâteau

3⊠504

⊠325

Fraiture

Regne

Hebronval

Provedroux

Otre

Baraque-de-
Fraiture

0	5 Miles

☐ U.S. Unit	⌐¬ Initial position	X X Division	⊠ Parachute Infantry
◼ German Unit	☐ Final position	I I I Regiment	⊠ Glider Infantry
◠ U.S. Positions	⟹ German attacks	I I Battalion	⬭ Panzer
⇠-- Movement of 82nd Airborne Units		I Company	⊠ Panzer Grenadier

E Company. The battalion CP was set up in a house about four hundred yards in rear of F Company, and the battalion aid station was located about one mile in the rear of the MLR in the vicinity of Trou de Bra."[9]

Late that night, Corporal Obie Wickersham and his squad of the 1st Platoon of Company C, 307th Airborne Engineer Battalion, received an order to establish a roadblock in front of the 3rd Battalion sector. "There were eight of us, each carrying two antitank mines. After going through our outposts into enemy territory and upon approaching the crossroad, we were preparing to lay our mines. I remember a flash and a huge explosion, which picked me up and hurled me into a ditch against a barbed wire fence. After the shock, I found that all the men were killed or wounded. Two [Private Elmer E. Bowers and Private First Class Albert C. Middlemiss] were killed instantly, and two [Private First Class Stanley F. Symin and Lieutenant Melvin C. Ullrich] died of wounds later. All the others were wounded. My platoon leader, Lieutenant Ullrich, lost both legs as well as other wounds and later died of shock. He most likely saved my life, because when the mine he was carrying exploded, his body shielded me from most of the shrapnel. My first thoughts after the explosion was that a tank had fired at us, but we later found out that it was a German 120mm mortar round that hit in our midst and set off that mine that my platoon leader was carrying.

"If this wasn't bad enough, the next morning, Christmas Day, although slightly wounded, I had to go up to the site of the explosion to identify and collect the bodies of my friends. That Christmas Day, I sat in shock and in tears, thinking of what had happened the night before. I had seen my friends killed and wounded before, and that was sad enough, but to have this happen on Christmas Eve, and then to go back to the site the next morning, on Christmas day, to recover the bodies, was just too much. These men were not just men in my squad, but some of them had gone through jump school with me, and were some of the twenty-five of us that volunteered to go to the 82nd in Italy, and fought and died beside me. They were like brothers to me."[10]

Around 10:00 a.m. on Christmas morning, Colonel Tucker visited the 2nd Battalion command post, where Captain Campana had been working continuously since the prior night. "The battalion commander was out at that time checking for battalion defensive system. He asked for and was shown the disposition of the battalion defensive system. He noticed the village of Floret about one thousand yards to our front and astride the Bergifaz-Lierneux road and inquired as to what the battalion had done to outpost that town. When I replied that nothing had been done as yet, Colonel Tucker instructed me to tell Lieutenant Colonel Wellems to outpost the town immediately."[11]

At 3:00 p.m. on December 25, the 1st Platoon of Dog Company, led by Lieutenant Harry W. Rollins and his assistant platoon leader, Lieutenant Leonard Greenblatt, moved south of the main line of resistance to establish roadblocks on the main road from Lierneux to Bergifaz and a road running north through Floret toward the battalion's main line of resistance. They also established an outpost on the high ground at Romont between the two roads. Company C, 307th Engineers, laid antitank mines at the roadblock on the Lierneux-Bergifaz road, designated as Roadblock Number 1. Sergeant Harold M. Dunnagan's squad dug in on the high ground on both sides of the roadblock to cover it. Roadblock Number 2 was set up on the unimproved road which ran through Floret, converging with the Lierneux-Bergifaz road just north of Floret. Corporal Jack C. Larison's squad, positioned on high ground on both flanks, defended this roadblock. The platoon command post was set up in Floret, and the 60mm mortar squad was positioned about two hundred yards from the command post. The platoon set up sound-powered telephone wire communications from the Company D command post to the platoon CP and from the platoon command post to the outposts. The platoon had been equipped with an SCR-300 radio for the mission.

At about 4:30 p.m., Company H observed a company of panzer grenadiers moving northwest toward them on the high ground south of Bra. They called in artillery fire from the 376th Parachute Field Artillery and 81mm mortar fire from Headquarters Company, 3rd Battalion, with devastating effect.

About 1:50 a.m. the following morning, at the Company D platoon's outpost on the high ground at Romont, the squad defending Roadblock Number 1 observed a three-man enemy patrol coming up the Lierneux-Bergifaz road toward the roadblock. They allowed the patrol to walk into their kill zone and ambushed it, wiping it out. At 6:20 a.m., another three-man patrol attacked the squad defending Roadblock Number 1, but the troopers drove them off.

The D Company outpost observed two German half-tracks, motorcycles, and a company of panzer grenadiers moving up the road toward Floret at about 1:00 p.m. The squad ambushed the enemy squad acting as the force's point element. The D Company squad was then hit by an estimated company of the 9th SS Panzer Division. The troopers called in artillery and withdrew back to the 1st Platoon, losing one killed and two wounded and leaving behind a light machine gun, bazooka, and rifle-grenade launcher. Shortly before 6:00 p.m., the 1st Platoon was attacked at Romont. The platoon requested artillery fire from the 376th. However, a few minutes later, the Company D command post lost both phone and radio contact with the platoon. About thirty minutes later, nine troopers from the platoon arrived at the company command post and reported that the platoon was surrounded and advised not to transmit by radio unless necessary. Meanwhile, three more troopers from the platoon came through the Easy Company line, reporting that German infantry had used two Panzerschrecks to pin them down while they rushed the platoon. After overrunning Lieutenant Rollins' platoon, the 9th SS force pushed north up the road to Floret. The 75mm howitzers of the 376th and the 81mm mortars of Headquarters Company, 2nd Battalion, immediately plastered the road leading into and out of Floret and the village itself. By around 7:15 p.m., a total of thirteen survivors had made it back to the main line of resistance. Sergeant Dunnagan brought back eleven more shortly before 8:00 p.m. Of the twenty-five who returned, four had been wounded during the fighting and withdrawal. Privates Dominic T. Biello and Luther E. Krantz were killed during the fighting, and Lieutenant Harry W. Rollins, Corporal Jack C. Larison, and Privates First Class Edward C. Rosella and Kenneth M. Smithey were taken prisoner.

Meanwhile, on the 2nd Battalion's right flank, Fox Company met another attack by the 9th SS, including four or five Mark IV tanks, coming up the road to Xhout-si-ploux. After stopping the assault, troopers could hear moaning in front of their positions.

In the 3rd Battalion sector on the right, on the afternoon of December 27, an eight-man Company H outpost, under the command of Sergeant Robert A. Tague, was attacked by a numerically superior force of panzer grenadiers and was threatened with being overrun.

Company H platoon leader, Lieutenant Jim Megellas, was at the platoon command post of his best friend, Lieutenant Richard LaRiviere, whom everyone called Rivers. "I was with Rivers when he got the call. Without hesitation, taking several of his men [he] headed for his outpost like a man shot out of a cannon. It was his outpost; his squad, his sergeant, his men who needed help. Charging low and taking advantage of available cover, he was able to reach his beleaguered outpost.

"I waited anxiously for my closest buddy to return to our lines, not knowing the situation and concerned that he might not make it back. After an agonizing period, he returned with the six men from his outpost, bringing with them the bodies of Tague and Private First Class Clarence C. Smith, both killed in action.

"Corporal George D. Graves [with the Headquarters and Headquarters Company S-1 section] had known Tague for several years. He wrote the following in his diary: 'I got up at 0630. Upon going outside I looked in the death trailer of 'Judge' Vance's Grave Registration Jeep. To my horror, I recognized that carrot top of Red Tague along with three other corpses. He had just come back to duty the day before after having been wounded in the Waal River crossing in Holland. The last time I had seen him was in the aid station on the south bank of the river when he had weakly called my name and asked for a cigarette. He had been my squad sergeant for nine months in Fort Bragg. I stood staring at him for a full three minutes before I turned away with a bad frog in my throat. Somehow, the frozen bodies looked miserable even in death.'

"Because of his immediate, heroic action, and after a fierce firefight, Rivers was able to rescue the six survivors and returned to our lines at the risk of his own life. He could have sent one of his other squads to their rescue, but this was a job for a leader, not a commander."[12]

On December 28, Captain Frank Boyd was at the chateau in Bra when the 9th SS Panzer Division launched an infantry and armor attack in the 2nd Battalion sector. "I remember standing in a window of the heavy stone building directing artillery fire with a telephone in one hand and a radio microphone in the other as [Private Richard P.] Barr and [Private Abel J.] Fernandes killed German soldiers with their rifles, firing from the same window. They got that close. The 376th dropped a concentration only one hundred yards in front of the 504th line of foxholes and broke the assault."[13]

On the afternoon of January 3, Captain Victor Campana, the 2nd Battalion S-3, received word that the regiment would be relieved that night by elements of the U.S. 83rd Infantry Division. "We were relieved about 2100 hours, and the battalion moved out. Again, I was told where the unit was going. Snow had begun to fall, and the temperature dropped close to zero. The march by foot was slow and tedious. It was after midnight when we arrived in the wooded high ground in the vicinity of Derrière-le-Tige, tired, hungry, and cold. This was our assembly area, and word was passed around that we would be moving out early the next morning.

"The 2nd Battalion moved out at 0900 hours, 4 January, in a column of twos. The S-4 and his assistants passed out ammunition, K-rations, and heat tablets as we passed by. The battalion marched for hours over ice-coated roads, uphill and downhill, stumbling and cursing as the individual pack became heavier. By late afternoon, we arrived in the town of Fosse, which had been captured the day before by the 505th Parachute Infantry. The battalion commander reported to the regimental CP, which was set up in that town. The battalion commander received the regimental attack order, which was to seize the high ground southeast of Fosse, overlooking the crossings of the Salm River in the vicinity of Grand-Halleux.

"After receiving his attack order, Lieutenant Colonel Wellems issued his orders to his company commanders, who had been assembled by me. The battalion was to advance approximately four miles through dense woods, void of any good roads, except a few trails and firebreaks covered by waist-high snow. The formation for this advance was D, F, E, and Headquarters Companies, with a platoon of tank destroyers attached to D Company. One light machine gun section was attached to both D and F Companies. One platoon of 57mm towed antitank guns was attached to the battalion.

"The battalion commander led the way originally, attempting to find the trail leading to his objective. He finally discovered one trail, and the unit progressed for at least three hundred yards and then stopped. While the battalion commander was checking his map along with his compass, a mortar round landed next to the lead tank destroyers, killing one man and wounding the platoon leader of the advance party and the field artillery liaison officer.

"The battalion commander then dispatched Lieutenant [Stuart] McCash of F Company to take a patrol and reconnoiter another trail which he had just discovered. By this time, it had become dusk, and the cold air began to penetrate our clothing. Lieutenant McCash finally returned with the good news that it was the right trail.

"The battalion, after slight confusion, was turned around and proceeded along the trail. The trail was narrow and traversed with frequent streams. The attached tank destroyers and 57mm antitank guns could not advance and consequently were left behind. During the next seven hours, the battalion trudged along on deep, knee-high snow. The weather had suddenly turned very cold, and the wet, stiff web equipment stuck to one's outer garments.

"The battalion commander made frequent but short halts to check his route of march by compass. The battalion had now been marching for fifteen hours from the time it left the assembly area that morning, but not once did we have an opportunity to stop for any length of time to even eat a K-ration.

"At 0100 hours, 5 January, the battalion arrived at what we thought was the objective. It was a black, dreary, wooded area, void of everything but snow and one or two firebreaks. D Company was placed into position on the left flank and set up a roadblock across the trail, which was the boundary between the Second and Third Battalions. F Company was on the right flank, and it too set up a roadblock. E Company was put in reserve approximately two hundred yards from where the battalion CP was established. Since it was still dark, positions for the 81mm mortars were not set up. The battalion aid station was located in the town of Fosse, the only place where there were houses. Our bedrolls did not come up that night, and the men did not obtain any sleep. Everyone was completely exhausted by hunger and by the sixteen-hour march in intense cold over deep snow and ice-glazed trails. The situation was so bad that the men could not lie down in the cold snow for fear of freezing to death, nor could they move about too long to provide body circulation because of their exhausted condition. Fires were not possible because of the close proximity of the enemy.

"About 0300 hours, six mortar rounds dropped into the area occupied by D Company. Soon a phone call from Captain [Adam] Komosa was received, requesting several litters immediately. The mortar rounds had landed among his CP group. Unfortunately, no litters were on hand, nor were there any members of the battalion aid station present either. It was certainly a sad state of affairs. Half an hour later, the wounded men from D Company stopped at the battalion CP on the way to the rear. Captain Komosa's runner had been seriously wounded in the head and was being carried on a makeshift litter formed by tree limbs and an overcoat. Staff Sergeant [Ernest W.] Parks, the supply sergeant; Sergeant [Raymond A.] Kimball, the communications sergeant; Technician Fourth Grade [Lacy R.] Starbuck, the SCR-300 radio operator; and a first aid man had all been wounded. I immediately obtained some men from the 81mm mortar platoon to assist the wounded men back to the rear.

"As day broke on 5 January, all company positions were moved forward at least six hundred yards, when it was discovered that the 3rd Battalion on our left was unable to make contact with us because we were too far behind. That same morning, approximately sixty-five men from the battalion had to be sent to the rear because of trench foot. Later still, Lieutenant Colonel [Warren] Williams, the regimental executive officer, visited the battalion CP and wanted to know why the 81mm mortars had not been set up in position. He stated that German troops, consisting mainly of horsedrawn artillery, were reported to be leaving the town of Mont, some two thousand yards away. Lieutenant Colonel Williams wanted something done about that situation immediately. Accordingly, the 81mm mortars were set up approximately thirty yards from the battalion CP and began firing as soon as their observers were in position near D Company's observation post. After several minutes of firing and when no further lucrative targets had appeared, the mortars were displaced forward. Nothing exciting happened the remainder of the day."[14]

The following day, January 6, the division consolidated its positions and prepared to push the Germans out of the area west of the Salm River. The troopers were resupplied, and many got the first decent sleep since the night of January 1. This temporary respite gave the Germans the opportunity to reorganize somewhat on the high ground along the Salm. The coming day would be a tough one for many.

By nightfall on January 6, the 551st Parachute Infantry Battalion, which was now at about half strength, despite receiving some replacements, and had been involved in almost all of the heavy fighting in the 517th Parachute Infantry Regiment's sector, was now attached to the 504th. The 504th staff issued a warning order to be ready to capture the village of Rochelinval the following morning. Lieutenant Colonel Wood Joerg tried to convey to the 504th staff the exhausted and depleted condition of the 551st, but by that point, every battalion was in bad shape. A reconnaissance of the village reported it to be strongly held. Five hundred or so remaining survivors of the 183rd Volksgrenadier Regiment of the 62nd Volksgrenadier Division were defending the village, a fact unknown to anyone at division headquarters. Joerg knew that his battalion was facing annihilation if they made this assault. That night at his command post, in the back of a three-quarter-ton truck, the field telephone rang. Fearing it was the order to make the assault that would surely result in the destruction of his men, Joerg at first refused to take the call, saying, "You tell him I'm not moving another damned step until my men rest and get something to eat!"[15] The officer who answered the phone told Joerg that General Gavin wanted his battalion to move up. Joerg began to curse and started to cry, then took the phone. He firmly implored the unidentified caller to have his battalion withdrawn. Whoever the officer was on the other end of the line told Joerg they would attack Rochelinval in the morning. Joerg slowly put the receiver down on the hook.

That night, when Joerg relayed the order to his company commanders, they all told him it was suicide to make the attack with what they had. Lieutenant Donald Booth, in command of Company A, told Joerg, "We can't take that hill. You can hear the damn Germans digging in—clang, clang, clang. There's heavy machine guns—they're sandbagged. They could hit a fly one hundred yards away."[16]

The first sergeant of Company A, 551st, Roy McCraw, lined everyone up shortly before 6:00 p.m. on January 6. He began inspecting the men, looking for cases of trenchfoot, frostbite, malaria, respiratory infections, and wounds that were being concealed by those who refused to leave their buddies. He found fourteen men with serious medical conditions, including two running high fevers as a result of malaria contracted earlier when the battalion had been stationed in Panama, and most with frozen feet. This cut the strength to forty-nine men and five officers, including two new replacement officers assigned to the company earlier that day. Company B had around eighty-three men and officers. Company C had even fewer officers and men than Company A.

Lieutenant Richard Durkee, one of the Company A platoon leaders, introduced himself to the replacement officers, "Lieutenant [Charles] Dahl and Lieutenant [Joseph] Kienly, both fresh out of the quartermaster [company]. Neither had any experience in combat, and Lieutenant Dahl told me that all he wanted was to be awarded the Combat Infantryman's Badge. Our company had been divided into two platoons, one commanded by Lieutenant [Charles] Buckenmeyer, and the other by myself. Each new officer was assigned to [a] platoon—Lieutenant Dahl was assigned to me.

"On the night of the [6th] we had a meal of fresh steak. That afternoon I had a patrol out and saw a nice looking heifer, and Lieutenant Dahl, who had come along for the experience, had suggested that we bring it back and kill and eat her. We did just that, and Private First Class [William] McBee and Sergeant [Robert] Hill, who were former butchers, cut it up, and we sat around the fire and ate steak.

"At 21:00 hours, Lieutenant Booth called the officers in and informed us that we were to attack and hold the town of Rochelinval the following morning. The words I uttered at that time I can't print, but I was plenty mad. I had reconnoitered the area surrounding the town, and it was suicide to attack with our small company. I told him so, and also that there were plenty of Krauts in that town. He informed me that he had also told the battalion commander that, and was told they were orders handed down to him by General Gavin. So that was that.

"Lieutenant Booth then gave us his attack order, which included [that] the 2nd Platoon (my platoon) would bring up the rear with the 1st Platoon in front.

"That night, the men were instructed to make sure that their weapons were in shape. Sitting the 2nd Platoon around me while I ate a steak sandwich, I gave them my own attack order. The men knew it was a tough mission and that a lot of them would never see another night. They went to bed all feeling that they wouldn't be the one to give their life for Uncle Sam. Dahl seemed a little excited about the coming attack, not to mention my feelings, which [were] downright scared."[17]

The terrain around Rochelinval greatly favored the defenders who used it to their advantage. The village sat on a high bluff, which virtually precluded an assault from the north or east to the rear of the town. Pine trees to the northwest, west, and southwest ended about two to three hundred yards away, with open ground with sparse cover between the forest and the village. A deep gully ran through the middle of this open ground from the northwest side curving around to the west. From the gully a steep slope ran up the bluff to a stone wall that bordered the town. The Germans had close to a dozen machine guns dug in behind that wall and on the road approaching the village; their artillery and mortar units had the edge of the forest and the open ground in front of the village zeroed in.

The plan of attack by the 551st called for Company A to lead the assault from the left, approaching the village from the northwest, with Company B moving through the woods to attack from the southwest along both sides of the road leading into the hamlet. Company C would be in reserve just inside the edge of the woods to the west. Three tanks from the 740th Tank Battalion would support the attack, and an artillery liaison was attached to provide artillery support.

The officers and men of the 551st tried to get what sleep they could. At 3:00 a.m. on January 7, Lieutenant Durkee woke up his Company A troopers and got them ready to move out. "Mail had come in the night before, and the men seemed more cheerful than they had for the last few days. The officers checked the men to be sure that all ammunition was being carried and all weapons were in good condition. At 0400 hours, we started out; the 1st Platoon was in the lead, under the command of Lieutenant Buckenmeyer, and the 2nd Platoon was in the rear. We got all the available men for this attack, including the company clerk and the supply sergeant. On our way to the line of departure, Lieutenant Booth was in the rear of the company. Lieutenant Buckenmeyer and his platoon went straight ahead when they should have turned left, and by the time I had sent ahead word that he was wrong, I had led my platoon down the right trail. So, Lieutenant Booth told me to lead the way, and my platoon took the lead in the attack. At the fork of the trail, we picked up Lieutenant McNair, who was in command of the light machine gun section, which we were told to use for supporting fire.

"At 0435 hours, we arrived at our LD and sent up our yellow flare to signal the other companies that we had reached our LD. Lieutenant Booth had the forward observer, who had been attached to us for artillery support, ask for a concentration to be laid down on our objective. There was plenty of static on our SCR-300, and contact was very poor, but we finally managed to get two concentrations on the village. However, only one shell landed in the town. One artillery unit had argued with the forward observer that the target was out of their area, and they said they wouldn't fire on it. But, after considerable arguing and the interference of our colonel, they consented. But, for all the work to get them to fire on the town, when they did, the help wasn't much good and only warned the Germans that they were about to be attacked."[18]

As the time for the attack neared, Lieutenant Colonel Joerg hadn't seen any sign of three tanks that were supposed to support the attack. Furious, Joerg sent Lieutenant John Belcher, the battalion liaison officer, to find them.

As the seconds ticked by, Lieutenant Durkee waited nervously with his men for the signal to attack. "By the time we were ready to jump off on the attack, it had started to get light—all the time we could hear the Germans preparing the defenses. Just before we jumped off, Sergeant Hill told me that it was going to be a bloody fight and a hell of a lot of men would never get there. Our route of attack was a little country lane, and on each side there was a scattering of bunches of bushes. It was about two hundred fifty yards from where we were to the town. There was a fence on the left side of the lane and a few scattered stumps of trees on the right. That was the setup, and the Germans were sitting up in the town just waiting for us. But orders were orders.

"So when Lieutenant Booth gave me the nod to attack, we set out. I had one squad led by Sergeant Hill, to go down the lane on the left of the fence and one squad led by Sergeant Courtney to go down the right side. Lieutenant Dahl and myself were in the lane behind the two scouts."[19]

The Germans waited for Companies A and B to get out in the open about half way across the open ground, and then as if on a signal, unleashed a wall of lead straight into their thin skirmish lines.

Lieutenant Durkee's understrength platoon was decimated, as crisscrossing tracers from enemy machine gun positions on the high ground traversed the bare slope. "One scout, Private [Robert R.] Mowery, who was carrying the BAR, was the first; he was hit in the stomach and the head. I immediately put my machine gun in action behind a stump. They no sooner got set up than the Germans opened up on our left flank. They were directly in the crossfire, and before they got off their second burst, they were both dead. Sergeant Hill, seeing Private Mowery die, ran over to his body and picked up his fallen BAR and stood there and fired two magazines at the Germans before he was finally killed, after being wounded several times.

"Meanwhile, I had become the second scout and Lieutenant Dahl the first scout; and we continued the attack, taking with me up the hill the two bazooka men. Halfway up the slope, which on the top was the outskirts of the town, we put the bazooka in action and completely obliterated a machine gun nest. We four crawled on up, and a sniper at a corner of a building opened up on us. Knowing where he was, I knew I could lob a grenade behind it and get him. So, I told Lieutenant Dahl to fire on the sniper, and I would expose myself and toss the grenade. He did, but my toss was short. So, I told him to continue to fire, but he didn't. I looked over to his position a few feet away and he was kneeling there—his eyes closed. He was dead—some Jerry had shot him through the side of the neck.

"At that point of the attack, my position was on the very outskirts of town. I had one bazooka man still with me. The other had been killed shortly after the death of Lieutenant Dahl. I saw one man fifty yards down the draw from my position. I recognized him as my runner; his name, Private [Pat] Casanova. I yelled to him to get those riflemen up here in a hurry so it would be possible to attack the town. His answer, I'll never forget, 'Sir, they're all dead.'

"Well, I figured we had had it and told the bazooka man to crawl back down the draw and I would cover him. I figured there was no sense to attack the town with two men. My rifle was unusable, because of the snow in the bore, so I took Lieutenant Dahl's .45 out of his holster and carried that with me. The bazooka man crawled so far, when he must have gotten tired and figured he could make it by running. So he jumped up and took off. He got about three feet when a machine gun opened up and sent a quarter of a box of machine gun bullets through him.

"Crawling around the bend in the lane, I saw the reason for Casanova's answer, that 'they're all dead,' because there in the same location of the machine gun were the men who, the night before, had such a great time eating steak sandwiches. They were lying in all kinds of postures, some face up, staring with sightless eyes into the sky; and others, face down, submerged in the snow. Looking on up the lane, I could see men lying along the trail every two yards. The men were not wounded, because their bodies were in plain view of the Krauts; who, just for practice, pumped their bodies full of German lead.

"From my position, I could not be seen by the Germans, and I could just reach the grip on our machine gun. So with the help of my trench knife, I took out the bolt and took it with me. I said a prayer to myself, and got up and ran for the woods and made it. How I ever came out of it alive, God only knows.

"When I was up in front, things were happening in my rear, which I didn't know about till I got back there. I found out I was the company commander of a company of nine men. Lieutenant Buckenmeyer had been severely wounded, and Lieutenant Booth had been killed."[20]

The Company A commander, Lieutenant Don Booth, had been almost cut in half by German machine gun fire as he attempted to take out a machine gun that was firing directly down the footpath. His wounded radio operator, Sergeant Harry Renick, had managed to transmit a mayday distress call to Joerg's radioman over the battalion net.

About that time, a heavy barrage of artillery and mortar fire hit the woods, severing the antenna of Joerg's SCR-300 radio. A tree burst critically wounded Joerg, as he observed the assault from the edge of the woods west of the village, only three hundred yards away. Suffering a terrible head wound from shrapnel that went through the top of his helmet, penetrated his skull, and lodged in his brain, Joerg was put on a stretcher, carried to a nearby jeep, and driven to a 504th aid station, where he was placed outside. Word of Joerg getting hit quickly spread through the battalion, stunning officers and men alike.

By 8:30 a.m., Company A was a fighting force of just ten; their attack had failed. Despite intense machine gun and mortar fire, Company B pressed its attack on Rochelinval from the southwest along the road. The battalion executive officer, Major William Holm, took command after Joerg was hit and immediately committed the reserve, Company C, which was now under the command of Lieutenant Leroy Sano. The battalion mortars and machine guns from Headquarters Company kept up a constant fire on the German positions, inflicting a great many casualties. Around 9:30 a.m., 113 smoke rounds began landing in the area, to cover the withdrawal of Company A, which had been virtually wiped out an hour earlier.

Company C, which was around twenty men by this time, came out of the woods and attacked a German squad manning a roadblock that barred the way into the town, wiping it out. This opened the way for Company B to move forward and destroy another German squad in hand-to-hand fighting.

The fighting raged throughout the morning, but around noon, an M5 Stuart light tank was seen down the road behind the 551st. Lieutenant Sano, the Company C commander, ran back and ordered the tank to move forward to assist in the attack. The tank's turret was damaged and couldn't rotate. It was stuck with the gun pointing at an angle to the right. However, Sano brought the tank forward, and as it moved up the road toward Rochelinval, firing two of its three .30-caliber machine guns, the remnants of Companies B and C moved forward with it. Together, the small tank and the paratroopers moved into the edge of the hamlet, where a close-combat, house-to-house fight began. After fighting all morning against these tenacious paratroopers who would not quit, the sight of the tank evidently unnerved the Germans holding the town. They came out of houses and barns, and from behind stone walls with their hands up, shouting, 'Kamerad!' By 3:00 p.m. the fighting was over. The 551st had destroyed the German force and captured the village, but had itself been destroyed.

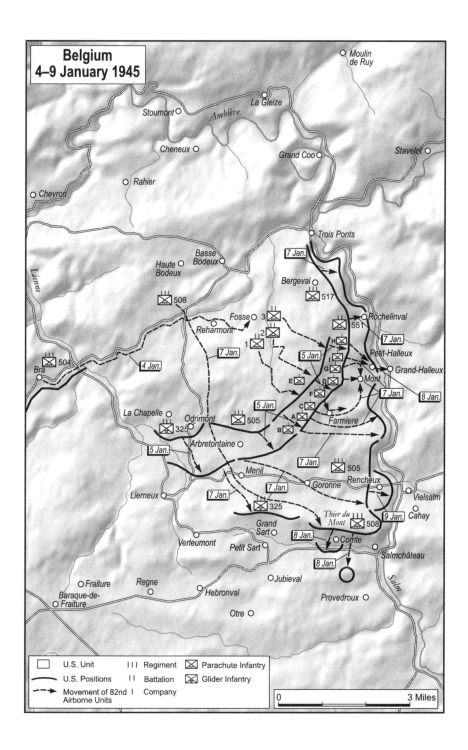

**Belgium
4–9 January 1945**

Moulin
de Ruy

La Gleize

Stoumont

Amblève

Cheneux

Grand Coo

Stavelot

Rahier

Chevron

Trois Ponts

7 Jan.

Basse
Bodeux

Haute
Bodeux

Bergeval

517

Lienne

508

Fosse 3

Rochelinval

Reharmont

2

551

7 Jan.

504

1

7 Jan.

H

Petit-Halleux

Bra

4 Jan.

5 Jan.

I

G

Grand-Halleux

E

D

Mont

7 Jan.

8 Jan.

La Chapelle

Odrimont

5 Jan.

505

C

F

A

Farmiere

325

B

Arbretontaine

5 Jan.

Menil

7 Jan.

505

Lierneux

7 Jan.

Goronne

Rencheux

Vielsalm

7 Jan.

325

Thier du
Mont

508

9 Jan.

Cahay

Grand
Sart

8 Jan.

Comte

Salmchâteau

Verleumont

Petit Sart

8 Jan.

Salm

Fraiture

Regne

Jubieval

Provedroux

Baraque-de-
Fraiture

Hebronval

Otre

	U.S. Unit	III	Regiment	Parachute Infantry
	U.S. Positions	II	Battalion	Glider Infantry
	Movement of 82nd	I	Company	
	Airborne Units			

0   3 Miles

To the right of the 551st, in the 3rd Battalion sector, on the regiment's left flank, Companies H and I moved southeast toward Petit-Halleux. As Company I on the right advanced into the town, Germans in one of the houses opened fire on Sergeant Darrel D. Edgar's squad. Edgar instantly returned fire, killing one of the Germans and forcing the others to take refuge in the cellar of the house. Sergeant Edgar directed the squad's light machine gun into position to cover the front of the house, then worked his way around to the back of the house, and tossed a grenade into the cellar, causing eight Germans to surrender. Edgar together with another trooper and stormed the house across the street, taking six more Germans prisoner. Next, he directed a tank destroyer to fire at an enemy roadblock further down the road, then led his squad in an assault on the strongpoint, capturing another twenty-three enemy soldiers. Sergeant Darrel Edgar received the Silver Star for his bravery.

Company G on the 3rd Battalion's right flank advanced south toward Mont, while Company C, to the south, advanced northward in a pincer movement to capture the village. To the right of G Company, in the center of the 504th sector, one platoon each from Dog and Fox Companies made a diversionary attack to tie up enemy forces west of Mont. Lieutenant Hanz Druener's 2nd Platoon, Company D, on the left, attacked east toward Mont, while Lieutenant Richard A. Harris' F Company platoon attacked eastward on the right toward Farnieres, capturing that hamlet, southwest of Mont, and turning it over to the 1st Battalion, then continued east toward the Salm River. Moving over open terrain, Harris's platoon ran into a well-concealed enemy strongpoint of twelve men and two machine guns, which opened up at close range on the point element of the platoon, killing Harris, wounding several others, and pinning down the remaining troopers. They returned fire to cover several men who attempted to go to the aid of Harris and the wounded men, but were themselves killed.

Private William L. Aston, Jr., the platoon's bazooka gunner, courageously moved in the open under intense and accurate small-arms and machine gun fire in an effort to locate the enemy position and bring his bazooka fire to bear. Seeing two of his comrades who had been wounded, Aston advanced about a hundred yards in an effort to go to their aid, but was wounded by three bullets. He returned to his squad, retrieved a rifle from another wounded man, and continued to fight until loss of blood and exhaustion forced his evacuation.

When the ammunition supply of one of the platoon's machine guns ran low, Private Fred L. Kincaid voluntarily rushed forward to retrieve cans of ammo from a dead ammunition bearer. Despite being hit as he advanced, Kincaid retrieved the ammunition and carried it back, allowing his squad to continue firing the machine gun at the enemy strongpoint.

Upon receiving word of the situation of Harris' platoon, Lieutenant Martin Middleton organized and led a group of Company F troopers on a flanking attack on the German positions. Intense enemy fire pinned down the patrol. Middleton spotted one well-protected machine gun, which he personally knocked out by firing several rifle grenades. Nonetheless, both Harris' platoon and Middleton's patrol remained pinned down under the heavy German fire. Middleton got up and ran back under fire over the exposed ground, then made his way back to the main Company F positions, where he secured a number of smoke shells for the rifle grenade launcher. Middleton then returned once more, braving the heavy enemy fire to rejoin his men. Middleton fired the smoke shells in front of the German strongpoint to cover the evacuation of the wounded men from in front of the position.

When the smokescreen began, the Germans, realizing that an evacuation was imminent, opened fire on the wounded. Seeing this, one of Harris' squad leaders, Sergeant Frank J. Salkowski, immediately jumped to his feet and began moving to draw the enemy fire away from the wounded.

Sergeant John C. Chamberlin, another of Lieutenant Harris' squad leaders, along with Private Kincaid and two other troopers, moved forward and picked up two of the wounded men. As they moved them back, a German mortar barrage began exploding all around them. Despite this, they got the wounded men to partial cover and returned to their squad's position. When the mortar barrage subsided, Chamberlin once again started across the open field, as the smokescreen was clearing, to evacuate another wounded man, but was hit and seriously wounded in the arm, forcing him to return to his squad.

Sergeant Salkowski then moved to an exposed position with a BAR and laid down a base of fire from the front. Lieutenant Middleton directed his patrol to lay down a heavy flanking fire, then moved across the open ground to the area where the remaining casualties lay. There, he killed two Germans who were looting the dead troopers. He then directed the evacuation of the remaining wounded and dead, personally carrying one of the seriously wounded men to safety.

Despite his wound, Sergeant Chamberlin remained in the open and directed the withdrawal of his squad, after the evacuation of the wounded and dead. The other survivors of Harris' platoon withdrew as well. In addition to Lieutenant Harris, the platoon lost Sergeant Willard G. Tess, Corporal Robert L. Righthouse, and Privates Russell Christman, Robert H. Kerkemeyer, and William Meyer. For their individual acts of heroism and leadership under fire, Lieutenant Martin Middleton, Sergeants John Chamberlin and Frank Salkowski, and Privates William Aston and Fred Kincaid were each awarded the Silver Star.

As the 2nd Platoon of Company D, led by Lieutenant Druener, moved down a barren slope northwest of Mont, Private First Class William G. Lanseadel was acting as the platoon scout. The Company D commanding officer, Captain Adam Komosa, was informed that "three hundred yards from the platoon jumpoff point, the platoon was met by heavy enemy fire from a well concealed machine gun. Instead of taking cover, Private First Class Lanseadel moved aggressively and boldly forward in the face of this fire; his actions so upset the enemy that they abandoned the position. Six of the fleeing Germans were killed by members of the platoon."[21]

As the advance continued, snipers in the town opened fire, and an enemy mortar barrage began impacting the entire area. A short time afterward, Lieutenant Harold A. Stueland, a liaison officer and forward observer with the 376th Parachute Field Artillery Battalion arrived, having laid a half mile of wire through an area infested with enemy snipers, in which he had personally killed three and was instrumental in the capture of ten more. Stueland immediately called in the battalion's artillery on Mont, suppressing the enemy fire coming from the town.

As shells exploded and enemy snipers fired from Mont's houses, Lieutenant Druener reorganized his understrength platoon and aggressively led it down the slope toward the town, with the platoon scout, Private First Class Lanseadel, out in front. They moved toward the village ahead of the main attack from the north and south by Companies G and C.

Corporal John A. Schaebler, leading one of the squads, saw his machine gunner go down with a wound. Schaebler ran to the man's aid, carried him to defilade, then returned and picked up the wounded trooper's machine gun and fired it from the hip as he advanced. Inspired by the leadership of Druener and Schaebler and the extraordinary courage of Lanseadel, the platoon approached the western edge of the town, where two snipers in one of the houses opened fire at close range. Captain Komosa later learned that "while the platoon fired at the snipers, Private First Class Lanseadel ran fifty yards through a hail of bullets, into the house, and up the stairs, where he killed one of the snipers and captured the other.

"Further on, in town the platoon was temporarily halted by another machine gun nest. While his comrades poured heavy fire into it, Private First Class Lanseadel ran boldly forward to within hand grenade distance and with a Gammon grenade wiped out the nest, killing two of the enemy and wounding several more.

"While advancing further towards a house near the far end of the town, a cleverly concealed sniper wounded Private First Class Lanseadel. Despite the wound, he kept moving in advance of his platoon until hit again by the same sniper. Though seriously and painfully wounded, Private First Class Lanseadel was able to point out the location of the sniper to the leading rifle squad leader, who shortly thereafter killed the sniper. A few minutes later, Private First Class Lanseadel died.

"The platoon continued mopping-up operations in the town, capturing a total of forty-eight and killing forty others."[22]

The remaining Germans defending pulled out of the town and tried to escape.

Lieutenant Stueland brought down artillery fire on the enemy, pinning them down as they fled the town, contributing to the capture of over two hundred Germans by Companies G and C closing in from the north and south.

For his extraordinary heroism and sacrifice, Private First Class William G. Lanseadel was posthumously awarded the Distinguished Service Cross. Lieutenants Hanz Druener and Harold Stueland, as well as Corporal John Schaebler were each later awarded the Silver Star for their actions.

On the right flank of the 504th sector, Lieutenant Reneau Breard, a platoon leader temporarily transferred from Company A, and his seventeen-man Company B platoon were in position on the edge of the woods overlooking the railroad cut and the Salm River, southeast of Mont. Lieutenant Breard and his men scratched out holes in the deep snow, but the ground was too frozen to dig. "Up the hill from the cut, there was a small trail that paralleled the tracks. I had my CP up there. We had outposted along the bottom of the ridge looking down over the railroad."[23]

Suddenly the platoon was counterattacked by an estimated company of German Volksgrenadiers attacking out of the railroad cut. Lieutenant Breard was at his command post when the attack began. "We were thrown back. We got mortar fire. It happened so fast, my squads came back and went behind me up the hill. Well hell, I did, too. I called [Lieutenant Leo D.] van de Voort [Company B platoon leader] to my left, and I asked him if he could help me, and he said no."[24]

While under intense grazing fire from the Germans down the hill, Lieutenant Breard reorganized his men along a trail about thirty yards further up the hill. "There was another path running along parallel to the one where I had my CP. I had about four men from A Company, from my old platoon, 1st Platoon, that showed up. The boy's name [leading] that patrol was [Ignatius W.] Wengress. He came and asked, 'Do you want us to help you?'

"I said, 'I'd appreciate it. But, I don't want to get you involved, because I haven't got time to go to A Company through B Company and all of that crap.' So I asked, 'Can you give me some backup with your rifles?' I think they had a BAR as well. They gave me a base of fire.

"I took one squad, because I was spread out and went down the right hand side. We hit their left flank. We ran down toward them, everybody firing and yelling. I pulled them back up the hill to the first position.

"On the left side you went down the hill, and then it became flat and it went to the railroad cut. I don't know how many men I had, probably five. We came in from that direction because there was a lot of shooting going on there."[25]

One of the men with Breard was a new man in his platoon, a sergeant who had served earlier with the 2nd Battalion, 509th Parachute Infantry. "He got hit in the shoulder. I got all the way to an embankment, and I looked around and nobody but me was there. The snow was about waist deep.

"I crawled up to where you could look down on the railroad. That's when a German put the rifle over the embankment right in my face and fired. He shot underneath me. I don't know how it was that he missed me. All I could see was the gun. I pulled back—firing my Tommy gun—crawling back, and when I did, I left two grenades up there. They came loose, and I got the hell out of there. I backed out of there and ran into another German and got a prisoner and was taking him back. I must have gotten out too far ahead the squad, I guess, because when I was bringing him in, somebody behind me shot him. He was standing right in front of me. I don't know who it was, but I raised hell over it."[26]

After being struck on both flanks, the German company withdrew. Breard returned to his platoon's main position up the hill. He and his understrength platoon had killed fifteen, wounded another fourteen, and captured six of the enemy, while sustaining only two wounded. For his great courage and bold leadership, Lieutenant Breard received the Silver Star.

The attack by the 82nd Airborne on January 7 almost completed the destruction of the 62nd Volksgrendier Division. On January 8, the 504th cleaned out Petit-Halleux and put patrols over the river into Grand-Halleux. For Private First Class Leo Muri, with Company I, it had "been over two days since we had been idle long enough to grab a bite to eat, and had had little sleep. However, it was necessary to keep going—if anyone stopped to rest or sleep, he might have frozen."[27]

The conditions had been so bad that week that Corporal Ted Johnson, with Battery B, 376th Parachute Field Artillery Battalion, felt "the cold and the snow was almost unbearable. At times, a person did not care if he lived or died."[28]

On the night of January 10–11, the 75th Infantry Division relieved the 82nd Airborne Division along the Salm River. The various divisional units moved by truck to billets in small Belgian towns a few miles behind the lines. The exhausted survivors of almost a month of tough combat against some of the best troops in the German military, and of brutal winter conditions the previous week, pulled into the 504th rest area. Private First Class Ed Bayley, a replacement who had joined Company A in France, stepped down off the back of a deuce-and-a-half truck "just after daylight in the town of Remouchamps, Belgium. This town is located in a deep valley surrounded by low mountains. As we unloaded, we were given our Combat Infantryman's Badges.

"About six or eight of us were assigned to share a small, two-story house with Belgian civilians—a husband and wife, a couple of kids, and an older person or two. They made us very welcome. My first memory is going upstairs to a bedroom with no furniture, laying my sleeping bag on a bare board floor, and passing out in deep sleep. The house did not have central heat, but there was plenty of heat in the kitchen and other downstairs rooms. The soldiers in our group were extremely well behaved and shared what we could in the way of food and other luxuries such as candy or cigarettes with the civilians.

"During our approximate two week stay in this town, most of us shaved off our beards and went shopping in stores, all of which were in normal business, even though the war was going on at full-tilt only a few miles away.

"One day in Remouchamps, we were taken to a mobile shower unit for a good cleaning. This was our first shower or bath any of us had for about four weeks. We stood outdoors in a long line in the cold snow and were told to take off all our clothing and throw it in a heap. Somehow, we retained our boots. After a warm shower, we were passed through a line for refitting with reprocessed clothing that others had discarded and had been cleaned. This was the first time in my life that I wore secondhand clothing.

"On another day, we were given instruction and hands-on training in operating light tanks in the event that we got some or found them otherwise unattended on the battlefield. We ran the tank up and down the steep and winding mountain road into and out of the town.

"While in the house at Remouchamps, we had a chance to learn a lot more about the soldiers we were serving with. Letters were read and photos and stories shared. We were able, in spite of language difference with our hosts, to converse reasonably well and have a good time. We had one paratrooper with us that I had never seen before, nor after leaving Remouchamps, that was thirty-nine years old. We named him grandpa."[29]

On the night of January 26–27, the 504th loaded into trucks, as the citizens of Remouchamps gathered to wish them good-bye. The 82nd Airborne Division was going back into combat.

Chapter 14

"No Amount of Hardship Or Loss Could Affect Its Morale"

T he division detrucked on January 27 around St.-Vith behind the 7th Armored Division lines, where the 504th bivouacked near Wallerode. Two of the very best divisions in the U.S. Army, the 1st Infantry and 82nd Airborne, would spearhead a drive to pierce the German border and the Siegfried Line. General Gavin planned an attack with two regiments abreast: the 325th on the left and the 504th on the right. The 505th would move behind the 325th, and the 508th would follow the 504th. Those regiments would pass through and continue the attack on the second day. The following day, the 325th and 504th would pass through the 505th and 508th and keep the momentum of the attack going.

That night before moving out, the men left behind musette bags, overcoats, blankets, bedrolls, and sleeping bags, hopefully to be brought up later. The men were now better clothed for winter weather than when they left France. Most now had white snow capes, pullovers, bed sheets, or mattress covers. They had been issued long-john underwear, wool sweaters, gloves, and shoe-pacs, but they were going into weather and snow depths much worse than before.

The following morning at 6:00 a.m., the 325th and 504th passed through the lines of the 7th Armored Division and jumped off on time in bitterly cold conditions and knee-deep snow. The usual artillery barrage prior to attack was foregone, and it worked. The Germans were caught eating breakfast in their billets when the 325th and 504th hit them.

The 504th moved northeast from Wallerode toward the village of Herresbach four miles away. Before Company A moved out, Private First Class Ed

Bayley and the men in his platoon gathered around their platoon leader, where they learned of their mission. "About dawn of January 28, we were informed that we were invading Germany and heading for the Siegfried Line. We were moving out with the 1st Division on our left and the 87th Division, Third Army, on our right.

"We proceeded into the woods and waited. Finally, a flare was seen in the sky, and we moved out. We met no opposition as we moved through the woods and finally onto a road in a wide cut in the heavy woods on both sides. The snow was deep, and it also began snowing heavily, and it became very cold. Men sent into the woods to patrol for the enemy had it very rough, as they had to walk through about twenty-four-inch-deep snow. Some of our officers were trying to ride at the head of the line in a jeep. They weren't doing too badly at first, being dug out now and then. I think they finally had to abandon it. Some of the Germans must have anticipated a long stay in the woods, as some very substantial log cabins had been constructed. There were signs that Germans had been there and left sometime before we arrived.

"There was sporadic artillery fire bearing down on us in the road. Once in a while, someone would be hit by a several-inch-sized piece of shrapnel. Often the hits were in the abdomen. Some of these men immediately lost consciousness. Someone would stop, open the man's clothing, and look at the large wound, which usually was not bleeding externally. Sulfa drug would be powdered over and into the wound, a gauze compress applied and stuck down, and the man tagged for a medical pickup, hopefully before he died. Usually, we never saw these men again."[1]

The men could only advance in columns, with one man breaking a trail through the snow. Lieutenant Reneau Breard, who had temporarily transferred from Company A to Company B after Cheneux, moved out at the head of his 1st Platoon troopers, breaking the trail. "You couldn't go very far before you wore yourself out. In traveling through the snow, when you'd just fall over to the side and let the next man break the path. You'd come back at the rear of the platoon and start all over again."[2]

At the point of the regimental attack, Company H, accompanied by two tank destroyers, arrived in the woods about a half mile outside of Herresbach after making an arduous twelve-hour march against little enemy resistance. It was nearly dusk, and Company H put out security, and the men were digging the snow out for shelter and opening their cold K-rations. Suddenly, the familiar sound of an American jeep approaching from the direction of Herresbach could be heard. Company H platoon leader, Lieutenant Richard LaRiviere, known as Rivers to everyone, waited until the jeep was close enough to identify four Germans in the vehicle. Rivers opened fire with his M1, killing the driver. The other three were taken prisoner and interrogated. They indicated that a large German force was following them on foot. One of the other Company H platoon leaders, Lieutenant Jim Megellas, heard Colonel Tucker's deep voice behind him say, "Greek, Rivers. Take those two cans [the tank destroyers] and get into that town."[3]

Megellas had twenty-seven men in his platoon and Rivers had about the same, some of whom were replacements with no prior combat experience who had joined the company in the last two weeks. Megellas and Rivers began getting their men ready to move into the town. Megellas got the two tank destroyer commanders to start their vehicles. Private Harold J. Sullivan was waiting for orders as Rivers approaching the platoon to fill them in. "He came back and told us that we would be able to sleep inside if we could take this little place up ahead. [Lieutenant] Colonel [Julian] Cook was in the middle of the road, and when I passed him, he saw a German gas mask canister under the white bed sheet we had for camouflage, and he stopped me, thinking he had a German soldier in the mix. When he heard I had my stove in the canister, he was all right."[4]

The two Company H platoons were deployed in tactical columns on each side of the tank destroyers, which were moving down the road. The visibility was poor—it was almost dark, and a low fog shrouded the surrounding area. As Sullivan was moving along the road, he saw figures suddenly emerge out of the fog ahead of him. Immediately, the veterans opened fire on the approaching figures, who seemed to be momentarily surprised. Sullivan was briefly startled as well, but within just a second or two, recovered and began shooting. "I don't know who was more surprised, but I know who had more firepower. I was on the left-hand side of a tank destroyer, and everybody was firing to the side and out front. Clips seemed to pop out of the M1 very fast. A lot of dead Germans were on the road and alongside the road."[5]

Lieutenant Megellas, at the front of the column, engaged the Germans at close range. "We were firing at almost point-blank range. The enemy was so close that I did not have to put my gun to my shoulder to aim it; I just pointed and fired in their direction. My Tommy gun was red hot, rapid-firing clip after clip. It was a killing frenzy unlike any other I experienced in the war; we were shooting everything in sight."[6]

The two platoons of Company H and the two tank destroyers had run into an entire battalion of German infantry, supported by a Mark V Panther tank moving at the rear of their column. Sergeant Jimmie Shields was with his squad at the front of the Company H column when suddenly the huge Mark V tank opened fire on them. "One of our TDs had gotten into a snow bank and was not moving. I was carrying a Browning Automatic Rifle, and at this point we were 150 yards from the German Mark V. Lieutenant Megellas broke out of the company formation and started firing at the tank. As he approached the enemy tank, my squad was in a position that we could return fire on the troops around the Mark V tank."[7]

As Staff Sergeant Charles H. Crowder and his men from Rivers' platoon moved up past the immobilized tank destroyer, he saw Megellas doing something he almost couldn't believe. "He and his platoon advanced on the enemy firing from the hip. The Germans were being killed in all directions. I saw the tank firing its machine guns and saw Lieutenant Megellas running toward the tank, shooting from the hip."[8]

Sergeant Lawrence H. Dunlop, an original member of the company, could see Megellas out in front of everyone running toward the tank. "Lieutenant Megellas went alone from tree to tree."[9]

Another platoon leader, Lieutenant Ernest P. Murphy, saw Megellas "throw a Gammon grenade at the tank, which stopped its movement. I then observed Lieutenant Megellas move up to the immobile tank and toss a hand grenade into the open turret, which killed the crew."[10]

As Staff Sergeant Crowder and his men advanced, the surviving German infantry down the road broke and ran. "Seeing the Germans running back into town, Lieutenant Megellas and some of his men followed, fighting from house to house."[11]

Private Sullivan was one of the troopers who helped clear the houses. "We found loads of German soldiers in the houses, and they seemed to give up quickly. I don't know what happened to my night inside, but after a short warmup and rest in a house, [Sergeant] Shields came in and said, 'My guys outside'—another night in the snow watching to make sure we wouldn't be surprised."[12]

The Company H executive officer, Lieutenant Ed Sims, helped to get the company reorganized after the attack. "A hasty defense was established in preparation for counterattacks by the Germans.

"Our forces had no casualties. An individual count [of enemy casualties] by a staff member of the 504 had 138 killed and two hundred captured. We in Company H, who did not stop to count enemy casualties, believe the count to be much higher, such as over 250 killed and over 250 captured. Lieutenant Megellas was personally responsible for twenty-five of those killed."[13]

Lieutenant Megellas was recommended for the Congressional Medal of Honor. However, due to a paperwork mistake, mention of his heroic single-handed destruction of the Mark V tank was omitted, and he was awarded an oak leaf (second award) to his Silver Star medal.

Two parachute rifle platoons had destroyed the entire German battalion. That night the 3rd Battalion repulsed three counterattacks. The fight for Herresbach was a victory of overwhelming proportions for the 504th.

THE FOLLOWING DAY, THE 504TH CONSOLIDATED ITS POSITIONS while the 508th passed through the regiment and continued the attack eastward. At 5:00 a.m. on January 30, the 504th took over the advance once again. After a grueling march through deep snow, Company D approached the village of Eimerscheid,

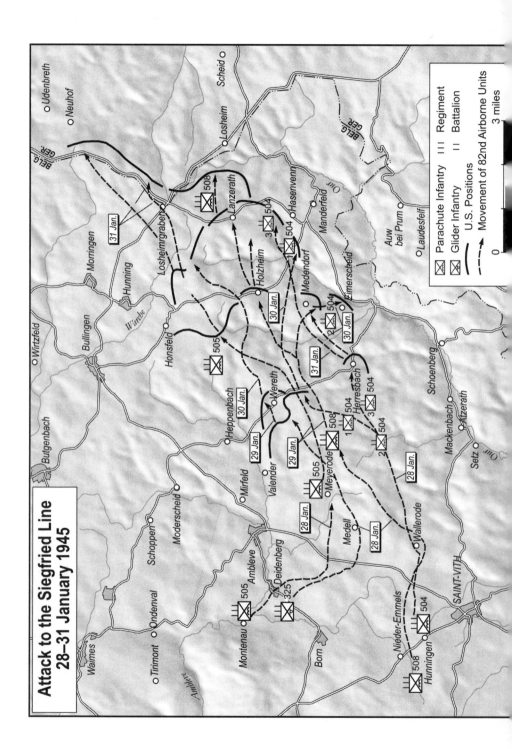

**Attack to the Siegfried Line
28–31 January 1945**

Udenbreth

Neuhof

Scheid

Losheim

BELG.
GER.

BELG.
GER.

Morringen

Hunning

Losheimergraben

31 Jan.

508 Lanzerath

505 Hasenvenn

3 504 Medendorf

Manderfeld

Auw
bei Prum

Laudesfelf

Wirtzfeld

Bullingen

Warche

Honsfeld

505

Holzheim

30 Jan.

504

30 Jan.

2 504

30 Jan.

Emerscheid

Schoenberg

Butgenbach

Heppenbach

30 Jan.

Wereth

31 Jan.

504 Herresbach

3 504

Mackenbach

Alzerath

Setz

Mirfeld

29 Jan.

29 Jan.

Valender

29 Jan.

1 504

508

2 504

Moderscheid

505 Meyerode

28 Jan.

Schoppen

28 Jan.

Medell

28 Jan.

Wallerode

28 Jan.

Trimont

Ondenval

Ambleve

Deidenberg

325

Born

SAINT-VITH

Waimes

Montenau

505

6

Nieder-Emmels

504

Ambleve

508 Hunningen

Legend:

Parachute Infantry	III	Regiment	
Glider Infantry	II	Battalion	
		U.S. Positions	
		Movement of 82nd Airborne Units	

0   3 miles

Belgium, across open ground, where it came under crossfire from four enemy machine guns, pinning down the company. The commanding officer, Captain Adam Komosa, knowing the company would be decimated if it remained on this open terrain, stood up and ran forward through the deep snow as tracers crisscrossed the air all around him. Running for short distances, then diving into the deep snow before enemy gunners could zero-in on him, Komosa was under concentrated automatic weapons fire for some five minutes before getting close enough to rake one of the machine gun nests with his Thompson submachine gun, killing the crew. He then waved one of the company's machine gun crews forward, where he directed it to an advantageous position. Komosa directed the fire of his machine gunners at the remaining three well-camouflaged enemy machine gun positions, destroying each them. Captain Komosa then led Company D in an assault of the village, capturing approximately eighty Germans. For his courageous leadership, Captain Komosa was later awarded the Silver Star.

To the south, the 1st Battalion moved east to Holzheim, where it passed through the 508th, then turned southeast toward Manderfeld. Company A was in the lead as the battalion moved eastward along the same road that the 508th had taken the previous day as it headed toward Holzheim. Private First Class Ed Bayley was near the front of the company column. "A small group of six of us or so, including myself, was selected to lead the single-file line of advance. Staff Sergeant Frank Heidebrink (a person with an always upbeat attitude who was respected and liked by all who knew him in the company), with two others following him, took the lead. I was the fourth man in the column. As we rounded a sharp right-hand bend in the road, a volley of tracer bullets rang out. Staff Sergeant Heidebrink and the second man were instantly killed. I managed to drop and roll into a shallow ditch, while several more tracers passed just above my body. Several of the troopers tried to shoot rifle grenades in the direction of the shots, only to have them fail to detonate as they landed short in the soft snow. Another two soldiers who were very close friends of Heidebrink ran forward to see if they could help him, while I yelled for them to stay down, as he was already gone, and that they too might get killed. Both were shot dead.

"By now, while lying in the snow, my hands and feet began to get real cold. I crawled back some distance where there was a Weasel with the motor running. I went to this with two or three others to get thawed out, and while there, spoke to a major and tried to have mortars fire at the approximate area from which the shots had come. He said that he had been by the area earlier in the day and that there were no Germans there and refused to take any action. We told him that Germans were definitely there, because they had yelled at us in German. We told him that Germans could have moved in after he had gone by earlier.

"At this time, a foreign-appearing person that I had seen earlier with the division and in an American uniform came forward. He yelled something toward the direction from which the shots had come, and two German soldiers emerged and came to him. At first, they would not talk. He had whipped them across the face several times, and they finally talked. We found out that they were the only ones there.

"We now had lost by death four more of our veterans. After a delay of maybe two or so hours, we moved on and came to a crossroads and a small village, Holzheim. We halted here for awhile. American troops had been here earlier, as there were a number of dead Germans lying about in the snow and a German vehicle destroyed. We were told to advance down one of the roads to find what was down there and to launch an attack against the bridge. The snow banks at the sides of the road were several feet high, where the Germans had plowed the road. The snow in the fields was about twenty-four inches deep.

"As we went forward and started a small descent down toward the Our River, rifle shots from the high ground beyond the river valley snapped and buzzed over our heads. No one was hit. As we advanced down a shallow hill toward a curve in the road, additional and more intense rifle firing began, and our troopers, finding targets, began to shoot back. I guess some of the troopers were hit, as I could not see all of them. Some had spread out as skirmishers in the field to the left. Then artillery shells began falling. Some hit the road and exploded. Some, landing in the soft snow in the fields, did not explode. Others, hitting the snow, skipped across, like small stones skipping on water.

"All the time, a captain I had never seen before (not our company commander) on the top of the road rise, kept yelling for the troopers to advance under withering rifle and deadly artillery fire. Suddenly, the captain was seen no more, and a lieutenant ordered us to pull back, as nothing but death and grievous wounds were being obtained.

"As we turned and as I was running, I saw some of my close friends lying dead in the road, their bodies having been torn asunder by the artillery. At that time, a heavy shock lifted me off the road and several feet in the air. My backside stung as if from a hornet, and I suddenly landed on it on the icy road surface, and quickly got up and ran again with the other troopers to get out of there. Later, I realized that an artillery shell had exploded beneath my feet and that I had survived without even a cut. We pulled back and regrouped, while the Germans continued to shoot 20mm antipersonnel flak shells over our heads. Shortly, the medics and volunteers with a big Red Cross flag went down into the shootout area to retrieve the wounded. We couldn't believe it, but the Germans shot and wounded several of these men. We were supposed to have had an artillery barrage and a couple of tanks assist us with this operation, but this did not occur.

"During the several minutes of this tragic event, we lost several more of the long-term veterans to death. It seemed a shame that some of them had come all the way from Africa, Sicily, Italy, France, and Holland to be killed in what would be the last days of the war. Taking into account Cheneux and other battles of the previous weeks, a large number of the old-time veterans had been killed. Some had been badly wounded but were still alive, although we never saw them again."[14]

When Company A pulled back, Lieutenant Reneau Breard, with Company B, received an order to flank the German positions. "I was sent off to the left through the snow, through the woods, maybe a hundred yards around to their left, crossed the creek, and came up on the other side. By that time, some [American] tanks had come up into Holzheim and could see these artillery units shooting direct fire at A Company on the road. The tanks cut loose with their guns, and by the time we got there, there weren't any Germans left—they were all dead. They just knocked the woods down; the guns were lying around everywhere, turned over. They just killed those artillerymen right at their guns. We came in from the north and crossed the road, and A Company got in the woods to the right and went up."[15]

With his platoon leader hit and Sergeant Heidebrink killed, Staff Sergeant John H. Stubbs took command of the platoon, which was now down to just a handful of men. He ordered Private First Class Bayley, a BAR gunner, to take the point of the Company A attack. "There was nothing I could do but go. Rifle bullets were coming in, but I could not take this into account. I had to lead the attack. Not trusting anything for snipers, et cetera, I shot up everything I saw, including electric transformers on the poles and vehicles beside the road. Nothing was left to chance—I briefly saw two or so German soldiers in the road near a truck. I completely shot up the truck, as there might be someone that didn't like me hiding in there. I learned later where the Germans I had seen had gone. They had gotten into the truck, and I had gotten them.

"There was a large farmhouse and several farm buildings on the heights. We stopped our attack at that point."[16]

Sergeant Stubbs and his platoon, now down to just four men, cornered sixty-five Germans in the farm buildings. Stubbs ran back through six hundred yards of heavy enemy fire to guide the supporting tanks forward. As he approached the farm buildings with the tanks, he spotted some Germans in concealed positions about to ambush him and the tanks. Stubbs flushed six from their concealment and killed them as they attempted to escape. He then persuaded the remaining Germans in the buildings to surrender.

At the top of the hill, where the road curved to pass the farmhouse, Private First Class Bayley and other Able Company troopers "found and destroyed the artillery piece that had wreaked havoc among our troops earlier that day. We took well over one hundred prisoners.

"During this engagement, we had lost several men to wounds and had lost forever Staff Sergeant Heidebrink, Private Louis Bosher, Private First Class Charles Galitza, Private First Class Angus Giles, Jr., Private John McFadden,

Private Clarence Sonntag, Private Maurice Stone, Private Ignatius Wengress, and Lieutenant Henry Dunavant."[17]

Staff Sergeant John Stubbs was later awarded the Silver Star for his courageous leadership during the attack.

By late that afternoon, the 1st Battalion dug in on the high ground on the far side of the Our River, protecting the division's southern flank. The 2nd Battalion moved into Medendorf and relieved the 2nd Battalion, 508th, then moved south against light opposition and captured Eimerscheid to protect the southern flank as well. Attacking from Herresbach, the 3rd Battalion took the high ground overlooking the town after a short fight.

On January 31, the 3rd Battalion, 508th, was relieved at Lanzerath by the 504th, which set up roadblocks on all roads around the town. Private William L. Bonning had joined Company B shortly after Cheneux. He had been a staff sergeant with the 86th Infantry Division before volunteering for the airborne, and then reduced in rank to private in Remouchamps because there were as many non-coms as privates in the platoon. "The company moved up into this hilly area in some woods. It was daytime. They must have seen us move in. They started lobbing 88s in. A bunch of guys got hit. [Private First Class] Harold [E. Florey] got hit again. I remember a redheaded kid, I think his name was Dudley; he got hit near me, in the throat.

"We started moving out to get the hell out of there. We went by and here I saw a guy sitting there and he had a 500 radio on his back and his helmet off. I looked—God it's [Technician Fourth Grade William H.] Jandran. He got hit with a full burst of 88 behind him. It just took [off] the back of his head, and his 500 radio was totaled—it was just destroyed. Bill Jandran—one hell of a good, clean-cut guy."[18]

On February 1, the 517th Parachute Infantry Regiment was attached to the division and prepared to move into the division's area of operations. The attack planned against the Siegfried Line was postponed until the following day. The 325th Glider Infantry Regiment was brought forward to attack and capture the small German hamlets of Neuhof and Udenbreth. On the right flank of the 325th, the 504th would seize the Hertesrott Heights southeast of Neuhof, while the 505th would attack to the southeast.

Lieutenant Richard R. Hallock, a platoon leader with Company A and a former member of the now disbanded 551st Parachute Infantry Battalion, knew the attack would be a difficult one. "The terrain in the division zone consisted of rugged, forested heights, the most dominating of which, the Hertesrott Heights, extended in a ridgeline southeast across the division zone. This hill mass was deeply cut and cross-compartmented by the Wilsam River and numerous draws, along which had been sighted heavy concrete pillboxes of the permanent fortifications type. Open ground on the north was controlled by the fortified town of Neuhof, which was accessible by road from the line of departure and in turn, connected with Frauenkron, outside the division sector, by an unimproved road running across the Hertesrott Heights. Except in the Neuhof sector, there were no roads from the line of departure into the objective area; and because of terrain barriers, none could be constructed within the time and means available. Foot movement was difficult on steep and slippery forest trails. Fourteen inches of snow covered the ground; the temperature varied between ten degrees at night and twenty-five degrees during the day. Visibility was too poor for adjustment of artillery fire and for air observation.

"The morning's PW haul identified remnants of the 3rd Parachute Division, which had opposed the 82nd Division in its advance to the Siegfried Line, together with an assortment of alarm, fortress, and service units, and produced a report that a regiment of the 9th Panzer Division was closing into Frauenkron. Enemy morale was low. However, remnants of the 3rd Parachute Division were fighting tenaciously, the terrain favored the enemy, and the regiment of the 9th Panzer Division, should it be able to engage in time, would be a powerful reinforcement.

"Except for two weeks in corps reserve, the 82nd Airborne Division had seen continuous service in the bitter winter fighting of the Ardennes. Both the enemy and the cold had taken their toll. Battalion strengths were 45 percent throughout the division. However, the 82nd was an elite division and a veteran of five campaigns and two winters of fighting. No amount of hardship or loss could affect its morale. In the rugged and roadless terrain now confronting it, the division's light organization and tough, aggressive infantry would be used to maximum advantage. Combat efficiency was excellent.

"The division was adequately equipped and supplied when it left the line of departure [in Belgium]. Now, however, it was imperative that the 325 Glider and 504 Parachute Infantry seize their objectives with the utmost speed—and in the case of the 504, with rations and ammunition on its back—as the four-thousand-yard hand-carry distance to the 504 was prohibitive of an extended action and could be shortened only after the road through Neuhof was cleared. Evacuation for the 504, already difficult, was being accomplished with the aid of PWs en route to the rear."[19]

Lieutenant Edward F. Shaifer, a platoon leader with Company B, was concerned about the physical condition of the troopers of the regiment. "Much had been lost of the physical vigor of these traditionally fit troops as the result of this period of operations. Men were generally fatigued and underweight because of the extended periods of exposure and hunger. More than 60 percent suffered from the effects of a bloody winter dysentery, complicated by the twin agents of bad water and a generally insufficient diet. This latter shortcoming was due principally to the simple fact that the caloric value of the standard ration did not meet the daily heat and energy requirements of the individual soldier, who, in the ceaseless cold, expended heat energy at a prodigious rate.

"Another limiting consideration was the lack of winter clothing and gear."[20]

Shaifer was also concerned about the high number of recent replacements resulting from the decimation of Companies B and C at Cheneux a little over a month earlier. With so many replacements, the 504 would be sorely tested in the upcoming battle.

In the early darkness, Lieutenant Shaifer, assembled his platoon, and they loaded into a deuce-and-a-half truck for the ride to the assembly area just behind the 505th PIR frontline. "Arriving in its forward assembly shortly before dawn on the second of February, the 1st Battalion paused to shed [bed] rolls and draw extra ammunition. Grenades, armor-piercing cartridges, and the reliable German Panzerfausts were issued in plenty. However, no rations were available at this time. The last Class I issue had occurred on the 31st of January, and that had been two days late. The 82nd Division, limited in transportation, often found itself short of rations and medical supplies, as was the case. It was seldom, however, even in the tightest of situations, that it failed to come up with an ammunition resupply.

"The German Panzerfaust was a tremendously more potent weapon than the U.S. bazooka, and consequently had become almost a standard item of issue in the regiment. Men were regularly trained in its use, with the result that it had become a valued assault weapon.

"While troops were drawing ammunition, all officers were briefed on the mission. Reference was made to the reconnaissance report, which buoyed spirits and hopes that the fight would only be a light action, if it was a fight at all. All concerned were also advised that no supporting fires would be available and that a resupply would not be effective until the Neuhof road net was cleared by the 325th Glider Infantry."[21]

Shaifer and the other officers listened as the briefing turned to the overall attack plan. "The mission of the 2nd Battalion, led by Lieutenant Colonel Edward N. Wellems, was to strike due east through the Buchholz Forst Gerolstein, enter the Siegfried Line at a bend in the Wilsam Brook, attack up the prominent ridge leading to the Jagerhauschen Farm, cut the Scheid-Neuhof road at that point, and go into the defensive.

"Major John T. Berry, commanding the 1st Battalion, was directed to follow through the gap to be created by the 2nd Battalion, swing southeast, and seize the lower Hertesrott Heights, thus expanding and establishing the regimental penetration. Both units were to clear all fortifications in their respective zones of action.

"The 3rd Battalion, which would not close in its assembly area until well after the regiment had begun its attack, was designated as the regimental reserve. Additional orders were to be given upon its arrival in the new assembly area."[22]

Lieutenant Shaifer studied the map overlay showing each of the battalion's company's general route and objective on the lower Hertesrott Heights. "C Company would lead out in the tracks of the 2nd Battalion, turn right after entering the line, and center itself on the battalion objective. A and B Companies, following in column, would then position themselves on the left and right respectively, thus forming a battalion perimeter on the objective. Mortars and machine guns would remain under battalion control and be employed on opportunity."[23]

The 2nd Battalion crossed the line of departure at dawn, moving into the thick woods of the Forst Gerolstein. The regimental recon platoon, attached to Company E, led the battalion, followed by E, F, D, and Headquarters Companies, and a platoon of Company C, 307th engineers. The Company E troopers encountered extremely well camouflaged pillboxes and log-topped bunkers. The German gunners let the troopers come close to their emplacements before opening fire. As the lead platoon approached one of the unseen, snow-covered pillboxes, a machine gun opened up from short range. Captain Herbert H. Norman was mortally wounded, and platoon leader Lieutenant Roy L. James was killed. The executive officer, Lieutenant John Thompson, took command and continued to lead the assault.

When Company E bazooka gunner, Private First Class Louis H. Tuthill, saw his squad leader, Staff Sergeant Diego Lisciani, get killed, he zigzagged through intense machine gun fire to get within seventy-five yards of the pillbox. There, he fired all of his ammunition at the firing slits, then charged to within twenty-five yards, throwing a Gammon grenade at a slit. This convinced the five Germans in the pillbox to surrender. Tuthill returned to retrieve Sergeant Lisciani's Thompson submachine gun.

Held up by the well-hidden enemy defenses and strong counterattacks, Lieutenant Thompson sent a squad to conduct a reconnaissance to the right, but they ran into a heavily mined area. Thompson requested a mine detector, but was told there was not enough time to wait for it.

Lieutenant Colonel Wellems came forward and decided to slip Company F to the right and make a frontal assault against the pillboxes in that sector. Lieutenant William J. Sweet, Jr., the Company F commander, briefed his platoon leaders, and they moved out with Lieutenant Stuart McCash's platoon in the lead. As they approached the enemy-held ridge, McCash deployed his machine guns and bazookas where they could deliver strong fire on the firing slits of the pillboxes, and then McCash and Sweet personally led the troopers in assaulting the line of pillboxes and German infantry dug in behind them, protecting the rear of the pillboxes. Firing BARs and submachine guns from the hip as they struggled up the ridge, the troopers closed in. Some fired Panzerfausts, with their large, shaped-charge warheads, at the slits or the rear doors of the pillboxes and log-topped bunkers from close range. It was over in a few minutes, with German corpses strewn about behind the pillboxes and lying in destroyed bunkers. The rear doors of the pillboxes smoldered after being blown open by the Panzerfausts. Company F took thirty enemy prisoners.

As Company F was cleaning out the pillboxes, bunkers, and enemy fighting positions to their right, enemy fire had pinned down the Company E platoon led by Lieutenant William E. Sharp, Jr. He moved to the point and rallied his men while exposed to intense enemy fire. Sharp then led them down a wooded slope toward an open streambed as machine gun fire from pillboxes on the opposite slope raked the platoon, killing Sharp.

Technical Sergeant Robert Lemery, the platoon sergeant, took over and led the assault across the streambed and up the enemy-held slope, exposed to concentrated automatic weapons fire, where they captured five pillboxes and took twenty-seven Germans prisoners, while sustaining few casualties. For their courageous leadership, Lieutenant Sharp (posthumously) and Technical Sergeant Lemery received the Silver Star.

During the assault on the enemy ridgeline, the medics did what they always did—risked their lives to save the wounded. Private First Class Benjamin P. Walker left the comparative safety of his position to aid a seriously wounded trooper in one of the assaulting squads. With enemy machine gun and sniper fire cracking the air around him, Walker administered first aid and then picked up the wounded man to carry him to safety. As he did so, he was mortally wounded. Technician Fifth Grade Marvin Dixon crossed two hundred yards as tracers zipped by his head, striking trees around him. Dixon reached a wounded trooper lying in an exposed position, and as he tended to the man's wound, he was hit and killed instantly. For their courageous acts, Private First Class Walker and Technician Fifth Grade Marvin Dixon were each posthumously awarded the Silver Star.

A short time after Company F overran the fortifications in their area, two battalions of infantry moving along the ridge from the southeast struck its right flank, threatening to split the battalion. Lieutenant Sweet adeptly pivoted Lieutenant McCash's platoon to meet the threat from the right flank, then adeptly maneuvered the other two platoons to counterattack the enemy and convince them they were facing a much larger force. Lieutenant Sweet, wounded during this fighting, refused evacuation and continued to lead his company.

As Company F began to run low on ammunition, two platoons of Company E were committed to the fight. Company E bazooka man Private First Class Louis Tuthill fired his dead squad leader's Tommy gun as they attacked, using all of the ammunition, then picked up a BAR from a wounded gunner. Tuthill killed and wounded a number of Germans, exacting payback for Sergeant Lisciani's death. For their heroic actions and inspirational examples under fire, Lieutenants Sweet and McCash and Private First Class Tuthill each received the Silver Star.

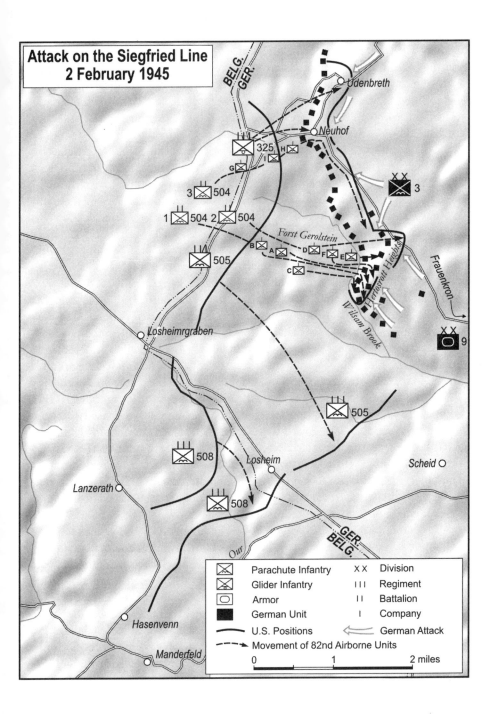

**Attack on the Siegfried Line
2 February 1945**

BELG.
GER.

Udenbreth

Neuhof

325
H

G

XX
3

3 504

1 504 2 504

Forst Gerolstein

B   A   D   F   E

505

C

Herbstein Hügble

Wilsan Brook

Frauenkron

XX
9

505

508   Losheim

Scheid

Lanzerath

508

Hasenvenn

Our

GER.
BELG.

Manderfeld

Parachute Infantry	X X	Division
Glider Infantry	I I I	Regiment
Armor	I I	Battalion
German Unit	I	Company
U.S. Positions		German Attack
Movement of 82nd Airborne Units		

0   1   2 miles

Following behind, the 1st Battalion moved out in a column of companies. As Private First Class Ed Bayley, with Company A, moved down an unimproved road that led toward the forest, an open-cab bulldozer plowed the snow in the road in front of him. "In front of the dozer, soldiers would take turns walking ahead with a mine detector. When a soldier got tired walking in the deep snow, another would take his place. We proceeded slowly down the road in a gentle downhill direction. There was fighting taking place elsewhere, but nothing in our immediate area.

"After several hours we saw German prisoners walking back parallel to our advance. That indicated that someone else was operating ahead of us, but having gone by a different route. Finally, we arrived at a clear area, through which a shallow and narrow river flowed. We were told to stay in the path through this area, because of the probability of mines. We had no problem crossing the river. Our feet didn't get wet as we stepped over the rocks. As we crossed the area, we could see a three-story reinforced concrete pillbox. It was empty. There were zigzag trenches on the sides of the pillbox. They were empty. We didn't know whether those ahead of us had taken the pillbox, or if it was not manned. We did not see soldiers from any other outfit.

"We were told to spread out in lines and to climb a steep hill. The hill was covered in icy snow, and we had to climb almost hand by hand, grabbing small trees. At the top of the hill there were countless log-covered gun emplacements that were high enough to use guns from, but with tops just above the ground level, so that they might be hard to see and to attack. They were empty.

"In a few minutes, we met in the heavy woods a large group of Germans who were apparently heading for these emplacements. We sensed that the enemy was close by and got ready to attack. I test-fired my brand-new BAR that I had picked up a few days ago, and it would not work. Nothing is scarier than facing imminent combat with a useless weapon. It was just about unbelievable; when I looked to my left, I found an old-issue BAR resting against a tree. Somebody must have been there some time before us and left the gun. Happily the gun worked well when test-fired.

"We met the Germans head on. A very intense and heavy firefight started. On both sides many soldiers were getting hit, as this was practically a hand-to-hand battle. I could see tracer bullets as they passed close to me. Finally, I got hit by a bullet, which made a long and deep wound in the left shoulder. About three paratroopers fired at the soldier who had shot me and killed him. I could not continue to fire my BAR, so I propped it against a tree and went looking for help.

"While walking back looking for medical assistance, I met a close friend who had been shot through the throat. He was not bleeding badly and could talk OK. We continued to walk back along the narrow road and came to the small river we had crossed about an hour or so before.

"On the far side was a group of airborne soldiers who had stopped before advancing into the battle behind our troops. A battalion doctor had set up a temporary treatment table and was ministering to those needing assistance. A group of German prisoners with a German medic was in line nearby. Several troopers were sitting in a circle just off the path eating field rations and chatting. Another trooper jumped over the heads of others and landed in the middle of the circle, apparently tripping a mine. He and several others were grievously injured. Pieces of metal also struck the battalion doctor. The German prisoner medic broke ranks and opened his medical case and began immediately administering to the fallen troops."[24]

Lieutenant Shaifer and the troopers of the 3rd Platoon of Company B struggled up and down the steep, rough, snow-and-ice-covered ground, cut by small creeks and ravines. "All men were heavily burdened with ammunition and the high proportion of automatic weapons always carried by parachute units. For all individuals the constant climbing and sliding was a hardship. Progress in many places was made on hands and knees through the ice and snow. Some men, had they not been closely supervised, would have thrown away the extra ammunition they carried. However, leather-lunged noncommissioned officers kept up a ceaseless, vocal snarl at the end of each sub-column, preventing this, and preserving for their commanders both a rapid rate of march and essential control.

"Proceeding in this fashion for some three thousand yards, word came back from the regimental commander, who was well forward with his lead battalion, that despite earlier reconnaissance reports, the Siegfried Line was occupied by the enemy in force. The 2nd Battalion had shot its way through the first line of bunkers, suffering heavy casualties, but was now moving forward to its objective against increasing resistance. It was also seriously tied up with heavy counterattacks from the south. The 325th Glider Infantry to the north had stirred up a hornet's nest and was fighting for its life in a pitched battle against massed armor counterthrusts. With this news, the attack on the Siegfried Line changed from a cross-country hike to a fight in earnest.

"As a consequence, the 1st Battalion was then given definite orders to attack through the line, relieve the pressure on the 2nd Battalion from the south, and then seize its original terrain objective. To implement these instructions, the battalion commander decided to lead out with B Company, then in column to the rear. Calling forward its company commander and one platoon leader, he explained the situation and gave orders as follows: 'I want B Company to enter the line through the gap created by the 2nd Battalion and attack to the south to take the pressure off that battalion. Your specific objectives [as indicated on the map overlay] are these two pillboxes. Knock them out, then change direction to the southwest and drive to the Wilsam Brook, clearing any installations in your path.

" 'To assist your lead platoon, I am going to attach a section of machine guns to it. Use those guns to fire on the apertures. I also want you to take this interpreter and have him talk to the occupants of any box your may surround into surrender.

" 'C Company will enlarge the gap made by the 2nd Battalion by turning on the shoulder of the Siegfried Line and attacking south along the Wilsam Brook, clearing out all installations as it goes. C Company will contact you on the Wilsam Brook at this pillbox [pointing to the map overlay]. A Company will follow you until you turn to the Wilsam Brook. At that point it will take up your old direction of assault and will make a limited attack to the east.' "[25]

Having received his orders, Lieutenant Shaifer returned to his troopers and the 3rd Platoon moved out. "[Captain] John [M.] Randles, able commander of Company B, making decisions where he stood, seized upon the following scheme of action. He would push the 3rd Platoon as far as it could go on the circuit just outlined by the battalion commander, and, if necessary, he would reinforce its actions with the 2nd Platoon, which he held out as his support element. The 1st Platoon would protect the company's open left flank after the turn to the Wilsam Brook had been made. He, himself, would keep well forward, observing the action of his leading 3rd Platoon, and prepared to direct the employment of his mortar and support elements.

"The 3rd Platoon moved on to the Siegfried Line and passed through the two bunkers which had been reduced by the 2nd Battalion. In this area, signs of a recent violent fight remained. Dead Germans were spread everywhere, and interspersed among the enemy dead were a few American bodies. Sporadic mortar and artillery fire was interdicting the area. To prevent casualties and prepare itself for the assault, the platoon was organized into sort of a dispersed column. Thousands of antipersonnel mines had been sown in the vicinity, and initially the troopers were forced to move in a single file. The heavy snow also served to prevent lateral employment of the unit at a time when this deployment was specifically indicated. Although hampering movement, the snow proved to be a silent friend. Alternate melting and freezing had immobilized the firing mechanisms of many mines, with the result that only a very few ever exploded.

"Owing to the denseness of the timber in the area, and the thorough concealment of the German positions, it was a certainty that contact with the enemy would come by surprise. The option of opening fire first would be all his."[26]

Lieutenant Shaifer wanted to make sure his entire platoon didn't walk into an enemy kill zone, so he "chose two men for scouts and placed them diagonally to my front, frankly realizing that they made perfect targets. Both were recent replacements from the regimental Service Company.

"These two men to the front looked like targets, and they knew it. They refused to move rapidly, and I was forced to drive them forward from vantage point to vantage point.

"As the platoon moved diagonally forward across the south part of the big ridge just cleared by the 2nd Battalion, a continuous check was made of the route by map. It soon became obvious that the wintry terrain corresponded little with the details of the map. This area had never before been occupied by Allied troops, and all charting had been done from aerial photographs. As a consequence, each map contained numerous errors. Pillboxes appeared where none were supposed to be and vice-versa. The maps were so inaccurate, in fact, that it became impossible for units to identify their objectives.

"The farther the platoon went into the Hertesrott Heights the more inaccurate the maps seemed to become. The 3rd Platoon was half across a second ridge and had progressed into a forward draw when sweeping rifle fire from a smaller ridge just to the front drove most of the exposed men to the ground. There was no time to turn and regain the cover behind the ridge just traversed. To do so would have been to get shot in the back. One course only was open. This consisted of a single straight rush at the enemy. The logic was simple. Drive them off the ridge and they wouldn't fire at you."[27]

Lieutenant Shaifer yelled to his understrength platoon of mostly recent replacements, "Come on you guys, let's get 'em!" With that, Shaifer jumped to his feet and ran toward the enemy, firing on the move. Only two of the veterans in Shaifer's platoon followed him. "The rest lay where they had hit the ground, not moving and not firing.

"Suddenly, from the heights to the left, a powerful, sustained burst of fire from an American light machine gun ripped into the German position to the front, enfilading the entire ridge."[28]

Recognizing it as friendly fire, Shaifer and the two troopers instinctively hit the ground "to wait for a lull in the flying bark and armor-piercing ricochets. The enemy fire ceased completely."[29]

As the enemy firing ceased, Lieutenant Shaifer turned his head to the rear and yelled, "'When I stand up, all you guys get up here and help us out!' Individual instructions were also shouted to two non-coms at the rear to police up the tail of the platoon. The two men who had gone forward with me were two of the platoon's three squad leaders. The thing that had sent them forward was the same thing that had made them squad leaders.

"The remainder of the men to the rear were a study in contrasts. Two new machine gunners were crawling backwards from their gun assemblies as if they were more afraid of [them] than the enemy. Only one of the scouts was visible. He lay in a trench of snow with a look of unbelieving horror on his face. At the top of the ridge to the rear appeared two faces of the platoon's veteran sergeants coolly reviewing the situation.

"Abruptly, the flanking machine gun fire ceased, and I cautiously got up, hoping that the lull was a long one. It was."[30]

Shaifer then once more exhorted his men, "'Come on, 504, let's get 'em!' Accompanying shouts and yells rose up and the platoon sprinted forward—

about half of it, that is. Many men did not get up until the situation on the top of the hill was proven safe.

"As a matter of fact, it was so safe that the platoon had to waste few rounds improving it on the few shadowy forms disappearing into the trees to the front. On the position itself, only one German moved. He was in a sitting position with his hands in the air, screaming for his life. He couldn't get up. One of his legs was a twisted, bleeding shambles.

"Every other German on the ridge lay dead, arrayed in a perfect skirmish line, each behind a tree, many with their brains leaking out of their helmets. The machine gun had been decisive and accurate. It is not often that such completely effective use can be made of an automatic weapon. This cooperative move prevented the 3rd Platoon from receiving a single casualty."[31]

Lieutenant Shaifer decided that he had moved too far to the east, estimating that the platoon was about one thousand yards into German lines, and he thought he had bypassed the two pillboxes that were the platoon's objective. Shaifer "dressed down the men who had failed to attack," then decided to turn the platoon to the southwest and move out for the Wilsam Brook.

Only minutes after the 3rd Platoon of Company B moved out, Company A arrived at the same draw. Lieutenant Richard Hallock and his 3rd Platoon were bringing up the rear of Company A, which "arrived at the draw as a two platoon company, with its platoons in column, 1st, 3rd. It had reorganized into two platoons earlier in the attack. Its strength now was three officers and fifty-nine enlisted men, including an aid man.

"As the company commander arrived at the head of his column, he noted that F Company on his left, deployed on the right flank of the 2nd Battalion objective, was receiving small-arms fire from across the draw. He was temporarily out of radio contact with battalion. Knowing that speed was paramount, he decided to proceed with the battalion mission. He ordered the 1st Platoon to attack across the draw at once.

"The 3rd Platoon, in support, arrived at the draw in platoon column between F Company and the 1st Platoon. Sporadic fire from a machine gun and several rifles was being received from the area in front of Company A. This fire seemed unaimed and was not sufficient to deter movement, most of it being directed at F Company. No enemy could be seen."[32]

Lieutenant Hallock, a combat veteran, but new as platoon leader of the 3rd Platoon, was seeing his first action with these troopers. "In the attack to the Siegfried Line the platoon had lost two officers and six out of eight NCOs and two-thirds of its numbers. Squad identities had been lost, and the men were suffering from frozen feet, hunger, and exhaustion from the hard climb over slippery trails. However, it was a veteran platoon, proud of its fighting record, proud of its regiment and division, and long inured to change and hardship.

Although understrength, it was a balanced team, high in firepower. Combat efficiency was good.

"The platoon consisted of an officer, a platoon sergeant, and twenty-one enlisted men organized as an eight-man rifle squad (the 1st Squad), a ten-man rifle squad (the 2nd Squad), and a three-man light machine gun team. The 1st Squad, armed with two Browning Automatic Rifles, one Thompson submachine gun, and five rifles, had been organized the day before from remnants of all of the rifle elements of the platoon. The 2nd Squad, armed with two Thompson submachine guns and eight rifles, had been organized a half a mile down the trail from remnants of the platoon's mortar squad and six men from the company's dissolved 2nd Platoon.

"The draw in front of the platoon was about one hundred yards wide and fifty feet deep, with gently sloping sides. It came to a head about eighty yards to the left, in front of F Company. The ground on both banks of the draw was covered moderately densely with pine trees, with boles up to thirty inches in diameter. The trees thinned out down the sides of the draw, becoming open along the bottom. Observation from the top of one bank to the other was limited due to the trees, and the bottom of the draw was not visible to the far bank because of the contour of the ground. The head of the draw was thinly wooded and open to observation from the enemy side. The draw deepened toward the south, and the woods on the far side extended more toward the bottom on A Company's right."[33]

Lieutenant Hallock quickly developed a plan of attack and organized his platoon for the assault. "The formation would be two pairs of scouts abreast, followed by a skirmish line consisting of the 1st Squad, followed by the light machine gun team, followed by a second skirmish line consisting of the 2nd Squad. Each squad would furnish two scouts, and the 2nd Squad would give two men to the 1st Squad, to give each squad a strength of eight men without scouts."[34]

In order to control the attack, Hallock decided he would be positioned in the middle of the first skirmish line, with the squad leader and assistant squad leader positioned on each side about midway to the flanks. The two BAR gunners of the 1st Squad would be positioned on each end of the first skirmish line. The platoon sergeant would be positioned in the middle of the second skirmish line.

As Lieutenant Hallock was giving his platoon sergeant and squad leaders the information, "The 1st Platoon jumped off and disappeared into the trees at the foot of the far slope. Light firing broke out, and a PW drifted back. The firing continued, but it became apparent that the 1st Platoon was halted short of the objective. The company commander then ordered the 3rd Platoon to jump off.

"The 3rd Platoon immediately formed as planned, broke back the bolts on its weapons to make sure they were not frozen, and moved out from the tree line."[35]

Hallock let the scouts clear the tree line by about thirty yards before he and the first skirmish line moved out of the woods, followed by the second skirmish line about forty yards behind. Hallock ordered the first skirmish line to begin a light marching fire as it advanced, taking care not to hit the scouts to their front. As the platoon started up the slope to the other side of the draw, it came under light fire. As the scouts approached the tree line on the far side, they came under fire first. The scouts stopped to return fire while the first skirmish line closed up. Together they moved forward, closing on the enemy positions, firing as they advanced. Hallock could now see "enemy heads and rifles protruding from behind the bases of large pine trees. The first skirmish line, now reinforced by the scouts, on which it had closed, advanced into an area of scattered trees. As the men continued forward, bark flew from the trees around them, and the sharp crack of bullets past their ears became more distinguishable in the racket of the firefight than the duller report of enemy weapons. As the enemy fire became heavier and the range closed, the first skirmish line tended to bend back at the flanks, but the aggressive firing of the Browning Automatic Rifle gunners on the flank extremities and the exhortations of the leaders brought the flanks on line again. I saw that the Germans were not dug in, but were firing from prone positions behind the trees, using the tree trunks as cover; and I yelled to the men to fire into the boles of the trees. Whether in the noise and confusion the order was heard or not, Private First Class [Harold J.] Freeman, the left Browning Automatic Rifle gunner, fired into the tree trunks, and his tracers set the example for the rest.

"The progress of the line became slower as individuals advanced a step or two, fired two or three aimed shots, and advanced again—each man firing at those Germans most threatening him. The Browning Automatic Rifle gunners fired from the hip, aiming by their tracers, and in spite of the confusion, carefully returned the empty magazines to their belts. Magazines were difficult to replace, and consequently, had taken on a value almost as great as the BAR itself. The line was building up fire superiority and continuing to move in."[36]

Lieutenant Hallock now "moved abreast of the right lead scout who was crouching by a tree. The scout shouted that his rifle would not fire. I told him to wait and get another from a casualty. Suddenly the scout's helmet flew off and he slapped his head as though he had been stung. A stream of blood an inch in diameter arched out from his temple and continued to run like an open spigot, melting a hole in the snow. The scout gradually relaxed and died in his crouching position.

"In a few yards the [skirmish] line reached level ground above the draw. About forty Germans could be seen prone behind trees, their positions exposed to the advancing line. The skirmish line almost halted as the men fired flatfooted into the nearest Germans, who were only a few feet away, some returning the fire and some already dead. On the right, a German crawled forward, pushing an MG-34 ahead of him in the snow, and was killed as he tried to put it into action. A second German, moving as though in a trance, tried to man the gun, but it was kicked out of his hands, and he was killed as he reached for it a second time.

"Looking back to check the progress of the second skirmish line, I saw that it had closed on the first and was adding its fires to the fight. [Staff Sergeant John H.] Stubbs, the platoon sergeant, was steady as a rock as he pushed his men forward."[37]

As Lieutenant Hallock turned back around, he saw a German pointing a rifle at him from a distance of about fifteen feet. Hallock stepped sideways and fired his carbine at the German, seemingly without effect. When he tried to fire again, his carbine jammed. He cleared the malfunction and fired two more times, the carbine jamming after each round. Hallock then moved on. "The platoon had gained positive fire supremacy, and the men spontaneously slacked off their fire and called, 'Kamerad! Kamerad!' to the enemy to give him a chance to surrender, took up the fire again when he did not, and then repeated the process; but no German availed himself of the opportunity.

"The line advanced among the most forward of the Germans, most of whom were dead, and fired into [the] enemy deeper in the position."[38]

Hallock decided to get his light machine gun into action. "Turning to call up the light machine gun team, I found the gunner at my elbow, carrying the entire mounted and loaded machine gun. The gunner calmly moved to the left and slightly to the rear of the enemy, set down his gun in the snow, and from a kneeling position, fired systematically into the German backs, his tracers ripping into one exposed prone figure after another.

"Suddenly, two Germans at the rear of the group got up and made a break for the woods to the left. A rifle grenadier from the 1st Platoon, just joining the fight, ran forward cursing, took deliberate aim from his shoulder, and stuck one of the Germans squarely between the shoulder blades with a grenade. The right Browning Automatic Rifle fired four or five long bursts at the second running German at a range of forty yards and missed. The German's flapping Geneva Red Cross apron became visible as he disappeared into the edge of the woods—the only man to escape.

"In the center of the enemy group, a German lieutenant got to his knees, looked about at his dead comrades, and quit hesitatingly as though reluctant to live. He lurched by, dazed, with bullet holes showing through the nape of his helmet and laced through the back of his overcoat. Suddenly, all firing ceased and the woods were still. The time was 1230; the assault had taken about twenty minutes.

"Inspection of the position showed forty Germans of the 3rd Parachute Division—all dead—most of them shot more than once through the head. The bases of the trees behind which they had taken up firing positions had served well as aiming points for the platoon. Thirty-caliber bullets had penetrated the thirty-inch pine trunks without even slowing up. The fact that the enemy had fought to the last man even though repeatedly given the opportunity to surrender was mute testimony to the quality of this group.

"From the tracks in the snow it was apparent that the German group had been moving forward when they encountered the right flank of F Company. Initially, they had crawled to the edge of the draw and disposed themselves to fire across it. The arrival of A Company and the assault of the 1st Platoon had caused them to redispose themselves to their left, and then the assault of the 3rd Platoon caught them in their right flank."[39]

As Company A was attacking at the draw, Company B moved toward the Wilsam Brook. The 3rd Platoon, led by Lieutenant Shaifer was still leading the Company B advance. "Its command party was following the 3rd Platoon, staying sufficiently far to the rear to avoid any other firefights that the 3rd Platoon might develop. The 1st Platoon was shifted to the left to guard the 3rd Platoon's flank."[40]

One of the 3rd Platoon troopers, Private Bill Bonning was carrying a BAR, and a new replacement, Private John W. McLaughlin, whom he didn't know, was up ahead carrying another BAR. Bonning was unable to see McLaughlin in the thick fog. "We were moving slowly, and [Frank] Amendola was behind me. On the snow was [an empty BAR] magazine, and then you would hear a burst of fire from a BAR, you would recognize it right away. We'd be moving slowly, and there would be another magazine. I said, 'Man, this is a good BAR man.'

"And then I saw an image ahead of me . . . moving forward . . . moving forward, and holy mackerel here's the BAR man. He's partially kneeling and partially standing, and he's got a bullet right through the helmet—a sniper got him right in his forehead—killed instantly. His BAR was stuck in the snow—he was propped against it. It was like a movie set—unbelievable, like a dummy."[41]

As 3rd Platoon advanced, Lieutenant Shaifer heard the crack of small-arms fire coming from the front. "The enemy was more distant than in the previous encounter, and thereby allowed the platoon more cover and time to prepare a coordinated attack. I called for my platoon sergeant to come forward.

"The platoon sergeant ran up with the platoon guide and the interpreter, a trooper [Jack J. Cocozza] who had formerly been a Czechoslovakian national, and who was now too impatient to remain in the rear."[42]

When the firing began, Private Bill Bonning and the other troopers had hit the ground and waited for orders. "Lieutenant Shaifer sent Ortega out [to scout the enemy positions]. Ortega was walking slowly and the Krauts let him through. One of the Krauts fired and shot him through the back of the helmet into his head. The Kraut moved back, and we got to Ortega, and the medic couldn't do anything for him, except send him back. Ortega walked back with a bullet in his head.

"There were about six or eight of us. Lieutenant Shaifer pointed to me to go out as scout. I had [Frank] Amendola behind me with the ammo. And—this is something I have regretted for sixty years—I raised up and showed him I had the BAR and I shouldn't go out as scout with the BAR. So, he pointed to [Private Sydney J.] Redburn. Redburn didn't have much experience in combat. This was his first time, really, because they had broken up Service Company when we were at Remouchamps and put all of these guys in different companies.

"So he sent Redburn out, and a machine gun opened up. Redburn hit the ground, and instead of lying there behind a tree, he rolled over and raised his rifle up, that old basic training crap. When he did that, the machine gun hit him in the shoulder. He screamed his head off.

"Then, Shaifer sent me, Amendola, and [Robert E.] Waldon to circle around and flank the pillbox. It was deep snow, there was Waldon, and I was on the left and a little bit behind him, and Amendola was a little bit behind and to the left of me. All of a sudden, we saw two Krauts carrying a litter with a Kraut on it. So, Waldon held up his hand, because he thought it was two Kraut medics. Well, it was a Kraut on a litter with a burp gun. He rolled off the litter and he sprayed us. He didn't hit any of us. Waldon fired his M1, and I fired my BAR, and it went, 'klunk.' It had spent all morning ice cold, and the slide just slid forward. I cleared the slide and fired at the crest of snow where they were, but didn't hit any of them, and they got back to the pillbox. They were outside the pillboxes to resist any attack. The pillboxes were totally covered with snow, including any slits. They would retreat into the pillboxes and hide out."[43]

As Lieutenant Shaifer was getting the attack coordinated, "suddenly, the interpreter [Jack J. Cocozza] could stand it no longer. He began to rush straight to the pillbox, which he had initially located, spraying fire with his Thompson submachine gun."[44]

Lieutenant Shaifer, seeing this, shouted to his platoon to follow him and jumped to his feet and charged toward the enemy, swinging wider to the left and firing from the hip as he moved. "The platoon assault was on, with two men and a volley of yells. This small thrust momentarily caused the Germans to reduce their fire. Several others began to move forward. The impasse was broken and the platoon began to get into action. A group of men came up carrying Panzerfausts. One of the light machine guns from the rear began to fire into the tops of the trees in the direction in which I had gone. There wasn't much chance of this gun hitting anybody, but its fire, combined with the riflemen now in action, was effective firepower, for field-gray-clad soldiers could be seen abandoning their positions and fleeing through the trees.

"Suddenly, from an open concrete fire pit just to the left of the pillbox which the interpreter had located and attacked, a group of trapped Volksgrenadiers led by a parachute captain rushed from behind each side of a concrete apron. Somebody let a 150mm Panzerfaust go perfectly in their midst, and pieces of German soldiers were splattered in liberal quantities all over the landscape. Those of the enemy who were able, surrendered on the spot.

"The interpreter, in the meantime, almost sprayed his way into the pillbox, which he had rushed all alone, but the Germans who had been out of it defending its rear, shut it in his face as he jumped for the entrance.

"Screaming in German, he fired a full clip into the outer passage in which he was standing, completely unaware of any danger from his own ricochets. He was unharmed.

"Several more Panzerfausts were brought up, and security elements were placed to the north and south. The surrender of the bunker which had been assaulted single-handedly by the interpreter became a cat-and-mouse game. The two embrasures were blown in with Panzerfausts in a hurry, but the Germans inside would not readily surrender, because their officer would not permit it.

"Several B Company men were standing on top of this pillbox when two bazooka rounds were fired at them by C Company, which had come from the north. This was a mistake in identification. One round exploded in the center of the group, but wounded nobody. Recognition was made through the medium of 'loud protests' voiced by B Company.

"In the rear, the platoon sergeant was asking the occupants of the pillbox silenced by the platoon guide to surrender. He was successful shortly thereafter, and a total of four prisoners were taken. One German was dead inside—hit full in the face by the fire which the platoon guide had delivered through the aperture. The pillbox surrendered soon after and swelled the company's total for this single action to twenty-two Germans taken prisoner.

"B Company then moved out again for the battalion objective on new orders given by radio. This time the 1st Platoon took the lead. The 3rd Platoon would follow as soon as it was reorganized. No men were spared to guard the recently captured boxes, owing to the company's limited strength. The company commander made this decision, choosing the lesser of two evils. He was well aware of the consequences should the enemy decide to attack and reoccupy them."[45]

After getting his platoon reorganized, Lieutenant Shaifer and his troopers moved out, following the 1st Platoon of Company B. "Advancing rapidly to the battalion objective, B Company had traveled some fifteen yards, observing enemy movement, but making no real contact, when a halt was called. The company was now astride what appeared to be the objective. All features shown on the map could be located on the ground, including a road, two bordering brooks, and cleared area to the south.

"Verification was requested from the battalion headquarters group. However, it was found that B Company had moved so rapidly that the head-quarters group was outdistanced, and that Germans had infiltrated back into the installations between the rifle units and the command group, with the result that there was now no physical contact between the fighting elements and the command elements of the battalion.

"Company B was soon followed by Company C, which had been following, and a lively discussion soon began among the officers present as to whether the objective had or had not been reached. The platoon leader of Company B's 1st Platoon [Lieutenant Reneau Breard], which had set the rapid pace to the objective, averred that it had not yet been reached. However, he was outvoted, and the battalion rifle units began to organize the ground into a perimeter defense. Company A arrived soon after, and a report was radioed back to the battalion command group that the objective had been taken and all units were in position.

"As a matter of fact, the battalion had failed by some six hundred yards to reach its proper objective. This error, however, gave little tactical advantage to the enemy, for the 2nd Battalion had successfully cut the Neuhof road. More-over, the 1st Battalion in its present location could do a fair job of defending the regimental sector from the south.

"Company B went into position on the south flank of the battalion perim-eter, and immediately dispatched patrols to its front. These patrols were short lived, however. They had gotten no farther than 125 yards when one of the patrols caught a group of Germans in the open between two pillboxes. These, they drove inside one of the bunkers and returned with the story that a line of the fortifications lay to the south. What was serious, as a result of this false report, lay in the fact that a supply-carrying Weasel, riskily squeezed through Neuhof by B Company's supply sergeant, was trapped by the enemy, as it searched for the misplaced battalion on the Neuhof road. This vehicle carried a trailer loaded with ammunition and the odds and ends of a few ration boxes scavenged from the 740th Tank Battalion, which supported the division. Food was beginning to become a real problem. Every man's belly was gnawed by hunger.

"Little progress was made in the digging of holes on the position. It was not that the men didn't want to dig the holes; it was due to the fact that each man was so tired and too weak from hunger to do more than scrape the snow away from the ground. A little rut in the ground was to be his abode for the night."[46]

THAT AFTERNOON, THE 3RD BATTALION PASSED THROUGH THE 325TH at Neuhof and attacked southeast along the high ground astride the road from Neuhof to Scheid, perpendicular to the defenses to roll up the flank of the defenders and link up with the 2nd Battalion. The battalion encountered extensive minefields, but fortunately the snow and cold rendered most of those inoperable. Lieutenant Ed Sims, the executive officer of Company H, found the going a little tougher moving through their less heavily wooded sector. "Our attempts to seize these bunkers became difficult. Those inside would, initially, not surrender and would call for their own artillery fire on their bunker while we were outside, trying to get in. We used rocket launchers and Composition C to blast our way through the heavy steel doors that were below ground level. Once we were inside, the occupants surrendered. Fortunately for us, the fortifications in the Siegfried Line were not fully manned."[47] The 3rd Battalion pushed southeast until it linked up with the 2nd Battalion late that day.

Casualties had been light during the attack by the 504th, although trench-foot and frostbite continued to take a toll among the troopers. Getting ammunition, water, food, and medical supplies up to the rifle companies was difficult because of the heavily wooded landscape and steep hills. Even the Weasel had difficulty negotiating this terrain. The Company C, 307th, engineers and Service Company performed yeoman work in moving badly needed supplies up to the rifle companies.

As daylight was fading in the 1st Battalion area, Company B platoon leader Lieutenant Ed Shaifer heard the sound of incoming heavy artillery. "The northern half of the company was plastered with salvo after salvo of 155mm artillery fire, which burst continuously in tree tops. Undoubtedly, this fire was being called for by the occupants of the pillboxes earlier contacted by B Company's patrols. Several men were wounded in this initial barrage, one man losing most of his lower legs and receiving other wounds seconds later, even while others were bent closely over him. This shook the morale of some, for the wounded man was one of the legendary heroes of the unit.

"This fire was to last incessantly all night, perhaps because the enemy had few other targets. The volume of fire was so heavy that when dawn arrived, the forest which Company B had occupied the night before was now only an open clearing of slashed and jagged stumps. There was a continuous shower of branches and tree limbs all night long. Wounded were evacuated by strong patrols, which made contact with the enemy both coming and going.

"That night the temperature dropped considerably, and the wet clothing of the men froze on their bodies. There was no warmth of any kind. Blankets, shelter halves, and raincoats had all been left in the assembly area. Many men slept with their arms around each other, trying to keep warm. Company officers were to endure all night the moaning of their men who were fighting the cold.

"The next day brought apt testimony of the price that the past day's operation had wrought. The labor of traversing areas without coats in blinding snowstorms, through waist deep drifts, in sub-zero temperatures without rest, shelter, or food took its inevitable toll. Men's feet were beginning to bleed and ooze fluid from the alternate freezing and friction of halts and marches. Both the feet and hands of many were beginning to turn the blue-black of frostbite, or trenchfoot, as it may be called. Some of the more serious cases were questioned and asked to return to the rear. This they refused to do, claiming that they were good for at least a few days more. Some men had removed their boots and found that they could not put them back on again. They wrapped their feet in parts of enemy uniforms, asking that they not be evacuated.

"Feet went bad despite the highest type of discipline. All troops had been well briefed on the evils of trenchfoot and kept their feet in the best condition they knew how. One of the surgeons recommended rubbing the feet with Barbasol Brushless Shaving Cream."[48]

Private Bill Bonning was one of the Company B troopers who received the treatment. "They would send two or three guys at a time. From the company, we would go back fifty yards to the company CP. Then they had little flags stuck in the snow, and you went back another fifty yards, then you'd turn left, and you'd go another fifty yards, then you'd turn left again and you'd go another fifty or hundred yards following these flags to this pillbox where the battalion CP. was located. The reason why we were going back there was they were going to give us two pairs of socks, and they were putting Molle Shaving Cream on our feet—smearing these tubes of shaving cream on our feet. They put all of this damned shaving cream on our feet, put our socks, on and we'd go back to the line.

"This major said, 'Anyone here read maps?'

"Because I had been a staff sergeant and had map reading and all of that, I said, 'Yes sir, I can read maps.'

"He said, 'Which company are you from?'

"I said, 'B Company.'

"He said, 'Show me on here, show me which way you came to where B Company is right now.'

"I looked at the map and I said, 'Sir, if I go out this door and I turn left, I'm right on the front line. You're right here where B Company is—B Company is on your left.'

"He said, 'It can't be.'

"I said, 'Yes, sir, you are—you're on the front line. I went back fifty yards, I went left fifty yards and I went forward fifty yards. I'm right back on the front lines.'

"They put this damned Molle Shaving Cream on us. It was supposed to keep the moisture out. They thought that the shaving cream had oils in it, but the shaving cream was all moisture. That stuff froze that night. Everybody was taking newspapers, *Stars and Stripes*, and trying to rub this stuff off of our feet in the middle of the night."[49]

On the morning of February 3, 1945, Lieutenant Shaifer, the platoon leader of the 3rd Platoon of Company B, checked on his troopers, anticipating an enemy counterattack. "During the night the enemy had not been idle. He had fully developed the battalion's position, and with daylight he launched heavy coordinated counterattacks, preceded by masses of artillery fire against A and C Companies principally. These were repelled only after severe fighting.

"Company B was struck by a flanking unit of about a platoon in size, and this attack was quickly repelled, mainly by the actions of one of the attached machine gun crews. Their reward for their performance was to be blasted to pieces by a well arched Panzerfaust, which fell exactly in their hole.

"This eventuality was the key that ended the enemy effort against Company B, however. The 1st Platoon fired two Panzerfausts back from where the first had come, with the result that all fire and other evidences or enemy activity in this area evaporated completely.

"Artillery fire began to fall in the area with negligible results. Still, some few men began to show concern for their personal safety. The company's prize 'goldbrick' developed a suspicious limp, claiming he had been struck in the anklebone, and that he couldn't walk. A heart-to-heart talk by one of the company officers straightened him out. Another of the company officers was hit and refused to evacuate himself. The medic who treated him, a veteran with over three hundred days' combat, lost his nerve and went AWOL to the rear, never to return to the outfit. Little things, these, but the strain and physical deterioration were becoming noticeable in Company B.

"Another patrol was put out by the company to its front in order to determine whether or not the pillboxes were occupied."[50]

One of the troopers on the patrol was Private Bill Bonning, who moved out under an overcast sky as broken fog hung low in the ravines. During the patrol, Bonning and the others saw eight or ten Germans moving through the woods toward them. "We could see them two or three hundred yards away. We waited until they were about a hundred yards away then opened fire on them. We were in higher ground, firing down on them. Then there was fire coming back at us, and it kept getting more intense. I kept thinking, 'This doesn't sound right. I'm hearing a BAR.' We knew it was Krauts down there, because we could tell by the shapes of their helmets and their weapons. The Krauts were in between us, firing both ways. But, there were guys on the other hill firing across at us. I was screaming and hollering, and finally we discovered they were Americans, and they discovered we were Americans."[51]

The Company B patrol captured a number of prisoners and returned without further incident. Otherwise, the Company B area was relatively quiet, except for sporadic enemy artillery fire. But, Lieutenant Shaifer heard that "back at the regimental CP, however, the situation was not as peaceful. The failure of the battalion to secure its objective the day before was a sin of the worst sort, and much commotion was caused thereby. A platoon of tanks seeking the 1st Battalion had made a dangerous four thousand–yard sweep into enemy lines looking for the wayward battalion in vain, but had luckily escaped intact. The battalion ammunition resupply had been lost there also, in the unfortunate Weasel incident. Throughout its colorful history, the 504 had excused many understandable shortcomings in its subordinate units, but failure to deliver the results called for on the field of battle had not been one of them. In one way or another, the unit had always accomplished its mission, and from the moral standpoint, it was going to accomplish this one. A wide gap existed between the 1st and 2nd Battalions, and because of the unremitting German counterattacks, it was essential that the 1st Battalion's position be improved.

"Having had the major portion of its front pinched out by the 508th, Company B was free to be used for this purpose. It constituted the only unit in the entire regiment that could be spared. The 3rd Battalion was completely employed in mopping up the defenses between Neuhof and the Jagerhauschen Farm. Both A and C Companies were desperately resisting well-supported counterattacks from the south and could not possibly be disengaged. They were to be under constant pressure for the next thirty-six hours.

"It was now apparent that there were two kinds of enemy in this sector. Poorly organized fortress units—whose resistance varied inversely as the proximity of their officers—manned the indefensible pillboxes, and better outfitted Wehrmacht troops comprised the counterattacking units, with which the 1st and 2nd Battalions had been embroiled since yesterday. In cracking the Siegfried Line, the troopers had actually run head-on into an estimated reinforced regiment which was moving to meet the 325th Glider Infantry's threat at Neuhof. If the 504 could hold as it had been against this more able-bodied threat, its mission would be fully accomplished.

"Company B was then ordered to withdraw deep into the regimental area, swing through the 2nd Battalion, and attack south along the Frauenkron [Scheid-Neuhof] road to the edge of the Forst Gerolstein. It was now hoped that this movement would outflank the assaulting enemy now being beaten off by A and C Companies. Returning, the company waded through the bodies of Germans who littered most of the regimental zone of action. The enemy's move to reinforce Neuhof had, up to this point, failed entirely. Tracing its route by following wire lines, tied in one instance around the upthrust frozen arm of a dead German, the company passed through the 2nd Battalion. There, the 2nd Battalion supply officer, a provider of no mean ability, issued every third or fourth man a single 'K' ration unit, the first food in the hands of the company in over three days. Men ate ravenously, and even the infamous 'corned pork loaf with apple flakes' portion of the ration tasted good."[52]

After moving through the 2nd Battalion, Company B advanced down the unimproved road, with Lieutenant Reneau Breard's 1st Platoon in the lead. "I had a tank destroyer with us. We were out in front of that tank destroyer. We got into a shallow part of the woods. It looked like a lot of it had been cut. It reminded me of where they gathered logs to put on trucks. The trail was

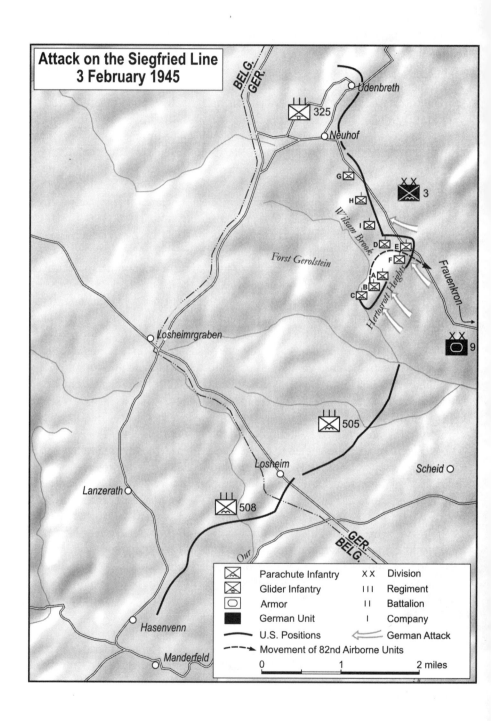

**Attack on the Siegfried Line
3 February 1945**

BELG.
GER.

Udenbreth

325

Neuhof

G

3

H

William Brook

I

D E

Forst Gerolstein

F

Frauenkron

A

Hertgsrott Heights

B

C

9

Losheimrgraben

505

Losheim

Scheid

Lanzerath

508

GER.
BELG.

Our

Hasenvenn

Manderfeld

	Parachute Infantry	X X	Division
	Glider Infantry	I I I	Regiment
	Armor	I I	Battalion
	German Unit	I	Company
	U.S. Positions		German Attack
	Movement of 82nd Airborne Units		

0   1   2 miles

going through there. All of a sudden, my whole platoon got mortared. The tank destroyers pulled back. I didn't know what to do, so I pulled back, too, and got them out of there. I had one man killed and everybody wounded except me and four people. The area was mortared real hard, and we had to take cover. I just evacuated them real fast. There was nobody to get up, but me and four people. We got all of my wounded back and the one dead person. We got mortared again on the way back. I left the four men on an outpost.

"I went back to [Captain John] Randles and told him what had happened."[53]

Private Bill Bonning was nearby and listened as Captain Randles radioed battalion. "He's arguing back and forth. 'We can't go farther—we've got to dig in—the attack is failing—we're getting too many casualties.' "[54]

Lieutenant Breard listened to Captain Randles argue with Major John Berry. Then, there was a pause, and Breard was handed the radio handset. "Major Berry got me on the phone, and he wanted me to take the 2nd Platoon up. I told him that I would do it, but that I didn't know too much about the 2nd Platoon.

"He said, 'Are you refusing to?'

"I said, 'No, sir, I'll take them. I don't have but four men from getting mortared. They're on outpost.'

"He said, 'Well, let me talk to Randles again.'

"So they called it off."[55]

Lieutenant Shaifer knew the company couldn't take much more attrition. "Two platoons remained. One consisted of twelve men, including five attached machine gunners; the other platoon had eleven. Company strength numbered about thirty, including the skeletonized mortar unit.

"Artillery fire began to fall a round at a time in the area. One of the aid men became hysterical. An officer talking in reasoned sentences brought him under control. The company commander argued again and again with his battalion commander that he could not succeed if he was required to continue the attack. There was no route to employ the tanks where they could be supported by infantry. The troopers who heard him knew that too, and their knees shook with something else beside cold. Yet, most of the junior officers were ready, and if the order were given, they would go. They began to reconnoiter the flanks."[56]

After Company B received the order to defend its present position, Lieutenant Shaifer deployed his 3rd Platoon troopers to stop an anticipated enemy counterattack. "The company went into position that night and repelled enemy patrols and a counterattack, which at one time enveloped its two flanks. This attack did not succeed because of the excellent sound-powered telephone outpost system, which fully alerted all members, and the inability of the Germans to withstand the close-range fire of the [740th Tank Battalion] tanks. During this effort, thousands of rounds of ammunition were fired. The area was so lit up from tracers that a man could have read a newspaper by their light had he been so inclined.

"That night the enemy could be heard moving up tracked vehicles. This was reported, and two tank destroyers were sent forward to join the company. Because of the open tops of the vehicles and tree bursts which the enemy was throwing in, the crews spent more time under their tanks than they did in them. The narrow road caused a difficult problem in dispersing of vehicles in a defensive array, but this was accomplished after much difficulty.

"Early on the morning of the fourth [of February], the enemy poured four distinct calibers of fire on Company B, including flat-trajectory fire. None of these weapons could be located except through the medium of shells bursts. They were too well concealed.

"Slowly, Company B was getting another forest shot down over its head. Heavy tree trunks were being sheared off like grass stalks. One man was pinned in his hole by the sixteen-inch bole of a falling tree. A tree burst killed two occupants of a tank destroyer. It was as safe standing in the open as to remain in holes. Men, unable to find room under a tank, became resigned to the fact that they were going to be hit, and their sense of self-preservation began to disappear. One man working, fully exposed, kept trying to repair a telephone line that was continuously being shot out. Farther away from him, one of the platoon leaders stood out in full view of everybody, moving from shell crater to shell crater as they occurred, writing down data for shell reports.

"That night the company was relieved twenty-four hours late by elements of the 99th Division, who many times lost their way coming up from the rear over complex terrain."[57]

On the morning of February 5, Staff Sergeant William L. Reed and his squad of Company C troopers were holding an isolated position, awaiting relief by the 99th Infantry Division, when they were attacked by a reinforced company of German infantry. Instructed to withdraw, Reed asked for permission to stay, because four of his men were wounded in the initial attack. Sergeant Reed inspired his remaining troopers to repulse the enemy assault. When the Germans temporarily pulled back, Reed quickly withdrew his squad, including the four wounded troopers, to an alternate position. Staff Sergeant Reed received the Silver Star for his leadership.

Later that day, the 504th Regimental Combat Team was trucked to the village of Grand-Halleux, Belgium for rest.

Chapter 15

"Big Six-Foot Jerries, In Waves Of Skirmish Lines As Far As The Eye Could See"

On February 8, the 504th Regimental Combat Team was trucked to Schmidthof, on the edge of the Hürtgen Forest—the meat grinder that had chewed up so many U.S. Army divisions during the previous fall. By this time virtually the entire area was one of almost complete devastation, reminiscent of the battlefields of the First World War. The towns were ruins, the trees were stumps, and the ground was churned up with countless craters from the terrific number of artillery and mortar rounds fired by both sides during the earlier fighting.

The regiment was held in division reserve until February 13, when the 1st Battalion relieved the 1st Battalion, 508th Parachute Infantry Regiment, southeast of Bergstein. Over the following four days, elements of the regimental combat team participated in assault-boat training in preparation for an assault crossing of the Roer River. Fortunately, the crossing was canceled, and on February 18 the regiment was relieved by the 9th Infantry Division. Except for organic transportation units, the division was put on trains and moved mostly in 40 & 8 boxcars, first to Aachen and then to its base camps in the Rheims, France, area. The Sissonne camp had been taken over by a hospital unit, so the 504th was moved to accommodations at nearby Laon.

The 504 rested at Laon over the following month and a half, receiving and integrating replacements, conducting training, as well as getting veterans back from hospitals.

ON APRIL 2, THE 504TH RCT, as part of the 82nd Airborne Division, boarded troop trains, mostly consisting of 40 & 8 boxcars, and traveled to Stohlberg, Germany, arriving the following day. That day, division headquarters issued Field Order Number 19, which called for relieving the U.S. 86th Infantry Division along the west bank of the Rhine River from the town of Worringen, eight miles north of Cologne, south through Cologne, then another thirteen miles south to Graurheindorf. The total frontage was about thirty-two miles. The relief began that evening and was completed by 8:30 a.m. the next morning. The 504th sector extended north from Cologne, while the 325th occupied Cologne, and the 505th sector spanned from just south of Cologne to just north of Bonn.

The units established positions in factories, homes, and commercial buildings along the riverfront of the Rhine, and set up listening posts along the edge of the river that were manned during darkness. Any movement observed by the Germans resulted in artillery, mortar, and 20mm antiaircraft fire from the eastern side of the river.

On April 5, the 504th received an order to put one company across the Rhine River after midnight to seize and hold the town of Hitdorf, which extended for a mile along the eastern shore of the Rhine River, north of Cologne. The operation was a feint to draw German forces in the Ruhr Pocket toward the river to stop a potential crossing of the Rhine River on the western side of the pocket. Corporal George Graves, with the regimental S-1 section, received a copy of the attack order issued by regimental headquarters: " 'A' Company, 504th Parachute Infantry, to attack with attachments of demolitionists, a light machine gun section, and the routine additions of artillery liaison and intelligence personnel, across the Rhine in four waves, because of the limited availability of assault boats. The 3rd Platoon, constituting the first wave, would attack, seize, and prepare for defense the southeastern portion of Hitdorf. The 1st Platoon in the second wave would pass through Hitdorf from the south, clearing the town as they advanced, to establish a defensive perimeter around the northern outskirts of the town. The 2nd Platoon would arrive in the third wave to clear and defend the eastern flank of Hitdorf. The fourth and last wave, composed of company headquarters, demolitionists, and the light machine gun section, would clear and defend the area surrounding the CP, which was to be established in a church located near the center of the town."[1]

At 2:30 a.m. on April 6, Company A, commanded by Captain John N. Pease, and led by the 3rd Platoon, loaded into assault boats and began crossing the swollen and fast-flowing Rhine River. When the first wave of boats touched down on the east side of the river, withering enemy automatic weapons fire pieced the night air as tracers came from several points along the beach area. The 3rd Platoon also landed in the midst of a minefield. It quickly organized into two combat teams and moved out. When one of the troopers stepped

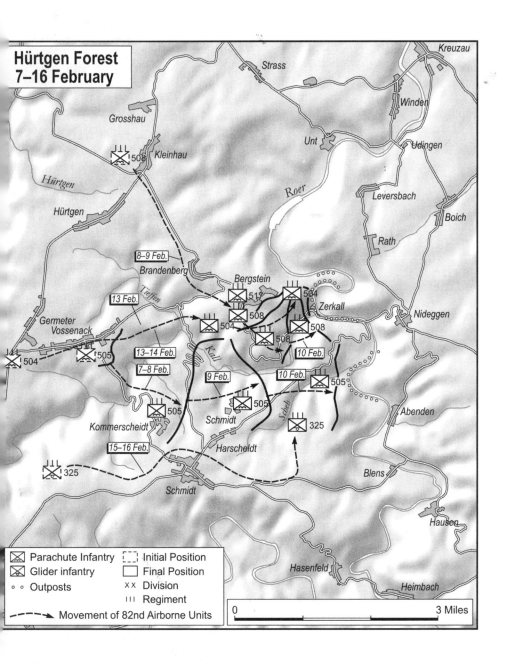

**Hürtgen Forest
7–16 February**

Strass

Kreuzau

Winden

Grosshau

Unt

Udingen

Kleinhau

506

Hürtgen

Roer

Leversbach

Boich

Hürtgen

Rath

8–9 Feb.

Brandenberg

Bergstein

504

Zerkall

Nideggen

13 Feb.

512

508

Germeter
Vossenack

504

508

504

505

13–14 Feb.

508

508

10 Feb.

7–8 Feb.

9 Feb.

10 Feb.

505

505

505

Kommerscheidt

Schmidt

Scheb

325

Abenden

15–16 Feb.

Harscheidt

Blens

325

Schmidt

Hausen

Hasenfeld

Heimbach

0   3 Miles

on a mine, illuminating the area, it caused momentary confusion, and the two teams lost contact. One team, led by Lieutenant Richard Hallock, moved out toward the southwest end of the town, where it ran into enemy machine gun and small-arms fire. The other group, led by Lieutenant Miars, infiltrated through the town to the church, where a firefight broke out. Six enemy were killed and three captured, and the area was cleared.

The 1st Platoon, in the next wave, landed a few hundred yards south of where the 3rd Platoon had come ashore. As it landed, it spontaneously split into two combat teams and ran toward the flashes of the enemy automatic weapons, firing from the hips and throwing grenades as explosions from enemy Panzerfausts burst around them. The 1st Platoon troopers knocked out several machine guns and forced the surviving enemy troops to retreat to the east. The platoon then moved north toward the south end of the town. From there it fought its way north through the town with the axis of advance up the main street. It reached the north edge of Hitdorf, where it established blocking positions on the street and set up an outpost in a factory.

The 2nd Platoon, under the command of Lieutenant James A. Kiernan, was split into two groups that fought their way eastward, where it contacted the 3rd Platoon element in the vicinity of the church. The 2nd Platoon then pushed on toward the northeastern edge of the town, where it established defensive positions. During this assault, the 2nd Platoon knocked out four machine guns and captured twelve Germans, but Lieutenant John W. Spooner, Kiernan's assistant platoon leader, was hit. Kiernan immediately went to Spooner's assistance, administering first aid as explosions from artillery and mortar fire as well as enemy tracers lit up the darkness all around him. Kiernan carried Spooner to the village church.

After ferrying the first three waves across the river, the assault boats returned to take the last wave across. Lieutenant Reneau Breard, the Company A executive officer, stepped into one of the boats with a group of company headquarters troopers. "Just before I got ready to shove off, here came a captain down with two radio operators.

"He said, 'Are you going across the river?'

"I said, 'Yeah.'

"He said, 'Can I go?'

"I said, 'Well you could, we've got a whole company over there, trying to find out something about what the hell is going on.'

"He said, 'I'm an artillery officer with the 20th Armored Division.'

"I said, 'You're welcome to go. What are you shooting?'

"He said, 'I can shoot the whole division artillery if I have to.'

"So I took him across. You had to start upriver and then paddle across; we all had to paddle. The current was strong and would take you down opposite the town. I went over in the last boat, with mostly communication equipment, wire, etc. I didn't have any extra radios though."[2]

After landing, Lieutenant Breard made his way to the company command post. "At that time Pease had the company CP in the church, which was right about in the middle of town. It faced the river, a beautiful little church. When I walked in, there was a body there. I said, 'Who is that?'

"Pease said, '[Lieutenant John] Spooner—he was killed. He was wounded, and died in the church.'

"I introduced Pease to this [artillery] captain, and the captain went off and started shooting."[3]

Lieutenant Breard then checked to make sure the three rifle platoons were moving to the correct positions to secure Hitdorf and establish an outpost line just outside of the hamlet. "One platoon went to the north, one was out in front of us east of us, and one went to the right, south of us. We had two machine gun sections from Headquarters Company.

"When daylight came we moved the CP into the town. There were two main streets. We got into one of the houses on the southwest corner. That's where we set up the CP the second time."[4]

About 8:45 a.m., a company of German infantry approached from the south. Private First Class Francis L. Eisemann, at one of the 3rd Platoon outposts, fought off this strong enemy force until the position was about to be overrun, then he and the others at the outposts withdrew to the edge of the village. The German infantry continued to advance, the 3rd Platoon letting them come to within fifty yards of their positions before cutting loose with devastating fire.

Sergeant William H. Consigny and his machine gun squad on the platoon's left flank, holding a roadblock, killed seventeen Germans in a matter of seconds. The 3rd Platoon took thirty-three prisoners. The rest of the German force were killed or wounded; no one was seen to have escaped.

Captain Pease left the company command post to check on each of the three platoons when he got the word that a German attack was underway. Meanwhile, Breard was ordered to get the prisoners evacuated to the other side of the river so Company A wouldn't have to continue to guard them. "About noon we put the prisoners in the boats and sent them back across. And then, we didn't have boats to get back. If we had any wounded, we couldn't send them back."[5]

As Company A evacuated the prisoners across the river, the Germans opened up with an extremely heavy artillery barrage on the village, cutting the field-telephone wires running from the platoons to the company command post and across the river to battalion headquarters. Thick smoke billowed over the town. The Germans used flat-trajectory 88mm fire to take out the church steeple, knocking out the artillery observation post. When enemy artillery fire wounded a trooper, one of the Company A medics, Technician Fifth Grade Francis F. Phelps, moved under the rain of shrapnel to the trooper's aid, carrying him to safety at a covered position.

About 3:30 p.m. the Germans began laying a smoke screen on the southeastern portion of the village, followed immediately afterward by an attack from the south and the east with another company of infantry, this time backed by two tanks. This attack was met by the 3rd Platoon and supporting artillery fire from the 376th Parachute Field Artillery Battalion.

Lieutenant Rex E. Hazen, a forward observer with the 376th, directed devastating fire on the enemy. The accurate and effective artillery, mortar, small-arms, and machine gun fire broke up the attack, and the Germans withdrew to regroup. After about fifteen minutes, the Germans attacked again with renewed fury. Lieutenant Hallock sent a runner back to the company command post, requesting additional Panzerfausts. This was the last communication that Captain Pease had with the 3rd Platoon. Pease sent his runner, Private First Class Charles A. Burton, to make contact with the 3rd Platoon. As Burton made his way south, he moved through heavy artillery fire and was subjected to enemy sniper fire. After he was unable to find the 3rd Platoon, three German paratroopers tried to ambush him on his way back to the company command post. Burton took them prisoner and brought them back with him.

At his outpost, Sergeant Harry N. Smith, with the attached light machine gun section with Headquarters Company, 1st Battalion, "heard tanks rumbling towards our roadblock, and the biggest thing I've ever seen on tracks roared at us. Our gun position was in a strongly built house basement of a stone house, so we felt pretty safe. At fifty yards, we opened up on its open hatch and vision slits. The bullets bounced off the sides like they were ping-pong balls. We gave a couple of sweeps at the infantry behind, and after the tank blew down our house, we shagged back towards our main line of resistance. Our section chief [Staff Sergeant John I. Kaslikowski] picked us up; we fought our way a couple of blocks towards the command post, but decided to take over a house and fortify it. How we got that far is more than I can understand. We escaped a half-dozen ambushes and killed at least twenty Jerries. By this time, we had gathered another ten of our boys, and for the next three hours we really gave it to them."[6]

Under his leadership, Sergeant William Consigny's machine gun squad on the left flank of the 3rd Platoon conducted a skillful fighting withdrawal and was one of the few groups to make it back to the company command post. Sergeant Consigny was awarded the Silver Star for his bravery under heavy mortar and small-arms fire.

When the German infantry overran Lieutenant Hazen's artillery forward observation post and knocked out his radio, he infiltrated back to the Company

A command post, where he used the company's radio to continue to direct the 376th's effective artillery fire. Lieutenant Hazen would receive the Silver Star for his courageous actions during the operation.

After the German tanks and infantry overran the 3rd Platoon, they moved through the village toward the center of town. Staff Sergeant Kaslikowski and his men withdrew from the house and joined other troopers from Company A and Headquarters Company, 1st Battalion, in a factory. There, Kaslikowski's leadership helped to throw back several enemy attacks.

From the second floor, Lieutenant Breard saw German tanks lumbering down the street toward the command post. "They had some tanks that came in right down, underneath the company CP. They were probably Panthers or type IVs."[7] The tanks were accompanied by about thirty German paratroopers. From an upper floor window, the company runner, Private First Class Charles Burton, shot and killed three of the enemy infantry, driving them away, then dropped a Gammon grenade on the tank below, immobilizing it. The rest of the German paratroopers near the tank were shot down as they sought cover. Private First Class Burton received the Silver Star for his action at Hitdorf.

Another reinforced company hit the 2nd Platoon from the east at about the same time. Staff Sergeant John H. Stubbs watched as German infantry "moved in again—big six-foot Jerries, in waves of skirmish lines as far as the eye could see. Our light machine guns killed beaucoup and pinned down the force to our front."[8]

One of Sergeant Stubbs' machine gunners, Private First Class Maurice O. Bledsoe, and his team let one platoon of German paratroopers with the 3rd Fallschirmjäger Division approach to within fifteen yards of his position, while a second platoon moved in on his flank, before opening fire. The enemy infantry returned fire with MP-44s and Panzerfausts as Bledsoe moved from position to position to direct the defense of his squad. Lieutenant Kiernan personally covered them as they pulled back in good order, despite the overwhelming number of Germans attacking them from all sides. For his extraordinary bravery, Lieutenant James A. Kiernan received the Distinguished Service Cross.

Simultaneously, as the other platoons were attacked, approximately two hundred German infantrymen attacked the 1st Platoon on the north end of town. The platoon withdrew southward under the overwhelming weight of the enemy force.

At the command post in the center of the village, Captain Pease received a couple of messages just as artillery fire cut the telephone lines. "The situation became critical at 1900. The 2nd and 3rd Platoon positions were overrun by Tiger tanks and infantry, and we lost all communications with them."[9]

Lieutenant Breard left the command post to make contact with Lieutenant Kiernan's platoon. "Pease sent me down to find the 2nd Platoon, and I couldn't find the 2nd Platoon. When I came back to the Company CP, I ran into Germans. I was lying in a flowerbed—all I had was a .45."[10]

Staff Sergeant William Bullock was dispatched to find the 3rd Platoon. "Little groups of soldiers were walking all over town. I stepped over at least fifty dead men—only two were GIs. I came to a mangled pile of torn-up Jerry corpses, and as I was stepping over them, I heard a cool voice ask, 'Is that a GI?' Two demolition men in the second story of a house had been up there since dark, letting small groups pass and dropping Gammon grenades on every large bunch of Krauts that came within their range. We pulled back to the command post."[11]

When Lieutenant Breard returned to the company command post, he learned that Kiernan had been badly wounded. "Somebody [Private First Class James McNamara] dropped a grenade behind a tank [disabling it and killing seven German paratroopers], and Kiernan must have been near it. It landed in a pile of glass; he was wounded, just perforated all over his body. We got him out, but [Lieutenant Larkin S.] Tully, we couldn't find him, and a lot of his people were captured, some were killed."[12]

At 6:00 p.m., Captain Pease received a radio message from Colonel Tucker, ordering him to hang on. Tucker told him that two platoons of Company I would cross the river that night to reinforce them.

Captain Pease ordered the 1st and 2nd Platoons to fall back to the beach, where they formed a horseshoe-shaped defensive perimeter. Staff Sergeant John Stubbs and a squad and a half of the 2nd Platoon established a defended corridor to the beach for the withdrawal. The enemy attacked Stubbs and his men with approximately two platoons of infantry firing automatic weapons and Panzerfausts, and supported by two tanks, cutting off his small force. Stubbs personally directed his troopers so effectively that they repulsed the enemy attack. As Stubbs led his men in an attack to reach the beach, his machine gun team, led by Private First Class Bledsoe, covered the withdrawal, displacing his gun only twenty to thirty yards at a time. For their actions at Hitdorf, Staff Sergeant John Stubbs later received an oak leaf for the Silver Star, and Private First Class Maurice Bledsoe was awarded the Silver Star.

That night at 1:30 a.m., the 1st and 2nd Platoons of Company I crossed the river in nine steel boats. They got less than half way when four spotlights illuminated them. Private First Class Leo Muri was in the same boat with the company commander, Captain T. Moffatt Burriss. Fortunately for Muri, the boat was at the rear of the column of boats and had not gone too far across the river. "The bottom fell out of our boat, so I went for a swim. Of course, I let my rifle and ammo drop to the bottom, as it was too much of a load for swimming. The remainder of the men who made it over had quite a scrap, but all got back safely."[13]

Landing on the eastern shore just south of the village, the two platoons left one squad to guard the boats and sent another along the railroad tracks running parallel to the road into the village to clear that, while the remainder moved along the river road. The Company I troopers ran into several machine gun nests positioned along the railroad tracks, which they flanked and eliminated, then moved on to the Company A perimeter. Captain Pease, being the senior officer, sent one squad of Company I north to set up a roadblock, another south to set up a roadblock into town from that direction, and another to the northeast to set up a roadblock along the main north-south road running through the village. With the remaining squad of Company I, Pease moved back into town to evacuate wounded they had been forced to leave in the church and who were fighting off the Germans who had surrounded them. Company A would maintain their defensive perimeter to which the Company I squads would withdraw upon evacuation of the wounded in the church.

Each one of the Company I squads engaged superior numbers of German troops in carrying out their assignments, and inflicted heavy casualties on the enemy. However, a reinforced company of German infantry supported by two tanks hit the roadblock on the road south of the village. The lone squad fought a delaying action, slowly giving ground, while being blasted by the tanks. As the squad was driven back, the squad that had earlier been assigned to clear the railroad hit the German force on the flank, forcing the enemy infantry and tanks to fall back in disorder, abandoning some of their weapons in the process. Burriss' men used Gammon grenades to knock out one of the tanks.

The squad, led by Captain Pease and guided by Private First Class Francis Eisemann, used a back alley to come up on the rear of the German infantry surrounding the church, where they opened fire, killing twenty-three and wounding seven enemy soldiers. Eisemann personally killed three of the enemy and wounded several more. "I Company men swarmed all over the big tank in our yard; opening the hatch, they killed all the Jerries inside."[14] Private First Class Eisemann received the Silver Star for his actions at Hitdorf. After destroying the enemy around the church, the squad moved inside and evacuated the wounded to the Company A perimeter on the beach.

At 0300, Staff Sergeant John Kaslikowski led a breakout from the factory through the enemy-held area to the beach, where he helped tend to the wounded. For his heroism, Staff Sergeant Kaslikowski received the Silver Star.

Runners were sent out to recall each of the Company I squads, which pulled back to the Company A perimeter. The Company I squads then attacked and cleared the area around the Company A perimeter. The 3rd Platoon of Company I manned more boats on the west side and paddled them across the river under heavy fire, touching down at a point inside the beach perimeter. They evacuated the wounded and the prisoners and took them back across, returning again and picking up the members of the two Company I platoons, then crossed again to evacuate the two Company A platoons. The withdrawal of all troopers was accomplished before daylight on the 7th of April.

Lieutenant Breard would later learn what had happened to the 3rd Platoon of Company A which had been overrun earlier. "They ganged themselves up in one building. The Germans surrounded it and took what were left of them all prisoner."[15]

One of those captured, Technician Fifth Grade Francis Phelps, a medic, was shot in the chest by one of the Germans, but the bullet was deflected by one of his ribs. Phelps fell to the ground and played dead, and the German left him for dead. That night, Phelps made his way through the village swarming with enemy troops to the beach and was evacuated.

Companies A and I killed and wounded around 350 and captured a total of eighty prisoners, who were all taken back across the river, while suffering nine killed, seventy-nine missing (mostly captured), and twenty-four wounded in action. Company A would later receive a Presidential Unit Citation for the fighting it did at Hitdorf. Captain John Pease was awarded the Silver Star for his gallant and inspirational leadership during the operation.

On the night of April 7–8, Corporal Obie Wickersham, an assistant squad leader with Company C, 307th Airborne Engineer Battalion, led a patrol across the Rhine. "Lieutenant [Michael] Sabia came down and said, 'You've got to go across and pick up some GIs left across the river.' At this time, I was getting leery of water. We had been patrolling two times before this and once had got shot up pretty badly. That was the only time I left my wallet with my medic because I knew something was going to happen. The 504 had about five men, and Sergeant [Raymond H.] Slocum, myself, and another engineer [were on the patrol].

"We went across, and just as we got to the other side of the river, just at dusk, I could see these figures. I heard click-click. 'That is not an M1.' It probably saved my life. They opened up with everything they had. There was an infantryman beside me in the front of the boat. He went out [of the boat,] and they hit him. I bailed out on the left side and got behind a pile of rocks.

"Sergeant Slocum knew it was an ambush, so he pulled the boat out. Just as they were pulling out, he asked where Wickersham was. One of the guys said, 'Oh, he was cut half in two by a machine gun.' I guess when I bailed out of the boat they thought I was hit. So they went back across the river and reported me killed in action.

"So I was lying there with just me and the Germans. I finally tried to play possum. They never came down to the water, unless they thought they had killed me. They were kind of up on a levee. I laid there about an hour. I was half-in and half-out of the water, and it was April, and it was cold. So well, I thought, 'I'm going to swim this river.'

"I took off my clothes, all but my old GI olive drab shorts and tee-shirt. I tried swimming, and I got about twenty or thirty yards out, and every limb on my body cramped. So I floated back into the bank down below about a hundred yards. I lay there all night, and the Germans were chattering away. I know a couple of them had been hit because you could hear them screaming and everything.

"The next morning, they left their dugouts on the levee and pulled up into the village and could look right down on the Rhine and see across to the 504. It was foggy, so daylight came, and they pulled out, and I saw them. Well, I crawled up and crawled into their dugout, and there was a machine gun in there they had left. They just left it there because they were going to come back. There was a shelter-half and some straw. I rolled up in that straw and that shelter-half, and I went to sleep. I was so beat up, and I had crawled on the rocks all that night.

"I woke up probably late afternoon, and I came to my senses and I thought, 'Where the hell am I? My God, they're going to be back down here at dusk. What am I going to do? They're going to really get me this time.' So I thought, 'Well—hell.' So I went barreling over that levee down toward the water, and the 504 saw me.

"I was supposed to be dead—I'm not supposed to be over there. But, they knew it was a GI because of the olive drab tee-shirt and shorts.

"So I got down to the water, and I thought, 'I'm going to go upstream a little on the bank because the current is going to carry back into the German side.' The Germans saw me, too. I would go about fifteen yards, and the Germans would lay a mortar [shell] over. I crawled back up the bank, and I found where I had left my uniform, my M1, and my dog-tags. I got up there and I thought, 'Well, I'm going to try it again.'

"I'm not a good swimmer—[but] I could swim. I got in that water, and I would dog paddle, and I would float, and I would crawl, and I would get on my back and try to rest. The Germans would shoot at me, and the 504 was shooting over my head. I never remember getting tired.

"I remember hitting the bank, and this time I thought, 'Man, I've got it made.' I jumped out. There were two 504 guys who came down to get me, and I said, 'Hey, I'm OK.' I went about ten steps, and I turned blue, and I just collapsed. Hypothermia had set in.

"They carried me over the levee, put me in a Volkswagen bus, and took me up to regimental headquarters in a building. They tried to interview me—my teeth were chattering—I couldn't even talk. By the stretcher were two big burners on each side, and they were pouring coffee down me, because they wanted to know what was over there and if there were any guys left over there. Finally, they got me thawed out, and I told them all I knew. They were going to send me back to a hospital. My knees and my hands were all chewed up from crawling over the rocks. So they said, 'You're going to the hospital.'

"I said, 'No, no,' because you knew you were airborne, and if you went back to a hospital in the rear, you don't know where you were going to end up.

I said, 'Let me go back to my outfit, and I won't do anything for a few days, and I'll be all right.'

"So they put me in a jeep with no top on it—me and the driver. I had an old overcoat on with jump boots and the same old wet underwear. They didn't phone or radio the company. We went down to where the platoon was dug in. Here, these guys, you knew them all personally. Just to see their expressions—'Wickersham, you're supposed to be dead!'

"When a guy was killed, they went through his barracks bags and took all of his stuff out and sent his personal stuff home. I looked over and I saw a guy cleaning his M1 with my toothbrush.

"Captain Spike Harris said, 'Bring him in here.' He was in a dugout there with a lamp, and he had a footlocker. The letter was lying there written to my mother saying I was killed in action. He wanted to know what all had happened, and I told him. So he dug out a bottle of Scotch, and he said, 'Wickersham, have a drink.' Now, I was nineteen at this time. I would have a beer every now and then and some gin the British had or some rum. So, I turned it up and kind of palmed it a little bit. He said, 'Damn it! I said have a drink!' Well, about an hour later, they carried me out of there, put me in a sleeping bag, and I think I slept for two days. I was sorer than hell for a long time."[16] Corporal Obie Wickersham was later awarded the Silver Star for his actions.

The following day, April 9, Captain Frank Boyd, with Headquarters Battery, 376th Parachute Field Artillery Battalion , received a telephone call from the battalion commander who "said that we had several battalions of medium and heavy artillery from Corps behind us and the division artillery commander wanted to shoot a TOT; did I have an appropriate target. TOT stands for 'time on target.' Each battery calculates the time of flight of its projectiles to the target and fires on a schedule that makes the entire concentration arrive on target at the same instant. I suggested Hitdorf, since we had a particular grudge against the Germans, and that night we demolished that town in about three minutes.

"Every artillery unit has extensive tables of figures covering all of its characteristics; sight settings for every range, based on the propelling charge; deflections per thousand yards of range for each mill change on the sight; maximum height of trajectory for each range; and time of flight (muzzle to ground burst) for every range. This last figure is used in computing TOT firing times. The biggest TOT we ever fired was into Hitdorf. We had several battalions of corps artillery (medium and heavy—155mm howitzers, 8-inch gun howitzers, 155[mm] Long Toms, and 240mm howitzers). Each computed its range to the target and looked up the time of flight. The time on target was 2100 hours. As the TOT began, we could hear the deep booms of the Long Toms and the 240s away back in our rear, then the 155 howitzers, the 105 howitzers, and finally our little 75s. The whole devastating tonnage of shells landed in the middle of Hitdorf within a period of two or three seconds. You can imagine the damage. I selected 2100 hours because we knew that was the time that they changed reliefs and sent out hot meals to the frontline troops, who usually came out of their holes to eat."[17]

ON THE NIGHT OF APRIL 12–13, PRIVATE FIRST CLASS BILL BONNING, with Company B, manned an outpost along the river at the very farthest point on the left of the division line, a half a mile away from the company command post. "We heard footsteps, like a light trot coming toward us. So we kept watching and waiting. We hollered, 'Halt.' [It was] one of our guys. We thought, 'Oh man, we're getting out of here. They're going to pull us out.'

"He came out there to tell us President Roosevelt died, so everybody would know on the line. We were a half a mile away, and they sent a guy out that night to tell us."[18]

On April 15, the U.S. 97th Infantry Division cleared the east side of the Rhine River across from the 82nd Airborne Division line, and the 82nd was relieved the following day. From April 17 to 25, the 504th and other units of the division carried out occupation duties in the Cologne area: rounding up POWs, locating and guarding weapons and ammunition caches, guarding key infrastructure such as bridges, administering and guarding displaced persons camps, and marking minefields.

On April 23, the division was alerted for possible movement northeast to the Elbe River. The division was relieved two days later, and from April 26 to 28, elements of the division moved by train and motor convoy to Lehrte and Weyhausen.

In the early hours of April 30, the 505th made an assault crossing of the Elbe River. The 2nd Battalion began arriving by train that night and crossed the bridge, moving into the bridgehead at 4:30 a.m. The battalion immediately went into an attack, jumping off at 5:00 a.m. on May 1. The other two battalions of the 504th arrived during the day and joined the attack, driving eastward nine miles against light resistance. Major John T. Berry and the 1st Battalion crossed the river last. "After crossing the Elbe, the situation was rather fluid, as we were moving rapidly away from the river. I was attempting to locate Colonel Tucker, who was out ahead with elements of either the 2nd or 3rd Battalion. I kept getting info from the troops that Colonel Tucker was up ahead. Eventually, and quite accidentally, I found myself ahead of any U.S. troops. Suddenly, we came upon a large convoy of German double-decker buses, which were stopped in the road. In front of the buses stood a group of German officers. Not realizing that they had not surrendered, we stopped a few yards away. My driver, suddenly realizing that they were not captive, grabbed his Tommy gun. Realizing this was foolish, I made him put it away. I got out of the jeep and engaged an officer in conversation. It seems they were staff officers from Berlin trying to make their way to Hamburg. I advised them they could not reach

Routes of the 82nd Airborne Division to Cologne and the Elbe River Areas

Kiel

Lübeck • Wismar •

Hamburg •

Wilhelmshaven

Emden • Lünburg •

Groningen • Oldenburg • Bremen • Weyhausan

Emmen • Celle

Amsterdam • Lehrte

NETHERLANDS Minden • Hannover

The Hague • Utrecht Brunswick Magdeburg

Rotterdam •

Münster

G E R M A N Y

Tilburg •

Essen • Dortmund

Antwerp • Kassel •

Ghent • Dusseldorf Erfurt •

Brussels • Cologne

BELGIUM Aachen Modrath Marburg •

Liege • Stolberg • Bonn

Charleroi • Fulda •

Koblenz •

Weisbaden • Frankfurt

LUX. Mainz • Darmstadt • Würzburg

Charleville Trier Manheim •

Laon • Sissonne • Luxembourg Nürnberg •

Ansbach •

Reims •

Saarbruken

Suippes • Verdun • **C**

Chalons-sur-Marne Metz **E**

Motor route ----▶

Rail route ········▶

0 100 Miles

Hamburg. Their only alternative seemed to be to surrender to us or get caught by the Russians. They wanted to do neither, so I got into the jeep and started to leave. They then changed their minds. I brought them back and left them just outside of our front lines. The amazing part of that little incident was the manner in which they parked the buses—hub-to-hub, with bumpers exactly lined up. If any bus was two or three inches out of line, they made the driver being it exactly into line."[19]

Even as the war in Europe reached its final days, death stalked the troopers, seemingly everywhere. That afternoon of May 1, Technician Fifth Grade Jack Bommer, a wireman with regimental headquarters company, was with his best friend, T/4 Rockwell R. "Rocky" Easton. "He and I were standing in a ditch repairing a line to regiment. We were commenting on the number of mines our equipment were setting off, when about twenty-five feet behind our equipment, a tank [struck a mine] and overturned and burned fiercely. Rocky and I heard the cries of the tank crew and went immediately to help get them out. We pulled three GIs from the tank, and the medics took over. Rocky and I returned to our wire and were taping up the splice, standing facing each other, when a shell inside the burning tank exploded and a fragment of the shell casing ripped through my left sleeve and into Rocky's chest. He leaped about three feet up and did a complete flip, landing on his back. Blood was spurting from his chest no less than six inches. I rushed to him and jammed my hand into the wound and seemed to shut off the gushing of the blood. I sat with Rocky's head in my lap for a full ten minutes, while he talked to me. I cried. He cried. He smiled. I smiled. Many of the things he said were of events we had both participated in—our women in Naples, our women in England, the 'drunks' in Naples, the 'parties' in England. Then, he proceeded to tell me what I should take from his musette bag and keep, and with that, Rocky drew his last breath. The war was over for Rocky."[20]

Also that day, the 2nd Platoon, Company C, 307th Airborne Engineer Battalion, led by Lieutenant John Holabird, was assigned to find and remove mines along a road, after interrogation of a German prisoner revealed the existence of the mines. "We found some wires leading to the center of the road from the ditch alongside. Word came down from someone more experienced that these were sea mines used against naval warships and they could be set electrically so they would explode at the fourth or fifth or sixth or whatever, metal object passing by. The controls seemed to be in the ditch.

"Part of my platoon had their shovels out, digging in a likely spot at the center of the road. When I got within sight and hearing range as I ran toward them, I yelled to 'stop—wait for me!' I was too late—evidently the shoveling was enough to detonate the mine. Two or three of the squad [Technician Fifth Grade Max E. Albert and Private First Class William R. Prescott] just disappeared; one other [Private First Class Harold G. Herbert] blown about twenty yards away by the blast; two others, further away, were spared. It was a terrible thing to have happened [six] days before the end of the war."[21]

The platoon medic, Technician Fifth Grade Richard E. Shumaker, had been talking with Albert and Prescott, and had walked down the road about a hundred feet away when the explosion occurred. "I was thrown about twenty feet through the air and landed hard on the ground. I looked back and saw what seemed to be a man spinning through the air about a hundred feet up. Then, big chunks of macadam and rocks began falling all around me from the sky. Some of the rocks were six or eight inches in diameter. They were half buried by the impact. One big chunk of macadam, about three feet square, slammed into the ground six feet from me. The impact shook the ground. I suddenly became fearful for my life. I pulled my arms and legs close, to make as small a target from the sky as possible. I thought that my helmet would protect my head from the small, falling rocks. For a few seconds, it rained rocks and chunks of macadam. Then clouds of sand and dirt fell, and slowly drifted away."[22]

Shumaker jumped to his feet and ran back toward the site of the explosion. "Where they had been standing a few seconds before, there was a large hole about thirty feet across. They had vanished from the face of the earth.

"About fifty feet beyond the crater, a man [Private First Class Harold Herbert] lay up against a fence post. Apparently, he had been approaching Bill [Prescott]'s mine when it exploded. He was writhing in pain. His leg was bent where there was no joint. I surmised that the blast had thrown him against the fence post. The impact had broken his leg when he struck the fence post. There was a small dead tree nearby. I broke it up to make two splints for his leg.

"A jeep came racing down the road. It was our company truck driver. He wanted to know what had happened. I explained and asked him to take the injured man, Harold Herbert, to the hospital, as his legs looked badly broken. I pulled out of my kit a tube of morphine and gave him a shot. I told him, 'There, that will ease the pain a little.'

"I then walked to the farmhouse to tell the captain of our accident. He was saddened to hear of the loss of two good men.

"The next day, the entire platoon went out to search for the two missing men. 'Joe' [Technician Fifth Grade Max Albert] was found about two hundred feet from the crater. The top of his head above the eyes had been ripped off by the blast. We searched for Bill [Prescott] for several hours with only a little success.

"One man found a big toe. Another man found his wallet. Another found one of his fingers. I found a piece of his intestine hanging on the barbed wire fence. I placed all of these parts in a cigar box and carried it back to the farmhouse to give to the captain. Our captain called Graves Registration to arrange for burial."[23]

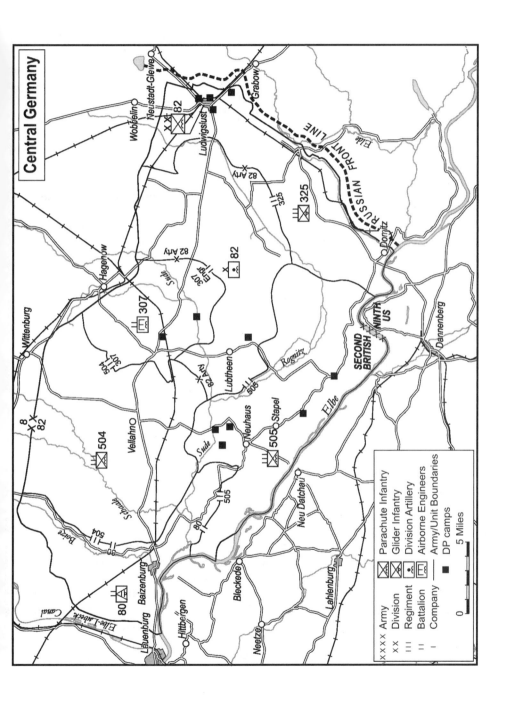

Central Germany

Private First Class Harold Herbert's knees, ankle, and back were seriously injured. He was unconscious for three days and "woke up in a field hospital. The next thing I knew after I came to, they put me on a plane and flew me to England. They tried to set my ankle nine different times in England. It needed an operation instead of just setting the bone. They would put the cast on, and it would swell up. They would have to relieve the cast, and they would have to do again. I got back in the States in June. I spent the next eighteen months in the hospital."[24]

AT 5:00 A.M. ON MAY 2, THE 504TH PUSHED RAPIDLY EAST on the right flank of the 325th against light opposition, reaching their objective by 8:15 a.m. Lieutenant James R. Allmand and his Company G platoon moved out along with two light tanks. "We started out sitting on top of the two tanks—half with me and the other half with Technical Sergeant Thomas J. Patterson from Randolph, New York. All morning we pushed on as rapidly as possible, taking very little precautions; seeing every now and then loose Germans hightailing it for the woods to stay clear of us. We were taking potshots with rifles at them on the move, as we were in an extreme hurry. I kept the tanks on a route that would give them the most concealment, staying off the main roads. By the time I moved upon a main road to Eldena, the countryside was more open and the highway was tree-lined."[25]

Later that afternoon, General Gavin met with the commander of the German 21st Army Group at the town of Ludwigslust, where the surrender of 144,000 troops was accepted. That day and the next, a flood of prisoners was disarmed and sent westward through the division's lines for processing. Displaced persons and German civilians also were moving west, frantic to escape the Red Army.

On May 3, the first contact took place with the Red Army, which triggered many impromptu celebrations among the troopers and Soviet troops. Two days later, a horrific discovery was made four miles north of Ludwigslust—the Wöbbelin concentration camp. The Germans running the camp had pulled out in a hurry, leaving piles of dead inmates. The 504th's assistant adjutant, Lieutenant Charles L. Wroten, visited the camp after it was found and wrote about the sights one would see upon visiting Wöbbelin. "Inconspicuously situated one hundred yards off the highway, the camp was built by slave laborers less than a year earlier to 'accommodate' American PWs, though none were found there. The inmates were Russian (sixty percent), French, Spanish, Belgian, Polish, Dutch, and recalcitrant Germans. The high barbed wire fence enclosed perhaps ten acres of sandy soil with a dozen one-story red brick buildings consisting of nothing more than four walls and a roof. The prisoners built triple-deck bunks of pine saplings or slept on the dirt floor. Their mattresses were of saplings and barbed wire."[26]

Corporal Clayton W. Blankenship, with Battery B, 376th, was one of the troopers who visited the camp. "I was shocked at what I saw. Dead people were piled head and tails on top of each other. Many were still dying. There were dead in trenches. It looked like they were just thrown in head and tail. It was an awful sight. Women were housed in a place where the bunks were three-four high. Many were too sick to move and were messing on the ones below. They were making German flags. One lady made me a large German flag while I was there, and I brought it home. I kept it for years. While I was there, the Red Cross was escorting a high-ranking German general and putting questions to him. The American authorities made them dig the bodies out of the trenches and had them turn out and walk by to see the bodies. The bodies were given a decent burial."[27]

Lieutenant Wroten visited the camp as the inmates' bodies were being removed for burial. "Several hundred yards from this enclosure, in communal graves, rectangular and perhaps eight feet deep, if you can stand the stench, you can see where German civilians are being compelled to exhume the naked skeletons of the dead. The death rate was sixty-five to one hundred daily, mostly from starvation, some from failure to survive 'corrective treatment.' These bodies, almost void of flesh, are sometimes gashed and sliced and battered and broken into hardly recognizable human pulp.

"Allied Military Government compels every local German to walk through the building, a typical one, in which we now stand. You will do well to light a cigarette. It deadens the sense of smell. And one precaution: If, as you look at the piles of mangled corpses, one should seem to slightly breathe or feebly move, do not be surprised.

"Your eyes gradually adjust to the gloom which pervades this room."[28]

In the early hours of May 7, at SHAEF Headquarters in Rheims, France, German General Alfred Jodl, representing Hitler's successor, Admiral Karl Dönitz, signed the documents of unconditional surrender of all German forces to the Allied nations. General Eisenhower sent the following telegram to the Combined Allied Chiefs of Staffs: "The mission of this Allied Force was fulfilled at 0241 hours, local time, May 7, 1945. Eisenhower"

That same day, a funeral service was held at Ludwigslust for two hundred of the camp inmates. German civilians of the town were required to provide the labor of handling the bodies and digging the graves. The entire adult population of the town was required to attend the funeral ceremony, conducted by the division's chaplains.

The surrender of all German forces took effect at 11:01 a.m. on May 8, 1945. Corporal Joe Watts, with Fox Company, reacted with "disbelief. It couldn't just end like that. No more night patrols, no more fear."[29]

While the Allied victory in Europe was something to celebrate, General Gavin put that victory in the proper perspective. "We had come to the end of the war in Europe. It had been costly. More than sixty thousand men had passed through the ranks of the 82nd Airborne Division alone. We had left in our wake thousands of white crosses from Africa to Berlin. And when it came to an end, there was not a man in the ranks of the 82nd Airborne Division who did not believe that it was a war that had to be fought."[30]

Staff Sergeant Ross Carter, who had served the 504 as a member of Company C, was one of the very lucky men who had served in a rifle company from North Africa to Germany. "My friends call me a refugee from the law of averages. My regiment still exists as a name, but the regiment in which I trained, fought, and almost died, now lies buried in obscure army cemeteries in ten countries."[31]

Captain Frank Boyd, with Headquarters Battery, 376th Parachute Field Artillery Battalion, also felt the loss of his comrades very deeply. "In Picher, just two days after the war ended, the 376th held a memorial service for all of our men who had been killed; we had thirty-five men killed in Sicily, sixteen in Italy, fourteen in Holland, and four in Belgium. Thirty of the thirty-five killed in Sicily were from C Battery, killed by nervous gunners of the U.S. Navy as their planes flew over the invasion fleet."[32]

The 504th performed occupation duties over the next three weeks, primarily guarding German prisoners. On June 1, the division was relieved and moved by rail, primarily in the ubiquitous 40 & 8 boxcars, and by organic transport to Camp Chicago, near Laon, France, arriving June 5th. Private First Class Ed Bayley had caught up with Company A only a few weeks earlier, after being released from the hospital, where he had been treated for a wound during the attack on the Siegfried Line. "We climbed aboard 40 & 8 freight cars and began a several-day journey. It was a long and slow trip, as some of the destroyed tracks meant that we had to detour, or we would go to a siding and wait for other trains to pass. Whenever we knew that we were on a several-hour stop, some of the troopers would explore the area. One morning we came to a provisions train scheduled for another airborne outfit. This was considered fair game by the more ambitious troopers. When a guard challenged them and threatened to shoot, some of troopers said if he as much as tried to shoot, they would twist the gun barrel around his neck. The guard took off as if running for his life. The result was that many of our cars now had big wooden cases of York Peppermint Patties. Most of us really enjoyed these, as we had not had anything like this for months. We finally arrived back in the Laon barracks [on June 5] and after a few days' rest, did a bit of training, got new Eisenhower dress jackets, polished our boots, and went to town and to other cities on passes.

"During this short stay in Laon, several of the veteran troopers who had accumulated enough points were detached and sent back to the U.S.A. After a few days, we boarded trains again and headed for some place only known by the officers. We enlisted personnel were only along for the ride. The officers were riding in regular passenger coaches. We were in freight cars as usual, on the hard wooden floors, with no padding. A short while out of Laon the train stopped in a large rail yard.

"Our usual scroungers went to work. The first thing they found was rail cars [containing] hay and straw. This they stole, and brought back to several of the freight cars. We had about a twenty-four-inch-deep hay base in our car after that. Later, some of the officers came to the hay-padded freight cars so they could rest and sleep more comfortably than in the coaches. The hay made the cars fairly comfortable.

"The next thing they went looking for was ration cars. They found some. They brought back wooden cases of something which we quickly stashed under the straw and hay. About that time, a very irate lieutenant colonel or major from some other outfit, probably in charge of the provision train, started raving and ranting to the airborne officers and demanding that all stolen stuff be immediately returned. Some was—but not ours.

"Our officer pretended to search our cars, but did not bother to comb through the hay. After we got under way again, we opened the wooden cases. Mostly, we had gallon cans of sliced peaches. They sure tasted good. In a few hours, we paid the penalty—the runs. This meant hanging out the door of the car and trying to go without falling out, or waiting for a stop and relieving ourselves, hopefully before the train started again. I don't remember that we lost anyone, but more than one trooper had to sprint to catch the train before it got away.

"After an all-night ride, we arrived in the small town of Rambervillers, France, about twenty miles or so southeast of Nancy, in the Vosges Mountains. We spent one of two nights in a large French army barracks. We did some drill and physical exercises and got some rest. Some of the soldiers went into town and fraternized to their regret with some of the women and caught a disease or two which required antibiotic treatment.

"A few days later, many of us were trucked a few miles out of town to a big, empty field and told to erect tents for an encampment. This included squad tents that slept about six men and huge tents for the mess hall. We got these up before dark and had wood and canvas cots delivered.

"We received crowd- and riot-control drill, along with physical training and double time route marches to keep us in condition. While in this tent city, we gathered some new members who had been transferred over from the 13th and 17th Airborne, some of the outfits to which 82nd veterans were assigned for their trip back to the U.S.A.

"One day we were trucked to Epinal, a large French town about twenty miles or so distant, paraded, and had a mass formation so General Gavin could speak to the division. He told us what a great history the division had written in its relatively short life of about three years and that sixty thousand men had been involved in its ranks. This meant the equivalent of about five airborne divisions had served in one unit in its three years' existence. We were informed that our next assignment was to be occupation troops in Berlin. This was a relief, as we expected that he was going to tell us we were headed for the Pacific war.

"We spent several more days outside of Rambervillers. Along about the end of July, we boarded the train for Berlin. Some of the officers abandoned their passenger coaches for the increased comfort of the freight cars, where they could spread out in their sleeping rolls and rest in comfort, rather than riding upright in the coach passenger seats.

"I remember stopping in Magdeburg, which had been captured by the Americans, but was now in Russian hands. At this stop, our scroungers remained close to the train, because they were not sure what the Russians might do. As we started to leave Magdeburg, the coupling broke loose, so we stayed another hour or two while it was repaired.

"After we left Magdeburg, we went past vast fields of abandoned American tanks and trucks, for which there was no more use. We saw long trains of Russian soldiers headed back home. They had ripped plumbing such as toilets out of houses and were taking it back with them. We wondered if they had any running water back home and if they would know how to install the stuff anyway. Long trains of open-top cars of potatoes were seen carrying this staple for the local populations. We found when we got to Berlin and were invited into peoples' homes that some had found innovative ways to prepare potatoes to give a good variety of tastes. They had to—it was all they had."[33]

Upon arriving in Berlin, Bayley found the city in ruins. "The entire city of Berlin was a horrible mess—very few buildings escaping at least some bombing damage. Large groups of women were employed in many streets gathering bricks and cleaning them off for recycling for reconstruction. At the time of our service in Berlin, many dead were still buried in the rubble and lying in the flooded subway stations where they had drowned. Some parts of the city were not very pleasant to be in.

"We had to guard public utility installations to prevent them from being pilfered by the Russians. This was one of the duties our platoon had for several days. The Russians would steal almost anything they could, whether they had a real use for it or not.

"Part of our first day in Berlin was taken up by orientation—the things to do and not to do. One must not have anything but official business or duty contacts with a German. We were each issued three condoms and an emergency prophylactic kit. The condoms were to be used if one fraternized, and the kit was to be used if one did not use a condom. If a military policeman or an officer stopped a soldier and one of the three condoms or the prophylactic kit was missing or apparently used, this was a criminal offense subject to court-martial and possible confinement. Obviously, with thousands of soldiers and hundreds of thousands of lonesome girls and women not having had any sexual contact for a long time or ever, this was a no-win situation. There was no way that fraternization and sexual activity could be prevented. The results were predictable for both officers and enlisted personnel—venereal disease for some, pregnancies for others, and lots of fun and amusement, and in some cases, eventual marriage for others.

"We took over blocks of multi-story apartment houses for our Berlin residence. I have no idea where the families went. We took over the apartments and the furniture and fittings within them. The bombing damage wasn't so heavy in our area. We had some guard and light training duty, but most of the time we were free to roam about as we wished.

"For the most part, Berlin duty was very pleasant. We were mostly on our own, except for morning roll call, when in barracks. If there were no specific duties for that day, we were essentially free to do what we pleased. If we were assigned to specific guard duties within the city, we usually had a squad leader with us. Our company contacts were with the food trucks which visited three times per day. When not on guard shifts, we were on our own, so most of us were able to see much of Berlin night and day.

"Families would invite us to their homes for visits and dining with them. This is when we found that they had ways of making ordinary potatoes taste really good. We usually tried to bring them a gift of some sort, maybe cigarettes, candy bars, wines, et cetera.

"We rode on the trolley cars into the Russian zone. The people in that zone seemed to be more stressed than those in our zone. It seemed that we saw more displaced persons in their striped dress clothing in the Russian zone than in ours. In those early days of occupation, there was open, unrestricted transport and communication for civilians among all of the military occupation zones.

"My platoon's first assignment was guard duty at a bombed office building on Wilhelmstrasse, down the road from the Tiergarten. We took over from a U.S. armored division, which had been assigned occupation duty until the 82nd arrived. The purpose of the guard was security of a big supply of wines and liqueurs in the cellar. Some military officers had found this cache, and it was used for the enjoyment of military government officers. Each day, two or three German laborers came and grubbed out the liquor from among the rocks and concrete debris. A military government vehicle would come by to pick up the liquor each day after verifying that some was available. We soldiers thought that it was a real waste for senior officers to have this great liquor when we and our friends could enjoy it, so we gradually produced decreasing amounts for the military government, keeping most of it for ourselves and friends.

"A subway rail tunnel and station near [the office building we were guarding] had been flooded. Thousands of people had to walk by our post every day during working hours. This was a great way to meet girls. We lived in an apartment next to the office building.

"Some of the older people would comment that Hitler was going to return and that we would be thrown out of Germany. They were completely convinced that this would happen. They refused to believe that Hitler was dead.

"We made friends with several families living in the small apartment complex built around a small courtyard. We would give them cigarettes and candy now and then. There were several small children living there. After a while, they began congregating near the chow truck when our hot food was delivered. There was always more food than we needed, so one day we started feeding the kids. They had never had food like this, so they developed real hurting stomachs. When their systems changed to suit this new food, they ate happily with us.

"Many of the Germans had had no supply of tobacco for a long time. They were crazy for cigarettes. We could buy them for fifty cents per ten-pack carton at the army post exchange. We sold them to the Germans for two hundred dollars per carton of regulars and three hundred dollars for king-size such as Pall Mall.

"Chocolate bars were also in big demand. We could sell a single Hershey's bar for at least twenty-five dollars. Mickey Mouse watches were especially in big demand. The Germans would pay large amounts of money for these. Fine Leica cameras were available for trades of cigarettes and candy, and many soldiers took advantage of this.

"Due to the large amounts of German occupation money being acquired by the more adventurous in the black-market trade and the conversion of that into U.S. currency being shipped back to the U.S.A., orders were issued that no more than the soldier's pay plus ten percent could be converted to U.S. currency. The more resourceful found ways of getting around this.

"Another interesting assignment was supervision of a central railroad station, where long lines of displaced people were trying to board trains to take them to their homes, assuming they would find them standing when they got there. Trains were going to both West German and Russian-dominated destinations. The trains were mostly boarded during daylight hours. Some people stood in long lines all night long for a place, hopefully on a next-day train. The crowd could get a bit unruly at times, so we would fire a rifle into the air to make a loud noise, which always quieted them.

"We lived in a small hotel near the station during this session. Some of the troopers would take girls back to the hotel for the night on the promise that the girls would go to the head of the line the next day. This promise was always kept. This gave a willing girl a clean, comfortable place to sleep after she did what came naturally.

"One night we received a complaint that a group of Russian soldiers was bothering the local burgomeister. We said that we couldn't do anything about that, as it was not on our beat. Later that night, we heard strange noises coming from one of the bombed-out storefronts. Since we did not have good lights, we decided to wait until the periodic armored car patrol came around, as they had good lights and a .50-caliber machine gun. They arrived, and we told them of our problem. Nobody answered their challenge, so they lined up the jeep and prepared to fire the machine gun. I asked them to turn on the lights, as maybe there were some displaced civilians or former German war prisoners there, taking shelter. When the headlights were turned on, there were about twenty Russian soldiers sleeping there."[34]

Each regiment of the division formed an honor guard company to perform ceremonial duties during its occupational duty in Berlin. Each trooper selected for the 504th honor guard was at least six feet tall and possessed the best characteristics of military bearing. The 504th honor guard company was commanded by Captain Howard A. Stephens, with Headquarters and Headquarters Company. Each battalion supplied a platoon of thirty-two men, a platoon sergeant, and a platoon leader. Lieutenant Jack Wolf, with Headquarters Company, 1st Battalion, commanded the 1st Battalion platoon. Lieutenant William J. Hardy, with Headquarters Company, 2nd Battalion, was the platoon leader of the 2nd Battalion platoon. Lieutenant Nathan J. Thomas, with Company G, led the 3rd Battalion platoon.

In mid-November, the 82nd Airborne Division was notified that it was to return to the United States to march up Fifth Avenue in New York City in a great victory parade in January 1945. It was relieved of occupation duty in Berlin on November 19, and moved by train to Camp Chicago, near Rheims. There, the division practiced almost full time for the upcoming parade, holding as many as three parades daily. The division moved to Camp Lucky Strike, near Le Havre, where it was ferried to England. Billeted in British Army barracks, the division celebrated its third Christmas overseas. A few days later, it was moved to Southampton, where it boarded the converted passenger liner the *Queen Mary*. On December 29, the 504th and the rest of the division left England for the United States.

On January 3, troopers stood silently on the deck of the ship as it passed the Statue of Liberty. Tugboats pulled it up the East River, where it docked. Later that day, the division disembarked and was transported by train to nearby Camp Shanks in the Hudson Valley. The division conducted daily practice over the next week and, on the morning of January 12, boarded trains for New York City.

Later that day, with newsreel cameras rolling and throngs of people watching, the 504th Regimental Combat Team, as part of the 82nd Airborne Division, marched proudly up Fifth Avenue in the New York City Victory Parade. George Leoleis, one of the high-point men who had returned to the United States earlier, came to watch the parade with his new wife. "Diana and I worked our way to the front so we could see better. By this time the people were ten deep on both sides of the street; you could hardly move. It was estimated that about two million people watched the biggest parade in history. The bands played, confetti flying from open buildings on both sides of the street. It was a sight to behold. Everyone was screaming, everyone was clapping, people had small children on their backs, no one wanted to miss this parade. It made everyone proud to be an American. People were talking about the 82nd Airborne Division and their accomplishments. The papers for days were full of pictures and stories about the history of the 82nd. One woman's remark that stands out in my mind was when she spoke to someone next to her, 'How wonderful and brave these men were, the suffering they must have gone through.' This was about the same sentiments being expressed all along the parade route. I looked at her and smiled, and she took it as an agreement to what she had just said.

" 'Lady, if you knew. If you only knew.' Diana took my hand and squeezed it, as if she knew what I was thinking and feeling right then. We looked at each other, and my thoughts went back to April 29, 1943, when we left the harbor of New York City and how everyone was looking at the Statue of Liberty, and a lot of us wondered how many of us were coming back and if we would ever see her again. I thought of when we landed in Casablanca, Africa, of the days we spent getting ready to invade Sicily, the jump there, and the boys we left behind, and our navy shooting down [twenty-three] planes of our own men, who died not by the enemy, but their own men. I thought of the landings at Salerno and the boys we left there. I thought of the assault to take Naples and the men we lost there. I thought of the drive up beyond Naples to Venafro and the surrounding towns and mountains and that we pushed so far that we were twenty-two miles ahead of everyone, and they pleaded with us to stop because the Fifth Army and the British Eighth Army couldn't keep up with us. Just one regiment, the 504, all alone up there, not even General Patton had spearheaded that far ahead of support. I thought of the men we left behind there. I thought of the landings at Anzio, and that disaster and of the good men we left behind there.

"I thought of the men we left behind in France, in Belgium, in Holland, and the men we left in Germany. I thought of all these men, and even though I didn't remember their names, I remembered their faces. I thought of the few who made it back and wondered where they were at the moment."[35]

Epilogue

"No Braver, More Loyal, Or Better Fighting Men Ever Lived"

*T*he combat record of the 504th Regimental Combat Team was incredible. It had jumped into Sicily, spearheading the invasion. It had been the first to jump at Salerno, and had stabilized and saved the beachhead there. Company H was awarded the first of four Presidential Unit Citations the regiment would be awarded for its defense of the Chiunzi Pass area as part of the Ranger Force. The 504th RCT went on to fight in the Italian mountains, then came ashore at Anzio, where the 3rd Battalion stopped the breakthrough by the Hermann Göring Panzer Division and was awarded another Presidential Unit Citation. It had jumped in Holland and captured the Grave bridge and the bridge over the Maas-Waal Canal. Three days later, it made the assault crossing of the Waal River to capture the north ends of the two huge bridges at Nijmegen, in one of the greatest feat of arms of the war. It had fought side-by-side with the 505th in Belgium, stopping the three best-equipped and most powerful SS Panzer divisions in the entire German Army. Together with the 325th, it had cracked the Siegfried Line, then defended the western side of the Rhine River, and pushed east of the Elbe River to save Denmark from Russian domination.

Darrell Harris had served with the regimental demolitions platoon from Fort Bragg through the end of the war. "In the beginning, we were so young and full of life that it never occurred to us that we wouldn't live forever. But when we began to see our comrades die, we were forced to accept our own mortality and to reflect on the value of life. This, in turn, could raise questions about taking of another human's life.

"There are many ways of killing people during a war. A B-17 pilot, or even an artillery gunner, never sees his victims. To an infantryman, killing is more up front and personal. In the heat of battle, there is no time for questions, and when you are being shelled and bombed, you are not inclined to contemplate these matters. Later, in retrospect, you can justify, or at least rationalize, the taking of life by remembering such things as the trooper whose finger was cut off for his ring—'Maybe one of the bastards who did that was the one I killed.'

"Then you think about your friends and comrades who were killed, and you wonder what kind of lives they would have had if they had not died so young. It seems the first ones to go were somehow easier to take than the ones who went later. That is, the ones who fell in Sicily did not hurt as much as those who made their last stand at the Battle of the Bulge. I suppose it was because you had been friends longer and been through more together with the later ones. They came from the breadth of our country; Glenn Faust from Montana, Joe Nino from Texas, Kenneth Henderson from North Carolina. Why were some chosen to die while others were spared?"[1]

All of the returning officers and men had at one time or another asked themselves this question: Were the terrible costs in lives, crippling wounds, mental trauma, frostbite, trench foot, and malaria worth it? Walter E. Hughes, who had served in Company I, thought about his experiences this way: "I had seen many of my fellow troopers die right next to me. I had seen many of them grievously wounded, with legs split open and huge chunks of flesh torn from their torsos. It was a horrible feeling, and we seemed to justify it by the so many German dead everywhere you looked. No eighteen year old should have to experience that kind of carnage. It would take the death camp at Wobbelin to convince me it was all worth it. Up to that time the enemy was soldiers from another country, Germany. With Wöbbelin, it became the whole German race. How could people be led so that they could destroy generations of people just because they were of a different religion or race? To this day, I have never forgotten it."[2]

Ross Carter spoke for all 504th RCT combat veterans when he described the dead comrades and friends he had left behind in those cemeteries; "tough-fibered, hard-living, and reckless; but no braver, more loyal, or better fighting men ever lived."[3]

MOST OF THE VETERANS OF THE 504TH REGIMENTAL COMBAT TEAM were discharged after being wounded, sent home on points, or after the Victory Parade. A few stayed with the division, but most moved to the next stage of their lives, that of being civilians. A good number took advantage of the greatest investment that the federal government ever made, the GI Bill, which gave them the opportunity to attend college. As a result, many enlisted men became successful businessmen, physicians, teachers, attorneys, and scientists. One common theme is, they approached their civilian lives like they did the army. If they were going to do something, they wanted to be the best. Men courageous enough to jump out of an airplane at night, under fire, in enemy territory weren't frightened by the challenges of starting a new business or getting an advanced degree.

Many of the men were severely wounded during the war. Walter S. Van-Poyck had lost a leg, with the other badly injured, in Holland, but returned to his job at Eastern Airlines, where he had a successful career. Despite being terribly injured and given a 100 percent disability by the Veterans Administration, Harold Herbert worked for the U.S. Postal Service until 1972, when he had to retire because his fused spine could no longer take the strain.

Some stayed in the army and made it a career, becoming the backbone of the army, supplying key officers and senior non-commissioned officers during the Korean and Vietnam Wars. Frank L. Dietrich, a platoon sergeant with Company C, rose to the rank of colonel and retired with three Combat Infantryman Badges in three wars as well as every medal awarded for valor except the Congressional Medal of Honor.

Almost to a man, they felt that as a member of the 504th RCT, they experienced things they never would have had the opportunity to do, otherwise. Clayton Blankenship, who had served with D Battery, 376th, "saw and learned more the next four years than I would have ever dreamed. I had never been very far from Kentucky, where I was born, or West Virginia, where I had spent most of my life. The following four years I was to be in Africa, Sicily, Italy, England, France, Holland, Belgium, Luxemburg and Germany. All had many things I enjoyed seeing, but the war was always before us. Had it not been for the war, it would have been experiences and education to cherish forever."[4]

The opportunity to serve his country as a member of the 504th Parachute Infantry had transformed Joe Watts. "Before the war, all I knew was what I experienced and read. Radio was not that informative then. At CMTC [Citizens Military Training Camp] in '39, I learned something about people from other walks of life. In the army, I learned something about people from other parts of the country and world. World War II was an extreme mind and body expansion for me. I literally grew up in the army of '41–45. From a pseudo-sophisticated urban high school kid of 5'8", 145 pounds to a well-traveled and knowledgeable young man of 6', 185 pounds."[5]

Milton Knight had served with the regiment from its formation to the end of the war. "Every man in our outfit was a hero, because he may not have received the highest decorations—he may not have received any decorations at all—but in our outfit our commanding officer, Colonel Tucker, didn't believe in passing out medals by the basketful. His philosophy was that that was our job; we had been trained for it, we were being paid for it, and that's what we were supposed to do."[6]

Joe Watts believed that the magnificent performance of the 504th RCT during World War II was the result of all the necessary ingredients: leadership at all levels, self-discipline, and camaraderie that lingers to this day. "We had our share of Silver Stars, but to read these citations, one believes they could have been upgraded once or twice. 'Heroic' in other infantry units was business as usual in the 504! Every man in the unit knew what the mission was and how it was to be accomplished. That is what the World War II Airborne soldier was all about: initiative, determination, courage. 'Strike and Hold' was our regimental motto; and we did, by regiment, battalion, company, platoon, squad, or individual."[7]

Notes

Introduction

1. Captain Edward F. Shaifer, "The Operations of Company B, 504th Parachute Infantry (82nd Airborne Division) in Piercing the Siegfried Line, near Losheimergraben, Germany, 2–4 February 1945" (Rhineland Campaign) Personal Experience of a Platoon Leader, courtesy of the Donovan Research Library, Fort Benning, Georgia, p. 11.
2. James M. Gavin, *On To Berlin*, Viking Press, 1978, p. 67.
3. Headquarters, Third Infantry Division, Office of the Assistant Chief of Staff, G-2, and Special Service, "The Parachutists," March 22, 1944.
4. Lieutenant William D. Mandle and Private First Class David H. Whittier, comps., *The Devils In Baggy Pants, Combat Record of the 504th Parachute Infantry Regiment April 1943–July 1945*, Draeger Frères, Paris, 1945.

Chapter 1: "I'm Going To Be A Paratrooper"

1. Ross S. Carter, *Those Devils In Baggy Pants*, Buccaneer Books, 1976, Preface.
2. Major Reuben H. Tucker, as quoted in "Prop Blast," February 1943, reprinted in *Prop Blast: Chronicle of the 504th Parachute Infantry Regiment*, Steven J. Mrozek, compiler and editor, 82nd Airborne Division Historical Society, 1986.
3. Louis E. Orvin, Jr., interview with author.
4. Joseph C. Watts, Jr., response to "WWII Army Service Experiences Questionnaire," U.S. Army Military History Institute, p. 2.
5. Ibid., p. 4.
6. Ibid., pp. 4–5.
7. Robert W. Zost, as quoted in Jan Bos, *Circle and the Fields of Little America*, Voices of the Veterans, A Battery, courtesy of Jan Bos.
8. Lawrence H. Dunlop, written account, courtesy of Alex Kicovic.
9. Milton V. Knight, response to questionnaire by Alex Kicovic, courtesy of Alex Kicovic.
10. Thomas J. McCarthy, as quoted in *In Their Own Words, WWII: The European Theater*, audio book, Topics Entertainment, Cassette 1, Side A.
11. Reneau Breard, interview with author.
12. Wesley Pass, as quoted in Bos, *Circle and the Fields of Little America*, Voices of the Veterans, Headquarters Battery.
13. Darrell G. Harris, *Casablanca to VE Day*, Dorrance Publishing, 1995, p. 1.

14. Lawrence Warthman, as quoted in Bos, *Circle and the Fields of Little America*, Voices of the Veterans, B Battery.
15. Orvin, interview.
16. Breard, interview.
17. Warthman, quoted in Bos, *Circle and the Fields of Little America*.
18. Le Vangia, written account.
19. Warthman, quoted in Bos, *Circle and the Fields of Little America*.
20. Ibid.
21. Breard, interview.
22. Le Vangia, written account.
23. Leo M. Hart, interview with the author.
24. Ibid.
25. Breard, interview.
26. Knight, questionnaire.
27. Major Reuben H. Tucker, as quoted in "Prop Blast," September 1, 1942, reprinted in *Prop Blast*, Mrozek, compiler and editor.
28. Knight, questionnaire.
29. Ibid.
30. Ross Pippin, "A Paratrooper's Story: My World War II Experiences as told to Gary Shaffer," courtesy of Ross Pippin and Gary Shaffer, p. 3.
31. Orvin, interview.
32. Ibid.
33. Frank D. Boyd, as quoted in Bos, *Circle and the Fields of Little America*, Voices of the Veterans, Headquarters Battery.
34. Frank W. Moorman, as quoted in Clay Blair, *Ridgway's Paratroopers*, Dial Press, 1985, p. 43.
35. Ibid.
36. Ibid.
37. Maxwell D. Taylor, as quoted in ibid., p. 43.
38. Lawrence Warthman, as quoted in Bos, *Circle and the Fields of Little America*, Voices of the Veterans, B Battery.
39. Moorman as quoted in Blair, *Ridgway's Paratroopers*, p. 44.
40. Lieutenant Colonel Reuben H. Tucker, as quoted in "The Prop Blast," January 1943, reprinted in *Prop Blast*, Mrozek, compiler and editor.
41. Le Vangia, written account.
42. Edward P. Haider, *Blood In Our Boots*, Trafford, 2002, p. 13.
43. Haider, *Blood In Our Boots*, pp. 16–18.
44. Fred J. Baldino, as quoted in, James McNamara, "Fred J. Baldino's War Story," p. 2.
45. James Emory Baugh, M.D., *From Skies of Blue*, iUniverse, 2003, p. 33.

Chapter 2: "Another Hellhole"

1. Henry D. Ussery, Jr., as quoted in, Jan Bos, *Circle and the Fields of Little America*, Voices of the Veterans, Headquarters Battery.
2. Francis W. McLane, "Francis W. McLane a.k.a. 'Mac' World War II, Journal," courtesy of Francis W. McLane, p. 2.
3. Baugh, *From Skies of Blue*, p. 33.
4. William R. Leonard, memoirs, courtesy of William R. Leonard.
5. Baugh, *From Skies of Blue*, pp. 33–34.
6. Robert H. Neptune, quoted in Bos, *Circle and the Fields of Little America*, Voices of the Veterans, Headquarters Battery.
7. Baugh, *From Skies of Blue*, p. 35.
8. Henry Ussery, quoted in Bos, *Circle and the Fields of Little America*, Voices of the Veterans, Headquarters Battery.
9. Arthur Foster, as quoted in Bos, *Circle and the Fields of Little America*, Voices of the Veterans, C Battery.
10. Neptune, as quoted in Bos, *Circle and the Fields of Little America*, Voices of the Veterans, Headquarters Battery.
11. Ibid.
12. Breard, interview.
13. Ussery, as quoted in Bos, *Circle and the Fields of Little America*, Voices of the Veterans, Headquarters Battery.
14. Ibid.
15. Neptune, as quoted in ibid.
16. Breard, interview.
17. Ussery, as quoted in Bos, *Circle and the Fields of Little America*, Voices of the Veterans, Headquarters Battery.
18. Neptune, as quoted in ibid.
19. T. Moffatt Burriss, *Strike And Hold*, Brassey's Inc., 2000, p. 30
20. Neptune, as quoted in Bos, *Circle and the Fields of Little America*, Voices of the Veterans, Headquarters Battery.
21. Ussery, as quoted in ibid.
22. Burriss, *Strike And Hold*, p. 30.
23. Arthur Foster, as quoted in Bos, *Circle and the Fields of Little America*, Voices of the Veterans, C Battery.
24. Captain Adam A. Komosa, "Airborne Operation, 504th Parachute Infantry Regimental Combat Team (82nd Airborne Division), Sicily, 9 July–19 August, 1943, Personal Experience of a Regimental Headquarters Company Commander," pp. 4–5.
25. Ussery, as quoted in Bos, *Circle and the Fields of Little America*, Voices of the Veterans, Headquarters Battery.
26. Knight, questionnaire.

27. Clayton Blankenship, as quoted in Bos, *Circle and the Fields of Little America*, Voices of the Veterans, D Battery.

28. Reuben H. Tucker, as quoted from William B. Breuer, *Drop Zone Sicily*, Presidio Press, 1983, p. 3.

29. Komosa, "Airborne Operation, 504th Parachute Infantry Regimental Combat Team," p. 6.

30. Ibid., pp. 7–8.

31. Ibid., pp. 9–10.

32. Omar N. Bradley and Clay Blair, *A General's Life*, Simon and Schuster, 1983, pp. 175–76.

33. Reed S. Fassett, as quoted in Bos, *Circle and the Fields of Little America*, Voices of the Veterans, A Battery.

34. Leonard D. Battles, as quoted in Bos, *Circle and the Fields of Little America*, Voices of the Veterans, Headquarters Battery.

35. Komosa, "Airborne Operation, 504th Parachute Infantry Regimental Combat Team," p. 7.

36. Lawrence H. Dunlop, written account, courtesy of Alex Kicovic.

37. Watts, response to "WWII Army Service Experiences Questionnaire," pp. 23, 31.

38. Roy M. Hanna, response to author's questionnaire.

39. Orvin, interview.

40. Darrel G. Harris, *Casablanca to VE Day*, Dorrance Publishing, 1995, p. 5.

41. Shelby R. Hord, interview with author.

42. "82nd Airborne Division In Sicily And Italy, Part II—Sicily," courtesy of the 82nd Airborne Division War Memorial Museum, p. 34.

43. Dunlop, written account.

44. Ibid.

45. Lieutenant James C. Ott, as quoted in "82nd Airborne Division In Sicily And Italy, Part II—Sicily," p. 34.

46. Charles W. Kouns, as quoted in Doyle R. Yardley, *Home Was Never Like This*, Yardley Enterprises, 2002, p. 115.

47. Lieutenant George J. Watts, as quoted in "82nd Airborne Division In Sicily And Italy, Part II—Sicily," p. 34.

48. Ibid., p. 36.

49. Ibid., p. 35.

50. Ibid., p. 36.

51. Hord, interview.

52. Ibid.

53. Ibid.

54. Ibid.

55. Dunlop, written account.

56. Knight, questionnaire.

57. Komosa, "Airborne Operation, 504th Parachute Infantry Regimental Combat Team," pp. 11–12.

Chapter 3: "The Sky Was Full Of Tracers And Bursting Shells"
1. Leonard D. Battles, as quoted in Jan Bos, *Circle and the Fields of Little America*, Voices of the Veterans, Headquarters Battery.
2. Albert B. Clark, response to author's questionnaire.
3. Lieutenant John S. Thompson, "Individual Report on Operation Husky," courtesy of the 82nd Airborne Division War Memorial Museum.
4. Le Vangia, written account.
5. Captain Willard E. Harrison, as quoted in "82nd Airborne Division in Sicily and Italy, Part II—Sicily," courtesy of the 82nd Airborne Division War Memorial Museum, p. 7.
6. Clark, questionnaire.
7. Thomas J. McCarthy, as quoted in *In Their Own Words, WWII: The European Theater*, audio book, Topics Entertainment, Cassette 1, Side A.
8. Robert H. Neptune, as quoted in Bos, *Circle and the Fields of Little America*, Voices of the Veterans, Headquarters Battery.
9. "82nd Airborne Division in Sicily and Italy, Part II—Sicily," pp. 7–8.
10. Ibid., p. 9.
11. Thompson, "Individual Report on Operation Husky."
12. Watts, Jr., response to "WWII Army Service Experiences Questionnaire," pp. 27–28.
13. Edward J. Sims, "Enclosure 1 To Army Service Experience Questionnaire For Edward J. Sims, Sicily," U.S. Military History Institute, pp. 1–2, courtesy of Edward J. Sims.
14. "82nd Airborne Division in Sicily and Italy, Part II—Sicily," p. 8.
15. Le Vangia, written account.
16. Leonard D. Battles, as quoted in Bos, *Circle and the Fields of Little America*, Voices of the Veterans, Headquarters Battery.
17. Ibid.
18. Paul D. Donnelly, as quoted in ibid.
19. Henry D. Ussery, Jr., as quoted in ibid.
20. Bill Roberts, Jr., as quoted in ibid.
21. Tom Shockley, as quoted in ibid.
22. Stanley Galicki, as quoted in Bos, *Circle and the Fields of Little America*, Voices of the Veterans, A Battery.
23. Robert W. Zost, as quoted in ibid.
24. James F. Crosbie, letter to Jan Bos, courtesy of Mr. Richard Claeys, p. 2.
25. Neil D'Avanzo, as quoted in Bos, *Circle and the Fields of Little America*, Voices of the Veterans, B Battery.

26. Roy Pack, as quoted in Bos, *Circle and the Fields of Little America*, Voices of the Veterans, C Battery.
27. Larry Reber, as quoted in ibid.
28. Russell Long, as quoted in Bos, *Circle and the Fields of Little America*, Voices of the Veterans, Headquarters Battery.
29. Alphonse Czekanski, as quoted in Bos, *Circle and the Fields of Little America*, Voices of the Veterans, D Battery.
30. Frank D. Boyd, as quoted in Bos, *Circle and the Fields of Little America*, Voices of the Veterans, Headquarters Battery.
31. Private Keith K. Scott, as quoted in "82nd Airborne Division in Sicily and Italy, Part II—Sicily," p. 10.
32. Le Vangia, written account.
33. Sims, "Enclosure 1," pp. 1–2.
34. Thompson, "Individual Report on Operation Husky."
35. Shelby R. Hord, interview with author.
36. Ibid.
37. Lawrence H. Dunlop, written account, courtesy of Alex Kicovic.
38. Hord, interview.
39. Dunlop, written account.
40. Kouns, quoted in Yardley, *Home Was Never Like This*, p. 115.
41. Major William R. Beall, as quoted in "82nd Airborne Division In Sicily And Italy, Part II—Sicily," p. 36.
42. Thompson, "Individual Report on Operation Husky."
43. Hord, interview.
44. Major William R. Beall, as quoted in "82nd Airborne Division In Sicily And Italy, Part II—Sicily," p. 36.
45. Sims, "Enclosure 1," p. 2.
46. Ibid.
47. Knight, questionnaire.
48. Dunlop, written account.
49. Komosa, "Airborne Operation, 504th Parachute Infantry Regimental Combat Team," p. 26.

Chapter 4: "Retreat Hell! Send Me My 3rd Battalion!"
1. Milton V. Knight, response to questionnaire from Alex Kicovic, courtesy of Alex Kicovic.
2. Thomas J. McCarthy, as quoted in *In Their Own Words, WWII: The European Theater*, audio book, Topics Entertainment, Cassette 1, Side A.
3. Knight, questionnaire.
4. McCarthy, as quoted in *In Their Own Words*.
5. General Maxwell Taylor, as quoted in "The 82nd Airborne Division In Sicily And Italy, Part III—Italy, Section IV," courtesy of the 82nd Airborne Division War Memorial Museum, p. 62.

6. General Maxwell Taylor, as quoted in "The 82nd Airborne Division In Sicily And Italy, Part III—Italy, Section III," p. 56.
7. Ibid., p. 57.
8. Ibid., p. 57.
9. Joe Watts, as quoted in Patrick K. O'Donnell, *Beyond Valor*, The Free Press, 2001, p. 66.
10. Edward J. Sims, "Enclosure 2 To Army Service Experience Questionnaire For Edward J. Sims, Italy," pp. 1–2.
11. Robert S. Hutton, as quoted in Bos, *Circle and the Fields of Little America*, Voices of the Veterans, B Battery.
12. Sims, "Enclosure 2," pp. 1–2.
13. James M. Gavin, *On To Berlin*, Viking Press, 1978, p. 65.
14. Matthew B. Ridgway and Harold H. Martin, *Soldier: The Memoirs of Matthew B. Ridgway*, Greenwood Press, 1956, pp. 84–85.
15. Reneau Breard, interview with author.
16. Albert B. Clark, response to author's questionnaire.
17. Ridgway and Martin, *Soldier*, p. 85.
18. "Unit Journal of the 2nd Battalion, 504th Parachute Infantry, 82nd Airborne Division," courtesy of the 82nd Airborne Division War Memorial Museum, p. 21.
19. Regis J. Pahler, as quoted in Lou Hauptfleisch, "Devils in Baggy Pants" column, *The Static Line*.
20. Ibid.
21. Breard, interview.
22. Ibid.
23. Major John S. Lekson, "The Operations of the 1st Battalion, 504th Parachute Infantry (82nd Airborne Division) In The Capture Of Altavilla, Italy, 13 September–19 September, 1943," courtesy of the Donovan Research Library, Fort Benning, Georgia, p. 8.
24. General Mark Clark, as quoted in "The 82nd Airborne Division In Sicily And Italy, Part III—Italy, Section I," p. 49.
25. Colonel Reuben H. Tucker, as quoted in, Ibid.
26. Lekson, "Operations of the 1st Battalion," p. 8.
27. Lieutenant William G. Kellogg, "Report of the 2nd and 3rd Sticks, 1st Platoon, Company C, 307 Engineer on Avellino Jump," National Archives, p. 2.
28. Lekson, "Operations of the 1st Battalion," p. 9.
29. "Unit Journal of the 2nd Battalion, 504th Parachute Infantry," p. 21
30. Kellogg, Report of 2nd and 3rd Sticks," p. 2.
31. Lekson, "Operations of the 1st Battalion," p. 11.
32. Ibid., p. 15.
33. "Unit Journal of the 2nd Battalion, 504th Parachute Infantry," p. 22.

34. First Lieutenant Otto W. Huebner, "The Operations of Company A, 504th Parachute Infantry (82nd Airborne Division) In The Defense Of Hill 424 Near Altavilla, Italy, 17 September–19 September 1943," courtesy of the Donovan Research Library, Fort Benning, Georgia, pp. 10–11.

35. Huebner, "The Operations of Company A, 504th Parachute Infantry," pp. 11–12.

36. Kellogg, "Report of 2nd and 3rd Sticks," p. 2.

37. Richard Tregaskis, *Invasion Diary*, Random House, 1944, pp. 116–117.

38. Ibid, p. 117.

39. Lekson, "Operations of the 1st Battalion," pp. 17–19.

40. Tregaskis, *Invasion Diary*, pp. 118, 120.

41. Huebner, "Operations of Company A, 504th Parachute Infantry," pp. 11–13.

42. Lekson, "Operations of the 1st Battalion," pp. 23–24.

43. "Unit Journal of the 2nd Battalion, 504th Parachute Infantry," p. 22.

44. Ross S. Carter, *Those Devils In Baggy Pants*, Buccaneer Books, 1976, p. 38.

45. The 504 was called the "Legion" by some of its troopers.

46. Carter, *Those Devils In Baggy Pants*, p. 41.

47. Huebner, "Operations of Company A, 504th Parachute Infantry," pp. 13–14.

48. Lekson, "Operations of the 1st Battalion," pp. 27–29.

49. "Unit Journal of the 2nd Battalion, 504th Parachute Infantry," p. 22.

50. Huebner, "Operations of Company A, 504th Parachute Infantry," pp. 14–15.

51. Reneau Breard, interview.

52. Huebner, "Operations of Company A, 504th Parachute Infantry," pp. 15–18.

53. Albert Clark, response to author's questionnaire.

54. Huebner, "Operations of Company A, 504th Parachute Infantry," pp. 18–20.

55. Lekson, "Operations of the 1st Battalion," p. 30.

56. Huebner, "Operations of Company A, 504th Parachute Infantry," pp. 20–22.

57. Fred J. Baldino, as quoted in "Fred Baldino's War," James McNamara, p. 3.

58. George F. Taliaferro, sworn statement, September 24, 1943, Major Robert B. Acheson awards file, National Archives.

59. "Unit Journal of the 2nd Battalion, 504th Parachute Infantry," p. 22.

60. Lekson, "Operations of the 1st Battalion," pp. 34–35.

61. Huebner, "Operations of Company A, 504th Parachute Infantry," pp. 22--25.

62. Breard, interview.

63. Huebner, "Operations of Company A, 504th Parachute Infantry," p. 25.

64. Breard, interview.
65. Huebner, "Operations of Company A, 504th Parachute Infantry," p. 25.
66. "Unit Journal of the 2nd Battalion, 504th Parachute Infantry," p. 22.
67. Ibid.
68. Huebner, "Operations of Company A, 504th Parachute Infantry," p. 25.

Chapter 5: "The Germans Were Always On The High Ground Looking Down Our Throats"
1. Lieutenant William G. Kellogg, "Report of the 2nd and 3rd Sticks, 1st Platoon, Company C, 307 Engineer on Avellino Jump," National Archives, p. 2.
2. George Leoleis, *Medals*, Carlton Press, 1990, p. 85.
3. Kellogg, "Report of 2nd and 3rd Sticks," p. 3.
4. Edward J. Sims, "Enclosure 2 To Army Service Experience Questionnaire For Edward J. Sims, Italy," p. 2.
5. Kellogg, "Report of 2nd and 3rd Sticks," p. 3.
6. Ibid.
7. Ibid.
8. Ibid., p. 4.
9. James F. Crosbie, letter to Jan Bos, courtesy of Mr. Richard Claeys, p. 2.
10. Kellogg, "Report of 2nd and 3rd Sticks," p. 4.
11. Robert Tallon, as quoted in Burriss, *Strike And Hold*, Brassey's, 2000, pp. 55–56.
12. Burriss, *Strike and Hold*, p. 56.
13. Tallon, as quoted in ibid., p. 56.
14. Burriss, *Strike and Hold*, p. 56.
15. Ibid.
16. Ibid.
17. Ibid.
18. Ibid.
19. Reed S. Fassett, as quoted in Jan Bos, *Circle and the Fields of Little America*, Voices of the Veterans, A Battery.
20. Clark, questionnaire.
21. Neil D'Avanzo, as quoted in Jan Bos, *Circle and the Fields of Little America*, Voices of the Veterans, A Battery.
22. Knight, questionnaire.
23. Ridgway and Martin, v*Soldier: The Memoirs of Matthew B. Ridgway*, pp. 89–90.
24. Breard, interview.
25. Ridgway and Martin, *Soldier*, pp. 91–92.
26. Mark W. Clark, *Calculated Risk*, The Citadel, the Military College of South Carolina, 1964, p. 236.
27. Sims, "Enclosure 2," p. 2.

28. "Unit Journal of the 2nd Battalion, 504th Parachute Infantry, 82nd Airborne Division," courtesy of the 82nd Airborne Division War Memorial Museum, p. 34.
29. Ted C. Johnson, as quoted in Jan Bos, *Circle and the Fields of Little America*, Voices of the Veterans, B Battery.
30. Knight, questionnaire.
31. Lieutenant Payton F. Elliott, statement in "Factual Account of the Actions of Elements of Companies H and I, 504th Parachute Infantry, Leading to the Capture of Hill 1017," AGF Board, AFHQ, NATO, 4 December 1943.
32. Lieutenant Willis J. Ferrill, statement in "Factual Account of the Actions of Elements of Companies H and I, 504th Parachute Infantry, Leading to the Capture of Hill 1017," AGF Board, AFHQ, NATO, 4 December 1943.
33. McLane, "World War II, Journal," p. 10.
34. Ibid., p. 11.
35. Carter, *Those Devils In Baggy Pants*, p. 67.
36. McLane, "World War II, Journal," p. 11.
37. Carter, *Those Devils In Baggy Pants*, p. 67.
38. McLane, "World War II, Journal," p. 11.
39. Carter, *Those Devils In Baggy Pants*, pp. 69–70.
40. Sims, "Enclosure 2," p. 3.
41. Carter, *Those Devils In Baggy Pants*, p. 74.
42. James Megellas, *All The Way To Berlin*, The Ballantine Publishing Group, 2003, p. 28.
43. Ibid., pp. 28–29.
44. McLane, "World War II, Journal," p. 14.
45. "Unit Journal of the 2nd Battalion, 504th Parachute Infantry, 82nd Airborne Division," courtesy of the 82nd Airborne Division War Memorial Museum, p. 44.
46. Breard, interview.
47. McLane, "World War II, Journal," p. 14.
48. Breard, interview.
49. Leoleis, *Medals*, pp. 109–110.
50. McLane, "World War II, Journal," pp. 14–15.
51. Leoleis, *Medals*, p. 112.
52. McLane, "World War II, Journal," p. 15.
53. Joseph W. Lyons, response to author's questionnaire.
54. "Unit Journal of the 2nd Battalion, 504th Parachute Infantry," pp. 45–46.
55. Ibid., p. 46.
56. Harry A. Corbin, interview with author.
57. Delbert Kuehl, as quoted in T. Moffatt Burriss, *Strike and Hold*, Brassey's, 2000, p. 59.
58. "Unit Journal of the 2nd Battalion, 504th Parachute Infantry," p. 46.

59. Jack L. Bommer, questionnaire, Cornelius Ryan Collection, Alden Library, Ohio University.
60. Megellas, *All The Way To Berlin*, p. 34.
61. Ibid.
62. William B. Breuer, *Geronimo!*, St. Martin's Press, 1989, p. 157.
63. Breard, interview.
64. Ibid.
65. Leo P. Muri, letter to sister, May 24, 1945, courtesy of William R. Leonard.
66. Russell T. Long, "My Life in The Service, The Diary of Cpl. Russell T. Long," courtesy of Jan Bos.
67. Breard, interview.
68. Hord, interview.

Chapter 6: "Seems Like The Black-Hearted Devils Are Everywhere"
1. Robert S. Hutton, as quoted in Bos, *Circle and the Fields of Little America*, Voices of the Veterans, B Battery, courtesy of Jan Bos.
2. Leo M. Hart, interview with author.
3. Leo P. Muri, letter to sister, May 24, 1945, courtesy of William R. Leonard.
4. Harry A. Corbin, interview with author.
5. William R. Leonard, written account, courtesy of William R. Leonard
6. Muri, letter.
7. Leonard, written account.
8. Louis E. Orvin, Jr., interview with author.
9. Edward J. Sims, "Enclosure 2 To Army Service Experience Questionnaire For Edward J. Sims, Italy," pp. 3–4.
10. Muri, letter.
11. George Leoleis, *Medals*, Carlton Press, 1990, p. 133.
12. Ibid., pp. 133–35.
13. Orvin, interview.
14. Leonard, written account.
15. Muri, letter.
16. Leonard, written account.
17. Ibid.
18. Albert Clark, response to author's questionnaire.
19. Milton V. Knight, response to questionnaire by Alex Kicovic, courtesy of Alex Kicovic.
20. Captain William J. Sweet, Jr., "Operations of the 2nd Battalion, 504th Parachute Infantry Regiment (82nd Airborne Division) on the Anzio Beachhead, 22 January–23 March 1944," courtesy of the Donovan Research Library, Fort Benning, Georgia, pp. 6–10.
21. Albert Clark, questionnaire.
22. Darrell G. Harris, *Casablanca to VE Day*, Dorrance Publishing, 1995,

p. 10–11.
23. John A. Holabird, letter to author.
24. Colonel Reuben H. Tucker, Recommendation for Award, Lieutenant Colonel Warren R. Williams, Jr., June 18, 1945, courtesy of Mike Bigalke.
25. Captain John N. Pease, sworn statement, June 18, 1945, Recommendation for Award, Lieutenant Colonel Warren R. Williams, Jr., courtesy of Mike Bigalke.
26. Captain Albert E. Milloy, sworn statement, June 18, 1945, Recommendation for Award, Lieutenant Colonel Warren R. Williams, Jr., courtesy of Mike Bigalke.
27. Tucker, Recommendation for Award.
28. Landon Chilcutt, response to author's questionnaire.
29. Tucker, Recommendation for Award.
30. Sweet, Operations of the 2nd Battalion, 504th," pp. 13–14.
31. Tucker, Recommendation for Award.
32. Sims, "Enclosure 2," p. 4.
33. Ibid.
34. Orvin, interview.
35. Holabird, letter.
36. Ibid.
37. James Megellas, *All The Way To Berlin*, The Ballantine Publishing Group, 2003, p. 61.
38. Ibid., p. 62.
39. Ibid.
40. Ibid., pp. 63–64.
41. Roy M. Hanna, written account, courtesy of the 82nd Airborne Division War Memorial Museum.
42. Orvin, interview.
43. Hanna, written account.
44. Orvin, interview.
45. Megellas, *All The Way To Berlin*, pp. 64–65.
46. John Granado, interview, courtesy of Terry Poyser.
47. Hanna, written account.
48. Granado, interview.
49. Leoleis, *Medals*, pp. 143–144.
50. Granado, interview.
51. John Granado, as quoted in Megellas, *All The Way To Berlin*, The Ballantine Publishing Group, 2003, p. 67.
52. Granado, interview.
53. Granado, quoted in Megellas, *All The Way To Berlin*, p. 67.
54. Megellas, *All The Way To Berlin*, p. 67.
55. Hanna, written account.

56. Leonard, written account.
57. Hanna, written account.
58. Orvin, interview.
59. Robert H. Neptune, as quoted in Bos, *Circle and the Fields of Little America*, Voices of the Veterans, Headquarters Battery, courtesy of Jan Bos.
60. C. L. Tackel, as quoted in "21 Years Ago, 82nd Troopers Faced Death," *Army Times*, February 3, 1965, p. 9.
61. Lieutenant William D. Mandle and Private First Class David H. Whittier, compilers, *The Devils In Baggy Pants, Combat Record of the 504th Parachute Infantry Regiment April 1943–July 1945*, Draeger Frères, Paris, 1945.

Chapter 7: "The Regiment Was Probably At The Peak Of Its Fighting Efficiency"

1. Fred J. Baldino, as quoted in "Fred Baldino's War," James McNamara, p. 5.
2. Carl Mauro, memoirs, courtesy of Carl Mauro.
3. Ibid.
4. Ibid.
5. James L. Ward, response to author's questionnaire.
6. Mauro, memoirs.
7. Ibid.
8. Lieutenant Harold A. Stueland, "Patrol Report—March 18, 1944," courtesy of Mike Bigalke.
9. James F. Crosbie, letter to Jan Bos, courtesy of Mr. Richard Claeys, p. 2.
10. Holabird, letter to author.
11. Ted C. Johnson, as quoted in Jan Bos, *Circle and the Fields of Little America*, Voices of the Veterans, B Battery, courtesy of Jan Bos.
12. Leonard D. Battles, as quoted in ibid., Voices of the Veterans, Headquarters Battery.
13. Carl Mauro, memoirs, courtesy of Carl Mauro.
14. Johnson, as quoted in Bos, *Circle and the Fields of Little America*, Voices of the Veterans, B Battery.
15. Wesley Pass, as quoted in ibid., Voices of the Veterans, Headquarters Battery.
16. Battles, as quoted in ibid, Voices of the Veterans, Headquarters Battery.
17. Ridgway and Martin, *Soldier*, p. 92.
18. Blair, *Ridgway's Paratroopers*, Dial Press, 1985, p. 242.
19. Robert H. Neptune, as quoted in ibid, Voices of the Veterans, Headquarters Battery.
20. Thomas J. McCarthy, as quoted in *In Their Own Words, WWII: Europe*, audio book, Topics Entertainment, Cassette 1, Side A.
21. Thomas J. McCarthy, as quoted in, David R. Berry, letter to Rodgers and

Jacobs families, courtesy of Ed Dodd.
22. Captain John T. Joseph, "The Operations of a Regimental Pathfinder Unit, 507th Parachute Infantry Regiment (82nd Airborne Division) in Normandy, France 6 June 1944 (Normandy Campaign)," Advanced Infantry Officers Course, Fort Benning, Georgia, courtesy of the Donovan Research Library, Fort Benning, Georgia, pp. 8–9.
23. Ibid.
24. Dan Serillo, as quoted in David R. Berry, letter to Rodgers and Jacobs families, courtesy of Ed Dodd.
25. McCarthy, as quoted in ibid.
26. Gavin, *On To Berlin*, p. 103.
27. Ibid.
28. McCarthy, *In Their Own Words, WWII: Europe*, Cassette 1, Side A.
29. Serillo, as quoted in Berry letter to Rodgers and Jacobs families.
30. Ibid.
31. McCarthy, as quoted in ibid.
32. Ibid.
33. Serillo, as quoted in ibid.
34. Edwin M. Clements, written account, www.marketgarden.com (Topics/ Veterans Memories).
35. Joseph C. Watts, Jr., response to "WWII Army Service Experiences Questionnaire," U.S. Army Military History Institute, p. 13.
36. Julian A. Cook, questionnaire, Cornelius Ryan Collection, Alden Library, Ohio University.
37. Frank D. Boyd, as quoted in Bos, *Circle and the Fields of Little America*, Voices of the Veterans, Headquarters Battery.
38. Blair, v*Ridgway's Paratroopers*, p. 360.
39. The James M. Gavin Papers, Personal Diaries, Box 8, Folder–Diary Passages, courtesy of the U.S. Army Military History Institute.
40. Ibid.
41. Robert Wienecke, questionnaire, Cornelius Ryan Collection, Alden Library, Ohio University.
42. HQ 82nd Airborne Division, APO 469, US Army, September 11, 1944, "Order of Battle Summary."
43. Ibid.
44. Ibid.
45. Ibid.
46. Major General James M. Gavin, letter to Capt. John C. Westover, July 25, 1945, courtesy of the 82nd Airborne Division War Memorial Museum.
47. Alphonse Czekanski, as quoted in Jan Bos, *Circle and the Fields of Little America*, Voices of the Veterans, D Battery.
48. Herman Swope, as quoted in ibid., Voices of the Veterans, C Battery,

courtesy of Jan Bos.

49. Carl W. Kappel, interview, Cornelius Ryan Collection, Alden Library, Ohio University.

50. Captain Carl W. Kappel, "The Operations of Company H, 504th Parachute Infantry, (82nd Airborne Division) in the Invasion of Holland 17–21 September 1944, (Personal Experience of a Rifle Company Commander)," Advanced Infantry Officers Course 1948–1949, Academic Department, The Infantry School, Fort Benning, Georgia, courtesy of the Donovan Research Library, Fort Benning, Georgia, p. 15.

51. Ibid., pp. 10–11.

52. Walter VanPoyck, questionnaire, Cornelius Ryan Collection, Alden Library, Ohio University.

53. Hubert A. Wolfe, interview, courtesy of Robert Wolfe.

54. Clayton I. Thurman, as quoted in Jan Bos, *Circle and the Fields of Little America*, Voices of the Veterans, D Battery.

55. Kappel, "Operations of Company H," pp. 12–14.

56. Philip Nadler, questionnaire, Cornelius Ryan Collection, Alden Library, Ohio University.

Chapter 8: "Let's Get Across The Bridge!"

1. Hanz K. Druener questionnaire, Cornelius Ryan Collection, Alden Library, Ohio University.

2. Nicholas W. Mansolillo questionnaire, Cornelius Ryan Collection, Alden Library, Ohio University.

3. Edwin M. Clements, written account, www.marketgarden.com.

4. Ibid.

5. Bommer, questionnaire, Cornelius Ryan Collection, Alden Library, Ohio University.

6. Jack Alexander, as quoted in Jan Bos, *Circle and the Fields of Little America*, Voices of the Veterans, D Battery, courtesy of Jan Bos.

7. George Willoughby, written account, courtesy of George Willoughby.

8. Virgil Carmichael, questionnaire, Cornelius Ryan Collection, Alden Library, Ohio University.

9. Willoughby, written account.

10. James Megellas, questionnaire, Cornelius Ryan Collection, Alden Library, Ohio University.

11. Chilcutt, questionnaire.

12. Albert A. Tarbell, written account, Cornelius Ryan Collection, Alden Library, Ohio University.

13. Arthur W. Ferguson, questionnaire, Cornelius Ryan Collection, Alden Library, Ohio University.

14. Paul A. Mullan, written account.

15. Earl S. Oldfather, questionnaire, Cornelius Ryan Collection, Alden Library, Ohio University.

16. John R. Duncan, questionnaire, Cornelius Ryan Collection, Alden Library, Ohio University.

17. Louis A. Hauptfleisch, questionnaire, Cornelius Ryan Collection, Alden Library, Ohio University.

18. Colonel Warren R. Williams, Jr., questionnaire, Cornelius Ryan Collection, Alden Library, Ohio University.

19. Frank L. Dietrich, questionnaire, Cornelius Ryan Collection, Alden Library, Ohio University.

20. Clements, written account.

21. Wolfe, interview.

22. Chilcutt, questionnaire.

23. Mansolillo, questionnaire.

24. Druener, questionnaire.

25. Victor Campana, questionnaire, Cornelius Ryan Collection, Alden Library, Ohio University.

26. Philip H. Nadler, questionnaire, Cornelius Ryan Collection, Alden Library, Ohio University.

27. VanPoyck, questionnaire.

28. Lieutenant John S. Thompson, "Holland Jump," courtesy of the 82nd Airborne Division War Memorial Museum.

29. VanPoyck, questionnaire.

30. Harold G. Herbert, interview with author.

31. Ibid.

32. Robert S. Hutton, as quoted in Jan Bos, *Circle and the Fields of Little America*, Voices of the Veterans, B Battery.

33. Ted C. Johnson, as quoted in Jan Bos, *Circle and the Fields of Little America*, Voices of the Veterans, D Battery.

34. Pat A. Fusaro, response to author's questionnaire.

35. Ibid.

36. Clayton Blankenship, as quoted in Jan Bos, *Circle and the Fields of Little America*, Voices of the Veterans, D Battery.

37. Alphonse J. Czekanski, as quoted in Jan Bos, *Circle and the Fields of Little America*, Voices of the Veterans, D Battery.

38. Walter A. Barbour, as quoted in Jan Bos, *Circle and the Fields of Little America*, Voices of the Veterans, Headquarters Battery.

39. Robert A. Lally, as quoted in Jan Bos, *Circle and the Fields of Little America*, Voices of the Veterans, Headquarters Battery.

40. Arthur Fransosi, questionnaire, Cornelius Ryan Collection.

41. Thompson, "Holland Jump."

42. Carl Mauro, memoirs, courtesy of Carl Mauro.

43. Staff Sergeant Alek Misseres, combat interview, courtesy of the Cornelius Ryan Collection, Alden Library, Ohio University.

44. Colonel Reuben H. Tucker, combat interview, courtesy of the Cornelius Ryan Collection, Alden Library, Ohio University.

45. Philip Nadler, interview, courtesy of the Cornelius Ryan Collection Alden Library, Ohio University.

46. Ibid.

47. Ibid.

48. Thompson, "The Holland Jump."

49. Nadler, interview.

50. Carl Mauro, memoirs.

51. Leo M. Hart, interview with author.

52. Mauro, memoirs.

53. Thompson, "The Holland Jump."

54. Corporal John G. Branca, Jr., combat interview, "Company E, 504th Parachute Regiment, 82nd Airborne Division," courtesy of the Cornelius Ryan Collection, Alden Library, Ohio University.

55. VanPoyck, questionnaire.

56. Ibid.

57. Lieutenant John H. Murphy, interview, 160th General Hospital, National Archives.

58. VanPoyck, questionnaire.

59. Captain Albert E. Milloy, combat interview, courtesy of the Cornelius Ryan Collection, Alden Library, Ohio University.

60. Captain Thomas B. Helgeson, combat interview, courtesy of the Cornelius Ryan Collection, Alden Library, Ohio University.

61. Wolfe, interview.

62. Ibid.

63. Ibid.

64. Helgeson, combat interview.

65. Ibid.

66. Ibid.

67. Ibid.

68. Robert D. Stern, oral history transcript, courtesy of Robert Wolfe.

69. Helgeson, combat interview.

70. Stern, oral history.

71. Edwin M. Clements, written account, www.marketgarden.com

Chapter 9: "Somebody Has Come Up With A Real Nightmare"

1. Captain Carl W. Kappel, "The Operations of Company H, 504th Parachute Infantry, (82nd Airborne Division) in the Invasion of Holland 17–21 September 1944, (Personal Experience of a Rifle Company Commander)," Advanced Infantry Officers Course 1948–1949, Academic Department, The Infantry School, Fort Benning, Georgia, courtesy of the Donovan Research Library, Fort Benning, Georgia, pp. 18–19.
2. Ibid., pp. 20–21.
3. Leo P. Muri, letter to sister, May 24, 1945, courtesy of William R. Leonard.
4. Robert W. Zost, as quoted in Jan Bos, *Circle and the Fields of Little America*, Voices of the Veterans, A Battery, courtesy of Jan Bos.
5. Gorman S. Oswell, as quoted in Jan Bos, *Circle and the Fields of Little America*, Voices of the Veterans, Headquarters Battery.
6. Frank D. Boyd, as quoted in Jan Bos, *Circle and the Fields of Little America*, Voices of the Veterans, Headquarters Battery.
7. Roy Pack, as quoted in Jan Bos, *Circle and the Fields of Little America*, Voices of the Veterans, C Battery.
8. Boyd, as quoted in ibid., Voices of the Veterans, Headquarters Battery.
9. Willard Strunk, questionnaire, Cornelius Ryan Collection, Alden Library, Ohio University.
10. James M. Gavin, *On To Berlin*, Viking Press, 1978, pp. 161–162.
11. Walter S. VanPoyck, questionnaire, Cornelius Ryan Collection, Alden Library, Ohio University.
12. Ibid.
13. Ibid.
14. Ibid.
15. Earl S. Oldfather, questionnaire, Cornelius Ryan Collection, Alden Library, Ohio University.
16. Captain Fred E. Thomas, "Holland Mission," courtesy of the Cornelius Ryan Collection, Alden Library, Ohio University.
17. James Megellas, questionnaire, courtesy of the Cornelius Ryan Collection, Alden Library, Ohio University.
18. Colonel Reuben H. Tucker, written account, courtesy of the Cornelius Ryan Collection, Alden Library, Ohio University.
19. George Chatterton, as quoted in Cornelius Ryan, *A Bridge Too Far*, Simon and Schuster, 1974, pp. 432–33.
20. James M. Gavin, as quoted in ibid., p. 433.
21. Frederick M. Browning, as quoted in ibid., p. 433.
22. Tucker, written account.
23. Ibid.
24. John Holabird, interview, courtesy of the Cornelius Ryan Collection, Alden Library, Ohio University.

25. Thomas McLeod, questionnaire, courtesy of the Cornelius Ryan Collection, Alden Library, Ohio University.
26. Thomas, "Holland Mission."
27. Robert M. Tallon, Sr., interview notes, March 6, 1968, courtesy of the Cornelius Ryan Collection, Alden Library, Ohio University.
28. Roy M. Hanna, telephone interview notes March 5, 1968, courtesy of the Cornelius Ryan Collection, Alden Library, Ohio University.
29. Lieutenant Chester A, Garrison, "Unit Journal of the 2nd Battalion, 504th Parachute Infantry, 82nd Airborne Division," courtesy of the 82nd Airborne Division War Memorial Museum.
30. Julian A. Cook, questionnaire, courtesy of the Cornelius Ryan Collection, Alden Library, Ohio University.
31. Hanz K. Druener, questionnaire, courtesy of the Cornelius Ryan Collection, Alden Library, Ohio University.
32. Megellas, questionnaire.
33. Ibid.
34. Julian A. Cook, as quoted in Cornelius Ryan, *A Bridge Too Far*, Simon and Schuster, Inc. 1974, p. 459.
35. Captain Henry B. Keep, letter to mother, November 20, 1944, courtesy of the 82nd Airborne Division War Memorial Museum.
36. T. Moffatt Burriss, *Strike And Hold*, Brassey's, 2000, p. 109.
37. Boyd, as quoted in Bos, *Circle and the Fields of Little America*, Voices of the Veterans, Headquarters Battery.
38. Robert S. Hutton, as quoted in Bos, *Circle and the Fields of Little America*, Voices of the Veterans, B Battery.
39. Hanna, interview.
40. Kappel, "Operations of Company H," p. 26.
41. Keep to mother, November 20, 1944.
42. Reverend Delbert Kuehl and Allan Taylor, "Frontline," privately published, pp. 39–40.
43. Francis X. Keefe, written account, courtesy of Francis X. Keefe and William R. Leonard.
44. Ibid.
45. Virgil F. Carmichael, questionnaire, courtesy of the Cornelius Ryan Collection, Alden Library, Ohio University.
46. Kenneth S. Nicoll, questionnaire, courtesy of the Cornelius Ryan Collection, Alden Library, Ohio University.
47. James Megellas, *All The Way To Berlin*, The Ballantine Publishing Group, 2003, pp. 114–15.
48. Keep to mother.
49. Holabird, interview, Cornelius Ryan Collection.
50. Walter E. Hughes, written account, courtesy of Walter E. Hughes.

51. Kuehl and Taylor, "Frontline," p. 39.
52. Megellas, *All The Way To Berlin*, p. 116.
53. Patrick J. Mulloy, questionnaire, courtesy of the Cornelius Ryan Collection, Alden Library, Ohio University.
54. Tucker, written account.
55. Alfred Hermansen, as quoted in Jan Bos, *Circle and the Fields of Little America*, Voices of the Veterans, Headquarters Battery.
56. Robert M. Tallon, Sr., questionnaire, courtesy of the Cornelius Ryan Collection, Alden Library, Ohio University.
57. Burriss, *Strike And Hold*, p. 131.
58. Carl W. Kappel, interview, courtesy of the Cornelius Ryan Collection, Alden Library, Ohio University.
59. Keep, letter to mother.
60. McLeod, questionnaire, Cornelius Ryan Collection.
61. Carmichael, questionnaire, Cornelius Ryan Collection.
62. William R. Leonard, written account, courtesy of William R. Leonard.
63. Albert A. Tarbell, questionnaire, courtesy of the Cornelius Ryan Collection, Alden Library, Ohio University.
64. Ibid.
65. Holabird, interview, Cornelius Ryan Collection.
66. Keep to mother.
67. Virgil Carmichael, as quoted in William B. Breuer, *Geronimo!*, St. Martin's Press, 1989, p. 352.
68. Tucker, written account.
69. Keefe, written account.
70. Leonard, written account.
71. Leonard G. Trimble, questionnaire, courtesy of the Cornelius Ryan Collection, Alden Library, Ohio University.
72. Louis E. Orvin, Jr., interview with author.
73. Harold G. Herbert, interview with author.
74. Megellas, questionnaire.
75. Kuehl and Taylor, "Frontline," p. 40.
76. Patrick J. Mulloy, questionnaire, Cornelius Ryan Collection.
77. Keep to mother.
78. Tallon, interview.
79. Megellas, questionnaire.
80. Jimmie Shields, as quoted in James Megellas, *All The Way To Berlin*, The Ballantine Publishing Group, 2003, p. 121.
81. James L. Ward, response to author's questionnaire.
82. McLeod, questionnaire.
83. Carmichael, questionnaire.
84. Keefe, written account.
85. Burriss, *Strike And Hold*, pp. 113–15.

Chapter 10: "I Have Never Seen A More Gallant Action"
1. Leo P. Muri, letter to sister, May 24, 1945, courtesy of William R. Leonard.
2. Kenneth S. Nicoll, questionnaire, courtesy of the Cornelius Ryan Collection, Alden Library, Ohio University.
3. Muri, letter.
4. Francis X. Keefe, written account, courtesy of Francis X. Keefe and William R. Leonard.
5. William R. Leonard, written account, courtesy of William R. Leonard.
6. Ibid.
7. Matthew W. Kantala, Jr., questionnaire, courtesy of the Cornelius Ryan Collection, Alden Library, Ohio University.
8. Mulloy, questionnaire.
9. Julian A. Cook, questionnaire, courtesy of the Cornelius Ryan Collection, Alden Library, Ohio University.
10. George Leoleis, *Medals*, Carlton Press, 1990, pp. 175, 179.
11. Ibid., p. 179.
12. Keefe, written account.
13. Ernest P. Murphy, questionnaire, courtesy of the Cornelius Ryan Collection, Alden Library, Ohio University.
14. James L. Ward, questionnaire, courtesy of the Cornelius Ryan Collection, Alden Library, Ohio University.
15. Clark Fuller, questionnaire, courtesy of the Cornelius Ryan Collection, Alden Library, Ohio University.
16. Carl Kappel, interview, courtesy of the Cornelius Ryan Collection, Alden Library, Ohio University.
17. Ibid.
18. James Megellas, questionnaire, courtesy of the Cornelius Ryan Collection, Alden Library, Ohio University.
19. Giles Vandeleur, interview, courtesy of the Cornelius Ryan Collection, Alden Library, Ohio University.
20. Herbert P. Keith, questionnaire, courtesy of the Cornelius Ryan Collection Alden Library, Ohio University.
21. Ibid.
22. Walter E. Hughes, written account, courtesy of Walter E. Hughes.
23. Obie Wickersham, interview with author.
24. Leonard G. Trimble, oral history, courtesy of Mrs. Leonard G. Trimble.
25. Henry B. Keep, letter to mother, November 20, 1944, courtesy of the 82nd Airborne Division War Memorial Museum.
26. Edward J. Sims, "Enclosure 4 To Army Service Experience Questionnaire for Edward J. Sims–Holland," courtesy of Edward J. Sims, p. 2.
27. Albert A. Tarbell, questionnaire, courtesy of the Cornelius Ryan Collection, Alden Library, Ohio University.
28. Louis E. Orvin, Jr., interview with author.

29. Keep, letter to mother.
30. Robert M. Tallon, Sr. interview notes, courtesy of the Cornelius Ryan Collection, Alden Library, Ohio University.
31. T. Moffatt Burriss, *Strike And Hold*, Brassey's, 2000, p. 115.
32. Megellas, questionnaire.
33. Orvin, interview.
34. Keefe, written account.
35. Ibid.
36. Ibid.
37. James Megellas, *All The Way To Berlin*, The Ballantine Publishing Group, 2003, p. 127.
38. Sims, "Enclosure 4," p. 2.
39. Burriss, *Strike And Hold*, pp. 120–121.
40. John Holabird, interview, courtesy of the Cornelius Ryan Collection, Alden Library, Ohio University.
41. Keep to mother.
42. Frederick M. Browning, as quoted in Ryan, *A Bridge Too Far*, Simon and Schuster, 1974, p. 463.
43. Hanz K. Druener, questionnaire, courtesy of the Cornelius Ryan Collection, Alden Library, Ohio University.
44. Roy M. Hanna, telephone interview notes March 5, 1968, courtesy of the Cornelius Ryan Collection, Alden Library, Ohio University.
45. Earl S. Oldfather, questionnaire, courtesy of the Cornelius Ryan Collection, Alden Library, Ohio University.
46. Allen F. McClain, III, questionnaire, courtesy of the Cornelius Ryan Collection, Alden Library, Ohio University.
47. Kuehl and Taylor, "Frontline," p. 40.
48. Dr. Hyman D. Shapiro, questionnaire, courtesy of the Cornelius Ryan Collection, Alden Library, Ohio University.
49. Keefe, written account.
50. Theodore Finkbeiner, as quoted in James Megellas, *All The Way To Berlin*, The Ballantine Publishing Group, 2003, p. 131.
51. Megellas, ibid., p. 129.
52. Ibid.
53. Ibid., p. 130.
54. Captain Carl W. Kappel, "The Operations of Company H, 504th Parachute Infantry, (82nd Airborne Division) in the Invasion of Holland 17–21 September 1944, (Personal Experience of a Rifle Company Commander)," Advanced Infantry Officers Course 1948–1949, Academic Department, The Infantry School, Fort Benning, Georgia, courtesy of the Donovan Research Library, Fort Benning, Georgia, pp. 31–32.
55. Ibid., pp. 32–33.

56. Hughes, written account.

57. Thomas, "Holland Mission."

58. Ross Pippin, as quoted in, Ross Pippen and Gary Shaffer, "A Paratrooper's Story," p. 34.

59. Thomas McLeod, questionnaire, courtesy of the Cornelius Ryan Collection, Alden Library, Ohio University.

60. Nicholas W. Mansolillo, questionnaire, courtesy of the Cornelius Ryan Collection, Alden Library, Ohio University.

61. Edwin M. Clements, written account, www.marketgarden.com (Topics/ Veterans' Memories).

62. Sims, "Enclosure 4," pp. 2–3.

63. Richard G. LaRiviere, as quoted in Cornelius Ryan, *A Bridge Too Far*, Simon and Schuster, 1974, p. 467.

64. Allen F. McClain, questionnaire, courtesy of the Cornelius Ryan Collection, Alden Library, Ohio University.

65. Kappel, "Operations of Company H," p. 34.

66. McClain, questionnaire.

67. Sims, "Enclosure 4," p. 3.

68. Charles B. McDonald, *The U.S. Army in World War II: The Siegfried Line Campaign*, Office of the Chief of Military History, U.S. Army, 1963, p. 181.

69. Thomas, "Holland Mission."

70. Keep to mother.

71. Jack L. Bommer, questionnaire, courtesy of the Cornelius Ryan Collection, Alden Library, Ohio University.

72. Richard G. LaRiviere, as quoted in T. Moffatt Burriss, *Strike And Hold*, Brassey's, 2000, p. 121.

73. Burriss, *Strike And Hold*, pp. 121–122.

74. Leoleis, *Medals*, pp. 175, 180.

75. Burriss, *Strike And Hold*, p. 122.

76. Ibid.

77. James J. Musa, as quoted in James Megellas, *All The Way To Berlin*, The Ballantine Publishing Group, 2003, 134.

78. Megellas, Ibid.

79. Kappel, "Operations of Company H," pp. 35–36.

80. Vandervoort, in "Echoes of the Warriors," pp. 365–366.

81. Heinz Harmel, as quoted in Cornelius Ryan, *A Bridge Too Far*, Simon Schuster, 1974, p. 473.

82. Ibid., p. 473.

83. Ibid., pp. 473–474.

84. Burriss, *Strike And Hold*, p. 123.

85. Ibid.

86. Thomas, "Holland Mission."

87. Colonel Edward N. Wellems, letter to Heather Chapman, March 8, 1968, courtesy of the Cornelius Ryan Collection, Alden Library, Ohio University.
88. Keep to mother.
89. Reuben H. Tucker, written account, courtesy of the Cornelius Ryan Collection, Alden Library, Ohio University.
90. Abdallah K. Zakby, questionnaire, courtesy of the Cornelius Ryan Collection, Alden Library, Ohio University.
91. Wickersham, interview.

Chapter 11: "Our MOS Was Still, Kill Germans"
1. Henry B. Keep, letter to mother, November 20, 1944, courtesy of the 82nd Airborne Division War Memorial Museum.
2. Reuben H. Tucker, written account, courtesy of the Cornelius Ryan Collection, Alden Library, Ohio University.
3. James M. Gavin, *On To Berlin*, Viking Press, 1978, pp. 181–182.
4. Captain Henry B. Keep, letter to mother, November 20, 1944, courtesy of the 82nd Airborne Division War Memorial Museum.
5. Ross Pippin, as quoted in, Ross Pippen and Gary Shaffer, "A Paratrooper's Story, p. 34.
6. Keep to mother.
7. Miles Dempsey, as quoted in James M. Gavin, *On To Berlin*, Viking Press, 1978, p. 185.
8. Harold G. Herbert, interview with author.
9. Warren R. Williams, Jr., questionnaire, courtesy of the Cornelius Ryan Collection, Alden Library, Ohio University.
10. Julian A. Cook, questionnaire, courtesy of the Cornelius Ryan Archive, Alden Library, Ohio University.
11. Robert H. Neptune, as quoted in Jan Bos, *Circle and the Fields of Little America*, Voices of the Veterans, Headquarters Battery.
12. Ibid.
13. Lieutenant James H. Nelson, interview, 97th General Hospital, National Archives.
14. Albert Tarbell, interview, courtesy of the Cornelius Ryan Collection, Alden Library, Ohio University.
15. Virgil F. Carmichael, letter to Cornelius Ryan, October 13, 1967, Cornelius Ryan Collection, Alden Library, Ohio University, p. 5.
16. Cook, questionnaire.
17. Paul A. Mullan, written account.
18. Earl S. Oldfather, questionnaire, courtesy of the Cornelius Ryan Collection, Alden Library, Ohio University.
19. Virgil F. Carmichael, letter to Cornelius Ryan, October 13, 1967, courtesy of the Cornelius Ryan Collection, Alden Library, Ohio University.

20. Louis E. Orvin, Jr., interview with author.
21. T. Moffatt Burriss, *Strike And Hold*, Brassey's, 2000, p. 148.
22. Ibid., p. 149.
23. George Leoleis, *Medals*, Carlton Press, 1990, p. 192.
24. Ibid.
25. Ibid.
26. Ibid., p. 193.
27. Orvin, interview.
28. Ibid.
29. Nelson, interview.
30. Raymond E. Fary, written account, courtesy of Raymond E. Fary.
31. Kenneth S. Nicoll, questionnaire, courtesy of the Cornelius Ryan Collection, Alden Library, Ohio University.
32. Nelson, interview.
33. Walter S. VanPoyck, questionnaire, courtesy of the Cornelius Ryan Collection, Alden Library, Ohio University.
34. Nelson, interview.
35. James Megellas, questionnaire, courtesy of the Cornelius Ryan Collection, Alden Library, Ohio University
36. Ibid.
37. John A. Holabird, letter to author.
38. Carl Mauro, memoirs, courtesy of Carl Mauro.
39. VanPoyck questionnaire.
40. Alfred Hermansen, as quoted in Jan Bos, *Circle and the Fields of Little America*, Voices of the Veterans, Headquarters Battery.
41. Reneau Breard, interview with author.
42. Ibid.
43. Ibid.
44. Leo M. Hart, questionnaire, courtesy of the Cornelius Ryan Collection, Alden Library, Ohio University.
45. Ibid.
46. Ibid.
47. Breard, interview.
48. Ibid.
49. Leoleis, *Medals*, pp. 186, 187.
50. Holabird, letter to author.
51. Edwin R. Bayley, written account.
52. Captain Victor W. Campana, "The Operations of the 2nd Battalion, 504th Parachute Infantry (82nd A/B Div) in the German Counter-offensive, 18 December 1944–10 January 1945 (Ardennes Campaign) (Personal Experience of a Battalion S-3)," courtesy of the Donovan Research Library, Fort Benning, Georgia, p. 5.

Chapter 12: "Far Worse Than Any Nightmare"

1. Captain Victor W. Campana, "The Operations of the 2nd Battalion, 504th Parachute Infantry (82nd A/B Div) in the German Counter-offensive, 18 December 1944–10 January 1945 (Ardennes Campaign) (Personal Experience of a Battalion S-3)," courtesy of the Donovan Research Library, Fort Benning, Georgia, p. 6.
2. Reneau Breard, interview with author.
3. Campana, "Operations of the 2nd Battalion," pp. 6–7.
4. John A. Holabird, letter to author.
5. Edwin R. Bayley, written account, courtesy of Edwin R. Bayley.
6. Breard, interview.
7. Bayley, written account.
8. Breard, interview.
9. Malcolm Neel, memoirs, courtesy of Bob Burns.
10. Campana, "Operations of the 2nd Battalion," p. 8.
11. Holabird, letter.
12. Bayley, written account.
13. Mike Holmstock, written account, courtesy of Mike Holmstock
14. Thomas R. Holliday, interview with author.
15. "The Story of the 82nd Airborne Division in the Battle of the Belgian Bulge, in the Siegfried Line, and of the Roer River, Section II—Division Commander's Report," courtesy of the 82nd Airborne Division War Memorial Museum, pp. 1–2.
16. Campana, "Operations of the 2nd Battalion," pp. 8–9.
17. Bayley, written account.
18. Campana, "Operations of the 2nd Battalion," pp. 9–12.
19. Captain Marshall W. Stark, "The Operations of the 1st Platoon, Battery C, 80th Airborne Antiaircraft Battalion, (82nd Airborne Division), In the Battle of the Bulge, 17 December–3 January 1945," courtesy of the Donovan Research Library, Fort Benning, Georgia, pp. 13–14.
20. Captain Thomas C. Helgeson, "Action of the First Battalion, 504th Parachute Infantry at Cheneux, Belgium, on December 20–21, 1944," courtesy of Mike Bigalke.
21. Stark, "Operations of the 1st Platoon, Battery C," pp. 14–15.
22. Holliday, interview.
23. Charles Battisti, interview with author.
24. Helgeson, "Action of the First Battalion, 504th Parachute Infantry," states, "Enemy SP mortar fire swept the two leading elements of the attack, killing six men and knocking out the company's radio." However, only two B Company men were KIA during the attack on Cheneux. Therefore, "killed" should have read, "wounded."
25. Ibid.

26. Holliday, interview.

27. Helgeson, "Action of the First Battalion, 504th Parachute Infantry."

28. Holliday, interview.

29. Ibid.

30. Ibid.

31. Stark, "Operations of the 1st Platoon, Battery C," pp. 14–15.

32. Charles Butler, interview with author.

33. Mike Holmstock, interview with author.

34. Frank L. Dietrich, interview, courtesy of Raymond E. Fary.

35. Holmstock, interview.

36. Holmstock, written account.

37. Dietrich, interview.

38. Ross Pippin and Gary Shaffer, "A Paratrooper's Story," courtesy of Ross Pippin and Gary Shaffer, p. 37.

39. Battisti, interview.

40. Holmstock, interview.

41. Sergeant William L. Clay, sworn statement, January 13, 1945, William P. Walsh awards file, National Archives.

42. Staff Sergeant James M. Boyd, sworn statement, January 13, 1945, William P. Walsh awards file, National Archives.

43. Clay, sworn statement.

44. Ibid.

45. Boyd, sworn statement.

46. Private Edward Focht, sworn statement, January 13, 1945, William P. Walsh awards file, National Archives.

47. Holmstock, interview.

48. Dietrich, interview.

49. Butler, interview.

50. Holliday, interview.

51. Butler, interview.

52. Holmstock, interview.

53. Ibid.

54. Holmstock, written account.

55. Robert M. Kinney, as quoted in Patrick K. O'Donnell, *Beyond Valor*, The Free Press, 2001, p. 245.

56. Ibid.

57. Holliday, interview.

58. Pippin and Shaffer, "A Paratrooper's Story," p. 38.

59. Obie Wickersham, interview with author.

60. Ibid.

61. Holmstock, interview.

62. Holmstock, written account.

63. Ibid.
64. James Megellas, *All The Way to Berlin*, The Ballantine Publishing Group, 2003, p. 188.
65. Albert Tarbell, as quoted in, Megellas, *All The Way to Berlin*, The Ballantine Publishing Group, 2003, p. 189.
66. Megellas, *All The Way to Berlin*, p. 191.
67. Donald Herndon, response to author's questionnaire.
68. Megellas, *All the Way to Berlin*, p. 192.
69. Corporal George Graves, Regimental S-1 Journal, December 21, 1944, courtesy of Mike Bigalke.

Chapter 13: "At Times A Person Did Not Care If He Lived Or Died"
1. Captain Victor W. Campana, "The Operations of the 2nd Battalion, 504th Parachute Infantry (82nd A/B Div) in the German Counter-offensive, 18 December 1944–10 January 1945 (Ardennes Campaign) (Personal Experience of a Battalion S-3)," courtesy of the Donovan Research Library, Fort Benning, Georgia, pp. 12–13.
2. Ibid., pp. 13–14.
3. "The Story Of The 82nd Airborne Division In The Battle Of The Belgian Bulge, In The Siegfried Line And On The Roer River, Section II – Division Commander's Report," courtesy of the 82nd Airborne Division War Memorial Museum, pp. 5–7.
4. Campana, "Operations of the 2nd Battalion," pp. 14–15.
5. Bernard L. Montgomery, as quoted in Clay Blair, *Ridgway's Paratroopers*, Dial Press, 1985, p. 468.
6. Ibid., p. 448.
7. "The Story Of The 82nd Airborne Division In The Battle Of The Belgian Bulge, In The Siegfried Line And On The Roer River, Section II – Division Commander's Report," p. 7.
8. Frank D. Boyd, as quoted in Jan Bos, *Circle and the Fields of Little America*, Voices of the Veterans, Headquarters Battery.
9. Campana, "Operations of the 2nd Battalion," pp. 16–17.
10. Obie Wickersham, "Christmas Eve 1944—The Loneliest One," courtesy of Obie Wickersham.
11. Campana, "Operations of the 2nd Battalion," p. 17.
12. James Megellas, *All The Way To Berlin*, The Ballantine Publishing Group, 2003, pp. 202–203.
13. Frank D. Boyd, as quoted in Jan Bos, *Circle and the Fields of Little America*, Voices of the Veterans, Headquarters Battery.
14. Campana, "Operations of the 2nd Battalion," pp. 22–26.
15. Gregory Orfalea, *Messengers of the Lost Battalion*, The Free Press, 1997, p. 296.

16. Ibid., p. 298.
17. Richard Durkee, written account, courtesy of Doug Dillard.
18. Ibid.
19. Ibid.
20. Ibid.
21. Captain Adam A. Komosa, Recommendation for Award (Posthumous), Private First Class William G. Lanseadel, January 19, 1945, courtesy of Mike Bigalke.
22. Komosa, Recommedation for Award.
23. Reneau Breard, interview with author.
24. Ibid.
25. Ibid.
26. Ibid.
27. Leo P. Muri, letter to sister, May 24, 1945, courtesy of William R. Leonard.
28. Ted C. Johnson, as quoted in Jan Bos, *Circle and the Fields of Little America*, Voices of the Veterans, B Battery.
29. Edwin R. Bayley, written account, courtesy of Edwin R. Bayley.

Chapter 14: "No Amount Of Hardship Or Loss Could Affect Its Morale"

1. Edwin R. Bayley, written account, courtesy of Edwin R. Bayley.
2. Reneau Breard, interview with author.
3. James Megellas, *All The Way To Berlin*, The Ballantine Publishing Group, 2003, p. 224.
4. Harold Sullivan, written account, courtesy of Harold Sullivan.
5. Ibid.
6. Megellas, *All The Way To Berlin*, p. 225.
7. Jimmie Shields, sworn statement for Congressional Medal of Honor award effort for James Megellas, courtesy of Colonel Edward J. Sims.
8. Charles H. Crowder, sworn statement for Congressional Medal of Honor award effort for James Megellas, courtesy of Colonel Edward J. Sims.
9. Lawrence H. Dunlop, letter to President George W. Bush, August 29, 2002, for Congressional Medal of Honor award effort for James Megellas, courtesy of Colonel Edward J. Sims.
10. Ernest P. Murphy, sworn statement for Congressional Medal of Honor award effort for James Megellas, courtesy of Colonel Edward J. Sims.
11. Crowder, sworn statement.
12. Sullivan, written account.
13. Edward J. Sims, letter to President William J. Clinton, May 18, 1999, for Congressional Medal of Honor award effort for Megellas, courtesy of Colonel Edward J. Sims.
14. Bayley, written account.
15. Breard, interview.

16. Bayley, written account.
17. Ibid.
18. William L. Bonning, interview with author.
19. Captain Richard R. Hallock, "The Operations of the 3rd Platoon, Company A, 504 Parachute Infantry (82nd Airborne Division) in an Assault Across a Draw on the Hertesrott Heights, in the Siegfried Line, Near Neuhof, Germany, 2 February 1945" (Rhineland Campaign), Personal Experience of the Platoon Leader, courtesy of the Donovan Research Library, Fort Benning, Georgia, pp. 4—5.
20. Captain Edward F. Shaifer, "The Operations of Company B, 504 Parachute Infantry (82 Airborne Division) in Piercing the Siegfried Line, near Losheimergraben, Germany, 2–4 February 1945" (Rhineland Campaign) (Personal Experience of a Platoon Leader), courtesy of the Donovan Research Library, Fort Benning, Georgia, p. 10.
21. Ibid., pp. 12–13.
22. Ibid., p. 12.
23. Ibid., p. 13.
24. Bayley, written account.
25. Shaifer, "Operations of Company B," pp. 14–15.
26. Ibid., pp. 15–16.
27. Ibid., pp. 16–17.
28. Ibid., p. 17.
29. Ibid.
30. Ibid., p. 18.
31. Ibid.
32. Hallock, "Operations of the 3rd Platoon," pp. 4–5.
33. Ibid., pp. 7–8.
34. Ibid., p. 9.
35. Ibid.
36. Ibid., p. 11.
37. Ibid., pp. 11–12.
38. Ibid., p. 13.
39. Ibid., pp. 13–14.
40. Shaifer, "Operations of Company B," p. 19.
41. Bonning, interview.
42. Shaifer, "Operations of Company B," pp. 19–20.
43. Bonning, interview.
44. Shaifer, "Operations of Company B," p. 22.
45. Ibid., pp. 22–23.
46. Ibid., pp. 24–25.
47. Edward J. Sims, "Enclosure 5 To Army Experience Questionnaire— Belgium "Battle of the Bulge," courtesy of Colonel Edward J. Sims, p. 3.
48. Shaifer, "Operations of Company B," pp. 25–26.

49. Bonning, interview.
50. Shaifer, "Operations of Company B," pp. 26–27.
51. Bonning, interview.
52. Shaifer, "Operations of Company B," pp. 28–29.
53. Breard, interview.
54. Bonning, interview.
55. Breard, interview.

56. Shaifer, "Operations of Company B," p. 30.
57. Ibid., pp. 31–32.

Chapter 15: "Big Six-Foot Jerries, In Waves Of Skirmish Lines As Far As The Eye Could See"

1. Corporal George D. Graves, "A Preface to Narrative of Events of Action of Company A, 504th Parachute Infantry at Hitdorf, Germany on April 6–7th, 1945," courtesy of Mike Bigalke.
2. Reneau Breard, interview with author.
3. Ibid.
4. Ibid.
5. Ibid.
6. Harry N. Smith, as quoted in, *Saga of the All-American*, compiled and edited by W. Forrest Dawson, 82nd Airborne Division Association, Inc., 1946.
7. Breard, interview.
8. John H. Stubbs, as quoted in "Prop Blast," April 23, 1945, reprinted in *Prop Blast*, Mrozek, compiler and editor.
9. John Pease, as quoted in, *Saga of the All-American*, compiled and edited by Dawson.
10. Ibid.
11. William Bullock, as quoted in *Saga of the All-American*, compiled and edited by Dawson.
12. Breard interview.
13. Leo P. Muri, letter to sister, May 24, 1945, courtesy of William R. Leonard.
14. Francis Eisemann, as quoted in *Saga of the All-American*, Forrest W. Dawson, compiler and editor, 82nd Airborne Division Association, 1946.
15. Breard, interview.
16. Obie Wickersham, interview with author.
17. Frank D. Boyd, as quoted in Jan Bos, *Circle and the Fields of Little America*, Voices of the Veterans, Headquarters Battery.
18. William L. Bonning, interview with author.
19. John T. Berry, questionnaire, courtesy of the Cornelius Ryan Collection, Alden Library, Ohio University.
20. Bommer, questionnaire.
21. John A. Holabird, letter to author.

22. Richard E. Shumaker, "A Deadly Boom Near the Elbe River, Germany, 1945," courtesy of Harold G. Herbert.
23. Ibid.
24. Harold G. Herbert, interview, with author.
25. James R. Allmand, letter to Cornelius Ryan, courtesy of the Cornelius Ryan Collection, Alden Library, Ohio University.
26. Charles L. Wroten, written account, courtesy of Mike Bigalke.
27. Clayton Blankenship, as quoted in Jan Bos, *Circle and the Fields of Little America*, Voices of the Veterans, D Battery.
28. Wroten, written account.
29. Joseph C. Watts, Jr., response to "WWII Army Service Experiences Questionnaire," U.S. Military History Institute, p. 37.
30. James M. Gavin, *On To Berlin*, Viking Press, 1978, pp. 289–290.
31. Ross S. Carter, *Those Devils In Baggy Pants*, Buccaneer Books, 1976, Preface.
32. Frank D. Boyd, as quoted in Jan Bos, *Circle and the Fields of Little America*, Voices of the Veterans, Headquarters Battery.
33. Edwin R. Bayley, written account, courtesy of Edwin R. Bayley.
34. Ibid.
35. George Leoleis, *Medals*, Carlton Press, 1990, pp. 249–250.

Epilogue: "No Braver, More Loyal, Or Better Fighting Men Ever Lived"
1. Darrell G. Harris, *Casablanca to VE Day*, Dorrance Publishing, 1995, p. 26.
2. Walter E. Hughes, written account, courtesy of Walter E. Hughes.
3. Ibid.
4. Clayton Blankenship, as quoted in Jan Bos, *Circle and the Fields of Little America*, Voices of the Veterans, D Battery.
5. Joseph C. Watts, Jr., response to "WWII Army Service Experiences Questionnaire," U.S. Army Military History Institute, p. 40.
6. Milton V. Knight, response to questionnaire by Alex Kicovic, courtesy of Alex Kicovic.
7. Watts, response to "WWII Army Service Experiences Questionnaire," p. 30.

Bibliography

Published Sources

Baugh, James Emory. *From Skies of Blue*. Bloomington, IN: iUniverse, 2003.

Biello, D. Thomas. "The 82nd Airborne Division during WW II." www.ww2-airborne.us/division/82_overview.html.

Blair, Clay. *Ridgway's Paratroopers*. Garden City, NY: Dial Press, 1985.

Bos, Jan, *Circle and the Fields of Little America*. Baltimore: Gateway Press, 1992.

Bowditch, John III. *Anzio Beachhead 22 January–25 May 1944*. Washington, D.C.: U.S. Army Center of Military History, 1990. First published 1948 by U.S. War Department, Historical Division. www.army.mil/cmh-pg/books/wwii/anziobeach/anzio-fm.htm.

Bradley, Omar N., and Blair, Clay. *A General's Life*. New York: Simon and Schuster, 1983.

Breuer, William B. *Drop Zone, Sicily*. Novato, CA: Presidio Press, 1983.

———. *Geronimo!* New York: St. Martin's Press, 1989.

Burriss, T. Moffatt. *Strike and Hold*. Washington, D.C.: Brassey's, 2000.

Carter, Ross S. *Those Devils in Baggy Pants*. Cutchogue, NY: Buccaneer Books, 1976. First published 1951 by Appleton-Century-Crofts.

Clark, Mark W. *Calculated Risk*.New York: Harper & Brothers, 1950.

Clemens, Edwin M. "My Memories of Market Garden 1944." www.marketgarden.com.

Cole, Hugh M. *The Ardennes: Battle of the Bulge*. Washington, D.C.: U.S. Army Center of Military History, 1990. First published 1965 by Office of the Chief of Military History, Department of the Army. www.army.mil/cmh-pg/books/wwii/7-8/7-8_cont.htm.

Dawson, Buck, ed. *Saga of the All American*. Atlanta: Albert Love Enterprises, 1946.

Dugdale, J. *Panzer Divisions, Panzergrenadier Divisions, Panzer Brigades of the Army and the Waffen SS*. Johannesburg, South Africa: Galago Publishing, 2000.

Fifth Army Historical Section. *Fifth Army at the Winter Line (15 November 1943–15 January 1944)*. Washington, D.C.: U.S. Army Center of Military History, 1990. First published 1945 by U.S. War Department, Historical Division. www.army.mil/cmh-pg/books/wwii/winterline/winter-fm.htm

———. *From the Volturno to the Winter Line (6 October-15 November 1943)*. Washington, D.C.: U.S. Army Center of Military History, 1990. First published 1945 by U.S. War Department, Historical Division. www.army. mil/cmh-pg/books/wwii/volturno/volturno-fm.htm

———. *Salerno: American Operations From the Beaches to the Volturno (9 September-6 October 1943)*. Washington, D.C.: U.S. Army Center of Military History, 1990. First published 1944 by U.S. War Department, Historical Division. www.army.mil/cmh-pg/books/wwii/salerno/sal-fm. htm

Gavin, James M. *On to Berlin*. New York: Viking Press, 1978.

Haider, Edward P. *Blood in Our Boots*. Victoria, BC: Trafford, 2002.

Harris, Darrell G. *Casablanca to VE Day*. Pittsburgh, PA: Dorrance Publishing, 1995.

Kershaw, Robert J. *It Never Snows in September*. New York: Sarpedon, 2001.

Leoleis, George. *Medals*. New York: Carlton Press, 1990.

MacDonald, Charles Brown. *A Time for Trumpets*. New York: Morrow, 1985.

———.*The Siegfried Line Campaign*. Washington, D.C.: Office of the Chief of Military History, Department of the Army, 1963.

Mandle, William D., and David H. Whittier, eds. *Combat Record of the 504th Parachute Infantry Regiment, April 1943–July 1945*. Paris: Draeger Freres, 1945.

Margry, Karel. *Operation Market-Garden Then and Now.*Essex, U.K.: After the Battle, 2002.

Marshall, S. L. A. *Night Drop*. Boston: Little, Brown, 1962.

McCarthy, Thomas J. *In Their Own Words—WWII.*Renton, WA: Topics Entertainment, 2002. Compact discs.

Megellas, James. *All the Way to Berlin.*New York: Ballantine Books, 2003.

Mrozek, Steven J., ed. *Prop Blast*. Fort Bragg, NC: 82nd Airborne Division Historical Society, 1986.

O'Donnell, Patrick K. *Beyond Valor*. New York: Free Press, 2001.

Orfalea, Gregory. *Messengers of the Lost Battalion*. New York: Free Press, 1997.

Pahler, Regis J. "Devils in Baggy Pants." *The Static Line*, Private collection of Lou Hauptfleisch.

Pallud, Jean-Paul, *Battle of the Bulge Then and Now*. Essex, U.K.: After the Battle, 1999.

Ridgway, Matthew B., and Martin, Harold H. *Soldier: The Memoirs of Matthew B. Ridgway, as told to Harold H. Martin*. Westport, CT: Greenwood Press, 1956.

Ruppenthal, Maj.Roland G. *Utah Beach to Cherbourg*. Washington, D.C.: U.S. Army Center of Military History, 1990.

Ryan, Cornelius. *A Bridge Too Far*. New York: Simon and Schuster, 1974.

Saunders, Tim. *Nijmegen, Grave, and Groesbeek*. Barnsley, U.K.: Leo Cooper, 2001.

Tregaskis, Richard. *Invasion Diary.* New York: Random House, 1944.

Turnbull, Peter. *I Maintain the Right: The 307th Airborne Engineer Battalion in WWII.*Milton Keynes, U.K.: AuthorHouse, 2005.

Warren, John Cushman. *Airborne Operations in World War II, European Theater.* Maxwell Air Force Base, AL: USAF Historical Division, 1956.

Yardley, Doyle R. *Home Was Never Like This.* Evergreen, CO: Yardley Enterprises, 2002.

Unpublished Sources

Allmand, James R., to Cornelius Ryan. Cornelius Ryan Collection, Alden Library, Ohio University.

Baldino, Fred J. "Fred J. Baldino's War Story." Private collection of James McNamara.

Battisti, Charles. Interview by author.

Bayley, Edwin R. Papers. Private collection.

Bedell, Allen. Written interview by author.

Berry, David R., to Rodgers and Jacobs families. Private collection of Ed Dodd.

Berry, John T. Written interview by author.

Bommer, Jack L. Written interview by author.

Bonning, William L. Interview by author.

Boyd, James M. Sworn statement, January 13, 1945. William P. Walsh awards file, National Archives.

Branca, John G. Jr. Interview. Cornelius Ryan Collection, Alden Library, Ohio University.

Breard, Reneau. Interview by author.

Burriss, T. Moffatt. Written interview by author.

Butler, Charles. Interview by author.

Campana, Victor W. "The Operations of the 2nd Battalion, 504th Parachute Infantry (82nd A/B Div) in the German Counter-offensive, 18 December 1944–10 January 1945 (Ardennes Campaign) (Personal Experience of a Battalion S-3)." Advanced Infantry Officers Course, Infantry School, 1946–1947. Donovan Research Library, Fort Benning, GA.

Campana,Victor W. Written interview by author.

Carmichael, Virgil F., to Cornelius Ryan, October 13, 1967. Cornelius Ryan Collection, Alden Library, Ohio University.

Carmichael, Virgil F. Written interview by author.

Chilcutt, Landon. Written interview by author.

Clark, Albert B. Written interview by author.

Clay, William L. Sworn statement, January 13, 1945. William P. Walsh awards file, National Archives.

Cook, Julian A. Written interview by author.

Corbin, Harry A. Interview by author.

Crowder, Charles H. Sworn statement for Congressional Medal of Honor award effort. Private collection of Col. Edward J. Sims.

Crosbie, James F., to Jan Bos. Private collection of Richard Claeys.

Dietrich, Frank L. Interview by Raymond E. Fary.

——. Written interview by author.

Distinguished Service Cross citations and Presidential Unit citations. Facsimiles. 82nd Airborne Division War Memorial Museum, Fort Bragg, NC.

Distinguished Service Cross citations, maps, photos, and after-action reports. Facsimiles. Cornelius Ryan Collection, Alden Library, Ohio University.

Dodd, Gilbert E. Written interview by author.

Druener, Hanz K. Written interview by author.

Duncan, John R. Written interview by author.

Dunlop, Lawrence H., to President George W. Bush, August 29, 2002, for Congressional Medal of Honor award effort. Private collection of Col. Edward J. Sims.

——. Papers. Private collection of Alex Kicovic.

Durkee, Richard. Papers. Private collection of Douglas Dillard.

80th Airborne Antiaircraft (Antitank) Battalion. Various documents and reports. Private collection of Raymond E. Fary.

"82nd Airborne Division in Sicily and Italy." 82nd Airborne Division War Memorial Museum, Fort Bragg, NC.

82nd Airborne Division. "World War II Casualties, Decorations, Citations." 82nd Airborne Division War Memorial Museum, Fort Bragg, NC.

"Factual Account of the Actions of Elements of Companies H and I, 504th Parachute Infantry, Leading to the Capture of Hill 1017." AGF Board, AFHQ, NATO, December 4, 1943.

Fary, Raymond E. Written interview by author.

——. Papers. Private collection.

Ferguson, Arthur W. Written interview by author.

Focht, Edward. Sworn statement, January 13, 1945. William P. Walsh awards file, National Archives.

Fransosi, Arthur. Written interview by author.

Fuller, Clark. Written interview by author.

Fusaro, Pat A. Written interview by author.

Gavin, Maj.Gen.James M., to John C. Westover, July 25, 1945. 82nd Airborne Division War Memorial Museum, Fort Bragg, NC.

——. Papers. Cornelius Ryan Collection, Alden Library, Ohio University.

Granado, John. Interview by Terry Poyser.

Graves, George D. "A Preface to Narrative of Events of Action of Company A, 504th Parachute Infantry at Hitdorf, Germany, on April 6–7th, 1945." Private collection of Mike Bigalke.

——. Regimental S-1 journal, December 21, 1944. Private collection of Mike Bigalke.

Hallock, Richard R. "The Operations of the 3rd Platoon, Company A, 504 Parachute Infantry (82nd Airborne Division) in an Assault Across a Draw on the Hertesrott Heights, in the Siegfried Line, Near Neuhof, Germany, 2 February 1945 (Rhineland Campaign), Personal Experience of the Platoon Leader." Advanced Infantry Officers Course, Infantry School, 1949–1950. Donovan Research Library, Fort Benning, GA.

Hanna, Roy M. Interview. Cornelius Ryan Collection, Alden Library, Ohio University.

——. Papers. 82nd Airborne Division War Memorial Museum, Fort Bragg, NC.

——. Written interview by author.

Hart, Leo M. Interview by author.

——. Written interview by author.

Hauptfleisch, Louis A. Written interview by author.

Headquarters IX Troop Carrier Command. "Operation Market, Air Invasion of Holland." Cornelius Ryan Collection, Alden Library, Ohio University.

Headquarters, Third Battalion 504th Parachute Infantry, APO 469, U.S. Army. "Battle of the Bulge (Belgium and Germany) 17 Dec. 1945 – 21 Feb. 1945."

——. "Holland Campaign 17 Sept. – 15 Nov. 1944."

——. "The Anzio Beachhead, Italy."

——. "Watch on the Rhine and the Push Across the Elbe from 2 April to 2 June 1945."

Headquarters, Third Infantry Division, Office of the Assistant Chief of Staff, G-2, and Special Service. "The Parachutists." March 22, 1944.

Helgeson, Thomas C. "Action of the First Battalion, 504th Parachute Infantry at Cheneux, Belgium, on December 20–21, 1944." Private collection of Mike Bigalke.

——. Interview. Cornelius Ryan Collection, Alden Library, Ohio University.

Herbert, Harold G. Interview by author.

Herndon, Donald. Written interview by author.

Holabird, John A. Interview. Cornelius Ryan Collection, Alden Library, Ohio University.

——. Letter to author.

Holliday, Thomas R. Interview by author.

Holmstock, Mike. Interview by author.

——. Papers. Private collection.

Hord, Shelby R. Interview by author.

HQ 82nd Airborne Division, APO 469, U.S. Army. "Order of Battle Summary." September 11, 1944. Cornelius Ryan Collection, Alden Library, Ohio University.

Huebner, Otto W. "The Operations of Company A, 504th Parachute Infantry (82nd Airborne Division) in the Defense of Hill 424 Near Altavilla, Italy, 17 September –19 September 1943, (Naples-Foggia Campaign), (Personal Experience of the Company Operations Sergeant)." Advanced Infantry Officers Course, Infantry School, 1948–1949, Donovan Research Library, Fort Benning, GA.

Hughes, Walter E. Papers. Private collection.

Jacobus, George, ed. "Echoes of the Warriors." Private collection.

James M. Gavin Papers, Personal Diaries, Box 8, Diary Passages Folder. U.S. Army Center of Military History, Washington, D.C.

Joseph, John T. "The Operations of a Regimental Pathfinder Unit, 507th Parachute Infantry Regiment (82nd Airborne Division) in Normandy, France 6 June 1944, (Normandy Campaign), (Personal Experience of a Regimental Pathfinder Leader)." Advanced Infantry Officers Course, Infantry School, 1947–1948. Donovan Research Library, Fort Benning, GA.

Kantala, Matthew W. Jr. Written interview by author.

Kappel, Carl W. Interview. Cornelius Ryan Collection, Alden Library, Ohio University.

——. "The Operations of Company H, 504th Parachute Infantry, (82nd Airborne Division) in the Invasion of Holland 17–21 September 1944, (Rhineland Campaign), (Personal Experience of a Rifle Company Commander)." Advanced Infantry Officers Course, Infantry School, 1948–1949, Donovan Research Library, Fort Benning, GA.

Keefe, Francis X. Papers. Private collection of Francis X. Keefe and William R. Leonard.

Keep, Henry B., to mother, November 20, 1944. 82nd Airborne Division War Memorial Museum, Fort Bragg, NC.

Keith , Herbert P. Written interview by author.

Kellogg, William G. "Report of the 2nd and 3rd Sticks, 1st Platoon, Company C, 307 Engineer on Avellino Jump." National Archives.

Kicovic, Alex. Papers. Private collection.

Knight, Milton V. Papers. Private collection of Alex Kicovic.

Komosa, Adam A. "Airborne Operation, 504th Parachute Infantry Regimental Combat Team (82nd Airborne Division), Sicily, 9 July–19 August, 1943, Personal Experience of a Regimental Headquarters Company Commander." Advanced Infantry Officers Course, Infantry School, 1946–1947. Donovan Research Library, Fort Benning, GA.

——. Recommendation for award (posthumous), Pfc. William G. Lanseadel, January 19, 1945. Private collection of Mike Bigalke.

Kuehl, Delbert, and Allan Taylor. "Frontline." Private collection of Delbert Kuehl.

Lekson, John S. "The Operations of the 1st Battalion, 504th Parachute Infantry (82nd Airborne Division) in the Capture of Altavilla, Italy, 13 September – 19 September, 1943, (Naples-Foggia Campaign), (Personal Experience of a Battalion Operations Officer)." Advanced Infantry Officers Course, Infantry School, 1947–1948, Donovan Research Library, Fort Benning, GA.

Leonard, William R. Papers. Private collection.

LeVangia, Warren J. Papers. Private collection of Alex Kicovic.

Long, Russell T. "My Life in the Service: The Diary of Cpl. Russell T. Long." Private collection of Jan Bos.

Lyons, Joseph W. Written interview by author.

Mansolillo ,Nicholas W. Written interview by author.

Mauro, Carl. Papers. Private collection.

McClain, Allen F. III. Written interview by author.

McLane, Francis W. "Francis W. McLane a.k.a. 'Mac,' World War II, Journal." Private collection.

McLeod , Thomas. Written interview by author.

Megellas, James. Written interview by author.

———. Papers. Private collection.

Milloy, Albert E. Interview. Cornelius Ryan Collection, Alden Library, Ohio University.

———. Sworn statement, June 18, 1945. Recommendation for award, Lt. Col. Warren R. Williams Jr. Private collection of Mike Bigalke.

Misseres, Alek. Interview. Cornelius Ryan Collection, Alden Library, Ohio University.

Mullan, Paul A. Papers. Private collection.

Mulloy, Patrick J. Written interview by author.

Muri, Leo P., to sister, May 24, 1945. Private collection of William R. Leonard.

Murphy, Ernest P. Written interview by author.

———. Sworn statement for Congressional Medal of Honor award effort. Private collection of Col. Edward J. Sims.

Col. Murphy, John H. Interview, 160th General Hospital. National Archives.

Nadler, Philip H. Interview. Cornelius Ryan Collection, Alden Library, Ohio University.

———. Written interview by author.

"Narrative of Action of the First Battalion, 504th Parachute Infantry at Cheneux, Belgium on December 20–21, 1944."

Neel, Malcolm. Papers. Private collection of Bob Burns.

Nelson, James H. Interview, 97th General Hospital. National Archives.

Nicoll, Kenneth S. Written interview by author.

Oldfather, Earl S. Written interview by author.

"Operation Market, a Graphic History of the 82nd Airborne Division." 82nd

Airborne Division War Memorial Museum, Fort Bragg, NC.

Operation Market orders and reports. Cornelius Ryan Collection, Alden Library, Ohio University.

Orvin, Louis E. Jr. Interview by author.

Pease, John N. Sworn statement, June 18, 1945. Recommendation for award, Lt. Col. Warren R. Williams Jr. Private collection of Mike Bigalke.

Pippin, Ross. "A Paratrooper's Story: My World War II Experiences as told to Gary Shaffer." Private collection of Ross Pippin and Gary Shaffer.

"Report of the 504th Parachute Infantry Combat Team in Operation Avalanche." 82nd Airborne Division War Memorial Museum, Fort Bragg, NC.

Ridgway, Matthew B. Oral history, Part 2. U.S. Army Military History Institute, Carlisle, PA.

Ryan, Edward R. Written interview by author.

Shaifer, Edward F. Jr. "The Operations of Company B, 504th Parachute Infantry (82nd Airborne Division) in Piercing the Siegfried Line, near Losheimergraben, Germany, 2–4 February 1945 (Rhineland Campaign) (Personal Experience of a Platoon Leader." Advanced Infantry Officers Course, Infantry School, 1948–1949. Donovan Research Library, Fort Benning, GA.

Shapiro , Hyman D. Written interview by author.

Shields, Jimmie.Sworn statement for Congressional Medal of Honor award effort. Private collection of Col. Edward J. Sims.

Shumaker, Richard E. "A Deadly Boom Near the Elbe River, Germany, 1945." Private collection of Harold G. Herbert.

Sims, Edward J. "Army Service Experience Questionnaire for Edward J. Sims." U.S. Military History Institute.

Sims, Edward J., to President William J. Clinton, May 18, 1999. For Congressional Medal of Honor award effort. Col. Private collection.

Stark, Marshall W. "The Operations of the 1st Platoon, Battery C, 80th Airborne Antiaircraft Battalion, (82nd Airborne Division), in the Battle of the Bulge, 17 December—3 January 1945, (Ardennes-Alsace Campaign), (Personal Experience of a Platoon Leader)." Advanced Infantry Officers Course, Infantry School, 1947–1948, Donovan Research Library, Fort Benning, GA.

Stern, Robert D. Oral history. Private collection of Robert Wolfe.

"The Story of the 82nd Airborne Division in the Battle of the Belgian Bulge, in the Siegfried Line, and of the Roer River." 82nd Airborne Division War Memorial Museum, Fort Bragg, NC.

Strunk, Willard. Written interview by author.

Stueland, Harold A. "Patrol Report—March 18, 1944." Private collection of Mike Bigalke.

Sullivan, Harold. Papers. Private collection.

Supreme Headquarters Allied Expeditionary Force, Office of Assistant Chief of Staff, G-2. "Weekly Intelligence Summary, for Week ending 16 September 1944." Cornelius Ryan Collection, Alden Library, Ohio University.

Sweet, Capt. William J. Jr. "Operations of the 2nd Battalion, 504th Parachute Infantry Regiment (82nd Airborne Division) on the Anzio Beachhead, 22 January – 23 March 1944, (Anzio Campaign), (Personal Experience of a Battalion Operations Officer and Company Commander)." Advanced Infantry Officers Course, Infantry School, 1947–1948. Donovan Research Library, Fort Benning, GA.Tackel, C. L. "21 Years Ago, 82nd Troopers Faced Death." Army Times, February 3, 1965.

Taliaferro, George F. Sworn statement, September 24, 1943. Maj. Robert B. Acheson awards file, National Archives.

Tallon, Robert M. Sr. Interview. Cornelius Ryan Collection, Alden Library, Ohio University.

Tarbell, Albert A. Interview. Cornelius Ryan Collection, Alden Library, Ohio University.

———. Papers. Cornelius Ryan Collection, Alden Library, Ohio University.

———. Written interview by author.

Thomas, Fred E. "Holland Mission." Cornelius Ryan Collection, Alden Library, Ohio University.

Thompson, John S. "Individual Report on Operation Husky." 82nd Airborne Division War Memorial Museum, Fort Bragg, NC.

———. "The Holland Jump." 82nd Airborne Division War Memorial Museum, Fort Bragg, NC.

Trimble, Leonard G. Written interview by author.

———. Oral history. Private collection of Mrs. Leonard G. Trimble.

Tucker, Reuben H. Interview. Cornelius Ryan Collection, Alden Library, Ohio University.

———. Papers. Cornelius Ryan Collection, Alden Library, Ohio University.

———. Recommendation for award, Lt. Col. Warren R. Williams Jr., June 18, 1945. Private collection of Mike Bigalke.

"Unit Journal of the 2nd Battalion, 504th Parachute Infantry, 82nd Airborne Division." 82nd Airborne Division War Memorial Museum, Fort Bragg, NC.

Vandeleur, Giles. Interview. Cornelius Ryan Collection, Alden Library, Ohio University.

VanPoyck, Walter S. Written interview by author.

Ward, James L. Written interview by author.

Watts, Joseph C. Jr. Response to "WWII Army Service Experiences Questionnaire." U.S. Army Military History Institute, Carlisle, PA.

Wellems, Edward N., to Heather Chapman, March 8, 1968. Cornelius Ryan Collection, Alden Library, Ohio University.

Wickersham, Obie. "Christmas Eve 1944—The Loneliest One." Private collection.

———. Interview by author.

Wienecke, Robert. Written interview by author.

Williams, Warren R. Jr. Written interview by author.

Willoughby, George. Papers. Private collection.

Wolfe, Hubert A. Interview. Private collection of Robert Wolfe.

Wroten, Charles L. Papers. Private collection of Mike Bigalke.

Zakby, Abdallah K. Written interview by author.

Index to Maps

Index